# In Between and Across

# In Between and Across

*Legal History without Boundaries*

*Edited by*
KENNETH W. MACK AND JACOB KATZ COGAN

OXFORD
UNIVERSITY PRESS

OXFORD
UNIVERSITY PRESS

Oxford University Press is a department of the University of Oxford. It furthers the University's objective of excellence in research, scholarship, and education by publishing worldwide. Oxford is a registered trade mark of Oxford University Press in the UK and certain other countries.

Published in the United States of America by Oxford University Press
198 Madison Avenue, New York, NY 10016, United States of America.



---

Library of Congress Cataloging-in-Publication Data
Names: Mack, Kenneth Walter, 1964– editor. | Cogan, Jacob Katz, editor.
Title: In between and across : legal history without boundaries / [edited by] Kenneth W. Mack, Jacob Katz Cogan.
Description: New York : Oxford University Press, 2024.
Identifiers: LCCN 2024021012 (print) | LCCN 2024021013 (ebook) |
ISBN 9780197680995 (hardback) | ISBN 9780197681015 (epub) |
ISBN 9780197681008 (updf) | ISBN 9780197681022 (online)
Subjects: LCSH: Law—History. | Jurisdiction—History.
Classification: LCC K150 .M33 2024 (print) | LCC K150 (ebook) |
DDC 340.09—dc23/eng/20240511
LC record available at https://lccn.loc.gov/2024021012
LC ebook record available at https://lccn.loc.gov/2024021013

---

DOI: 10.1093/oso/9780197680995.001.0001

Printed by Sheridan Books, Inc., United States of America

*For Dirk Hartog,*
*who taught us to inhabit the in between*

# Contents

## PART III: RETHINKING METHOD: LAW AND EVERYTHING ELSE

# Acknowledgments

We would both like to acknowledge all those whose generosity and dedication helped to produce the October 2018 conference at Princeton University entitled "Between Private and Public: A Celebration of Dirk Hartog," out of which this book emerged: Jennifer D. Loessy and Judy Hanson of the Princeton history department; Judith Ferszt of Princeton's program in American studies; Professor William Jordan, former chair of the history department at Princeton; Professor Paul Frymer, former director of the program in law and public affairs at Princeton; Professor Anne Cheng, former director of the program in American studies; Princeton University president Chris Eisgruber; Professor Angela Creager, former director of the Shelby Cullom Davis Center for Historical Study; and all the participants who were generous enough with their time and commitment to participate in the conference.

We would also like to extend our generous thanks to the anonymous readers at Oxford University Press, who helped us clarify and improve the central claims made in this book; Jacqueline Larabee and Paulina dos Santos Major at Oxford University Press, for their extreme patience, dedication, and wisdom in guiding this book through its stages of production; Kezia Johnson of Oxford University Press, for helping out with our contract and many other details; Merel Alstein, Alex Flach, and Jamie Berezin for their welcome support of this project. Kate Masur and Ariela Gross were kind enough to give our introduction a careful and insightful reading, which helped us tighten and focus its argument and narrative, although any errors that remain are no doubt our own.

We would also like to thank Andrew Matthiessen and Kathy McGillicuddy for their kind assistance, without which this book would not have reached publication, and Gilbert Placeres, who provided an outstanding read and correction of the final manuscript. Finally, we would like to thank both of our families, for putting up with how much this wonderful endeavor has taken up our time.

# Abbreviations

| | |
|---|---|
| ACLU | American Civil Liberties Union |
| ADL | Anti-Defamation League |
| AFDC | Aid to Families with Dependent Children |
| AFL | American Federation of Labor |
| AJC | American Jewish Committee |
| BEN | Records of Master of the Bench and Bench Committees, ITA |
| BTO | Bench Table Orders, ITA |
| CCNYR | Columbia University Rare Book and Manuscript Library |
| CIO | Congress of Industrial Organizations |
| CORE | Congress of Racial Equality |
| DIS | Records of Disciplinary Cases, ITA |
| GAMA | Gunnar and Alva Myrdal Archives |
| GEB | General Education Board |
| *IS* | *The Indian Sociologist* |
| ITA | Inner Temple Archives |
| JOBS | Job Opportunity and Basic Skills Training program |
| *JRKC* | *James River and Kanawha Company . . . Annual Report* |
| JTA | Jewish Telegraphic Agency |
| MHP | Melville Herskovits Papers |
| MOE | maintenance-of-effort |
| [NAACP's] LDF | Legal Defense Fund |
| NAACP | National Association for the Advancement of Colored People |
| NEPA | National Environmental Policy Act |
| NLRA | National Labor Relations Act |
| NWRO | National Welfare Rights Organization |
| PRWORA | Personal Responsibility and Work Opportunity Reconciliation Act |
| PSFR | Phelps Stokes Fund Records |
| PSID | Panel Study of Income Dynamics |
| RCA | Radio Corporation of America |
| SNCC | Student Nonviolent Coordinating Committee |
| SSI | Supplemental Security Insurance |
| SSRC | Social Science Research Council |
| TANF | Temporary Assistance for Needy Families |
| *TI* | *The Times of India* |
| *TL* | *The Times* (London) |
| UNIA | Universal Negro Improvement Association |
| WIN/WIP | Work Incentive Program of 1967 |

# Contributors

**Kenneth W. Mack** is the inaugural Lawrence D. Biele Professor of Law and Affiliate Professor of History at Harvard University. He is also the co-faculty leader of the Harvard Law School Program on Law and History. His 2012 book, *Representing the Race: The Creation of the Civil Rights Lawyer* (Harvard University Press), was a Washington Post Best Book of the Year, was a National Book Festival Selection, was awarded honorable mention for the J. Willard Hurst Award by the Law and Society Association, and was a finalist for the Julia Ward Howe Book Award. He is also the co-editor of *The New Black: What Has Changed—and What Has Not—with Race in America* (New Press, 2013). His work has been published in the *Harvard Law Review, Yale Law Journal, Journal of American History, Law and History Review*, and other scholarly journals. In 2010, he was awarded an honorary doctor of public service by Harrisburg University of Science and Technology. In 2016, President Obama appointed him to the U.S. Permanent Committee for the Oliver Wendell Holmes Devise. He began his professional career as an electrical engineer at Bell Laboratories before turning to law and history. More information available at: http://kennethwmack.com.

**Jacob Katz Cogan** is Judge Joseph P. Kinneary Professor of Law and affiliate faculty of the department of history at the University of Cincinnati. He was an attorney-adviser at the U.S. Department of State before joining Cincinnati Law. His research focuses on the hidden assumptions, informal rules, and constitutive decisions and structures that form the operational international legal system. He also writes about the history of international law. An author of many articles and essays, he is the co-editor of *The Oxford Handbook of International Organizations* (Oxford University Press, 2016) and *Looking to the Future: Essays on International Law in Honor of W. Michael Reisman* (Martinus Nijhoff Publishers, 2011). In 2010, he was awarded the Francis Deák Prize by the American Society of International Law.

**Matthew Axtell** is assistant counsel for historic preservation & ecosystem restoration, U.S. Army Corps of Engineers, focusing upon National Historic Preservation Act compliance during the planning and permitting of controversial infrastructure projects. Prior to rejoining the Corps in 2016 (where he worked from 2002 to 2006), he held research fellowships at the NYU School of Law and the Supreme Court of the United States. His work has appeared in the *Columbia Journal of American Studies*, the *Environmental Law Reporter*, the *Journal of Law and Politics, Law and Social Inquiry*, the *Hastings Race and Poverty Law Journal*, the *Minnesota Review*, and *Ohio Valley History*. Since 2017, Dr. Axtell has served as the program manager for his agency's civilian honors program, overseeing the recruitment of entry-level talent into the Corps' worldwide legal enterprise.

**Donna Dennis** is professor of law and Justice Frederick W. Hall Scholar at Rutgers Law School, where she teaches courses on legal history and corporate law. She is the author of

*Licentious Gotham: Erotic Publishing and Its Prosecution in Nineteenth-Century New York* (Harvard University Press, 2009).

**Catherine L. Evans** is associate professor at the Centre for Criminology and Sociolegal Studies at the University of Toronto. She is a historian of criminal law in the nineteenth-century British empire, with particular interests in forensic science, colonial psychiatry, and the professions. She is the author of *Unsound Empire: Civilization and Madness in Late-Victorian Law* (Yale University Press, 2021), a history of criminal responsibility and liberal legalism in the nineteenth-century British empire. From 2015 to 2017, she was a Prize Fellow at the Center for History and Economics at Harvard University. Her current project is a legal history of incendiarism in the British empire.

**Maeve Glass** is an associate professor at Columbia Law School and a legal historian of the United States. Her scholarship examines the development of constitutional law and its implications for today. She is currently completing her first book, *These United States: The Fracturing of America.* It is based on her Ph.D. dissertation, which won the American Society for Legal History's best dissertation prize in 2017. Glass has also published articles in the *University of Chicago Law Review*, *Law and Social Inquiry*, and the *Columbia Human Rights Law Review.* Before her appointment to the Columbia faculty in 2018, Glass was an academic fellow at the law school. She has also held fellowships in legal history at Harvard Law School and NYU Law.

**Felicia Kornbluh** is professor of history and gender, sexuality, and women's studies at University of Vermont. She is the author of *The Battle for Welfare Rights: Poverty and Politics in Modern America* (2007) and, with Gwendolyn Mink, *Ensuring Poverty: Welfare Reform in Feminist Perspective* (2018). She is at work on two books: *How to Win a War on Women: My Mother, Her Neighbor, and the Fate of Reproductive Rights and Justice*, and an essay collection titled, *Constant Craving: Identity Politics and Economic Justice.* Her articles on history, law, culture, and politics have appeared in the *American Historical Review, Journal of American History, Feminist Studies, Radical History Review, Labor, Law and Social Inquiry*, and many other journals, as well as in such periodicals as the *New York Times*, the *Los Angeles Times*, the *Nation, In These Times*, and the *Women's Review of Books.* Kornbluh teaches on the history of law, on the United States since 1945, and on the history of poverty.

**Jessica K. Lowe** is Visiting Scholar at the University of Virginia School of Law, and a scholar of early American legal history, criminal law, and religion in the American South. She has published in *Constitutional Commentary, Law and Social Inquiry*, and other journals, and her first book, *Murder in the Shenandoah: Making Law Sovereign in Revolutionary Virginia* (Cambridge University Press, 2019), was Finalist for the 2019 David J. Langum, Sr. Prize in American Legal History. Lowe earned a J.D. from Harvard Law School, a Ph.D. from Princeton University, and attended Yale Divinity School, and has held fellowships from, among others, the Center of Theological Inquiry in Princeton, N.J., and the Princeton University Program in Law and Public Affairs, as part of a Templeton Foundation grant in law and religious freedom, as well as the Princeton University Center for Human Values. Before entering academia, Lowe clerked at the U.S. District Court for the District of Connecticut and the U.S. Court of Appeals for the Fourth Circuit and practiced appellate litigation in Washington D.C. Her current project examines the rise of proslavery theology in the nineteenth century and its impact on American jurisprudence.

**Maribel Morey**, a historian of U.S. philanthropy and the social sciences, is executive director of the Miami Institute for the Social Sciences, a nonprofit whose work responds to the unique positionality of the city as a hub for international thought with global calls to bring to the center of academic scholarship perspectives and understandings of the Global Majority—of communities of Black and Indigenous and People of Color (BIPOC) around the world. Morey is also author of *White Philanthropy: Carnegie Corporation's* An American Dilemma *and the Making of a White World Order* (UNC Press, 2021) and of several other articles and chapters on the history of U.S. philanthropy and the social sciences on race in the United States, British Africa, and Europe during the twentieth century.

**Farah Peterson** is a professor of law at the University of Chicago Law School. Her scholarship focuses on constitutional theory and the history of statutory interpretation. Peterson clerked for Associate Justice Stephen Breyer at the U.S. Supreme Court and Judge Guido Calabresi at the U.S. Court of Appeals for the Second Circuit.

**Christina D. Ponsa-Kraus** teaches constitutional law and American legal history at Columbia Law School. She is the author of several articles on the constitutional history of U.S. imperialism and the extraterritorial application of the U.S. Constitution, and co-editor of *Foreign in a Domestic Sense: Puerto Rico, American Expansion, and the Constitution* (Duke University Press, 2001). She served as a law clerk to Judge José A. Cabranes on the Second Circuit Court of Appeals and to Justice Stephen G. Breyer on the U.S. Supreme Court.

**Sarah A. Seo** is a professor of law at Columbia University Law School. She is a legal historian of criminal law and procedure in the twentieth-century United States. Her book, *Policing the Open Road: How Cars Transformed American Freedom* (Harvard University Press, 2019), examines the history of the automobile to explain the evolution of Fourth Amendment jurisprudence and to explore the problem of police discretion in a society committed to the rule of law.

**Mitra Sharafi** is Evjue-Bascom Professor of Law at the University of Wisconsin–Madison, where she is affiliated with history, legal studies, and the Center for South Asia. Her first book, *Law and Identity in Colonial South Asia: Parsi Legal Culture, 1772–1947* was awarded the Law and Society Association's 2015 Hurst Prize. She is currently working on her second book project, *Fear of the False: Forensic Science in Colonial India*. She was a Davis Center fellow (Fall 2018) and an ACLS Burkhardt fellow (2018). Her research has been recognized by the Institute for Advanced Study, the Andrew W. Mellon Foundation, the National Endowment for the Humanities, the National Science Foundation, and the Social Science Research Council. Sharafi hosts the South Asian Legal History Resources website and has been a regular contributor to the Legal History Blog.

**Laura Weinrib** is the Fred N. Fishman Professor of Constitutional Law at Harvard Law School, Suzanne Young Murray Professor at the Harvard Radcliffe Institute, and a faculty affiliate in the Harvard University Department of History. A legal historian, her scholarship explores the intersection of constitutional law and labor law in the United States. She is the author of *The Taming of Free Speech: America's Civil Liberties Compromise* (Harvard University Press, 2016), which traces the emergence during the first half of the twentieth century of a constitutional and court-centered concept of civil liberties as a defining feature of American democracy. Her articles, essays, and book chapters have explored a wide range of subjects in American legal history, as well as constitutional law, labor law, and law and literature.

# Introduction

## Rewriting the Boundaries of Legal History

*Kenneth W. Mack and Jacob Katz Cogan*

What is legal history? Legal history is the historical study of something we call law, and the study of something we might call by the name of society, culture, institutions, practices, or many other things. As one recent essay by Hendrik Hartog, a leading practitioner in the field who has shaped the careers of the contributors to this volume, has termed it:

> [T]he law we study may become portraits and evocations of localized and particularized and plural understandings and ways of being, explorations of spaces and practices that are apart from what lawyers or legislators will ordinarily recognize as "law."[1]

The subject of legal history is, in short, the study of pluralism in law and life. It is the study of the multiple rules, norms, and customs with which we organize things such as families, communities, and the institutions of governance and economic life, as well as those that organize the more formal rules, politics, practices, ideas, and discourses that we often identify as law. It is legal *history*, so it is the study of all these things in the context of some past society that is not our own, but a past that can be made legible to us and that can be related, in some mediated way, to the pressing questions of the day. Legal history is the study of the multiple regimes of rules, norms, and customs encompassed in what we call law, and the study of those multiple regimes in all other domains of life. And it is the study of how all those things interact with one another. If you are doing history, it's likely that some aspect of what you are doing is legal history.[2]

In recent years, legal history has become a central field on which writers and scholars in disparate areas of historical scholarship inquire about the past. Law and legal study have become a field that unites the historical study of empires with microhistory, that links the revived study of political history with narratives of everyday life, and that connects the study of transnational things with the language of the irrepressibly

[1] Hendrik Hartog, "Four Fragments on Doing Legal History, or Thinking with and against Willard Hurst," *Law and History Review* 39 (2021): 835–65.

[2] Of course, one might offer multiple definitions of what it means to engage in the enterprise of legal history. The enterprise might be simply "just what legal historians (both those credentialed professionally and those who do legal history without formal credentials) do" as they teach and write about the subject. Hendrik Hartog, "Response: A Muddle in the Middle," *Law and Social Inquiry* 44 (2019): 534, 535. Or it might be both a more diffuse and more focused inquiry, for instance, "to understand legal sources—as existing in historical time." Hartog, "Four Fragments," 835.

Kenneth W. Mack and Jacob Katz Cogan, *Introduction* In: *In Between and Across.* Edited by: Kenneth W. Mack and Jacob Katz Cogan, Oxford University Press. © Oxford University Press 2024. DOI: 10.1093/oso/9780197680995.003.0001

local. Legal history, as one scholar notes, offers the chance to see "familiar impulses and practices—those we identify with Western families and market capitalism and contractualism and global mobility—become strange and slightly different."[3] It allows us to critique what is familiar and understand what is different. Works of legal history now win prestigious scholarly prizes and garner attention from publics far outside of scholarly circles.[4] The boundaries between the history of law and the history of everything else are now quite porous. Whether one is asking questions about the origins of the carceral state, the relationship between slavery and capitalism, the history of migration flows and empires, the longer story of human rights, the building of the straight state, the role of religion in public life, or many others, there is a shared belief that law and its history matter, and matter a great deal.[5]

It was not always so. A generation ago, legal historians were still trying to convince others of the simple proposition that law was an important object of study. Social history was then an insurgent field, having emerged in the context of the social movements and anticolonial struggles of the second half of the twentieth century. Its core claim was that historians should study those excluded from power rather than subjects such as law, which to many appeared to be simply the technology of the powerful.[6] Leftist scholars, by contrast, tended to see law as merely superstructural, with the real forces of protest, repression, continuity, and change located elsewhere. For them, law seemed to be a simple reflection of some other, more basic historical processes.[7] By that time, economists had come to dominate the study of capitalism and its relationship to larger societal forces. These scholars often took it for granted that the real action in economic life lay in markets, which were taken to be more or less autonomous from law, or as only needing simple, predictable legal rules to work their magic.[8]

[3] Hendrik Hartog, "Somedays, I Have Second Thoughts," *Law and Social Inquiry* 40 (2015): 519, 529.

[4] See, for example, John Fabian Witt, *Lincoln's Code: The Laws of War in American History* (New York: Free Press, 2012); Annette Gordon-Reed, *The Hemingses of Monticello: An American Family* (New York: W.W. Norton, 2008).

[5] See, for example, Elizabeth Hinton, *From the War on Poverty to the War on Crime: The Making of Mass Incarceration in America* (Cambridge: Harvard University Press, 2016); Sven Beckert and Christine Desan, *American Capitalism: New Histories* (New York: Columbia University Press, 2018); Claire Priest, *Credit Nation: Property Laws and Legal Institutions in Early America* (Princeton: Princeton University Press, 2021); Lauren Benton and Richard J. Ross, eds., *Legal Pluralism and Empires, 1500–1850* (New York: New York University Press, 2013); Samuel Moyn, *The Last Utopia: Human Rights in History* (Cambridge: Harvard University Press, 2010); Margot Canaday, *The Straight State: Sexuality and Citizenship in Twentieth-Century America* (Princeton: Princeton University Press, 2009); Sarah Barringer Gordon, *The Spirit of the Law: Religious Voices and the Constitution in Modern America* (Cambridge: Harvard University Press, 2010).

[6] See, for example, Hendrik Hartog, "Introduction to Symposium on 'Critical Legal Histories,'" *Law and Social Inquiry* 37 (2012): 147–54; Kenneth W. Mack, "Law and Local Knowledge in the History of the Civil Rights Movement (reviewing Tomiko Brown-Nagin, *Courage to Dissent: Atlanta and the Long History of the Civil Rights Movement*)," *Harvard Law Review* 125 (2012): 1018–40. Some groups of scholars, particularly in African American history, had long argued for the importance of law for the disempowered. See, for example, W. E. B. Du Bois, *Black Reconstruction: An Essay Toward a History of the Part in Which Black Folk Played in the Attempt to Reconstruct Democracy in America, 1860–1880* (New York: Harcourt Brace, 1935).

[7] Hartog, "Introduction to Symposium on 'Critical Legal Histories.'" One canonical work that had outsized influence in making the case for law's importance was Morton J. Horwitz, *The Transformation of American Law, 1780–1860* (Cambridge: Harvard University Press, 1977).

[8] Sven Beckert and Christine Desan, "Introduction," in *American Capitalism*. 1–34.

By the 1980s and early 1990s, a new generation of scholars had organized the modern field of legal history around what had once seemed like as a set of counterintuitive claims. Some argued that phenomena such as working-class consciousness, the cultures of subaltern communities, or the structure of family life were not independent of law, but rather that legal rules, doctrines, and institutions helped "constitute" them, in the language of the time. In turn, the consciousness of ordinary people worked its way into formal legal rules, doctrines, statutes, and institutions, as insurgent groups pressed their claims on the state. Institutions such as the American Society for Legal History and, later, the J. Willard Hurst Summer Institute for Legal History, played an important role in promoting a continuing conversation between legal historians with and without law degrees, and historians teaching in law schools and elsewhere, and to meld them into a common enterprise. Some scholars who did not identify as legal historians were drawn into the field by the allure of archival legal sources, while other scholars made the opposite journey. Legal historians settled on the proposition that law and everything else were mutually constitutive.[9] Pluralism became the order of the day, as one now-classic account framed legal history as a narrative of contending social orders, each of which presented itself as law.[10]

Indeed, legal historians began to focus on the blurring of boundaries that are now so familiar in the freshest of modern scholarship, such as those between markets and politics; between identity and state power; and between national borders and the flows of people, capital, and ideas around the world. Law became the technology—a set of innovative tools and new sources of knowledge—that allowed historians to imagine and think creatively across the boundaries of their fields. This is not to say that scholars had never thought past boundaries and borders, but rather that legal

[9] For summaries of these developments, see, for example, Robert Gordon, *Taming the Past: Essays on Law in History and History in Law* (New York: Cambridge University Press, 2017); Christopher Tomlins, "What Is Left of the Law and Society Paradigm after Critique? Revisiting Gordon's Critical Legal Histories," *Law and Social Inquiry* 37 (2012): 155–66; Michael Grossberg, "Social History Update: 'Fighting Faiths' and the Challenges of Legal History," *Journal of Social History* 25 (1991): 191–201; Daniel T. Ernst, "Law and American Political Development, 1877–1938," *Reviews in American History* 26 (1998): 205–19; Hendrik Hartog, "The Constitution of Aspiration and 'The Rights that Belong to Us All,'" *Journal of American History* 74 (1987): 1013–34; William E. Forbath, Hendrik Hartog, and Martha Minow, "Introduction: Legal Histories from Below," *Wisconsin Law Review* (1985): 759–66. For more recent work that pushes the argument forward, particularly in the ways that ordinary people help constitute the formal law, see Dylan C. Penningroth, *Before the Movement: The Hidden History of Black Civil Rights* (New York: Liveright, 2023); Kate Masur, *Until Justice be Done: America's First Civil Rights Movement: From the Revolution to Reconstruction* (New York: W. W. Norton, 2021); Alejandro de law Fuente and Ariela J. Gross, *Becoming Free, Becoming Black: Race, Freedom, and Law in Cuba, Virginia, and Louisiana* (New York: Cambridge University Press, 2020); Martha S. Jones, *Birthright Citizens: A History of Race and Rights in Antebellum America* (New York: Cambridge University Press, 2018); Michelle A. McKinley, *Fractional Freedoms: Slavery, Intimacy, and Legal Mobilization in Colonial Lima, 1600–1700* (New York: Cambridge University Press, 2018); Daniel J. Sharfstein, *The Invisible Line: Three American Families and the Secret Journey from Black to White* (New York: Penguin Press, 2011); Laura F. Edwards, *The People and their Peace: Legal Culture and the Transformation of the Transformation of Inequality in the Post-Revolutionary South* (Chapel Hill: University of North Carolina Press, 2009); William E. Nelson, *The Legalist Reformation: Law, Politics, and Ideology in New York, 1920–1980* (Chapel Hill: University of North Carolina Press, 2001).

[10] Hendrik Hartog, "Pigs and Positivism," *Wisconsin Law Review* 1985: 899–935. See also Hendrik Hartog, *The Trouble with Minna: A Case of Slavery and Emancipation in the Antebellum North* (Chapel Hill: University of North Carolina Press, 2018).

historians helped bring those kinds of projects into renewed focus and prominence as they modernized their own fields.[11]

That kind of transgressive practice was aided by larger trends, both within and outside of historical writing. By the 1980s, Theda Skocpol and others were mounting influential efforts to "bring the state back in," to make law and state power relevant again.[12] During the next decades, the field would weather, and incorporate, external challenges from legal scholarship, the humanities, and the humanistic social sciences, particularly from critical legal studies, feminist theory, subaltern studies, and what was then called the linguistic turn.[13] By the early years of the new millennium, revivals of entire fields of study were under way, including the history of capitalism, new forms of political history, and transnational history. Scholars in these newly prominent areas often viewed law as a field that united markets with politics, subaltern consciousness with the imaginations of the political elite, and local phenomena with global trends.[14] There were other insurgent modes of legal scholarship, such as critical race theory, which began as a movement of law professors of color but later acquired vast influence by foregrounding the role of law in reproducing racial inequality and in constituting the complex social identities with which we move through the world. Critical race theory also injected new terms, such as intersectionality, into the scholarly and popular discourse.[15] By the 2010s, many scholars and activists sought to reconstitute many of these trends into new formulations such as that of racial capitalism.[16]

[11] Kunal Parker persuasively argues, for instance, that the blurring of the boundary between law and everything else has a long and complex history. See Kunal M. Parker, "Approaches to the Study of Law as a Social Phenomenon," in Austin Sarat and Patricia Ewick, eds., *The Handbook of Law and Society* (Hoboken, N.J.: John Wiley & Sons, 2015), 56–70.

[12] Theda Skocpol, "Bringing the State Back In: Strategies of Analysis in Current Research," in Peter B. Evans, Dietrich Rueschemeyer, and Theda Skocpol, eds, *Bringing the State Back In* (New York: Cambridge University Press, 1985); Stephen Skowronek, *Building a New American State: The Expansion of National Administrative Capacities, 1877–1920* (New York: Cambridge University Press, 1982); Ernst, "Law and American Political Development."

[13] For some of that narrative, see Laura Kalman, *The Strange Career of Legal Liberalism* (New Haven: Yale University Press, 2008); William W. Fisher, III, "Texts and Contexts: The Application to American Legal History of the Methodologies of Intellectual History," *Stanford Law Review* 49 (1997): 1065–110; Hartog, "Introduction to Symposium on 'Critical Legal Histories'"; Hartog, "Response: A Muddle in the Middle."

[14] See, for example, William J. Novak, *New Democracy: The Creation of the Modern American State* (Cambridge: Harvard University Press, 2022); Meg Jacobs, William J. Novak, & Julian E. Zelizer, eds., *The Democratic Experiment: New Directions in American Political History* (Princeton: Princeton University Press, 2009); Paul A. Kramer, "Embedding Capital: Political-Economic History, the United States, and the World," *Journal of the Gilded Age and Progressive Era* 15 (2016): 331–62; Emma Rothschild, *An Infinite History: The Story of a Family in France Over Three Centuries* (Princeton: Princeton University Press, 2021); Rebecca J. Scott, *Freedom Papers: An Atlantic Odyssey in the Age of Emancipation* (Cambridge: Harvard University Press, 2012).

[15] For helpful guides, see Khiara M. Bridges, *Critical Race Theory: A Primer* (St. Paul, MN: Foundation Press, 2018); Kimberlé Williams Crenshaw, "Race Liberalism and the Deradicalization of Racial Reform," *Harvard Law Review* 130 (2017): 2298–2319; "Critical Race Theory/Law and Literature: Patricia Williams," in James R. Hackney, Jr., *Legal Intellectuals in Conversation: Reflections on the Construction of Contemporary American Legal Theory* (New York: New York University Press, 2012), 112–27. Early critical race theorists, in turn, built on the pioneering works of legal history such as Mary Frances Berry, *Black Resistance, White Law: A History of Constitutional Racism* (New York: Appleton-Century-Crofts, 1971); and A. Leon Higginbotham, Jr., *In the Matter of Color: Race and the Legal Process: The Colonial Period* (New York: Oxford University Press, 1978).

[16] Destin Jenkins and Justin Leroy, "Introduction," in their *Histories of Racial Capitalism* (New York: Columbia University Press, 2021); K-Sue Park, "Money, Mortgages, and the Conquest of America," *Law and Social Inquiry* 41 (2016): 1006–35.

The revival of interest in law across many fields was also spurred by trends beyond the confines of scholarly inquiry. In the post-9/11 world, suddenly the intersections of state power with surveillance and violence became the object of historical inquiry, and the histories of entire fields, such as those of human rights and international law, came to be rethought.[17] The aftermath of the 2007–2008 financial crisis helped reinforce and deepen the emerging trend to revive the study of political economy as a field of inquiry.[18] The growing consciousness of what came to be called mass incarceration spurred fresh inquiries into the long history of what was now being called the carceral state.[19] In addition, renewed debates over the presence of racial and religious minorities within many nations, and the movement of ethnic and racial outsiders across borders, prompted renewed attention to the role of law in policing what some called "the borders of belonging" within states, as well as the movement of persons across state borders.[20] Whether it is the emergence of an immigration regime, a constitution, a code of law for slavery, or a social policy regime, the formal rules of law have traditionally helped scholars mark off one thing from another, geographically, temporally, or conceptually. It is that very same feature of marking that has helped legal historians use law as a way of thinking past and across boundaries and borders.

The once-transgressive claims of legal history—about the permeability of borders of all kinds—have now been taken up across many fields and continue to generate novel reimaginations of the past and future. Many of the most pressing questions concerning the past and future of historical scholarship are now being asked through the prism of legal history, broadly conceived. What was once radical has become a commonplace assumption in historical writing across many fields. Legal history, broadly conceived, seems to mark much of the most exciting work that is redrawing the boundaries of historical scholarship in many areas of study. *In Between and Across: Legal History without Boundaries* gathers some of the newest and freshest work by both younger and established scholars who are carrying forward that project and extending it into new areas of historical inquiry. It captures the best of the new and innovative tools and questions that have made law a central plane of inquiry,

[17] See, for example, Lauren A. Benton and Lisa Ford, *Rage for Order: The British Empire and the Origins of International Law, 1800–1850* (Cambridge: Harvard University Press, 2016); Tamar Herzog, *Frontiers of Possession: Spain and Portugal in Europe and the Americas* (Cambridge: Harvard University Press, 2015); Witt, *Lincoln's Code*; Moyn, *The Last Utopia*; Lynn Hunt, *Inventing Human Rights: A History* (New York: W.W. Norton, 2007); Elizabeth Borgwardt, *A New Deal for the World: America's Vision of Human Rights* (Cambridge: Harvard University Press, 2005); Giorgio Agamben, *State of Exception*, Kevin Attell, trans. (Chicago: University of Chicago Press, 2005).

[18] Sven Beckert and Christine Desan, "Introduction," in *American Capitalism*, 1–34; Jeremy Adelman and Jonathan Levy, "The Rise and Fall of Economic History," *Chronicle of Higher Education*, December 1, 2014.

[19] See, for example, James Foreman, Jr, *Locking Up Our Own: Crime and Punishment in Black America* (New York: Farar, Straus, and Giroux, 2017); Hinton, *From the War on Poverty to the War on Crime*; Khalil Gibran Muhammad, *The Condemnation of Blackness: Race, Crime, and the Making of Modern America* (Cambridge: Harvard University Press, 2010).

[20] See, for example, Sunil S. Amrith, *Crossing the Bay of Bengal: The Furies of Nature and the Fortunes of Migrants* (Cambridge: Harvard University Press, 2013); Mae M. Ngai, *Impossible Subjects: Illegal Aliens and the Making of Modern America* (Princeton: Princeton University Press, 2004). On the borders of belonging, see Barbara Young Welke, *Law and the Borders of Belonging in the Long Nineteenth Century United States* (Cambridge: Cambridge University Press, 2010).

charts novel directions for the field, and poses broader questions concerning the past, present, and future.

*In Between and Across* had its origins in a conference on the past and future of legal history held at Princeton University in late 2018 to mark the retirement of the well-known historian Hendrik ("Dirk") Hartog. The conferees presented forward-looking papers based on original research, with commentary by senior scholars. The attendees resolved to push beyond the accepted modes of inquiry concerning the relationship between law and everything else, and to put forward new organizing metaphors, themes, and modes of inquiry for the field. The topics for the papers ranged in geographic focus across the globe from British-ruled Australia, to colonial India and Malaysia, to the United States. They ranged creatively from reimagining the role of law and lawyers in the long history of human rights, to rethinking the timelines that organize the bedrock narratives of constitutional history, to reworking the story of the origins of stockholder challenges to corporate transactions.

What unites the essays gathered in this book is a call to arms to sketch the future direction for scholars, teachers, and readers of history in which law provides a central plane on which to rethink the boundaries that often divide histories by region, subject, and method. What has made legal history into an exciting and productive subfield of the discipline has been the potential for law to become the technology that allows scholars to talk across the boundaries of their usual modes of inquiry. Legal history provides the language to talk across national borders, with the realization that law flows across national borders along with peoples, ideas, goods, and capital. The history of law and legal institutions allows scholars to talk simultaneously about politics as well as societies and economies, with the realization that law provides the language of politics and at the same time constitutes, and is constituted by, markets and other social relations. Legal history was once imagined, both by its practitioners and by those outside the field, to be an enterprise with a significant degree of separation from the history of everything else, but it has now made itself into an innovative way of talking about phenomena, ideas, and institutions seemingly far from the reach of traditional legal institutions. Those who modernized the field, and their successors in the new millennium, helped make law itself into an innovative mode of inquiry by recasting legal history as a metalanguage—a way of talking about other things—that enables historians to see beyond the boundaries that have divided their disparate fields.

As captured in the title of this book, *In Between and Across*, the historiographical intervention that connects these essays is one that acknowledges the boundaries that have separated out different modes of historical inquiry, but views law as a way of talking across them. In so doing, it brings together and goes beyond the methodological innovations of recent years and pushes further against the bounds that still organize the field of historical inquiry. What made the legal history of the past generation so exciting was the potential for law to be a way of talking across important boundaries that helped constitute the field of history. Where we once talked about having conversations between political history and economic history, engagement with law helped steer the conversation into political economy.[21] Where there was

[21] See, for example, Beckert and Desan, "Introduction," in *American Capitalism*. 1–34.

once an effort to talk about society and politics together, analyses of law and legal institutions helped scholars talk about the new political history as something that incorporates rather than competes with social history.[22] Where once law and constitutions provided the means to talk across the geographic and jurisdictional borders that separated national histories from one another, legal history, broadly conceived, helped scholars constitute new fields, such as transnational history, that reimagined the limits of the nation-state.

Yet, in talking across these bounds, historians found themselves eventually redrawing the boundaries themselves. Law was the language of translation between one field and another, and eventually of the transformation of the fields themselves. The contributors to this book take up that challenge and push up against the new bounds that our reconstituted histories have erected for themselves—bounds of time, space, and methodology. The legal history that is set out in this volume is one that seeks to blur and rework those boundaries and to recognize and embrace the contradictions that disciplinary categories have sought to resolve. Each of the contributors to this book share a commitment to the exploration of law as a field of study that crosses boundaries of disciplines, geography, and methods. What unifies them is the proposition that law can play a unique role of translation, and eventually transformation, not just by moving beyond certain categories of analysis but by redrawing the categories themselves. By roving across boundaries and by embracing complications that are found in the "in between," legal history can be a method of reimagining the past and future of the writing of history.

As represented in the essays gathered in this book, the legal history of the future might be organized around three broad themes. These themes, of course, are merely illustrative organizational frameworks, and many of these essays encompass more than one of them, as well as other broad themes. The first of these themes might be called the political economy of time. Political economy has been a core subject in the revival of fields such as the history of capitalism and political history. But time (or more specifically the timing of economic development) in such accounts is often imagined as moving primarily in familiar directions—toward the creation of industrial capitalism for instance, or forward to the welfare state, or neoliberalism. Scholars often link these transitions to particular legal developments—stable legal rules for capitalism, for instance, or deregulation and the removal of legal constraints for neoliberalism. There have been many groundbreaking works that, for instance, have backdated the emergence of market economies, or that have shown that slavery was in fact a precursor to industrial capitalism rather than its antithesis. But the general direction of political economy is often taken for granted—moving from markets to industry to the welfare state to neoliberalism. The point of the essays in the book isn't just that developments occurred earlier or later than what is commonly assumed, but that the direction of developments in political economy is not always clear or even ultimately resolved in some clear way. The essays gathered here complicate both the timing and inflection points of economic development, and attempt to revise and rework core assumptions about the development of capitalism and the state.

[22] See, for example, Novak, *New Democracy*.

Matthew Axtell's "Views from Rathole Mountain: A Lawscape Journey through Old Virginia," takes as its project the nature of commerce in the nineteenth century, and challenges the usual expectation that the time of development moved forward, as commercial development pushed goods, ideas, and markets across the lines of geography that divided American states from one another. Taking as his subject a "lawscape"—encompassed in the political economy of economic development in early nineteenth-century Virginia—Axtell reworks the presumed direction of development in early capitalist transformation. Rather than moving in the direction of increased commerce and development (with the accompanying assumption that the alternative is "failure"), Axtell tells a story of ambivalence. To what extent is the ability to think up and complete a grand public works development project a unique triumph of modern democratic state-building, or a subversion of some of its processes? Axtell mines the archives of a state-backed Virginia canal company that found it difficult to leverage the state's power of eminent domain in Old Dominion courts when faced with folk opposition to the project on many fronts during the 1800s. All of the actors in his story believe that a proposed canal linking the eastern and western parts of Virginia is important, but they differ markedly on why this is so. Axtell's actors push a variety of projects that often have little to do with increased commerce and development. The story resolves itself into a studied ambivalence, which Axtell traces down to the present by walking along the present-day lawscape of the presumed canal himself. Historians have taken the direction of time for granted, he argues in his chapter, assuming that it leads to ever-expanding narratives of commerce. Axtell, by contrast, argues that for the participants in debates about the political economy of early nineteenth-century Virginia, the time of development and commerce moved in contradictory directions.

Donna Dennis, in "The Rise of Retail Stockholder Litigation and the Creation of the Plaintiff's Bar in American Business Law, 1930–1950," by contrast, focuses on the dyad of profit-making versus public interest in the story of lawyers in a developing capitalist economy. Her target is the familiar direction of time that leads from profit-making, whether of the corporate or the "ambulance-chasing" type, to the public-spirited ideas of civil and human rights that would dominate the second half of the twentieth century. Her vehicle is the retail stockholder suit, much criticized in legal literature as a simple vehicle for profit-making by enterprising attorneys. Dennis directly challenges the familiar narrative that leads from private to public interest, from profits to public service, and from self-interest to human rights. In contrast to the dominant, pejorative view of stockholders' attorneys—a perspective that persists to this day—Dennis argues that the pioneers of the field (a tight network whose leaders included David Podell and Abraham Pomerantz) were innovative, conscientious lawyers, who combined formidable trial skills with sophistication in corporate finance, accounting, and governance. Focusing on the lawyers who helped invent the modern stockholder suit, she argues that they traversed many boundaries, working to imbue that form of litigation with an ethical sensibility, and adopting a variety of positions on the complicated politics of the New Deal, socialism, and many other causes. By the time she reaches the Nuremberg trials, which typically serve as a convenient marker for the emergence of human rights ideas, one loses the sense that the trials are either the beginning or end of any particular narrative. Rather, they seem more of a midpoint in a narrative of public and private interest, of human rights and state power, that remains unresolved to this day.

Felicia Kornbluh's "Private Law, Public Welfare, Marital Ideals, and the Gender Binary ... or, What I Learned at the Socio-Legal Revolution," by contrast, takes on the familiar divide between the policy response to capitalism in the nineteenth century, when social provision was often made through the mechanism of the private family, and the twentieth, when historians have argued that such provision shifted partly away from the family and toward the growing welfare state. Kornbluh draws on current research about the gendered nature of domestic social policy, and particularly the ways in which racialized stereotypes about men and masculinity have shaped policy, to argue that much of what scholars have written about common-law coverture in the "long nineteenth century" is relevant today. Surveying more recent developments in social welfare policy, Kornbluh contends that the image of the private family as the primary means of social welfare provision has reappeared and become the organizing basis for much of recent policy. Kornbluh argues that even coverture, the legal idea that organized the nineteenth century family into a unit with the husband at its head, has reappeared in recent times. Motherhood and fatherhood have become the template for social welfare policy, which has focused on making citizens into good mothers and fathers. She directly challenges the political economy of welfare provision, which is commonly seen as moving from private social provision toward public and then perhaps to neoliberalism. Kornbluh focuses on the welfare reform law of 1996 and its legacy over the following twenty years, as a case study in the significance of gendered analysis for the interpretation of public policy and of the continuing relevance of ideas of husbandly and wifely obligation. Kornbluh explores this by invoking the landmark scholarship that was once thought to describe the nineteenth century, rather than the late twentieth or the twenty-first. The time of the welfare state, in her account, almost loops back on itself, repeating themes that had long been thought to have been banished from the political landscape. Along the way, Kornbluh is also making a point about method, blurring policy history with the social history of the family.

Maribel Morey's "Power of the Purse: How 'The Philanthropic North' Has Helped Determine Which Individuals, Groups, and Ideas in the Black Freedom Struggle Will Thrive Nationally," examines the long history of the Black Freedom and its intersection with the larger world of political economy in the form of elite white philanthropic foundations such as Carnegie, Rockefeller, and Ford foundations and the Phelps Stokes and Garland Funds. All the way back to the first glimmers of freedom for the formerly enslaved, she argues, men such as the banker George Foster Peabody cast their eye on Black education in the South, just as Blacks were engaged in efforts to establish their own educational institutions. By the turn of the century, such men had been joined in these efforts by industrialists such as John Rockefeller and Andrew Carnegie, even as some of these industrialists battled with labor organizers and contended with Black strikebreakers. That, in turn, Morey argues, intersected with a pitched debate among Black activists and leaders such as Booker T. Washington, W. E. B. Du Bois and Carter G. Woodson over how their own educational projects might affect Black life and racial equality. Ultimately, Morey argues, even Du Bois couldn't escape the disciplinary gaze of the philanthropists and the need to speak their language. The ultimate winner in that competition, however, was the Swedish economist Gunnar Myrdal, whose *An American Dilemma: The Negro Problem and Modern Democracy*, rather the proposed projects of Black activists like Du Bois, would be the text that would shape race relations in the mid-twentieth century. Morey shows how organizations such as the National Association for the Advancement of Colored People (NAACP) and their Legal Defense Fund (LDF) were profoundly shaped by the guiding hand of white philanthropy, as the influence of philanthropy would help determine which activists, agendas and organizations would gain national recognition and which would not. Morey explicitly invites those grappling with similar questions today to learn from the history of elite funders and their role in shaping the participants and objectives of movements along BIPOC peoples in the United States.

Sarah Seo's "'Kindred to Treason': Conspiracy Laws in the United States" challenges the presumed movement of time encompassed in a major organizing theme of recent historiography: state-building. The very term incorporates an implicit idea of the time of political economy within its contours—often assuming that the history of the modern state moves forward toward modern social welfare and disciplinary state bureaucracy. Seo offers a countervailing view in her interpretation of the early history of treason and conspiracy prosecutions in the aftermath of putative armed rebellions against the United States. In the early years of the republic, Seo argues, national political leaders struggled with the question of how to enforce federal authority in an era with little enforcement bureaucracy, and in which widespread flouting of federal law called into question the power of the national government. Seo traces the evolution of treason prosecutions, and later the creation of a general federal crime of conspiracy, finally achieved in the context of the Civil War and Reconstruction, as a response to this problem. By the early twentieth century, she argues, these developments had become so uncontroversial that few questioned the existence of conspiracy as a federal crime, and the long history of its contested creation was now forgotten. The development of conspiracy as a federal crime, she argues, should be seen as an episode of state-building, achieved without the extension of bureaucratic apparatus that might attach to such a project. Indeed, it is implicit in Seo's account that the contours of the familiar strong state/weak state debate should be completely rethought, as a state might be "strong" and "weak" along various dimensions.

The second major theme represented in this volume is law as a medium for rethinking and reorienting the spatial dimensions of history. Much recent scholarship has pushed the historical imagination across familiar geographic boundaries, such as those between nation-states, or between empires and colonies, or the bounds separating members of widely dispersed racial or ethnic groups. The essays gathered in this volume push that trend further and show the reorientation of historical space to be an even more complex and contested endeavor than it is often presumed to be. Spatial boundaries of many kinds remain important, but the point of the essays is to draw into question which boundaries are doing the work and which seem less important, as ideas, people, and practices flow across the conventional geographic boundaries that organize historical scholarship. Legal rules, norms, customs, and practices, as they simultaneously mark off boundaries and flow across them to erect new ones, seem particularly ripe for such an enterprise. Legal history foregrounds questions of multiple and overlapping geographies and jurisdictions, foregrounding, as well, the questions of pluralism that sit at the core of the modern field.

Catherine L. Evans's "The Case as Episode: Murder and Migration in Colonial Australia" examines the British Empire and the multiple discourses that constitute it through the prism of seemingly the smallest of things: a case about an attack on a pig-keeper in late nineteenth-century Australia. Evans is directly challenging several well-known boundaries that organize historical scholarship, such as those that separate the new global history and the familiar microhistory, and those that mark off novel approaches to transnational history from the history of the irrepressibly local. In her account, the global and transnational can be viewed through the most local of things, in particular through the use of law to discipline violence within the British Empire. In her story, a criminal trial prompted by an attack on Chinese migrants became a vehicle for extended commentary, within British Australia, on what it means to travel from other parts of the empire (such as Ireland or Tasmania) to Australia, on the status of white Australians within a global empire, and on the translation of Chinese migrants' testimony in the courts of the British Empire and in the worldviews of white Australians. Evans is also making a subtle point about time, and about the contradictory futures that the actors in her story imagine for British law—that it might be extended throughout the empire and incorporate various peoples, and simultaneously that the passage of time might be stopped and British law preserved from further change.

Maeve Glass's "The Chain and the Rope: Illuminating Constitutional Traditions" is a dramatic reworking of some of the core stories of American constitutional history—stories of a journey from slavery to freedom, from contested citizenship for racial others to full inclusion in American constitutional traditions, from the First Reconstruction to the Second, and from state-based citizenship to national rights. Glass argues that one can see all this in the case of a putatively enslaved woman named Jane Johnson who, in Philadelphia in 1855, with the help of several black porters and a white abolitionist, walked away from the man who claimed her as property. The subsequent contests involving the man who wanted to reclaim her as his property, Glass argues, curiously involved little talk that would sound familiar to readers of conventional constitutional history—talk of freedom, or of equal citizenship or of national rights. Instead, the arguments in and out of court focused on something that was asserted to predate the American colonies, that had traveled across the Atlantic to the New World, and that would continue long after the controversy over Johnson's body had ceased—republican citizenship for the white men whose lives were touched in various ways by her case. In that cacophony of citizenship talk, Glass argues, there was little room for a Black woman's claim to equal citizenship and belonging to be heard—although her voice does briefly break through here and there. Glass is posing the question of what, exactly, organizes the writing and telling of constitutional history. Is the main story one of change over time in which the un-righted acquire rights and citizenship in an expanding nation, or is it story of deep-seated continuity where local hierarchies persist even through revolutionary changes in the formal constitutional order? Glass is suggesting that it is easier to see change, but that the stories of persistence are also there in the archive if we are discerning enough to see them.

Mitra Sharafi's "South Asians at the Inns of Court: Empire, Expulsion, and Redemption circa 1900" tracks the movement of Indians to the English Inns of Court for their legal education, their movement from the Inns to England and back to the empire, and their movement back again to the Inns for cases of discipline. Sharafi has unearthed the long-neglected records of the perhaps five thousand students from the British colonies who studied at the Inns—which trained the elite British litigators known as barristers—between 1861 and 1948, highlighting the records of a select few who came in for discipline for alleged misconduct. The prospect of discipline, she argues, illuminates the larger project of the Inns' admission of applicants from the colonies, which was to create "imperial lawyers," colonial subjects who would serve the larger purposes of the imperial project. In particular, Sharafi highlights the accounts of several lawyers, one of whom was accused of unethical and deceptive behavior but ultimately forgiven, and another who was disbarred for anticolonial revolutionary activities but whose case was later revisited in the aftermath of decolonization and the Inns' partial reckoning with their colonial past. In Sharafi's account, racial and colonial identity in the empire was fluid, flowing across the boundaries between the various parts of the empire, but always with the discipline of the Inns, and their project of imperial lawyering, in the background. The "imperial lawyer" was a contested concept, and enterprising colonial attorneys might negotiate its bounds for their own purposes—albeit within limits. She is also making a point about private governance. The vastness of the empire was often administered through private governance, not only through the much-studied joint stock corporations such as the East India Company, but also through lesser-known entities such as the Inns.

The third theme for the future of legal history illustrated by the essays gathered in this book turns to questions of method. As legal historians pressed their claims on the broader corpus of historical scholarship, their core interventions have always sounded in themes of boundaries and methods. Social historians challenged the continued relevance of the study of institutions, states, governance, and professions. Legal history, in turn, made itself relevant by asking sophisticated questions about how scholars should unite the high with the low, the voices of the elite with those of the masses, the study of institutions and governance with that of social groups far outside the bounds of state power. Those questions might be summed up in the proposition that legal history made itself into an innovative branch of the discipline by asking methodological questions about how to analyze the boundaries between law and everything else. The essays gathered here take that question more or less for granted, and push questions about methods and boundaries into new terrain.

Jessica K. Lowe's "Our Experiences Make Us Who We Are": Lessons from Thomas Ruffin and Dirk Hartog," for instance, takes up one of the most fundamental of the boundaries that defines the historical method: that between experience, memory, and action. We tend to think of experience and memory as the raw materials for law, with law providing the technology that might translate them into political action. Lowe, however, argues that these things are far more closely intertwined. Focusing on *State v. Mann*, one of the two most infamous legal opinions concerning American slavery (the other being *Dred Scott*), and its equally infamous author, North Carolina Supreme Court Justice Thomas Ruffin, Lowe asks what we can learn of this emblematic case by questioning some of the bounds that historians still maintain in writing about it. In *Mann*, Ruffin reversed the criminal conviction of a white man who hired an enslaved person and then shot her, famously writing that "inherent in the relation of master and slave" is the fact that "the power of the master must be absolute to render the submission of the slave perfect." Ruffin and *Mann* have long been productive vehicles for the exploration of judicial duty and moral sentiment in the context of slavery, but Lowe mines Ruffin's life and career for another cause. Focusing on an 1804 letter that a young Ruffin wrote to his father grappling with the morality of slavery, Lowe asks questions about the relationship of the experience of Judge Ruffin, a slaveholder, writing his infamous opinion and his memory of his own letter to his father decades earlier. Lowe even goes further than this, foregrounding her own experiences as a young historian grappling with trauma and simultaneously writing about young Ruffin's encounter with his own trauma, effectively questioning the bounds that separate experience, memory, and action for the historian as well as the historical subject.

Farah Peterson's "Debtor Constitutionalism" questions some of the core methodological assumptions of constitutional history: that such history should reference some written text, and that political legitimacy is tied to a core text—at least in regimes with written constitutions. Even after the events of 1787–89, she argues, many Americans continued to believe in, and act upon, the existence of an unwritten constitution not encompassed in the texts and words prepared by the great white men who remain at the center of constitutional debates to this day. Peterson traces this unwritten constitution through the prism of the repeated use of Indian costume as part of a carnivalesque form of protest in which participants in these insurrectionary actions argued that the norms of the unwritten constitution were being violated, regardless of what the formal constitutional text or its privileged interpreters might say. E. P. Thompson described "counter-theatre" as one consistent element of English crowd actions of the late eighteenth century. American mobs engaged in their own form of theater, which included white men dressing as Native Americans. The symbol of the white man in native dress took on powerful symbolic meaning during the Revolution, and it persisted as a trope of popular protest long into the nineteenth century. Indeed, Peterson's analysis pushes constitutional history across the presumed boundary of 1787, which is supposed to separate an era in which Americans regarded extrajudicial mob protest as legal from one in which the new constitutional text assumed a monopoly on legality. In Peterson's story, the triumph of the written constitution may not have become complete until at least the 1840s (if it did even then).

Christina D. Ponsa-Kraus's "Roosters and Resistance" takes as its methodological challenge the writing of the history of an absence, in this case Puerto Rican social history in the absence of empire. The idea for this chapter occurred after Ponsa-Kraus went looking for the sound of roosters while visiting Puerto Rico. Taking as her subject the legality of cockfighting, a popular pastime in Puerto Rico since at least the eighteenth century, Ponsa-Kraus tells the story of her search for a way of writing the history of this phenomenon, but also asking, "[W]here would I find a description of cockfighting in Puerto Rico that wasn't about Puerto Rico being a colony?"

Ponsa-Kraus's story is, in the end, about the power of the received bounds of a particular historical enterprise—in this case the history of empire—to overwhelm even the capacity of the historian to bring alternative methods to bear on her subject. In the context of Puerto Rico, she argues, the law of empire seems to dominate such that it is difficult to get beyond its bounds. The answer to her question, in the end, is "*nowhere*."

Laura Weinrib's "Law, History, and the Interwar ACLU's Jewish Lawyers," examines the American Civil Liberties Union's turn away from its politically engaged defense of mass picketing, strikes, political dissent, and its antipathy for courts, and toward the modern constitutional and juridical ideas of civil liberties for which it is now known. During that period, many of the ACLU's leading lawyers—who increasingly defined the organization's agenda and steered its activity from direct action to litigation—were Jewish. To many of them, the best bulwark against totalitarianism in America was to prohibit state-sanctioned orthodoxy, whether religious or ideological, even if the target of state suppression was hateful or dangerous speech. That principle, however, manifested itself in vastly differing visions of how civil liberties should be understood and implemented. This chapter considers the influence of ACLU lawyers' religious identities and corresponding concerns about anti-Semitism on the organization's strategies and goals. What did the increasing presence of lawyers, and in particular the Jewish lawyers who had a substantial role in bringing it about, have to do with this turn, she asks? Weinrib surveys the usual methodological approaches to this kind of question and finds them incomplete—at least as applied to the influence of two lawyers in particular, Arthur Garfield Hays and Morris Ernst, on the ACLU's evolution. Weinrib focuses on the vigorous debate, within early twentieth-century Jewish communities, concerning group rights and individual identity, Jewish identification and national belonging. Civil liberties, she argues, was a "badge of belonging" for Jewish lawyers navigating a world of labor collectivism, New Deal bureaucracy, civil rights activism and, above all else, a world that seemed to be slipping into illiberal anti-Semitism, particularly in Europe. Civil liberties advocacy was a way of navigating the cross-currents of the world of the 1930s, which oddly enough, might bear a family resemblance to our own. Weinrib foregrounds that question through the story of her own experience as a public voice on matters of civil liberties and racial prejudice—and that experience's relationship to her own Jewish identity—in the present day.

Taken as a whole, the essays gathered in this volume sketch new boundaries for the history of law to traverse, new organizing metaphors for the study of legal history, and novel ways for legal history to continue to remake itself as an innovative field of study of the past that also points toward the future. Legal history once sketched the bounds of the future of historical inquiry for many reasons. Law and legal institutions were one feature of society that united the quotidian lives of ordinary people and social movements with state power. Law drew the formal boundaries that separated states and nations from each other—and that scholars sought to traverse. Law provided scholars with a sense of movement of historical time, as legal changes marked off the development of capitalism, the modern state, and ideas of civil and human rights. Law and legal changes also helped sketch the development of more ominous features of state power as well, such as surveillance, incarceration, and public violence.

The essays in this volume gather some of the richest work in legal history to sketch new boundaries for the field to cross—boundaries of time, of geography, and of method. Law, broadly conceived, continues to be a technology that crosses borders of many kinds. This book is dedicated to the proposition that, in addition to gathering evidence of its past achievements, legal history should continue to define the future direction of historical inquiry.

# PART I
# THE POLITICAL ECONOMY OF TIME

# 1
# Views from Rathole Mountain
## A Lawscape Journey through Old Virginia

*Matthew Axtell*

> *Poseidon became bored with his sea. He let fall his trident. Silently he sat on the rocky coast and a gull, dazed by his presence, described wavering circles around his head.*
>
> —Franz Kafka, Diaries 1910–1923

In the beginning, the project almost seemed to consist of a lone 57-year-old man in a boat. The man was John Marshall, chief justice of the Supreme Court of the United States. He was charged with the following under Virginia state law: (1) to ascend the James River as it rolled down Virginia's mountains; (2) to mark out a turnpike route between the headwaters of the James and the Greenbrier, the James's nearest counterpart in the west; and (3) to assess the feasibility of navigating along the Greenbrier as it flowed first into the New River, then the Kanawha River, and eventually the mighty Ohio. With U.S. troops fighting Britons in the interior, Marshall set out from Richmond in the fall of 1812. The season had been "remarkably dry," Marshall reported, the traveling "attended with some difficulty." On the James, he removed stones and dragged the boat over boulders, at one point only traveling three miles in two days. A few days later, Marshall hoisted and dragged his vessel over the rocks again, this time over the whole extent of the Greenbrier, only to encounter a waterfall. Finally, after raising the boat by rope over two other unruly spots, he lifted it out one last time to evade a 24-foot drop near the falls of the Kanawha. Entering Virginia's west, the water suddenly lost its "wild and savage aspect." Marshall glided the rest of the way to the Ohio River trouble-free.

Warming his toes by the fire, casting aside the strains of his physical ordeal, John Marshall transmitted a report to the Virginia Assembly in late 1812 declaring success. His work had not really been the effort of one man; as Marshall noted, he traveled with "experienced and judicious boatmen," a "number of hands usually employed in navigation" (probably slaves), and other well-placed white men handpicked by the legislature. For accurate readings of river depths, hazards, and the best route, Marshall also relied upon "testimony" from the inhabitants of the hills and valleys he traversed. Synthesizing his experiences with theirs, Marshall found that a hybrid canal/turnpike connection between the James and Kanawha Rivers was practicable over most sections, well worth the Commonwealth's time and money. Human ingenuity could overcome the river's most "awful and discouraging" segments. Almost every problem

Matthew Axtell, *Views from Rathole Mountain* In: *In Between and Across*. Edited by: Kenneth W. Mack and Jacob Katz Cogan, Oxford University Press. © Oxford University Press 2024. DOI: 10.1093/oso/9780197680995.003.0002

had a technological fix: a sluice system could remove all danger of rocks near the water's surface; a system of locks and canals with horse-drawn boats could overcome the waterfalls; early steamboats could tame the New River. And even if the legislature's interests were "limited to the conveyance of articles," Marshall opined, a mountain waterway could pay for itself as a benevolent act of social engineering. Carrying goods from Richmond over the mountains could connect Virginia "to her sister States in the west," the mobile, hardscrabble shepherds of the mountains gradually transforming themselves into sedentary, governable grain-growers. The "augmentation of the wealth" in western Virginia would add to Virginia's wealth as a whole, "bind[ing] together individuals of different counties" through the creation of a shared "line of communication," the "interchange of good offices," and the exchange of "mutual interest," Marshall predicted.[1]

All that was needed to complete the picture now, Marshall concluded in his report, was a new law, namely a statute from the legislature to authorize a grand public canal connecting Virginia's eastern and western halves. Several years later, Virginia's lawmakers obliged, enacting a new Board of Public Works to oversee a reinvigorated waterway project being built sporadically by a state-chartered corporation since the days of George Washington. Rebranded the "James River and Kanawha Canal Company" in 1835, this company's central aim was to build and extend a canal along the James River from Richmond to the base of the Alleghenies in the middle of the state, connecting then to the Kanawha River by a canal, railroad, or turnpike while clearing river obstructions all the way to the Ohio. Eight million dollars and nearly a half-century later, the company partially met this goal. Through slave and European immigrant labor, a tow-path canal was built from Richmond to Maiden's Adventure, 24 miles west of Richmond, between 1820 and 1824. The waterway extended another 150 miles to Lynchburg by 1840 and then stretched past the Blue Ridge by locks and dams to the mountain town of Buchanan, 198 miles west of Richmond, by 1851. While railroads eventually took its place, the canal was the major commercial thoroughfare through Virginia in its day, carrying salt, plaster, fish, nails, and fertilizer to grain-producers, tobacco-growers, stock-raisers, and colliers in Virginia's west while shipping tobacco, wheat, corn, pig iron, stone, and wood down to Richmond in the east. Prior to 1860, the company's works carried more tonnage than all of Virginia's railroads combined.[2]

Through heroic waterway projects such as these, visionary statesmen across time and space have occasionally attempted to do what Chief Justice Marshall attempted in 1812: to legislate a particular set of legally proscribed land uses practices—what Australian legal scholar Nicole Graham would later call a particular type of

[1] See River Commission Report (December 26, 1812), reprinted in *The Papers of John Marshall, Vol. 7*, ed. Charles Hobson (Chapel Hill: University of North Carolina Press, 1993), 355–9. Marshall's confidence in the ability of long-distance trade to smooth out regional political differences had antecedents in the Early Modern era. See Albert O. Hirschman, *The Passions and the Interests: Political Arguments for Capitalism before Its Triumph* (Princeton: Princeton University Press, 1977).

[2] The signature history of the canal is Wayland F. Dunaway, *History of the James River and Kanawha Company* (New York: Columbia University Press, 1922). See also Ronald Shaw, *Canals for Nation: The Canal Era in the United States* (Lexington: University of Kentucky Press, 1990), 112–17, 269–70.

"lawscape"—into being.[3] In Marshall's era, the idea was already at least as old as the seventeenth-century Enlightenment, where large public works such as France's Canal du Midi began to appear. Long-distance canals sent a very specific message, providing what historian Clarence Glacken called "conspicuous and dramatic evidence" of a particular state or ruling class's ability to tame nature, link populations, and to re-order a series of organically occurring, helter-skelter commercial trade routes into a single, straight, taxable line.[4] The tools to achieve this were often legal in form, centering upon public law statutes chartering corporations to execute the project, usually empowering this entity to condemn land, raise funds, and collect tolls while shielding it from private liability.

Like earlier canal builders, John Marshall and other nineteenth-century Virginians saw the need to wield the state's full array of legal tools to complete this work as a pressing matter of statecraft. "Beyond the Allegheny, an unexpected revolution threatens the Atlantic States in general, the accomplishment of which will create new interests and views in that flourishing and important section of America," a Virginia Assembly committee warned in 1815 while endorsing Marshall's report. A water connection across the mountains, both brought into being and protected by law, provided "the best means of arresting the progress of this revolution," tethering Virginia's west to Richmond once and for all.[5]

And yet, three decades after Marshall's report, a former University of Virginia student named Edgar Allan Poe could still write a believable story titled "A Tale of the Ragged Mountains," telling of "uncouth and fierce races of men" tenanting Old Dominion "groves and caverns" that the Chief Justice's waterway project never reached. While the state's canal company attempted a final extension of locks and dams underneath the Alleghenies between 1853 and 1856, this segment was never completed. Closer to Richmond, some wealthy planters resisted the canal line crossing their land, winning sizeable damage claims against the canal company in court. River traders beyond the mountains often followed suit, holding the company to the letter of its charter to require improved navigation in western waters before the company could collect tolls. All the while, older competing lines of trade flourished, and competing transportation modes appeared, similarly protected by Virginia law. By 1858, the Baltimore and Ohio Railroad shot across the Potomac in the state's north, running parallel to the Chesapeake and Ohio Canal and the federal turnpikes of "the National Road." Farther south, from Richmond, travelers could hitch a ride

[3] See Nicole Graham, *Lawscape: Property, Environment, Law* (New York: Routledge, 2011), 2. Special thanks to Emmanuel Kreike for introducing me to this book.

[4] On the Canal du Midi, see Clarence Glacken, *Traces on the Rhodian Shore: Nature and Culture in Western Thought from Ancient Times to the End of the Eighteenth Century* (Berkeley: University of California Press, 1967), 496. For other examples, see Edward Said, *Orientalism* (New York: Pantheon, 1978), 88–91 (Suez Canal); Michael Adas, *Dominance by Design: Technological Imperatives and America's Civilizing Mission* (Cambridge: Cambridge University Press, 2006), 185–216 (Panama Canal); J. R. McNeill, *Something New Under the Sun: An Environmental History of the Twentieth-Century World* (New York: Norton, 2000), 120–83 (twentieth-century "heroic-scale" water infrastructure). My understanding of the state-building function of large-scale public works projects is indebted to James C. Scott, *Seeing like a State: How Certain Schemes to Improve the Human Condition Have Failed* (New Haven: Yale University Press, 1998).

[5] See Report of the Committee of Roads and Internal Navigation (1815), reprintedin Carter Goodrich, *The Government and the Economy, 1783–1861* (Indianapolis: Bobbs, 1967), 59–77.

with railways such as the Virginia and Tennessee Railroad, taking them as far south as Georgia. By this time, Virginia legislators had imposed multiple water and rail routes on top of the sputtering canal project still in use, running state-financed lines of transport from a Potomac River navigation project in the north to a Roanoke River project stretching to Danville in the south.[6]

As residents and visitors to nineteenth-century Virginia could often attest, the lawscape of the James River and Kanawha Canal was not universal, instead always existing awkwardly alongside other counterparts of both earlier and later provenance. If Justice Marshall had helped to legislate a new lawscape into being, his work was nevertheless fallible, incomplete, easily revised. And if, as historians such as Willard Hurst and William Cronon once noted, legal institutions have often played an important but often hidden role in shaping environments in the American past,[7] the result has not always been in one direction, trending only toward increased state centralization, corporate control, or more concentrated forms of resource extraction. Instead, in some corners, a decentralized set of legal concepts, arguments, and procedures has persisted, allowing less severe environments to remain and sometimes even to appear for the first time. Because of this, while studying the legal and business records of the old James River and Kanawha Canal Company, several years ago I decided to retrace some of John Marshall's old footsteps, to document some of the lawscapes left behind in his unfinished river project's shadow.[8] Here, annotated by some of the legal records that I also came across, is a summary of what was found. If studied with the granularity of a historical ecologist, each river mile that I encountered could probably reveal itself to be the product of a novel set of legal permutations and outcomes carried into the water and imprinted upon the land. For brevity's sake, here are three contrasting but equally representative lawscapes glimpsed over the course of my own abbreviated river journey: one from the canal's beginning, one from its middle, and one from its end.

## I. Lawscape No. 1: Richmond Canal Walk (River Mile 0.0)

Down the hill from Richmond's courthouse district, near the preserved law offices of John Marshall, stands the ideal lawscape that the great chief justice sought to conjure

[6] For a map of the rail network circa 1858, see William Link, *Roots of Secession: Slavery and Politics in Antebellum Virginia* (Chapel Hill: University of North Carolina Press, 2003), 31. For the water network, see William Trout, *A Guide to the Works of the James River and Kanawha Company from the City of Richmond* (McLean: Virginia Canals and Navigation Society, 2002).

[7] SeeWilliam Cronon, *Changes in the Land: Indians, Colonists, and the Ecology of New England* (New York: Hill and Wang, 1983), 54–81; Cronon, "Kennecott Journey: The Paths out of Town," in Cronon et al., eds., *Under an Open Sky: Rethinking America's Western Past* (New York: Norton, 1992), 280, n. 39 (citing James Willard Hurst, *Law and Economic Growth: The Legal History of the Lumber Industry in Wisconsin, 1836–1915* (Cambridge: Harvard University Press, 1964)); Theodore Steinberg, *Nature Incorporated: Industrialization and the Waters of New England* (Cambridge: Cambridge University Press, 1991; 2004).

[8] The physical portion of this journey, taken with my very patient parents, was taken by following the excellent maps and directions found in W. E. Trout, *A Guide to the Works of the James River & Kanawha Company*.

forth in his 1812 river report, artfully restored in miniature form. Seeking out the James River from underneath the highway overpasses in Shockoe Slip, the "Richmond Canal Walk" emerges through a burst of sunlight, protected behind a flood wall built by the U.S. Army Corps of Engineers. Here, you can step onboard a freshly painted canal packet and cruise along a gently curving one-mile line of the restored James River and Kanawha Canal, armored on both sides by modern concrete blocks. And if proceeding by foot is your fancy, you can walk along the tranquil waters of the preserved canal, inspecting historical markers fixed into the bonded gravel pavement over the same distance.

In John Marshall's time, the pleasantly linear commercial lawscape of Richmond's Canal Walk would have taken a great deal of law to build and defend. Not surprisingly, in Virginia's historical tradition the idea of a transmontane canal is said to have a military origin, thought up by General George Washington himself, who in 1784 petitioned the state "to incorporate & encourage private Adventurers" to improve navigation on the state's river. Washington became a founding stockholder of the "James River Company," chartered in 1784 by Virginia's Assembly to achieve this purpose.[9] Private funds alone eventually proved inadequate to extend work, and by 1823 the state legislature had passed a series of laws rechartering the company into a state agent under the complete control of Virginia's Board of Public Works. This version of the James River Company was equipped with formidable government powers, including the ability to condemn land along its canal's route and to proceed with construction without the possibility of being enjoined by any affected landowner.[10] When the company was rechartered again in 1832 as a "mixed enterprise" joint stock company, reverting back to private management, the legislature voted for the company to retain these privileges in essentially the same form.[11]

Nowhere was the way-clearing legal power of the "James River and Kanawha Canal Company" and its predecessors on clearer display than alongside Richmond's riverfront, near the current site of the city's present-day Canal Walk. In 1838, for example, the company condemned one side of a city street serving Richmond's warehouse district to widen the canal, draining the waterway and its turning basin to allow space for the work. Nearby property owners and businessmen who relied upon both the street and the canal to bring their goods to market brought a nuisance suit to stop construction, alleging that a private company had no right to occupy "public highways" and restrain the city's trade. Virginia's Supreme Court of Appeals dismissed their claim. Between 1820 and 1832, the court reasoned in a decision reported as *James River and Kanawha Company v. Anderson*, when the company was solely state-owned, "the company had full power to pass through the city," a power that it had used to build and operate a great canal. In 1832, when the state company was wound up and a new

[9] See Letter from George Washington to Benjamin Harrison, Oct. 10, 1784, reprinted in *The Papers of George Washington, Confederation Series, vol. 2* (Charlottesville: University of Virginia Press, 1992), 86–99 (on Washington's petition); "An act for clearing and improving the navigation of James River" of 1784; "An act for clearing and improving the navigation of Potowmack River" of 1784, reprinted in *A Collection of All Such Acts of the General Assembly of Virginia, of a Public and Permanent Nature, as are Now in Force* (1802), 440–6; app. at 3.

[10] See 1819–20 *Va. Acts* 38–47; 1822–23 *Va. Acts* 50–58.

[11] See 1831–2 *Va. Acts* 73–87.

"mixed enterprise" joint stock company took its place, "everything owned by the old company was transferred to the new," including the power to condemn land and enlarge the canal upon company discretion. Even though it was now managed by a private board and only answerable to its shareholders, the company could still act with relative impunity to take riverfront land as it needed, and to close and reopen its canal when it chose, clothed as it was in a residual public purpose. "The legislature did not consider it proper," Justice John Allen scolded, "that a great public work, intimately connected with the wealth and prosperity of the whole state, should be arrested."[12]

In actuality, especially in its most lasting iteration as a privately managed joint stock company beginning in 1832, the James River and Kanawha Company was far from the impartial agent of the "whole state" as imagined by the Virginia Supreme Court of Appeals in the *Anderson* case. By 1835, even though the state's shares in the company were increased by statute from holding a 40% to a 60% ownership stake, the legislature also voted to retain the voting control of private shareholders over company affairs.[13] Eventually, the governance rules of corporate law allowed a smaller collection of planter/shareholders from central Virginia, a group that one of its members called "the James River Interest,"[14] to steer the company's work, generally shielded from public oversight. For example, even though its 1832 charter required the company to start its work across the mountains, clearing the Kanawha River and then possibly building a railroad back over the mountains to Richmond, its shareholders voted in 1835 to build an all-water route, conveniently serving plantations along the James River, and to start this work in the east. As for the western railroad segment, company leaders decided to delay work until "after the execution of the water parts of the line."[15]

In public, the "James River Interest" portrayed its company's narrow geographic focus, insisting upon an all-water mode of transport, as a matter of democratic principle. A canal, the company's president argued, was merely a man-made extension of a river, a form of aquatic roadway that everyone could always cross. Choosing instead to build a railway, with its costly machinery, "would be the means of exchanging a free highway for a close monopoly."[16] After all, one company engineer asserted, canals were always open to the public, places where "every man is his own carrier, if he chooses to be so."[17] Writing in 1832, at a moment when Virginia's legislators were openly debating whether to abolish slavery, William & Mary's Thomas Dew even went so far as to theorize that the canal "diminish[ed] the evils" of the peculiar institution within the Old Dominion. In the east, he predicted, the canal would build

[12] James River and Kanawha Canal Co. v. Anderson, 39 Va. 278, 301–307 (1841).

[13] See 1834–5 *Va. Acts* 70–1.

[14] See, e.g., Letter from Joseph C. Cabell to John H. Cocke, Aug. 30, 1831, University of Virginia Special Collections, Cabell Family Papers, Collection No. 38-11 [hereinafter "Cabell Papers"], Box No. 23 (justifying a run for political office because of being "compelled to defend the James River Interest," educating voters on the need to accept "the policy of connecting the waters without delay").

[15] See *James River and Kanawha Company, 1835 Annual Report* [hereinafter "[year reporting] *JRKC Report* [year published, if different]", i–xix.

[16] See 1845 *JRKC Report*, 587–8, 602–4, 607. Company president John C. Cabell's reasons against an all-railroad line first appeared in 1835. See 1835 *JRKC Report*, xi–xii.

[17] See Claudius Crozet, *Remarks on the Most Urgent Improvements in the State of Virginia*, in *Virginia House of Delegates*, 1827 *Va. House Journal*, at app. 24–5 [hereinafter "[year] *Va. House J.*"] (quoting canal engineer Benjamin Wright).

up new cities and towns, calling for "less slave and more free labor." As water from the canal flowed up the western mountains, the state's most inexcusable exception to freedom and democracy would gradually wash itself away: hardscrabble grazers and shepherds would transform into small farmers, presumed by Dew to prefer relying upon the labor of other free white men rather than upon the work of slaves.[18]

In practice, however, the James River and Kanawha Company seemed focused upon replacing Virginia's naturally flowing riverways with a single, stagnant artificial waterway under private day-to-day control, inevitably carrying western trade and tribute back to Richmond. For instance, as construction crept slowly west, the company became not only the builder of a canal, but also its nascent administrator. In 1840, the James River and Kanawha Canal Company published detailed printed regulations for the waterways that it deemed were under its legal domain, stretching from the Tidewater in the east to the Ohio River in the west, offering a glimpse at the closely held lawscape that it intended to create. Tolls would be collected as far west as Charleston, the capital of present-day West Virginia, all the way eastward to Richmond. All along the line, a fleet of "lock-keepers," "toll gatherers," and "inspectors" were to register boats, weigh their cargoes, collect revenues from freight and passengers, and impound vessels and other rivergoing property in the event of nonpayment. Other officers would be responsible for "police of the canal," enforcing rules on maximum speeds, how to pass other vessels, where to embark, even where to stop.[19] If put into practice, the orderly legal aesthetic of Richmond's Canal Walk would extend approximately four hundred linear river miles, encompassing the entire length of the Old Dominion.

The rules meant to reorganize Virginia's ancient routes of river trade into a single line of tribute flowing inexorably toward downtown Richmond came with some new social costs: tolls would be demanded from—and traffic rules forced against—journeys that had once been taken out of sight from any centralized corporation's watch, for free. But inconveniences to small-time river traders paled in comparison to strains imposed upon an even less powerful class of people alongside the river. Within Virginia, the digging, grubbing, and other manual business of building a canal resembled the planting and tending of crops, and most often fell to enslaved people of African descent. According to white canal advocates, the project's construction ensured the full employment of the state's enslaved population after the growing season. After all, posited one businessman euphemistically, "[T]he labouring classes in the southern states are stationary, and not a migratory class as in the northern states."[20] And so, perhaps not surprisingly, the canal that Thomas Dew once claimed could "diminish slavery's evils" came to be built, maintained, and operated mainly by Virginia's slaves, working under a canal company's day-to-day legal control.

18 See Thomas Dew, "Review of the Debate in the Virginia Legislature of 1831–1832," reprinted in *Pro-Slavery Argument* (Philadelphia: Shepherd and Cohn, 1853). The proslavery Dew made this argument in a speech opposing state-managed abolition.

19 See *Regulations for the James River and Kanawha Canal and For its Protection Together With Tables for Tolls, Weights, and Distances* (Richmond: Shepherd and Cohn, 1840).

20 SeeEdward Kenna, *Supplementary Report to the President and Directors of the James River and Kanawha Company on the Improvement of the Kanawha River and Resources of the Kanawha Valley* (1856), 4.

Early on, the predecessor of the James River and Kanawha Canal Company owned slave property of its own. This placed the majority of the company's workforce more or less at the mercy of white canal administrators. "[Y]ou can command their service when you please," one company officer explained when describing his enslaved laborers, and "when your work is completed, if you have not further occasion for them, they can be sold for nearly as much, or probably more than they cost you."[21] However, by the 1830s, with the company having repeatedly sold off its slaves for cash during lean economic times, most slaves working on the canal came to be supplied through seasonal contracts with slaveholders or third-party contractors. Under prevailing legal understandings, such arrangements were adjudged under the "law of bailments," as being rentals of a thing. While the canal company may have owed a general duty to a slave's owner to act prudently with their hire, Virginia law gave slaves themselves no formal option to bargain with the canal company directly, much less to complain or walk away.[22] Digging and outfitting a canal was hard physical labor, making this arrangement favorable to the white men directing the work under tight schedules. By 1838, the company president remarked that the company's workforce included around 95 slaves, consisting of a "manageable and stable" cadre of about two-thirds of the workforce. Slightly more than a decade later, this number had grown, with one officer noting that 27 slaves were working at just one of the canal's many different active locks, tallying 7,065 of the 8,587 days (82%) of the total labor worked at the construction site that year.[23]

Taking a comprehensive tour of the canal under construction in 1837, the James River and Kanawha Canal Company's president reported seeing "contractors and their throngs of laborers forming a line almost unbroken … for 120 miles."[24] Viewed from the perspective of the slave laborers this sight would have encompassed, such an orderly procession takes on the sinister appearance of a forced march. Back at Richmond's Canal Walk, beside plaques to George Washington and John Marshall, we can also imagine rudiments of what some scholars have called a "hydraulic society" being summoned forth—reflections of a system where "a few supreme individuals wielded absolute control over the common people as they did over the rivers that coursed through their territory." Here, perhaps, is the recreation of a specific type of legal zone where "power over canals converts itself into power over people."[25]

[21] See Letter from John Bosher to Robert Pollard, Nov. 11, 1822, quoted in Peter Way, *Common Labour: Workers and the Digging of North American Canals, 1780–1860* (Cambridge: Cambridge University Press, 1993), 88.

[22] See Thomas Morris, *Southern Slavery and the Law, 1619–1860* (Chapel Hill: North Carolina, 1996), 132–58 (law of bailments as governing the "slave hireling contract" beginning in 1830s).

[23] See 1836 *JRKC Report* 1837, 92–5 (95 slaves); 1838 *JRKC Report* 1839, 330–2; Way, *Common Labour*, Table 6 (7,065 of 8,587 worked). The day-to-day work was overwhelmingly performed by a core group of slaves at this spot: while 87 free laborers passed through, each only worked an average of 18 days per year at the site. In comparison, each slave worked an average of 262 days at the same location.

[24] See 1837 *JRKC Report* 1838, 250.

[25] See Donald Worster, *Rivers of Empire: Water, Aridity, and the Growth of the American West* (New York: Oxford University Press, 1992), 23 ("absolute control"); Lon Fuller, "Irrigation and Tyranny," *Stanford Law Review* 17 (1965) 1021–42, 1023 ("power over people"). Worster discusses the limits of the hydraulic society thesis at *Rivers*, 22–63.

## II. Lawscape No. 2: Hollywood Cemetery and Environs (River Mile 2.0)

Except for the segments now occupied by Richmond's Canal Walk, the lawscape envisioned in the company's 1840 canal regulations—a simplified central waterway extending from Virginia's Tidewater to the Ohio River under the total extractive control of a single corporation—never fully materialized on a statewide scale. Today, when attempting to track John Marshall's route from Richmond, a more complex lawscape quickly begins to emerge. Right around Tredegar Iron Works, Richmond's Canal Walk ends, forcing the traveler into riskier spaces. Cement eventually gives way to dirt, the concrete-armored downtown causeway becoming a ragged urban ditch. One section is reconditioned to provide water to a power plant, but by Hollywood Cemetery, it becomes necessary to climb over fences and ignore "No Trespassing" signs to chase remnants of John Marshall's canal on Richmond's outskirts. Beyond town, the task of chasing the canal largely becomes an even more challenging archeological pursuit, involving the search for crumbling stone culverts, retaining walls, and archways under highway overpasses, kept at arm's length by barbed wire fencing behind CSX Railway rights-of-way at the edge of small river towns like Irwin, Scottsville, and Buffalo Station.

The presence of a second more provisional lawscape starting within Richmond's own confines, raising new questions to the traveler about ownership, jurisdiction, and rights of access, suggests that not everyone within nineteenth-century Virginia chose or was forced to play along with the James River and Kanawha Company's proffered rules. If we take a break from our journey to review the business and court records attached to the company, this indeed appears to be the case.

Throughout the entire history of the James River and Kanawha Canal, construction never proceeded at what the company considered its optimum pace, due in part to legal problems in acquiring a sufficient workforce. In 1839, while the company estimated that one thousand workers were necessary for the "vigorous and efficient movement" of the line from the east to west, it reported having as few as three hundred workers executing the project.[26] Because it relied so heavily upon hiring out from the state's existing plantation-based slave labor pool, the company's perceived worker shortage may have been due to the fact that under existing legal precedents in Virginia, slave hirers such as the company were not strictly responsible in every case for every conceivable mishap that may befall a slave in their care.[27] According to the canal company's president, some Virginia planters sustained an "aversion" for contracting out their slaves, concerned that their property would either be "improperly exposed" to the elements while working in stagnant waters during very hot or cold months, or otherwise could be more profitably deployed on their own land during the planting or harvesting seasons.[28]

[26] See 1838 *JRKC Report* 1839, 329.

[27] See Morris, *Southern Slavery*, 134–35 ("the custom in Virginia was that slave hirers were not insurers against all contingencies").

[28] See 1836 *JRKC Report* 1838, 94–5.

In Virginia, when the company attempted to offset labor shortfalls by hiring free white men from overseas, this proved to be largely ineffective. As in other parts of the United States before the Civil War, hiring free white laborers imposed a different set of legal expectations on business concerns such as the James River and Kanawha Canal Company, subjecting employers to an alternate contractual system where workers themselves could formally bargain over terms of service. In 1838, for instance, the canal company's president reported having 346 German "laborers and citizens" on his employment rolls, men who first passed between contractors searching for the highest wage, then vanished from the route altogether. Irish laborers were temporarily hired to supplement their ranks. But the Irish, the company president found, "were men who war against our institutions." Unlike slaves working under tight legal restraints, they "roam among the various public works in progress, and are constantly arriving and departing upon the different lines, as interest or caprice dictates a change." In 1838, when "the incongruous mass struck for higher wages, accompanying the demand with demonstrations of intended force," they received a 20% raise. But when twenty Irishmen were worked to death shortly afterwards, hundreds simply "left the work and moved north." The company's workforce shrunk in size, once again.[29]

When and if a canal segment was actually finished under these conditions, legal challenges did not necessarily end for Virginia's canal company. Take, for example, the fraught business of collecting tolls from river traders along the Kanawha River, the main waterway across the mountains serving Charleston in present-day West Virginia. As one Charleston-based toll gatherer testified in 1850, rivergoing vessels first needed to stop on the city's steamboat dock, locate a James River and Kanawha Company representative, and then provide a shipping manifest of what they were carrying. This was toll collection implemented under the honor system: "I have no knowledge of the goods except what I get from such manifests," the toll gatherer admitted.[30] Among repeat players or first-time travelers, papers could easily be altered, figures rounded up or down by mutual agreement, or Charleston's dock could be avoided altogether. "The boatmen often descend in the night," the company president lamented to shareholders in 1842, "and although the officers of the company are frequently on the watch all night, they are constantly evaded."[31]

For some of the most sophisticated western rivermen and business concerns, simple fare evasion or riverfront negotiation proved unnecessary. Instead, Virginia's formal legal system provided an impressive array of arguments, procedures, and institutions that could be deployed to mitigate exposure to the company's tolling power. By 1817, for instance, more than thirty industrial furnaces, owned and operated by a group of lawyers and businessmen that had organized themselves into one of America's first commercial cartels, sat alongside the Kanawha River, processing salt and running

[29] See 1837 *JRKC Report* 1838, 246–7 (German laborers); 1838 *JRKC Report* 1839, 330–2 (Irish). Some white laborers bargained for the upfront payment of their wages before commencing work; others left a construction site "en masse" when their pay was reduced. See Way, *Common Labour*, 89, 111.

[30] See Deposition of John J. Manin (Feb. 1850) in James River and Kanawha Canal Company v. Wood, et al. (1849), Kanawha County Circuit Court Records, West Virginia and Regional History Collection, University of West Virginia, Morgantown, WV.

[31] See 1842 *JRKC Report* 370–5.

boats for the Ohio River's lucrative pork trade headquartered in Cincinnati.[32] These men regularly adjudicated their business in local county circuit courts, leading to verdicts that could only be appealed in rare circumstances to Richmond's Supreme Court under Virginia's constitution. Not surprisingly, the members of western Virginia's salt trade used Charleston's local court, the Kanawha County Circuit Superior Court, as an alternate center of jurisdictional power, launching a sustained campaign against toll collection by the James River company.

The power of the James River and Kanawha Company to levy tolls on salt—"part of the commerce between the states"—was "unconstitutional and void," argued the attorneys for salt magnates Joel and William Shrewsbury in Kanawha County's circuit court in 1840. A few years earlier, a local jury asserting that it was acting on behalf of the entire "Commonwealth of Virginia" had presented a bill of "three summonses and two indictments" against the company in this local court, arguing that the state-funded company's limited set of river modifications was actually a nuisance in the west. "The Kanawha river is in worse state, and more difficult for navigation than when they commenced working on it," the jury alleged. Now, with their clients facing a bill of $22,677 in unpaid tolls, the Shrewsbury lawyers repeated this claim. The Kanawha had not, in fact, been improved by the canal company; much of the Shrewsbury family's salt had been "wrecked, sunk, and wholly lost" on account of the company's works. The river was essentially returning to its natural state, and "in the natural conditions of the streams, every citizen of the United States ha[d] a right to pass and repass therefrom, free from charge or hindrance." The Shewsburys owed nothing to the company for continuing to use the Kanawha River to carry their goods to market. If anything, their lawyers asserted, the company owed the Shewsburys compensation for the salt they had lost along the way.[33]

The idea that a salt trader could collect damages from the James River and Kanawha Company in local courts to offset, or even eliminate, assessed tolls was more than just a rhetorical flourish on the part of creative defense counsel. Both Kanawha River steamboats and the salt that they carried were someone's property, and Virginia's legal system entertained claims in both law and equity brought against parties that damaged this property's commercial use. Thus, in 1846, when the canal company sought to collect tolls from one western boat operator, he could bring a trespass suit for damages in Kanawha's circuit court, alleging that at the time the tolls had allegedly accrued, his boat was in fact lost on account of "the negligence of said company in making its repairs." After securing an award of more than $1,000, this boat operator could go to equity, securing an order from the county sheriff to "detain" all of the canal company's property within his respective bailiwick until this full amount was paid.[34]

32 See, e.g., John Stealey, *The Antebellum Kanawha Salt Business and Western Markets* (Lexington: University of Kentucky Press, 1993), 8–16; Matthew Maury and W. M. Fontaine, eds., *Resources of West Virginia* (Wheeling: Register, 1876), 280–5.

33 See pleas in James River and Kanawha Company v. Shrewsbury, et al. (1841), Kanawha County Circuit Court Records, West Virginia and Regional History Collection. The 1828 indictment is found at Commonwealth v. James River Company, Kanawha County Superior Court, Kanawha County, West Virginia, Microfilm KAN 58, Env. 34 1900 (1828), University of West Virginia, Morgantown, WV.

34 See McMullin v. James River and Kanawha Company (1846), Kanawha County Circuit Court Records, West Virginia and Regional History Collection.

And in 1848, after the canal company was able to fend off another damage claim in an adjacent county (with a decision issued by a judge who turned out to be a company shareholder), a Kanawha jury stepped in to overturn the verdict, awarding $1,800 to a river ferry operator who stood to lose his livelihood after the company built a competing toll bridge alongside his business.[35]

By the 1850s, Virginia's constitution had been revised to award more representation to Kanawha's west.[36] Even the state's highest court was beginning to reflect this shift in power away from Richmond's canal company when similar cases were brought to its bar. In 1850, another western boatman owing tolls brought suit in a county court against the canal company, again seeking to recover the value of his boat and salt cargo, both of which he alleged had been lost when striking a snag in the Kanawha River. After he secured an award in local court, the company appealed to the Virginia Supreme Court of Appeals, arguing that as an agent of the Commonwealth, the company had succeeded to the state's powers as a sovereign to collect tolls while being immune from private suit. Unfortunately for the company, the case came before a court that included Justice George H. Lee, a former commercial lawyer from across the mountains who had once served as the U.S. Attorney for Virginia's Western District. Justice Lee issued an opinion in *James River and Kanawha Canal v. Early* rejecting the company's immunity claim, declaring the company's arguments "grievously unjust." The company may have stood in the shoes of the state when choosing to enlarge its canal in downtown Richmond in the *Anderson* case, but in this western dispute, it was "not a public corporation representing the public and administering public funds for the benefit of the public." Instead, it was a private "joint stock company which has undertaken the construction of a work useful to the public certainly but intended for the private emolument of the stockholders in dividends of the profits." In the west, the company's right to collect tolls, and its liability for any failure to improving the Kanawha River as Virginia's legislature had authorized, were "reciprocal and correlative." "[T]he tolls are the remuneration to the company for its expenditures on its works," Justice Lee reasoned, "and the consideration and basis for any legal liability that may be cast upon it." As such, the transfer of the state's "privileges and immunities" to the company under the 1832 statute did *not* include the Commonwealth's exemption from private suit. The Virginia Assembly, Justice Lee concluded, had not "intended to place the James [R]iver and Kanawha company above the law and to leave individuals who might be specially injured by the neglect of its corporate duties without remedy or redress."[37]

If the canal company was not "above the law" in western Virginia, and thus was required to answer for any damages that it may have caused to rivergoing property because of its limited work to clear obstructions in that section of the state, this was also the case along the James River, where even more invasive canal construction could

35 See Thompson v. James River and Kanawha Co. (1848), Kanawha County Circuit Court Records, West Virginia and Regional History Collection.

36 See William Shade, *Democratizing the Old Dominion: Virginia and the Second Party System, 1824–1861* (Charlottesville: University of Virginia Press, 1996) (comprehensive study of Virginia's evolving constitutional history and its impact on political representation during the antebellum era, including the state's 1850–1 constitutional amendments).

37 See James River and Kanawha Co. v. Early, 54 Va. 541, 551–6 (1856).

permanently impact tobacco farms and plantations. Throughout the nineteenth century, the majority of eastern Virginia's commercial classes, outside of Richmond-based promoters like John Marshall and the officers of the canal company itself, maintained limited support for the idea of a grand east-to-west canal connecting the state's two halves. The main complaint had always been fiscal; in 1785, around the same time that George Washington was lobbying for the project, for instance, Thomas Jefferson wrote that it was doubtful whether the "great and numerous rapids" of the Kanawha River could ever sustain navigation, except at great "expence."[38]

If John Marshall's canal company was eventually seen in Kanawha County as seeking to siphon revenues away from the western river trade and toward Richmond, some eastern planters saw things in reverse. For them, the James River and Kanawha Company, funded in part by government dollars, was little more than an example of "actual efforts to tax the lowlands for the benefit of western interests." "[T]he people of the west," one eastern planter warned during a statewide constitutional convention that was considering greater western representation, "want to make some Appian, or some Flaminian way, or some Roman aqueduct, or some other splendid Internal Improvement," charging it to the east "against our consent."[39] Even along the James River, where the canal provided the most immediate financial benefits, patience for the canal company ran thin. "I find from all quarters of the legislature prejudice," wrote one political observer in 1843. Within the Virginia Assembly, there was a "determined hostility to [the canal] company, a settled purpose it seems... to break it down entirely." Remarkably, this opposition was "greatest among the eastern members," including even some living along the line of the canal: "They have got the improvement now along their own plantations. They care nothing about it extending beyond the Blue Ridge... some of them would be willing to prostrate the company with the hope of getting rid of the tolls."[40]

Eastern opponents of the James River and Kanawha Company used the full force of Virginia's legal system to limit the company's canal and to restrain the power of its officers to collect tolls. As public lawmakers working out of the state legislature, they eventually passed statutes freezing all construction contracts on "the mountain section of the James river canal" and the further extension of Kanawha River improvements,[41] halting "the continuation or extension of the canal beyond the extent to which it (was) now under contract," and chartering competing railroads that drew freight and passengers away from the line.[42] Most important, while Virginia statute prevented landowners from enjoining the James River and Kanawha Company should it choose to run the canal across their land, James River planters leveraged Virginia laws to

[38] See Thomas Jefferson, *Notes on the State of Virginia* (1785; London: Penguin, 1999), 15.

[39] See*Proceedings and Debates of the Virginia State Convention of 1829–30, Vol.* 1 (Richmond: Ritchie, 1830), 63, 114. See also Dickson Bruce, *The Rhetoric of Conservativism: The Virginia Convention of 1829–30 and the Conservative Tradition in the South* (Ann Arbor: Michigan, 1982).

[40] See Letter from Andrew Parks to Lewis Summers, Jan. 12, 1843, Folder 3, A&M 1791, Summers Papers, West Virginia and Regional History Center, West Virginia University, Morgantown, WV.

[41] See 1825–6 *Va. Acts* 26–30.

[42] See 1841–2 *Va. Acts*, at 72–4 ("continuation or extension"). In 1843, the Assembly added insult to injury by resolving that the salary of the company's officers should be reduced. See 1842–3 *Va. Acts* 117. For an example of railroad legislation, see 1848–9 *Va. Acts* 101–3 (authorizing state purchase of stock in Lynchburg-to-Tennessee railway, completed in 1856).

increase the company's cost of doing so. Under every charter authorized by Virginia's legislature, the canal company was required to negotiate just compensation awards on a parcel-by-parcel basis whenever it exercised its powers of eminent domain. Under this process, property assessors visited affected lands in advance. By statute, they were then required to take into account the quantity and quality of the to-be-condemned property, the additional fencing required and all other "inconveniences," and then weigh these considerations against the "advantages" the landowner was said to derive from the canal. From this, they calculated a money settlement. Under this process, some landowners were able to open up the company's coffers and negotiate higher rewards. In 1836, for instance, one fellow named James Robertson initially informed the company of his plan to "avail himself of all legal talent" to prevent the canal from entering his land. Eventually he entered an agreement to increase his compensation for sundry "inconveniences" inflicted by the company on his land, including increased flooding, "the throwing up of dirt," the removal of coopershops, and the pain of "having lockkeepers and lock lots in the heart of the proprietor's estate."[43]

When the company approached the largest plantations along the James to build its central canal, Virginia's most defiant proprietors could also count upon the state's court system if they refused to give way at all. In 1836, for example, canal company assessors eyed the riparian property of Mrs. A. D. Turner, who owned land south of Lynchburg along the approaching canal line. Company assessors decided that her "advantages" of being close to the canal outweighed her "inconveniences," and awarded her nothing. Turner ran to a sympathetic courthouse and appealed, a local judge finding that the company needed to show "particular advantages" instead of merely "general" and "speculative" ones to offset her damages. Two of three judges on the Virginia Supreme Court of Appeals agreed. Judge William Brockenbrough, an ancient rival of John Marshall, twisted one of the arguments made by Marshall in years past, insisting that the river trade of the company's works only ran between Richmond and the Ohio River, bypassing individual landowners like Mrs. Turner altogether. Paying tolls already offset her "general advantages," effectively leaving the company in debt to her. Despite pro-canal propaganda, Brockenbrough was not prepared to see any "special advantages" attaching to Turner at all, especially because the company was only half-public in its ownership. In fact, he was inclined to support damages to *any* dissenting private landholder along the line: "Why should he pay for an advantage which is in some sort forced upon him by the public, and which it confers on him, not with the particular view of benefiting him, but for its own purposes?"[44]

The success of Turner's courtroom gambit indicated that open canal resistance was tolerated in even the state's highest tribunals. The floodgates of dissent opened. In 1836, a landowner from Lynchburg named John Percival launched a sustained campaign against the incoming canal. The company built a fence across his property, removed a barn, and cut his land "into two pieces." Then assessors arrived to offer him

[43] See Extraction of Minutes (1835–1840) Regarding Location of Canal and Names of Owners of Condemned Land, Jan. 20, 1836, p. 9, James River and Kanawha Company Business Records, Library of Virginia, Accession No. 23369a.

[44] See James River and Kanawha Company v. Turner, 36 Va. 313, 331–7 (1838).

"only" $808.[45] Percival had other plans and started holding up construction. Under an old law, the state could not condemn "private gardens" for public use. Percival leveraged this by planting a garden, flowers and the like, up to the edge of the river. While the canal company's president had the Assembly repeal this law, Percival refused to back down. When company agents attempted to enter his land to survey and assess damages, "he prevented them from doing so by the use of force and arms, threatening certain and immediate death to any agent of the company who should enter his lands."[46] The company brought suit against Percival, but they avoided his land until the company president engineered another act specifically designed for his arrest. In the meantime, local canal users were not required to pay tolls near Percival's property until 1841, starving the company of critical revenue during this time.[47]

The combined weight of such legal opposition eventually left the state's central canal line impoverished, unfinished, and vulnerable to whims of nature, which to nineteenth-century residents often felt like being subject to the overpowering dictates of an even more powerful sovereign. As early as the 1820s, the French engineer employed by the state's Board of Public Works criticized the canal company's habit of collecting water and trapping it behind fragile wooden gates that could never hold during periods of high rainfall; such work, Claudius Crozet wrote, was in direct opposition to "natural causes and effects," and would "soon yield to the irresistible laws which govern the operation of streams."[48] During heavy floods in 1838 and 1841, his prediction proved correct, time and again.[49] By 1842, with state appropriations dwindling, the company started turning against itself. That year, after a flood near Lynchburg, state assessors rendered sizable damage awards to adjoining landowners on the grounds that "the company's works caused the mischief." The canal company president took this as a fatal omen. "Alas! I fear that the scheme will sink under the weight of the never ending... claims of the proprietors, who seem really to think it a most serious and dangerous price of liberality to do anything as to yield anything to a great work... What in the name of God has got into the James River people!?"[50] In 1860, when a French business firm unsuccessfully offered to purchase the insolvent canal in its entirety, its offer sheet contained the following: "The present company shall do away, either by payment or amicable settlement, with all suits in law now pending. We cannot take any litigation, but the concern entirely free of any litigation whatever."[51] This was a poison pill and the sale never went through; by this time, the company's courtroom liabilities were simply too expansive to bring off the books.

[45] See Extracts from Proceedings of Board of Assessors (1836–40), Nov. 10, 1836 (1835–40) Regarding Location of Canal and Names of Owners of Condemned Land, Jan. 20, 1836, p. 7, James River and Kanawha Company Business Records, Library of Virginia, Accession No. 23369b.

[46] See 1839 *JRKC Report* 510-5.

[47] See 1839–40 *Va. Acts* 63-6; 1839 *JRKC Report* 515.

[48] See Claudius Crozet, "Report on the Survey of the James River," in *Virginia Board of Public Works, 1828 Annual Report*, 3–4.

[49] See e.g., 1838 *JRKC Report* 347–8; 1839 *JRKC Report* 503; 1840 *JRKC Report* 1841, 655–6.

[50] Letter from Cabell to Cocke, Nov. 8, 1842, Cabell Papers, Box No. 33.

[51] See Ernest De Bellot des Minieres to Col. Thomas Ellis, president of the James River and Kanawha Company, Richmond, May 2, 1860, in Robert Alonzo Brook Collection, Reel 4329, Huntington Library, San Marino, CA.

## III. Lawscape No. 3: Rathole Mountain (River Mile 274.5)

Today, perhaps the best way to view what precisely had "gotten into" nineteenth-century "James River people" when they simultaneously used Virginia's legal system to build and obstruct a grand canal to the west is not from Richmond, but from a more remote spot nestled in the state's windy mountain borderlands near West Virginia. Here, close to Rathole Mountain on State Route 220, near a severe bend in the James before it changes its name to the Jackson River, is the final lawscape in our river journey: Near a few abandoned cement kilns at the terminus of "the river where America began,"[52] amidst the shade and mosquitoes, is a parking lot overlooking a deep cut in the earth that seems to be eroding back into time. Moving closer reveals that this crevasse is held together by stone blocks of irregular shape and size, now overgrown with weeds. This, it turns out, is the final lock ever built by the James River and Kanawha Company, designed to feed water from Eagle Creek to supply the river line's abandoned march up the hills. Here, near the West Virginia border, is Virginia's canal in its rawest form, still searching out the best way to cross the Alleghenies, still awaiting a builder's next move, a lawyer's next response.

What are we to make of the view of Virginia's canal from Rathole Mountain? If we look at the site from the perspective of John Marshall, or from the standpoint of the James River and Kanawha Company and its supporters, it is certainly a lawscape of defeat. This is the most common assessment that can be found in most secondary literature to this day. Because the project "failed to reach its destination," one later historian concluded in 1977, it could not be seen as a success.[53] As early as the 1940s, when the Social Science Research Council (SSRC) commissioned statewide studies of "attempts to apply the instrument of the state or its agencies to control or develop a phase of the state economy," Virginia was seen as a case study in one state's unfortunate "lack of action." A paper on Virginia's "internal improvements" system, originally expected to produce a monograph alongside similar studies of Pennsylvania and Massachusetts, was rejected for further funding by SSRC leadership.[54] Today, for several economic historians, trained under a tradition to judge historical actors for the

[52] This phrase is from Bob Deans, *The River Where America Began: A Journey Along the James* (New York: Rowman, 2007).

[53] See David Goldfield, *Urban Growth in the Age of Sectionalism: Virginia: 1847–1861* (Baton Rouge: LSU, 1997), 228–31.

[54] The genesis and historiography of this Rockefeller-funded set of "Commonwealth School" of state studies funded is further discussed in Harry Scheiber, "Review: Government and the Economy: Studies of the 'Commonwealth' Policy in Nineteenth-Century America," *The Journal of Interdisciplinary History*, 3.1: (Summer 1972), pp. 135–51. For the fate of a Virginia study within the Commonwealth School, see Minutes of Meeting of Committee on Research in Economic History, Sept. 27–28, 1944, Box 146, Folder 804 ("not exuberant"); Minutes of Meeting of Committee on Research in Economic History, Feb. 23–24, 1946, Box 146, Folder 804, SSRC Collection, Rockefeller Archive Center (rather than a monograph, the historian who produced a draft history of Virginia's "internal improvements" would need to revise his work on his own time, then fashion it into "an article or articles [for] some journal"). Some of this work was published at Wiley Hodges, "Pro-Governmentalism in Virginia, 1739–1836: A Pragmatic Liberal Pattern in the Political Heritage," *The Journal of Politics* 25.2: (May 1963), 333–60. See also Carter Goodrich, *Government Promotion of American Canals and Railroads, 1800–1890* (New York: Columbia University Press, 1960), 87–101.

profit-maximizing potential of their decisions, Virginia's inability to complete a central canal line was a "short-sighted" failure of political economy, leading to a supposed "lack of central place" in the Old Dominion, especially to blame for squandering the "wasted potential" of the state's western coalfields.[55]

As an early antecedent of a New Deal or World Bank development project, as a type of nineteenth-century predecessor of modern heroic-scale water infrastructure projects like the Grand Coulee Dam or the re-engineering of the Nile River, the James River and Kanawha Canal most assuredly came up short. But maybe this is not so terrible. In studying the law and politics behind grand water projects, the environmental historian Richard White has suggested, the goal can sometimes be "to understand rather than denounce."[56] To complete a canal over the mountains in the early 1800s, an artificial waterway stretching from Richmond to the Ohio River under the administration of a single corporation, Virginia would have had to be a far more authoritarian place than it was. Such a project, at least as envisioned by canal boosters such as John Marshall, relied mainly upon slave labor and would have likely turned more of present-day West Virginia into an industrial zone. Completing the canal would have involved working more laborers to death while expropriating more dollars from river traders, all while draining the state of its financial flexibility to shift into later modes of transportation. Most important for our purposes, it would have required a far more severe legal system to reach its destination, requiring the equivalent of a "high modernist" juridical regime offering little room for dissent. Gone would be the possibility to offset the company's tolls or collect damages for a lost vessel, or for damaged farmland, with a strategic trespass claim in a rural county court. Gone too would be the chance to temper the project's physical impacts by limiting the canal's budget, or by revising its charter, under Virginia's legislative process.

In a way, the pre-existing legal system that the James River and Kanawha Canal project found itself operating within, unequal and pluralistic as it was, operated as a type of disaggregated statewide environmental planning law at the time. In nineteenth-century Virginia, while some were left at the command and control of others, the law gave others a chance to comment upon, influence, and in some instances prevent major changes to their physical world before these changes were set to take place.[57] If, as the political anthropologist James C. Scott has documented, certain utopian public works visions have the capacity to go awry when they are prosecuted with little

[55] See John Majewski, *A House Dividing: Economic Development in Pennsylvania and Virginia before the Civil War* (Cambridge: Cambridge University Press, 2000), 31–5, 124–8 ("lack of a central place"); Sean Adams, *Old Dominion, Industrial Commonwealth: Coal, Politics, and Economy in Antebellum America* (Baltimore: Johns Hopkins University Press, 2004), 86–102 ("wasted potential"). My critique of some econometric approaches to writing antebellum political economy, as being disproportionately influenced by presentist concerns, has been informed by D. N. McCloskey, *The Rhetoric of Economics* (Madison: University of Wisconsin Press, 1985), 114–32.

[56] Richard White, *The Organic Machine: The Remaking of the Columbia River* (New York: Hill and Wang, 1996), 57.

[57] A modern analogue aggregating some of these functions under federal law would be the National Environmental Policy Act (NEPA), 42 U.S.C. § 4321 et seq. See, e.g., Richard J. Lazarus, *The Making of Environmental Law* (Chicago: University of Chicago Press, 2004) (NEPA as an "early warning system about major environmental modifications and proposals, permitting public comment and criticism before the event"), 48. On the pluralistic, decentralized nature of nineteenth-century American law, see Hendrik Hartog, "Pigs and Positivism," *Wisconsin Law Review* (1985): 899–935.

commitment to democratic processes or private rights, Virginia's common law legal system of "courts and parties" prevented the state's central canal project from taking a consistently despotic turn.[58] In the end, as some historians of technology have suggested, the nineteenth-century Virginia of Thomas Jefferson and John Marshall was a special place where competing sets of Americans fretted with "tragic ambivalence" over their industrial future, promoting change in only the most "hesitant and equivocal" ways.[59] In this light, the rough and unfinished lawscape found at Rathole Mountain—a jumble of human-laid stones slowly melting back into an engineered crack in the earth—perhaps leaves us with the most permanent, and evocative, physical monument to the law of a lost age.

[58] See Scott, *Seeing like a State*, 89. The venerable understanding of nineteenth-century American political systems being dominated by "courts and parties," since qualified but in my view never entirely disproven by later scholars, was originally introduced in Stephen Skowronek, *Building a New American State: The Expansion of National Administrative Capacities, 1877–1920* (Cambridge: Cambridge University Press, 1982), 19–36.

[59] See Leo Marx, *The Machine in the Garden: Technology and the Pastoral Ideal in America* (New York: Oxford University Press, 1964), 117–44 ("tragic ambivalence"); Merritt Roe Smith, *Harper's Ferry and the New Technology: The Challenge of Change* (Ithaca: Cornell University Press, 1977), 22–23 ("hesitant and equivocal").

# 2

# The Rise of Retail Stockholder Litigation and the Creation of the Plaintiff's Bar in American Business Law, 1930–1950

*Donna Dennis*

For many years, corporate law scholars have focused extensive, mostly critical attention on virtually every aspect of representative stockholder litigation.[1] Despite this vast, ever-burgeoning body of literature, commentators have generally overlooked the origins of retail (or "Main Street") stockholder suits and the creation of the plaintiff's bar in business law.[2] Retail stockholder litigation, initially centered in New York City, was distinguished by the presence of ordinary shareholders with small holdings of publicly traded securities as representative plaintiffs, the assertion of claims involving breach of fiduciary duty against elite officers and directors of large public companies, and the emergence of a specialized cadre of stockholders' lawyers, working on a contingency basis, as the architects of such cases. This novel form of legal practice, along with the plaintiff's bar that masterminded it, first appeared as a major phenomenon in the 1930s and remains a fundamental feature of American corporate law today.[3]

[1] In representative stockholder litigation, an investor sues on behalf of the corporation as a whole (in a derivative suit) or on behalf of a class of similarly situated shareholders (in a class action). For a comprehensive review of the scholarly literature challenging the value and merits of representative shareholder litigation as well as the motivations and ethics of the plaintiff's bar in business law, see Charles R. Korsmo and Minor Myers, "The Structure of Stockholder Litigation: When Do the Merits Matter?," *Ohio State Law Journal* 75.5 (2014): 837–58. In general, this scholarship has highlighted the asserted "pathologies" of modern stockholder litigation and the stockholders' bar. See Korsmo and Myers, "Structure of Stockholder Litigation," 836. For illustrative critiques, see Roberta Romano, "The Shareholder Suit: Litigation Without Foundation?," *Journal of Law, Economics, and Organization* 7.2 (Spring 1991): 63; Jessica Erickson, "Corporate Governance in the Courtroom," *William and Mary Law Review* 51.5 (2010): 1823 (supporting "the view of scholars and commentators that many derivative suits are strike suits in which the real winners are not corporations or their shareholders, but attorneys").

[2] For notable exceptions, see John C. Coffee, Jr., *Entrepreneurial Litigation: Its Rise, Fall, and Future* (Cambridge: Harvard University Press, 2015), 33–51; Eric A. Chiappinelli, "The Underappreciated Importance of Personal Jurisdiction in Delaware's Success," *DePaul Law Review* 63.4 (2014): 915–18, 925–29; Harwell Wells, "'No Man Can Be Worth $1,000,000 a Year': The Fight over Executive Compensation in 1930s America," *University of Richmond Law Review* 44.2 (2010); Lawrence E. Mitchell, "Gentleman's Agreement: The Antisemitic Origins of Restrictions on Stockholder Litigation," *Queen's Law Journal* 36.1 (Fall 2010).

[3] In the last third of the twentieth century, spurred on by revisions to Rule 23 of the Federal Rules of Civil Procedure, many high-profile shareholders' lawyers began to shift away from derivative litigation and into securities class actions. See Coffee, *Entrepreneurial Litigation*, 45–46, 52–85; Jessica Erickson, "The Lost Lessons of Shareholder Derivative Suits," *Washington and Lee Law Review* 77.3 (2020): 1143 ("Securities class actions stepped in to address many of the same types of claims that derivative suits had traditionally addressed"). While the use of derivative suits on behalf of retail investors has declined in importance relative to class actions over time, such litigation has hardly withered away. On the continuing significance of

Donna Dennis, *The Rise of Retail Stockholder Litigation and the Creation of the Plaintiff's Bar in American Business Law, 1930–1950* In: *In Between and Across*. Edited by: Kenneth W. Mack and Jacob Katz Cogan, Oxford University Press.
 DOI: 10.1093/oso/9780197680995.003.0003

This essay seeks to shed light on several significant but largely unexplored aspects of the history of Main Street stockholder litigation in the United States. Focusing on the shareholder derivative suit—the only legal mechanism available to minority stockholders to protect themselves from breaches of duty by directors until the growth of securities class actions in the late 1960s[4]—it first explains the genesis of retail shareholder actions and the emergence of the stockholder's lawyer. It then analyses the harsh attacks by corporate leaders and lawyers on the legitimacy of derivative suits and the ethics of plaintiff-side attorneys. In conclusion, the essay assesses the contributions of the first generation of retail shareholder suits and the early plaintiff's bar. It explores the important role played by Main Street stockholder litigation in policing corporate management, ferreting out wrongdoing, and protecting minority investors. And it demonstrates that many pioneering shareholders' lawyers, in particular David Podell and Abraham Pomerantz, developed professional identities that were considerably more influential, accomplished, and ethical than the conventional, pejorative narrative of the plaintiff's bar conveys.

## I. The Birth of Retail Shareholder Litigation and the Occupation of the Stockholder's Lawyer

American stockholder litigation was not invented in the 1930s; rather, the classic derivative action first appeared in the early 1830s.[5] Specifically, it arose as an equitable device to allow stockholders of a corporation to commence litigation to protect the firm in situations where it was faced with harm or had suffered an injury, such as when directors breached fiduciary duties of care or loyalty they owed to the corporation. Stockholders could only resort to the derivative remedy if they showed that the corporation's directors had improperly refused to take legal action against the parties harming the company or could not be trusted to do so because the alleged wrongdoers were in control of the entity. Because the cause of action on which shareholders were permitted to sue "derived" from the rights of the corporation, early derivative cases established that the corporation itself, rather than the plaintiff-stockholders, was entitled to any recovery.[6]

derivative suits in twenty-first-century American corporate law, see Erickson, "Corporate Governance," 1754; Deborah A. DeMott, *Shareholder Derivative Actions: Law and Practice* (Thomson Reuters, 2021–2022 ed), § 1:5.

[4] Bayer v. Beran, 49 N.Y.S.2d 2, 4 (N.Y. Sup. Ct. 1944) (the derivative suit "is, at present, the only civil remedy that stockholders have for breach of fiduciary duty on the part of those entrusted with management and direction of their corporations").

[5] Commentators have generally identified Robinson v. Smith, 3 Paige Ch. 222 (N.Y. Ch. 1832), decided by the Chancery Court of New York in 1832, as the first case to recognize the right of minority shareholders to file a derivative suit against corporate directors for breach of fiduciary duty. On derivative litigation in nineteenth-century America, see generally Bert S. Prunty, Jr., "The Shareholders' Derivative Suit: Notes on Its Derivation," *New York University Law Review* 32.5, (1957): 985–92; Ann M. Scarlett, "Shareholder Derivative Litigation's Historical and Normative Foundations," *Buffalo Law Review* 61.1 (2013): 871–86; Donna I. Dennis, "Contrivance and Collusion: The Corporate Origins of Shareholder Derivative Litigation in the United States," *Rutgers University Law Review* 67.6 (2015): 1479–513.

[6] Garrard Glenn, "The Stockholder's Suit—Corporate and Individual Grievances," *Yale Law Journal* 33.6 (1924): 580–81.

In the early 1930s, a novel style of stockholder litigation emerged, chiefly developed by a small circle of lawyers in New York City.[7] This twentieth-century version of the derivative suit had four distinguishing characteristics. First, practitioners began to file complaints on behalf of retail investors with small holdings of stock. Second, the defendants were generally affluent directors of large, publicly traded corporations rather than privately held companies. Third, the attorneys for plaintiffs, given the modest means of their clients, typically took such cases on contingency, hoping to receive a fee award out of any recovery obtained for the corporation. Fourth, the lawyers for plaintiffs, rather than the shareholder-clients, usually acted as the animating force in the initiation, prosecution, and resolution of the litigation.[8]

What produced the surge of retail derivative suits in 1930s New York? In essence, their proliferation stemmed from a confluence of three nineteenth-century doctrines about the costs of litigation and attorney's fees and three twentieth-century transformations in securities markets. These factors, together with New York's status as a financial metropolis and home to a cluster of lawyers with the diligence and daring to litigate complex financial cases against the directors of giant corporations, galvanized the rise of Main Street stockholder litigation in the United States.

## A. Legal Doctrines Governing Costs of Litigation

The first doctrine that underpinned the growth of retail stockholder suits in the 1930s was the longstanding "American rule" on the costs of litigation, under which each side of a lawsuit bore its own legal expenses. This rule developed in contrast to the British, common-law approach to attorney's fees, under which the losing party was responsible for the costs of the action (including the winning party's legal expenses).[9] In the context of shareholder litigation, the American rule had the effect of protecting small investors from having to pay the potentially overwhelming legal expenses of corporate defendants if their suits proved unsuccessful.

The second development was legal acceptance of contingency-fee arrangements for lawyers. In the last half of the nineteenth century, American judges and legislators gradually ceased to view such arrangements as a violation of the traditional common-law prohibition on champerty.[10] This shift was spurred in part by an egalitarian

[7] On the "prolific rise" of a new style of derivative action in 1930s New York, see Mortimer Hays, "A Study in Trial Tactics: Derivative Stockholders' Suits," *Columbia Law Review* 43.3 (April 1943): 275. See also Franklin S. Wood, *Survey and Report Regarding Stockholders' Derivative Suits, authored on behalf of the Special Committee on Corporate Litigation of the Chamber of Commerce of the State of New York* (New York: New York Chamber of Commerce, Special Committee on Corporate Litigation, 1944): 26–29 (sharply contrasting the characteristics of derivative litigation before and after 1930) [hereinafter *Wood Report*]; George D. Hornstein, "Rights of Stockholders in the New York Courts," *Yale Law Journal* 56.6 (June 1947): 949.

[8] Chiappinelli, "Underappreciated Importance," 915–16.

[9] Coffee, *Entrepreneurial Litigation*, 22–23; John Leubsdorf, "Toward a History of the American Rule on Attorney Fee Recovery," *Law and Contemporary Problems* 47.1 (Winter 1984): 9.

[10] Black's Law Dictionary defines "champerty" as an "agreement between an officious intermeddler in a lawsuit and a litigant by which the intermeddler pursues the litigant's claim as consideration for receiving part of any judgment proceeds." Bryan A. Garner, ed., *Black's Law Dictionary*, 11th ed. (St. Paul, MN: Thomson Reuters, 2019).

impulse to expand legal recourse for individuals of the lower classes who were injured in early industrial or transportation accidents.[11] In response, courts and legislatures began to allow lawyers to pursue cases against large corporations, such as railroad companies and their insurance carriers, on contingency.[12] In personal injury litigation in New York City, for instance, provisions for contingency fees in retainer agreements, while still rare in 1870, were common by 1890 and widespread by 1910.[13]

The third development—one that acquired particular importance for the plaintiff's bar in stockholder suits—was the recognition of the "common fund" doctrine. This policy, first approved by the U.S. Supreme Court in *Trustees v. Greenough* (1881), permitted plaintiffs who created a fund that resulted in a common benefit for others to recoup any attorney's fees they incurred out of that fund. In the context of retail stockholder litigation, the common fund doctrine provided the legal justification for compensating plaintiffs' counsel, who typically worked on contingency, by awarding them a portion of any financial recovery or other benefit obtained for a corporation (and indirectly for all its shareholders).[14]

## B. Transformations in Securities Markets

Significant changes in early twentieth-century securities markets also laid the groundwork for the rise of retail stockholder actions in the 1930s. First, the shares of publicly traded companies became increasingly dispersed among small investors in the 1910s and 1920s. This process began during World War I, when the marketing of Liberty Bonds first convinced average American households to buy securities.[15] In the 1920s, the strategies used to sell Liberty Bonds were retooled into campaigns for marketing common stock in publicly traded corporations to working-class and middle-class customers.[16] The effort was a dramatic success, as millions of ordinary Americans, including large numbers of women, began to buy the stock of public corporations for the first time.[17] While only a few hundred thousand individuals owned stocks or bonds before World War I, nearly eight million American households (approximately

[11] Peter Karsten, "Enabling the Poor to Have Their Day in Court: The Sanctioning of Contingency Fee Contracts, A History to 1940," *DePaul Law Review* 47.2 (Winter 1998): 244–45.

[12] Coffee, *Entrepreneurial Litigation*, 20.

[13] Randolph E. Bergstrom, *Courting Danger: Injury and Law in New York City, 1870–1910* (Ithaca and London: Cornell University Press, 1992), 89.

[14] George D. Hornstein, "The Counsel Fee in Stockholder's Derivative Suits," *Columbia Law Review* 39.5 (May 1939): 786–88. The common fund doctrine later permitted stockholders to recover attorney's fees even when the mutual benefit created was nonmonetary in nature. Coffee, *Entrepreneurial Litigation*, 27.

[15] Julia C. Ott, *When Wall Street Met Main Street: The Quest for an Investors' Democracy* (Cambridge: Harvard University Press, 2011), chap. 3.

[16] Ott, *When Wall Street Met Main Street*, 105–26.

[17] Mary O'Sullivan, "The Expansion of the U.S. Stock Market, 1885–1930: Historical Facts and Theoretical Fashions," *Enterprise & Society* 8.3 (September 2007): 524; John H. Sears, *The New Place of the Stockholder* (New York: Harper & Brothers, 1929), 215 (noting newly broad distribution of stocks among many small investors of moderate means in the 1920s); Sarah C. Haan, "Corporate Governance and the Feminization of Capital," *Stanford Law Review* 74.3 (March 2022): 542–50 (describing increasing numbers of women investors in securities during the "great bull market" of the 1920s).

25%) owned stock in 1929.[18] Scholars have attributed this steep increase in shareholding to expansive marketing techniques and aggressive, often deceptive efforts by large corporations and the securities industry to persuade average Americans that investing in securities was a safe activity.[19]

Second, the stock market crash of 1929 and the ensuing Great Depression inflicted staggering losses on investors and generated widespread hostility to managers of financial institutions and other giant corporations. These economic disasters at once created an ample pool of sympathetic plaintiffs and sowed pervasive mistrust about the competence and trustworthiness of business executives. They also encouraged a new breed of lawyers to formulate cases on behalf of small stockholders seeking to hold corporate managers personally accountable for the massive losses experienced by investors.[20]

Third, government hearings in the early 1930s widely publicized fraud and abuses on the part of officers and directors of public companies. As George Hornstein, the leading commentator on retail shareholder suits in the mid-twentieth century, asserted, derivative actions "rapidly increased in number after 1933, when Congressional disclosures made known to stockholders how some directors and officers were looting their corporations."[21] Abraham Pomerantz, one of the founders of Main Street shareholder litigation, recalled the impact of Congressional hearings in more colorful terms: "Back in the nineteen-thirties, when the Senate Subcommittee on Banking and Currency disinterred quite a few smelly skeletons from the corporate closet, the era of the stockholders' derivative action commenced."[22]

## C. New York's Prominence

Early on, New York established itself as the preeminent jurisdiction for retail stockholder litigation. New York's dominance was in part a product of its status as the nation's financial and commercial capital. As such, the metropolis served as the headquarters for a broad array of major business enterprises. It was also the place where the greatest number of directors of large corporations resided. As a result, personal

[18] Ott, *When Wall Street Met Main Street*, 52–53, 152. In the 1920s, numerous commentators called attention to the vulnerability of widely scattered small investors and their potential for exploitation by corporate managers. One of the first was William Z. Ripley, a well-known Harvard economist, who wrote a series of articles in the *Atlantic Monthly* that were later reprinted in Ripley's *Main Street and Wall Street* (1927). The problem of executive unaccountability to relatively powerless, broadly dispersed shareholders was further explored in Adolph Berle and Gardiner Means's classic work, *The Modern Corporation and Private Property* (1932).

[19] Ott, *When Wall Street Met Main Street*, chaps. 7–8; Arthur E. Wilmarth, Jr., "Prelude to Glass-Steagall: Abusive Securities Practices by National City Bank and Chase National Bank during the 'Roaring Twenties,'" *Tulane Law Review* 90.5 (2016): 1285–329.

[20] Coffee, *Entrepreneurial Litigation*, 27.

[21] Hornstein, "Rights of Stockholders," 949. Hornstein joined the faculty of New York University law school in 1951, where he specialized in corporate law and published numerous articles defending derivative litigation in the *Harvard Law Review, Yale Law Journal*, and *Columbia Law Review*, among other publications. See "George D. Hornstein, Law Professor, 85," *New York Times*, Feb. 23, 1990, B5.

[22] Abraham Pomerantz, "Point of View, Class Suits Defended: Actions Protect Stockholder and Small Consumer," *New York Times*, April 25, 1971, F22.

jurisdiction over both corporations and directors was easiest to obtain in New York.[23] Indeed, the city continued to be the center of the most significant retail derivative actions through the 1950s. As late as 1958, financial writer J. A. Livingston remarked that New York was still the "home of the biggest and most important stockholder suits."[24]

New York's position at the center of stockholder litigation was also linked to the presence of innovative, highly motivated attorneys with the capacity to pursue complicated financial cases against the directors of huge public corporations on a contingency basis. Such cases presented enormous challenges and risks, but they also offered new possibilities for lawyers at a time of economic distress. These opportunities were especially appealing to practitioners who were typically excluded from employment at corporate law firms and from representing large organizational clients, such as Jewish lawyers who joined the New York bar in record numbers in the 1930s.[25]

The Great Depression placed heavy burdens on the New York legal profession. As Jerold Auerbach has written, "In 1933 the median income of lawyers in Manhattan was below $3,000; nearly half the members of the metropolitan bar earned less than the minimum subsistence level for American families."[26] Two years later, 1,500 unemployed lawyers in New York City took a pauper's oath administered by the Works Progress Administration to qualify for work relief.[27]

But the economic hardship fell particularly harshly on Jewish attorneys, who comprised slightly more than half of the metropolitan bar in the 1930s.[28] According to a 1939 study commissioned by the Committee on Law of the Conference on Jewish Relations, Jewish lawyers trailed their non-Jewish counterparts in every economic category. One attorney surveyed strikingly described the profession as "a dignified road to starvation."[29]

[23] George D. Hornstein, "Legal Controls for Intracorporate Abuse-Present and Future," *Columbia Law Review* 41.3 (March 1941): 405 n.5. See also Hays, "Study in Trial Tactics," 275 n.1; Chiappinelli, "Underappreciated Importance," 924–25.

[24] J. A. Livingston, *The American Stockholder* (Philadelphia: Lippincott, 1958), 56. On New York's continuing prominence in stockholder litigation, see also George D. Hornstein, "Legal Therapeutics: The 'Salvage' Factor in Counsel Fee Awards," *Harvard Law Review* 69.4 (February 1956): 667–68; Douglas G. Cole, "Counsel Fees in Stockholders' Derivative and Class Actions—Hornstein Revisited," *University of Richmond Law Review* 6.2 (1972): 283–85 (half of stockholder suits resulting in counsel fee awards between 1955 and 1970 were filed in New York courts).

[25] On the large numbers of Jewish lawyers joining the bar in 1930s New York, see Robert W. Gordon, "The American Legal Profession, 1870–2000," in *The Cambridge History of Law in America*, vol. 3, ed. Michael Grossberg (Cambridge: Cambridge University Press, 2008), 78 ("In New York City, most dramatically, Jewish lawyers rose from 26 percent of new bar admissions between 1910 and 1920 to 80 percent between 1930 and 1934, stabilizing thereafter at 50 percent."). On the exclusion of Jewish lawyers from firms that represented large corporations, see Gordon, "American Legal Profession," 80; Mitchell, "Gentleman's Agreement," 85–95.

[26] Jerold S. Auerbach, *Unequal Justice* (New York: Oxford University Press, 1976), 159. See also Richard L. Abel, *American Lawyers* (New York: Oxford University Press, 1989), 159, 302 table 38.

[27] Melvin M. Fagen, "The Status of Jewish Lawyers in New York City: A Preliminary Report on a Study Made by the Conference on Jewish Relations" *Jewish Social Studies* 1.1 (January 1939): 73.

[28] Fagen, "Status of Jewish Lawyers," 75.

[29] Ibid., 74.

## D. Early Cases and Strategies

Before the 1930s, the large expense of pursuing derivative litigation made shareholder suits against the management of a public company a rare occurrence. As Samuel Untermyer, a partner at Guggenheimer, Untermyer, & Marshall, then the nation's most successful Jewish law firm, told the New York County Lawyers' Association in 1911, "It is all very well to say that the minority stockholder has his redress if his company is being managed in an adverse interest. He hasn't--litigating against one of these powerful systems is an expensive business." Rather, such suits represented a "luxury reserved for the large holders and then only when they have plenty of money and infinite patience."[30]

As discussed above, several forces contributed to making stockholder suits less exclusive by the 1930s. In particular, the broad diffusion of securities, the collapse of the stock market, the wide dissemination of information about managerial misconduct, and the willingness of economically marginalized lawyers, often first- or second-generation Jewish immigrants, to pursue challenging financial claims on contingency helped to convert derivative litigation from a "luxury reserved for the large holders . . . with plenty of money" to a device that shareholders from middle and even working-class households could employ.

Two famous early cases in the history of retail shareholder litigation, *Gallin v. National City Bank of New York*[31] and *Bookbinder v. Chase*,[32] illustrate these forces at work. The first, *Gallin v. National City Bank*, was initially developed by 30-year-old Abraham Pomerantz in 1933.[33] The year before, Pomerantz had been contacted by Celia Gallin, the widow of his high school gym teacher.[34] As he later recalled, Gallin told him that her husband had left her 20 shares of the stock of National City Bank of New York (City Bank), then the largest bank in the United States and a predecessor of today's Citigroup, when he died. But the value of the stock had declined precipitously since the market crash. Once worth $585 a share, it had fallen to $17 by 1932. Gallin asked Pomerantz for his advice about whether there was anyone she could sue. His first reaction was that she had no recourse.[35]

But Pomerantz changed his mind after the Senate Banking Committee began a public investigation into abuses by City Bank and its high-profile president, Charles E. Mitchell.[36] Beginning on February 21, 1933, Mitchell faced harsh questioning by the Committee's counsel, Ferdinand Pecora, which revealed pervasive misconduct

[30] Samuel Untermyer, "Some Needed Legislative Reforms in Corporate Management" (Jan. 5, 1911), quoted in Harris Berlack, "Stockholders' Suits: A Possible Substitute," *Michigan Law Review* 35.4 (February 1937): 601 n.12. On Guggenheimer, Untermyer, & Marshall, see Auerbach, *Unequal Justice*, 122. On Untermyer's career, see "Untermyer Dead in His 82nd Year," *New York Times*, March 17, 1940, 1.

[31] Gallin v. Nat'l City Bank, 273 N.Y.S. 87, 119–20 (N.Y. Sup. Ct. 1934); Gallin v. Nat'l City Bank, 281 N.Y.S. 795, 807 (N.Y. Sup. Ct. 1935) (report of referee).

[32] "Bookbinder v. Chase Nat'l Bank," *New York Law Journal*, June 23, 1937, 3166.

[33] Spencer Klaw, "Abe Pomerantz is Watching You," *Fortune*, Feb. 1968, 156.

[34] Edward A. Gargan, "Abraham Pomerantz, 79, Pioneering Lawyer," *New York Times*, Nov. 21, 1982, 44.

[35] Klaw, "Pomerantz," 156. On the enormous size and catastrophic collapse of National City Bank, see Wilmarth, "Prelude to Glass-Steagall," 1297–1301.

[36] Klaw, "Pomerantz," 156.

and conflicts of interest at City Bank and incited extensive public outrage.[37] Early in his testimony, Mitchell conceded that he and other senior executives had received massive payments from an incentive-based profit-sharing plan in the years and months leading up to the stock market crash.[38] While many shareholders (like the widow Celia Gallin) lost their life savings when the price of City Bank's shares collapsed, the bank's board of directors failed to demand that Mitchell or other insiders return the millions of dollars in bonuses they received based on artificially inflated profits.[39]

The disclosures coming out of the 1933 Senate Banking Committee hearings prompted Pomerantz to revise his legal advice to Gallin. As a journalist from *Fortune* magazine recounted:

> [He] told her that if she would sue, he thought there was a chance of forcing Mitchell and the others to return some of their bonus money. He explained that, at best, this would increase the book value of her stock by only a few cents a share, but that she had nothing to lose.[40]

At the time he gave this opinion, Pomerantz was still relatively inexperienced and, like many lawyers in Depression-era New York, struggling both professionally and economically. The child of Jewish immigrants from Russia, the Brooklyn-born Pomerantz had aspired to practice law from an early age. Because there was then no need for a college degree to practice law, Pomerantz, along with many other first- and second-generation immigrants of his era, skipped college and enrolled in the night program at Brooklyn Law School after graduating from high school. While holding down a series of full-time day jobs, he completed the four-year program and entered the practice of law in 1924.[41]

As a young lawyer, Pomerantz found it difficult to obtain clients. Sharing office space with three other solo practitioners, he earned some money writing briefs for a personal injury attorney in Brooklyn and doing occasional real estate work for his father's small construction business. But both these sources of fees dissolved by 1929. Searching for income after the onset of the Depression, he tried to support himself, his wife, and their two young children by answering mail-order inquiries from other attorneys for five dollars a question.[42]

Given these circumstances, Pomerantz clearly lacked both the expertise in financial litigation and the economic resources to bring a complex, potentially protracted case involving charges of elaborate accounting fraud and mismanagement against

[37] On explosive revelations of deceptive and unscrupulous practices at City Bank in the 1920s, see generally Wilmarth, "Prelude to Glass-Steagall."

[38] On improper compensation practices at City Bank, see Wilmarth, "Prelude to Glass-Steagall," 1322–26. See also "Mitchell Avoided Income Tax in 1929 by '2,800,000 Loss,'" *New York Times*, Feb. 22, 1933, 1.

[39] Wilmarth, "Prelude to Glass-Steagall," 1323.

[40] Klaw, "Pomerantz," 156.

[41] Klaw, "Pomerantz," 156; Gargaran, "Abraham Pomerantz," 44. A 1939 study of Jewish lawyers in New York City found that only 44% possessed college degrees and that almost half graduated from either Brooklyn Law School or NYU Law, "where tuition is relatively low and where part-time courses are offered." Fagen, "Status of Jewish Lawyers," 81, 83.

[42] Klaw, "Pomerantz," 156.

the directors of a colossal banking institution like City Bank. Fortunately, Pomerantz was able to recruit a veteran New York trial lawyer, David L. Podell, to take the lead in the case. In 1933, Podell was already in the midst of a distinguished legal career. Like Pomerantz, he was of Russian Jewish heritage, having emigrated to New York with his family as a child. Unlike Pomerantz, Podell had elite academic credentials, holding degrees from Columbia College and Columbia Law School. After joining the New York bar in 1907, he soon gained a reputation as a consummate trial lawyer and an expert in antitrust and trade association law. In recognition of his accomplishments, Podell was named chief special assistant to the U.S. Attorney General in 1921 to direct the prosecution of major antitrust cases for the Department of Justice, where he secured a number of notable convictions for antitrust violations.[43]

In the 1920s, Podell formed Hays, Podell, & Shulman (1924–47), a firm that gradually grew in size and stature over time.[44] By the early 1930s, it had developed an orientation toward liberal and left-wing politics and a "reputation for having a social conscience."[45] For instance, the firm hired a series of talented, leftist young lawyers, including Felix Cohen, Benjamin Algase, and Victor Rabinowitz.[46] In his memoir, Rabinowitz, a self-described "unrepentant leftist" who got his first legal job at the firm in 1934, characterized the political orientation of Hays, Podell, & Shulman as progressive (though not entirely radical): "David Podell was an eminent Roosevelt supporter, and Morty Hays was, a few years later, president of the NYC chapter of the National Lawyers Guild."[47] He added that, despite the busy nature of the firm's practice: "No one complained when I took a few hours off now and then to do work for the ILD [International Labor Defense] or the American Labor Party."[48]

With Roosevelt's election in 1932, Podell, an enthusiastic advocate of Roosevelt and the New Deal, was tapped to advise the new administration. As an authority on antitrust law, he played an important role in drafting the National Industrial Recovery Act in early 1933.[49]

It was around the same time that Podell agreed to take Gallin's case on contingency, serve as lead counsel, and conduct the trial.[50] On February 27, 1933, the Gallin

[43] "D. L. Podell Dead; Noted Lawyer, 62; Former Special Assistant to U.S. Attorney General Had Helped to Draft NIRA," *New York Times*, Feb. 2, 1947, 57. The entries for Podell in the Martindale-Hubbell Law Directories identify his year of birth as 1883.

[44] See entry for Mortimer Hays in *Encyclopedia of American Biography: New Series* 11 (New York: The American Historical Company, Inc., 1940), 561–62.

[45] Dalia Tsuk Mitchell, *Architect of Justice: Felix S. Cohen and the Founding of American Legal Pluralism* (Ithaca: Cornell University Press, 2007), 63.

[46] "Biographical Sketch," *Rutgers Law Review* 9 (Winter 1954): 347; Victor Rabinowitz, *Unrepentant Leftist: A Lawyer's Memoir* (Urbana: University of Illinois, 1996), 13.

[47] Rabinowitz, *Unrepentant Leftist*, 13, 18.

[48] Rabinowitz, *Unrepentant Leftist*, 18. Rabinowitz left Hays, Podell for Louis Boudin's union-side labor law firm in 1938. Ibid., 13–14, 18. Felix Cohen joined Nathan Margold and other New Deal lawyers at the Department of the Interior in 1933. Mitchell, *Architect of Justice*, 59, 63–64. Benjamin Algase, who remained at Hays, Podell and its successor firms through the 1960s, played an active role in the National Lawyers Guild for many years, including during the McCarthy Era. See entry for Hays, Algase, Feuer, Porter, & Spanier in *The Martindale-Hubbell Law Directory* (1963), 4207 (noting Algase's membership on the National Executive Board of the National Lawyers Guild in the 1940s and 1950s and his service as an editor of the Lawyers Guild Review from 1940 to 1948).

[49] "D. L. Podell Dead," 57.

[50] Klaw, "Pomerantz," 156.

derivative action commenced. On behalf of Gallin and other similarly situated shareholders of City Bank, it charged the officers and directors of the bank and its securities affiliate, National City Company (City Company), with wide-ranging breaches of their fiduciary duties and sought to recover damages from the director-defendants for the benefit of the two corporations.[51]

The proceedings in Gallin unfolded laboriously over the course of two and a half years.[52] Fifteen corporate law firms represented the individual defendants. The roster of prestigious defense counsel included Wall Street fixtures such as Davis, Polk, Wardwell, Gardiner, & Reed, Donovan, Leisure, Newton, & Lumbard, and Chadbourne, Stanchfield, & Levy.[53] When the case came to trial before state court justice Edward Dore in 1934, he rejected several of Gallin's causes of action. But he also certified an array of "complicated issues of corporate accounting" relating to executive bonuses, which required "long, intricate, and difficult examination," for resolution by a referee, Frank Laughlin.[54] The subsequent referee's hearing extended over two months in late 1934 and early 1935, producing more than 1,600 pages of testimony.[55]

The conclusion of the hearing yielded a significant recovery for City Bank and City Company (and indirectly for Gallin and the other shareholders). Laughlin found the outside directors who approved the bonuses for Mitchell and two other bank officers based on the size of corporate profits personally liable for more than $1.8 million in inflated executive compensation. In effect, Laughlin concluded that the outside directors had been negligent in failing to supervise the execution of the profit-sharing plan and had improperly permitted Mitchell and other insiders to overstate corporate profits for the purpose of calculating their bonuses.[56]

The final judgment included an award of $450,000 in fees for plaintiffs' counsel and affiliated accountants, based on approximately 25% of the amount recovered for the corporations.[57] In hindsight, Pomerantz felt he "had made a poor bargain with Podell, [because] even though he had collaborated actively throughout the trial, his share of the fee amounted to only $60,000." Nevertheless, Pomerantz's earnings totaled "more than three times as much money as he had cleared during all of his first ten years at the bar" and represented a remarkable payday at a time when the typical New York City attorney earned less than $3,000 a year.[58]

The field of executive compensation proved to be a fertile one for plaintiffs' lawyers seeking to develop retail stockholder cases.[59] As Pomerantz put it, "The word

[51] Gallin v. Nat'l City Bank, 273 N.Y.S. 92 (because the "action is a representative one," any recovery "does not belong to the individual plaintiff stockholders, but belongs to and must be paid over to [City Bank] or [City Company]").

[52] The protracted course of the Gallin litigation soon became standard practice in complex derivative actions. See Hays, "Study in Trial Tactics," 300, n.40.

[53] Gallin v. Nat'l City Bank, 273 N.Y.S. 91–92.

[54] Gallin v. Nat'l City Bank, 273 N.Y.S. 119–20.

[55] Gallin v. Nat'l City Bank, 281 N.Y.S. 797.

[56] Gallin v. Nat'l City Bank, 281 N.Y.S. 807–808.

[57] "Lawyer's Award $450,000; Court Allows Sum to D. L. Podell in National City Case," *New York Times*, Aug. 2, 1935, 22.

[58] Klaw, "Pomerantz," 156. On lawyer salaries in 1930s New York, see Fagen, "The Status of Jewish Lawyers," 95; Auerbach, *Unequal Justice*, 159.

[59] In addition to Gallin and Bookbinder, see Winkelman v. General Motors Corp., 44 F. Supp. 960 (S.D.N.Y. 1942) (holding GM directors personally liable for improper bonus payments); Heller v. Boylan, 29 N.Y.S.2d 653 (Sup. Ct. 1941) (holding American Tobacco directors personally liable for overpayments of

got around.... People would call up and say, 'Hey, I've got a case like the one you just won against the National City Bank!"[60] Even before the Gallin matter was resolved, Pomerantz and Podell teamed up on a second action involving executive bonuses in the fall of 1933. This time, Pomerantz received a tip from a stockbroker about a possible lead plaintiff, a woman named Gertrude Bookbinder, who owned shares of The Chase National Bank of the City of New York (Chase), a predecessor of today's JPMorgan Chase & Co. Like City Bank, Chase was a huge banking and securities conglomerate with a lavish executive bonus plan in place in the 1920s. Like Charles Mitchell, Albert H. Wiggin, the president of Chase, came under harsh fire during the Senate Banking Committee hearings in 1933. Along with evidence of financial manipulation, insider trading, and self-dealing, the hearings revealed that Wiggin too had received improperly inflated bonuses that he retained even after Chase's stock collapsed.[61]

The stockbroker's referral eventually led to the filing of *Gertrude Bookbinder v. Chase National Bank of the City of New York* in October 1933.[62] Once again, David Podell and his firm served as lead counsel and chief trial lawyers. Once again, a cavalcade of white-shoe corporate law firms represented the defendant directors, prominently including Cravath, deGersdorff, Swaine, & Wood (a predecessor of today's Cravath, Swaine, & Moore), Sullivan & Cromwell, White & Case, and Simpson, Thacher, & Bartlett.[63] As the Cravath firm's biographer, Robert Swaine, described the case:

> It was a consolidation of a number of actions by stockholders of the Chase Bank and Chase Securities Corporation against the officers and directors of both corporations and holding companies controlled by Albert H. Wiggin, former president of the Chase Bank, to recover millions of dollars of alleged losses suffered by Chase Bank or Chase Securities Corporation, and alleged profits made by others of the defendants, as a result of a variety of transactions entered into during the 1920s.

After lengthy depositions and discovery, the suit proceeded to trial on April 2, 1937. Less than two weeks later, Wiggin and the estates of two other inside directors made formal settlement offers. Wiggin promised to return two million dollars of past compensation to Chase and Chase Securities Corporation, while the estates pledged to return $250,000 each, for a total corporate recovery of $2.5 million (equivalent to roughly $54 million today).[64]

bonuses to executives). On executive compensation cases in this era, see generally Wells, "'No Man Can Be Worth $1,000,000 a Year.'"

[60] Klaw, "Pomerantz," 156.

[61] Hearings before Committee on Banking and Currency on S. 84, 72nd Cong. Sess. (1932–1933). On improper compensation practices at Chase in the 1920s, see Wilmarth, "Prelude to Glass-Steagall," 1322–26.

[62] Bookbinder v. Chase Nat. Bank, N.Y. Co. Clk's Index No. 42665/1933.

[63] For a list of ten prominent New York firms representing the individual defendants, see Bookbinder v. Chase Nat. Bank of City of N.Y., 153 Misc. 899 (Sup. Ct. 1934).

[64] Robert T. Swaine, *The Cravath Firm and its Predecessors, 1819–1947* (Clark, NJ: Lawbook Exchange 2007), 680 & n.2. For the present value of the settlement, see https://www.usinflationcalculator.com (last checked June 10, 2024).

Although not required by New York law, counsel for plaintiffs and defendants agreed that the court should supervise and confirm the settlement. Accordingly, notice of the proposed offer was provided to all public shareholders of Chase (with 7,400,000 shares outstanding) and a referee was appointed to assess its adequacy and fairness.[65] After a month of hearings, the referee recommended approval of the settlement, which the court granted on June 24, 1937.[66]

The court's confirmation of the settlement included an award of $625,000, again representing 25% of the corporation's recovery, to plaintiffs' attorneys as compensation for their services.[67] This time around, Pomerantz negotiated with Podell for $150,000 of the fee, a substantial increase over the $60,000 he took home in the Gallin case two years earlier.[68] The remainder of the award, less payments for expert accountants and lawyers for co-plaintiffs and intervenors, went to Podell and his firm.

Podell and Pomerantz parlayed their considerable success in Gallin and Bookbinder into new retail shareholder cases during the late 1930s and 1940s. For instance, in *Litwin v. Allen*, Podell represented Eva Litwin, a holder of 10 of the 900,000 outstanding shares of Guaranty Trust Company of New York (Guaranty Trust), an affiliate of J. P. Morgan & Co. Podell also served as lead counsel in the litigation. The complaint, filed in the Supreme Court of New York County in 1938, charged the officers and directors of Guaranty Trust with misconduct in a range of transactions. The defendant-directors were chiefly represented by Wall Street powerhouse, Davis, Polk, Wardwell, Gardiner, & Reed.[69]

The trial that ensued in *Litwin v. Allen* led not only to another victory for Podell but also to a landmark in corporate governance on a director's fiduciary duty of care (and a staple of corporate law casebooks for years to come). In ruling that the directors of Guaranty Trust breached their duty of care, the court condemned one of the challenged transactions approved by the bank's board as "so improvident, so risky, so unusual and unnecessary as to be contrary to fundamental conceptions of prudent banking practice."[70] Pending appeal, all the defendants chose to settle in 1941. The court-approved settlement provided a $750,000 recovery for Guaranty Trust, with roughly one third of that amount earmarked for plaintiffs' attorneys and their accountants.[71]

Pomerantz also found success striking out on his own. Consider a derivative action he filed in 1938 against Radio Corporation of America (RCA) and the directors of RCA, Westinghouse, and General Electric on behalf of RCA shareholder George Saievetz, which later became consolidated as *Druckerman v. Harbord*.[72] Nearly forty

[65] Swaine, *The Cravath Firm*, 680. For the number of outstanding public shares, see *Wood Report*, 51.

[66] Swaine, *The Cravath Firm*, 680 & ns. 3–4.

[67] Ibid., n.4; "Bookbinder v. Chase Nat'l Bank," *New York Law Journal*, June 23, 1937, 3166 (reporting fee award).

[68] Klaw, "Pomerantz," 156.

[69] Litwin v. Allen, 25 N.Y.S.2d 667 (N.Y. Sup. Ct. 1940).

[70] Litwin v. Allen, 25 N.Y.S.2d 667, 699 (Sup. Ct. 1940).

[71] On the fee award in Litwin, see *Wood Report*, 50, 79. Criticizing Podell and his team for being overly thorough in the discovery phase, the Wood Report complained that "20 persons, fifteen of them directors and six senior officers of the bank, were examined for a total of 30 days, a total of 1370 pages of testimony being taken." *Wood Report*, 62.

[72] Druckerman v. Harbord, Sup. Ct., N.Y. Co. Clerk's Index No. 31307/1938.

other plaintiff-stockholders and intervenors brought separate actions involving the same claims. In such circumstances, veteran practitioners of derivative suits—a group that now included Pomerantz—stood the best chance of receiving a coveted appointment as lead counsel for all plaintiffs and intervenors once the cases were consolidated.[73] Acting as chief counsel had the benefit of giving such lawyers the ability to control strategy for the consolidated litigation; it also put them in line to secure the lion's share of attorney's fees if the case proved successful.

As a mark of his growing prominence, Pomerantz won appointment as lead counsel of the combined derivative actions in *Druckerman* in 1939.[74] Three years later, defendants offered to resolve the suit for $1,000,000. After the court approved the settlement, it set aside approximately 25% of the recovery obtained for the corporation for plaintiffs' attorney's fees. Pomerantz, as lead counsel, was allocated $100,000 of the total.[75]

David Podell died in 1947, bringing a long and remarkably successful legal career to an end. Three years later, a profile in *Time* magazine acknowledged Pomerantz as the "nation's top lawyer" in the then-flourishing field of retail derivative litigation.[76]

## II. The Corporate Bar Strikes Back

Historians of the legal profession often locate the birth of the modern corporate lawyer and modern corporate law firm around the turn of the twentieth century.[77] It was during this time that the "pinnacle of success at the bar" became defined as a partnership at a law firm that catered exclusively to a corporate clientele.[78] By the 1920s, business lawyers also dominated the leadership of the legal profession. In the words of Jerold Auerbach, "[C]orporate lawyers enjoyed unchallenged professional hegemony and unsurpassed opportunity to articulate their wishes as professional values."[79]

[73] On the preferred judicial approach to consolidating duplicative derivative actions in New York, see Dresdner v. Goldman Sachs Trading Corporation, 269 N.Y.S. 360 (N.Y. App. Div. 2d Dep't 1934). On the practice of appointing a lead or general counsel to control consolidated derivative actions, see George D. Hornstein, "Problems of Procedure in Stockholder's Derivative Suits," *Columbia Law Review* 42.4, (April 1942): 580–81.

[74] "Druckerman v. Harbord," *New York Law Journal*, March 8, 1939 (appointing Pomerantz as general counsel); *Wood Report*, 68 (describing consolidation).

[75] *Wood Report*, 84; Swaine, *The Cravath Firm*, 682 n.1.

[76] "D. L. Podell Dead," 57; "In the Stockholders' Interest?," *Time*, May 22, 1950, vol. 55, issue 21, 95. A firm founded by Pomerantz in 1940, Pomerantz, Levy, Haudek, & Block, continues to this day as Pomerantz LLP. See https://pomlaw.com/firm-history.

[77] Mark E. Steiner, "The Legal Profession" in *A Companion to American Legal History*, ed. Sally E. Hadden (Chichester: Wiley, 2013), 256.

[78] Gordon, "American Legal Profession," 93. On the growth of specialized corporate law firms and the occupation of the corporate lawyer, see also Lawrence M. Friedman, *A History of American Law* (New York: Touchstone, 2005), 484–90; Swaine, *The Cravath Firm*, 680; Robert W. Gordon, "'The Ideal and the Actual in the Law': Fantasies and Practices of New York City Lawyers, 1870–1910," in *The New High Priests: Lawyers in Post-Civil War America*, ed. Gerard Gawalt (Westport.: Greenwood, 1984); Robert W. Gordon, "Legal Thought and Legal Practice in the Age of American Enterprise, 1870–1920" in *Professions and Professional Ideologies in America*, ed. Gerald L. Geison (Chapel Hill: University of North Carolina Press, 1983).

[79] Auerbach, *Unequal Justice*, 130.

This legal elite was knit together by a profound identification with the interests of their institutional corporate clients. Corporate lawyers in New York and elsewhere worked tirelessly to enhance the power of managers of large corporations. They convinced state legislatures to amend business codes to eliminate prior restrictions on corporate size and powers and persuaded courts to grant directors virtually unfettered discretion over business decisions.[80] They also held a shared commitment to using the U.S. Constitution as a weapon to stave off government efforts to regulate, tax, or otherwise restrain the power of corporations.[81] This commitment became all the more fervent in light of the rising tide of corporate regulation ushered in by the New Deal.

Given this climate, it is perhaps predictable that the corporate bar greeted the sudden onslaught of retail derivative suits against powerful directors of prominent public companies with indignation. With their prized business clientele already besieged by New Deal measures that imposed new obligations on corporations, eminent law firms reacted to an avalanche of state court litigation, engineered by upstart lawyers for run-of-the-mill investors, with unsparing contempt. The frequent appearance of women with small holdings of shares as lead plaintiffs (such as Celia Gallin, Gertrude Bookbinder, and Eva Litwin) likely added to the scorn the business community heaped on retail derivative suits and the lawyers who pursued them.[82]

As early as 1937, one New York plaintiffs' lawyer, Harris Berlack, bemoaned how the retail stockholder suit was unfairly and "universally reviled and deplored" by corporate executives and their counsel.[83] Even more troubling to Berlack was the personal nature of the attacks on plaintiff-shareholders and their attorneys "in even the most thoroughly justified and socially praiseworthy" derivative cases. As he observed first hand:

> So intensified has become the rancor of this attitude [on the part of business leaders and the business bar], that the upstart who dares to question the conduct of corporate affairs is cast outside the pale of common decency. The opprobrium which may be heaped upon the plaintiff and counsel in a stockholders' action, by lawyers who have otherwise a reputation for calmness, courtesy, and fairness, would be unbelievable if so many examples were not recorded in stenographers' minutes and printed briefs.

According to Berlack, the smaller the holdings of the suing stockholders, the more severe was the "viciousness of such attacks."[84]

[80] Gordon, "The Ideal and the Actual," 58; Louis K. Liggett Corp. v. Lee, 288 U.S. 517, 541–80 (1933) (Brandeis, J., dissenting) (describing changes to state business codes to increase power of large corporations and expand discretion of corporate management). See also Gordon, "American Legal Profession," 95.

[81] Gordon, "American Legal Profession," 90.

[82] For evidence of the prevalence of women as plaintiffs in retail derivative suits and an illustration of contempt within the business community for the financial capacities of women, see *Wood Report*, 56, 46–47. On the dramatic increase of women as shareholders of public companies in the first half of the twentieth century and the derision they often provoked among corporate experts, see Haan, "Corporate Governance," 522–24.

[83] Berlack, "Stockholders' Suits," 599.

[84] Berlack, "Stockholders' Suits," 605–06.

By the early 1940s, corporate representatives moved beyond personal insults against plaintiffs' lawyers and their clients to legislative strategies to restrict the availability of derivative actions, especially for investors of modest means. In 1942, the New York Chamber of Commerce, a private organization comprised of "extremely conservative corporation and financial interests," commissioned an investigation into minority stockholder suits and the need for legislative reforms by a Special Committee on Corporate Litigation.[85] The resulting study, generally known as the Wood Report after its lead author, corporate lawyer Franklin S. Wood, stridently attacked the legitimacy of retail derivative suits and the ethics of stockholders' lawyers.

The Wood Report focused on what it portrayed as an explosion of groundless derivative actions in which the named plaintiffs were small investors and the individual defendants were officers and directors of public companies.[86] According to the Report, the plaintiff's bar that arose in the 1930s routinely exploited unwitting shareholders to concoct "vexatious," baseless claims against honest, faithful corporate managers.[87] As the Report charged, unscrupulous plaintiffs' lawyers were especially adept at finding purportedly unsophisticated investors, especially impressionable women who were alleged to have little or no understanding of the substance of the litigation and were "merely a catspaw for counsel."[88] Such lawyers then filed meritless "strike suits," essentially nuisance actions designed to extort settlements that provided generous payments of attorneys' fees but little or no relief for the corporation.[89] Driving home his point, Wood declared, "This shoddy burlesque of a professional relationship to clients makes the ambulance-chaser by comparison a paragon of propriety."[90]

But the Wood Report did not stop there. It went on to accuse stockholders' lawyers of pretending to provide a "social benefit" while in fact perpetrating a train of ethical abuses, including solicitation, champerty, and fraud. As the Report provocatively charged, "[D]erivative actions have come to harbor as a matter of course solicitation and inducement in bringing them, champerty and maintenance in their prosecution, the brokerage of litigation in their trial, and division of fees with laymen at their conclusion.[91] It concluded by condemning the entire field of retail shareholder litigation as "a business of irresponsible, vexatious, commonly ill-founded litigation for lawyer's profit, without any of the controls that a real relation of attorney and client assures."[92]

By the time the Wood Report was issued in 1944, corporate lawyers and lobbyists had already succeeded in enlisting the aid of New York Republicans to curb derivative

85 George D. Hornstein, "New Aspects of Stockholders' Derivative Suits," *Columbia Law Review* 47.1 (January 1947): 2 n.8.

86 *Wood Report*, 16, 26–29, 54.

87 Ibid., 56–57.

88 Ibid., 56, 46. For sarcastic effect, Wood added, "Presumably, these [women] stockholders flock to examine S.E.C. reports and studies, minutes of the Public Service Commission and the like for these have been the main source of information upon which stockholders' suits are based." Ibid., 47. For an important discussion of the relationship between rising numbers of purportedly passive women stockholders and the increasing power of corporate managers in this era, see Haan, "Corporate Governance," 525–26 ("The passivity thesis helped to justify the much-celebrated shift in corporate power away from shareholders, a group that included many women, to corporate managers, a group that was exclusively male.").

89 *Wood Report*, 49.

90 Ibid., 47.

91 Ibid., 48.

92 Ibid., 49.

suits.[93] First, in 1941, the legislature amended the state's business code to give corporations the power to indemnify directors for litigation expenses incurred in defending derivative actions.[94] The next year, it shortened the statute of limitations in derivative suits from ten to six years and mandated that such suits be filed within six years of the commission of a wrongful act rather than from the date of its discovery.[95] Then, in 1944, the legislature passed a contemporaneous ownership rule, which required that plaintiffs-shareholders in derivative cases own their stock at the time of the challenged act or transaction (thereby making it more difficult for lawyers to locate representative plaintiffs).[96]

The same year, the legislature enacted a fourth law, the nation's first "security-for-expenses" statute, plainly designed to insulate corporate managers from derivative suits by retail stockholders.[97] This measure, codified as Section 61-b of New York General Corporation Law, was the most controversial yet, drawing strong objections from the New York County Lawyers Association, the New York City chapter of the National Lawyers Guild, the American Investors Union, the American Federation of Labor, and the Congress of Industrial Organizations.[98] Section 61-b entitled corporations to require small shareholders (defined as those holding less than 5% of the outstanding shares of a corporation or stock valued at less than $50,000) to post a bond for all defendants' reasonable expenses, including attorneys' fees, incurred during the litigation.[99] Given the standard practice in derivative cases involving major public companies of having a separate prestigious Wall Street law firm represent each defendant-director, total defense costs could quickly reach staggering totals.

Together, these four amendments to New York's business code took sharp aim at the field of Main Street shareholder litigation. Advocates for investors bemoaned that such legislation, clearly designed to "strangle" and "kill off" stockholder suits at the behest of corporate interests, represented the "death knell" of shareholders' rights.[100] Indeed, in the immediate aftermath of passage of Section 61-b, such predictions seemed to ring true, as stockholder actions filed in New York state courts declined precipitously.[101]

However, to the frustration of corporate executives and their lawyers, prophecies about the demise of derivative litigation underestimated the persistence and ingenuity of the New York plaintiff's bar. Stockholders' lawyers soon developed a strategy to circumvent Section 61-b in many cases. If defendants moved for security, plaintiffs invoked the statutory right of shareholders to inspect corporate books and records

93 Hornstein, "New Aspects," 2, 4–10; Chiappinelli, "Unappreciated Importance," 927–29.

94 George D. Hornstein, "The Death Knell of Stockholders' Derivative Suits in New York," *California Law Review* 32.2 (June 1944):126 n.9.

95 Hornstein, "Death Knell," 126 n.9.

96 Ibid., 126 n.10; Chiappinelli, "Unappreciated Importance," 928.

97 N.Y. Gen. Corp. Law § 61-b. See Hornstein, "Death Knell," 123 (describing the security for expense statute as "virtually strangling stockholders' derivative suits"); Hornstein, "New Aspects," 3.

98 Sergei S. Zlinkoff, "The American Investor and the Constitutionality of Section 61-B of the New York General Corporation Law," *Yale Law Journal* 54.2 (March 1945): 360.

99 N.Y. Gen. Corp. Law § 61-b; Hornstein, "Death Knell," 124.

100 Hornstein, "Death Knell." See also Zlinkoff, "American Investor"; Victor House, "Stockholders' Suits and the Coudert-Mitchell Laws," *New York University Law Quarterly Review* 20.4 (October 1945).

101 Hornstein, "New Aspects," 5.

to gain access to the corporation's list of stockholders. They then provided information about the pending suit to other shareholders and invited newcomers to join the litigation so that the combined holdings of plaintiffs satisfied the $50,000 threshold for avoiding application of the security requirement.[102] Through such maneuvers, the New York plaintiff's bar largely managed to undercut the intended impact of Section 61-b. According to Abraham Pomerantz, by the 1960s, savvy corporate counsel realized that a motion to require a plaintiff to post a bond for defendants' expenses would prompt the plaintiff to move for a list of shareholders and, once the list was obtained, to disseminate information about managerial misdeeds to other stockholders.[103]

## III. Taking Stock of Retail Derivative Litigation and the Plaintiff's Bar in Business Law

### A. Social Benefits of Derivative Suits

In the face of relentless hostility from business leaders and the business bar, the founders of retail stockholder litigation strove to publicize its importance as the only private remedy available to protect small investors from the malfeasance of corporate officers and directors. Writing in 1943, in the aftermath of his firm's triumphs in the *Gallin, Bookbinder, Litwin*, and *Guth* cases, Mortimer Hays penned a vigorous defense of the "social justification" for retail derivative suits. He began by emphasizing the pressing need for such litigation in light of widespread evidence of blatant, otherwise unchecked managerial wrongdoing.[104] He then highlighted the unique role that derivative actions played in protecting shareholders and in deterring corporate executives from misconduct. The "minority stockholders' suit," Hays argued, was "often the only instrumentality by which this scattered majority of the stockholders can effectively exercise control over the management." The rise of retail derivative suits thus offered dispersed, otherwise powerless shareholders of public companies a rare opportunity to impose "a real measure of restraint upon faithless or reckless management."[105] In the same vein, Hay's and Podell's partner, Sergei Zlinkoff, warned that curbing the availability of Main Street derivative actions would "mean[] the complete disappearance of any equitable judicial check on fiduciaries to whom the public at large has entrusted tens of billions of dollars in assets."[106]

Abraham Pomerantz also championed the social benefits of derivative litigation. While acknowledging that successful cases often resulted in lucrative awards

[102] Note, "Security for Expenses in Shareholders' Derivative Suits: 23 Years' Experience," *Columbia Journal of Law and Social Problems* 4.1 (1968): 62–63. New York's highest court upheld this strategy in Baker v. McFadden, 300 N.Y. 325 (1950). Later on, plaintiffs' lawyers developed a second tactic to sidestep Section 61-b. They began to file suits in federal court containing claims based on federal securities statutes, which were exempt from New York's bond posting requirement, along with traditional state causes of action for breach of fiduciary duty. Note, "Security for Expenses," 59–60.

[103] Ibid., 64–65. See also Ralph C. Ferrara, Kevin T. Abikoff, and Laura Leedy Gansler, eds., *Shareholder Derivative Litigation: Besieging the Board*, § 4.06 (Law Journal Seminars-Press 2013).

[104] Hays, "Study in Trial Tactics," 275–76.

[105] Hays, "Study in Trial Tactics," 277.

[106] Zlinkoff, "The American Investor," 372.

of attorney's fees, he maintained that derivative suits provided critical safeguards to stockholders of modest means. In part, such suits protected ordinary investors by obtaining valuable recoveries for corporations harmed by wrongful actions of directors. In 1950, Pomerantz asserted that, as a result of the stockholder litigation he filed in the 1930s and 40s, "he and associates have forced corporate bigwigs to pay back more than $20 million to their companies."[107] Two decades later, he estimated that the universe of retail derivative actions filed since *Gallin* in 1933 had "resulted in recovering hundreds of millions of dollars for corporations despoiled by their fiduciaries."[108]

Even more important, according to Pomerantz and other advocates for derivative litigation, was the "socially indispensable" role such suits played in deterring wrongdoing and promoting corporate integrity.[109] As Pomerantz' longtime partner, Julius Levy, argued, "The stockholder's suit is the only avenue of redress not only for the stockholders, but for the corporations themselves against unfaithful managements in control of the corporations; and the threat of such suits is the only sanction restraining corporate fiduciaries otherwise free from any control or curb." Without such suits, directors would have "complete license to disregard their duties and to deal with the properties entrusted to them as their uncontrolled self-interest may dictate."[110] As Pomerantz succinctly put it: Many a dishonest "corporate scheme was not carried through because of fear of stockholder action."[111]

Judges overseeing stockholder litigation also praised its social value in protecting investors by deterring managerial wrongdoing. In 1942, Simon Rifkind, a judge in the Southern District of New York and future name partner of the esteemed corporate law firm Paul, Weiss, Rifkind, Wharton, & Garrison, maintained, "The measure of effectiveness of the stockholder's derivative suit cannot be taken by a computation of the money recovery in the litigated cases. The minatory effect of such actions has undoubtedly prevented diversion of large amounts from stockholders to managements and outsiders." According to Rifkind, such suits, properly viewed, *assisted* rather than thwarted the work of conscientious corporate lawyers by providing "an arsenal of authorities to support their cautioning advice to clients who may be disposed to risk evasion of the high standard the courts have imposed upon directors." Derivative actions thus played a critical role in developing a sophisticated body of caselaw that "educated corporate directors in the principles of fiduciary responsibility and undivided loyalty."[112]

In 1949, the U.S. Supreme Court likewise recognized the derivative suit as "long the chief regulator of corporate management." As the stock of public companies came to be held by "numerous and scattered holder of small interests" in the twentieth century, "directors were no longer subject to an effective accountability" and lax codes of corporation law "created strong temptation for managers to profit personally" at the

107 "In the Stockholders' Interest?," 95.

108 Pomerantz, "Point of View," 22.

109 Pomerantz, "Point of View," 22.

110 Brief by Julius Levy for amicus curiae William B. Weinberger in Cohen v. Beneficial Industrial Loan Corporation, 1949 WL 38655 (U.S.), 17.

111 "Companies in Court: Stockholders File More Suits, Sparking Debate among Lawyers; Plaintiffs' Attorneys Are Called Opportunists; They Claim They Deter Crime," *Wall Street Journal*, April 27, 1961, 1.

112 Brendle v. Smith, 46 F. Supp. 522, 525–26 (S.D.N.Y. 1942).

expense of shareholders. According to the Court, the derivative suit, "born of stockholder helplessness," provided a necessary check on abuses of trust and breaches of fiduciary duty by corporate managers.[113]

In an important 1959 essay, "To Whom and for What Ends Is Corporate Management Responsible?," Eugene Rostow, who had briefly practiced at the Cravath firm before joining the faculty of Yale Law School in 1938 and becoming its dean in 1955, similarly applauded the stockholders' suit as "an imaginative creation, particularly in its American forms, intended to protect the corporation against fraud, overreaching, and other breaches of fiduciary duty on the part of officers and directors." Expressing dismay over what he viewed as the unwarranted "distaste" and "repugnance" for the derivative suit that prevailed in the corporate world, he hailed the device as "the most important procedure the law has yet developed to police the internal affairs of corporations."[114]

## B. Justifications for Lucrative Fee Awards

As described above, the business community's hostility to the derivative suit was often merged with vitriolic attacks on stockholders' attorneys as greedy, disreputable extortionists. For instance, a common charge against members of the plaintiff's bar was that they received excessive fee awards based on frivolous "strike suits" rather than legal skill or merit.[115]

In response, advocates of retail stockholder litigation argued that the difficulties and risks of pursuing derivative cases justified generous fee awards in cases where plaintiffs prevailed. In their view, such suits involved arduous, fastidious preparation. They also required that practitioners possess a rare skill set that combined expertise in often arcane aspects of corporate law with dexterity in the courtroom. As Podell's longtime partner, Mortimer Hays, explained:

> Stockholders' suits ... comprehend, from the factual side, all of the complexities and intricacies of modern business and corporate finance; and from the legal side, every aspect of the relationships between management and stockholders, of stockholders *inter se*, and between parent corporation and subsidiaries. Their preparation often involves years of work by a large staff of experienced lawyers and accountants.[116]

Another prominent plaintiff's lawyer, Percival Jackson, similarly argued that there were "a limited number of lawyers who have the legal knowledge needed to maintain

[113] Cohen v. Beneficial Industrial Loan Corp., 337 U.S. 541, 547–48 (1949).

[114] Eugene V. Rostow, "To Whom and for What Ends Is Corporate Management Responsible?," in *The Corporation in Modern Society*, ed. Edward S. Mason (Cambridge.: Harvard, 1959), 48–49. On Rostow's brief tenure at Cravath, see "Review, Robert T. Swaine, The Cravath Firm and Its Predecessors, 1819–1948," *Yale Law Journal* 58 (1948–1949): 650, 655 n.5.

[115] Hays, "Study in Trial Tactics," 300 & n.40 (a stockholder's attorney "must be prepared to pit his abilities, not against one adversary, but usually against many, often including the leaders of the corporate and trial bars").

[116] Hays, "Study in Trial Tactics," 280; Berlack, "Stockholders' Suits," 601.

and prosecute and the financial ability to await the result of a stockholder's derivative suit."[117]

But members of the plaintiff's bar were not the only ones to defend their lofty fee awards in derivative actions. Judges supervising derivative suits also recognized that such cases constituted grueling, high-stakes pursuits for stockholders' counsel. As one New York court pointed out in 1942, "A stockholders' suit of this kind requires many months of concentrated and skilled work of preparation, examination, discovery, presentation, and legal and factual research." Moreover, even the most accomplished plaintiffs' lawyers "always took the risk that their time and efforts might go for naught."[118]

Some courts hearing derivative suits further noted that, in addition to the complexity of the cases and the risk of no recovery, stockholders' lawyers had to confront frequent roadblocks erected by hostile corporate attorneys and obstructionist defendants. The New York Appellate Division provided an unusually frank description of such tactics in connection with an early derivative case in which Podell represented the famous comedian and actor Eddie Cantor against the directors of Goldman Sachs Trading Corporation. As the Court explained in 1934, shareholders of large companies usually lacked the ability to pursue relief on their own:

> Stockholders are widely scattered and have no definite method of contact with each other. They usually know that the evidence is almost exclusively in the control of those who are charged with delinquency; that those same individuals are likewise in control of the funds of the corporation and may apply them in defense of their acts, whether those acts are innocent or wrongful; that *in seeking a remedy the stockholder will be met with every obstacle and procedural delay that the ingenuity of skilled [defense] counsel can devise, as is illustrated in the present case.*

Given the obstacles, minority investors naturally chose "to remain quiescent, accepting their misfortunes as a decree of relentless fate." Indeed, it was only "in times of general cataclysm or great stress, like those of the present, that indignation will flare up into some decisive action."[119] Even in times of economic crisis, the Court noted, the efforts of the plaintiff's bar to obtain redress for corporate malfeasance faced daunting hurdles, such as a "great reluctance" to turn over evidence, continual procedural delays to avoid trial on the merits, and myriad other "difficulties and discouragements created chiefly by those whose acts are attacked."[120]

Despite the steady stream of obstructionist tactics from opposing counsel, David Podell, Abraham Pomerantz, and other pioneers of the plaintiff's bar (a group that also included Milton Paulson and later long-time Southern District of New York

[117] Percival E. Jackson, "Reorganization of the Corporate Concept and the Effect of Section 61-B of the New York General Corporation Law" *American Bankruptcy Review* A5.1 (July 1944): 339.

[118] Neuberger v. Barrett, 39 N.Y.S.2d 575, 577 (N.Y. Sup. Ct. 1942).

[119] Dresdner v. Goldman Sachs Trading Corp., 240 A.D. 242, 245–46 (2nd Dept. 1934) (emphasis added).

[120] Dresdner v. Goldman Sachs, 240 A.D. 245–46.

Judge Milton Pollack[121]) managed to build practices that were not only profitable but also had a deep and lasting impact on the development of the law of corporate governance. For example, Podell and his firm were the lead lawyers in two canonical cases that expanded the common law of corporations to protect investors and hold directors responsible for breach of their fiduciary duties of care and loyalty. As noted above, Podell achieved a historic ruling on the personal liability of directors for violation of the fiduciary duty of care in *Litwin v. Allen* (1940).[122] In addition, he litigated a second landmark case establishing the personal liability of a director for theft of a corporate opportunity (and accompanying breach of the fiduciary duty of loyalty) in *Guth v. Loft* (1939).[123] Likewise, Abraham Pomerantz acted as the general counsel for the shareholder-plaintiffs in *Perlman v. Feldmann* (1955), another groundbreaking derivative suit holding a director and dominant shareholder liable for misappropriation of a corporate opportunity.[124]

## C. Ethical Standards of the Plaintiff's Bar

In response to the corporate bar's blanket, often self-serving condemnations of plaintiffs' lawyers as sinister and unscrupulous, Podell, Pomerantz, and other early experts in retail stockholder litigation strove to cultivate ethical norms for their new specialty. This is not to say that plaintiffs' lawyers never succumbed to ethical temptations or exploited moral ambiguities in their positions. It is also difficult to know what occurred in closed-door meetings with potential plaintiffs or in negotiations among co-counsel or with defense attorneys.[125] But leading shareholders' lawyers repeatedly emphasized the importance of pursuing meritorious claims and avoiding groundless nuisance suits. For instance, Podell's long-time partner, Mortimer Hays, stressed the imperative for successful plaintiffs' lawyers to weed out frivolous or dubious claims. In a 1943 guide on trial tactics in derivative suits, he underscored the necessity for plaintiffs' counsel to file "*meritorious* stockholders' suits" that accurately portrayed misconduct by corporate officers and directors.[126]

Similarly, veteran trial lawyer Victor House argued that the pursuit of baseless litigation by shareholders' lawyers in the hope of obtaining a quick settlement was doomed to failure because corporate directors routinely refused to settle claims unless they had some underlying merit. As House asserted, "[N]o stockholders' derivative suit

[121] On Pollack, see "Business and the Law: Insider Suits Face Struggle," *New York Times*, April 27, 1987, D2 ("Along with Abraham L. Pomerantz, who often worked with him in the 1940s, Mr. Pollack earned a reputation as an innovator in lawsuits brought by shareholders.")

[122] Litwin v Allen, 25 N.Y.S.2d 667.

[123] Guth v. Loft, Inc., 5 A.2d 503, 515 (Del. 1939).

[124] Perlman v. Feldmann, 219 F.2d 173 (2d Cir. 1955). At the time, Pomerantz helmed the firm of Pomerantz, Levy, Schreiber, & Haudek.

[125] For one perspective on possible ethical temptations and moral ambiguities in the field of stockholder litigation, see the memoir of plaintiffs' lawyer Sidney Silverman, which describes his practice in the 1960s. Sidney B. Silverman, *A Happy Life: From Courtroom to Classroom* (Bloomington: iUniverse, 2009), 1–15. For an insightful appreciation of the ambiguities of individual motivation and behavior in legal history, see Hendrik Hartog, *Someday All This Will Be Yours: A History of Inheritance and Old Age* (Cambridge.: Harvard University Press, 2012).

[126] Hays, "Study in Trial Tactics," 278 (emphasis in original).

has ever been settled or offered to be settled where legal or moral liability did not exist, and there was not fear either of plaintiff recovery, or the rattling of closeted skeletons, or the opening of a Pandora's box of grievances still unsuspected."[127] Pomerantz likewise insisted that retail stockholders' lawyers could only thrive by filing factually and legally sound cases. Indeed, he was well known for bringing only a small number of stockholder suits at a time so that he could thoroughly investigate and develop potential actions.[128] As a result, he dismissed the idea that plaintiffs' attorneys could make money by filing baseless "strike suits" and obtaining quick settlements as an "epithet bereft of reality" and a "fantasy" propagated by the corporate bar.[129]

Early practitioners of Main Street shareholder litigation also advocated making settlements transparent and having courts supervise the settlement process. In particular, they disavowed secret settlements that provided private payments or other benefits to named plaintiffs but were not disclosed to other stockholders or paid to the corporation. Sergei Zlinkoff, another partner at Podell's firm, lambasted secret settlements as a "genuine evil," which "have often enabled faithless fiduciaries to escape detection or accountability for illegal actions."[130] Likewise, Percival Jackson lamented the persistence of private settlements, which allowed corporate defendants to "'buy off' the complaining stockholder and his lawyer, rather than make proper and greater restitution to the corporation."[131]

## D. Government and Community Service

Furthermore, contrary to the corporate bar's portrayal of the plaintiff's bar as motivated solely by self-interest, leading proponents of retail stockholder litigation often led lives distinguished by government and community service. As noted above, Podell was a dedicated, passionate supporter of Roosevelt and the New Deal throughout Roosevelt's presidency. In addition to being tapped to assist in drafting the National Industrial Recovery Act in 1933, the Roosevelt administration again recruited Podell as a special assistant U.S. attorney for the antitrust division of the Department of Justice in 1938. Serving in that capacity until 1941, he supervised important antitrust prosecutions involving aluminum manufacturers and represented the United States in negotiations of consent decrees with the motion picture industry. During World

127 House, "Stockholders' Suits," 389.

128 Coffee, *Entrepreneurial Litigation*, 37.

129 Note, "Security for Expenses," 65; Robert J. Cole, "The Director at Bay," *New York Times*, Oct. 17, 1971, F1.

130 Zlinkoff, "The American Investor," 366. At the time he wrote this article, Zlinkoff was a junior partner at Hays, Podell, & Shulman. See biographical entry for Hays, Podell, & Shulman in *The Martindale-Hubbell Law Directory* (1944), 1154.

131 Jackson, "Reorganization of the Corporate Concept," 339. Despite the harms of private settlements, the New York corporate bar and corporate lobbyists repeatedly resisted legislative efforts to prohibit them. Hornstein, "New Aspects," 3–4 n.15. New York's business corporation law did not require notice to shareholders and judicial approval of derivative suit settlements in the discretion of the court until 1963. Note, "Security for Expenses," 58.

War II, Roosevelt turned to Podell again, nominating him as general counsel of the Smaller War Plants Corporation, a position he held from 1941 through 1945.[132]

Podell was also extremely active in philanthropy from the 1930s until his death in 1947. He was elected president of the board of trustees of Beth Israel Hospital in 1936, a position he held for many years. (The hospital's auditorium is still named in his honor.) In 1942, he acted as co-chairman of the Greater New York Campaign of the American ORT Federation, an organization closely allied with the Jewish labor movement. In addition, he served on the board of directors of numerous other charitable organizations, including the New York Federation of Jewish Philanthropies, the Educational Alliance, and the Council of Fraternal and Benevolent Organizations of the New York and Brooklyn Jewish Federations of Charities.[133]

Like David Podell, Pomerantz was an enthusiastic supporter of New Deal initiatives and was active in politics, though his political orientation was less mainstream than that of Podell. Identifying as a socialist since his late twenties, Pomerantz joined the National Lawyers Guild and enrolled in the American Labor Party, an alternative political party in New York formed by labor leaders, socialists, Communists, and progressive Democrats, during the 1940s.[134] In 1945, he forcefully advocated the rights of workers while campaigning (unsuccessfully) on the joint ticket of the American Labor Party and the Democratic Party as a candidate for New York State Supreme Court.[135]

In 1946, the Truman administration recruited Pomerantz to join the prosecution team at the Nuremberg trials. Based "on the strength of his familiarity with complicated financial transactions and his reputation as a tenacious trial lawyer," he was appointed deputy chief counsel at Nuremberg and put in charge of developing a theory to support the prosecution of German corporations for collaborating in Nazi atrocities.[136] After eight months at Nuremberg, however, Pomerantz resigned in protest over what he perceived as the lackluster commitment of the Truman administration to the prosecution of German corporations.[137] During 1947, he organized with other liberals and progressives to call out the U.S. government for its refusal to devote sufficient resources to holding German industrialists accountable for complicity in Nazi war crimes and its lack of political will at Nuremberg.[138] Pomerantz continued to publicize the failure of U.S. officials to pursue criminal accountability for international crimes committed by German corporations in 1948.[139]

132 "D. L. Podell Dead," 57. The entries for Hays, Podell, & Shulman in the Martindale-Hubbell Law Directories from 1943 to1947 describe Podell as of counsel to the firm and "with U.S. Government."

133 "Beth Israel Hospital Elects Podell," *New York Times*, April 20, 1937, 2; "D. L. Podell Dead," 57.

134 Klaw, "Pomerantz," 146. On the American Labor Party, see Rabinowitz, *Unrepentant Leftist*, 44.

135 On Pomerantz' pro-labor ideology, see Gargan, "Abraham Pomerantz," 44; Rabinowitz, *Unrepentant Leftist*, 45; "Appeals Court Backs Pomerantz Removal," *New York Times*, June 14, 1946, 14 (reporting appellate decision upholding Pomerantz's disqualification as arbitrator of dispute between Western Union workers and management based on his alleged pro-labor bias).

136 Klaw, "Pomerantz," 156; Jonathan A. Bush, "The Prehistory of Corporations and Conspiracy in International Criminal Law: What Nuremberg Really Said," *Columbia Law Review* 109.5 (June 2009): 1149 ("Pomerantz was brought to Nuremberg as a trial manager and big-picture strategist. With his broad experience taking on corporations... Pomerantz had been a prized catch for the recruiters.")

137 Klaw, "Pomerantz," 156; Bush, "Prehistory of Corporations," 1171.

138 Bush, "Prehistory of Corporations," 1197.

139 Bush, "Prehistory of Corporations," 1232.

The same year, further disillusioned with the general rightward shift of the Democratic Party in the Truman years, Pomerantz served as campaign treasurer for Henry Wallace in his third-party run for president on the ticket of a resurrected Progressive Party.[140] After 1948, Pomerantz largely retreated from electoral politics, though he occasionally published letters to the editor criticizing McCarthyism and American involvement in the Vietnam War.[141] Though less prominent in philanthropy than Podell, Pomerantz was also a generous contributor to civil rights and other progressive causes throughout his career.[142]

## IV. Conclusion

In 1959, Eugene Rostow, dean of Yale Law School, expressed shock at the scathing treatment of practitioners representing shareholders by business leaders and the business bar. As he remarked, "One would expect those concerned for the integrity and future of private business institutions to applaud the intrepid souls who ferret out corporate wrongdoing, and risk their own time and money against contingency of being rewarded, if in the end sin is found to have flourished." Unfortunately, Rostow concluded, "Such men are not treated as honored members of the system of private enterprise, but as its scavengers and pariahs."[143]

Even now, more than sixty years after Rostow's observations, the conventional narrative continues to depict shareholders' attorneys as irresponsible, self-interested interlopers, who cloak nuisance suits in the mantle of public interest to extort attorney's fees from corporations for their private benefit.[144] In contrast to this dominant, pejorative view of the plaintiff's bar in business law, this essay suggests an alternative narrative. A closer look at the origins of retail stockholder litigation reveals that its pioneers were often adroit, diligent, and innovative attorneys, who combined prodigious litigation skills with command of intricate aspects of corporate finance, accounting,

[140] Klaw, "Pomerantz," 156. On the Wallace presidential campaign, see John C. Culver and John Hyde, *American Dreamer: The Life and Times of Henry A. Wallace* (New York: Norton, 2000).

[141] Klaw, "Pomerantz," 156; Abraham Pomerantz, "Letter to the Editor," *New York Times*, Sept. 18, 1955, E10 (criticizing anti-Communist hysteria); Abraham Pomerantz, "Letter to the Editor," *New York Times*, Aug. 25, 1972, 32 (criticizing American aggression in Vietnam).

[142] Klaw, "Pomerantz," 156.

[143] Rostow, "To Whom and for What Ends Is Corporate Management Responsible?," 49. Rostow further remarked, "'Strike Suit' and 'blackmail' are among the kindest words heard in higher business circles to describe the most important procedure the law has yet developed to police the internal affairs of corporations." Ibid., 48.

[144] See Robert B. Thompson & Randall S. Thomas, "The Public and Private Faces of Derivative Lawsuits," *Vanderbilt Law Review* 47.5 (October 2004), 1748 ("[D]erivative suits today are regularly portrayed as nuisance suits whose 'principle beneficiaries … are attorneys.'"); Erickson, "Corporate Governance," 1792 (describing "widespread belief among corporate officers and directors that [derivative] suits are nothing more than strike suits"); Patrick Gallagher, "Merger Objection Lawsuits Getting Tougher for Plaintiffs' Attorneys," Dix & Eaton (blog), Aug. 6, 2018, https://www.dix-eaton.com/our-blog/merger-objection-lawsuits-getting-tougher-for-plaintiffs-attorneys/ (condemning most merger-objection stockholder suits as meritless "holdup cases" and "racket[s]" fabricated by plaintiffs' firms and "abhor[ed]" by both "corporate boards and their legal counsel").

and corporate governance. They also vigorously advocated the social benefits of derivative litigation and highlighted its essential role in protecting retail investors from managerial overreaching and abuse of corporate power. At the same time, they created influential precedents in the arena of corporate governance and strove to craft ethical norms for their new field of legal practice. Moreover, rather than embracing the pursuit of profit at any cost, the most successful plaintiffs' lawyers demonstrated a powerful sense of civic obligation and commendable records of public service.

# 3

# Private Law, Public Welfare, Marital Ideals, and the Gender Binary . . . or, What I Learned at the Socio-Legal Revolution

*Felicia Kornbluh**

As part of his bid to become president of the United States, Senator Barack Obama gave a memorable address about fatherhood. At a Baptist church on the South Side of Chicago on Father's Day 2008, Obama chastised fathers, especially Black fathers, who were "acting like boys instead of men." Acknowledging a role for government in enabling children's well-being, the candidate insisted, "[W]e also need families"—presumptively, procreative, two-parent, heterosexual families caring for biological progeny—"to raise our children.... We need them to realize that what makes you a man is not the ability to have a child—it's the courage to raise one."[1]

Candidate Obama's policy prescriptions involved both privileges for fathers and controls on them. "We should be making it easier for fathers who make responsible choices," he proposed, "and harder for those who avoid them." His ideas included giving low-income or unemployed fathers who paid child support special job and training opportunities, "and a larger Earned Income Tax Credit that can help them pay the bills."[2] But another portion of Obama's speech in effect blamed single motherhood and absent fatherhood for violent crime, addiction, and incarceration. "How many in this generation are we willing to lose to poverty or violence or addiction?" the candidate asked. Only properly behaving husbands and fathers, he suggested, could come to the rescue.

Obama's rhetoric reprised an often underappreciated aspect of legal and gender history from an earlier period. In what Hendrik Hartog, echoing and revising Eric Hobsbawm, has called the "long nineteenth century"—underlining the relative continuity in the law and culture of common-law coverture from perhaps the late

* My very sincere thanks to Karen Tani and Dirk Hartog for thinking through some of the questions raised by this essay with me. Thanks also to Gwendolyn Mink, my co-author for the book, *Ensuring Poverty* (Philadelphia: University of Pennsylvania Press, 2018), in which some of these thoughts first appeared (see discussion below).

[1] Father's Day speech by Senator Barack Obama (D-Illinois), June 15, 2008, to Apostolic Church of God, Chicago, Illinois, as released by his campaign, politico.com, http://www.politico.com/story/2008/06/text-of-obamas-fatherhood-speech-011094?o=4 (accessed July 21, 2016). In official fatherhood program materials, the Obama administration often reused the phrase "What makes you a father is not the ability to have a child." U.S. Office of Faith-Based and Neighborhood Partnerships, "Promoting Responsible Fatherhood and Strong Communities," https://www.whitehouse.gov/administration/eop/ofbnp/policy/fatherhood (accessed July 21, 2016). Ibid.

[2] Ibid.

Felicia Kornbluh, *Private Law, Public Welfare, Marital Ideals, and the Gender Binary . . . or, What I Learned at the Socio-Legal Revolution* In: *In Between and Across*. Edited by: Kenneth W. Mack and Jacob Katz Cogan, Oxford University Press.
 DOI: 10.1093/oso/9780197680995.003.0004

eighteenth century through the middle twentieth, despite shifts in statutory law and women's rights that appeared to change more than they did—coverture dominated legal understandings of family and gender roles. Men as husbands and fathers had great power relative to women as wives and mothers. But there were limits on men's power, enforced rarely by courts during intact marriages but enforced under conditions of legal separation and actively present in the United States thanks to the centrality of coverture as a cultural as well as a legal system.[3]

Given that common-law coverture is generally thought to have ended in the middle twentieth century, the assumptions about husbandhood and wifehood that it bequeathed to this society should have dissipated by the second decade of the twenty-first century. However, the (very) long life of coverture comes into new relief when we place legal histories such as Hartog's alongside the history of modern social welfare policy. By appreciating the historical ways in which U.S. law shaped gendered identities and family relationships, in all of the great complexity that foundational works of socio-legal historiography have captured, it is possible to see continuities that would otherwise be difficult to discern—across decades, generations, and even centuries. These continuities help us understand not only women's persistent subordination in a bivariate gender system anchored in law, but, counterintuitively, the limitations on men's power and their vulnerability to the sharp edge of state power when they fail to perform the roles of husband and father that are also anchored in law.

Obama's remarks in Chicago illuminate several of the arguments my coauthor, political scientist Gwendolyn Mink, and I formed after years of research on the history and politics of welfare reform in the late-twentieth and twenty-first-century United States. We focused particularly, although not exclusively, on the Personal Responsibility and Work Opportunity Reconciliation Act (PRWORA) of 1996, the signal "welfare reform" statute of the past half century, passed by a Republican-dominated Congress and signed by President Bill Clinton.[4] By privileging husbands and fathers, and prescribing their household economic dominance as a cure for poverty, Obama's rhetoric was patriarchal in the most literal sense. However, unlike familiar understandings of

[3] Hartog reorganized historical chronology around law and gender much as Hobsbawm's landmark works of Marxist social history reorganized late-eighteenth and nineteenth-century European history around economy and empire. Hendrik Hartog, *Man and Wife in America: A History* (Cambridge: Harvard University Press, 2000), Kindle edition locations 431, 440, 554, and, on the "very long nineteenth century" stretching into the 1950s or perhaps the 1970s, 3959 and 4282; Eric Hobsbawm, *The Age of Revolution: Europe, 1789–1848* (New York: New American Library, 1962), *The Age of Capital, 1848–1875* (New York: Scribner, 1975), and *The Age of Empire, 1875–1914* (New York: Pantheon, 1987); and Joseph Fronczak, "Hobsbawm's Long Century," *Jacobin*, June 9, 2017, https://jacobin.com/2017/06/eric-hobsbawm-historian-marxism-communist-party-third-reich-stalingrad (accessed August 11, 2022). For other scholarship of the breakout socio-legal history generation that placed common-law coverture at the heart of the legal and gender systems, see Carol Smart, ed., *Regulating Womanhood: Historical Essays on Marriage, Motherhood, and Sexuality* (London and New York: Routledge, 1992); Linda K. Kerber, *No Constitutional Right to be Ladies: Women and the Obligations of Citizenship* (New York: Hill and Wang, 1999), which illuminates the paradoxes of women's subordinated status under marriage law and associated cultural norms; and Michael Grossberg, *Governing the Hearth: Law and the Family in Nineteenth-Century America* (Chapel Hill: University of North Carolina Press, 1986). For a work in the next generation of socio-legal history that carries forward in the Hobsbawmian and Hartogian spirit of rethinking chronology, see Barbara Welke, *Law and the Borders of Belonging in the Long Nineteenth-Century United States* (Cambridge: Cambridge University Press, 2010).

[4] Kornbluh and Mink, *Ensuring Poverty*.

patriarchy that emphasize only the way it enables male dominance, this early-twenty-first-century version enabled both dominance and state-sponsored stigmatization of men who failed the standard of maleness and fatherhood that it announced—a standard that was inextricable from the ways race and class were mobilized and politicized by a wide swath of the period's political elites. At the same time, the privileging of male family dominance and suggestion that absent-father families were responsible for an array of social ills helped to normalize the economic immiseration of women and children who were themselves heads of families, and who lacked intimate connection to men who made "responsible choices."

Political historians of the recent past in the United States generally identify the kind of gender conservatism and antifeminism Obama displayed in 2008 as at the heart of Republican Party discourse. However, these sentiments, which reached both sides of the normative gender divide and two distinct dimensions of culturally sanctioned masculinity, also helped Obama win *Democratic* primary voters: the lines he drew between male and female, and, even more, between good and bad men, were familiar from the already-long history of welfare reform in the United States and its celebration by mainstream elected officials and intellectuals associated with both major political parties. The discourse of fatherhood among early-twenty-first-century Democrats was inseparable from contemporaneous efforts at promoting marriage, which became a ubiquitous symbol in this period of the moral and economic good.

In this essay, I reconsider my earlier reading of Obama's speech and years of social welfare policy that preceded and surrounded it to develop an argument about the utility of legal history writing about family relations to scholarship that seeks to interpret the modern U.S. welfare state—and look especially at ways in which this writing points to the place of common-law coverture in bequeathing to U.S. legal culture the gendered assumptions about husbands and fathers that Mink and I explored in our shared work. I find surprising continuities within U.S. legal history and historiography across long swaths of time, and unexpected points of connection between the legally constituted "private" realm of family life and the "public" welfare state. I find that legal-historical and socio-legal writing on the supposedly private law of marriage, divorce, child custody and inheritance, published as early as the 1980s, is an irreplaceable help in understanding the origins and full meanings of rhetoric like Obama's. It is an aid, too, to comprehending relatively recent innovations in statutory law such as the "welfare reform" legislation President Bill Clinton signed in 1996.

## I. The "Long Nineteenth Century" in the Twentieth-Century Welfare State

The history of political rhetoric like Obama's and of related social policies gains from the *longue durée* perspective imparted by a study of private law in the legal-historical long nineteenth century. If we were to read the policies and rhetoric of the Clinton and Obama presidencies solely as "neoliberal," we would capture significant aspects of their place in late-twentieth- and twenty-first-century political economy. However, we would fail to capture or explain elements of gendered and generational regulation that are also present in them, and that <u>are</u> captured in scholarship on family regulation within "private" law. To view these policies in the context of twentieth-century political or policy history might help in understanding them as departures from a New Deal–era norm of government responsibility for (a measure of) social and individual welfare and would participate in a narrative about "the rise and fall of the New Deal order" that does some important work.[5] By adding legal-historical approaches to family regulation that cover a longer time frame, however, Obama's rhetoric and policies related to it appear as less anomalous and more consistent with Anglo-American legal norms, including the norm of public welfare being constructed against background understandings of private family obligations that have been enforced both informally and formally.

I continue with a set of general remarks about the ways in which legal-historical scholarship on "private" family law illuminates aspects of U.S. history that are significant for historians of gender and social policy. Then, I explore further the specific ways in which this research links to the study of twentieth- and twenty-first-century welfare policy, with an emphasis on the ways masculinity was figured in policy debates and in the substance of policy.

## II. Socio-Legal Histories, Masculinity, and Welfare

First, this work teaches about the cultural as well as legal centrality of marital roles, norms, and obligations in the long shadow of common-law coverture, and about the ways in which gendered rights and obligations have been legally constructed on the masculine side of the binary as well as on the feminine side throughout U.S. history. The aggressive late-twentieth- and early-twenty-first-century effort by politicians to make national statutory law express an old common-law vision of fatherhood and husbandship had the effect of affirming disproportionate masculine economic and political power. It also had a constraining, even punishing, effect upon many individual men, and upon many women. It had a disproportionately negative effect on poor people and people of color, whose failure to reach the ideal was virtually assured.

Second, this scholarship points to many ways in which the study of the modern welfare state may be seen as a branch of legal history. Although much of the legal history scholarship that has been published in the United States since the era of Willard Hurst has been located in courtrooms, it has widened the purview of the field dramatically by decentering constitutional law and federal appellate courts. By assiduously studying legal events far from the U.S. Supreme Court, this socio-legal historical tradition has helped scholars of later generations understand the diversity and multiplicity of law, and the vast range of loci in which people have encountered it—from administrative-legal procedures, to state and local statutory and regulatory law, to the rights-leaning imaginings of low-income, female, and nonwhite people, in their daily family lives and encounters with the gatekeepers of public aid among many others.

Third, legal-historical scholarship on family regulation teaches about the deep interpenetration of legal and social history. This work has been widely influential within

[5] Steve Fraser and Gary Gerstle eds., *The Rise and Fall of the New Deal Order, 1930–1980* (Princeton: Princeton University Press, 1990).

U.S. history scholarship generally, and not just in subdisciplinary circles, because it builds powerfully and compassionately from the record of individual and familial lived experiences. While keeping law in view, scholars have taken social life on its own terms and explored it from the inside out, from the vantage point of those who lived. This work of course encompasses the understanding that, for example, propertied white men in a society we could call capitalist, white supremacist, and heteropatriarchal exercised disproportionate power vis-à-vis all of the others whom historians have learned to foreground in recent generations of work. Socio-legal history takes this as one strand in a complex skein that includes, too, the improvisations real people—including, for example, white married women living under common-law coverture—performed with the notes they were given, including those that were given by the authorized legal texts and actors in their societies. In other words, this scholarship persistently pursues an understanding of how people came to understand and to shape their lives as subjects rather than objects or victims of historical circumstance.

Fourth, despite what its practitioners have sometimes proclaimed, legal history scholarship on "private" family life has not simply been history "from below." Socio-legal studies of legally regulated family life in the "long nineteenth century" belie the eloquent, important, and yet insufficient description in William Forbath's, Hartog's, and Martha Minow's canonic essay, "Legal Histories from Below," that "law is not the formal banner, but its travels in the crowds grasping for it."[6] This scholarship certainly teaches historians to place emphasis on how law is understood and experienced, embraced or resisted, and the power that is or isn't arrayed on behalf of any exercise of force by governmental authorities. But it teaches as well that legal history requires looking and listening for the constraining formal dimensions of legal rules and norms.

This ambiguity or multiplicity of interpretative strategies is present in "Legal Histories from Below." It is also in Hartog's solo-authored piece from the same time, "Pigs and Positivism."[7] "Legal Histories From Below" reads, in lines that appear shortly before the ones usually quoted, that the authors were seeking "a perspective wide enough to glimpse the tugs and pulls between those who contributed to law's formal statements, those subjected to its enforcement and yet able at times to resist and/or reinterpret, and those who consciously reconstructed the law for their own purposes."[8] The history of law is, then, a chronicle of tugs and pulls, not just so-called ordinary people in their neighborhoods insisting that, for example, pig-keeping was legal no matter what.

Coauthor Karen Tani and I extended the understanding of "Legal Histories from Below" in our reflections on the law of poverty in U.S. history.[9] Tani and I underlined our understanding that in the history of poverty, law has indeed resided in both the formal banner and its travels in the crowd, and in the dynamic relationship between the two. We built upon this foundation in two ways: We claimed that the "tugs and

[6] William Forbath, Hendrik Hartog, and Martha Minow, "Introduction: Legal Histories from Below," *Wisconsin Law Review* 1985.6: 765.

[7] Hendrik Hartog, "Pigs and Positivism," *Wisconsin Law Review*1985.6: 899.

[8] Forbath et al., "Legal Histories from Below," 764.

[9] Kornbluh and Karen Tani, "Siting the Legal History of Poverty: Below, Above, and Amidst," *A Companion to American Legal History*, eds. Sally E. Hadden and Alfred L. Brophy (Malden, MA, Sussex, and Oxford: Wiley-Blackwell, 2013), 329–48.

pulls" of the legal past have occurred in specific socio-geographic contexts, and we found a third layer of legal activity, between law-making from "below" and "above," the "amidst" of lower level courts and public administrators with finite discretionary authority. "Poor people," Tani and I argued, "have met law in specific locations, institutional sites at which power has been exercised, interpreted, occluded, generated, contested, and transformed."[10] We concluded our consideration of the history and historiography of poverty law: "Neither elites nor 'the crowd' may claim exclusive credit or blame" for legal change. "Judges and legislators," we continued, "welfare claimants and needy strangers, low-level bureaucrats and neighborhood lawyers together have written the law of poverty."[11]

Fifth, contemporary historians of social welfare have learned from earlier generations of socio-legal historical practitioners to consider welfare states in relationship to (legally, publicly constituted) private family and family law. In other words, when studying an impoverished person's efforts to gain material aid from a local or national body at any point in U.S. history, one can understand that act and responses to it as occurring against a background understanding of the responsibilities of family members for one another. Whether explicitly marked in statute or regulations, or not, legalized understandings of what spouses, lovers, parents, and children owe one another have been woven into the administration and adjudication of poor people's claims upon their communities.[12] And the opposite has also been true: The private adjudication of familial relations has occurred against background understandings of what governmental authorities could do or were obliged to do—often, with an eye to averting public financial obligations that might be incurred if families failed to keep economic need "private."

The deep connections between economic transfers within families and from government authorities appear in *The Trouble with Minna*, Hartog's careful study of New Jersey law in the age of gradual emancipation. In the work, Hartog illuminated the ways in which judicial authorities sought to maintain Minna's status as a form of enslaved property, decades after emancipation began in her home state. This occurred in part, apparently, because it was thought preferable to the alternatives, that public resources would need to provide for an elderly, enfeebled woman, or, given the infant state of public welfare, that she would be without provision.[13]

Last, the legal history scholarship on so-called private family life has taught scholars much about how to pursue the gendered history of the welfare state. Among its

10 Kornbluh and Tani, "Siting the Legal History of Poverty," 342.

11 Ibid.

12 See histories of early American "warning out," such as Cornelia Dayton and Sharon V. Salinger, *Robert Love's Warnings: Searching for Strangers in Colonial Boston* (Philadelphia: University of Pennsylvania Press, 2014), and of twentieth-century "responsible relatives'" laws and regulations, discussed in Susan Stein-Roggenbuck, "Resisting a Right to Relief: States, Responsible Relatives Laws, and Old Age Assistance," *Journal of Policy History* 30/3 (July 2018): 400–28 and Jacobus tenBroek and Floyd Matson, *Hope Deferred: Public Welfare and the Blind* (Berkeley and Los Angeles: University of California Press, 1959), 70–72. As tenBroek and Matson wrote, in 1943 the Social Security Board noted 28 state programs of Old Age Assistance, 21 programs of Aid to the Blind, and 18 programs of Aid to Dependent Children that enforced financial responsibility for relatives (72).

13 Hendrik Hartog, *The Trouble with Minna: A Case of Slavery and Emancipation in the Antebellum North* (Chapel Hill: University of North Carolina Press, 2018), 7, 33–36.

important lessons has been that socially and legally constructed masculinity is an arena of compulsion and constraint as well as a sphere of privilege and power. In his study of family law and lives, *Governing the Hearth,* for example, Michael Grossberg illuminates men's nineteenth-century loss of presumptive child custody in formal marital separations and the ways in which wives could sometimes appeal successfully to the interests of judges in preserving social standards of masculinity, even against individual men (their husbands).[14] In *A Judgment for Solomon*, Grossberg offers a closely researched study of a single—and signal—antebellum custody case, which ended with maternal custody. The work underlined the facts that "Victorian marriage … imposed a set of mandatory sex-role specific duties upon husband and wife," and that, despite formal sex inequality, the husbands didn't always get what they wanted.[15] Hartog's *Man and Wife in America*, too, takes women's and men's roles, in a bivariate gender system defined through law, as equally constructed. He takes as one of his central subjects the ways men and women inhabit and improvise upon their gendered roles. Masculine power is real in this telling, but it is not the only notable thing about masculinity.[16]

## III. Men, Coverture, and Policy before the 1990s

In the remainder of this chapter, I apply these ideas to the history of welfare reform in the late-twentieth- and twenty-first-century United States. I pay particular attention to the ways in which treatments of men, masculinity, fatherhood, and husbandhood that echo those that were paradigmatic of common-law coverture persisted through the twentieth and early-twenty-first centuries.

Discourse and policy about welfare were particularly revealing of the long morning after common-law coverture in four particular periods of recent U.S. history: In the 1960s through the late 1980s; in 1996, in the ambit of the welfare reform statute President Bill Clinton signed days before the Democrats nominated him for reelection to the White House; the late Clinton and early George W. Bush years, rife with bipartisan congressional initiatives on behalf of fathers and a modern version of the marital ideal typical of the culture of common-law coverture; and the Obama years, characterized by a heteromarital (apparent) consensus that made the My Brother's Keeper program and the marriage mantras of Washington, D.C. –based policy intellectuals nearly immune to critique.

Rhetoric and policy in the 1960s were more divided than were the debates of later decades. The Kennedy and Johnson administrations, and many of their Democratic allies in Congress, evinced a kind of sympathy for welfare recipients but still pursued racialized and gendered reforms. Social Security amendments in 1962 turned the federal categorical aid program Aid to Dependent Children, created in the New Deal period, into Aid to Families with Dependent Children (AFDC). This move

[14] Grossberg, *Governing the Hearth.*

[15] Michael Grossberg, *A Judgment for Solomon: The D'Hauteville Case and Legal Experience in Antebellum America* (Cambridge: Cambridge University Press, 1996), 14.

[16] Hartog, *Man and Wife.*

recognized the labor of maternal care. However, legislators who created AFDC also did so in part because they saw impoverished mothers as deficient and government as an agent of rehabilitation.[17] Without spelling out this argument in detail, President Kennedy suggested that mothers who could not make the economic system work for their families could receive a course of professional social work intervention and then "get … off assistance and back into useful, productive roles in society."[18] While ostensibly sympathetic to impoverished parents, the emphasis upon rehabilitation was built upon an assumption that low-income and, according to the increasingly prevalent stereotype, nonwhite mothers belonged in the waged labor market even when their children were young.[19] And this rehabilitative approach to supporting parents who combined waged work with primary responsibility for children flowed all too easily into mandates for waged labor. Under Democratic leadership, and with the support of social welfare advocates, national policymakers introduced work mandates into public assistance policy within five years of privileging supportive services for welfare clients. Policymakers came to see waged work itself as a tool for reforming clients and readapting them to what was seen as a normal life.[20]

Policies that subjected low-income mothers to mandatory waged work did not go unchallenged. Urban Democrats outside the South opposed these restrictive welfare policies, even when their chief antagonists were others in their own party. A major welfare reform initiative from the Johnson era in 1967, for example, faced significant opposition within the Democratic congressional caucus. Under Democratic control, Congress had passed into law (and the president had signed) a welfare "freeze" that capped the national budget for public assistance. However, under pressure from Democrats such as Robert F. Kennedy, who was threatening a dissident presidential run, Congress repealed the freeze before the administration implemented it. President Johnson and the white Southern Democrats who chaired major committees also ushered into law a national work mandate under welfare policy. The Work Incentive Program of 1967 was known as "WIN" to policy makers and "WIP" to the activists who thought of it as just the latest in a long line of efforts to compel Black women to perform demeaned, low-wage (or no-wage) work.[21] Dissident Democrats did not force a repeal of "WIN," but they pressured the administration to implement

[17] Jennifer Mittelstadt, *From Welfare to Workfare: The Unintended Consequences of Liberal Reform, 1945–1965* (Chapel Hill: University of North Carolina Press, 2005) makes this point and discusses the slippery slope from here to policymakers seeing waged work as a form of rehabilitation for (effectively disabled) poor women. See details of the amendments in Wilbur J. Cohen and Robert M. Ball, "Public Welfare Amendments of 1962 and Proposals for Health Insurance for the Aged," *Social Security Bulletin*, October 1962: 3–15, https://www.ssa.gov/policy/docs/ssb/v25n10/v25n10p3.pdf (accessed August 30, 2017).

[18] John F. Kennedy, "Special Message to Congress on Public Welfare Programs" (1962), *Welfare: A Documentary History of U.S. Policy and Politics*, eds. Gwendolyn Mink and Rickie Solinger (New York: NYU Press, 2003), 212–13.

[19] On the stereotype, see Martin Gillens, *Why Americans Hate Welfare: Race, Media, and the Politics of Antipoverty Policy* (Chicago: University of Chicago Press, 1999). Also see aspects of its development in Mittelstadt, *Welfare to Workfare*, and Ellen Reese, *Backlash Against Welfare Mothers, Past and Present* (Berkeley and Los Angeles: University of California Press, 2005).

[20] Mink and Solinger, eds., *Welfare*, 197–98; and see discussion of the Work Incentive Program in Kornbluh, *The Battle for Welfare Rights: Poverty and Politics in Modern America* (Philadelphia: University of Pennsylvania Press, 2007), 96–100.

[21] Kornbluh, *Battle for Welfare Rights*, 96.

it in a way that guaranteed that few mothers would in fact lose access to financial aid if they failed to juggle waged work and parenting for young children in the way the program's designers had anticipated.

Democrats in the 1960s also placed new emphasis on men, masculinity, and fatherhood in public assistance. Although most mainstream Democrats agreed on this, serious splits emerged over how to translate it into policy. Congressional and administration officials offered a variety of provisions to utilize public means to re-engage noncustodial fathers in their children's and female partners' lives.[22] In addition, unemployed and underemployed men were increasingly a focus of public assistance policy. This was a masculinist response to the civil rights and Black Power movements, and to the perception that urban riots were driven by male unemployment. The work training and educational benefits sponsored under the "service" provisions of the 1962 welfare reforms discussed above went overwhelmingly to low-income men.[23] A demonstration program to enhance the access of two-parent families to welfare aid, which the Kennedy administration had initiated in 1961, was made, later in the decade, a permanent option the states could adopt. Such policies were a fit with an address President Johnson gave at Howard University in 1965 and a simultaneous Department of Labor report, which became known as the Moynihan Report (named for Daniel Patrick Moynihan, at this time a mid-level Democratic official who was its main sponsor). These texts described a crisis in Black masculinity caused by the twin scourges of discriminatorily high unemployment for men and Black women's excessive access to income.[24]

## IV. Resisting the Gender Scripts: Welfare Rights

In the late 1960s and early 1970s, organized groups of public assistance clients, mobilized as a movement for welfare rights, participated in the debates that shaped statutory and appellate law. The organization most closely associated with this movement is the National Welfare Rights Organization (NWRO).[25] NWRO members did not always agree with one another. However, for the most part they sought to persuade people who had the power to write and administer statutory law that maternal labor should not need to be combined with waged work—although mothers who sought work should be permitted to pursue it while receiving public assistance until they were no longer poor. Welfare rights organizations participated with activist attorneys in litigation that ultimately succeeded in influencing the U.S. Supreme Court to find that state statutes or regulations that deprived women and children of public aid because the women were in sexual relationships with men who were treated as

[22] Kennedy in 1962, for example, called for "more effective location of [deserting] parents." Mink and Solinger, *Welfare*, 213.

[23] Headnote, Mink and Solinger, *Welfare*, 195–96.

[24] Robert Self, *All in the Family: The Realignment of American Democracy Since the 1960s* (New York: Hill and Wang, 2012) discusses the Moynihan Report and the limited imagination of the Democratic Party in particular around issues of "family."

[25] Kornbluh, "Food as a Civil Right: Hunger, Work, and Welfare in the South after the Civil Rights Act," *Labor*, 12/1-2 (March–May 2015): 135–58.

the "substitute fathers" for their children, and therefore as financially responsible for their well-being, violated the Social Security Act of 1935, which authorized the AFDC program.[26]

Welfare rights activists added perspectives to the debates over gender and social welfare that could be characterized as feminist: Their politics included a demand for human dignity outside of marriage and for free sexuality. These welfare reformers from below further claimed the positive right of economic support to parent one's own children even if one were not attached to a man who earned a high wage. The earliest welfare rights groups on both coasts of the United States wanted to restrict the ability of local welfare departments to deny families benefits on the basis of women's sexual and romantic behavior.[27] NWRO members argued that efforts to force women aid claimants to name the fathers of their children, and to criminalize men's failure or inability to pay child support, were dangerous. They might lead either to men's further alienation from their children or bring them back, angrily, into the lives of women who had separated from them with good reason.

The diverse activist energies that brought the perspectives of poor people into the policy-making process launched into national politics the idea of a universal basic income, termed at the time a "negative income tax," "national minimum income," or "guaranteed income." The idea originated with intellectuals, such as economist John Kenneth Galbraith, Jr.[28] NWRO members amended the intellectuals' proposal and made a motherhood-centered argument for basic income: Why, they asked, should a woman work for wages in a child care center or another woman's kitchen when the social good was served as well by her raising her own children? Why was supplying them with a basic minimum income sufficient to support a parent and her children not an appropriate use of public tax monies? NWRO formalized the idea into a proposed Guaranteed Adequate Income (GAI), which members demanded that politicians consider.[29] They debated policy intellectuals, political leaders, and advocates who saw basic income as a supplement for (stereotypically men's) low wages, rather than as a potential substitute for waged work and support for (stereotypically women's) full-time parenting. Members of the Nixon administration, for example, unsuccessfully supported a kind of basic income but argued that their proposal would replace traditional public assistance, which they claimed unfairly privileged female-headed versus male-headed households. The Nixon White House's proposal, known as the Family Assistance Plan, included a mandate for waged work for recipients of the benefit (although only for one parent in a two-parent household, thus discriminating between married and unmarried mothers).[30]

[26] King v. Smith, 392 U.S. 309 (1968).

[27] Martha F. Davis, *Brutal Need: Lawyers and the Welfare Rights Movement, 1960-73* (New Haven: Yale University Press, 1993), 84–85.

[28] Felicia Kornbluh, "Is Work the Only Thing that Pays? The Guaranteed Income and Other Alternative Anti-Poverty Policies in Historical Perspective," *Northwestern Journal of Law and Social Policy*, 4/1 (Winter 2009): 61–84; Brian Steensland, *The Failed Welfare Revolution: America's Struggle Over Guaranteed Income Policy*, (Princeton: Princeton University Press, 2008).

[29] Kornbluh, *Battle for Welfare Rights*, 153–56.

[30] Felicia Kornbluh, "Who Shot FAP? The Nixon Welfare Plan and the Transformation of American Politics," *The Sixties: A Journal of History, Politics, and Culture*, 1/2 (December 2008): 125–50.

## V. Research Findings Nobody Wanted

After this wave of welfare reform and activism in the 1960s and 1970s, the next major phase began in the 1980s. It first established and then built upon a set of gendered and racialized antiwelfare ideas, and ended with a major welfare reform that was understood at the time by claimants and their allies as draconian. The new understanding of welfare gathered slowly in the aftermath of poor people's powerful assertion through NWRO and other groups. In addition to and intermixed with the collapse of a nationally coordinated welfare rights movement, the ebbing of Black and feminist activism by the end of the 1970s helped enable it.[31]

Two tributaries of research in the late twentieth century might have led the public conversation about welfare in a less moralistic and punishing direction than the one it ultimately took. However, in both cases, policy intellectuals neutralized this potential by reading the newly available data in antifeminist and racialist ways. After Congress and the White House deadlocked over the Nixon plan, the national government funded demonstrations of "income maintenance," basic income provided solely on the basis of economic need, in Seattle, Denver, and other locales. Preliminary data from these demonstration projects became available in the late 1970s. Researchers found that basic income security had a slight depressive effect upon recipients' willingness to do paid work—concerning in Washington although arguably exerting salutary pressure on employers, who would have to offer more decent working conditions to ensure a robust labor force. Among the variables researchers chose to study, the only sizable effect, and only in the Seattle-Denver study, was upon sexual and marital behavior[32]: women with a steady, nonstigmatized income source were more likely to leave intimate partnerships than were women without it.[33] Researchers in the Canadian province of Manitoba, which conducted a comparable experiment, found similar results. Later analysis of the data indicated that this kind of no-strings-attached welfare also limited women's exposure to domestic violence.[34]

Policymakers had ready to hand a second federally funded source of information about poverty and people's use of welfare benefits. With backing from the National Science Foundation, the Panel Study of Income Dynamics (PSID) began in 1968 to

[31] On welfare/feminist overlaps, see Wini Brenes, *The Trouble between Us* (New York: Oxford University Press, 2006); Ann Valk, *Radical Sisters: Second-Wave Feminism and Black Liberation in Washington, D.C.* (Champaign: University of Illinois Press, 2008), 38–59; and Marjorie Spruill, *Divided We Stand: The Battle over Women's Rights and Family Values that Polarized American Politics* (New York: Bloomsbury, 2017), 27–28, 58, 138, 221.

[32] Questions Submitted by Senator Daniel Patrick Moynihan to HEW Secretary Joseph Califano (1978), *Welfare*, eds. Mink and Solinger, 438; "Do Income Maintenance Programs Break Up Marriages? A Reevaluation of SIME-DIME," (University of Wisconsin-Madison, Institute for Research on Poverty, 1987–1988), 10/4 https://www.irp.wisc.edu/publications/focus/pdfs/foc104a.pdf (accessed Sept. 19, 2017); and discussions in Michael B. Katz, *The Undeserving Poor: From the War on Poverty to the War on Welfare* (New York: Pantheon, 1989), and Alice O'Connor, *Poverty Knowledge: Social Science, Social Policy and the Poor in Twentieth-Century U.S. History* (Princeton: Princeton University Press, 2001).

[33] In the Canadian study, conducted under the progressive (NDP) provincial government in Manitoba and a Liberal national government under Pierre Trudeau, researchers studied domestic violence, apparently not on the agenda of U.S. researchers.

[34] David Calnitsky, "'More Normal than Welfare': The Mincome Experiment, Stigma, and Community Experience," *Canadian Review of Sociology* 53/1 (February 2016): 26–71.

study a large, diverse sample of U.S. households.[35] By the early 1980s, researchers had evidence to share about family incomes over a decade. In *Years of Poverty, Years of Plenty* (1984), Greg J. Duncan and colleagues argued using PSID data that poverty was a normal, not anomalous, experience among U.S. families. They attributed this ubiquitous poverty to easily identified features of the economy (e.g., structural, that is, more or less permanent, unemployment) and government, such as a bare-bones welfare state that left families mostly on their own to accommodate the cost of raising young children. Along with ubiquitous poverty was a ubiquitous need for—and use of—welfare benefits. In the course of a decade, Duncan and colleagues wrote, over one quarter of households received government grants from the means-tested programs AFDC, food stamps, Medicaid, or Supplemental Security Income (or its predecessor programs).[36] These numbers suggested that welfare recipients should not be shamed, their economic dependence treated as an outrage or scandal, but as a normal phenomenon in a society that had made economic and political choices with certain predictable consequences.

In the policy circles that produced antiwelfare reforms, these data were either recruited into a war against welfare or ignored. In the 1980s, conservative intellectuals amplified gender-based arguments and made little of the contrary evidence they might have gleaned from the income experiments or the PSID. Writers such as George Gilder, Charles Murray, and Lawrence Mead utilized portions of the Seattle-Denver income maintenance project evidence in the touchstone texts of the Reagan presidency, *Wealth and Poverty* (1981), *Losing Ground* (1984), and *Beyond Entitlement* (1986).[37] They argued that AFDC and, by extension, all government antipoverty efforts, reduced sexual abstinence and fidelity, pointing men toward "deadbeat" fatherhood and women toward lone parenting.[38] The overall result, they suggested, was social chaos, with government policy at its source.

## VI. Common-Law Gender and Marital Ideals Redux

An antiwelfare consensus could not have formed without the participation of both major political parties, whose leading lights were all in thrall to a latter-day version of common-law marital and gender ideals. Daniel Patrick Moynihan, then U.S. senator from New York, helped set the tone, but he was hardly alone. In 1985, he was

[35] https://psidonline.isr.umich.edu/ (accessed September 7, 2015), and Katz, *Undeserving Poor*, 119–20.

[36] Greg J. Duncan, *Years of Poverty, Years of Plenty: The Changing Economic Fortunes of American Workers and Families* (Ann Arbor: Survey Research Center, Institute for Social Research, University of Michigan, 1984), 72–74. The predecessor programs of Supplemental Security Insurance (SSI) were Aid to the Blind, Old Age Assistance, and Aid to the Permanently and Totally Disabled.

[37] George Gilder, *Wealth and Poverty* (New York: Basic Books, 1982) ); Charles Murray, *Losing Ground: American Social Policy, 1950–1980* (New York: Basic Books, 1984); and Lawrence Mead, *Beyond Entitlement: The Social Obligations of Citizenship* (New York: Free Press, 1986).

[38] For critiques, see Felicia Kornbluh, "Feminism: Still Hazy after All These Years," *Tikkun*, 6/1 (Jan/Feb 1991): 23–26)+ and Felicia Kornbluh, "Subversive Potential, Coercive Intent: Women, Work, and Welfare in the 1990s," *Social Policy*, 21/4 (Spring 1991): 23–39. And see discussion of these texts in Marisa Chappell, *The War on Welfare: Family, Poverty, and Politics in Modern America* (Philadelphia: University of Pennsylvania Press, 2010); Katz, *Undeserving Poor*; and O'Connor, *Poverty Knowledge*.

invited to give a major address at Harvard University that he later published as the book *Family and Nation*.[39] In this work, he focused on gender, sex, and poor people's choices about intimacy. He claimed that a tight link that had once prevailed between overall prosperity and the poverty rate had broken since 1965, and that the phenomenon could only be explained by behavioral or moral phenomena—chiefly, the propensity of poor and nonwhite people to bear and raise children outside of wedlock. The "Black family" of *Family and Nation* needed simple economic assistance less than it needed rehabilitative social policy to create or restore normal family, sexual, and gender roles. Moynihan muted other explanations for the gap between average economic well-being since the middle 1960s and that of African American families, such as racial discrimination, disproportionate rates of incarceration, and the hyper-exploitation of many working women of color by their employers.

Moynihan's perspective on marriage and women's and men's roles prevailed through the welfare reform debates of the 1980s. It shaped the last major national legislative change in AFDC before the 1990s. Moynihan himself was the primary author of this legislation, the Family Support Act of 1988. A major difference between Republican and Democratic approaches to gender and welfare in this period was that Republicans, echoing policy intellectuals Gilder, Murray, and Mead, blamed government programs themselves for producing the supposed gender crisis in impoverished families and communities, while Moynihan and his allies who leaned Democratic blamed gendered arrangements for producing the need for government programs.

The debates that helped produce the Family Support Act were not only gendered. They were, simultaneously, racialist. Sociologist William Julius Wilson, whose influence on the debate is difficult to overstate, bypassed many of the factors that produced poverty and the need for public assistance. He wrote compellingly about the sometimes illegal and self-destructive behavior that occurred in small, statistically aberrant, communities in which few people had decent jobs. Wilson's book, *The Truly Disadvantaged* (1987), and interviews with the journalist Nicholas Lemann that spurred a series in the *Atlantic* magazine, did as much as anything else to fuel antiwelfare reformism by changing the subject from poverty to the behavior of poor people—behavior that readers inevitably interpreted through the lens of their stereotypes about women, African Americans, and poor people.[40] As they were for Moynihan, men and masculinity were for Wilson both the center of the problem and the source of its solution: economic conditions and men's bad choices, together, left poor, African American neighborhoods with a paucity of what he termed "marriageable males" and

[39] Daniel Patrick Moynihan, *Family and Nation: The Godkin Lectures* (New York: Harcourt Brace Jovanovich, 1986), 138–39.

[40] William Julius Wilson, "The Black Underclass," *The Wilson Quarterly*, 8/2 (1984): 88–99); "Cycles of Deprivation and the Underclass Debate," *Social Service Review*, 59/4 (1985): 541–59); and *The Truly Disadvantaged: The Inner City, The Underclass, and Public Policy* (Chicago: University of Chicago Press, 1987). Also see Nicholas Lemann, "The Origins of the Underclass Part I," *Atlantic Monthly* 257, 31–61; "The Origins of the Underclass Part II," *Atlantic Monthly* 258 54–68; and *The Promised Land: The Great Black Migration and How It Changed America* (New York: Knopf, 1991). The period saw a metastasis of journalistic writing on views such as Wilson's, often far less subtle than his own work. See Mortimer B. Zuckerman, "The Black Underclass," *U.S. News & World Report*, April 14, 1986: 78; Mickey Kaus, "The Work Ethic State," *New Republic*, July 7, 1986, 22–33; and Ken Auletta, *The Underclass* (New York: Random House, 1982).

therefore created women's and children's distress.[41] Rather than defend the antipoverty policies that extended what lifeline there was in urban communities awash in postindustrial poverty, Wilson saw the solution to women's circumstances in an ambitious, and perhaps unrealistic, social-democratic program of education, training, and employment directed at men.

The Family Support Act of 1988 emerged from a Democratic Congress and was signed by a Republican president. It received critical support from a self-styled centrist Democratic group, the Democratic Leadership Council, and from the National Governors Association, both led by Governor Bill Clinton of Arkansas.[42] Its most distinctive feature followed William Julius Wilson's emphasis on masculinity and paternity without the social investments he recommended: The Family Support Act dramatically increased the involvement of the national government in paternity establishment and child support enforcement. The statute expanded the power of the national Office of Child Support Enforcement, which Congress had created in 1974. It required states to withhold money from the wages of absent fathers to support their children; states administering AFDC were penalized for failing to establish paternity in a substantial number of cases.[43] The other major portion of the legislation, less distinctive but equally significant for poor people, was a program of work mandates and promised investments in education and services. The Job Opportunity and Basic Skills Training (JOBS) program replaced and reprised WIN/WIP from the 1967 welfare law. Like that earlier effort, it both federalized and placed a rehabilitative gloss upon mandates for waged work applied primarily to impoverished mothers. However, one bright spot of the law from many participants' perspectives was that it contained a definition of "work" that included full-time participation in work training or school, including in advanced programs and four-year colleges.[44]

## VII. The Masculinity of Welfare Reform

After 1988, the next major transformation of U.S. welfare policy occurred in 1996. In this case, a Republican majority in Congress and a Democratic president shared responsibility for the statute, the Personal Responsibility and Work Opportunity

[41] Wilson, *Truly Disadvantaged*, 82–92, 95–106.

[42] Clinton headed the National Governors Association in 1986–87 and had before that been the head of the organization's welfare committee. Peter Edelman Interview, by Russell Riley, Ed Berkowitz, and Kent Germany, May 24–25, 2004, William J. Clinton Presidential History Project, Miller Center, University of Virginia, 128 (transcript copyright 2014, Miller Center Foundation and Pryor Center for Arkansas Oral and Visual History), http://millercenter.org/president/clinton/oralhistory (accessed October 15, 2015); and Jonah Edelman, "The Politics of Welfare Reform and the Family Support Act of 1988" (M.A. thesis, Oxford University, 1994) and "The Passage of the Family Support Act," (doctoral dissertation, Balliol College, Oxford University, 1995).

[43] Committee on Finance, United States Senate, *Family Security Act of 1988: Report* (Washington, D.C.: U.S. Government Printing Office, 1988; 100th Cong., 2d Session, Report 100–377); Kornbluh, "Subversive Potential, Coercive Intent." A summary of the law appears in Katz, *The Price of Citizenship*, (Philadelphia: University of Pennsylvania Press, 2008), 71–76; and Edelman, "The Politics of Welfare Reform" and "The Passage of the Family Support Act."

[44] Kornbluh, "Class Dismissed! Welfare Recipients Fight to Stay in College," *In These Times* October 5, 1997: 18–20.

Reconciliation Act (PRWORA). What I see, through the lens of socio-legal histories of family law, as a recrudescence of the cultural template associated with common-law coverture—or as simple continuity with the past—was this statute's defining aspect.

The text of PRWORA reveals the long arm of the gendered and marital understandings that lay at the heart of common-law coverture. The statute began with three "findings" that revealed this emphasis: "(1) Marriage is the foundation of a successful society. (2) Marriage is an essential institution of a successful society which promotes the interests of children. (3) Promotion of responsible fatherhood and motherhood is integral to successful child rearing and the well-being of children."[45] With breezy definitude, the text later declared the change for which it is best known, the end of the "individual entitlement" to aid for impoverished children and their custodial parents.[46] These two aspects of the law are closely linked to one another. Both announce a public priority for the legally constituted "private" family over the legally constituted national public sector, the realm in which policy makers in the early and middle twentieth century had acknowledged the distinctive vulnerability of parenting women to economic disaster.

In the world Hendrik Hartog describes in *Man and Wife*, most free white women of means could not see beyond the curtain of common-law coverture. They simply lived behind it. By the late twentieth century, legislators understood that aid from the national government represented an alternative to conventional marital, gender, and parenting norms—not coverture exactly, but certainly norms, like those woven through the Blackstonian description of domestic relations, that structured systematic gender inequality. PRWORA may be understood in part as an effort to restrict women's options. Examined through low-income mothers' eyes, secure government aid in the form of an entitlement increased a woman's bargaining power with men in her life. It may therefore have enabled her greater happiness, her ability to avoid or escape abuse, and opportunity to build a better intimate partnership when she chose to enter one.[47] Reliable and accessible government assistance also assigned social worth to the family work poor mothers did, while recognizing the double burden of wage work and care work that so many faced in an inflexible, low-wage labor market.

The members of Congress who voted for PRWORA mobilized negative masculine stereotypes and endorsed policies that aimed to change men who came under the law's jurisdiction, even as they also suggested that women should relinquish their claims for self-sovereignty and focus on heterosexual marriage instead.[48] So, for example, the fourth finding in the statute's preamble directed attention to the fathers of poor children. Here, policymakers offered quantitative data about the percentages of families that had child support orders and received payments under them.[49] This

[45] Personal Responsibility and Work Opportunity Reconciliation Act of 1996, P.L. 104–193, Title I, Sec. 101.

[46] Personal Responsibility and Work Opportunity Reconciliation Act of 1996, P.L. 104–193, Title I, Sec. 103 (A) 401 (b).

[47] See the exploration of the terms of women's citizenship in Nancy Fraser, *Fortunes of Feminism: From State-Managed Capitalism to Neoliberal Crisis* (New York: Verso, 2013).

[48] For masculinity and the history of U.S. public policy, see Alice Kessler-Harris, *In Pursuit of Equity* (New York: Oxford University Press, 2001).

[49] Personal Responsibility and Work Opportunity Reconciliation Act of 1996, P.L. 104–193, Title I, Sec. 101 (4).

emphasis on child support, calling to mind the stereotype of the so-called deadbeat dad, ushered in extensive changes under PRWORA to the national child support system that had been enhanced in 1988.[50] Likewise, the seventh finding revisited the subject of masculine behavior by invoking the stereotype of the so-called "statutory" rapist, the man who has consensual intercourse with a woman below the legal age of consent, placing her at risk of becoming a teenage mother.[51]

The debate over poverty shifted gears somewhat after the dust settled from what had been a bitter fight among Democrats about President Clinton's decision to sign PRWORA. Progressives such as Representative Patsy T. Mink in the U.S. House of Representatives and Paul Wellstone (D-Minnesota) in the Senate continued to call for substantial changes in the statute. But most others in Congress and the White House shifted gears, from debating PRWORA to building upon its gendered and pro-marital foundations. Not a few Democrats joined Republicans in bipartisan homage to the so-called traditional family. Even some progressive Democrats supported legislation to incentivize husband- and father-centered "family formation."

## VIII. Regulating Fathers after "Welfare Reform"

The idea that social provision could be reprivatized, that low-income men could be made to bear the burden of reducing women's and children's poverty, drove policies that might appear to be in tension with one another. Policymakers privileged fathers as primary earners who needed help to succeed in the labor market and whose wages were the ultimate solution to the problem of poverty. At the same time, legislators and members of Bill Clinton's administration singled out low-income fathers for opprobrium and possible prosecution. Supporting fathers, the administration and some congressional Democrats sought specifically to set aside training or educational grants for low-income fathers of children on welfare—if the fathers signed "personal responsibility contracts committing them to work and child support."[52] Disciplining fathers, the administration launched a Fatherhood Initiative to improve paternity establishment rates, thus subjecting more men to criminal sanctions should they default on child support obligations.[53]

[50] Discussed in Mink, *Welfare's End* (Ithaca: Cornell University Press, 1998), 69–93, and, regarding the 1980s, Kornbluh, "Subversive Potential, Coercive Intent," 23–39. Also see U.S. House of Representatives, Committee on Ways and Means, *Green Book: Background Material and Data on Programs within the Jurisdiction of the Committee on Ways and Means*, "Child Support Enforcement Legislative History" (Washington, D.C.: Government Printing Office, 2012), http://greenbook.waysandmeans.house.gov/2012-green-book/child-support-enforcement-cover-page/legislative-history (accessed August 1, 2017).

[51] Personal Responsibility and Work Opportunity Reconciliation Act of 1996, 19 P.L. 104–193 (1996), Title I, Sec. 101 (7). By critiquing the way PRWORA mobilized stereotypes, I do not of course mean to endorse the sexual or physical abuse of young women.

[52] U.S. Department of Labor, "Welfare-to-Work Reauthorization," January 28, 1999, and attached, "Memorandum, from CAN [?], to P[atsy] T[akemoto] M[ink], on the Administration's Welfare-to-Work Proposal Briefing," February 2, 1999, Patsy T. Mink papers, box 1654/F4, Manuscripts Division, Library of Congress, Washington, D.C. Also see text of S. 1317, introduced by Senator Akaka of Hawaii, with cosponsors Moynihan, Feinstein, Wellstone, Murray, and Lautenberg, July 1999, 106th Cong., 1st sess. (not enacted), https://www.govtrack.us/congression/bills/106/21317/text (accessed January 20, 2016).

[53] Gwendolyn Mink, "Violating Women: Rights Abuses in the Welfare Police State," *Annals of the American Academy of Political and Social Science* 577/1 (September 2001): 84.

In Congress, the signal legislation that revealed the ambivalent treatment of low-income men by post-PRWORA policy makers was called "Fathers Count." Republicans led the way on this initiative. However, it had the support of the Clinton administration and other Democrats. Various fatherhood bills would have dedicated funds to noncustodial fathers of impoverished children to improve the men's success at getting and staying married, and at gaining and keeping employment. The chief congressional sponsor of Fathers Count legislation was Representative Nancy Johnson, Republican from Connecticut.[54] Similar bills were introduced by liberal Democrat Jesse Jackson, Jr., in the House, and Democrat Evan Bayh (D-Indiana) in the Senate.[55] The House version of the bill enjoyed support from the generally liberal Children's Defense Fund, Center on Budget and Policy Priorities, and Center on Law and Social Policy.[56]

Representative Johnson's bill did not make it to the Senate. However, as an indication of how widespread political support for this combination of privileging and regulation toward men had become, the Johnson legislation passed with a hefty 328 bipartisan votes.[57] It would have established fatherhood grant programs "to: 1) promote marriage ... 2) promote successful parenting ... and 3) help fathers and their families avoid or leave cash welfare."[58] Seventy-five percent of the funds were reserved for nongovernmental and even sectarian agencies, which the American Civil Liberties Union (ACLU) warned could proselytize with governmental imprimatur. The Fathers Count Act would have made funds available to private groups that focused on fatherhood and which tended to be antifeminist. It would have heightened child support enforcement beyond the level authorized by PRWORA.[59]

This legislative effort demonstrated ways in which regulation of men as fathers and husbands could also affect women as wives and mothers: Congresswoman Patsy T. Mink cautioned that the Fathers Count bill would harm mothers who would be excluded from its benefits and might encourage women in violent relationships to stay in those relationships. In a statement on the floor of the House, Mink argued, "I have nothing against fathers. I have lived with one for the last 49 years. However, we need to provide assistance to custodial parents," that is, to mothers raising children, "in order to make them self-sustainable." She expressed surprise at the idea that the bill implicitly told "women that the way to get out of poverty is find a husband!"[60]

[54] Fathers Count Act of 1999, H.R. 3073, 106th Cong. (1999).

[55] Responsible Fatherhood Act of 2000, H.R. 4671, 106th Cong. (2000); Responsible Fatherhood Act of 1999, S. 1364, 106th Cong. (1999).

[56] Democratic Policy Committee, "H.R. 3073, 'The Fathers Count Act'—Floor Update," November 9, 1999, Mink papers, box 1654/F6. The National Organization for Women opposed the bill.

[57] Clerk of the House of Representatives, roll call 586, http://clerk.house.gov/evs/1999/roll586xml (accessed May 26, 2016).

[58] Fathers Count Act of 1999, H.R. 3073, 106th Cong. (1999), Title I, Sec. 403A (pp. 3–4), https://www.govtrack.us/congress/bills/106/hr3073 (accessed May 27, 2016).

[59] Democratic Policy Committee, floor update, H.R. 3073, the "Fathers Count Act," November 9, 1999, Mink papers, box 2090/F6; American Civil Liberties Union, "Dear Representative Letter," re: H.R. 3073, the "Fathers Count Act," November 9, 1999, Mink papers, box 1654/F4; statement of Congresswoman Patsy T. Mink of Hawaii, on her Parents Count Amendment to H.R. 3073, November 10, 1999, Mink papers, box 2090/F6; and National Organization for Women, "The Fathers Count Act of 1999, H.R. 3073—Talking Points," November 9, 1999, Mink papers, box 1654/F4.

[60] Statement of Congresswoman Patsy T. Mink of Hawaii, on her Parents Count Amendment to H.R. 3073, November 10, 1999 (on her stationery), Mink papers, box 1654/F6. Mink used the same language in

## IX. The Long Nineteenth Century in the Early Twenty-First Century?

In the early 2000s, Republicans in the White House and Congress debated Congressional Democrats over what was slated to be the first reauthorization of PRWORA. Although there were meaningful differences between members of the two major parties, there were also enormous differences among Democrats (and, to a lesser degree, among Republicans) about the statute and its gendered foundations. Conservative Republicans argued the need for more systematic marriage promotion and greater enforcement of the waged work ethic. Although PRWORA had declared marriage "the foundation of a successful society," conservative critics argued that neither the national nor state governments had invested enough resources in attempting to change the marital lives of impoverished Americans. Robert Rector from the Heritage Foundation think tank led the way, supporting his push for greater emphasis on the marital and gendered dimensions of welfare policy with claims that "illegitimacy [was] ... passed, like a virus, between generations" and that mothers who received welfare payments were "sit[ting] idly on the rolls."[61]

In the political mainstream, most leading Democrats endorsed the idea of using at least a portion of public antipoverty funds for marriage promotion, or "family formation," instead of for direct poverty reduction. Wendell Primus, who had resigned from the Clinton administration in protest over PRWORA, helped sustain the marriage agenda when he declared that "progressives should [not] be scared of this issue" because "we also believe in marriage and two-parent families."[62] In congressional testimony, a senior fellow of the liberal-leaning think tank, the Urban Institute, admitted that there was no research to support the idea that tweaks in antipoverty programs could reverse long-term trends in marital or sexual behavior. But "independently from whether [they would] significantly affect behavior in a narrow sense," he believed government should pursue them.[63]

Efforts at welfare reauthorization in 2002 fizzled, and PRWORA was sustained by a series of continuing resolutions that made no major changes in the program for several years. But the maritally oriented and fatherhood-based discourses surrounding welfare were firmly entrenched and overwhelmingly bipartisan well before Obama made his Father's Day speech in 2008. As with other aspects of the political and intellectual surround of welfare reform, not all Democrats participated in this bipartisanship. But many did. Primus, for example, described as a "liberal lion" in a piece

Patsy T. Mink, member of Congress, letter to colleagues, "Fathers Count Act Ignores the Needs of Mothers," November 8, 1999, Mink papers, box 2090/F6.

[61] Robert Rector, senior policy analyst, Heritage Foundation, statement, Welfare Reform: Hearing Before the Subcommittee on Human Resources of the Committee on Ways and Means, U.S. House of Representatives, 107th Cong., 1st sess., March 15, 2001. Copy in Mink papers, box 1775/F3.

[62] Laura Meckler, Associated Press, "Marriage to Be Welfare Focus," *Boston Globe*, February 12, 2001, A5.

[63] C. Eugene Steuerle, senior fellow, Urban Institute, statement, Hearing on Welfare and Marriage Issues, U.S. House of Representatives, Committee on Ways and Means, Subcommittee on Human Resources, 107th Cong., 1st sess., May 22, 2001.

about his later work as senior advisor to Speaker Nancy Pelosi,[64] argued that fatherhood promotion should hold a major place in antipoverty policy. A 2001 briefing paper Primus coauthored with conservative researcher Ron Haskins included a full-throated call for direct government assistance to poor fathers and the reassignment of poor mothers to father-headed households. They cautioned that single motherhood had not been proved to *cause* poverty, but still built their argument upon assorted correlations between single motherhood and adverse child outcomes. Therefore, they maintained, publicly funded marriage promotion "would be a good way to reduce child poverty and to promote child and adult well-being more generally."[65]

In their rush to restore a version of the Blackstonian ideal of marital unity to antipoverty policy, neither Democrats nor Republicans who favored fatherhood promotion reconciled their assumptions with those of advocates for victims of domestic violence. This was not surprising: A feminist interpretation of domestic violence would include the notion that any policy that enhanced the economic power of men over women was also likely to enhance abusers' ability to mistreat their partners. One of the best policies to help those who had experienced violence was a generous cash welfare program for single parents, with supportive services they could access at will. One egregious example of the bipartisan unwillingness to comprehend the feminist and violence-sensitive perspective was an attempt at rapprochement between fatherhood policy activists and antiviolence advocates, led by the Ford Foundation. The report on this effort chronicled the "barriers to collaboration" between fatherhood promoters and feminist antiviolence advocates. It made no recommendations for antipoverty policies that would better protect women or support the underfunded feminist domestic violence infrastructure. It concluded with only a weak endorsement of the idea that fatherhood programs, themselves, should address the issue of violence.[66]

In the George W. Bush era, there was as much regulation and underfunding of "traditional" families as there was celebration of them in rhetoric. PRWORA reauthorization, which finally occurred in 2005–06, privileged heterosexuality and masculinity in their ideal or archetypal forms but did not grant benefits unequivocally to heterosexual couples or individual men. A new requirement that states place 90% of two-parent families in approved work activities, for example, was likely to drive bureaucrats and politicians to keep two-parent families off their caseloads—even as the Bush administration sang the praises of fatherhood and married child-rearing.[67] Similarly, the child support policies written into reauthorization were *more* punitive toward noncustodial parents (fathers) than the original version of PRWORA had

[64] Mary Ann Akers, "In the Speaker's Office, a Quiet Liberal Lion: Wendell E. Primus," *Washington Post*, June 21, 2010, http://www.washingtonpost.com/wp-dyn-content/article/2010/06/20/AR2010062003442_2.html (accessed August 11, 2016).

[65] Ron Haskins and Wendell Primus, "Welfare Reform and Poverty," Policy Brief No. 4, July 2001, Washington, D.C.: The Brookings Institution: Welfare Reform and Beyond project.

[66] Marguerite Roulet, "Fatherhood Programs and Domestic Violence," Center on Fathers, Families, and Public Policy, Technical Assistance Series, n.d. [2002], filed as "Fatherhood programs and dv-crfpp," in Gwendolyn Mink files on fatherhood promotion.

[67] Deficit Reduction Act of 2005, P.L. 109–171, 120 Stat. 135 (2005), Title VII, Subtitle A, Sec. 7102.

been: for example, lowering the amount of money in owed child support that would trigger the invalidation of a parent's passport.[68]

Welfare reform reauthorization created a new funding stream of $150 million per year in grants to promote "Healthy Marriage" and "Responsible Fatherhood." These grants were to be distributed by the Department of Health and Human Services to state and local governments, nonprofit agencies, and profit-making companies.[69] Supportable activities included "public advertising campaigns on the value of marriage," "education in high schools on the value of marriage," and "divorce reduction programs."[70] The law permitted states to use money earmarked for welfare for parents and children to cover state contributions to the "healthy marriage" program.[71] The Wisconsin-based welfare rights group Welfare Warriors, one of the few to survive long after the heyday of NWRO, responded to this with an angry article in their newspaper *Welfare Mothers' Voice*. Milwaukee public aid recipient Pat Gowens informed readers that Congress and the White House had cut funds for nutrition and health care programs, but made them available for those she termed "marriage poverty pimps," who would "earn living wages to teach us poor folks how to stay with our batterers and abandoners."[72]

In the run-up to the 2008 elections, a rising generation of Democratic leaders resisted some of the Republican specifics on welfare reform but continued to participate in the neo-coverture discourse of fatherhood promotion. In 2006, for example, then-Senator Barack Obama cosponsored a fatherhood bill with Democrat Evan Bayh. The proposed law lingered in the Senate Finance Committee through Obama's presidential run. But it helped define fatherhood as what a writer for the *New York Times* called a "signature" issue for him and formed the basis for the speech

[68] Deficit Reduction Act of 2005, P.L. 109–171, 120 Stat. 135 (2005), Title VII, Subtitle C, Sec. 7903. Also see discussion of this and other proposals prior to congressional reconciliation of the different House and Senate versions of the Deficit Reduction Act in Vicki Turetsky, "Side-by-Side Comparison of Child Support and Fatherhood Program Provisions in Welfare Reauthorization Bills Passed by the Senate Finance Committee and House Human Resources Subcommittee," Center for Law and Social Policy, Washington, D.C., June 6, 2005, document titled, "clasp—billscomparisonfatherhood and cse-05," Gwendolyn Mink files on fatherhood promotion.

[69] P.L. 109–171, 120 Stat. 135, Subtitle A, Sec. 7103; Parrott, Schott, et al., "Implementing the TANF Changes in the Deficit Reduction Act," 107; Elizabeth Lower-Basch, Evelyn Ganzglass, Elisa Minoff, Sharon Parrott, and Liz Schott, "Analysis of New Interim Final TANF Rules," 33; and "Reauthorization of the Temporary Assistance for Needy Families Program, Interim Final Rule," 45 CFR Parts 261, et al. (Part IV, Department of Health and Human Services, Administration for Children and Families), *Federal Register* 71/125 (June 29, 2006): 37470–71.

[70] P.L. 109–171, 120 Stat. 135, Subtitle A, Sec. 7103.

[71] When the Temporary Assistance for Needy Families program (TANF) was created in 1996, each state was required to continue spending at least 80 percent of the amount it had spent on the predecessor program, Aid to Families with Dependent Children. This funding was known in late twentieth- and twenty-first-century social policy argot as the state's "maintenance-of-effort (MOE)" amount. By 2005, states were spending only a minority of MOE money on cash aid to TANF families. Most of the funds were going to child care assistance and child welfare programs that reached non-TANF as well as TANF families, and to filling budget holes. Allowing states to use the money for marriage promotion was an extension of the federal government's loose reading of the requirement that states maintain the effort they had once devoted to alleviating the poverty of mothers and children who lacked other means of economic sustenance. Parrott, Schott, et al., "Implementing the TANF Changes in the Deficit Reduction Act,", 108–9.

[72] Pat Gowens, "Poverty Pimps 'Floating on Ceiling' after $50 Billion Cut," *Welfare Mothers' Voice*, Winter 2006, archived at http://www.welfarewarriors.org/mwv_archive/w06/w06_pimp.htm (accessed October 3, 2016).

he ultimately gave on Father's Day.[73] Senate bill 3607, the Bayh-Obama bill "to ensure funding for grants to promote responsible fatherhood and strengthen low-income families," was more internally consistent than the welfare reauthorization law had been; it was fatherhood promotion without as much father discipline.[74] Obama and Bayh would, for example, have eliminated the mandate that states place 90% of two-parent families in work activities and therefore removed that disincentive to states and localities serving married people. However, they did not question the other party's treatment of child support as a morally better source of mothers' income than government grants. Obama and Bayh departed from the bipartisan consensus when they included male unemployment and low wages, and parents' incarceration, among the reasons some fathers were not in their children's lives. And their bill required that agencies receiving fatherhood funds consult with domestic violence experts. The senators also authored a new grant program for domestic violence prevention and services for people who had experienced violence.[75]

In the same period, former president Clinton shared his thoughts on the reauthorized cash welfare program and on how to move forward. He took PRWORA's tenth anniversary in August 2006 as an opportunity to express paternal pride for the statute rather than ring a tocsin of alarm. He celebrated the child support enforcement his administration pursued against low-income fathers as "the toughest … in history."[76] While acknowledging criticism he had received from liberals, Clinton nonetheless argued that "welfare reform worked because we all worked together" and "never betrayed our principles."[77] Regarding the Republican-driven reauthorization, he did not mention the gender-specific fatherhood program or other shortcomings identified by advocates for low-income people. However, he did criticize the Bush administration for narrowing recipients' access to education. The fix he proposed was a bipartisan coalition to pass additional legislation that would give state governments the option to count higher education as work under the PRWORA work requirement.[78]

## X. The New Old Conversation about Fatherhood

During the season when Barack Obama first ran for president, many Democrats remained wedded to a bipartisan set of ideas about poverty's behavioral causes and

73 The tie between them was sufficiently strong that Bayh was spoken of during the 2008 campaign as a potential vice-presidential running mate for Obama. Carl Hulse, "Indiana Senator Offers Obama Risks and Rewards," *New York Times*, August 11, 2008, http://www.nytimes.com/2008/08/12/us/politics/12bayh.html (accessed September 21, 2016). On the connection between the Senate bill and his campaign rhetoric, see Adam Serwer, "Democrats Find Their Footing on Fatherhood," *American Prospect*, September 22, 2008, http://prospect.org/article/democrats-find-their-footing-fatherhood (accessed September 21, 2016).

74 S. 3607, 109th Cong., 2nd sess., introduced June 29, 2006, https://www.congress.gov/bill/109th-congress/senate-bill/3607 (accessed August 15, 2017).

75 S. 3607, 109th Cong., 2nd sess., Title I, Sec. 101 (2) (b) and Sec. 102.

76 Bill Clinton, "How We Ended Welfare, Together," *New York Times*, August 22, 2006, A19.

77 Ibid.

78 Ibid.

cures. These ideas shared a privatizing impulse, locating economic security in the efforts of individuals and, even more, within families organized along heteromarital lines. Many liberals and Democrats were enthused about the Obama approach, with a writer for the left-of-center *American Prospect* magazine, for example, celebrating a new Democratic "political conversation about fatherhood" that promised a solution to poverty in African American communities. "Ultimately all the money in the world fails to fill the emotional void left by an absent father," Adam Serwer wrote.[79]

As president, Obama's policies were consistent with his campaign commitments to welfare reform and fatherhood promotion. His administration never tried to remove welfare work requirements. (It did invoke the emergency measures included in the 1996 welfare reform legislation to extend time limits for receiving benefits during the recession and offered states the option of waivers to increase flexibility regarding clients' work activities.) The Obama White House maintained a signal Bush-era domestic policy initiative, renamed the Office of Faith-Based and Neighborhood Partnerships, and made "Promoting Responsible Fatherhood and Strong Communities" one of four "key priorities" for that office.[80] In 2009, the president hosted forums around the country on "fatherhood and personal responsibility."[81] He followed in 2010 with the President's Fatherhood and Mentoring Initiative, which called for added investment in job training and economic incentives for noncustodial, but not for custodial, parents, as well as "a new and expanded Fatherhood, Marriage and Families Innovation Fund" to "scale up" the "network of support for men" throughout the United States.[82] "Nurturing families come in many forms," read the administration's 2010 Father's Day Proclamation, "and children may be raised by a father and mother, a single father, two fathers, a stepfather, a grandfather, or caring guardian."[83]

The administration continued its emphasis on men and boys through the end of Obama's second term.[84] In 2014, the White House initiated My Brother's Keeper, a set

[79] Serwer, "Democrats Find Their Footing."

[80] White House, "Promoting Responsible Fatherhood and Strong Communities," https://www.whitehouse.gov/administration/eop/ofbnp/policy/fatherhood (accessed July 21, 2016).

[81] Marjorie Kehe, "Obama Fatherhood Initiative: A Rare Issue of Bipartisan Accord?" *Christian Science Monitor*, October 19, 2009, http://www.csmonitor.com/USA/Politics/2009/1019/obama-fatherhood-initiative-a-rare-issue-of-bipartisan-accord (accessed July 21, 2016); and discussion of 2009 efforts in [White House], "President Obama Launches Next Phase in Fatherhood Efforts with the President's Fatherhood and Mentoring Initiative—Press Release," June 21, 2010, https://www.whitehouse.gov/the-press-office/president-obama-launches-next-phase-fatherhood-efforts-with-presidents-fatherhood-a (accessed July 21, 2016).

[82] [White House], "President Obama Launches Next Phase"; "President Obama Promotes Responsible Fatherhood: 'No Excuses,'" https://obamawhitehouse.archives.gov/blog/2010/06/21/president-obama-promotes-responsible-fatherhood-no-excuses (accessed October 23, 2017).

[83] Administration of President Barack Obama, "Proclamation 8537, Father's Day 2010," June 18, 2010, Government Publishing Office, https://www.gpo.gov/fdsys/pkg/DCPD-201000511/pdf/DCPD-201000511.pdf (accessed October 11, 2017); Fred Lucas, "Obama Fatherhood Proclamation Mentions Families with 'Two Fathers,'" *Christian News Service*, June 21, 2010, http://www.cnsnews.com/news/article/obama-fatherhood-proclamation-mentions-families-two-fathers (accessed July 21, 2016).

[84] I differ from political scientist and commentator Melissa Harris-Perry, who found President Obama's practice of publicly acknowledging the contributions of women of color a "meaningful discursive practice" that earned him "genuine intersectional bona fides." Melissa Harris-Perry, "Obama Proves, Yet Again, That He Is Our Most Black, Feminist President to Date," *Elle Magazine*, May 9, 2016, http://www.elle.com/culture/career-politics/a36255/obama-our-most-black-feminist-president/ (accessed July 21, 2016).

of public-private partnerships to promote the educational and career success of men and boys of color, which were shepherded into being following the killing of the unarmed Black teenager Trayvon Martin in Florida. Under pressure, the administration made some of the language in its My Brother's Keeper materials gender-neutral and supportive of nonwhite girls. But the project continued to skew male. And, although it skewed male, it did not address the need for criminal justice reform, the gendered and racist causes and effects of mass incarceration, or, indeed, the politics of paternal responsibility both within and outside of the welfare system that had burdened many low-income fathers with stigma and overwhelming financial obligations.[85]

Eli Saslow's Pulitzer Prize–winning reporting for the *Washington Post* revealed the contradiction between Obama's rhetorical endorsement of a private-law ideal of husbandhood and fatherhood, and the disappointments faced by impoverished twenty-first-century fathers who sought public support in their efforts to be good parents and partners: Fathers such as Paul Gayle, a high school graduate from Milwaukee, attended fatherhood classes approved by the White House. Gayle hoped for help to pay for things his baby needed ("he had been buying Pampers one at a time," Saslow reported). But he received nothing but bromides, invocations of a common-law marital ideal that did little to overcome economic, racial, and geographic barriers to being the husband and father whose role was celebrated.[86]

Meanwhile, fathers such as Walter Scott in South Carolina suffered for nonpayment of child support in the context of a bipartisan war against "deadbeat dads" that had started in the late twentieth century and was seemingly stronger than ever in the twenty-first. Scott was one of those low-income Black fathers whose ex-partner relied in part on public assistance. Obama's fatherhood address during his campaign for president had promised to make things "harder" for such men because they failed to make "responsible choices." Scott served six months in jail during the year of Obama's electoral victory, supposedly the post-racial apotheosis of U.S. politics. At the time of Scott's killing by police in 2015, there was a warrant out for the arrest of

[85] Obama White House Archives, "About My Brother's Keeper," n.d. [2016], https://obamawhitehouse.archives.gov/node/279811#section-about-my-brothers-keeper (accessed October 11, 2017) ("President Obama launched the My Brother's Keeper initiative to address persistent opportunity gaps faced by boys and young men of color and ensure that all young people can reach their full potential."); White House, *My Brother's Keeper—2016 Progress Report: Two Years of Expanding Opportunity and Creating Pathways to Success*, n.d. [2016], https://www.whitehouse.gov/sites/whitehouse.gov/files/images/MBK-2016-Progress-Report.pdf (accessed January 17, 2017); and Nia-Malika Henderson, "Obama Announces $100 Million Expansion of 'My Brother's Keeper,'" She the People blog, *Washington Post*, July 21, 2014, https://www.washingtonpost.com/blogs/she-the-people/wp/2014/07/21/obama-announces-100-million-expansion-of-my-brothers-keeper/?utm_term=.ab5bde35e38e (accessed October 11, 2017).

[86] Eli Saslow, "A Father's Initiative—Paul Gayle Had No Job, No Money, a New Baby and 16 Lessons from the Obama Administration to Teach Him What to Do Next," *Washington Post*, May 16, 2015, http://www.washingtonpost.com/sf/national/2015/05/16/a-fathers-initiative/?utm_term=.9f9d2d1e0aa0 (accessed October 11, 2017).

this fifty-year-old father of four—the latest in a string of warrants, which had caused him to lose jobs but had never resulted in him meeting what the state treated as his child support obligations. When he was stopped for a broken taillight, Scott's family theorized, he probably ran because he was unwilling to rejoin the one-eighth of South Carolina prison inmates jailed for overdue child support.[87] Things had indeed gotten hard for him, and for his children.

[87] Frances Robles and Shaila Dewan, "Skip Child Support. Go to Jail. Lose Job. Repeat," *New York Times*, April 19, 2015, https://www.nytimes.com/2015/04/20/us/skip-child-support-go-to-jail-lose-job-repeat.html (accessed April 9, 2023); Christopher Mathias, "One-Eighth of South Carolina Inmates Were Jailed over Child Support Payments. Walter Scott Was One of Them," *Huffington Post*, April 10, 2015, https://www.huffingtonpost.com/2015/04/10/walter-scott-child-support-_n_7036174.html (accessed October 10, 2017); and Alan Blinder, "Charleston Jury Gets Case of Officer Who Killed Walter Scott," *New York Times*, November 30, 2016, http://www.nytimes.com/2016/11/30/us/michael-slager-walter-scott-killing.html?_r=0 (accessed December 1, 2016). The U.S. Supreme Court has acknowledged, to a limited degree, the relationship between aggressive child support enforcement and mass incarceration, concluding that a South Carolina man who served twelve months in jail for nonpayment of child support after a civil proceeding in which he had no attorney, and in which there was little discussion of his indigence, should have been provided counsel by the state. Turner v. Rogers, 546 U.S. 431 (2011). The vote on the opinion was 5–4.

# 4
# Power of the Purse
## How "The Philanthropic North" Has Helped Determine Which Individuals, Groups, and Ideas in the Black Freedom Struggle Will Thrive Nationally

*Maribel Morey*

> *"[T]he Negro who shows the slightest independence of thought or character is apt to be read out of all possible influence not only by the white South but by the philanthropic North."*
>
> —*W. E. B. Du Bois,* The Crisis *(1918)*[1]

In *Courage to Dissent* (2011), U.S. legal historian Tomiko Brown-Nagin vividly recounts how Black civil rights activists in mid- to late-twentieth-century Atlanta had differing and contesting visions on how best to address Jim Crow in the United States—whether directly through civil disobedience, such as sit-ins and boycotts, or more indirectly through private dialogues with influential white Americans within the city's white power structure.[2] Brown-Nagin explains:

> Long before 'black power' emerged and gave black dissent from the mainstream civil rights agenda a name, disagreement flourished between civil rights lawyers and civil rights activists, between civil rights organizations and their client communities, between gradualists and advocates of 'Freedom Now!' and between proponents and skeptics of integration.... Blacks played out these disagreements in the courts, in the streets, and in the informal and formal arena of politics.[3]

Brown-Nagin writes against a national narrative of the Black freedom struggle in the United States long assuming that, with the exception of a fringe group of Black Americans supporting Black nationalist groups such as the Black Panther Party and, before it, Marcus Garvey's Universal Negro Improvement Association (UNIA), most if not all Black Americans long have pined for assimilation into white institutions

[1] W. E. B. Du Bois, "Negro Education," *The Crisis* (February 1918), 177.
[2] Tomiko Brown-Nagin, *Courage to Dissent: Atlanta and the Long History of the Civil Rights Movement* (New York: Oxford University Press, 2011).
[3] Brown-Nagin, *Courage to Dissent*, 8–9.

Maribel Morey, *Power of the Purse* In: *In Between and Across.* Edited by: Kenneth W. Mack and Jacob Katz Cogan, Oxford University Press. © Oxford University Press 2024. DOI: 10.1093/oso/9780197680995.003.0005

and norms. In this spirit, the country's national narrative has assumed that Black Americans full-heartedly stood behind the school desegregation efforts of the NAACP Legal Defense and Educational Fund (LDF) in the 1940s and 1950s and, for example, the efforts of college students in the 1960s to desegregate lunch counters.

Writing a bottom-up narrative of the U.S. civil rights movement in Atlanta, Brown-Nagin pushes against this national narrative long simplifying the Black community and Black Americans' varying calls for action—and she does so (not by complicating the national narrative's assumption that all Black Americans have aimed for inclusion into white-led institutions in the United States as the very definition of equality and freedom, but) by detailing generational disagreements on the best means of arriving at this assimilationist goal. To this point, Brown-Nagin in *Courage to Dissent* describes middle-aged Black Atlantans' hesitations with a younger generation's direct-action approach to addressing white supremacy in the city. She underscores, for example, how an older generation of Black Atlantans, which she characterizes as "pragmatists," were skeptical of Black college students' sit-ins and doubted the wisdom of school desegregation efforts. She writes that "the black middle class's concerns about workplace discrimination overtook the school desegregation litigation, just as the U.S. Court of Appeals for the Fifth Circuit committed itself to desegregating schools 'root and branch.'"[4] And as far as the sit-ins, Brown-Nagin explains that these Atlanta pragmatists doubted the efficacy of such direct action.[5]

Similarly complicating the country's general narrative of the Black freedom struggle in the twentieth century, though with an eye toward questioning all Black Americans' supposed support for racial assimilation, other scholars have underscored the sheer popularity of Black nationalist groups within Black communities. Historian Keisha Blain writes in *Set the World on Fire* (2018) that Black nationalist leader Marcus Garvey, with the assistance of Amy Ashwood, established the UNIA in Jamaica in 1914, which became "the largest and most influential Pan-Africanist movement of the twentieth century."[6] By the early 1920s, Blain notes that the UNIA "attracted millions of followers in more than forty countries around the world," including the United States.[7] Moving ahead to later decades in the twentieth century, sociologist Alondra Nelson's *Body & Soul* (2011) details the Black Panther Party's community health care initiatives in Oakland, California, in the 1970s, suggesting just how this Black nationalist group was neither a fringe group in Black communities nor a group singularly or principally made up of "aimless youth with violent tendencies."[8] Taking on the perspective of Black Americans throughout the twentieth century, these scholars complicate white Americans' long assumption that the NAACP LDF's school desegregation efforts and racial assimilationist agendas generally have long reflected most if not all Black Americans' expectations for freedom and equality in the United States.

[4] Brown-Nagin, *Courage to Dissent*, 14.

[5] Brown-Nagin, *Courage to Dissent*, 13.

[6] Keisha Blain, *Set the World on Fire: Black Nationalist Women and the Global Struggle for Freedom* (Philadelphia: University of Pennsylvania Press, 2018), 11.

[7] Blain, *Set the World on Fire*, 12.

[8] Alondra Nelson, *Body and Soul: The Black Panther Party and the Fight against Medical Discrimination* (Minneapolis: University of Minnesota Press, 2011), 4.

Moving beyond the Black freedom struggle, other freedom movements in indigenous and other people of color (BIPOC) communities in the United States are equally cacophonous and oversimplified by our national narratives. It seems so simple and obvious to note that we disagree within our BIPOC communities on what collective grievances we might have in the face of white Anglo-American supremacy in the United States and how best to address them. As a Cuban-American woman living in the Latino-dominant city of Miami, for example, I see and experience vividly every day how we Latinos disagree on how best to go about collectively addressing white Anglo-American supremacy. This is all to say that the very act of figuring out how to collectively respond to white Anglo-American supremacy in the United States is contentious and, within our BIPOC communities, we disagree on how best to respond to it and what to expect as successful outcomes for our collective actions. We also disagree on what it means to be free in this country—whether it means accessing the existing white Anglo-American power structure or disrupting or rejecting it to varying degrees.

Seeing the complexities of our freedom movements from the ground up, the question then becomes: Why have certain activists, groups, and visions for equality in our communities gained such positive attention at the national level? One simple reason could be that these particular activists, groups, and visions for equality (more than their competitors with some support on the ground) simply enjoy more support within our communities across the country. So even if we sympathize with certain local leaders, organizations, and visions for equality, the majority of people in our communities across the country might not. As to why certain individuals, groups, and ideas end up winning the imaginations of our communities at a national level, scholars long have stressed the gender, racial, and class inequities that lead certain BIPOC movement activists and organizations to achieve more influence and attention within and beyond our communities. Scholars, for example, have noted that U.S. society at large—and our own BIPOC communities too—long have privileged the work and ideas of men over women, lighter- over darker-skinned people, the richer over the poorer, and all activists' pragmatic over radical theories of change that reinforce, rather than substantially challenge, the political economic status quo in this country.

To this point, scholars have repeatedly acknowledged that BIPOC male activists in the United States have tended to garner more of a following within and beyond our BIPOC communities, helping to explain, for example, why more Americans know about the work of Martin Luther King Jr. and Thurgood Marshall than that of Ella Baker and Constance Baker Motley in the Black freedom movement.[9] Explaining the absence of Motley in most national accounts of the movement, for example, Brown-Nagin reasons in *Civil Rights Queen* (2022), "In Western societies, historical significance is coded male. The lives of men are deemed worthy of study and remembrance."[10] Even when women are remembered in our communities and country, scholars have noted too that lighter-skinned women tend to attract more lasting

[9] See e.g., Barbara Ransby, *Ella Baker and the Black Freedom Movement: A Radical Democratic Vision* (Chapel Hill: University of North Carolina Press, 2003), 4; Tomiko Brown-Nagin, *Civil Rights Queen: Constance Baker Motley and the Struggle for Equality* (New York: Penguin Random House, 2022).

[10] Brown-Nagin, *Civil Rights Queen*, Introduction.

national attention than darker-skinned women.[11] Even more, scholars too have documented how middle-class rather than working-class activists tend to gain more attention within and beyond our communities, not only because the former have at their disposal more economic and political resources than the latter, but also because their activist goals tend to be more pragmatic and seemingly less threatening to the existing white power structure and to many within our own communities who feel most comfortable with pragmatic (rather than revolutionary) means towards greater freedom and equality.[12] This helps explain why the NAACP, rather than the Black Panther Party, for example, found a comparably more receptive audience among the white elite during the Black freedom struggle and, relatedly, why the NAACP generally has been remembered more fondly in the country's historical recounting of the struggle in the twentieth century.[13]

And yet, as this chapter stresses, our own BIPOC communities and the general U.S. public at large are not the only groups shaping which activists and ideas have gained (and will gain) national attention as key representative figures in our communities' freedom movements. Rather, prominent U.S. philanthropic organizations also have played critical roles in this process.

Focusing on the Black freedom struggle during the twentieth century, this chapter underscores the role played by an elite network of white Anglo-American funders based in New York City—particularly those at leading philanthropic organizations such as the Carnegie, Rockefeller, and Ford foundations and their colleagues in smaller funds such as the Phelps Stokes and Garland Funds—in shaping which Black freedom activists, organizations, and agendas would flourish nationally.

To present the long-standing role of white-led philanthropic organizations in shaping which activists, ideas, organizations, and agendas from the Black freedom struggle would thrive nationally in the United States, this chapter spotlights the work of various scholars who have researched the specific roles played by different white funders at various moments in the struggle—from the Rockefeller, Carnegie, Phelps Stokes, and Garland funds to the Ford Foundation. Bringing together our various analyses of white funders' influence in the Black freedom struggle throughout the twentieth century, this chapter provides a bird's eye view of the long-standing role of white funders in shaping which activists and organizations in the struggle would gain national attention. The chapter concludes with a look to the present, cautioning us to remain attentive to the ways that elite funders can continue to shape how we collectively imagine and define the key players and agendas in BIPOC-led movements in the United States.

In this first section, I discuss the chapter's temporal framing of the Black freedom struggle in the United States. Subsequent sections then outline the role of white funders in shaping which activists, groups, and ideas from the Black freedom struggle would thrive at the national level.

[11] See e.g., Serena Mayeri, *Reasoning from Race: Feminism, Law, and the Civil Rights Revolution* (Cambridge: Harvard University Press, 2011), 222.

[12] See e.g., Aldon Morris, *The Origins of the Civil Rights Movement* and Brown-Nagin, *Courage to Dissent*.

[13] See e.g., Nelson, *Body and Soul*, xiii.

## I. The Long Black Freedom Struggle

In the past decades, U.S. historians have been chipping away at various assumptions in the country's telling and retelling of the Black freedom struggle in the United States. As noted earlier in this chapter, some scholars have questioned the assumptions that Black Americans long have presented a united front on their grievances and hopes in the United States, with racial integration being the assumed policy goal of an oversimplified presentation of "the Black community" in the singular. Equally so, U.S. historians also have been chipping away at the relatively narrow timespan that the national narrative provides the U.S. Black freedom struggle. To this point, U.S. historian Jacqueline Dowd Hall's 2005 piece in the *Journal of American History*, "The Long Civil Rights Movement and the Political Uses of the Past," shook many fellow U.S. historians' subsequent telling of the U.S. civil rights movement or, rather, of the Black freedom struggle.[14] As Dowd Hall recounted in 2005, many U.S. historians generally had assumed that the U.S. civil rights movement in the U.S. launched following the U.S. Supreme Court's school desegregation decision *Brown v. Board of Education* (1954) and most poignantly with the Montgomery bus boycotts in 1955, and that the movement generally came to a close with the passage of the Civil Rights Act of 1964 and Voting Rights Act of 1965. With this 2005 article, Dowd Hall directly challenged this national myth that the movement was a short, successful bid to overcome racial segregation in the Jim Crow South.

Since then, and in dialogue with this 2005 article, many U.S. historians have expanded both the timeline of the U.S. civil rights movement back in time to include antislavery work in the United States in the nineteenth century and the geographic scope to include regions beyond the U.S. South. As could be expected, some scholars since 2005 have debated whether a U.S. civil rights movement in fact existed across geographies in the United States and over the span of decades, with others thus suggesting that perhaps the "long civil rights movement" should be termed the long Black freedom struggle instead. Because while a cohesive social "movement" for Black freedom might not have existed across the United States since the age of white Americans' enslavement of Black Americans, a "struggle" indeed has. To this point, historian Jeffrey Helgeson writes that "movements grow out of fertile ground of everyday struggle, yet they are also embattled, highly contingent, and temporary events."[15] It is in this spirit that this chapter applies the term and concept of a *long Black freedom struggle* to describe Black Americans' centuries-long effort and fight to achieve freedom in the United States.

Though even when embracing the term "struggle" rather than "movement" to describe Black Americans' long-standing battle in the United States to challenge deeply engrained white supremacy and anti-Black discrimination in nearly all aspects of life, we are still left with the question of why exactly certain Black freedom activists and agendas have been able to thrive in the United States and, relatedly, been able to define

[14] Jacqueline Dowd Hall, "The Long Civil Rights Movement and the Political Uses of the Past," *Journal of American History* 91.4 (March 2005).

[15] See, e.g., Jeffrey Helgeson, "Beyond a Long Civil Rights Movement," *The Journal of African American History* 99.4 (Fall 2014).

the means and goals of the movement. To this point, and as this next section of the chapter stresses, it is critical to acknowledge not only the role of the U.S. public generally and Black communities specifically in elevating to the national level certain Black freedom activists, organizations, and ideas over others, but also of elite white funders in the northern United States. In exercising the power of the purse, U.S. philanthropies and their staff and board members have played consequential roles in encouraging certain individuals, groups, and organizations over others to flourish nationally.

Though before arriving at historical examples of this powerful dynamic throughout the twentieth century, it is important to pause and acknowledge the use of "philanthropy" and "philanthropic" in this chapter. This is because, while I use these words in the context of elite white Anglo-American institutions, we should shy away from assuming that white Americans' funding practices define *philanthropy* in the United States. In this vein, historian Tyrone Freeman underscores that "there is not a single era in U.S. history in which African Americans were not engaged in their own philanthropic actions as a matter of daily survival, religious or cultural practice, or social change at scale."[16] In line with Freeman's caution, the next sections of this chapter analyze the critical role played by elite U.S. funders in the long Black freedom struggle without assuming that these actions were necessarily *more philanthropic or benevolent*—or even *particularly philanthropic or benevolent*—compared to Black Americans' own acts of benevolence and generosity at the time. That said, there is value in studying the behavior of elite white funders in the United States and its effects on the Black freedom struggle, for example, because their privileged political and economic positions in the United States have facilitated these Americans' ability to impact precisely which movement actors and ideas will have the best chances of thriving and, relatedly, of being remembered fondly in national memory. In this way, this chapter's critical lens on white U.S. funders owes much to the work of critical race theory scholars such as Kimberlé Crenshaw, Derrick Bell, and Carol Anderson.[17] As political scientist Megan Ming Francis highlights in her own study of a white-led foundation—the Garland Fund—in shaping the agenda of the NAACP in the 1930s, "Critical race theorists have made plain that racial domination can be reproduced in liberal institutions by well-meaning actors."[18]

Building upon the work of past and present scholars such as Francis, W. E. B. Du Bois, Carter Woodson, Kenneth J. King, Aldon Morris, Noliwe Rooks, David Levering Lewis, Karen Ferguson, Robert Allen, Jayne Beilke, Emma L. Thornbrough, and myself, who have researched the role of white-led foundations in the long Black freedom struggle in the United States, this chapter stresses that these organizations have helped to determine which individuals, groups, and ideas in the Black freedom

[16] Tyrone Freeman, "7 Ways to Read Around the History of Philanthropy's Diversity Program This Black History Month," *HistPhil* (February 25, 2019), at https://histphil.org/2019/02/25/7-ways-to-read-around-the-history-of-philanthropys-diversity-problem-this-black-history-month/ (last accessed August 30, 2022).

[17] *Critical Race Theory: The Key Writings that Formed a Movement*, eds. Kimberlé Crenshaw, Neil T. Gotanda, and Kendall Thomas (New York: New Press, 1996); Derrick Bell, *And We Are Not Saved: The Elusive Quest for Racial Justice* (New York: Basic, 1987); and, Carol Anderson, *White Rage: The Unspoken Truth of Our Racial Divide* (New York: Bloomsbury, 2016).

[18] Megan Ming Francis, "The Price of Civil Rights: Black Lives, White Funding, and Movement Capture," *Law and Society Review* 53.1 (March 2019): 280.

struggle would thrive nationally. This history of white Anglo-American funders' influence in the Black freedom struggle starts before the advent of modern U.S. foundations, which many scholars situate at the start of the twentieth century. After all, any discussion of white funders in the Black freedom struggle of the twentieth century needs to acknowledge the centrality of the Reconstruction Era as critical context from which a concentrated group of powerful white funders and their philanthropic organizations in the North became invested in financing certain freedom activists and ideas over others.

At the time of Reconstruction, former Black slaves in the United States were defining freedom in their lives—what it might mean for themselves and their families and friends to be *free*. For many Black Americans, key markers of freedom would include paid labor, marriage, and an education, all of which white Americans had denied them during slavery. And as far as former slaves' emphasis on education as a defining component of freedom, elite white Anglo-American funders would play a critical role in defining the content and purpose of this developing symbol of freedom.

## II. The U.S. Reconstruction Era and White Funders' Support for Booker T. Washington's Tuskegee Model of Education for Black Americans

U.S. historians have recounted how the country's Civil War, lasting from 1861 to 1865, was fought over the legality of the South's decision to secede from the Union and, in the process, continue Black Americans' enslavement in the region. With a northern victory, a Republican-run U.S. federal government subsequently overruled U.S. legal doctrine such as *Dred Scott v. Sandford* (1857), which had established that Black people had no claims to U.S. citizenship, and amended the U.S. Constitution to address the differentiating legal and constitutional status of white and Black people in the United States. In this vein, the U.S. Congress passed the Reconstruction amendments abolishing slavery and declaring, specifically in the Fourteenth Amendment, that Black Americans were U.S. citizens with equal protection of the laws. The Fifteenth Amendment to the U.S. Constitution furthermore declared that Black men had a right to vote (Black women would have to wait until the passage of the Nineteenth Amendment in 1920).

Historians refer to this period after the U.S. Civil War as the Reconstruction era, which not only saw the passage of the Reconstruction amendments, but also saw Black men participate as elected political officials in state and national bodies. Beyond these spaces in the public realm and throughout the private and social realms, Black Americans negotiated their new status as free people. In *To 'Joy My Freedom* (1998), for example, historian Tera Hunter excavates the records of Black women in Atlanta—living decades before Tomiko Brown-Nagin's narrative of Black life in the city—to illustrate how women defined freedom and reacted to the resistance they faced from white Americans as they, for example, reconstituted their family lives after being denied as slaves the right to marry or to retain their children; redefined themselves as paid laborers after being denied the right to demand payment for their labor; and, pursued educations after being denied the simple learning goals of reading and writing.[19] As Hunter writes, "Sheer survival and the reconstruction of family, despite all the difficulties, were the highest priorities of ex-slaves in the postwar period. But the desire for literacy and education was closely related to their strategies for achieving economic self-sufficiency, political autonomy, and personal enrichment."[20]

Newly free families sacrificed parts of their own earnings to build schoolhouses for themselves and for their children and to provide books, supplies, and pay teachers' salaries. Without the support of their states, which increasingly were providing schooling for all white Americans, Black southerners found themselves paying for their own schooling and, at times too, leaning on the support of northern missionaries and the U.S. federal government. Though in contrast to many Black families emphasizing classical education as means for greater political and economic empowerment, wealthy white northerners with interest in supporting education for Black southerners largely sympathized with the efforts of former Union Army general and founder of the Hampton Institute in Virginia, Samuel Armstrong, and especially that of his student and future principal of Tuskegee Institute, Booker T. Washington.[21] While Hampton and Tuskegee (along with other schools built in their images) continued to underscore the importance of a strong foundation in elementary education, at least in public, Washington stressed to potential white funders that this particular model of education first and foremost would emphasize the training of Black southerners for jobs that would not challenge white supremacy and anti-Black subordination in the region and would thus favor the economic and political interests of white people.[22] As historian Emma L. Thornbrough writes, "The views expressed by Washington on education and the position of Negroes in American society and politics were so much in harmony with the views expressed by the white philanthropists who supported Tuskegee and other public men of the day that their speeches and writings frequently sound like paraphrases of each other."[23]

Illustrating the developing symbiosis between the rising dominance of the Hampton-Tuskegee educational model for Black Americans in the southern United States and white northern philanthropists' developing interest in funding this particular model of Black education, George Peabody established the Peabody Education Fund in 1867, a year before Samuel Armstrong founded Hampton Institute. Historian Jayne R. Beilke notes, "Convinced that education was instrumental to reconciling the North and South during the Reconstruction period, this New England merchant and banker chartered the fund to encourage 'intellectual, moral, and industrial education' in the South and Southwest by stabilizing the public education system and fostering the growth of common schools."[24] Within ten years of operating the

[19] Tera Hunter, *To 'Joy My Freedom: Southern Black Women's Lives and Labors after the Civil War* (Cambridge: Harvard University Press, 1998).

[20] Hunter, *To 'Joy My Freedom*.

[21] Hunter, *To 'Joy My Freedom*, 41; Ron Chernow, *Titan: The Life of John D. Rockefeller, Sr.* (New York: Vintage, 1998), 483.

[22] W. Manning Marable, "Booker T. Washington and African Nationalism," *Phylon* 35.4 (4th Quarter, 1974), 400; Pero Gaglo Dagbovie, "Exploring a Century of Historical Scholarship on Booker T. Washington," *The Journal of African American History* 92.2 (Spring 2007): 257–59.

[23] Emma L. Thornbrough, "Booker T. Washington as Seen by His White Contemporaries," *The Journal of Negro History* 53.2 (April 1968): 166–67.

[24] Jayne R. Beilke, "Peabody Education Fund," in *Organizing Black America: An Encyclopedia of African American Associations*, ed. Nina Mjagkij (New York: Garland, 2001), 553.

Peabody Education Fund, Peabody met Armstrong and was sufficiently impressed by Armstrong to accept the invitation to join the Hampton board of trustees.[25]

Following Armstrong's lead, the Peabody Fund specialized in funding country schools offering vocational and agricultural education to Black southerners and in teacher training for these schools. The Peabody Fund supported Armstrong's Hampton Institute alongside the Tuskegee Institute, which Washington, a former slave and Hampton graduate, founded as the Tuskegee Normal School for Colored Teachers in Alabama in 1881. Much like the Hampton Institute, Booker T. Washington's Tuskegee Institute trained Black teachers and officially taught practical skills that would help Black students succeed at farming and in other manual trades in the South such as construction and domestic work. Unlike Hampton's faculty and staff, however, most of the faculty and staff at Tuskegee were Black. In an effort to advance this form of manual education for Black Americans, the Peabody Fund worked hand in hand with yet another philanthropic organization, the John F. Slater Fund, established by a textile manufacturer from Connecticut in 1882.[26]

In the 1860s and 1870s, Black schools controlled by missionary societies and Black religious organizations generally had been "indifferent or opposed to the Tuskegee model of industrial training," while those funded by this network of white northern philanthropists tended to argue that this pedagogy for Black students comfortably served the interests of both former Black slaves and white leaders in the South.[27] During the next decades, this latter educational model funded by key white philanthropists only gained momentum in the southern United States, though as this chapter later explains, its meteoric rise also met with public criticism and particularly from Black scholars such as W. E. B. Du Bois and Carter Woodson.

A turning point in this history of competing models for Black education in the South would be Booker T. Washington's address at the 1895 Atlanta Exposition. With this speech—and this national platform—he gained the attention and allegiance of even more leading white northern industrialists, including Gilded Age steel titan Andrew Carnegie. Faced with an audience of Black Americans and prominent white Americans from the North and South, Washington began the address by noting how vocational and agricultural education for Black southerners "would cement the friendship of the races and bring about hearty cooperation between them."[28]

When Washington delivered his address in Atlanta, Georgia, it had been nearly two decades since white northern Republicans had withdrawn federal troops from the region.[29] And since then, southern states such as Georgia had been passing laws demarcating a subordinate status for Black people and a superior one for whites. Just

[25] James D. Anderson, "Northern Foundations and the Shaping of Southern Black Rural Education, 1902–1935," *History of Education Quarterly* 18.4 (1978): 373. See also Anderson, *The Education of Blacks in the South, 1860–1935* (Chapel Hill: University of North Carolina Press, 1988).

[26] Beilke, "John F. Slater Fund," in *Organizing Black America: An Encyclopedia of African American Associations*, ed. Nina Mjagkij (New York: Garland, 2001), 291–92; Michael Fultz, "Teacher Training and African American Education in the South, 1900–1940," *Journal of Negro Education* 64.2 (1995).

[27] Anderson, "Northern Foundations," 378.

[28] W. Fitzhugh Brundage ed., *"Up from Slavery" by Booker T. Washington with Related Documents* (Boston: Bedford/St. Martin's, 2003), chap. 14.

[29] See, for example, Eric Foner, *Reconstruction: America's Unfinished Revolution, 1863–1877* (New York: Harper & Row, 1988).

four years prior to Washington's lecture in Atlanta, for example, Georgia's legislature had passed a law allowing the city to delineate the color line "in public conveyances 'as much as practicable.'"[30] A year after Washington's speech, the U.S. Supreme Court condoned such laws with its decision in *Plessy v. Ferguson* (1896), holding that state-imposed laws calling for the segregation of white and Black people were not necessarily discriminatory, and thus, did not violate the Fourteenth Amendment's Equal Protection Clause of the U.S. Constitution.

Speaking from the southern United States in 1895, Washington proposed the Tuskegee model of education for Black Americans as a public policy recommendation reflecting a compromise between three groups of Americans: southern whites, northern whites, and Black Americans. Likely because he was speaking in front of a white southern audience gaining ever more dominance in the region and support from white northerners, he first addressed the fears and anxieties of southern whites. In particular, he acknowledged white southerners' distress that education would empower Black Americans to expect equality with white Americans.

Washington took it upon himself to explain to southern whites, who had outlawed literacy and education to Black people during slavery, how and why any form of Black education was necessary. He first noted that Black people had been misguided in their efforts to achieve the same accomplishments as white people after the Civil War: "Ignorant and inexperienced, it is not strange that in the first years of our new life we began at the top instead of at the bottom; that a seat in Congress or the state legislature was more sought than real estate or industrial skill; that the political convention or stump speaking had more attractions than starting a dairy farm or truck garden."[31] Placating white Americans' anxieties that education for Black Americans would disrupt white supremacy, he echoed many white southerners' perspectives that Black Americans would need to work their way toward proving their equality. And he noted that Black Americans could begin to do so by showing white people that they found dignity in their manual work.

Illustrating how his thinking complemented that of his white southern audience, Washington then explained that the Tuskegee model not only would help Black Americans find pride in manual labor, but also help the southern U.S. economy advance after the catastrophe of the Civil War. Washington declared, "One-third of the population of the South is of the Negro race. No enterprise seeking the material, civil, or moral welfare of this section can disregard this element of our population and reach the highest success."[32] While acknowledging that white southerners remained hesitant to support Black Americans' education, (after all, many states had outlawed Black slaves' ability to learn how to read and write), Washington noted that agricultural and industrial education was necessary for the region's economic rehabilitation and growth after the Civil War.

Washington foresaw his white audience's misgivings about Black education and emphasized that the Tuskegee model of education would not encourage Black Americans to think of themselves as equals to white Americans in the South; but

[30] Hunter, *To 'Joy My Freedom*, 99.
[31] Washington, *Up from Slavery*, 142.
[32] Washington, *Up from Slavery*, 142.

rather, it would train them to accept entry-level work in southern agriculture and industry.[33] Even more, he stressed that this was entry-level work that would not upset the color line that southern whites were establishing at the time, pointing out, "In all things that are purely social we can be as separate as the fingers, yet, one as the hand in all things essential to mutual progress."[34]

Washington further clarified that the Tuskegee model of education not only played into the interests of southern whites, but also those of northern white industrialists. Just three years prior to Washington's Atlanta address, for example, the deadly Homestead Strike had taken place in one of Andrew Carnegie's steel plants near Pittsburgh, Pennsylvania, leaving several steelworkers and members of the Carnegie Steel Company police force dead and hundreds of others in both groups injured. Historian Nell Painter explains, "Most Americans, shocked at the bloodshed and the passion displayed by the workers, blamed the Carnegie management for provocation through wage cuts and the fortification of the mill."[35] The Pennsylvania governor had sent 8,000 militiamen to maintain order, but the chaos continued. That summer, there was an attempted assassination of the plant manager, Henry Clay Frick; and in the early fall, numerous strike workers were indicted on 167 counts of murder, rioting, and conspiracy.[36] All were found not guilty, but they had remained in jail awaiting trial for a month. While the Carnegie Steel Company succeeded in bringing an end to the strike, it was a signal to many Americans that there would be equally tense labor struggles in the future.

Alluding to the fact that many strikers in this infamous strike had been white and some strikebreakers Black, Booker T. Washington further noted in his Atlanta address that northern industrialists should support the Tuskegee model of education for Black Americans because it would help strengthen a laboring class that was loyal to them. To this point, he called northern industrialists: "Cast down your bucket among these people who have, without strikes and labour wars, tilled your fields, cleared your forests, builded your railroads and cities, and brought forth treasures from the bowels of the earth, and helped make possible this magnificent representation of the progress of the South."[37] To white northerners in the audience, Washington thus stressed that Black Americans were loyal laborers who would not strike. Instead, they would simply serve to maximize white Americans' profits with their continued hard work. And for these reasons, Washington urged northern industrialists, precisely such as Carnegie and his northern peers in philanthropy, to support and help fund the Tuskegee Institute and complementary groups in its orbit.

At the same time, Washington also spelled out why Black Americans should support this particular form of education. He argued that their future was in the South among southern whites, and that they should make the best of it: "To those of my race who depend on bettering their condition in a foreign land or who underestimate the importance of cultivating friendly relations with the southern white man, who is

[33] Washington, *Up from Slavery*, 142–143.
[34] Washington, *Up from Slavery*, 143.
[35] Nell Irvin Painter, *Standing at Armageddon: The United States, 1977–1919* (New York: Norton, 1987), 113.
[36] Painter, *Standing at Armageddon*, 114.
[37] Washington, *Up from Slavery*, 143.

their next-door neighbor, I would say: 'Cast down your bucket where you are'—cast it down in making friends in every manly way of the people of all races by whom we are surrounded."[38] Washington urged Black Americans to accept that they belonged in the South, that they were southerners, and that they could achieve freedom by learning "that there is as much dignity in tilling a field as in writing a poem."[39]

Before Washington's 1895 speech in Atlanta, northern white philanthropists such as George Peabody, John Slater, and John D. Rockefeller already had been funding the Hampton-Tuskegee educational model for Black Americans.[40] But their support would increase thereafter. A few years after the Atlanta address, , the Rockefellers wrote directly to Washington and asked how they could help in expanding the work of the Tuskegee Institute throughout the South; within a few months, John D. Rockefeller Jr. himself was on a train south to visit Hampton in Virginia and Tuskegee in Alabama. "After visits to Hampton and Tuskegee Institutes and from many discussions with the school campaigners, Rockefeller Jr. became sufficiently impressed with the southern education movement to approach his father about establishing a new foundation to reinforce the reformers' efforts."[41] In 1903, the Rockefellers founded the General Education Board (GEB). Though the organization was initially to be called the "Negro Education Board," advisors close to the Rockefellers suggested that a more neutral name would not alienate white southerners as much.[42] The Rockefellers incorporated the General Education Board with the general mission of promoting education in the United States irrespective of race, sex, or creed.[43]

After his 1895 Atlanta speech, and in these last years of the nineteenth century, Washington also attracted Andrew Carnegie's philanthropic support and greater commitment from the Rockefellers. Since Washington in 1895 had appealed to northern industrialists by underscoring ways that the Tuskegee educational model encouraged Black Americans to be and remain docile laborers loyal to capital, it is little surprise that he attracted the attention of even more northern white industrialists, including Carnegie, who only three years prior had experienced a violent labor dispute in one of his steel plants. Even more, Washington's 1895 speech only further clarified for northern industrialists such as Carnegie how helping to fund a particular model of Black education could serve the political and economic interests of white northerners such as himself and his peers who were eager to see a stronger southern—and by extension, national—economy.

In 1903, Carnegie made a substantial contribution of $600,000 to the Tuskegee Institute—a gesture further inspired by Washington's visit to New York City that year.[44] In a letter to a Tuskegee trustee published in the *New York Times*, Carnegie

[38] Washington, *Up from Slavery*, 142.

[39] Washington, *Up from Slavery*, 143.

[40] Ron Chernow, *Titan*, 239–242, 482.

[41] Anderson, "Northern Foundations," 378.

[42] Anderson, "Northern Foundations," 379.

[43] "The General Education Board." For more information on the smaller Peabody, Slater, and Jeanes Funds, see, for example, Will W. Alexander, *The Slater and Jeanes Funds: An Educator's Approach to a Difficult Social Problem* (Washington, D.C.: The Trustees of the John F. Slater Fund, Occasional Paper, no. 28) (1934), 2; "Administrative History," Phelps Stokes Fund Records, Schomburg Center for Research in Black Culture, New York Public Library (hereinafter PSFR); Earl H. West, "The Peabody Education Fund and Negro Education, 1867–1880," *History of Education Quarterly* 6.2 (1996).

[44] "$600,000 for Tuskegee and B. T. Washington," *New York Times*, April 24, 1903.

wrote, "I am satisfied that the serious race problem of the South is to be solved wisely only through Mr. Washington's policy of education—which he seems to have been specially born—a slave among slaves—to establish and in his own day greatly to advance. Glad am I to be able to assist this good work in which you and others so zealously labor."[45]

While enthusiastic about Washington's Tuskegee Institute, Carnegie never created an organization inspired by it such as the Rockefellers' GEB; nor did he play a leading role in financing Black schools. In the early 1910s, Andrew Carnegie—and by extension, Carnegie Corporation of New York, which inherited its founder's funding practices in Black education—was rather on the periphery of this network of philanthropic organizations dedicated to funding Black education within and beyond the United States.[46]

In the early decades of the twentieth century, after Washington's 1895 speech, the GEB was the wealthiest philanthropic organization dedicated to funding education for Black Americans, and it gained the cooperation of other philanthropic organizations invested in this field, such as the older Slater and Peabody Funds and the newer Jeanes and Phelps Stokes Funds.[47] The Jeanes Fund, or the Negro Rural School Fund, was established in 1907 by Anna T. Jeanes, a Philadelphia Quaker, who directed that the income from her estate, valued at about $1 million, be used to assist rural schools for Black Americans.[48] Three years later, the GEB also gained the cooperation of the Slater Fund and the support of the Peabody Education Fund's various state agents overseeing education in the South.[49]

In 1911, the Phelps Stokes Fund joined this network of foundations and it would play a sizeable role as advocate of the Tuskegee educational model for Black Americans and Africans alike. Founded by the estate of the deceased Caroline Phelps Stokes, the fund was established with the complementary goal of improving housing and education for Black Americans, Native Americans, and "deserving white students, through industrial schools, the founding of scholarships, and the erection or endowment of school buildings or chapels."[50] Within a year after its founding, however, Caroline Phelps Stokes's nephew Anson Phelps Stokes steered the organization to focus more heavily on education than on housing. Writing to Booker T. Washington, Stokes asked him to imagine the best use of five to ten thousand dollars. In response, Washington wrote that "such a sum could be instrumental in accomplishing what he had long regarded as a necessity: distinguishing the worthy from the unworthy

45 "$600,000 for Tuskegee and B. T. Washington."

46 It is also worth noting that John D. Rockefeller founded the Rockefeller Foundation two years later, in 1913, with a $100 million endowment. See Barbara Shubinski, "Finding a Footing," in *Evolution of a Foundation: An Institutional History of the Rockefeller Foundation, RE:source* (Rockefeller Archive Center, August 3, 2022), at https://resource.rockarch.org/story/rockefeller-foundation-history-origins-to-2013/.

47 Jayne R. Beilke, "General Education Board," in *Organizing Black America: An Encyclopedia of African American Associations*, ed. Nina Mjagkij (New York: Garland, 2001), 242–43.

48 Jayne R. Beilke, "Negro Rural School Fund," in *Organizing Black America: An Encyclopedia of African American Associations*, ed. Nina Mjagkij (New York: Garland, 2001), 507–508.

49 Beilke, "Peabody Education Fund," 553.

50 Thomas Jesse Jones, *Negro Education: A Study of the Private and Higher Schools for Colored People in the United States* (2 vols) (Washington, DC: Government Printing Office, 1917), vol. 1:xi.

small denominational Negro schools."[51] Stokes took this suggestion to the organization's trustees, and the following year, the fund's board of trustees recorded, "The trustees, believing that such a report of existing conditions would prove invaluable to southern educators and legislators, to philanthropists interested in Negro education, to the principals and trustees of schools for colored youth, and to various educational boards, adopted the recommendations and asked the Commissioner of Education if he would accept the cooperation of the Phelps Stokes Fund in making such a study on condition that the expenses of the agents should be paid by the fund."[52] As the trustees reasoned, such a report on schools for Black southerners would help educators, legislators, philanthropists, educational boards, principals, and trustees of schools assess the quality of high schools, colleges, and universities for Black Americans, and in the process, help steer public and private funding accordingly.

In 1912, Anson Phelps Stokes began a search for the study's director. Stokes had his sights particularly on the 39-year-old Thomas Jesse Jones, who was a specialist in community education at the U.S. federal government's Bureau of Education. In his correspondence with Booker T. Washington, Stokes explained that "the mere fact that Dr. Jones is at present connected with the Bureau of Education and that they would in all probability allow him to continue to occupy his office there, would be an important consideration."[53] It would be a study with the full sanction and prestige of the U.S. federal government behind it.[54]

Jones's survey of Black education in the United States would help this first generation of trustees and philanthropic staff at the Carnegie and Rockefeller organizations confirm that their support of the Tuskegee educational model for Black Americans was not only in line with their founders' intentions for Black Americans, but also a sound funding decision supported by contemporary data collected and analyzed by an increasingly trusted adviser, Thomas Jesse Jones.

## III. Leaning on Thomas Jesse Jones, White Funders Continue Their Support of the Tuskegee Model of Education for Black Americans

Published in 1917, Thomas Jesse Jones's two-volume study, *Negro Education: A Study of the Private and Higher Schools for Colored People in the United States* endorsed the Tuskegee model of Black education. Within the first page of his report, Jones mentioned Booker T. Washington (who had passed away two years earlier) and echoed this former Tuskegee principal's arguments for a particular model of education for Black Americans. Like Washington, Jones expressed that Black Americans' education would need to incorporate the interests of northern whites, southern whites, and

[51] Booker T. Washington to Phelps Stokes, May 15, 1911, quoted in Kenneth J. King, *Pan-Africanism and Education* (New York: Diasporic Africa Press, 2016) (originally published, 1971), 31.

[52] Jones, *Negro Education*, 1:xi.

[53] Anson Phelps Stokes to Booker T. Washington, November 12, 1912, in Louis R. Harlan and Raymond W. Smock eds., *The Booker T. Washington Papers: Vol. 12, 1912–14* (Urbana: University of Illinois Press, 1982).

[54] Commissioner P. P. Claxton to Anson Phelps Stokes, January 21, 1913, box 44, folder 1, PSFR.

Black Americans alike: "Democracy's plan for the solution of the race problem in the Southland is not primarily in the philanthropies and wisdom of northern people; nor is it in the desires and struggles of the colored people; nor yet in the first-hand knowledge and daily contacts of the southern white people."[55] As Jones explained, white northerners, white southerners, and Black Americans needed to work together to create a comprehensive educational policy for Black Americans.

In the study, Jones noted that Black Americans' education should focus on providing this group of Americans with skills adapted for the expectations and needs of rural communities in the South. Such an educational model, he argued, would help Black Americans learn the "sound habits of hand and head" that would help them become self-sustaining and, equally important, a well-trained and efficient labor force for white southerners. With a nod to white people in the North, and echoing claims of Washington in his 1895 Atlanta address, Jones stressed that educated Black labor would help strengthen the southern, and by extension the national, economies.[56]

Providing a "suggested program of educational development" for Black Americans from the elementary to college and professional levels, Jones argued in *Negro Education* that public school authorities needed to meet their obligations to educate Black Americans at the elementary level, with specific emphasis on their responsibility to increase literacy among this group of Americans. With respect to secondary schools, he considered their main purpose to be training teachers for elementary education and believed that private philanthropists and public-school authorities could continue working together in achieving this end. The highest level of education in Jones's educational program for Black Americans included college and professional education. Much as in the other two levels, Jones argued that this form of education should reflect the needs of the pupil and the community. Since a segregated society required Black doctors, teachers, and religious leaders, he stressed that Black colleges should provide for their training.[57]

Of this two-volume study, historian and editor of the NAACP's *The Crisis* and early critical scholar of U.S. foundations' grant-making practices both within and beyond the United States, W. E. B. Du Bois, would write that fellow Black people and "persons who know the problem of educating the American Negro will regard the Jones report, despite its many praiseworthy features, as a dangerous and in many respects unfortunate publication."[58] As Du Bois detailed, this was because Jones's study further cemented the already-dominant insistence "on manual training, industrial education, and agricultural training" among Black Americans in the region.[59] More specifically, Du Bois wrote:

[55] Jones, *Negro Education*: 1:22.
[56] Jones, *Negro Education*, 1:12.
[57] Ibid.
[58] Du Bois, "Negro Education," *The Crisis* (February 1918). For a discussion of Du Bois as an early critical scholar of U.S. foundations' domestic and international funding practices, see, e.g., Maribel Morey, "W. E. B. Du Bois's International Lens on Modern US Philanthropy and His Fleeting Hopes for Reform," *The Oxford Handbook of W. E. B. Du Bois*, eds., Aldon Morris, Walter Allen, Cheryl Johnson-Odim, Dan S. Green, Marcus Hunter, Karida Brown, and Michael Schwartz (Online Publication Date: June 2022).
[59] Du Bois, "Negro Education."

> This is an unfortunate and dangerous proposal for the simple reason that the great dominating philanthropic agency, the General Education Board, long ago surrendered to the white South by practically saying that the educational needs of the white South must be attended to before any attention should be paid to the education of Negroes: that the Negro must be trained according to the will of the white South and not as the Negro desires to be trained. It is this board that is spending more money today in helping Negroes learn how to can vegetables than in helping them to go through college.[60]

Under such a policy carried out by leading U.S. philanthropies, Du Bois predicted that Black Americans would have few options in traditional, liberal arts, and civic-minded education. Even when a few Black Americans could amass the funds to establish such schools, Du Bois also noted that a teacher financed by these foundations was probably not far away trying to change its curriculum.[61] In fact, Du Bois rightly foresaw that Jones's recommendations would lead to further entrenchment of white philanthropists' theory that a particular type of vocational and agricultural education for Black Americans was key to improving the condition of Black Americans in the South, and even more importantly to them, to improving the economic strength of the region and country.

Much like Du Bois, Black historian Carter Woodson perceived that the 1917 study was a menacing tool that could potentially undermine the proper education of Black Americans in the South. Woodson also acknowledged that some Americans had received the report with open arms. In "1917 assembled in Washington the outstanding Negro educators to discuss the two-volume report," Woodson recalled. "Some of the educators assembled who had given their approval took pride in defending it as a great achievement."[62] Referring to the conference that U.S. Commissioner of Education Philander Claxton had organized in Washington, D.C., months after the publication of *Negro Education*, Woodson reflected nearly two decades later in 1936 on the significance of Jones's project and its impact among powerful Americans shaping Black Americans' education: "The worst of all the results of his biased report was that the system of education which it endorsed produced a miseducated class of Negroes who are the greatest liability of the race."[63]

Woodson wrote these reflections on Thomas Jesse Jones's *Negro Education* nearly two decades after its publication, and in the context of protesting Du Bois's decision in the 1930s to collaborate with elite white foundations—and particularly the foundation

[60] Ibid.

[61] Ibid.

[62] Carter G. Woodson to "Gentlemen," June 26, 1936, 1.1. projects, series 200 United States, box 9, folder 81, Rockefeller Foundation Records, Rockefeller Archive Center, Tarrytown, NY. See also, for example, D. O. W. Holmes, "Twenty-Five Years of Thomas Jesse Jones and the Phelps Stokes Fund," *Journal of Negro Education* 7.4 (1938). For discussion of the conference, see, e.g., Thomas Jesse Jones to Wallace Buttrick, July 7, 1917 (with attached memorandum "Tentative Plans for a Conference on Negro Education"), series 1, subseries 2, box 264, folder 2728, General Education Board Records, Rockefeller Archive Center, Tarrytown, NY.

[63] Woodson to "Gentlemen," June 26, 1936.

funding Jones—in organizing and planning an "Encyclopedia for the Negro." In his open letter addressed to the network of northern philanthropies considering collaboration with the Phelps Stokes Fund and Du Bois, Woodson would make public his disappointment in Du Bois's decision to collaborate with a foundation they both long had criticized for its corrosive role in the lives of Black Americans. In writing such an open letter, Woodson viewed himself as being consistent in his stance against the Phelps-Stoke Fund. By contrast, he argued that Du Bois—whom he outed in this open letter for once calling Jones "that evil genius of the Negro race"—had compromised his integrity as a Black scholar in "the hope of a few dollars."[64]

As Du Bois once imagined and Woodson continued to press well into the 1930s, Jones's report on Black education in the United States strengthened the perception of white philanthropists and of their organizations' staff and trustees that the Hampton-Tuskegee model of education for Black Americans was worth supporting. Building upon his open letter to northern philanthropies in 1936 and just weeks after Jones's passing in January 1950, Woodson wrote:

> Jones's judgment led most Negroes to consider him an evil in the life of the Negro; but he was nevertheless, catapulted into fame among the capitalists and government officials supporting the education of Negroes. They made Jones the almoner of the despised race with the title of Educational Director of the Phelps Stokes Fund which he served from 1913 to 1946. When he said do not give here and do not help yonder the "philanthropic" element heeded his biddings.[65]

During the 1910s and well into the next two decades, this first generation of white U.S. philanthropic trustees and staff members found in the recommendations of Jones's *Negro Education* legitimation for their founders' funding patterns in Black education. As Du Bois and Woodson looked on in the 1920s and 1930s, Jones and his educational model for Black Americans—very much supported by these elite funders—gained traction in the United States as leading means for Black Americans to achieve equality with white Americans in the United States. In other words, this network of white funders in the U.S. was critically important for determining which set of actors and ideas speaking on behalf of Black freedom would dominate in the United States during the early decades of the twentieth century. In this same spirit, these funders elevated the prominence of Thomas Jesse Jones to the point that neither Woodson nor Du Bois could ignore him. Some decades later, they also would elevate the prominence of another white man—Gunnar Myrdal—as a key voice defining Black freedom in the United States, while simultaneously further marginalizing the aspirations of Du Bois to further amplify his own voice and vision for Black equality in the United States.

[64] Woodson to "Gentlemen."
[65] Woodson, "Thomas Jesse Jones," *Journal of Negro History* 35.1 (1950), 107.

## IV. White Funders' Support for the Carnegie-Myrdal Study of Black Americans over W. E. B. Du Bois's Proposed *Encyclopedia Africana*

On April 7, 1938, 70-year-old W. E. B. Du Bois had invited his assistant editor to wait with him for the telephone call that would bring news that the board of trustees of the Rockefellers' General Education Board had voted favorably to fund his *Encyclopedia Africana*. This assistant remembers that Du Bois was so confident that the funding would go through that the senior scholar had with him a chilled bottle of champagne. However, the phone never rang and the money would never come. Instead of blessing Du Bois's project, this network of white funders would support white Swedish economist Gunnar Myrdal's study of Black Americans—with lasting consequences for which and whose ideas about Black Americans' equality would dominate in the United States during the next decades.

To this point, Du Bois would soon find out during that spring of 1938 that neither the GEB nor the other foundation that he had been courting, Carnegie Corporation, would fund the encyclopedia project. Adding insult to injury, the Corporation would be commissioning a comprehensive, policy-oriented social scientific study of Black Americans of the size, scope, and budget previously unseen in the United States—and they would not be inviting him to direct it. Rather, they had chosen Swedish economist, Gunnar Myrdal, for the task, and they would afford him unlimited funds to conduct his own research and to commission data collections and analyses from other social scientists across the country.

For decades, Du Bois had hoped to materialize his vision for a large-scale encyclopedia project, which required significant financial support to achieve—a goal he would maintain throughout his life and would never really achieve. Illustrating his long-standing excitement for such a project, for example, he wrote to a colleague in 1909, "I am venturing to address you on the subject of a Negro Encyclopedia. In celebration of the 50th anniversary of the Emancipation of the American Negro, I am proposing to bring out an *Encyclopedia Africana* covering the chief points in the history and condition of the Negro race."[66] The project stalled, but twenty years later, the Phelps Stokes Fund brought together fellow Foundation officials and white and Black U.S. scholars to discuss plans for coordinating an encyclopedia of Africans and African Americans. Its plan was to fund a multivolume encyclopedia that would include phases of Black life and history, from "anthropological, ethnographical, biographical, historical, [and] educational" aspects to "industrial, economic, political, religious, psychological (including race relations, artistic, etc., etc.)."[67]

In the 1930s, Du Bois found himself willing to work alongside an organization he long had admonished, in order to bring about the encyclopedia project. Again, this was the same philanthropic organization for whom Thomas Jesse Jones still served

[66] Henry Louis Gates, Jr., "King of Cats: Albert Murray, *The New* Yorker," in *The Henry Louis Gates, Jr. Reader*, ed. Abby Wolf (New York: Basic *Civitas*, 2012), 314.

[67] Social Science Research Council Archives, Rockefeller Archive Center, Tarrytown, NY, Minutes of the Committee on Problems and Policy, March 17, 1934, SSRC, Accession 1, Series 2. Committee on P&P, Subseries 1. Minutes, Box 3113, Folder 1781.

as leading education advisor and that had financed Jones's *Negro Education* (1917), which Du Bois had criticized in the pages of *The Crisis*. But again, Du Bois was particularly committed to seeing through to publication an encyclopedia project on the African diaspora. From his end, Anson Phelps Stokes had reasoned with the GEB's Jackson Davis that Du Bois—whose role as editor-in-chief was unanimously supported by all Black colleagues planning the encyclopedia—would need to colead the project with "a white man of high standing and conservative reputation," leading them to pick the white sociologist Robert E. Park who had served "for many years at Tuskegee helping Booker Washington."[68] And as far as Du Bois himself, Anson Phelps Stokes explained to Davis, "Ten years ago, or even five years ago, it would not have been possible to consider Dr. Du Bois for this position in spite of the fact that he is recognized as the outstanding Negro scholar. He had become such an aggressive protagonist that his name created a lack of sympathy in various conservative circles. This is, of course, all partially still true but all who have met him in the last year have been amazed at how much he has mellowed."[69]

Given the Phelps Stokes Fund's grant-making practices in Black education, Du Bois most likely knew that the organization's reasons for financing an encyclopedia on Black people were distinct from his or Woodson's reasons for dreaming of a pan-African encyclopedia. To know the Phelps Stokes Fund at the time meant knowing that the organization was particularly invested in preserving white leadership over its initiatives on Black Americans and in analyzing and quantifying the benefits of the Tuskegee educational model for Black people, which the fund promoted and financed on both sides of the Atlantic as a means to principally appease the economic and political interests of white, rather than Black, people. As to its focus on preserving white leadership in its funding programs, historian Sam Klug notes that the Phelps Stokes Fund continued its "founding belief that Black uplift required white leadership" well into the 1940s.[70] So rather than a pan-African encyclopedia likely hoped by Du Bois, to be led by a team of Black scholars and intended both to cultivate pan-African pride and counter prejudicial assumptions about Black people's accomplishments and capabilities, this version of the encyclopedia on Black people shaped by the Phelps Stokes Fund would incorporate white scholars and maintain white peers as its main audience. In this version of the pan-African encyclopedia, Du Bois would thus work alongside a white coeditor, in dialogue with an advisory board of white and Black Americans and a team of Black and white contributors.[71]

Without the necessary resources to execute a project of this scale, and eager to solicit the collaboration of its main intended audience of white philanthropic peers, the

[68] Anson Phelps Stokes to Jackson Davis, March 31, 1932, box 39, folder 2, PSFR.

[69] Phelps Stokes to Davis.

[70] Sam Klug, "The Phelps Stokes Fund and the Institutional Imagination of Black Internationalism, 1941–1945," *Diplomatic History* 46.4 (September 2022), 679. Rather than being unique in this view, the Phelps Stokes Fund reflected founding beliefs shared by its network of northern U.S. foundations, from the Carnegie and Rockefeller organizations to the Julius Rosenwald Fund. Of the latter organization, for example, Black lawyer Loren Miller wrote in the 1930s, "The Fund is entirely controlled by whites and it was not until 1935 that a Negro, Charles S. Johnson, was placed on its board of trustees." See Loren Miller, "Mail-Order Dictatorship: The Rosenwalds and 12,000,000 Negroes," *New Masses* (April 16, 1935).

[71] For more on the Phelps Stokes Fund and the encyclopedia, see Morey, *White Philanthropy*, Chapter 7, Section 3.

Phelps Stokes Fund sought the support of the Rockefeller organizations and Carnegie Corporation. This was ultimately a frustrating and fruitless process consuming the attention of Du Bois and the Phelps Stokes Fund during the greater part of the 1930s and overlapping with Carnegie Corporation's decision to finance its own national study of Black Americans.

During these years, board members at the GEB, the Rockefeller Foundation, and Carnegie Corporation would continue receiving news from staff members and colleagues that the Phelps Stokes Fund's project was bound to fail. Not only had the Social Science Research Council (SSRC) declined the invitation to appoint two representatives on the advisory board of the encyclopedia, but the representatives whom these philanthropic managers sent to the group's meetings continued to return with negative impressions of the project's development.[72] From what these philanthropic managers could gather, the team of Black and white scholars under the directorship of Du Bois and Park (later to be replaced by white sociologist Guy B. Johnson) was fraught with tensions and antagonism.[73]

Reflecting these long-standing interpersonal strains among the planners of the encyclopedia, and even before Woodson's press release, SSRC staff member and sociologist Donald Young had complained to the anthropologist Melville Herskovits that he saw "no hope that the Encyclopedia can be turned into the sort of work in which you and I would be interested," and told him that he would not be attending the next meeting.[74] "If I had any hope that you and I by our attendance at the meeting could exert 'a restraining influence,' as you put it, I'd be there with bells on, but I do not believe that a dozen of us could do more than make nuisances of ourselves without swerving the leaders of the project a fraction of an inch from the course they have planned. These are hard words, but I suspect that you rather agree with me."[75] In response, Herskovits echoed Young's dissatisfaction, sharing that he too would miss the next meeting: "I think you're right at that, and so I too am sending regrets. As a matter of fact I was thinking of the jaunt in terms of that peculiar type of recreation obtained from fighting a lost cause."[76]

That is to say that Herskovits and Young would walk away from the "Encyclopedia of the Negro," even before Woodson's press release further aggravated elite foundations' negative perceptions of the project. Far from alone, Young and Herskovits would be joined by the Rockefeller and Carnegie organizations, which two years later, formally declined the Phelps Stokes Fund's request for support. In November 1938, Carnegie Corporation president Frederick Keppel would write to Anson Phelps Stokes to share the disappointing news. Keppel assured Stokes "that the trouble in my Board did not

[72] SSRC Minutes of the Committee on Problems and Policy, March 17, 1934, accession 1, series 2, Committee on P&P, subseries 1, Minutes, box 313, folder 1781, Social Science Research Council Records, Rockefeller Archive Center; "Memorandum on the Negro Encyclopedia," III.A. grant files, ca. 1911–1988, box 139, folder 139.11, Carnegie Corporation of New York Records, Columbia University Rare Book and Manuscript Library, NY (hereinafter CCNYR).

[73] "Encyclopedia of the Negro Memorandum," August 2, 1938, series 35:6, box 7, folder 19, Melville Herskovits Papers, Northwestern University Archival and Manuscript Collections (hereinafter MHP).

[74] Donald Young to Melville Herskovits, April 7, 1936, series 35:6, box 22, folder 3, MHP; Herskovits to Young, April 13, 1936, series 35:6, box 22, folder 3, MHP.

[75] Young to Herskovits; Herskovits to Young.

[76] Young to Herskovits; Herskovits to Young.

rise from memories of Du Bois as a firebrand, but from a general feeling that the idea of a specialized Negro Encyclopedia at all was a mistake."[77] While the Phelps Stokes Fund saw value in the encyclopedia project, its philanthropic peers at Carnegie Corporation saw the study as a "mistake," because funding a study that could have the effect—even indirectly—of increasing racial pride among Black people and thus contributing to escalating Black consciousness was reinforcing one of Keppel's and his white Anglo-American advisers' most basic fears since the 1920s. Instead, Carnegie Corporation would finance its own national study of Black Americans, inspired by its own funding of Malcolm Hailey's *An African Survey* (1938), which was being coordinated through Chatham House in London.[78] By contrast to the "Encyclopedia of the Negro," Carnegie Corporation intended this U.S. version of the *African Survey* to consider Black people as a societal problem and to offer white policymakers across governments in the United States with an opportunity to understand the problem and its solutions at the national level.

Commissioned and financed by Carnegie Corporation—and receiving the support of colleagues at the Rockefeller organizations which lent staff and made introductions for Myrdal among colleagues and policy contacts—Gunnar Myrdal's *An American Dilemma* soared to national significance and would define discussions of racial equality in the United States for several decades while Du Bois's encyclopedia project stalled and never came to fruition (though Du Bois kept his hopes to achieve its publication well into his last living days). To this point, historian David Levering Lewis writes, "On February 15, 1961, a few days shy of his ninety-third birthday, Du Bois received a cable from [Ghanaian President Kwame] Nkrumah informing him that the *Encyclopedia Africana* project had been 'accepted and endorsed by the Ghana Academy of Learning.'"[79] Living in Ghana during his final years of life, Du Bois ultimately would write solemnly to Nkrumah, noting that he only had one regret: "I failed you—my strength gave out before I could carry out our plans for the encyclopedia."[80]

Gunnar Myrdal's *An American Dilemma: The Negro Problem and Modern Democracy* (1944) would become, according to U.S. sociologist Aldon D. Morris, "the most famous and influential study of race ever produced."[81] Indeed, as fellow U.S. sociologist Stephen Steinberg points out, "Monumental is the modifier most commonly attached to Gunnar Myrdal's study, *An American Dilemma*."[82] Supporting the significance of Myrdal's book, political scientist Naomi Murakawa writes that it has been "the touchstone book of racial politics." Historian Daryl Michael Scott concurs that

[77] Frederick Keppel to Anson Phelps Stokes, November 17, 1938, III.A. grant files, box 139, folder 139.11, CCNYR.

[78] See Morey, *White Philanthropy*.

[79] David Levering Lewis, W. E. B. Du Bois: The Fight for Equality and the American Century, 1919–1963 (New York: Holt, 2000), 566.

[80] Levering Lewis, *W. E. B. Du Bois*, 570.

[81] Aldon D. Morris, *The Scholar Denied: W. E. B. Du Bois and the Birth of Modern Sociology* (Oakland: University of California Press, 2015), 198.

[82] Stephen Steinberg, "An American Dilemma: The Collapse of the Racial Orthodoxy of Gunnar Myrdal," *Journal of Blacks in Higher Education* 10 (Winter 1995–1996), 64.

*An American Dilemma* was "the era's most important study of Black life" in the United States.[83]

Historian Thomas J. Sugrue has similarly noted the continued influence of *An American Dilemma* in U.S. life. For example, referring to former president Barack Obama's Martin Luther King Day speech in 2008, Sugrue comments that "Obama's high-minded words echo those of Swedish economist Gunnar Myrdal, whose 1944 book *An American Dilemma* still defines the basic dynamics of racial politics in America."[84]

Throughout the two volumes of *An American Dilemma*, Gunnar Myrdal argues that anti-Black discriminatory policies and behavior run counter to Americans' national egalitarian ideals, which he refers to as the "American Creed."[85] The author subsequently encourages his white American readers to meet such ideals. Assuming that white Americans' non- discriminatory treatment of Black Americans meant opening up the way for Black Americans to achieve "white levels" in all aspects of life in the United States—from "land, credit, jobs" and treatment "in law courts, by the police, and by other public services" to the "use of public facilities such as schools, churches, and means of conveyance," "personal relations," and the legal right to marry and have "sexual intercourse" with white people—Myrdal stresses that white Americans could make use of an increasingly strong and centralized national government in the United States to expedite Black Americans' assimilation into white U.S. life; prioritizing first the forms of anti-Black public policies to which white Americans were least committed.[86] He argues that doing so will help white Americans prove to themselves and to the world that they are a particularly egalitarian people.[87] Myrdal furthermore encourages Black Americans to accept assimilation as equality, underscoring that "it is to the advantage of American Negroes as individuals and as a group to become assimilated into American culture, to acquire the traits held in esteem by the dominant white Americans."[88]

Gunnar Myrdal's analysis of anti-Black discrimination as a moral problem in the hearts and minds of white Americans, to be solved by urging these dominant white Americans to mobilize the national government to assimilate Black Americans into dominant white U.S. life, resonated with many Americans. Over sixty-five glowing reviews of the work were published in U.S. newspapers and magazines when it appeared in 1944. In that first year, the lengthy study went through four editions. Shorter summaries were also published, reviewed in newspapers, and sold to the U.S. public.[89] In 1944, the *Amsterdam Star-News* awarded *An American Dilemma* the runner-up book of the year, and the *Virginian Pilot* determined that it was the

[83] Naomi Murakawa, *The First Civil Right: How Liberals Built Prison America* (New York: Oxford University Press, 2014), 15; Daryl Michael Scott, *Contempt & Pity: Social Policy and the Image of the Damaged Black Psyche* (Chapel Hill: University of North Carolina Press, 1997), 54.

[84] Thomas J. Sugrue, "Hearts and Minds," *The Nation*, April 24, 2008.

[85] Gunnar Myrdal, *An American Dilemma: The Negro Problem and Modern Democracy* (New York: Harper, 1944), xliii. Unless otherwise noted, all references are to the 1944 edition of this work.

[86] Myrdal, *An American Dilemma*, 60–61, 437, 1066.

[87] Myrdal, *An American Dilemma*, 1015–1024.

[88] Myrdal, *An American Dilemma*, 929.

[89] See, for example, Maxwell Stewart, "The Negro in America," (*Public Affairs* Pamphlet no. 95) (New York: Public Affairs Committee, 1944).

best study of U.S. life. The following year, the *Saturday Review of Literature* gave it the Anisfield-Wolf Award for the best book on "race relations."[90] The *New York Post* described Myrdal's book as "outstanding" and "the most illuminating study on the Negro in this country that has ever been made."[91]

Beyond the general U.S. public, *An American Dilemma* both reflected and penetrated social scientific scholarship on race in the United States.[92] Historian Lee D. Baker writes, for example, that "*An American Dilemma* effectively reshaped the discussion of race and culture in the United States for the next fifteen years. It became a guide for an array of social policies, a standard text in university curricula, and a dominant reference in nearly every forum on race relations."[93] Likewise, historian Alice O'Connor notes that in the 1940s U.S. social scientists "crystallized the elements of an emerging liberal orthodoxy on race," an orthodoxy "drawn together in a sweeping synthesis in Gunnar Myrdal's *An American Dilemma* (1944)."[94] "This new synthesis," she explains, "defined 'the race problem' within a black/white paradigm, traced the roots of racial inequality to a wide range of social and cultural disadvantages rooted in white prejudice, and embraced integration and racial assimilation as desirable social goals."[95]

Moving beyond the project's intellectual context to its future impact in the social sciences, historian Leah Gordon argues that *An American Dilemma* "exemplified and aided a shift in research on the race issue in much social scientific, as well as popular and social policy, discourse."[96] For example, Gordon argues that Myrdal's study encouraged U.S. social scientists during the next two decades to focus on the white psyche, or rather, on white prejudice when analyzing racial injustice in the United States.[97]

In the 1940s and well into the 1960s, *An American Dilemma* dominated discussions of Black Americans in the United States not only among social scientists but also among policymakers. For this latter group, Myrdal's study helped frame and justify the U.S. federal government's reengagement in shaping a national policy program on Black Americans; a role from which the federal government generally had shied away since the end of the Reconstruction Era in the 1870s. In 1946, for example, U.S. president Harry S Truman convened by executive order a committee "to make recommendations with respect to adoption or establishment by legislation or otherwise of

[90] S. W. Garlington, "Newsettes," *Amsterdam Star News*, December 1944; Harry Hansen, "First Reader," *Virginian Pilot*, December 27, 1944; newspaper clipping, *Call*, March 10, 1945; "Documents from Gunnar Myrdal's Work," vol. 4.2.05:004, folder "An American Dilemma 1945," Gunnar and Alva Myrdal Archives, Arbetarrörelsens Arkiv och Bibliotek, Stockholm, Sweden (hereafter GAMA).

[91] Dorothy Norman, "World to Live In: Recent Books on Race Relations," *New York Post*, September 17, 1945; "Documents from Gunnar Myrdal's Work," GAMA.

[92] David W. Southern, *Gunnar Myrdal and Black-White Relations: The Use and Abuse of "An American Dilemma"* (Baton Rouge: Louisiana State University Press, 1994).

[93] Lee D. Baker, *From Savage to Negro: Anthropology and the Construction of Race, 1896–1954* (Chapel Hill: University of North Carolina Press, 1998), 194–95.

[94] Alice O'Connor, *Poverty Knowledge: Social Science, Social Policy, and the Poor in Twentieth-Century U.S. History* (Princeton: Princeton University Press, 2001), 76.

[95] O'Connor, *Poverty Knowledge*, 76.

[96] Leah Gordon, *From Power to Prejudice: The Rise of Racial Individualism in Midcentury America* (Chicago: University of Chicago Press, 2015), 36.

[97] Gordon, *From Power to Prejudice*, 38.

more adequate means and procedures for protection of civil rights of the people of the United States."[98] Written most immediately in response to white Americans' fatal violence against Black veterans returning from service during the Second World War, historian Kenneth Mack writes that the report produced by Truman's Committee on Civil Rights "was guided ... by a Myrdalian framework that by now had become second nature to its members."[99] In its report, the president's committee not only explained how white Americans' discrimination against Black Americans was an affront to U.S. ideals, but also emphasized the central role that the federal government could play in bringing about more equitable treatment for Black Americans in various aspects of U.S. life. Much like Myrdal, the committee members listed the numerous ways that Black Americans experienced white Americans' unequal and discriminatory treatment. In 1954, the U.S. Supreme Court also made explicit mention of *An American Dilemma* in its school desegregation case, *Brown v. Board of Education*. Years before, Supreme Court Justice Felix Frankfurter had told a U.S. journalist that "Myrdal's book was 'indispensable' for understanding the race problem."[100]

In many ways, *Brown* was a manifestation of the very theory of change that Myrdal proposed in *An American Dilemma*: not only because Myrdal had centered the U.S. federal government as an agent of change in his analysis of anti-Black discrimination in the U.S., but also because—among Black "improvement and protest organizations"—he centered the NAACP as "the most important agency for the Negroes in their struggle against caste."[101]

Years before the publication of *An American Dilemma*, NAACP director Walter White was attentive to the importance of Myrdal's Carnegie-sponsored project and to Myrdal's ultimate analysis of the role of the NAACP in the long Black freedom struggle. In correspondence with a colleague in 1940, for example, White described the Carnegie-backed study as "undoubtedly the most comprehensible study of the status of the Negro in America ever made" and urged colleagues to assist Myrdal in his data collection on the "experience of lawyers both white and Negro, when they have fought for justice under the law for Negroes."[102] Two years later, in July 1942, White sent Myrdal a detailed, four-page response to the latter's draft analysis of the NAACP in the struggle, which only further underscored the weight that White placed on Myrdal's research in the United States and, specifically, Myrdal's analysis of the NAACP.[103] To this point, just a month later in August 1942, White followed up with yet another letter to Myrdal, underscoring that he was willing to cancel his holiday that month if Myrdal intended to be in town: "I am hoping during August to get a

[98] Steven F. Lawson ed., *To Secure These Rights: The Report of President Harry S Truman's Committee on Civil Rights* (Boston: Bedford/St. Martin's, 2004), 14.

[99] Kenneth Mack, *Representing the Race: The Creation of the Civil Rights Lawyer* (Cambridge.: Harvard University Press, 2012), 244.

[100] John Gunther, *Inside U.S.A.* (New York: New Press, 1947), 683, 926, quoted in Southern, *Gunnar Myrdal and Black-White Relations*, 129.

[101] Myrdal, *An American Dilemma*, 819.

[102] Letter from Walter White to Carol Weiss King, April 23, 1940, New York Public Library, Carnegie-Myrdal Papers, Box M6514.

[103] Letter from Walter White to Gunnar Myrdal, July 29, 1942, "Negro Study Correspondence," CCNYR.

few days away for some rest—I have had no vacation for three years—and for some writing. But I will drop any of that if you are going to be here."[104]

At the time, Walter White was particularly anxious that political scientist Ralph Bunche, who served on Myrdal's staff and whom Myrdal had tasked with providing a memorandum on Black organizations including the NAACP, was too critical of the NAACP as a particularly bourgeois organization with little public support in the Black community and especially among working class Black Americans. Compared to White, NAACP assistant secretary Roy Wilkins was less anxious about this criticism of the NAACP, writing to Myrdal that same summer month that he thought that the "Association's case has been presented rather fairly [in the working draft he read of *An American Dilemma*]. Unlike some of my colleagues I do not believe that a study of this kind would be valuable if it did nothing except to present the viewpoint of the Association and its officers."[105] That said, and equally reflecting the importance Myrdal himself placed on his description of the NAACP in *An American Dilemma*, Myrdal would share with White later in August 1942 that he was rewriting the chapter on the NAACP.[106]

Ultimately, Myrdal's description in *An American Dilemma* of the NAACP would be highly favorable, with the author mainly underscoring the organization's centrality for his theory of change, which emphasized the importance of mobilizing white Americans to address anti-Black discriminatory behavior and policies—and to use the U.S. federal government, including the courts, in this process. In other words, and while Myrdal indeed centered white northerners and New Dealers in his theory of change in *An American Dilemma*, he left room for a "Black improvement and protest organization" such as the NAACP to play a complementary role in helping these white Americans (and by extension, the U.S. federal government) to expedite Black Americans' assimilation into white U.S. life.

Attracting a broad readership across the United States, and especially too within a network of elite foundations, their advisers, and grantees, this Carnegie-Corporation-financed study on Black Americans would serve to amplify the centrality of the NAACP's legal strategies in the Black freedom struggle—and the NAACP took notice. During the summer of 1948, a group of Americans coming together as the "Committee of 100" coordinated a dinner in New York City to honor Myrdal, "as an expression of the gratitude of Americans for the great contribution he has made toward the solution of the tragic racial division in our land through his brilliant study 'An American Dilemma.'"[107] The Committee intended the dinner to serve as a fundraising event for the NAACP Legal Defense and Educational Fund (LDF); urging fellow "friends and admirers of Dr. Myrdal" attending the dinner "to provide a gift" to the organization.[108]

104 Letter from Walter White to Gunnar Myrdal, August 3, 1942, "Negro Study Correspondence," CCNYR.

105 Letter from Roy Wilkins to Gunnar Myrdal, August 11, 1942, "Negro Study Correspondence," CCNYR.

106 Letter from Walter White to Gunnar Myrdal, August 26, 1942, "Negro Study Correspondence," CCNYR.

107 Committee of 100 Dinner Invitation, "Documents from Gunnar Myrdal's Work," June 2, 1948, vol. 4.2.05:003, folder "Klipp," GAMA. For a discussion of the Committee of 100, see Mark Tushnet, *Making Civil Rights Law: Thurgood Marshall and the Supreme Court, 1936–1961* (New York: Oxford University Press, 1994), 34–35.

108 Committee of 100 Dinner Invitation, "Documents from Gunnar Myrdal's Work."

Former first lady Eleanor Roosevelt, who had agreed to cooperate with Myrdal's team of researchers years earlier, was a speaker at the event. She was joined by other contributors to Myrdal's study, NAACP executive secretary Walter White, as well as Roy Wilkins, who had replaced W. E. B. Du Bois as editor of the NAACP's official journal *The Crisis*.

As this next section underscores, Myrdal's *American Dilemma* celebrated and amplified the significance of the NAACP at a moment when white funders were increasingly finding interest in the organization and helping to transform it into a nationally dominant and key figure of the Black freedom struggle.

## V. White Funders Center the NAACP's Litigation Strategies in the Black Freedom Struggle

As political scientist Megan Ming Francis has noted, "the NAACP shifted its agenda to a now-celebrated campaign against segregated education" in the 1930s, just a decade before the publication of *An American Dilemma*, and thanks to the American Fund for Public Service (many times referred to as the Garland Fund after its founder Charles Garland).[109] Francis argues that "the Garland Fund was a principal cause in the shifting of the NAACP's agenda away from racial violence to education," explaining that the "NAACP's landmark campaign against segregated education did not develop independently nor was it a collaborative endeavor with the Garland Fund. Rather, the NAACP's early civil rights litigation agenda was *captured* by the Garland Fund and redirected away from the issue of racial violence to the issue of education segregation."[110]

The version of the NAACP that Gunnar Myrdal celebrated in his Carnegie-Corporation-financed study for being particularly central to the Black freedom struggle was an NAACP already transformed by yet another white-led foundation also based in New York City, the Garland Fund.

Francis notes that the Garland Fund was able to play such an outsized role in directing the NAACP's attention towards a litigation plan to challenge segregated schools precisely because the NAACP did not have comparably large donors in the 1930s. At the time, the organization relied heavily on its membership base to support its work. "To provide some perspective on the significance of the Garland Fund's first grant to the NAACP," Francis writes, "no foundations or large donors ($1000 and over) contribute[d] to the NAACP before the Garland Fund got involved. Wealthy donors stayed away from the NAACP because it was viewed as too radical."[111]

After the Garland Fund financed the NAACP and transformed the organization's focus on litigating school segregation—a version of the NAACP that Myrdal then celebrated in *An American Dilemma*—even more elite white funding would follow suit. Aside from fundraisers such as the one organized by the "Committee of 100" to honor Myrdal, attracting the "who's who" in national policy circles, the NAACP

[109] Francis, "The Price of Civil Rights," 277.
[110] Francis, "The Price of Civil Rights," 278–79.
[111] Francis, "The Price of Civil Rights," 298.

increasingly received attention and trust from elite white funders such as the Carnegie and Rockefeller organizations and (new to the national scene after the Second World War) the Ford Foundation.

As historian Ellen Condliffe Lagemann writes in *The Politics of Knowledge* (1989), elite foundations' support for organizations like the NAACP increased in the 1960s. "This was part of a general movement among foundations toward increased financing of civil rights organizations."[112] Writing specifically about the Ford Foundation in the 1960s, Karen Ferguson notes in *Top Down* (2013) that Ford Foundation President McGeorge Bundy re-engaged the organization in "racial politics in the United States." This re-engagement "included what would become a long-term and large-scale commitment to mainstream black organizations—the NAACP and its Legal Defense and Educational Fund (NAACP LDF), as well as the even more mainstream and venerable National Urban League."[113] More broadly, Ferguson notes:

> The black freedom struggle's turn from the turbulence of the 1960s to the mediated conflicts of public-interest judicial activism of the 1970s can be attributed in part to the [Ford] Foundation's funding of organizations like the NAACP LDF along with other comparable organizations—including the Mexican American and Puerto Rican Legal Defense and Educational Funds (MALDEF and PRLDEF), both created out of whole cloth by the Foundation as Latino versions of the NAACP LDF. The Foundation founded these advocacy organizations, which had no grassroots membership, to extend the legal civil rights strategy that had resulted in the *Brown* decision, postwar racial liberalism's greatest achievement.[114]

From the Ford Foundation in the 1970s to Carnegie Corporation and the Garland Fund some decades earlier, U.S. philanthropic organizations played critical roles in elevating the national prominence—and shaping the work—of the NAACP LDF in the Black freedom struggle.

All that said, Tomiko Brown-Nagin and Megan Ming Francis both stress, in *Courage to Dissent* and "The Price of Civil Rights," respectively, that the NAACP's school desegregation agenda in the 1940s and 1950s did not define Black Americans' varying definitions and desired means for equality in the United States. In *Set the World on Fire*, Keisha Blain adds to this understanding about the richness and diversity of views within the Black freedom struggle, uncovering "the previously hidden voices of black nationalist women activists and intellectuals whose ideas and activities differed significantly from their counterparts in well-known organizations such as the National Association of Colored Women (NACW), the National Association

[112] Ellen Condliffe Lagemann, *The Politics of Knowledge: The Carnegie Corporation, Philanthropy, and Public Policy* (Middletown: Wesleyan University Press, 1989), 248, citing J. Craig Jenkins and Craig M. Eckert, "Channel Black Insurgency: Elite Patronage and Professional Social Movement Organization in the Development of the Black Movement," *American Sociological Review* 51 (December 1986): 812–29; and David J. Garrow, "Philanthropy and the Civil Rights Movement," Center for the Study of Philanthropy, Graduate School and University Center, City University of New York, October 1987.

[113] Karen Ferguson, *Top Down: The Ford Foundation, Black Power, and the Reinvention of Racial Liberalism* (Philadelphia: University of Pennsylvania Press, 2013), 70.

[114] Ferguson, *Top Down*, 81–82.

for the Advancement of Colored People (NAACP), and the National Urban League (NUL)."[115] In reality, that is, Black Americans in the Black freedom struggle worked across organizations and had varying and conflicting views on what it meant to achieve freedom and how best to work toward these goals across the country.

At the expense of these various organizations and activists, there are several reasons why the NAACP and especially the NAACP's Legal Defense and Educational Fund (LDF) gained dominance as the quintessential organization representing the Black freedom struggle in mid-twentieth-century United States. For starters, as Blain underscores, "[C]onventional historical narratives tend to privilege the political activities of the black middle class and elite" at the expense of those of "working-poor women activists" detailed in Blain's book. And a large segment of the NAACP's membership included the Black middle class.[116] With respect specifically to the centrality of the NAACP's LDF in national narratives of the Black freedom struggle, this chapter stresses that another key factor was that an increasing number of white funders and their grantees (most prominently, Gunnar Myrdal) came to embrace the NAACP's shifting agenda toward fighting school desegregation in the courts, at the expense of funding other organizations, activists, and agendas in the Black freedom struggle.

As this chapter thus has stressed, white funders long have played critical roles amplifying certain individuals, groups, and ideas over others in the Black freedom struggle-—encouraging the centrality of individuals such as Booker T. Washington, Thomas Jesse Jones, and Gunnar Myrdal and of organizations such as the Tuskegee Institute and the NAACP at the expense of marginalizing or co-opting other voices in the struggle such as that of Marcus Garvey, the Congress of Racial Equality (CORE), the Student Nonviolent Coordinating Committee (SNCC), and the Black Panther Party.[117]

Writing of the Ford Foundation under McGeorge Bundy's leadership in the 1960s and 1970s, for example, sociologist Robert Allen notes in *Black Awakening in Capitalist America* (1969) that the "Ford Foundation was on its way to becoming the most important, though least publicized, organization manipulating the militant black movement. Housed in an ultramodern headquarters building on East Forty-third Street in New York, the Foundation is deeply involved in financing and influencing almost all major protest groups, including CORE, [the Southern Christian Leadership Conference], the National Urban League, and the NAACP. Working directly or indirectly through these organizations, as well as other national and local groups, the Foundation hopes to channel and control the black liberation movement and forestall future urban revolts."[118] Citing Aldon Morris's complementary book, *The Origins of the Civil Rights Movement* (1986), Megan Ming Francis furthermore argues that "the NAACP was not alone in negotiating for greater control of its agenda with funders. SNCC, CORE, and many organizations large and small fought and sometimes split over questions of white influence over radical black politics

115 Blain, *Set the World on Fire*, 1–2.
116 Blain, *Set the World on Fire*, 8.
117 Francis, "The Price of Civil Rights," 298.
118 Robert Allen, *Black Awakening in Capitalist America: An Analytic History* (Garden City: Doubleday, 1969), 72–73.

including, specifically, the role that foundations would play in financing and shaping the struggle."[119] Such caution and debate within movement organizations were warranted since, as Karen Ferguson writes in *Top Down* (2013), U.S. philanthropic organizations such as the Ford Foundation intended "to domesticate black power and its challenge to liberalism, reforging a social consensus on race."[120]

In the later decades of the twentieth century, that is, the Ford Foundation followed colleagues' practices at peer white-led foundations of elevating the public prominence of the NAACP's LDF at the expense of other movement activists and organizations. More broadly, the Foundation also shaped which individuals, groups, and ideas in the Black freedom struggle would thrive nationally. It did so by deciding to finance the NAACP's LDF above that of CORE or SNCC. And even when funding the latter organizations, the Ford Foundation along with the Taconic and Field foundations shaped these movement organizations' foci away from mobilizing communities for protest and toward voter registration, which these white funders (in dialogue with President John F. Kennedy's administration) deemed to be more pragmatic.[121]

The Ford Foundation further curated what would become mainstream ideas in the Black freedom struggle by financing and shaping the content of Black Studies in universities across the United States. As Noliwe Rooks writes in *White Money, Black Power* (2006), Ford Foundation President McGeorge Bundy's "grants to African American Studies programs totaled more than ten million dollars and supported two dozen programs between 1968 and 1972."[122]

Rising in the wake of Black student revolts across more than fifty campuses calling for such departments, the organization's funding practices in Black Studies ultimately would be shaped by its own (not students') visions for these programs.[123] As far as the intensity of student protests, Rooks underscores Cornell University as an example. "Most tellingly," Rooks writes, "in April of 1969 at Cornell University, armed Black students occupied and took over Willard Straight Hall. In the course of the occupation, the students made a series of demands that included a new department of African American Studies that should function as an autonomous all-Black college, the hiring of Black faculty and administrators, and the recruitment of poor urban students to the Ivy League university."[124] As far as building departments of African American Studies both within and beyond Cornell, Rooks furthermore explains in *White Money, Black Power* that the Ford Foundation played a critical role in shaping their agenda: "Despite the various factions jockeying for position, only one rationale would come to dominate the field of Black Studies as it assumed its position in academic institutions. Although it clearly did not pioneer the approach, the Ford Foundation wholeheartedly supported an integrationist rationale and refused wholeheartedly to

[119] Aldon Morris, *The Origins of the Civil Rights Movement* (New York: Simon and Schuster, 1986), cited in Francis, "The Price of Civil Rights," 306.

[120] Ferguson, *Top Down*, 5.

[121] Noliwe Rooks, *White Money, Black Power: The Surprising History of African American Studies and the Crisis of Race in Higher Education* (Boston: Beacon, 2006), 83; Morris, *The Origins of the Civil Rights Movement*, 234–235.

[122] Rooks, *White Money, Black Power*, 77.

[123] Ibid., 17.

[124] Ibid., 20.

fund programs and groups that couched their requests for assistance within the rhetoric of Black Power."[125] The Ford Foundation thus would be financing a form of Black Studies that disassociated itself from anything like a "new black assertiveness" and would serve instead to help both Black Americans integrate into the dominantly white university culture and white Americans better understand Black Americans.[126]

## VI. Conclusion

Looking at the span of the twentieth century, it is not coincidental that the activists, organizations, and agendas in the Black freedom struggle that were financed and shaped by influential white-led philanthropic organizations would gain national attention and achieve heightened impact as key players in the struggle—and that many Americans within and beyond Black communities would come to equate these activists', scholars', and organizations' work with the struggle itself. And yet, there was and remains a difference between what leading white Anglo-American funders have deemed worthy of financing and amplifying in the Black freedom struggle in the United States and what the struggle was and remains in reality: a body of people with varying (at times, overlapping and, at other times, discordant) activities, viewpoints, and perspectives on how best to achieve Black freedom in the United States.

Today, in the twenty-first century, we can learn from this history by maintaining a critical lens on which BIPOC activists, organizations, and agendas seem most dominant among us, acknowledging that the activists and ideas for BIPOC freedom that we assume to be central to our movements might simply be prominent precisely because leading funders in the United States find them palatable or, rather, less threatening to the status quo than other, more marginalized activists and ideas. And if we *actually* intend to think through and move toward our collective freedom in the United States, it would behoove us to find and identify who is financing our community members and organizations and, subsequently, to find inspiration beyond the movement activists, organizations, and ideas most valued and centered (applying here W. E. B. Du Bois's own critical analysis in 1918 of the "philanthropic North" )by influential Americans with the power of the purse.

[125] Ibid., 22.
[126] Ibid., 21.

# 5

# "Kindred to Treason"

## Conspiracy Laws in the United States

*Sarah A. Seo*[*]

Situated about midway between the Great Lakes and the Atlantic Ocean and between Montreal and Albany, a body of fresh water has long served as a border lake. The Wabanaki Nation called it "lake in between"; the Iroquois referred to it as "lake that is the gate of the country."[1] In 1609, the Frenchman Samuel de Champlain entered the lake from one of the many rivers that flowed into it and admired the "many fine trees . . . with many vines finer than any I have seen in any other place," as well as "some very high mountains," where, he was told, "were beautiful valleys . . . with plains productive in grain, such as I had eaten in this country, together with many kinds of fruit without limit."[2] In short order, Europeans took the land and the lake and the rivers that fell into the lake from the indigenous peoples, as well as the abundance that the land and the waters produced. By the late eighteenth century, they had partitioned Lake Champlain's water basin with boundaries that today separate Canada and the states of New York and Vermont.

For those who lived in these borderlands, lines drawn on official maps did not determine with whom they traded nature's largesse. But boundaries did influence the routes they took and the prices they fetched, especially in times of global wars. For Vermonters, the area's Norway pines became one of their most lucrative exports to Canada and beyond. The winter season was the time for felling, clearing, chopping, rolling, burning, and carting. Logs were gathered and tied together to form acre-sized rafts that required many men to maneuver when the lake thawed in springtime. It was a backbreaking business made more profitable by the other commodities that the rafts could haul on their way to market.[3]

This thriving commerce was threatened in March 1808, when Congress supplemented the Embargo Act that was hastily enacted in December the previous year, after the British *Leopard* attacked the American *Chesapeake*, prompting calls for

* I am indebted to Amy Chazkel, Antony Duff, Lindsay Farmer, Kellen Funk, Dirk Hartog, Anna Lvovsky, Jane Manners, Sara Mayeux, Lev Menand, Dan Richman, David Sklansky, Karen Tani, and the participants of The Political Turn(s) in Criminal Law Theory, Columbia Law Faculty Workshop, Northeastern University Law School Faculty Colloquium, University of Connecticut Law School Faculty Workshop, Yale Legal History Forum, and Cornell Law Faculty Workshop for their comments. I'm also grateful for research assistance from Jane Park, Allyson Ping, and Nicolas N. Rodriguez.

1 Gary G. Shattuck, *Insurrection, Corruption, and Murder in Early Vermont: Life on the Wild Northern Frontier* (Charleston: History Press, 2014), 27; Peter S. Palmer, *History of Lake Champlain: From Its First Exploration by the French in 1609, to the Close of the Year 1814* (Albany: J. Munsell, 1866), 12.

2 Samuel de Champlain, *Voyages of Samuel de Champlain* (Boston: Prince Society, 1878), 2:215–217.

3 Shattuck, *Insurrection*, 36–38.

Sarah A. Seo, *"Kindred to Treason"* In: *In Between and Across.* Edited by: Kenneth W. Mack and Jacob Katz Cogan, Oxford University Press. © Oxford University Press 2024. DOI: 10.1093/oso/9780197680995.003.0006

retaliation. The "land embargo" clarified that in addition to the prohibition of exports transported on ships, it would also be illegal to export "in any manner whatever any goods, wares, or merchandise."[4] Those in the Lake Champlain region, who were confident that the 1807 "O-grab-me" ("embargo" spelled backwards) didn't apply to the overland trade with Canada, were up in arms. Four-hundred-thousand dollars' worth of lumber, already processed and awaiting the spring season, had suddenly become contraband.[5]

A few months later, a Vermont lumber trader by the name of Van Dusen shipped a raft about two acres in size and valued at $25,000.[6] En route to the Canadian market, near the Isle of Mott in Lake Champlain, a deputy customs official seized the raft. Van Dusen hired a man to take back the raft, promising $800 upon successful delivery to Canada. The hired man assembled a crew of about 60, including one named Frederick Hoxie and his two sons, who armed themselves with muskets, clubs, and spike poles.[7] Reclaiming the raft was not too difficult, as the sentinel had wandered from his post (perhaps in cahoots with the embargo violators). But about an hour later, the group encountered federal troops shooting at them from the shore. The men fired back. No one was injured in the skirmish, and the smugglers were able to make their way to Canada. They returned to Vermont and received their bounty.

Once back at home, Hoxie was charged not for violating the embargo, but, curiously, with treason for levying war against the United States. His case appears briefly in Willard Hurst's compendium *The Law of Treason in the United States*, which was first published as a series in the *Harvard Law Review* in 1945.[8] Hurst mentioned *Hoxie* to illustrate how "the scope of treason by levying war was narrowed" through "a strict definition of the intent element."[9] As circuit justice Henry Brockholst Livingston had instructed the jury, "the forcible rescuing of a raft from the custody of a military guard" for "the sole purpose of private gain" was wholly different from doing so with the intent to make war against one's own country.[10] Given this instruction, the jury acquitted Hoxie, after which the court dismissed treason charges against his sons.[11]

*United States v. Hoxie* is also included in another compendium, *Digest of Decisions of the United States Circuit and District Courts, from 1789 to 1880*, published by West

[4] Embargo Act, 2 Stat. 451 (December 1807); Supplementary Embargo Act, 2 Stat. 475 (March 12, 1808); see Peter Andreas, "Contraband and Embargo Busting in the New Nation," chap. 4 in *Smuggler Nation: How Illicit Trade Made America* (New York: Oxford, 2013); Gordon S. Wood, *Empire of Liberty: A History of the Early Republic, 1789–1815* (New York: Oxford University Press, 2009), 653; H. N. Muller, "Smuggling into Canada: How the Champlain Valley Defied Jefferson's Embargo," *Vermont History* 38.1 (Winter 1970): 6, https://vermonthistory.org/journal/misc/SmugglingIntoCanada.pdf. On the embargo in Maine, see Joshua M. Smith, "The Rascals of Passamaquoddy," chap. 4 in *Borderland Smuggling: Patriots, Loyalists, and Illicit Trade in the Northeast, 1783–1820* (Gainesville: University Press of Florida, 2019).

[5] Shattuck, *Insurrection*, 95.

[6] Ibid., 125.

[7] United States v. Hoxie, 26 F. Cas. 397 (C.C.D. Vt. 1808) (No. 15,407); Shattuck, *Insurrection*, 116, 118, 124, 257.

[8] J. Taylor McConkie, U.S. Department of Justice, Civil Division, "State Treason: The History and Validity of Treason Against Individual States," *Kentucky Law Journal* 101.2 (2013): 284, n.19.

[9] J. Willard Hurst, *The Law of Treason in the United States* (Westport: Greenwood, 1945, 1971), 195.

[10] Hoxie, 26 F. Cas. at 399.

[11] Shattuck, *Insurrection*, 259–260.

in 1898. The case is listed in the section on conspiracy, which is, again, curious.[12] Conspiracy—that is, an agreement to commit an unlawful act—wasn't a federal crime until over fifty years after Hoxie was tried.[13] Also curious is that West's *Digest* placed the *Hoxie* case under the subsection "treasonable conspiracies." A few months before Hoxie's trial, Congress had debated and declined to enact a treasonous conspiracy law.[14]

This chapter will try to solve the many puzzles of *Hoxie*: why the government brought treason charges, why more appropriate charges seemed inadequate, why the case later served to elucidate conspiracy doctrine, and how the offenses of treason and conspiracy were related. And by contextualizing these questions with the histories of critical but deeply contested policies from the Revolutionary period to Reconstruction, this chapter will examine why the federal government in the 1860s finally enacted general conspiracy laws—"general" in that they punished agreements to violate *any* federal law—and why it took so long, at least compared with England, which had criminalized conspiracies since the thirteenth century.[15]

The evident need to punish unlawful agreements goes to the heart of what criminal law is and what it is for. Criminal law is conventionally understood as a necessary condition of ordered society, keeping us from a state of nature.[16] But it has also been necessary for the *state*; specifically, conspiracy laws have been necessary for the *American* state. The case of *United States v. Hoxie* was tried at a time when the fledgling new nation lacked effective enforcement mechanisms to carry out national goals. The problem was existential; the American Civil War made clear, if the War of 1812 after the embargo's demise didn't already, that noncompliance could threaten government itself, even if it didn't amount to treason. Building the state was one way of solving the enforcement problem, but it was significantly constrained in a federal system that was politically and philosophically wedded to limited government. Criminal law offered an alternative. Albeit unintentionally, the *Digest* pointed to the state-building role of conspiracy laws, from protecting government functions to preventing rebellions—all without a bureaucracy that seemed too big.

## I. The Embargo Act and a Crisis of Enforcement

The British impressment of Americans on the high seas during its ongoing hostilities with France threatened the independence and honor of the young nation. President Jefferson believed that economic sanctions, not war, could compel European powers,

[12] *Digest of Decisions of the United States Circuit and District Courts, from 1789 to 1880* (Eagan: West, 1898), 702.

[13] See An Act to define and punish certain Conspiracies, 12 Stat. 284 (July 31, 1861). Before then, Congress had passed few, very specific conspiracy provisions, such as Section 12 of the 1790 Crimes Act, which prohibited individuals from joining a "confederacy to become pirates." 1 Stat. 115 (1790).

[14] 18 Annals of Cong. 2279 (1808).

[15] Frank P. Blair, "The Judge-Made Law of Conspiracy," *American Law Review* 37.1 (1903): 35.

[16] This explanation, of course, doesn't apply to the federal government, which does not exercise general police powers. Studying the history of federal criminal laws, as opposed to state laws, is one way to isolate the functions of criminal law that are not essential to what has often been referred to as "ordered society."

especially the British, to respect American neutrality and to leave its sailors alone.[17] After the British attack on the USS *Chesapeake*, the wave of patriotic outrage, plus faith in republican virtue and self-sacrifice, led Jefferson to have confidence that the people would forgo trade, at least temporarily. Put differently, American foreign policy depended on voluntary compliance with commercial restrictions, for the U.S. Customs Service did not have enough manpower—personnel numbered just a little over a thousand for the entire Atlantic coast.[18]

President Jefferson, however, had overestimated how much support there would be for the embargo laws. The embargo was a widespread failure, for he never considered how to enforce a decree that seemed, to many, to require a great deal of personal self-sacrifice.[19] The Vermont borderlands relied heavily on agricultural exchange "for many of the conveniences, and even necessaries of life," as residents of St. Albans, Vermont, explained to Jefferson in an appeal to end the embargo.[20] Other towns all along the Champlain Valley drafted similar letters demanding that trade restrictions be lifted.[21] Merchants throughout the country were furious and tried to sabotage the embargo before it even took effect, according to historian Gautham Rao.[22] The main consequence of the embargoes may have been to cut off a significant source of the federal government's revenue, for smuggling was rampant. Canadians reported that trade was "proceed[ing] as usual from the ports on the Lake to Montreal."[23] According to a local historian, commodities trading from the Champlain Valley to Canada increased 70% from 1807 to 1808.[24] Flagrant violations of the embargo augured violence. An informant enlightened the Canadian governor that "the clamour [sic] against the Government and the measure particularly is such that you may expect to hear of an engagement between the officers of Government and the sovereign people on the first effort to stop the introduction of that vast quantity of timber and produce which is prepared for the Montreal market."[25]

Anticipating a violent clash, Vermont's collector of customs asked Treasury secretary Albert Gallatin for "an adequate force" to enforce the new law.[26] Gallatin, in an

[17] Wood, *Empire of Liberty*, 626–633, 641–651; Gautham Rao, *National Duties: Custom Houses and the Making of the American State* (Chicago: University of Chicago Press, 2016), 132–33; George C. Herring, *From Colony to Superpower: U.S. Foreign Relations Since 1776* (New York: Oxford, University Press, 2008), 119–20; Muller, "Smuggling into Canada," 5–6.

[18] Carl E. Prince and Mollie Keller, *The U.S. Customs Service: A Bicentennial History* (Washington, D.C.: Department of the Treasury, 1989), 71, 79.

[19] Jefferson to Gallatin, August 11, 1808, Founders Online ("This embargo law is certainly the most embarrassing one we have ever had to execute. I did not expect a crop of so sudden & Rank growth of fraud & open opposition by force could have grown up in the US.") See Rao, *National Duties*, 156; Herring, *From Colony to Superpower*, 120.

[20] Inhabitants of St. Albans to Jefferson, May 21, 1808, Founders Online; see also Joshua Smith, "Patterns of Northern New England Smuggling, 1783–1820," in *The Early Republic and the Sea: Essays on the Naval and Maritime History of the Early United States*, ed. William S. Dudley and Michael J. Crawford (Sterling, VA: Potomac, 2001), 44 (on the economic circumstances of timber smugglers during the embargo).

[21] Muller, "Smuggling into Canada," 7–9.

[22] Rao, *National Duties*, 139, 141.

[23] *Connecticut Courant*, May 25, 1808, quoted in Muller, "Smuggling into Canada," 11.

[24] Muller, "Smuggling into Canada," 17; see also Smith, "Patterns of Northern New England Smuggling," 40.

[25] John Henry to Herman Witsius Ryland, 1808, quoted in E. A. Cruikshank, *The Political Adventures of John Henry: The Record of an International Imbroglio* (Toronto: Macmillan, 1936), 18.

[26] Muller, "Smuggling into Canada," 7.

admission of defeat, wrote Jefferson that "the stoppage of intercourse [was] so unpopular" that revenue agents were "afraid to act," an observation that surely called to his mind recent history, when threats to government officials posed threats to government itself.[27] During the American Revolution, colonial mobs had attacked customs officials in protest against British taxes. Parliament's mismanagement of the outcry had led to the ultimate rebellion: secession.

After Jefferson heard about the uproar in Vermont, he issued a proclamation decrying "sundry persons ... combining and confederating together on Lake Champlain ... for the purposes of forming insurrections against the authority of the laws of the United States."[28] He conceded that the protests "may not be an insurrection in the popular sense of the word" but nonetheless insisted that forcible opposition to federal law fell "fully within the legal definition of an insurrection."[29] Jefferson had to be legalistic about the matter because the Insurrection Act required the president to first order "insurgents" to "disperse and retire peaceably" before summoning regular troops and the militia.[30]

The proclamation backfired.[31] After Vermonters received the president's indictment, they indignantly penned a retort that they were "TRUE AND FAITHFUL CITIZENS."[32] They were shocked to learn that attempting to avoid the "ruin and wretchedness" of their families could amount to insurrection. Believing that it was, in fact, the government that was infringing their "right of disposing of our property in time of peace, to whomever we please," they sought "redress of our grievances" as "guaranteed to us by our constitution."[33]

The executive's charge of insurrection and the people's countercharge that they were comporting with true republicanism mirrored the dispute between Parliament and the colonists on the eve of the Revolution. From the perspective of imperial law, the mobs that attacked customs officials had engaged in unlawful rebellion.[34] But from the perspective of American colonists, according to historian John Phillip Reid, "they were far from being rebels and traitors" because they rioted and tarred-and-feathered the crown's agents for the purpose of protesting unconstitutional laws.[35] They justified their acts of violence as a last-resort measure to persuade Parliament to

[27] Gallatin to Thomas Jefferson, May 28, 1808, in *The Writings of Albert Gallatin*, ed. Henry Adams (Philadelphia: Lippincott, 1879), 1:393.

[28] Thomas Jefferson, A Proclamation, April 19, 1808, in *A Compilation of the Messages and Papers of the Presidents*, ed. James D. Richardson (Washington, D.C.: Bureau of National Literature and Art, 1910), 1:438.

[29] Jefferson to Daniel D. Tompkins, August 15, 1808, Founders Online.

[30] Jefferson Proclamation, in Richardson, *Compilation of the Messages*, 439; see Insurrection Act, 2 Stat. 443 (1807); see also Stephen I. Vladeck, "Emergency Power and the Militia Acts (Note)," *Yale Law Journal* 114.1 (2004): 164.

[31] Muller, "Smuggling into Canada," 8–9; see also Shattuck, *Insurrection*, 98, 100; Smith, *Borderland Smuggling*, 57; Wood, *Empire of Liberty*, 656.

[32] Inhabitants of St. Albans to Jefferson, May 21, 1808, Founders Online.

[33] "Copy of a Memorial, Addressed to the President of the United States, relative to the Embargo—By the Inhabitants of Castleton, Vermont," *Vermont Centinel*, July 15, 1808 (on file with author).

[34] John Phillip Reid, "In a Defensive Rage: The Uses of the Mob, the Justification in Law, and the Coming of the American Revolution," *New York University Law Review* 49.6 (1974): 1044.

[35] Ibid., 1053, 1063.

repeal laws that infringed colonial rights.[36] As important, Reid argued, all institutions of local government constituted under the British constitution, from juries to magistrates, condoned the mob's actions, which rendered their understanding of legality to be "law," albeit a contested one.[37]

Embargo protesters believed they were having the exact same fight; they revived revolutionary songs, compared President Jefferson unfavorably to King George, and even talked openly of secession.[38] While Jefferson characterized the Vermont protests as an insurrection that could undermine the new nation, Vermonters viewed their efforts to nullify or evade the laws as within their rights as American citizens.[39] And local institutions supported their views.[40] Despite Gallatin's direct orders to the federal prosecutor in Vermont "to institute prosecutions," hardly any enforcement actions were taken.[41] When a few Canadians were arrested and charged for smuggling rafts on Lake Champlain, the jury—a Democratic-Republican one at that—refused to return the indictments.[42] Even the state militia could not be trusted. Militiamen refused to shoot at violators and released the few prisoners they had taken.[43] Some, after serving their requisite three months, joined the smugglers.[44] Others went so far as to advocate murdering federal customs officers.[45] By the time of Hoxie's trial in October 1808, the governor had so little faith in the militia's loyalty that he relied on regular troops instead.[46]

Local allegiances explain why Hoxie believed that he would not encounter opposition when retaking the raft.[47] Even though he had talked big about taking troops as prisoners "if necessary" and "fighting his way through" the blockade, Hoxie likely did not expect to use force.[48] Though he did end up using force, he would have justified it as a necessary and legitimate challenge to the embargo laws. His lawyers were so confident in this position that they declined to put forth a defense.[49] Lawyers for

[36] Ibid., 1064. See also John Phillip Reid, "The Irrelevance of the Declaration," in *Law in the American Revolution and the Revolution in the Law*, ed. Hendrik Hartog (New York: New York University Press, 1981) (arguing that the Declaration was a legal document claiming a constitutional right).

[37] Reid, "Defensive Rage," 1089–1091.

[38] Herring, *From Colony to Superpower*, 120.

[39] See Farah Peterson, "Constitutionalism in Unexpected Places," *Virginia Law Review* 106.3 (May 2020) (arguing that mob action, with protesters often dressing in Indian costume, was understood to be an unwritten constitutional right to express economic grievances against the government that existed before, during, and after the ratification of the U.S. Constitution).

[40] Prince and Keller, *U.S. Customs Service*, 75.

[41] Gallatin to Jefferson, May 28, 1808, in Adams, *Writings of Albert Gallatin*, 393; Shattuck, *Insurrection*, 106, 107.

[42] Gallatin to Jefferson, July 29, 1808, in Adams, *Writings of Albert Gallatin*, 397. See also Smith, *Borderland Smuggling*, 29 (observing that even magistrates in Maine engaged in smuggling).

[43] Muller, "Smuggling into Canada," 9-10.

[44] Shattuck, *Insurrection*, 111.

[45] Ibid., 25.

[46] Ibid., 104.

[47] Hoxie, 26 F. Cas. at 396. To be sure, not all Vermonters opposed the embargo. See, e.g., "Incidents at Home," *The World*, June 13, 1808 (accusing the *St. Albans Adviser* for having "ridiculed the feeble arm of the officer of the customs, who has been constant in season and out of season in the faithful discharge of his duty" and criticizing that the *Adviser* had "never yet *advised* the people to support the laws of their country") (on file with author).

[48] Hoxie, 26 F. Cas. at 396.

[49] Shattuck, *Insurrection*, 257.

another individual in the same smuggling enterprise likened the men to "the soldiers of Washington," invoking the spirit of 1776.[50]

At issue in *United States v. Hoxie* was the validity of the smugglers' constitutionalism, that is, the validity of their obstruction of validly enacted federal laws. Conversely, the issue for the Jefferson administration was its ability to enforce laws and policies essential to the stability and standing of the nation.

## II. Treason as Enforcement Strategy

Given the import of the embargoes, Attorney General Caesar Augustus Rodney recommended that Hoxie's indictment for smuggling, which was punishable, at most, with a fine of $400, be changed to treason, which could be punished with death.[51] The chance of getting caught and fined hadn't been enough to deter the likes of Hoxie. It certainly wasn't sufficient to discourage the money men whose fortunes were at stake. To them, a fine was a mere rebuke for sabotaging national foreign policy. So long as they hired others to do the deed, then they would never face more serious criminal charges of rioting or, if things got out of hand, murder. Moreover, both rioting and murder were state crimes, which meant that the federal government had to rely on state courts to enforce federal laws—hardly a reliable option with hostile local institutions. Accordingly, Attorney General Rodney wanted to make an example of Hoxie by bringing the only effective criminal charge available. Otherwise, he wrote to Jefferson, "a system of evasion will defeat & prevent the good effects, expected to flow" from the embargo.[52]

Jefferson, however, had misgivings. "If all these people are convicted," he wrote Gallatin, "there will be too many to be punished with death."[53] The embargo was unpopular enough, especially in Federalist territory.[54] To try opponents of the embargo for treason risked alienating the populace and losing the electorate.[55] Jefferson was in a tight spot. On the one hand, treason was the only effective criminal sanction to those determined to defy federal authority.[56] On the other, treason was such a powerful tool that it could work to erode federal authority. The main legal device to enforce federal laws was both too aggressive and too ineffectual.

[50] Amos Marsh, quoted in Shattuck, *Insurrection*, 234.

[51] Carl Cummings and Homer McFarland, *Federal Justice: Chapters in the History of Justice and the Federal Executive* (New York: Macmillan, 1937), 68; Hurst, *Treason*, 198; An Act to regulate the Collection of the Duties by law on the tonnage of ships or vessels, and on goods, wares and merchandises imported into the United States, 1 Stat. 44 (July 31, 1789); see also Shattuck, *Insurrection*, 248, 251.

[52] Augustus Rodney to Jefferson, April 22, 1808, Founders Online.

[53] Jefferson to Gallatin, September 9, 1808, Founders Online.

[54] See Andrew Wender Cohen, *Contraband: Smuggling and the Birth of the American Century* (New York: Norton, 2015), 28.

[55] See "A Republican" to Jefferson, March 22, 1808, Founders Online ("[O]ur friends are fast falling off & the Federalists gaining ground upon us in every direction and our prospects ar [sic] really most unpromising. so [sic] severely is the effects of the embago [sic] felt that no arguments are sufficient to retain our weaker Brethren.").

[56] Smith, "Patterns of Northern New England Smuggling," 37 (smuggling was widely accepted and treated as a civil offense and not as a criminal offense until the late nineteenth century).

President Washington had faced a similar predicament during the Whiskey Rebellion that erupted in western Pennsylvania after his administration levied a tax on domestic liquors in an effort to repay the federal government's assumed debts from the American Revolution—an important component of Alexander Hamilton's financial program.[57] The new taxes especially burdened small farmers along the Monongahela River, who regarded whiskey as "an indispensable necessity to life, healthy, and happiness," according to an early historian.[58] They sold whiskey, they bartered with whiskey, they drank whiskey the way Europeans drank beer or wine. Farmers responded to the federal incursion on their way of life by reviving "the doctrines of the Declaration of Independence."[59] They raised their own flag, built mock guillotines, and established their own courts.[60] The invocation of revolutionary principles roused 7,000 armed men to march onto Pittsburgh, provoking Washington to send 13,000 militiamen to quash the rebellion. Afterwards, two participants were found guilty of treason, but the juries accompanied their verdicts with a petition that the president show mercy, describing the defendants as simpletons who did not play significant roles in the uprising.[61] Similar petitions arrived from throughout the country. These were fairly easy cases for clemency. But Washington went further and extended a blanket pardon to everyone who had been involved if they agreed to submit to the authority of the United States.[62] Some historians have argued that the rebellion's defeat demonstrated the new federal government's strength.[63] But from a law-enforcement perspective, the national government remained weak and unable to collect its taxes.

Indeed, the next president, John Adams, confronted the very same issue during Fries's Rebellion, another tax revolt that arose after Congress for the first time levied a direct tax on land, houses, and slaves to pay for the national defense amid growing hostilities with France.[64] Like Washington, Adams had just a few options at his disposal. And like his predecessor, Adams sent the military and brought treason charges. He also pardoned the three men convicted of treason, contrary to his cabinet's unanimous advice and notwithstanding his own condemnation of the rebellion.[65] "What good, what example," he later queried, "would have been exhibited to the nation by

[57] Leland D. Baldwin, *Whiskey Rebels: The Story of a Frontier Uprising* (Pittsburgh: University of Pittsburgh Press, 1968), 56; William Hogeland, "Spirits Distilled within the United States," chap. 3 in *The Whiskey Rebellion: George Washington, Alexander Hamilton, and the Frontier Rebels Who Challenged America's Newfound Sovereignty* (New York: Scribner, 2006).

[58] Baldwin, *Whiskey Rebels*, 10, 27–28; see also United States v. Insurgents of Pennsylvania, 26 F. Cas. 499, 500 (C.C.D. Pa. 1795) (No. 15,443) ("Not only were whisky and rum articles of commerce and of consumption, but from the natural deficiency of specie in a wild country they also were used universally as currency.").

[59] Baldwin, *Whiskey Rebels*, 13.

[60] Wood, *Empire of Liberty*, 137.

[61] Carlton F.W. Larson, *The Trials of Allegiance: Treason, Juries, and the American Revolution* (New York: Oxford University Press, 2019), 239–40.

[62] George Washington, Proclamation of Pardons in Western Pennsylvania, July 10, 1795.

[63] See Wood, *Empire of Liberty*, 138.

[64] Case of Fries, 9 F. Cas. 924 (C.C.D. Pa. 1800) (No. 5,127).

[65] Larson, *Trials of Allegiance*, 248 (on cabinet's advice); Hurst, *Law of Treason*, 269 (on Adams's abhorrence).

the execution of three or four obscure, miserable Germans, as ignorant of our language as they were of our laws, and the nature and definition of treason?"[66]

But Fries was not so ignorant as Adams claimed. He was a veteran of the Revolutionary War who fought on the side of tax protesters; he had also marched with Washington to put down tax protesters during the Whiskey Rebellion.[67] Now, as leader of a group of tax protesters, Fries argued that unconstitutional taxes justified their actions. He had heard this argument before and knew that it could ultimately lead to secession, an oft-bandied idea in the back country during the post-Revolutionary period.[68] Fries posed a threat to the still-young republic, and—to answer Adams's question of "what good, what example" would result—punishing him would have shown the entire nation that the laws must be respected.

Punishment, however, could also stoke the wrong feelings. Both Washington and Adams backed down and granted pardons after defeating those who flirted with the subversion of government. If recent experience with England provided additional perspective, it was that charging treason to enforce tax laws actually reflected an inability to accomplish imperial, or national, goals. Jefferson undoubtedly learned from history, for he attenuated his desire to punish the Vermont smugglers. "[M]y hope," he explained, was "that the most guilty may be marked as examples, & the less so suffer long imprisonment under reprieves from time to time."[69]

The government, however, faced an uphill task. As Professor Carlton Larson has pointed out, the U.S. Constitution's requirement of two witnesses to the same overt act and prohibition of out-of-court confessions made treason prosecutions significantly harder than under the British common law.[70] Practically, it was difficult to find two people who would cooperate and appear in court. Grand juries frequently declined to return indictments, and petit juries often acquitted defendants. For example, after the Whiskey Rebellion, the attorney general sought indictments against thirty-six individuals. The grand jury issued indictments against twenty-four; eleven defendants were never found; three successfully argued that they were entitled to amnesty under Washington's proclamation, leaving only ten defendants who were tried. Eight were acquitted. Only two—out of the thousands who took up arms—were convicted.[71] The results after Fries's Rebellion were likewise dismal. The grand jury returned nine indictments, but the prosecutor then declined to bring some of the cases, and a few defendants absconded, leaving only five to face trial. The jury acquitted two and convicted three.[72]

Charging Hoxie with treason was a risky enforcement strategy. The case was difficult to prove and difficult to win and, even if successful, it would have been difficult to go forward with the death sentence. But charging treason was the only way to send an unequivocal message that the United States government meant business when it

[66] Adams to James Lloyd, March 31, 1815, in *The Works of John Adams, Second President of the United States*, ed. Charles Francis Adams (Boston: Little, Brown, 1856), 10:153.
[67] Larson, *Trials of Allegiance*, 243.
[68] Wood, *Empire of Liberty*, 134–135.
[69] Jefferson to Gallatin, September 9, 1808, Founders Online.
[70] Larson, *Trials of Allegiance*, 231, 239.
[71] Ibid., 236, 239.
[72] Ibid., 246–247.

imposed a trade restriction. Unfortunately, Justice Livingston took that option off the table.

## III. *United States v. Hoxie* (1808)

Henry Brockholst Livingston received a recess appointment to the U.S. Supreme Court from President Jefferson in November 1806 and was renominated for a permanent position a month later.[73] Jefferson, in an effort to break Chief Justice John Marshall's Federalist stronghold on the high court, sought to appoint loyal Democratic-Republicans and believed he had found one in the patrician New Yorker who had supported him in the 1800 presidential election.[74] Livingston, friend of both Alexander Hamilton and Aaron Burr, had once been private secretary to John Jay, his sister's husband. But a personal dislike of his brother-in-law had turned into a political repudiation.

Jefferson should have examined Livingston's judicial record more closely. As a state judge, Livingston had repeatedly held customs officials personally liable for wrongful seizures and, in fact, had done so the very year he was appointed to the Supreme Court.[75] Politically he may have chosen to ally with Republicans, but his sympathies still lay with the merchant class. Predictably, Livingston soon disappointed Jefferson. As circuit justice of the Second Circuit, Livingston presided over *United States v. Hoxie* and admitted to the jury that it was "impossible, to suppress the astonishment which is excited at the attempt which has been made to convince a court and jury of this high criminal jurisdiction, that, between [the defendant's conduct] and levying war, there is no difference."[76]

Notwithstanding Livingston's certainty that Hoxie did not commit treason, the definition of treason was in flux during the age of revolutions.[77] American colonists had described their rebellion not as treason but as resistance to tyranny, then turned around and accused crown officials and loyalists of treason not against the king but against liberty itself. What, exactly, was the difference between political opposition, justified protest, unlawful rebellion, and treason if they all shared the goal of attacking those in power?[78] What constituted treason during civil war had to be hammered out, and what would constitute treason against the newly formed United States had to be decided.[79] Recalling how King George had tried to use treason charges to oppress

[73] "History of the Federal Judiciary: Judges," Federal Judicial Center, accessed July 20, 2022, https://www.fjc.gov/history/judges/livingston-henry-brockholst.

[74] Henry J. Abraham, "President Jefferson's Three Appointments to the Supreme Court of the United States: 1804, 1807, and 1807," *Journal of Supreme Court History* 31 (July 2006): 141, 147, 150–151.

[75] Rao, *National Duties*, 153.

[76] Hoxie, 26 F. Cas. at 399.

[77] Larson, *Trials of Allegiance*, 3–4, 31–34, 37–40; Robert A. Ferguson, *Reading the Early Republic* (Cambridge: Harvard University Press, 2004), 120 ("Nothing conveys the utter fluidity in Revolutionary American Culture more dramatically than the concept of treason.").

[78] These questions swirled in the 1790s with the emergence of Democratic-Republican Societies that challenged the political establishment and maintained that "the people had a continual right to organize and protest." Wood, *Empire of Liberty*, 163.

[79] See Larson, *Trials of Allegiance*, especially chapters 6–8.

them—and how the newly independent states had pursued treason charges against friends and family who assisted the British during the Revolution—those who gathered at the Constitutional Convention defined treason narrowly: "Treason against the United States, shall consist only in levying War against them, or in adhering to their Enemies, giving them Aid and Comfort."[80] By defining treason in the Constitution, the framers prevented all three branches of government from expanding its scope beyond the two instances of levying war against the United States and of giving aid to its enemies. These limitations reflected a concern, based on experience, that accusations of treason could be wielded as "an instrument of competition for political power," as Willard Hurst put it.[81]

Although the drafters sought to distinguish ordinary political struggles from treasonous conduct, it was more difficult to clarify the difference between rioting and high treason when both involved the use of force against government officials. Shortly after the ratification of the Constitution, James Wilson—to whom some scholars have given credit for the Treason Clause—remarked that the "line of division" between levying war and "an aggravated riot is sometimes very fine and difficult to be distinguished."[82] Twenty years of case law only somewhat clarified matters. Livingston surveyed all the treason trials that had taken place in the United States, including the recently tried case against Aaron Burr.[83] His jury charge, however, focused on a series of cases that came out of the Whiskey Rebellion and Fries's Rebellion in which the defendants were found guilty of treason by levying war against the United States. "If you look at the insurrections in 1794, and in 1799," Livingston's charge instructed, "you will be struck with the great difference between the cases which arose out of those occurrences, and the one on which you are now to decide."[84]

The cases of *United States v. Mitchell* and *United States v. Vigol* that Livingston cited were part of the Whiskey Rebellion, when rebel farmers assaulted and, in a symbolic gesture, tarred and feathered excisemen, looted their homes, and threatened their families to force their resignation. In July 1794, between four hundred and eight hundred men burned down the home of an excise collector, resulting in several deaths. Then in August came the march to Pittsburgh. The attorney general declared that the insurrection was "a well formed and regular plan for weakening and perhaps overthrowing the General Government."[85]

The third case that Livingston consulted, the *Fries* case, came out of the 1799 tax uprising during President Adams's administration, which followed the modus operandi of previous tax revolts: threats, harassments, and assaults to coerce tax assessors into resigning. After some protesters were arrested, nearly four hundred armed men, led by John Fries, demanded the release of the prisoners.[86]

80 U.S. Constitution, art. III, § 3, cl. 1.

81 Hurst, *Law of Treason*, 165–166; see also Hurst, *Law of Treason*, 141–143.

82 James Wilson, "Of Crimes, Immediately Against the Community" (lecture, College of Philadelphia, 1790–1791), in *The Works of the Honourable James Wilson*, ed. Bird Wilson (Philadelphia: Lorenzo, 1804), 3:104. See Larson, *Trials of Allegiance*, 231; Hurst, *Law of Treason*, 135, 142.

83 See Ex parte Bollman, 8 U.S. (4 Cranch) 75 (1807).

84 Hoxie, 26 F. Cas. at 400.

85 William Bradford quoted in Wood, *Empire of Liberty*, 137; see generally Baldwin, *Whiskey Rebels*; Larson, *Trials of Allegiance*, 235–236.

86 Larson, 243.

According to Livingston, there was "hardly a feature of resemblance" between what previous traitors had done and what Hoxie had done, that is, "forcing some lumber from the possession of a collector."[87] But, in truth, Hoxie had done more than that. He and the other men fired about a hundred shots at federal troops. Although no one was injured or killed, many bullets had struck the trees on the shore where the soldiers were standing, which suggested that the shots were "intended for execution," as the district attorney had alleged.[88] The differences between the cases were in scale, not in kind. The earlier episodes implicated more participants and resulted in more damage and injury to persons and property. Still, Hoxie and his men used deadly force against federal officers in order to obstruct the law, just as Mitchell, Vigol, and Fries had done.

The crucial distinction for Livingston lay not in the acts themselves, but in what we would today refer to as mens rea. Livingston identified the "essential ingredient" of treason as the "quo animo," that is, the intent "to prevent the execution of an act of congress, by force and intimidation."[89] Quoting *Vigol*, Livingston pointed out that treasonous acts were committed with the purpose to "suppress the office of excise," to "compel the resignation of the officer," and to "render null and void in effect an act of congress." These were objects "of a general nature and of national concern," as *Mitchell* explained. The *Fries* case phrased this principle conversely, that "the assembling bodies of men, armed and arrayed in warlike manner, for purposes only of a private nature, is not treason." Livingston maintained that, unlike prior defendants, Hoxie was a hireling. Although he was armed and acted in a warlike manner, Hoxie obstructed the embargo laws "for the single object of personal emolument."[90] The distinction that Livingston drew thus depended on public versus private motivations.

But determining whether the object of a mob's violence was public or private wasn't always clear cut. In the *Fries* case, the defense had argued that because the object was to rescue only certain prisoners, the rebellion was "not of a general nature."[91] Justice Chase had rejected the argument. Chase's broader view of Fries's intent could arguably apply to Hoxie as well. He was not merely rescuing a certain raft of lumber, but, more broadly, he was opposing "a great national and Constitutional object," as one senator declared when denouncing the "unprincipled Americans" engaging "in this scandalous traffic."[92] Prosecutors introduced evidence that Hoxie had undertaken several smuggling ventures and "had occasionally talked about fighting his way through," belying Livingston's claim that Hoxie had opposed the law "only in this instance, and for his own private emolument."[93] In all likelihood, Hoxie had taken part in the plot with a dual intent: he both detested the embargo and sought profit.

Livingston granted that it "may not be very easy ... to fix the exact boundary between treason and some other offenses, which partake, more or less, of an opposition to government."[94] But "if every opposition to law be treason," he reasoned, then "who

87 Hoxie, 26 F. Cas. at 400.
88 Ibid., 396.
89 Ibid., 401.
90 Ibid., 400.
91 Fries, 9 F. Cas. at 887.
92 19 Annals of Cong. 275–276 (1808) (Senator William B. Giles).
93 Hoxie, 26 F. Cas. at 396, 402.
94 Ibid., 400.

can say how many of them will in time become ranged under the class of treason."[95] There simply had to be a difference between treasonous and nontreasonous protest, and for Livingston, neither the mere violation of law nor the use of force, nor the two together, could be a sufficient factor to prevent treason prosecutions from becoming "as common as indictments for petit larcenies, assaults and batteries, or other misdemeanors." Certainly, it was difficult to state the principle for determining when the intent motivating the act was sufficiently universal or general, but Livingston was sure that Hoxie never believed that he had a war on his hands.

And so, Livingston advised the jury that "the proofs on trial have fallen very far short" of demonstrating treason.[96] He concluded his charge around eleven o'clock at night, and the jury quickly returned a verdict of acquittal.[97] The next morning, the court dismissed the treason charges against Hoxie's two sons. When the government brought a new indictment against the Hoxies for violating the embargo, they fled to Michigan.

## IV. Conspiracy as Enforcement Strategy

The Jefferson administration promptly lobbied Congress for stricter enforcement provisions. In a letter to Democratic-Republican senator William Giles from Virginia, Treasury Secretary Gallatin bemoaned that "every degree of opposition to the laws which falls short of treason is now, with but few exceptions, an offense undefined and unprovided for by the laws of the United States; whence it follows that such offenses remain unpunished."[98] Helpfully, Gallatin made a few suggestions to remedy this situation, such as additional forfeitures, which, he explained, was "the most efficient penalty." Gallatin was even more direct and aggressive about his legislative wishes in a private letter to Jefferson. "Congress must either invest the Executive with the most arbitrary powers and sufficient force to carry the embargo into effect, or give it up altogether," he wrote.[99] Gallatin spoke from personal experience. During the Whiskey Rebellion, he had represented the rebels in negotiations with the government.[100] But not everyone would agree to submit to federal laws in exchange for amnesty and, in the end, Washington had to muster federal troops to quell the rebellion. Having lived this history, Gallatin meant it when he urged Jefferson that a "sufficient force" was necessary "to carry the embargo into effect." Gallatin toned it down in his letter to Senator Giles, writing politely and passively, "It is with regret that the necessity of authorizing ... an immediate call for the local physical force of the country must also be stated."[101]

95 Ibid., 402.
96 Ibid., 403.
97 Shattuck, *Insurrection*, 259–260.
98 Gallatin to William B. Giles, November 24, 1808, in Adams, *Writings of Albert Gallatin*, 432.
99 Gallatin to Jefferson, July 29, 1808, in Adams, *Writings of Albert Gallatin*, 399.
100 Hogeland, *Whiskey Rebellion*, 122–123.
101 Gallatin to Giles, November 24, 1808, in Adams, *Writings of Albert Gallatin*, 431.

Congress responded to the Administration's entreaties by enacting "An Act to enforce and make more effectual [the embargo] act" in January 1809.[102] It included new forfeitures accompanied by expanded search-and-seizure provisions. Congress also authorized the president to employ forces or the militia "for the purpose of preventing and suppressing any armed or riotous assemblage of persons, resisting the custom-house officers in the exercise of their duties, or in any manner opposing the execution of the laws laying an embargo, or otherwise violating, or assisting and abetting violations of the same."[103] Previously, the president could not call troops during domestic strife without first issuing a proclamation ordering insurgents to disperse.[104] Although this procedural requirement was not too onerous[105] (notwithstanding Gallatin's complaint about the "circuitous manner" of calling for the public force[106]), it had a counterproductive effect: calling protesters insurgents made them even more belligerent, as Jefferson learned during the Vermont affair.[107] Now, under the 1809 Act, the president no longer needed to take the potentially inflammatory step before taking action.

Alas, the enforcement measures that Gallatin sought, and received, weren't enough. For one thing, forfeitures, which may have been "the most efficient penalty" for contraband in shipping vessels, unfortunately provided no solution to embargo violations "along our land frontier."[108] As Gallatin explained, the offense of smuggling "is not consummated till after the property has actually been carried beyond the lines, where, being in a foreign jurisdiction, it cannot be seized, so that forfeiture ... can never apply to exportations by land." The Van Dusens of the world remained untouchable. They well knew that they faced little meaningful sanction and acted accordingly. As a result, Gallatin concluded, "[T]he only remedy is the uncertain one of recovering penalties against apparent offenders, who either abscond" (like Hoxie) "or have no property," which was no remedy at all. More fundamentally, the necessity of military action amounted to an admission that the government had no good options. By the time the president had to call the militia, the problem was no longer simply about law enforcement; the government was dealing with rebellion or civil war.

In his letter to Senator Giles, Gallatin wondered "how far it may be practicable to make the act of preparing the means of exportation punishable" so that the government could take action before smugglers successfully thwarted its national policies.[109] But Gallatin wasn't certain how such proactive, preventative measures could be achieved, for Congress had rejected a law that would have criminalized preparatory acts back in April—just a little over a month after it had decided to extend the embargo

102 An Act to enforce and make more effectual an act intituled [*sic*] "An act laying an embargo on all ships and vessels in the ports and harbors of the United States," and the several acts supplementary thereto, 2 Stat. 506 (January 9, 1809).

103 2 Stat. 506, at 510 (Section 11). See also Wood, *Empire of Liberty*, 656; Jerry L. Mashaw, "Reluctant Nationalists: Federal Administration and Administrative Law in the Republican Era," *Yale Law Journal* 116. 8 (June 2007): 1666–1667.

104 Act to provide for calling forth the militia to execute the laws of the Union, suppress insurrections, and repel invasions and to repeal the act now in force for those purposes, 1 Stat. 424 (February 28, 1795).

105 Vladeck, "Militia Acts," 162–63.

106 Gallatin to Giles, November 24, 1808, in Adams, *Writings of Albert Gallatin*, 431.

107 See Dumas Malone, *Jefferson the President: Second Term, 1805–1809. Jefferson and His Time* (Boston: Little, Brown, 1974), 5:587.

108 Gallatin to Giles, November 24, 1808, 431–432.

109 Ibid., 432.

to the overland trade with Canada.[110] Senator Giles, along with Representative John Randolph, also from Virginia, had worked on a bill to punish "conspiracy to commit treason against the United States" with a fine of up to five-thousand dollars and a sentence between two to ten years.[111] As Randolph justified the proposal, "the public peace may be disturbed and the public safety endangered, by the previous preparations for such an event," that is, treason.[112] Because the essence of conspiracy is an agreement to commit a crime—which is a separate offense, and separately punished, from the crime itself—an individual need not have committed the crime or have attempted it. It's the act of agreeing that's criminalized. Punishing both the target offense and the unlawful agreement to commit that offense may seem redundant. But it authorized the government to prosecute someone like Van Dusen, who had orchestrated the operation without getting his hands dirty. The government could also initiate prosecution as soon as there was an unlawful agreement. That is, a conspiracy law would have allowed a fledgling state with a minimal enforcement apparatus to pursue action before the offending deed took place, or even before resentment against the law became unmanageable and turned into an insurrection.

But there were several limitations and concerns with Giles and Randolph's bill. First, it prohibited treasonous conspiracies, not smuggling conspiracies. It would have still been difficult to prove mens rea, or intent, to commit the target offense of treason, especially after Livingston's jury charge in *Hoxie*. Second, opponents of the bill argued that a treasonous conspiracy law was an end run around the Treason Clause.[113] Congress simply could not change, or add to, the Constitution's definition of treason—especially after the Supreme Court had just ruled that a conspiracy to commit treason without an accompanying overt act (namely, levying war or aiding the enemy) could not be punished as treason.[114] It was an open, and controversial, question whether Congress could prohibit treason-like conduct so long as it did not call it treason.

Notwithstanding the Senate's strident and long-winded debate, it passed the conspiracy bill, 18 to 10.[115] Meanwhile, the House appears not to have discussed the bill at all, but postponed its consideration "indefinitely," and there it died.[116] There is one likely guess as to why. Memories of the notorious 1798 Sedition Act were very fresh.[117] During the "Quasi-War" with France—waged by embargoing trade and abrogating all treaties—President Adams's pro-British party, in control of Congress, had passed the Act and used it to prosecute pro-French, Republican journalists and editors for seditious libel. Less known, the Act also prohibited conspiracies to oppose or impede U.S. policies, including, especially, its foreign policies. Federalists had acted out of a

110 18 Annals of Cong. 2279 (1808).

111 S. 10, 10th Cong. (1808).

112 18 Annals of Cong. 1717–1718 (1808).

113 See, e.g., 17 Annals of Cong. 109 (1808) (Senator Samuel Mitchell).

114 See Ex Parte Bollman and Ex Parte Swartwout, 8 U.S. (4 Cranch) 75 (1807); Catherine M. Tarrant, "To 'insure domestic Tranquility': Congress and the Law of Seditious Conspiracy, 1859–1861," *American Journal of Legal History* 14.2 (April 1971): 110–11.

115 17 Annals of Cong. 207 (1808).

116 18 Annals of Cong. 2279 (1808).

117 An Act for the Punishment of Certain Crimes Against the United States (Sedition Act), 1 Stat. 112 (July 14, 1798).

deep fear of a Jacobin conspiracy to infiltrate American politics and destroy American society. But the tyrannically factional exercise of power so sullied them that they never recovered after they lost the presidency and both houses of Congress in what Thomas Jefferson called the "revolution of 1800."[118] For the Democratic-Republicans in power in 1808, the treasonous conspiracy bill probably seemed like the reincarnation of the 1798 seditious conspiracy law.

With Congress having just rejected the preventative measures that would have helped to enforce the embargo, Gallatin wasn't sure what options were left and so asked Senator Giles to submit the issue "to the committee" to figure out.[119] The committee never did.

The lack of an enforcement mechanism that was nonviolent yet forceful, coercive but legitimate, and inexpensive but still effective, proved fatal to federal policies and nearly to government itself. Congress ended the embargo on Jefferson's last day in office.[120] Years later at Monticello, Jefferson recalled how he had "felt the foundations of the government shaken under my feet" during the embargo fiasco.[121] Jeffersonian Republicans had hoped to show the world that war, the scourge of monarchies, could be avoided. The failure of economic sanctions spelled the failure of republican diplomacy, and the United States declared war on Great Britain in 1812.[122]

## V. The Limitations of Seditious Conspiracy

The notoriety of the 1798 Sedition Act tainted conspiracy laws. Congress did not enact such a law again throughout the antebellum period, even as allegations of seditious activity abounded.[123] In 1851, when a Pennsylvanian Quaker by the name of Castner Hanway refused to help a slave owner execute an arrest warrant under the Fugitive Slave Act, a riot ensued that ended with the slave owner's death. Without a conspiracy law, and with a maximum sentence of just six months under the Fugitive Slave Act, the government resorted to charging Hanway with treason.[124] But the presiding judge, Supreme Court Justice Robert Grier (who, six years later, would vote with the majority in the *Dred Scott* case), instructed the jury that "the resistance of the execution of a law of the United States accompanied with any degree of force, if for a private purpose, is not treason"—citing *United States v. Hoxie*.[125] It took the jury only ten minutes to return a verdict of not guilty.[126]

[118] Wood, *Empire of Liberty*, 239–277.

[119] Gallatin to Giles, November 24, 1808, 432.

[120] See Wood, *Empire of Liberty*, 293, 657–658.

[121] Jefferson to Joseph C. Cabell, February 2, 1816, Founders Online.

[122] See Wood, *Empire of Liberty*, 630–633, 643, 662; Rao, *National Duties*, 156. See also Andreas, "Traitorous Traders and Patriotic Pirates," chap. 5 in *Smuggler Nation*; Stuart D. Brandes, *Warhogs: A History of War Profits in America* (Lexington: University of Kentucky Press, 1997), 56–57.

[123] See Joshua T. Carback, "Charging Riots and Insurrections at the Seat of Government," *American Journal of Criminal Law* 49.1 (2021): 20–21.

[124] Section 7 of the Fugitive Slave Act, 9 Stat. 462, 464 (1850).

[125] United States v. Hanway, 26 F. Cas. 105 (C.C.E.D. Pa. 1851) (No. 15,299).

[126] Andrew Delbanco, *The War before the War: Fugitive Slaves and the Struggle for America's Soul from the Revolution to the Civil War* (New York: Penguin, 2018), 289–92.

Then, in 1859, John Brown attempted a slave revolt at Harpers Ferry. In the tense aftermath, Democratic Senator Stephen A. Douglas set aside the fraught lessons of history and proposed a seditious conspiracy law, expressing the same concerns that had compelled the Federalists to pass the Sedition Act: "I have no hesitation in expressing my firm and deliberate conviction that the Harpers Ferry crime was the natural, logical, inevitable result of the doctrines and teachings of the Republican party, as explained and enforced in their platform, their partisan presses, their pamphlets and books, and especially in the speeches of their leaders in and out of Congress."[127] In Douglas's mind, abolition talk led directly to slave rebellion, and he sought to nip the former to prevent the latter. Congress "must punish the conspiracy," Douglas maintained; "then," he explained, "you will suppress it in advance."

Notwithstanding the terror and turmoil that the Harpers Ferry raid had unleashed, Congress didn't take up Douglas's bill. Jefferson Davis, then a senator, doubted whether the federal government could ensure domestic peace within the states.[128] Others feared that hyperpartisan uses of criminal law could backfire. A Republican senator warned that "there may be a time when the Federal action that you are now invoking for the protection of slavery" may be "employed for freedom as well as for slavery."[129] It "will be a dangerous precedent to set," he cautioned.[130]

It took the ultimate rebellion, civil war, to overcome constitutional and political scruples. In 1861, Congress, without its Southern section, passed "An Act to define and punish certain Conspiracies," which punished "two or more persons" if they

> shall conspire together to overthrow, or to put down, or to destroy by force, the Government of the United States, or to levy war against the United States, or to oppose by force the authority of the Government of the United States; or by force to prevent, hinder, or delay the execution of any law of the United States; or by force to seize, take, possess any property of the United States against the will or contrary to the authority of the United States; or by force, or intimidation, or threat to prevent any person from accepting or holding any office, or trust, or place of confidence, under the United States.[131]

Tellingly, the word "sedition" was left out of the text. So was the word "treason." The 1861 Act was, at its heart, a seditious, or treasonous, conspiracy law. Some congressmen saw right through it, repeating arguments made before that the law was a circumvention of the Constitution's strict requirements for a treason conviction. The Treason Clause, they maintained, was intended "to restrict the power of Congress in the creation of a political crime kindred to treason."[132] In response, Senator Lyman Trumbull argued that the law simply sought "to punish persons who conspire together to commit offenses against the United States not analogous to treason."[133] Both

127 Cong. Globe, 36th Cong., 1st Sess. 553 (1860) (Stephen A. Douglas).
128 Tarrant, "To 'insure,'" 115.
129 Cong. Globe, 36th Cong., 1st Sess. 8 (1859) (John Parker Hale).
130 Ibid., 9.
131 12 Stat. 284 (1861).
132 Protest of the minority of the Senate of the United States against the passage of the House bill No. 45, entitled "An act to define and punish certain conspiracies," Cong. Globe, 37th Cong., 1st Sess. 276–277.
133 Cong. Globe, 37th Cong., 1st Sess. 277 (Lyman Trumbull).

sides could point to some part of the text for support. Conspiracies to "overthrow" or to "levy war" against the government sounded in treason, while punishing conspiracies "to prevent, hinder, or delay the execution of any law" seemed more like an enforcement measure.

In wartime, the value of a seditious conspiracy law seemed obvious, and the law easily passed. Nevertheless, there was evidence of unease. According to one scholar, not a single indictment under the 1861 Act resulted in a conviction during the Civil War.[134] Another indication of misgivings comes after the war, during congressional debates about a bill to enforce the Fourteenth Amendment against Ku Klux Klan efforts to deprive black citizens of their life, liberty, and property. It ultimately passed as the Enforcement Act of 1871 (also known as the Civil Rights Act or the Ku Klux Klan Act) and is today known for creating a private cause of action against state actors who violate federal rights, the foundation of modern civil rights legislation. The Act also contained a conspiracy provision—the first third of which was practically identical to the 1861 conspiracy law—which received heavy criticism. Opponents of the 1871 Act, like opponents of the 1861 Act, expressed concerns that conspiracy prosecutions would be used for "political warfare" and pointedly brought up Senator Douglas's efforts to pass a seditious conspiracy law to uphold slavery.[135]

Supporters responded to the argument with legal precedent and experience. First, the 1861 law already punished conspiracies to violate U.S. laws, and the 1871 Act was no different.[136] Moreover, as the Republican senator from Nevada maintained, "If the power to preserve this Union, to suppress rebellion, to suppress Ku Klux organizations ... is not in the Constitution, we have no Government [and] secession is a fixed fact."[137] In other words, without a conspiracy law, the result would be another civil war. Ultimately, the provision survived and became Section 2 of the Enforcement Act.[138]

In 1883, however, the Supreme Court struck down Section 2, concluding that Congress had exceeded its authority to legislate under the Fourteenth Amendment, which applied only to state actions and not to private individuals.[139] The 1861 conspiracy law, by contrast, is still on the law books today, but rarely used.[140] As scholars have recently explained, "To label something sedition goes beyond normal criminality, suggesting that the conduct strikes at the heart of American democracy and falls within the same conceptual category as the most serious political crimes, such as rebellion, insurrection, and treason."[141]

[134] Tarrant, "To 'insure,'" 119–122.

[135] Cong. Globe, 42nd Cong., 1st Sess. 688 (1871) (Carl Schurz).

[136] When Congressman John F. Farnsworth voiced concerns about the constitutionality of Section 2, his colleague Samuel Shellabarger interrupted to point out that "he and I were both in Congress when [the 1861 conspiracy law] passed" and that "I think the gentleman voted" for that law. Cong. Globe, 42nd Cong., 1st Sess., app. 113 (1871).

[137] Cong. Globe, 42nd Cong., 1st Sess. 830 (1871) (Senator Stewart).

[138] See, e.g., Cong. Globe, 42d Cong., 1st Sess. 686–688 (1871) (Senator Carl Schurz).

[139] United States v. Harris, 106 U.S. 629 (1883).

[140] See 18 U.S.C. § 2384.

[141] Scott R. Anderson et al., "Seditious Conspiracy: What to Make of the Latest Oath Keepers Indictment," *Lawfare*, January 14, 2022, https://www.lawfareblog.com/seditious-conspiracy-what-make-latest-oath-keepers-indictment.

## VI. General Conspiracy and the American State

The American Civil War also marked a watershed in the structure of the U.S. fiscal state, which, in turn, transformed federal criminal law. To be sure, extending and protecting the civil rights of the formerly enslaved required new and enlarged federal criminal bureaucracies, like the Department of Justice.[142] But the most significant cause of change in criminal law came not from civil rights enforcement but from tax enforcement.

The Union's financial needs in 1861, the first year of war, was six times the previous year's budget and only grew as fighting continued.[143] At one point, expenses reached $2.5 million per day.[144] To pay for war, the government needed to borrow unfathomable sums. When interest in U.S. notes waned, Congress made their acceptance mandatory (these "greenbacks" were the precursor to contemporary paper bills, which have no intrinsic value other than the full faith and credit of the U.S. government).[145] Borrowing and printing money, however, would have been impossible without an income stream to bolster credit, and so the government imposed new taxes for the first time since the War of 1812.

The 1862 Revenue Act was "the longest and most detailed statute the country had ever seen," according to financial journalist Roger Lowenstein.[146] It also instituted the nation's first federal income tax.[147] In two years, internal revenue surpassed duties on foreign trade and raised a record $110 million.[148] But as war dragged on, Congress raised taxes again in 1864, seeking to double the nation's tax receipts.[149] By the time Confederate general Robert E. Lee surrendered at Appomattox in 1865, Union debt amounted to $2.68 billion, forty-one times as much as at the start of hostilities.[150] The American public did not like taxes any more than it did before war, but the government needed more revenue. To reconcile these two conflicting imperatives, Congress reduced income tax rates in the 1867 Revenue Act such that 90% of all revenue came from taxes on whiskey and tobacco.[151]

The decision to target whiskey and tobacco can be explained. Both were considered luxury goods, and as the House Ways and Means Committee chairman reasoned

[142] Act to Establish the Department of Justice, 16 Stat. 162 (1870); see Jed Handelsman Shugerman, "The Creation of the Department of Justice: Professionalization without Civil Rights or Civil Service," *Stanford Law Review* 66.1 (2014).

[143] Roger Lowenstein, *Ways and Means: Lincoln and His Cabinet and the Financing of the Civil War* (New York: Penguin, 2022), 50.

[144] Ibid., 262.

[145] Ibid., 90.

[146] Ibid., 128.

[147] Technically, the 1861 Revenue Act included the first income tax, but it was never implemented. See Lowenstein, *Ways and Means*, 126; "Historical Highlights of the IRS," IRS, last modified November 2, 2021, https://www.irs.gov/newsroom/historical-highlights-of-the-irs.

[148] Lowenstein, *Ways and Means*, 262, 286.

[149] Ibid., 286.

[150] Ibid., 314.

[151] An Act to Amend Existing Laws relating to Internal Revenue and for other Purposes, 14 Stat. 471 (March 2, 1867); Lowenstein, *Ways and Means*, 328; Romain Huret, "The Contested State: Revenue Agents, Resistance, and Popular Consent in the United States from the Early Republic to the End of the Nineteenth Century," *The Tocqueville Review/La revue Tocqueville* 33.2 (2012): 101; IRS, "Historical Highlights of the IRS."

in 1866, "[A]ll civilized nations requiring large revenues" sought to "squeeze out of those articles considered as luxuries by mankind."[152] The United States, he concluded, "should doubtless conform to that of the world." The temperance movement also helped to keep whiskey taxes in place. And not coincidentally on the heels of Union victory, taxing whiskey and tobacco disproportionately burdened the former Confederate states.[153] Certainly, both were produced and sold throughout the country. But taxing the production of goods affected small-time farmers and producers more than large manufacturers, and the former were concentrated in the South.

But there the similarities ended between whiskey and tobacco taxes; enforcement was altogether a different matter. The government negotiated its authority with tobacconists, while it dealt punitively with distillers.[154] A simple explanation for the differential treatment has to do with class and politics. The tobacco industry was dominated by established manufacturers, many of whom were prominent citizens. They were critical of federal tax policy not because they had to pay taxes—they accepted that luxuries would be taxed—but because rampant tax evasion resulted in an inequitable revenue system.[155] In other words, a government without an effective enforcement mechanism made fools out of those who paid their taxes. So tobacco manufacturers organized and formed trade associations, which lobbied Congress to revise the 1867 Revenue Act. As one industry leader declared, "We are the taxpayers of tobacco and must be protected."[156] The subsequent 1868 Revenue Act implemented a licensing system, which not only facilitated the payment of tobacco taxes but also protected manufacturers from competition and kept prices of raw leaf tobacco low. To their delight, the new system worked as intended. Federal regulations allowed large manufacturers to control the nation's supply of tobacco and to extract record profits. In turn, the federal government saw its tobacco receipts increase. Between 1868 and 1869 (a comparison that captures the difference between the 1867 and 1868 revenue laws), tobacco taxes jumped from $18.7 to $23.4 million.[157] A year later, that number jumped again to $31.3 million. By the early 1880s, the *U.S. Tobacco Journal* declared that tobacco tax frauds had become nonexistent.[158] Regardless of the verity of that observation, the fact that it was made is indicative of the cozy relationship between the Bureau of Internal Revenue and the tobacco industry. In fact, a leading New York cigar manufacturer later became a revenue collector who embarked on raids against "moonshine" distillers.[159]

That the federal government—whose agents included a tobacconist—relied on searches and seizures to collect whiskey taxes shows how differently it treated distillers. Unlike the tobacco industry where manufacture was completed in factories owned by businessmen, farmers could make their own alcohol. Actually, many preferred to

152 Cong. Globe, 39th Cong., 1st Sess. 2436 (1866) (Justin Morrill).

153 Lowenstein, *Ways and Means*, 258 (temperance), 328 (disproportionate burden).

154 The phrase "negotiated authority" comes from Gautham Rao's *National Duties*.

155 Patrick Mulford O'Connor, "Tobacco Politics and the Reconstruction of American Governance, 1862–1933" (PhD diss., University of Montana, 2019).

156 Ibid., "Tobacco Politics," 54.

157 Commissioner of Internal Revenue, *Annual Report: Fiscal Year Ended June 30, 1900* (1900), https://www.irs.gov/pub/irs-soi/1900dbfullar.pdf, 387.

158 O'Connor, "Tobacco Politics," 79.

159 Ibid., 71–72.

do it themselves because they could carry a lot more corn or fruit in liquid (or, er, liquor) form, liquor was not perishable, and it fetched more profit. Small-time distillers didn't form national associations whose leaders wined and dined Washington bureaucrats. Their relationship with the federal government was not a cooperative one.[160]

Those from the mountain regions of the former Confederacy were particularly hostile to federal authority and, as an extension, to federal taxes. To them, whiskey taxes not only curtailed what they deemed an economic necessity (rather than a luxury); taxes on their "traditional mountain dew" also undermined what they viewed as an inalienable right that they had long enjoyed—grievances that echoed the protests of the Vermont embargo evaders, insurrectionists during the Whiskey Rebellion and Fries's Rebellion, and, before them, America's founding fathers.[161] In 1870, a Raleigh, North Carolina, publication directly compared the liquor tax to the hated taxes of the British empire.[162]

Their grievances also mirrored the objections of slaveowners and secessionists. In fact, during the Civil War, many mountain distillers had embraced the confederate cause and, after the war, opposed Reconstruction and aligned with the Ku Klux Klan.[163] Moonshiners and Klansmen intimidated and attacked revenue collectors, who were often also tasked with enforcing civil rights laws.[164] Revenuers reported that they dared not attempt to collect taxes for fear of being "Ku-kluxed."[165] Although the federal government had emerged from the Civil War with a muscular taxing power, it had not yet developed a comparably muscular enforcement mechanism.

Rather than negotiating its authority as it had successfully with tobacco manufacturers, the government instead turned to criminal prosecutions—but not with treason charges that had to be tempered with pardons. As part of the 1867 Revenue Act, Congress included a provision, in Section 30, that criminalized conspiracies to defraud or violate the laws of the United States.[166] It set punishment at a fine of $1,000 to $10,000 and a sentence of not more than two years—much less than the

160 See Bruce E. Stewart, "Distillers and Prohibitionists: Social Conflict and the Rise of Anti-Alcohol Reform in Appalachian North Carolina, 1790–1908" (PhD diss., University of Georgia, 2007); Huret, "The Contested State."

161 See Gordon B. McKinney, "Moonshiners, Law Enforcement, and Violence: Legitimacy and Community in Western North Carolina, 1862–1882" (unpublished manuscript, November 1995, on file with author), 4; Wilbur R. Miller, "The Right to Make a Little Licker: Moonshiner Resistance to Federal Authority," chap. 3 in *Revenuers & Moonshiners: Enforcing Federal Liquor Law in the Mountain South, 1865–1900* (Chapel Hill: University of North Carolina Press, 1991).

162 Stewart, "Distilleries and Prohibitionists," 143.

163 Ibid., 149–154; Huret, "The Contested State"; Miller, *Revenuers & Moonshiners*, 43–44, 53–54; see also Allen W. Trelease, *White Terror: The Ku Klux Klan Conspiracy and Southern Resistance* (New York: Harper & Row, 1971).

164 During the 1871 debate on a bill to enforce the Fourteenth Amendment and eliminate the Ku Klux Klan, Senator William Morris Stewart mentioned the murder of revenue officers as a reason for the bill. Cong. Globe, 42d Cong., 1st Sess. 830 (1871); see also Stewart, "Distilleries and Prohibitionists," 122; McKinney, "Moonshiners," 9.

165 J. B. Eaves to Pinkney Rollins, April 20, 1871, quoted in Stewart, "Distilleries and Prohibitionists," 151.

166 An Act to Amend Existing Laws relating to Internal Revenue, and for other Purposes, 14 Stat. 471, at 484 (March 2, 1867). In 1866, Congress passed a law specifically punishing government inspectors who conspired with distillers "to defraud the United States of the revenue or tax arising from distilled spirits." 14 Stat. 159 (July 13, 1866). But this provision was overshadowed by Section 30 of the 1867 Revenue Act. Abraham S. Goldstein, "Conspiracy to Defraud the United States," *Yale Law Journal* 68.3 (1959): 418.

punishment for treason, but more serious than the penalty for embargo violations or tax evasion. Not only did Section 30 set forth real consequences for violations, but it also authorized the government to go after individuals simply for agreeing to violate the Revenue Act.

The reception of Section 30 was completely different from the 1798 Sedition Act, the 1861 conspiracy law, and the 1871 Enforcement Act. For one thing, Section 30 appears to have been uncontroversial. According to one scholar, there were no hearings or debate, and no reports, on Section 30 (in contrast to the 300-page report on internal revenue frauds).[167] Moreover, the Supreme Court did not just uphold the 1867 conspiracy provision; it ruled that Section 30 applied to all federal laws, even though the historical and statutory contexts suggested that Section 30 was intended to address the nonpayment of taxes.[168] While many conspiracy cases in the late nineteenth century involved tax prosecutions, they also included a conspiracy to steal money from the national bank and even a conspiracy to commit voting fraud.[169] In the 1898 West's *Digest* of federal cases, 16 of the 33 reported conspiracy cases involved taxes (of those 16, 13 involved whiskey taxes). Section 30, which arose from the need to enforce the revenue laws, thus became the federal government's first general conspiracy statute, the predecessor to the contemporary "catch-all" conspiracy law found in 18 U.S.C. § 371.[170]

That the first two conspiracy laws enacted right after the Civil War were intended to enforce whiskey taxes and the rights of Black citizens makes sense given that Southern malefactors tended to violate both. But legislators clearly did not view the Revenue Act's conspiracy provision as a partisan measure, in part because it didn't target politicians or newspaper editors and in part because resistance to whiskey taxes didn't seem to pose a serious threat of renewed civil war. To be sure, farmers and distillers could have political impact when acting in concert. This was Justice Livingston's dilemma when trying to distinguish between public and private intent, between treasonous and nontreasonous opposition. A resolution to the dilemma appeared by 1867, in the Revenue Act: distinguish prosecutions for treasonous conspiracies, which would be rare and hard to prove, from prosecutions for general conspiracies, which would be used as an enforcement mechanism. If *Hoxie* had come up at the end of the nineteenth century rather than at the beginning, the defendant would have been charged not with treason or conspiracy to commit treason, but with smuggling and conspiracy to evade the embargo.

[167] Goldstein, "Conspiracy to Defraud the United States," 418; Cong. Globe, 39th Cong., 2d Sess. 1920 (1867); *Report of the Select Committee on Internal Revenue Frauds to the House of Representatives*, 39th Cong., 2d Sess. (Washington: Government Printing Office, 1867).

[168] United States v. Hirsch, 100 U.S. 33 (1879).

[169] United States v. Martin, 4 Cliff. 156, 26 F. Cas. 1175 (C.C.D. Mass. 1870) (No. 15,728) (conspiracy to steal money from national bank); United States v. Wrape, 4 Cin. Law. Bul. 433, 28 F. Cas. 780 (C.C.D. Ind. 1879) (No. 16,767) (voting fraud).

[170] Section 30 became section 5440 of the Revised Statutes, which then became section 37 of the 1909 Crimes Act, 35 Stat. 1096 (March 4, 1909), which in 1934 became 18 U.S.C. § 88, which in 1948 became 18 U.S.C. § 371. See also Goldstein, "Conspiracy to Defraud the United States," 418–419; Congressional Research Service, "Federal Conspiracy Law: A Brief Overview" (April 3, 2020), https://fas.org/sgp/crs/misc/R41223.pdf, 4.

Of course, the government would still have had to prove that an unlawful agreement existed, which can be difficult. It's much easier to show that a tax was unpaid or that a raft was taken to Canada than it is to prove that two or more people had agreed to evade the revenue laws or the embargo. After all, "conspiracies are usually entered into in secret," as a nineteenth-century judge explained to a jury, and conspirators typically don't put their agreement in writing.[171] The utility of conspiracy laws would have been limited without sufficient investigatory agencies, which Americans on the whole loathed.[172] And they certainly did not want to be taxed to pay for such a bureaucracy.

Cognizant of the reasons for federal conspiracy liability, judges relaxed the government's evidentiary burden. Even as the state was growing in other areas, increasingly easy conspiracy prosecutions substituted for larger prosecutorial forces. For example, in the 1875 case *United States v. Ulrici*—another case listed in West's *Digest*—Justice Samuel Miller, sitting as circuit justice, explained that "the collection of the internal revenue tax in this country has required a system of legislation for its enforcement harsh beyond everything known to our history."[173] And still, he deplored, "the government is cheated out of perhaps one-half of its revenue, especially that from the tax on whisky and tobacco." After pointing out the futility of the enforcement system, he concluded that Congress may punish, as a felony, the failure to efface excise stamps on whiskey casks—so as to prevent their reuse without payment of taxes—without requiring criminal intent.

Miller's observations and decision in *Ulrici* highlighted a turning point in the development of the American state. To collect taxes or, more generally, to enforce its laws, the president could not always use military force against wayward citizens, at least not without diminishing the people's trust in government. Nor could the government rely on treason charges that had to be softened with pardons, especially after *Hoxie* narrowed the definition of "levying war." So the criminal laws provided an alternative to violence, a legal tool between treason and pardons. Those laws, in turn, were bolstered with conspiracy laws. Judicial decisions then made conspiracies much easier to prosecute than the target crime itself, helping to create a "system of legislation . . . harsh beyond everything known to our history," as Justice Miller described in *Ulrici*. So easy had conspiracy prosecutions become that just two generations later, in 1925, the Conference of Senior Circuit Judges reported that "the rules of evidence in conspiracy cases make them most difficult to try without prejudice to an innocent defendant."[174]

The argument that criminal law—specifically, conspiracy laws—compensated for relatively, and historically, small and underfunded government bureaucracies may seem at odds with much recent scholarship that has depicted "active and significant political institutions" from the beginning of the early republic.[175] In the past two

171 United States v. Wrape, 4 Cin. Law. Bul. 433, 28 F. Cas. 780.

172 Daniel Richman and Sarah A. Seo, "How Federalism Built the FBI, Sustained Local Police, and Left Out the States," *Stanford Journal of Civil Rights & Civil Liberties* 17 (Special Issue 2022).

173 United States v. Ulrici, 3 Dill. 532, 28 F. Cas. 328, 331 (C.C.W.D. Mo. 1875) (No. 16,594).

174 Attorney General of the United States, *Annual Report* (1925), 6.

175 Gautham Rao, "The New Historiography of the Early Federal Government: Institutions, Contexts, and the Imperial State," *William and Mary Quarterly* 77.1 (January 2020): 101.

decades, historians have corrected the "myth of the 'weak' American State," pointing to a flurry of federal activities, from postal services to land sales and western expansion.[176] But they have also been perplexed by a state "that seemed contradictorily strong and weak," and the historian Gautham Rao has called for more studies investigating "how federal governance worked in action."[177] To see government *in action*, we must look beyond laws that were enacted, policies declared, or even agencies created. We must look at how bureaucrats and officials actually collected revenue, regulated finance, supplied the military, and more. By doing so, we may find the weak/strong state dichotomy unhelpful in understanding the challenges of implementation. A "strong" state could prohibit trade with the two largest empires in the world but still be without sufficient manpower to nip the illicit traffic. More important than whether this ultimately belies a weak state is how, exactly, understaffed agencies tried to execute federal laws. Understanding criminal law as a state-building tool can illuminate how the U.S. government functioned with as minimal a bureaucratic apparatus as possible, which in turn explains the breathtakingly broad conspiracy liability in the United States.

The history of Frederick Hoxie's treason case in 1808 all the way through its appearance as a conspiracy case in West's 1898 *Digest* encourages this view of criminal laws. One way to understand conspiracy laws is to see how the law made up for an inadequately resourced American state. Another way to understand conspiracy laws is to see how the criminal laws laid the foundation of American governance in the modern era.

[176] William J. Novak, "The Myth of the 'Weak' American State," *American Historical Review* 113.3 (June 2008); Rao, "New Historiography," 101–102, 116; see also Richard R. John, *Spreading the News: The American Postal System from Franklin to Morse* (Cambridge: Harvard University Press, 1995).

[177] Rao, "New Historiography," 100, 117.

# PART II
# LAW, SPACE, AND PLACE IN HISTORY

# 6
# The Case as Episode
## Murder and Migration in Colonial Australia

*Catherine L. Evans*

In 1985, Dirk Hartog asked legal historians to consider the pig. His account of early nineteenth-century New York, and the ruder, rawer, smellier city that pigs and their keepers inhabited, challenged scholars to broaden their understanding of law. Over the past thirty years, historians of the United States have infused accounts of doctrine and procedure with the earthy details of everyday life. Scholars have used the tools of social and microhistory to frame legal cases as what Hartog called "episodes" of contact and conflict between competing normative orders.[1] Outside the United States, legal historians have been less eager to embrace the analytic potential of the metaphorical pig.[2] And yet, as I hope to show through a case tried in rural Australia in the 1870s, Hartog's perspective is built to travel. An approach that develops arguments about the nature of law and legal consciousness from social histories of superficially unremarkable cases is particularly well-suited to excavating the multiple meanings of law in colonial spaces.

When the case I consider here—*R v. Quin* (1871)—was tried in the colony of Victoria, Britons had been in Australia for less than a century. Victoria's bustling capital, Melbourne, had been founded only 36 years earlier, but was already a center of global finance, industry, and agriculture.[3] Victorian courts heard cases that dramatized the volatile relationships among new immigrant groups, more established British settlers, and Aboriginal Australians, which had been reconfigured by the discovery of gold deposits in 1851. The close study of individual cases reveals the dynamics among these communities as they navigated differences of class, race, and religion during a period of demographic and economic change.

In "Pigs and Positivism," Hartog began with *People v. Harriet* (1819): a misdemeanor case against a determined pig-keeper, Christian Harriet, orchestrated by a determinedly antipig New York City mayor, Cadwallader Colden. From that case, Hartog built a world—a vision of a metropolis on the brink of economic, social, and cultural transformation, in which the practice of fattening pigs on city streets represented the claims that rural, agricultural life still made on urban spaces and people. Hartog's reading of *People v. Harriet* showed how the legality of pig-keeping was

[1] Hendrik Hartog, "Pigs and Positivism," *Wis. L. Rev.* (1985): 899.

[2] Although social historians have long grasped the importance of literal pigs in rural and urban life. See, e.g., Jamie Kreiner, "Pigs in the Flesh and Fisc: An Early Medieval Ecology," *Past & Present* 236.1 (2017): 3–42; Bettina Bradbury, "Pigs, Cows, and Boarders: Non-Wage Forms of Survival among Montreal Families, 1861–91," *Labour/Le Travail* 14 (1984): 9–46.

[3] Asa Briggs, *Victorian Cities* (Berkeley, CA: University of California Press, 1993), 278.

Catherine L. Evans, *The Case as Episode* In: *In Between and Across.* Edited by: Kenneth W. Mack and Jacob Katz Cogan, Oxford University Press. © Oxford University Press 2024. DOI: 10.1093/oso/9780197680995.003.0007

a matter of perspective, at least until an outbreak of cholera in 1849 shifted public opinion radically against the urban pig. Histories in this vein therefore promise two things: the ability to capture the texture and complexity of everyday social life at a particular place and time; and the suggestion of an often-elusive plural legal order, in which questions of jurisdiction and authority were perpetually negotiated.

Like Hartog's early nineteenth-century New Yorkers, Victorians also had competing visions of modernity and social life that they brought with them to court. In the years after the south-east Australian gold rush, colonial authorities were preoccupied with the management of immigrant populations, especially the Chinese migrants and settlers who had arrived in large numbers in the 1850s and 1860s. As Victoria became a premier destination for migrants from across the world, from China to British India and Ireland, the Protestant Britons who had composed the first wave of European colonists questioned whether the colony would remain "British" or become something new. Law became a testing ground for colonial identity, where officials and the public debated the limits of liberalism and legal subjecthood. Unlike in Hartog's study, the core issue in *Quin* was not *what* was legal, but *who* was fit to participate in legal institutions, and to what degree. The formal exclusion of Chinese Australians from the protections of colonial criminal justice would have undermined the colony's liberal claims that its courts, like metropolitan British courts, took no cognizance of race. However, the integration of non-Britons into Australian criminal justice risked, some thought, compromising the integrity of British criminal law principles. Many Britons in the empire believed that the common law was vulnerable to plural legal understandings, even in the absence of formal challenges to established legal rules.

Hartog's approach is particularly germane to the history of law in the British Empire, including colonial Australia, because of its ability to unearth both individual experiences and the nuances of plural normative orders. The vastness of the empire often makes it difficult to say anything big without losing sight of everything small. The problem of scale at the heart of imperial histories is also present in the new wave of transnational, "hemispheric," "terraqueous," global, and oceanic histories.[4] As scholars explore the artificiality and permeability of national borders, they show movement and interconnection where others once saw fixity and isolation. But as the stories historians tell stretch across the globe, they can become attenuated—too thin for the kind of thick description that revealed the unruly hogs of New York. Scholars of the British Empire have worked to solve the problem of scale by following individuals and families in their travels around the world and by tracing imperial networks.[5]

[4] See, for example: David Armitage and Alison Bashford, eds., *Pacific Histories: Ocean, Land, People* (Basingstoke: Palgrave Macmillan, 2014); Sunil S. Amrith, *Crossing the Bay of Bengal* (Cambridge: Harvard University Press, 2013); David Armitage and Sanjay Subrahmanyam, eds., *The Age of Revolutions in Global Context, c. 1760–1840* (Basingstoke: Palgrave Macmillan, 2010); Alison Bashford, "Terraqueous Histories," *The Historical Journal* 60 (June 2017): 253–72; Bernard Bailyn, "The Idea of Atlantic History," *Itinerario* 20.1, (March 1996): 19–44; J. G. A. Pocock, "The New British History in Atlantic Perspective: An Antipodean Commentary," *The American Historical Review* 104.2 (1999): 490–500; Clare Anderson, *Subaltern Lives: Biographies of Colonialism in the Indian Ocean World, 1790–1920* (Cambridge: Cambridge University Press, 2012).

[5] For histories of families and networks in the British world, see David Lambert and Alan Lester, eds., *Colonial Lives across the British Empire: Imperial Careering in the Long Nineteenth Century* (Cambridge; New York: Cambridge University Press, 2006); Linda Colley, *The Ordeal of Elizabeth Marsh: A Woman in World History* (New York: Pantheon, 2007); Emma Rothschild, *The Inner Life of*

Accounts of the legal lives of communities of migrants, minorities, and seafaring merchants, among others, have enriched our understandings of law, subjecthood, and governance in colonial and international contexts.[6] But historians need not pursue their subjects across oceans or continents in order to discern the dynamism and complexity of nineteenth-century colonial societies. In a world marked by migration and colonization, even the most ordinary interactions engaged webs of personal, economic, and political connections that linked distant people and places. In this sense, every case is amenable to transnational analysis; the only question is how far to trace the threads that drew people, objects, and ideas to the courtroom. As Hartog showed in his study of New York, cases contain the world that generates them. Any legal conflict can be described as an "episode"'—a moment where normative orders, epistemologies, and borders of belonging are tested.[7] In the British Empire, then, the thick description of a single case can reveal how migration and movement inflected law and the form legal pluralism took during a period of demographic, economic, and political volatility. An embrace of the case as "episode" dares us to seek the meaning of law, including global and imperial legalities, in even the humblest case and the humblest court, from New York City to the Australian countryside.

Between 1850 and 1875, the demography and economy of Victoria had shifted. Migrants from across the British world poured into the colony in search of gold. The population grew from 97,000 in 1850 to more than a million by 1875.[8] Chinese and Irish migrants were two of the largest immigrant groups. From the mid-1850s to the end of the colonial period, 60,000–80,000 Chinese migrants arrived in the Australian colonies.[9] Mae Ngai estimates that there were 2,000 Chinese persons in the colony in

*Empires: An Eighteenth-Century History* (Princeton: Princeton University Press, 2011); Zoë Laidlaw, *Colonial Connections, 1815–45: Patronage, the Information Revolution, and Colonial Government* (Manchester: Manchester University Press, 2005); Miles Ogborn, *Global Lives: Britain and the World, 1550–1800* (Cambridge: Cambridge University Press, 2008); Felix Driver, *Geography Militant: Cultures of Exploration and Empire* (Oxford, Malden, MA.: Blackwell, 2000).

[6] See, e.g., Mitra Sharafi, *Law and Identity in Colonial South Asia: Parsi Legal Culture, 1772–1947* (Cambridge: Cambridge University Press, 2014); Fahad Ahmad Bishara, *A Sea of Debt* (Cambridge: Cambridge University Press, 2017); Julia Stephens, "An Uncertain Inheritance: The Imperial Travels of Legal Migrants, from British India to Ottoman Iraq," *Law and History Review* 32.4 (2014): 749–72; Renisa Mawani, *Across Oceans of Law: The Komagata Maru and Jurisdiction in the Time of Empire* (Durham: Duke University Press, 2018); Renisa Mawani and Iza Hussin, "The Travels of Law: Indian Ocean Itineraries," *Law and History Review* 32.4 (2014): 733–47.

[7] Barbara Young Welke, *Law and the Borders of Belonging in the Long Nineteenth Century United States* (Cambridge: Cambridge University Press, 2010).

[8] Briggs, *Victorian Cities*, 278.

[9] Alister Bowen, "The Merchants: Chinese Social Organisation in Colonial Australia," *Australian Historical Studies* 42, no. 1 (2008): 25. On the history of the Chinese in nineteenth-century Australia, see, for example: Kathryn Cronin, *Colonial Casualties: Chinese in Early Victoria* (Melbourne: Melbourne University Press, 1982); Mae M. Ngai, "Chinese Gold Miners and the 'Chinese Question' in Nineteenth-Century California and Victoria," *Journal of American History* 101, no. 4 (2015): 1082–105; Iain McCalman, Alexander Cook, and Andrew Reeves, *Gold: Forgotten Histories and Lost Objects of Australia* (Cambridge: Cambridge University Press, 2001); Keir Reeves and Tseen Khoo, "Dragon Tails: Re-Interpreting Chinese Australian History," *Australian Historical Studies* 42, no. 1 (2011): 4–9; Keir Reeves and Benjamin Mountford, "Court Records and Cultural Landscapes: Rethinking the Chinese Gold Seekers in Central Victoria," *Provenance: The Journal of Public Record Office Victoria*, no. 6 (2007); Mae M. Ngai, *The Chinese Question: The Gold Rushes and Global Politics* (New York: W. W. Norton, 2021).

1854 and 42,000 by 1859—20% of the adult male population of Victoria in that year.[10] When the rush was at its peak, there may have been as many as 50,000 Chinese immigrants in Victoria alone.[11] By 1861, there were more than 38,000 Chinese immigrants in the Australian colonies, mostly in and around the goldfields of Victoria, New South Wales, and Queensland. Many of these travelers were men who left their wives and children in the southern Chinese provinces of Fujian and Guangdong (Canton) to work on the goldfields.[12] However, a diminishing gold supply and an excess of claims meant that few could make a living entirely by digging gold just ten years after its initial discovery.[13] In the 1870s, the Chinese Australian population was in steady decline. One Australian statistician wrote that there were 17,935 Chinese people in Victoria in 1871, almost 30% fewer than had lived in the colony in 1861. He estimated that 36 were women.[14] By 1901, a series of restrictive immigration acts had reduced the Chinese population to just under 30,000—only 0.8% of the total.[15]

Large numbers of Irish immigrants also travelled to colonial Australia in the nineteenth century, first as transported convicts, then as subsidized migrants dispatched to increase free settler numbers, and eventually as fortune-seekers drawn by the mid-century gold rushes. Most settled in the eastern colonies of Victoria and New South Wales. While fewer Irish immigrants struck out for the Australian colonies than for the United States or Britain, they made up a larger share of the total settler population. At the time of Australian federation in 1901, approximately a quarter of white Australians were Irish born or descended.[16] Some Irish migrants were middle-class professionals, including a substantial population of lawyers chasing economic opportunity and political influence, but most were single men and women from rural areas. Young, unmarried women formed the majority of late nineteenth-century Irish emigrants, especially from the western counties.[17] Most migrants to Australia were Catholic and sought work and fellowship in farm communities and country towns.[18] The poverty and social dislocation many had fled in the wake of Ireland's Great Famine (1845–52) continued in the Antipodes. Elizabeth Malcolm notes that according to the 1891 census Victoria had both the highest proportion of Irish-born

[10] Mae M. Ngai, "Chinese Miners, Headmen, and Protectors on the Victorian Goldfields, 1853–1863," *Australian Historical Studies* 42.1 (2011): 11.

[11] Warwick Frost, "Migrants and Technological Transfer: Chinese Farming in Australia, 1850–1920," *Australian Economic History Review* 42.2 (July 1, 2002): 117.

[12] Ann Curthoys, "'Men of All Nations, Except China': Europeans and Chinese on the Goldfields of New South Wales," in *Gold: Forgotten Histories and Lost Objects of Australia*, eds. Iain McCalman, Alexander Cook, and Andrew Reeves (Cambridge: Cambridge University Press, 2001), 104.

[13] Brian Fitzpatrick, "The Big Man's Frontier and Australian Farming," *Agricultural History* 21.1 (1947): 9.

[14] Henry Heylyn Hayter, *Notes on the Colony of Victoria: Historical, Geographical, Meteorological, and Statistical* (Melbourne: George Skinner, Acting Government Printer, 1876), 58.

[15] Elizabeth Malcolm and Dianne Hall, *A New History of the Irish in Australia* (Cork: Cork University Press, 2019), 76.

[16] Elizabeth Malcolm, "Searching for the Irish and Irish Studies in Australia," *Estudios Irlandeses* 14 (March 2019): 207.

[17] Oonagh Walsh, "Gender and Insanity in Nineteenth-Century Ireland," in *Sex and Seclusion, Class and Custody: Perspectives on Gender and Class in the History of British and Irish Psychiatry*, by Jonathan Andrews and Anne Digby (Amsterdam, New York: Rodopi, 2004), 72.

[18] Malcolm, "Searching for the Irish and Irish Studies in Australia," 208.

immigrants in Australia, 38%, and the highest rate of committals to psychiatric institutions.[19]

These changes in colonial demographics meant that in the 1870s, Irish and Chinese immigrants were likely to cross paths in the rural settlements of colonial Victoria. With the exhaustion of the alluvial gold deposits, both groups sought new work and new places in agricultural communities and country towns, as well as in Melbourne. One historian describes the "clamor of a hundred thousand ex-miners for farm land" in the 1860s, as they competed with pastoralists who raised sheep for the lucrative wool trade on huge homesteads expropriated from Aboriginal communities.[20] Instead of small farmers, many former miners and new immigrants became wage laborers.[21] Others turned to petty trading or cultivated market gardens, a form of intensive, small-scale agriculture where gardeners grew vegetables, fruit, and herbs for commercial sale, often also keeping livestock or fowl—including pigs—as ready sources of fertilizer.[22]

In 1871, an Irish wage laborer attacked two Chinese entrepreneurs in the Ovens River basin, an agricultural region north of Melbourne. One of the victims was a market gardener and the other, like New Yorker Christian Harriet, was in the pig business. That August, Ah Woo and Ah Cow were on the road from Bright to Beechworth in the verdant Australian Alps.[23] Ah Woo, the gardener, owned the spring cart that he and his friend, the pig-dealer Ah Cow, were riding in that Sunday afternoon. The pair met two more Chinese pig-dealers driving a herd of pigs down the road. Minutes later, they encountered a white man, described in the press as a "European," who importuned them for a ride. They protested that the horse was too tired, but the man climbed in anyway, settling on a bag of chaff.[24] Suddenly, the stranger slashed the travelers with a tomahawk and beat them with their own whip, leaving Ah Woo to drown in an aqueduct, his empty pockets turned out. Ah Cow, also robbed and "terribly maimed," managed to wave his hat at the Chinese pig-dealers further down the road, who sent for the police in nearby Myrtleford.[25]

By late that night, news of the murder had reached the police. Newspapers reported that Alexander Brook Smith, the inspector assigned to the case, had leapt onto his

[19] Elizabeth Malcolm, "Irish Immigrants in a Colonial Asylum during the Australian Gold Rushes, 1848–1869," in *Asylums, Mental Health Care and the Irish: 1800–2010*, ed. Pauline M. Prior (Newbridge: Irish Academic Press, 2017).

[20] Fitzpatrick, "The Big Man's Frontier and Australian Farming," 11.

[21] Fitzpatrick, "The Big Man's Frontier," 12.; On market gardening, see also: Joanna Boileau, *Chinese Market Gardening in Australia and New Zealand: Gardens of Prosperity* (Cham, Switzerland: Springer, 2017).

[22] Boileau, *Chinese Market Gardening in Australia and New Zealand*, 2.

[23] Cantonese migrants generally gave only their personal names, and not their surnames, when interacting with Europeans in Australia. Moreover, those who had only one character in their personal name in Cantonese tended to add the sound "ah" to the beginning for aesthetic reasons. Many Chinese Australians therefore became known to Europeans, including colonial record keepers, as "Ah (name)", as Ah Cow and Ah Woo were. See: "Chinese Names in English," *Chinese Australian Historical Society*, https://chineseaustralianhistory.org/chinese-names/, accessed 3 October 2018.

[24] "The Myrtleford Murder: The Inquest," *Ovens and Murray Advertiser*, August 31, 1871, 3.; Judge's Notes of Evidence, Public Record Office of Victoria (PROV), VPRS 264, P0000, Unit 7, James Quinn, Capital Case File (1871).

[25] "The Myrtleford Murder," from the *Ovens Advertiser*, reprinted in the *Sydney Mail and New South Wales Advertiser*, September 9, 1871, 883.

horse and raced to the crime scene, while other members of the force fanned out across the region.[26] Smith rode through the night, arriving at 3 a.m. the next morning.[27] Police soon arrested James Quin (or Quinn), a stout, bearded, white man of about 30 who had left remote Tasmania for the hills of Victoria some months before. His wife worked as a servant in the town of Bright, where Quin visited her regularly between short-term engagements as a farm hand and millworker.[28] Newspaper reports and accounts of the inquest and trial that followed Quin's arrest emphasized his shabbiness, lingering on his frayed coat and filthy moleskin trousers. After his arrest, he said that he had drunk gin with a man named "Jack" on the night Ah Woo died, and that he had lost his horse and spent the night in the bush. Despite his efforts, Quin never found "Jack." He had no alibi.[29]

When Quin attacked Ah Woo and Ah Cow, there were over 100,000 Irish-born settlers in Victoria out of a total population of 729,014.[30] Clashes between Irish and Chinese miners were relatively common on the crowded goldfields of the 1850s and 1860s, as they jostled for resources and defended their claims. Irish Catholics, who also faced racial stigma in Protestant settler society, aligned themselves with "white Australia" policies, proclaiming their solidarity with white, Anglophone interests against an imagined Chinese threat in order to improve their social and political status.[31] The Irish antipathy to Chinese immigrants was widespread. It persisted into the twentieth century and crossed class lines among Irish Australians, uniting working-class miners with wealthy landowners and politicians.[32] By the end of the nineteenth century, the terms of white identity in Australia began to shift. Old divides between Catholic Irish and Protestant English and Scottish populations receded in favor of hardening lines between "white," "European" Australians and others, including Chinese, Indian, Pacific Islander, and Aboriginal Australians.[33]

While Quin was a relative stranger to Victoria, many recognized Ah Woo's "fine spring cart" and his light grey horse from his regular trips up and down the main road. A clutch of farmers' wives testified at Quin's trial that they knew the victims, if not their names, and could identify them even from over a hundred yards away.[34] The *Ovens Advertiser*, a local newspaper that reported extensively on the crime and its aftermath, described the men as "most respectable and well-to-do."[35] The papers made much of their wealth. At the inquest, Ah Cow testified that he had £40 tucked into his white calico sash when he was attacked.[36] Another witnessed averred that Ah Woo had £5/6 hidden under his own sash, suggesting both his relative wealth and the thief's lack of familiarity with Chinese customs, as he had only thought to turn out his victim's pockets.[37]

26 Ibid.
27 "The Myrtleford Murder," *Ovens And Murray Advertiser Supplement*, October 17, 1871, 1.
28 Ibid.
29 Judge's Notes of Evidence, James Quinn Capital Case File.
30 Hayter, *Notes on the Colony of Victoria*, 61.
31 Malcolm and Hall, *A New History of the Irish in Australia*, 77–78.
32 Ibid., 96.
33 Ibid., 100.
34 "The Myrtleford Murder," October 17, 1871.
35 "The Myrtleford Murder," September 9, 1871, 883.
36 "The Myrtleford Murder: The Inquest," August 31, 1871, 3.
37 Judge's Notes of Evidence, James Quinn Capital Case File.

As the investigation and trial proceeded, a detailed timeline of the killing emerged. On the afternoon of 27 August, the two Chinese victims had stopped at a shop run by Ah Shang, a local businessman and cook. They unharnessed their horse and fetched its feed from the cart just as James Quin arrived, on foot. Ah Shang and Mary Jane Cullen, who had also pulled over at the cookshop, recalled that Quin wanted to buy a new pipe, but that neither Ah Shang nor Ah Woo had one to sell. Five minutes later, Quin left the shop and continued down the road toward Bright.[38] The pig-dealers Kee Yet and Ming Ting later testified that they met Quin along the same road, followed closely by the victims. Kee Yet and Ming Ting encountered four white children on their way home from church, who agreed to climb a nearby hill to drive some wayward piglets back toward the herd. The children followed the little pigs along a raised bank. When they heard screaming, one boy, Thomas Cole, walked around a bend. In his testimony at Quin's trial, Ah Cow explained what Cole saw. Once Quin had climbed into the cart, he slashed at both men with "something like iron," knocking both off their seats. Somehow, Ah Woo fell or was dragged into the road, where Quin grabbed him by the hair and continued his assault. Quin yelled to Ah Cow to run for Kee Yet if he was able. As he went, Ah Cow turned to see Quin holding his friend by his braid. Ah Cow, giddy and covered with blood, raised the alarm. He said that he had been "stuck up by bushrangers and wounded with a tomahawk on the head." The blood-spattered cart was missing its seat, and bags were strewn about the road. One man tied the gray horse to a tree. Within an hour, Kee Yet found Ah Woo's body wedged under a log in the water of the aqueduct, coincidentally known as "Quinn's Race."[39]

The race, an aqueduct or wooden channel, in which Ah Woo drowned was one of many in the Murray-Darling basin, constructed to funnel water from the rivers to the goldfields.[40] Beechworth, the major settlement in the region, was approximately 275 kilometers northeast of Melbourne, deep inland. It is likely that Chinese laborers had built Quinn's Race. Most laborers traveled under the credit-ticket system, in which they borrowed money for their voyage to Australia from brokers in China in exchange for the proceeds of their first year's work.[41] On arrival in Australia, groups of between thirty and one hundred migrants, often from the same town or belonging to the same extended family, lived and worked together under the supervision of a headman or other comparatively wealthy Chinese leader.[42]

Not all Chinese migrants came to Australia to dig for gold.[43] Communities developed their own supply and merchant networks, building self-sufficient settlements where they worked as gardeners, grocers, traders, financiers, businessmen, spiritual leaders and, of course, gold diggers.[44] In the years after the rush abated, many settled

[38] Ibid.

[39] Redmond Barry to Governor of Victoria, 30 October 1871, James Quinn Capital Case File.; Judge's Notes of Evidence, James Quinn Capital Case File.

[40] Emily O'Gorman, *Flood Country: An Environmental History of the Murray-Darling Basin* (Collingwood: Csiro Publishing, 2012), 67.

[41] Bowen, "The Merchants: Chinese Social Organisation in Colonial Australia," 31.

[42] Curthoys, "'Men of All Nations, Except China,'" 105.

[43] Bowen, "The Merchants" 31.

[44] Bowen, "The Merchants," 32.

in the rural districts near the mines, especially near Beechworth, which had a thriving Chinatown, expanding their market gardening businesses or turning their skills to larger-scale commercial farming.[45] Chinese growers drew on their experiences planting and irrigating the arid land of Canton and developed new techniques that helped them prosper.[46] One commentator writing in 1888 credited the newcomers with revolutionizing agriculture in the drought-prone Australian colonies. In Victoria, he wrote, the Chinese had "hired barren wastes and sterile sands, and, by means of a system of irrigation . . .raised far better crops than the English farmers near them on the best of soil."[47] Ah Woo, a market gardener with a fine cart full of vegetables and ducks, and Ah Cow, an enterprising pig-dealer, were members of an established community of successful Chinese settlers, as were the other Chinese men they met on the road to Myrtleford. Their Anglo-Australian neighbors were also their customers. The testimony of the white farmers called as witnesses in Quin's trial, as well as the English-language newspaper coverage of the crime and its aftermath, reflected British Victorians' fascination with the victims' enviable wealth and entrepreneurial skill.

James Quin, in contrast to his victims, had little for Beechworth's farm wives to admire. Like Ah Woo and Ah Cow, he was an immigrant. He had made the eighty-day crossing to Launceston, Tasmania in 1855 from Liverpool aboard the *Montmorency* with his parents, a brother, and three sisters.[48] The ship brought 349 immigrants for the colony, of whom 44 were Irish.[49] The family had settled in Hobart Town, where they opened a lodging house for sailors. Quin had soon started work on a riverboat, and eventually saved enough money to buy his own cutter, which he christened *Wanderer*.[50] He worked for eight or nine years as a boatman in and around Hobart in the "river trade," ferrying goods and people along the Derwent River.[51] After the end of transportation to Tasmania in 1853, liberal land laws induced farmers to settle in the colony's outlying districts. But without adequate infrastructure, including roads and railways to bring goods to port, their crops rotted under the shade cast by, as one observer wrote, a "roadless forest" where "the rich vegetable mould was ever moist, and the tracks impassable."[52] The late 1860s brought some improvements, but the colony continued to struggle. Tasmanian agriculture had been frustrated by blight, other British colonies' protectionist tariffs, and a flood of oats and potatoes from New Zealand and South Australia. Although the discovery of tin deposits in 1871 would

[45] Frost, "Migrants," 118.

[46] Frost, "Migrants," 123.

[47] S. W. Silver & Co, *S.W. Silver & Co.'s Handbook for Australia & New Zealand: (Including Also the Fiji Islands) with New Map of the Colonies* (London: S.W. Silver, 1888), 159.

[48] "Ship News," *The Cornwall Chronicle*, June 30, 1855, 4. The *Montmorency* arrived in Launceston in June 1855 from Liverpool. While not certain, it is likely that this was Quin's voyage.; "Arrival of the 'Montmorency' at Launceston," *Courier*, June 26, 1855, 2.

[49] "Later English News," *Colonial Times* (Hobert, Tas.), June 29 1855, 2,

[50] Chief Constable of Police, Hobart Town, 26 September 1871, James Quinn Capital Case File (1871). The constable was unsure of whether Quin arrived in Tasmania in 1854 or 1855, but the *Montmorency* made her first passage to Australia in 1855.

[51] Petition for Clemency, September 1871, James Quinn Capital Case File.

[52] James Fenton and James Backhouse Walker, *A History of Tasmania: From Its Discovery in 1642 to the Present Time* (Hobart: J. Walch, 1884), 318.

radically improve the colony's fortunes, in 1870 its mines were failing. Of the ninety gold mining companies in operation there in 1870, only two remained in 1875.[53]

Quin sold his boat and left Tasmania for Victoria in 1870 or 1871. While the depression of 1870 might have encouraged him to leave Tasmania, the immediate cause was an "urgent request" by his wife, Anne. She urged him to follow her to Victoria, to join her brother in a business venture. The arrangement failed, and Quin returned to Hobart alone. Anne settled into service in the household of Miss Willoughby, the sister of an elderly police magistrate, William Willoughby. Back in Tasmania, Quin bought a horse and cab and worked as a driver for four months. He missed his wife, however, so he sold the horse and returned to Victoria.[54] Back in the Victorian Alps, he had no steady work, limited social connections, and few possessions. At the time of the killing, he had lived near Beechworth for only four months. He had no history of crime or disorderly behavior, with police reporting that his "habits [had] been sober, his pursuits industrious."[55] The local farmers knew him mostly because he had begged them for work, bread, or the occasional loan of a horse. Two weeks before the killing, Willoughby, the magistrate, died, and Quin came to collect his wife and all of her belongings.[56] Quin's reasons for robbing Ah Woo and Ah Cow were never explicitly addressed during his trial—his penury was apparently motive enough—but the abrupt change in his wife's situation might have thrust Quin from poverty to looming destitution.[57] On the day of the assault, he wrote to Anne to say that his search for work had been fruitless. "You need not expect me," he explained, "there is nothing doing down here now."[58]

The white community of the Ovens basin described Ah Woo and Ah Cow as "respectable," and certainly as more respectable than their Tasmanian attacker. However, the victims were also Chinese, and the object of racial animus among white settlers. White Britons' attitudes toward Chinese migrants were often contradictory. Chinese laborers were celebrated for their industry, but denigrated for their supposed willingness to tolerate living and working conditions that white laborers could not or would not accept. John Freeman, the author of a popular 1888 book about Melbourne, described Chinese Australians as "pushing in business matters, laborious, and persevering," but noted that "those very qualities which would be considered commendable in the Caucasian are looked upon [ ... ] as proofs of the natural depravity of the Mongolian."[59] This mix of what one scholar describes as "respect and derision" characterized white settlers' responses to Quin's crime.[60]

[53] Fenton and Walker, *A History of Tasmania*, 387.

[54] Chief Constable of Police, Hobart Town, 26 September 1871, PROV, VPRS 264, P0000, Unit 7, James Quinn Capital Case File (1871).

[55] Antecedents of James Quin, Hugh Barclay, Superintendent of Beechworth Police to Chief Commission of Police, Melbourne, 16 October 1871, James Quinn Capital Case File.

[56] "Bright," *Ovens and Murray Advertiser*, August 17, 1871, 3.

[57] "The Myrtleford Murder," October 17, 1871.

[58] James Quin to Anne Quin, 27 August 1870, James Quinn Capital Case File.

[59] John Freeman, *Lights and Shadows of Melbourne Life* (London: Sampson Low, Marston, Searle & Rivington, 1888), 145.

[60] Sascha Auerbach, *Race, Law, and "The Chinese Puzzle" in Imperial Britain* (New York: Palgrave Macmillan, 2009), 4.

Chinese Australians were acute critics of the hypocrisy of their Anglo neighbors. "It cannot be denied," wrote reformers and community leaders Lowe Kong Meng, Cheok Hong Cheong, and Louis Ah Mouy in 1879, "that our countrymen have been good colonists." Their pamphlet, *The Chinese Question in Australia, 1878–9*, protested a proposed restriction on Chinese immigration, and argued for the joint economic fortunes of China and the British Empire. Chinese gardeners' remarkable ability to coax life from "half an acre of apparently worthless land" with limited access to water or fertilizer was widely acknowledged, and had probably saved the lives of many children in the arid regions around the Victorian goldfields. Chinese fishermen and hawkers were equally essential to the survival of rural communities. Despite their success, or because of it, threats of violence against Chinese merchants were increasing, the authors warned, especially by working-class white men.[61] The authors concluded their entreaty with a reminder to Anglo-Australians not to "substitute arbitrary violence, hatred, and jealousy, for justice, legality, and right."[62] Not only did white Australians have a responsibility to ensure the safety of Chinese migrants at home, but also to guarantee their continued freedom of movement between China and the British Empire—an interpretation of the "unequal treaties" signed after the Opium Wars that emphasized reciprocity and mutual benefit, not exploitation.

By many measures, Chinese migrants were partners in British efforts to colonize and cultivate the Australian interior. They built commercial infrastructure in many small towns and farming communities and made scrublands bloom. Even as the Victorian goldfields became unproductive, Chinese merchants and farmers remained important to the provisioning of nearby settlements. Prominent Chinese Australians reminded their Anglo neighbors of their communities' interdependence, and of their equal rights under British law. Ngai writes that Lowe Kong Meng, one of the pamphlet's authors, belonged to a Southeast Asian Chinese elite "confident in their identity of belonging within both the British Empire and the Chinese diaspora."[63] And yet, racial and cultural stereotypes, as well as real differences in legal and social understandings, challenged this ideal of Anglo-Chinese integration.

British anti-Chinese discourse held that Chinese immigrants were uniquely incapable of integrating into British society, even compared to other nonwhite, non-Protestant groups.[64] Australian newspapers consistently portrayedChinese people as exotic and mysterious, and their culture as impenetrable to the white imagination. This presumption of difference had legal implications. Anglo-Australians were especially critical of Chinese Australians' reliability as witnesses.[65] One journalist wrote, "[T]he testimony of our Celestial brethren, however honestly meant, is desultory and spasmodic, and not altogether comprehensible to the average European mind."[66] In cases like *R v. Quin*, colonial authorities and members of the Anglo-Australian press

[61] Lowe Kong Meng, Cheok Hong Cheong, and Louis Ah Mouy, *The Chinese Question in Australia, 1878–79* (Melbourne: Bailliere, 1879), 7–8.

[62] Ibid., 30.

[63] Ngai, *The Chinese Question*, 57.

[64] Auerbach, *Race, Law, and "The Chinese Puzzle" in Imperial Britain*, 15.

[65] On how colonial Britons also cast Indians as innately mendacious, see Elizabeth Kolsky, *Colonial Justice in British India* (Cambridge: Cambridge University Press, 2010).

[66] "The Myrtleford Murder," September 9, 1871, 883.

expressed concern that Chinese immigrants would pervert the course of British criminal law by infusing it with their own legal and spiritual values, especially by lying to police or on the witness stand. The inherent flexibility of Anglo-Australian law made it vulnerable to reinterpretation. In addition, ample opportunities for discretion, in addition to outright lying, invited police, victims, witnesses, lawyers, and jurors to bend the law to their purposes. Anglo-Australians were keen to safeguard the Britishness of colonial law, even while extending its reach over an increasingly diverse population—a project that relied on the expertise and participation of people who were not archetypally "British."[67] The result was a deep ambivalence about the role of Chinese, South Asian, and Aboriginal people, among others, in the colonial legal order. So, although the white farmers of the Ovens basin sympathized with Ah Cow and condemned James Quin, they questioned a Chinese man's ability to participate in his attacker's judgment.

The idea that it was "difficult to get at definite facts from Chinese witnesses" permeated the press coverage of the murder, and was made worse by the fact that Ah Cow had suffered a severe head injury.[68] Just days after the attack, Ah Cow, accompanied by an interpreter, was roused from his hospital bed and brought to the Beechworth lock-up to identify Quin. Ah Cow's gaze flitted over the four other men in the identity parade before settling on Quin, at whom he stared for so long that "[Quin's] nervousness [became] painful to witness."[69] When pressed to name his attacker, however, Ah Cow demurred, telling the interpreter that he was not certain that Quin was the man. Soon, this brief encounter would be used to challenge Ah Cow's credibility in court.

In the weeks after Quin's arrest and before his trial, a petition arrived at the Beechworth jail. A group of more than thirty men from Hobart wrote to urge the court to have mercy on Quin, whom they described as a "hard-working, industrious man." The signatories included coal and lumber merchants, boat builders, a tanner, an iron founder, a saddler, a city inspector, and the chief clerk of the Public Works Department of Tasmania. A few added special pleas next to their names. One hoped that the Victorian court would be lenient for "his mother's sake," another pronounced Quin "upright" in his business dealings, and a third wrote that he had known Quin for fifteen years as a "hard-working, honest, and industrious, sober man."[70] While the denizens of the Ovens basin saw Quin as a rambler and a rascal, the Hobart petition suggests that he had once been a well-regarded member of the town's working class. Hobart police also reported that he had been married twice. His first wife had drowned, and his son, the child of this first marriage, lived in Hobart with Quin's mother.[71] Quin was a tragic figure who had twice forgone economic stability for love or loyalty to his second wife, Anne, leaving his son and mother behind. The petitioners likely understood Quin's violence as a response to the shame and disorientation of his abrupt loss of economic and social capital and community ties. He was a steady, hard-working man who had been reduced to begging farm wives for bread in dirty

67 On the relationship between Australian and British metropolitan law, see Bruce Kercher, *An Unruly Child: A History of Law In Australia* (St. Leonards: Allen & Unwin, 1995).

68 Ibid.

69 "The Myrtleford Murder," from the *Ovens Advertiser*, reprinted in the *Herald*, September 2, 1871, 3.

70 Petition for Clemency, September 1871, James Quinn Capital Case File.

71 Chief Constable of Police, Hobart Town, 26 September 1871, James Quinn Capital Case File.

moleskin trousers. They might have empathized with his jealousy of Ah Cow and Ah Woo, and their fine spring cart.

Quin was tried for murder at the Beechworth circuit court on 17 and 18 October 1871. The prosecutor and the judge in the case were both Irish-born and, like Quin, had come to Victoria to improve their prospects. Unlike Quin, however, they were professionals and Protestants, successful and respected. The prosecutor, Charles Alexander Smyth, had been educated at Gray's Inn, in London.[72] He immigrated to Victoria in 1853, a year or two before Quin did. From 1861, he had been the lead prosecutor for the Beechworth, Castlemaine, Sandhurst, and Maryborough circuits, in the farming and mining country around Melbourne.[73] Smyth enjoyed the country circuit, where he would spend most of his thirty-year prosecutorial career.[74] The judge, Sir Redmond Barry, had arrived in the colony in 1839 after struggling to make a career in the overcrowded Irish Bar. He had been elevated to the Supreme Court of Victoria in 1852, and had become the first chancellor of the University of Melbourne in 1853. As a judge, he was conservative and had a reputation for harshness, although he also had a history of representing Aboriginal defendants pro bono in criminal matters.[75]

During the trial, Quin's personal misfortune was clear. One farmer's wife, Caroline Dean, testified that she had chatted with Quin a few days before the attack when he had tried to buy a loaf of bread from her. He was traveling on foot, alone. She had no bread to sell, but gave him an old, soot-stained pipe of her husband's. The two talked about Quin's money troubles, as she remembered that he had lost some about nine months before, during his first stint in Victoria. Quin claimed that his wife and brother-in-law, Mr. Bruce, had stolen the money. Dean, like many of the witnesses, knew both Quin and his victims, Ah Cow and Ah Woo. In the tight-knit rural community, travelers often stopped at roadside farms to share news or to trade small favors. Two days before her conversation with Quin, she had given Ah Woo a bucket to water his horse. Just hours before the killing, she had seen Ah Woo and Ah Cow pass by in the cart, the gray horse at a trot.[76]

That white Australians considered Chinese witnesses unreliable or worse was evident during the trial. The prosecution's star witness, both at the pretrial inquest and at the trial itself, was not the surviving victim, Ah Cow, but Thomas Cole, the eleven-year-old boy who had stumbled upon the robbery. On the stand, he identified Quin as the man he had seen strike Ah Woo with the tomahawk while the merchant threw mud and stones to defend himself. Frightened, the boy ran up the hill to a clearing. He testified that he heard a "noise in the water [of] Quinn's race. I cannot tell what it was, it made a splash." He saw "the European" climb the hill and pass within several yards of where he stood. The man said something, but Cole could not say what.[77] Cole

[72] Joseph Foster, *Men-at-the-Bar: A Biographical Hand-List of the Members of the Various Inns of Court: Including Her Majesty's Judges, Etc.* (London: Reeves and Turner, 1885), 436.

[73] *Smyth v. The Queen, The Australian Law Times* (Sydney: Law Book Company of Australasia, 1898), 118.

[74] "Death Of Mr. C. A. Smyth," *Argus*, June 17, 1908, 7.

[75] Peter Ryan, "Barry, Sir Redmond (1813–1880)", Australian Dictionary of Biography, National Centre of Biography, Australian National University, http://adb.anu.edu.au/biography/barry-sir-redmond-2946/text4271. Barry was the judge in Ned Kelly's famous 1880 trial.

[76] Judge's Notes of Evidence, James Quinn Capital Case File.

[77] Ibid.

had also been to the Beechworth jail after Quin's arrest. While Ah Cow had equivocated, the boy had pointed directly at the prisoner and announced, "That's the man."[78] Although Quin's defense lawyer did his best to cast doubt on Cole's testimony, especially his memory, he admitted in his closing address that the child's evidence was "the clearest, and certainly the hardest to deal with, and the most difficult to controvert."[79] In a report on the case, Barry wrote that although the evidence of Quin's identity was circumstantial, it was "very strong" and there was "nothing to shake the belief which the jury attached to the testimony of these two eyewitnesses."[80]

Ah Cow's hesitation seven weeks before to identify Quin in the Beechworth lockup became a sticking point during the trial. When he was called to testify, Ah Cow was adamant that Quin was the man who had attacked him on the road to Beechworth. The judge, Barry, observed that Ah Cow testified with "firmness and consistency."[81] Quin's lawyers contrasted Ah Cow's confidence in court against his apparent confusion on encountering their client in jail, suggesting that the merchant was now lying. Ah Cow objected to the accusation, arguing that his recent head injury and changes in Quin's appearance, including a new beard, had initially made him doubt his judgment. "I was weak," said Ah Cow through an interpreter during the trial, "and sick, my eyes were weak and dim, and I was giddy when I was at the gaol." Facing his attacker in court after recovering from the assault, however, Ah Cow's confusion had dissipated, and he was sure that Quin was the man. According to Barry's notes of evidence, Ah Cow had even come to see Quin as physically extraordinary: a "strong big man 7 feet 8 inches high" whom Ah Cow, his senses restored, could not fail to identify accurately.[82]

One journalist, however, dismayed that the public of Beechworth was apparently inclined to accept Ah Cow's identification of Quin in court, pointedly related that the victim had also said, when first informed of Quin's arrest, "no good hang him, my £40 gone."[83] The statement's rough grammar implied that Ah Cow spoke in English rather than through an interpreter; his translated observations at the jail that Quin's "beard was too long, and the cheek bones not high enough" were in a noticeably smoother register.[84] It is not clear how the journalist knew what Ah Cow said in the hospital. While the remark about the £40 might have been invented, the journalist's account implied to his readers that the words were genuinely Ah Cow's, and that they communicated an ugly truth about Chinese-Australian visions of justice.

The mention of the stolen money would have been meaningful to Australian settlers. In this narrative, Ah Cow was unmoved by a desire for either vengeance or justice for himself or his dead friend; his attacker's conviction and execution could not restore what he had lost. The journalist's implication that Ah Cow was interested only in restitution and not in the vindication of the law as a public duty drew on stereotypes

78 "The Myrtleford Murder," September 2, 1871, 3.
79 Ibid.
80 Redmond Barry to Governor of Victoria, 30 October 1871, James Quinn Capital Case File.
81 Ibid.
82 Judge's Notes of Evidence, James Quinn Capital Case File.
83 "The Myrtleford Murder," September 2, 1871, 3.
84 Ibid.

that cast Chinese laborers as "hyper-capitalistic," as one historian puts it—motivated only by profit, not principle.[85] The article presented Chinese Australians as adherents of a normative order at odds with the moral core of British criminal jurisprudence. Ah Cow had been wronged, but he did not understand the true nature of the hurt. Where Ah Cow saw the attack and theft as personal affronts that only compensation could mitigate, Anglo-Australians imagined the crime as a transgression against public order that demanded exemplary punishment. The conclusion of this argument: Ah Cow could not be trusted to play his part in a judicial process that he did not understand. Quin's guilt would have to be proven some other way.

There is another means to interpret the statement attributed to Ah Cow. While some Britons repeated the canard that China was lawless and that Chinese migrants were motivated only by profit, others had long seen Chinese law as extraordinarily complex and its people as notably legalistic. In his influential 1810 digest of Chinese penal laws, Sir George Staunton, an English sinologist and official at the British East Indian Company's factory at Canton, argued that China had been unfairly maligned and misunderstood by Western observers. While not always just, Chinese penal law was "the most comprehensive, uniform, and suited to the genius of the people for whom it is designed, perhaps of any that ever existed."[86] In his preface, Staunton described what he saw as the key characteristics of Chinese criminal law. A distinctive feature was the gap between the severity of the formal law and the relative mildness of its execution.[87] It was quite difficult, he complained, to ascertain the true punishment a transgressor was likely to suffer, since this required "various references and considerable research."[88]

Later British officials echoed Staunton's views. In 1840, one writer described the Chinese criminal code as defined by its "characteristic love of order, and horror of tumults," including harsh punishments for killing in an "affray"—an approach to public violence that had brought unruly British subjects at Canton into conflict with local authorities.[89] Like Staunton, the author noted the importance of mercy in Chinese law, with lenience built into many punishments through the device of "imperial favor," comporting with the maxim, "in enacting laws, rigour is necessary; in executing them, mercy."[90] The idea that Chinese legal culture valued mercy also appeared in commentaries published after Quin's assault on Ah Cow. Ernest Alabaster, an English lawyer, published a new digest of Chinese criminal law based on research conducted by his late father, China-based administrator Sir Chaloner Alabaster, in 1899. Alabaster noted that no English-language compendium had been published since Staunton's nearly a century before. Like his predecessors, he wrote about the frequency with which capital sentences were commuted to terms of imprisonment,

[85] Christopher Bischof, "Chinese Labourers, Free Blacks, and Social Engineering in the Post-Emancipation British West Indies," *Past & Present* 231, (2016): 130.

[86] Sir George Thomas Staunton, *Ta Tsing Leu Lee; Being the Fundamental Laws, and a Selection from the Supplementary Statutes, of the Penal Code of China* (London: Cadell and Davies, 1810), xi.

[87] Staunton, xxvii.

[88] Ibid., xxviii.

[89] John Francis Davis, *The Chinese: A General Description of China and Its Inhabitants* (London: Knight, 1840), 114.

[90] Davis, *The Chinese*, 111.

transportation, or even to fines.[91] In China as in the British world, a convicted murderer had good cause to hope for clemency. Although he lingered on some of the more spectacular punishments, Alabaster summarized the Chinese penal system as "less Draconian" than the English.[92] If he said it at all, Ah Cow's remark about the pointlessness of hanging Quin might not have been about money. Instead, it might have signaled an appeal to mercy; neither his money nor his friend's life could have been recovered through Quin's death. English-language texts on Chinese law invited this interpretation, and white Australians would have understood clemency in capital cases, through the royal prerogative, to be a familiar feature of their own penal system. And yet, the Victorian press implied, however subtly, that Ah Cow's apparent ambivalence about punishing Quin showed a lack of commitment to justice, and perhaps to law itself.

The discussion in the press of Ah Cow's supposed reluctance to pursue Quin if it would not result in the recovery of his stolen money captures a core dynamic of the case. Ah Cow's white neighbors respected his wealth but suspected his character. Victorian farmers would buy a Chinese man's pigs and wave as he drove by while doubting his ability to internalize the values and logics of Anglo-Australian justice. Still, the law protected Chinese Australians. The Anglo-Australian farmers of the Ovens district celebrated the zeal with which authorities pursued the case against Quin, which they saw as proof of the colonial legal system's immunity to racial prejudice and of their own benevolence. "We are happy to say," wrote a local journalist, "that although we heard a man—if you can call him one—in a public bar in Beechworth declare that 'no man should be hanged for murdering a Chinaman . . . ' a very opposite feeling exists in the public mind." Instead, he continued, over 40 witnesses came forward at great inconvenience and expense to testify to what they knew about "this most ferocious and deliberate murder."[93]

The jury deliberated for nearly two hours, returning a verdict of "guilty" at nearly two o'clock in the morning. Barry warned Quin not to expect a commutation. This was not an empty threat. In his long career on the Victorian bench, Barry heard 358 capital cases, in which 53% of convicted defendants were later executed—a higher rate of completed executions than any other Victorian judge could claim in the period from 1852 to 1880.[94] After Barry delivered the sentence, Quin argued that he had been denied "fair play." He claimed that the governor of the Beechworth jail had perlustrated a private letter to his solicitor, instead delivering it to the Beechworth police. Barry was unmoved. He reminded Quin that he had been provided with legal counsel at public expense, and he agreed with the Crown Prosecutor that the defense lawyers' work "could not be impugned." Moreover, the judge declared that Quin's complaints had come too late. Quin was, in Barry's view, a capable advocate for his own

[91] Ernest Alabaster, *Notes and Commentaries on Chinese Criminal Law, and Cognate Topics: With Special Relation to Ruling Cases. Together with a Brief Excursus on the Law of Property, Chiefly Founded on the Writings of the Late Sir Chaloner Alabaster*... (London: Luzac & Company, 1899), lxv.

[92] Ibid., lxviii.

[93] "The Myrtleford Murder," from the *Ovens Spectator*, reprinted in the *Herald*, September 14, 1871, 3.; Some records estimate that more than fifty witnesses were examined. See Redmond Barry to Governor of Victoria, 30 October 1871, James Quinn Capital Case File.

[94] Malcolm and Hall, *A New History of the Irish in Australia*, 224.

interests, and "not the man to allow such a circumstance as that to pass by" during the trial, if it had actually happened.[95] Beechworth staff were keen to prove that Quin had suffered no injustice. The governor of the jail denied tampering with Quin's correspondence, forwarding a newspaper clipping describing Quin's exchange with Barry and a full account of the trial to the Beechworth sheriff, who sent the papers to the Melbourne authorities. Barry remained untroubled. Despite its minor irregularities, Quin's lawyer had mounted an able defense, and an impressive 49 witnesses had given evidence "with calmness and fairness." It had been a good trial.[96]

Quin was hanged in the second week of November at the Beechworth jail. The Irish-born made up a plurality of those executed in Victoria between 1865 and 1879. Of 43 total executions, 41.7% (18) were of prisoners born in Ireland, even though they made up just over a tenth of the population of the colony. By comparison, 9.3% (4) of executed prisoners were born in China, and 28% (12) in England or Scotland.[97] In a cryptic final statement, Quin blamed his wife, crying, "She brought me to this." The 60 or 70 people who had crowded into the prison to observe the execution were disappointed, officials having accidentally failed to admit them to the inner courtyard until it was too late.[98]

Hard-working Chinese merchants had a distinct, but circumscribed, place in rural Victorian society. In contrast, James Quin and men like him lived on the margins, marked by their dirty trousers and poverty. Chinese Australians forged social and economic bonds in their communities and enjoyed the protections of colonial justice. Their belonging was, however, incomplete. The suggestion in the case that Ah Cow and others like him could not fully appreciate the logics and aims of British justice, and might undermine the law even as it operated ostensibly in their favor, speaks to broader imperial concerns about governing diverse populations. The resort to "reliable" interlocutors, like the boy Thomas Cole, his story bolstered by the testimony of dozens of additional witnesses, allowed white settler authorities to demonstrate the power of British legal procedure. *R v. Quin* declared that the colonial legal order could discover truth and punish wrongdoing even when the surviving victim was Chinese and the assailant was white, and neither, for different reasons, could be trusted.

In a recent book on pigs in early medieval Europe, Jamie Kreiner describes the animals as "a sort of anti-synecdoche when it came to the way people thought about the world. [ . . . ] [P]igs called attention to the particularity of things."[99] Unglamorous and ubiquitous, pigs were often neglected in official medieval records. This belied, however, their importance to farms and families, and the many ways that the fates of pigs, ecosystems, and communities were intertwined. Pigs' stories are also the stories of the worlds they inhabited. But, Kreiner warns, the tales of pigs and the places they lived are specific, even unique, and cannot easily be translated into generalities. Instead, she argues, pigs can "move us from one scale to another," from the daily realities of

[95] Newspaper Clipping, *The Spectator*, 16 October 1871, James Quinn Capital Case File.
[96] "The Myrtleford Murder," October 17, 1871, 2.
[97] Malcolm and Hall, *A New History of the Irish in Australia*, 200–201; Arthur Patchett Martin, *Australia & the Empire* (Edinburgh: D. Douglas, 1889), 152.
[98] "Execution of Quin," *Argus*, November 11, 1871, 5.
[99] Jamie Kreiner, *Legions of Pigs in the Early Medieval West* (New Haven: Yale University Press, 2020), 1.

feeding and herding and slaughtering to metaphysical questions about the differences between humans and animals.

*People v. Harriet*, the subject of Hartog's influential study, was about pigs, but also about urbanization, city governance, and ultimately the nature of "law" itself. By starting with pigs, Hartog presented a theory of law, and a method that would influence generations of legal historians, that located the development of sophisticated, changeable understandings of rights and legal authority in intimate interactions at a profoundly human, even animal, scale. Seen this way, the microhistory of a legal case—a "pig"-based analysis, if we can call it that—is, to borrow from Kreiner, an "anti-synecdoche": a device for revealing the interconnections between people, places, and ideas through the infinite particularity of individual circumstance.

*R v. Quin* involves pigs but, unlike *People v. Harriet*, is not primarily about them. And yet, it remains amenable to the same (metaphorical) "pig" treatment. In fact, given the context of the global gold rushes and European imperialism in the Pacific that shaped the case, the problems of scale present in all academic histories are even more acute, and the solution represented by the pig, more necessary. Details of the case and discussions about it in the press—Quin's tattered trousers, Ah Woo's turned-out pockets, Ah Cow's comments about his lost £40, the farm wives' admiration for a fine spring cart—draw out aspects of everyday life in colonial Victoria that might otherwise be difficult to discern. The case shows the overlapping histories of Chinese and Irish migration to Australia, and of migration within the Australian colonies; the complexities of respectability and belonging; the distortions of white Australian visions of China; and the anxieties of settlers keen to assert the Britishness of colonial law during a period of rapid economic and demographic change. Pressed further, *R v. Quin* could yield even more, about gender and commerce, employment patterns, farming practices, food culture, religious identity, and news reporting, among other themes. As an episode in the legal history of the British Empire, *R v. Quin* captures the tension between claims that colonial law was impartial and fair, and the suspicion and denigration of difference that animated British colonialism. The conceptual and administrative infrastructure of law means that cases offer insights into the system that considered them, even as it evolved in response to new cases and shifts in social and political dynamics. The story of *R v. Quin* and the people with whose lives it intersected is small, but helps us to think big—but not so big that we lose sight of the pig.

# 7

# The Chain and the Rope

## Illuminating Constitutional Traditions

*Maeve Glass*[*]

On an autumn day in 1855, a federal judge received an unusual piece of paper.[1] Presented to him by two lawyers in the judge's Philadelphia courtroom, the paper was signed by a woman who, until that summer, had been held as chattel property in the nation's capital.[2] Undoubtedly, the judge would have recognized her name: Jane Johnson. Months earlier, he had issued a court order commanding that she be delivered to his courtroom by a local abolitionist accused of seizing her and her two children when they traveled with their self-proclaimed master through Pennsylvania en route from Washington to New York.[3] Not so, the woman now countered.[4] She had pursued freedom of her own volition, she declared; the abolitionist had nothing to do with the matter. It followed, she concluded, that the judge's writ directing the abolitionist to deliver her body and those of her children to the courts of the nation ought to be quashed.[5]

This remarkable document marks one of the rare moments in America's age of slavery when a woman of color formally petitioned a federal judge to set aside an existing command of law.[6] In recent years, scholars who have come across the paper trail that culminated in this petition have excavated what it reveals about Johnson's assertion of autonomy and personhood, as she set out to first escape from the man who claimed her as property, Colonel John Wheeler, and then challenge the authority of the federal official, Judge John Kane, who had commanded the return of her body to his courtroom.[7]

* The author thanks Jacob Cogan, Kellen Funk, Hendrik Hartog, and Kenneth Mack, as well as participants in the Columbia Law School Junior Faculty Workshop and the "New Perspectives on American Federalism" Panel at the American Society for Legal History's 2022 Annual Meeting. The phrase "the chain and the rope" is borrowed from a nineteenth-century case identified and analyzed by Kellen Funk in his seminal essay, "Equity's Federalism," *Notre Dame Law Review* 97.5 (2022): 2063. The subtitle "illuminating constitutional traditions" is inspired by the wonderful essay by Hendrik Hartog, "Imposing Constitutional Traditions," *William & Mary Law Review* 29.1 (1987): 75.

1 United States *ex rel.* Wheeler v. Williamson, No. 16-726, 28 F. Cas. 686, 687 (E.D. Pa. 1855).

2 Ibid.

3 United States *ex rel.* Wheeler v. Williamson (E.D. Pa. 1855), in *Case of Passmore Williamson: Report of the Proceedings on the Writ of Habeas Corpus, Issued by the Hon. John K. Kane* (Philadelphia: Uriah Hunt, 1856), 4.

4 *Wheeler*, No. 16-726, 28 F. Cas. at 687.

5 Ibid.

6 For a detailed history of enslaved women's experiences in the federal courts of Washington D.C., see Tamika Y. Nunley, *At the Threshold of Liberty: Women, Slavery, and Shifting Identities in Washington, D.C.* (Chapel Hill: University of North Carolina, 2021), 70–94.

7 For examples of scholarship that has analyzed the significance of Johnson's words, see Nunley, *At the Threshold of Liberty*, 86; Faith Barter, "Encrypted Citations: *The Bondswoman's Narrative* and the Case of

Maeve Glass, *The Chain and the Rope* In: *In Between and Across.* Edited by: Kenneth W. Mack and Jacob Katz Cogan, Oxford University Press. © Oxford University Press 2024. DOI: 10.1093/oso/9780197680995.003.0008

Despite the significance of Johnson's petition, a deceptively simple puzzle of legal procedure remains unsolved: How, why, and to what ends did a federal judge come to be involved in the first place? As lawyers who represented Passmore Williamson—the abolitionist accused of seizing Johnson and her children—pointed out, there was no constitutional text or federal statute that gave the court jurisdiction.[8] Nor was there any long line of judicial precedents that would allow a federal court to intervene in a dispute involving a man who had voluntarily traveled with the people he claimed as property across state lines.[9] To the contrary, as Johnson's lawyers argued, the writ of habeas corpus was traditionally deployed to "restore freemen to liberty."[10] How, then, did it come to be that a federal judge in 1855 could marshal the forces of the nation to lay claim to a woman's body?

The absence of inquiry into this puzzling exercise of federal jurisdiction is indicative of a broader asymmetry in our histories of the law and slavery. Propelled in part by the rightful recentering of the disenfranchised, recent scholarship has brilliantly illuminated the strategies of individuals who asserted claims to freedom and citizenship as well as the political structures of oppression in which these claims were made.[11] But while our view of an early American constitutional tradition of transformative, individual rights-seeking activity in the courts has sharpened—a view of what some might see as a constitutional tradition of liberalism[12]— much remains to be learned about the specific processes by which the law's appointed elite reconstituted structures of power in times of change.

In this essay, I invite us to read the paper trail that culminated in Johnson's petition by venturing beyond the well-mapped terrain of individuals staking a claim to their equal rights of liberty in the North, slowly paving the way to the end of slavery in the South.[13] Instead, I invite us to heed a legal historian's invitation, extended more than three decades ago, to construct and analyze an archive by pursuing two distinct interpretative strategies: first, visualizing the case as an instance of conflict between contending normative orders, and second, reading the case as a formal text that expounded legal doctrine by judges who spoke in languages that extended deep into a

Jane Johnson," *Melus* 46.1 (2021): 51; Edlie L. Wong, *Neither Fugitive nor Free: Atlantic Slavery, Freedom Suits, and the Legal Culture of Travel* (New York: New York University Press, 2009), 112; Nat Brandt & Yanna Kroyt Brandt, *In the Shadow of the Civil War: Passmore Williamson and the Rescue of Jane Johnson* (Columbia: University of South Carolina Press, 2007), 117.

[8] Commonwealth *ex rel.* Williamson v. Hortz (Pa. 1855), in *Case of Williamson*, 36.

[9] On the absence of precedent "upon which the jurisdiction can be sustained," see *Hortz*, in *Case of Williamson*, 40–41.

[10] *Wheeler*, No. 16-726, 28 F. Cas. at 687.

[11] On the historiography of civil rights in America, see Kate Masur, "Note on Historiography," *Until Justice Be Done: America's First Civil Rights Movement, From the Revolution to Reconstruction* (New York: W.W. Norton, 2021), 365–71.

[12] For a description of what some observers have referred to as a tradition of "classical liberalism" and its relationship to a tradition of republicanism, see Jack M. Balkin, "Which Republican Constitution," review of *Our Republican Constitution: Securing the Liberty and Sovereignty of We the People*, by Randy E. Barnett, *Constitutional Commentary* 32.1 (2017): 31–32; Hartog, "Imposing Constitutional Traditions," 76–77.

[13] On the need to move beyond a still dominant presumption of an "inevitable and linear progression from slavery to freedom," see Hendrik Hartog, *The Trouble with Minna: A Case of Slavery and Emancipation in the Antebellum North* (Chapel Hill: University of North Carolina Press, 2018), 6.

foreign historical past.[14] This shift in vantage point, I argue, offers a rare opportunity to see in granular detail an act of profound legal alchemy, one that enriches our understanding of America's constitutional traditions.

In particular, this archive reveals that at a time of growing uncertainty as to the extraterritorial reach of property rights in persons, a federal judge turned to the rigid forms of action at common law and the flexible fact-finding and remedies of equity—what some at the time called the "chain" and the "rope"[15]—to reframe the colonel's claim to Johnson from one of property to patriarchy. Overlooked for generations, this use of the chain and the rope allowed the judge to perform, and then celebrate in print, a constitutional tradition defined by an ancient custom of republican citizenship, one that predated the Constitution and promised that the courts of the sovereign would always protect the (white, male) property-owning citizens as they traveled with their movable households along the pathways of commerce in America.[16]

As these records make clear, when Judge Kane set out to assist Colonel Wheeler in the summer of 1855, he did so in a legal geography defined by enormous contestation as to the territorial reach of state laws of property in persons. Confronted with this tangled web of conflicting substantive rules governing Johnson's legal status, Judge Kane seized upon the multiple modes of legal reasoning that were available to him in his courtroom. He began by turning to the common law in the form of the prerogative writ of habeas corpus. By issuing this writ—a writ available for the recovery of people, but not property—the judge punted the thorny question of the colonel's title to Johnson and secured a (thin) jurisdictional foothold in the federal Judiciary Act of 1789.[17] When this deployment of the common law yielded a response from the abolitionist that Johnson was not and had never been in his possession—a response that, at common law, should have been enough to end the matter—the judge then picked up the rope, or language of equity, to satisfy his "conscience" and allow for additional discovery. After allowing the colonel to narrate a story of how the abolitionist had kidnapped Johnson and her sons, the judge then used this expanded fact pattern to exercise his equitable powers and jail the abolitionist for contempt.[18]

This seemingly banal use of law and equity had unexpected and far-reaching consequences. First, because the links of the common law chain required to establish a writ of habeas corpus required a showing that Johnson had been detained against her will, lawyers seeking to overturn the writ set out to name Johnson as an official party in the case. The result was one of the first petitions in American history by a woman of color to challenge the authority of a federal judge.[19] Of equal consequence, when

[14] Hendrik Hartog, "Pigs and Positivism," *Wisconsin Law Review* 4.1, (1985): 899. On the value of attending to "continuities of language" and the need to avoid anachronistic readings of the historical record, see Hartog, "Imposing Constitutional Traditions," 75.

[15] Funk, "Equity's Federalism," 2063.

[16] For a sketch of republican citizenship and its "intensely patriarchal" nature, see Hartog, "Imposing Constitutional Traditions," 79–81; see also Linda K. Kerber, "Making Republicanism Useful," *Yale Law Journal* 97.8 (1988): 1669.. For a classic history of republican citizenship, see J. G. A. Pocock, *The Machiavellian Moment: Florentine Political Thought and the Atlantic Republican Tradition* (Princeton: Princeton University Press), 361–401.

[17] See infra Part II.

[18] Ibid.

[19] See infra Part III.

confronted with this challenge to his authority, the judge shifted his mode of legal reasoning. In a remarkable opinion whose logic reverberated long afterwards, Judge Kane set aside the formalistic binaries of common law reasoning and the hallmark vocabulary of equity to land on the venerable language of ancient custom, one that he invoked to extend federal protection to the master's household and exclude Johnson's voice from the courts of the nation.[20]

The upshot was that even as the United States Supreme Court was carefully walling off federal equity from state rules of procedure that might have invited scrutiny into the institution of slavery,[21] a federal judge was quietly enlisting both the forms of common law and the language of equity to protect the intensely local sovereignty of the master's household, ultimately draping it in the timeless, borderless tradition of republican citizenship. To explore how and why this particular tradition emerged in print, this essay begins by exploring the multitude of competing visions of the legal order that existed outside the courtroom. It then shows how, in this context of substantive legal pluralism, the judge made use of the courtroom's procedural legal pluralism—the formalistic technicalities of common law reasoning, the narrative latitude and remedies of equity, and the lofty invocation of custom—to reframe the issue from one of an uncertain right of chattle property to a protected claim of household patriarchy. The essay concludes by showing how this assertion of jurisdiction inadvertently opened the courtroom door to a woman whose words of self-emancipation warned those who were listening that even their beloved republic could go up in flames.

## I. Of Borders & Meanings

The place where the train crossed over the state line into Pennsylvania would not have been immediately obvious from where the colonel sat on the morning northbound train from Washington to Philadelphia on July 18, 1855.[22] Hours earlier, the famed border between Maryland and Delaware that marked the Mason-Dixon line had announced itself with a great deal of fanfare. A gradual ascent up from the waters' edge to a hilltop, where the forest gave way to an open field and a yellow house. Just to the south of the yellow house were two stones, one labeled "M" and the other "D."[23] In contrast, no one had thought to mark this particular border that signaled the beginning of the free soil of Pennsylvania. This was a stretch of land said to be of "little interest" to the traveller: meadows and hills interrupted by creeks traversed by iron rails

[20] Ibid.

[21] Funk, "Equity's Federalism," 2072.

[22] This description is drawn from contemporary travel guides that narrated the train journey from Baltimore to Philadelphia. For a brief account of the state border, see Charles P. Dare, *Philadelphia, Wilmington and Baltimore Railroad Guide* (Philadelphia: Fitzgibbon & Van Ness, 1856), 98. For an account describing the country as "for the most part uninteresting," see William Ferguson, *America by River and Rail, or, Notes by the Way on the New World and its People* (London: James Nisbet, 1856), 98. For a map that marked the state border, see John C. Trautwine et al., "Map of the Philadelphia & Baltimore Rail Road," (Philadelphia: Watson's Lithographer, ca. 1853).

[23] Dare, *Railroad Guide*, 72.

that passed through a station surrounded by a white fence, where passengers waited beneath the eaves of a gabled roof for the incoming train.[24]

We have no way of knowing from the available record what the experience of this border crossing might have meant to the woman whom the colonel claimed as his property. We do know that, by her own account, Johnson had been planning this journey for quite some time. We also have good reason to speculate that whatever emotions the border crossing might have inspired in the moment, Johnson was clear in her assessment of the overall legal landscape: traveling from the enslaved soil of Washington D.C. where she boarded the train that morning to the free soil of Pennsylvania had not been enough to suddenly change her legal status, to suddenly extinguish the power that the man beside her named Colonel John Wheeler exercised over her and her children.[25]

As Johnson later explained, upon learning that the colonel intended to take her and her children with him to his diplomatic post in Nicaragua, she had begun making plans to escape once they reached New York.[26] Although Johnson never explained why she choose New York, her choice aligned with stories that may have sounded in the private homes of Washington's political elites where she had spent at least some portion of her life.[27]

Just over a decade earlier, for example, in a closely watched case, the Supreme Court had overturned the conviction of a slave-catcher named Edward Prigg who had been found guilty of kidnapping a family from their home in Pennsylvania.[28] In a town not far from the border that the train had just passed, a woman named Margaret Morgan and her husband had awoken to the sound of strangers at their door.[29] The children were still in their sleeping clothes when the men hauled the family out into an open wagon and traveled for miles through a cold rain to the house of the local justice of the peace,[30] before the children and their mother were taken to a jail in Bel Aire, Maryland.[31]

New York, in contrast, may have sounded more promising. Three years earlier, eight people had won their freedom under circumstances similar to that of Johnson's

[24] For this description of the countryside and a drawing of the train station, see ibid., 94–99.

[25] As Nunley puts it: "Johnson navigated outside the District with an understanding of the legal and geographical implications of travel to Philadelphia before her encounter with Williamson." Nunley, *At the Threshold of Liberty*, 87.

[26] *Narrative of Facts in the Case of Passmore Williamson* (Philadelphia: Pennsylvania Anti-Slavery Society, 1855), 14.

[27] On the sharing of information within enslaved communities, particularly among house servants, see Cynthia A. Kierner, *Scandal at Bizarre: Rumor and Reputation in Jefferson's America* (Charlottesville: University of Virginia Press, 2006), 69.

[28] Prigg v. Pennsylvania, 41 U.S. 539 (1842). As Nunley argues, "The Supreme Court not only sent a clear message to Pennsylvania, but enslaved women in the Chesapeake too intercepted the dispatch that freedom remained contested even on free soil." Nunley, *At the Threshold of Liberty*, 60.

[29] *Argument of Mr. Hambly, of York (Penn.), In the Case of Edward Prigg, Plaintiff in Error, v. The Commonwealth of Pennsylvania, Defendant in Error: In the Supreme Court of the United States* (Baltimore: Lucas and Deaver, 1842), 8, in Paul Finkleman, ed., *Fugitive Slaves and the American Courts: The Pamphlet Literature*, ser. 2, vol. 1 (New York: Garland, 1988), 128.

[30] Ibid.

[31] Thomas Culbreth to Thomas W. Veazey, June 28, 1837, in Governor Thomas W. Veazey Letterbook, Maryland State Archives.

family.[32] In a case that had generated a great deal of publicity,[33] a man who claimed the eight people as his property had brought them from Virginia to New York to catch a steamship bound for the Gulf of Mexico.[34] While the steamship was docked, a local Black abolitionist had filed a writ of habeas corpus in state court on the group's behalf.[35] Adopting the principle that a master in transit who voluntarily brought his property to a free state was bound by the laws of that jurisdiction, the court declared the people to be free.[36]

If, then, Johnson had at least some reason to conclude that her pursuit of freedom was more likely to be successful in New York than in Pennsylvania, it was by no means clear that others saw the legal landscape passing by the train window in the same way. There was, to begin with, their fellow passenger on the train that afternoon: a thirty-three-year-old lawyer named David Webster who may have taken it upon himself to expound upon the meaning of the border crossing to his fellow travelers.[37] Surveying the white gentleman from North Carolina and the young Black woman and her two children at his side, the lawyer perhaps began to explain the way of things as they traveled northwards.[38] There is no record of the conversation, but according to the colonel, the lawyer's analysis left him deeply uneasy. As the colonel later put it, "he rather excited my fear."[39]

Perhaps the lawyer had told them of what had happened not long ago in New York, when that respectable family from Virginia had stopped in Manhattan to catch the steamship that would take them down the coast.[40] Perhaps the lawyer had explained that if this *Lemmon* rule from New York were to be adopted in Pennsylvania, the event of the train crossing over the otherwise unremarkable state border had had the immediate effect of changing the legal status of the people at the colonel's side. Perhaps the lawyer had told the colonel about the "wild phrensy of negro adoration and negro idolatry" that was at work in Philadelphia.[41] And perhaps, as the train heaved to its final stop in Philadelphia and the lawyer rose to say farewell, he had given the colonel his card, asking him to look him up if the colonel should run into any difficulty.[42]

32 People *ex rel.* Napoleon v. Lemmon, 5 Sand. 681 (N.Y. Super. Ct. 1852).

33 Sarah L. H. Gronningsater, "'On Behalf of His Race and the Lemmon Slaves': Louis Napoleon, Northern Black Legal Culture, and the Politics of Sectional Crisis," *Journal of the Civil War Era* 7.2 (2017): 207.

34 Ibid., 206–7.

35 Ibid.

36 *Lemmon*, 5 Sand. at 68.

37 On the presence of the lawyer on the train, see John H. Wheeler, Diary Entry, July 18, 1855, John H. Wheeler Diary, John H. Wheeler Papers, Library of Congress, quoted in Henry Louis Gates Jr., "Introduction: *The Bondwoman's Narrative*: A Novel by Hannah Crafts," in *The Henry Louis Gates Jr. Reader*, ed. Abby Wolf (New York: Basic Books, 2012), 103 .

38 As Johnson later explained, "[B]efore leaving Washington, coming on the cars … a number of persons had told [the colonel] that in bringing his slaves in Pennsylavnia they would be free." "The Wheeler Slave Case. Statement by the Slave. Testimony of Another Witness," *Evening Post*, Aug. 1, 1855.

39 "The Wheeler Slave Case," *New York Semi-Weekly Tribune*, Sept. 4, 1855.

40 For the suggestion that "[t]he Lemmon case cannot have escaped [the colonel's] notice," see "Runaway Negroes," *National Anti-Slavery Standard*, July 28, 1855.

41 "The Wheeler Slave Case," *Daily Union*, Aug. 1, 1855.

42 This speculation comes from the fact that Webster later represented the Commonwealth in prosecuting the men whom Wheeler accused of kidnapping Johnson and her children. On Webster's role in opening the case for the Commonwealth, see "The Wheeler Slave Case," *New York Semi-Weekly Tribune*, Sept. 4, 1855.

Indeed, when the colonel disembarked at the Philadelphia train station to await the ferry that would bring him to New Jersey for the last leg of the journey to Manhattan, the litany of meanings as to what had happened when the train crossed over the border into Pennsylvania continued to sound. When, for example, the colonel stopped in for a brief visit with his father-in-law, a well-known artist named Thomas Sully, he heard confirmation of the lawyer's prediction. "[You] could not have done a worse thing," Johnson overheard the man say to his son-in-law, who had come to collect a trunk that belonged to the colonel's wife.[43] Perhaps best to leave immediately, Sully may have said, observing the Black woman who was not his daughter and the Black children who were not his grandchildren, children who were then having lunch and who called the colonel "Master John."[44]

For Johnson, meanwhile, these confident declarations from the lawyer and the colonel's father-in-law that she was now "free" had merely antagonized the colonel and intensified the control he exercised over her body. "To use Jane's own language," recalled the abolitionist William Still some time later, "he was '*on her heels ever minute*.'"[45] When, for example, they arrived at Bloodgood's Hotel for the colonel to get something to eat before the five o'clock ferry, he had ordered Johnson to stay still and not move from the porch.[46] And when, in the few minutes that he was gone, Johnson stopped one of the housekeepers, she did not introduce herself as a newly freed woman. "I told her I was a slave woman," she later testified. The woman likewise did not congratulate her on her newly granted status; instead, she offered Johnson her sympathies. "Poor thing," she had said. "I pity you."[47]

This multitude of meanings continued when one of the hotel's staff, possibly at Johnson's request, dispatched a hastily scribbled note to Still, the clerk and manager of the local Vigilance Committee.[48] Undated, the note referred to Johnson and her boys as "fugitive slaves," whose "master" was with them at the hotel.[49] As Still and his colleague, the white abolitionist Passmore Williamson, read over the note in Williamson's office, it was clear that they too were unsure as to how to proceed with this family of "fugitive slaves." As Williamson later explained, he believed they ought to obtain a writ of habeas corpus from the state courts.[50] Given the lack of time, however, he thought it best to simply gather what information they could and forward it on to their contacts on the Underground Railroad in New York. As Williamson later testified, "I told [Still]

[43] "The Wheeler Slave Case. Statement by the Slave. Testimony of Another Witness," *Evening Post*, Aug. 1, 1855.

[44] For the "Master John" reference, see William Still, "Trial of the Emancipators of Col. J.H. Wheeler's Slaves, Jane Johnson and her Two Little Boys," in William Still, *The Underground Railroad: A Record of Facts, Authentic Narratives, Letters, Etc.* (Philadelphia: People's Publishing Company, rev. ed. 1878), 89. For the lunch at Mr. Sully's, see "The Wheeler Slave Case," *New York Semi-Weekly Tribune*, Sept. 4, 1855.

[45] William Still to the Editor, July 30, 1855, ["Philadelphia Slave Case"], *New York Semi-Weekly Tribune*, Aug. 3, 1855.

[46] On the distance between Bloodgood's Hotel and the train depot, see Dare, *Railroad Guide*, 124.

[47] "The Wheeler Slave Case," *Boston Herald*, Aug. 1, 1855.

[48] On Still's role in managing the Philadelphia Vigilance Committee, see Andrew Diemer, "The Business of the Road: William Still, the Vigilance Committee, and the Management of the Underground Railroad," *Journal of the Early Republic* 42.1 (2022): 83–113.

[49] "William Still to the Editor, July 30, 1855, ["Philadelphia Slave Case"], *New York Semi-Weekly Tribune*, Aug. 3, 1855.

[50] *Wheeler*, in *Case of Williamson*, 10.

to go down and get such information as might be necessary to telegraph to New York, as it was too late to obtain a writ of habeas corpus here."[51] Still, meanwhile, wondered if a writ was even necessary. "What was there," Still asked Williamson, "to hinder them from leaving their master without the aid of legal process?"[52]

By the time Williamson and Still arrived at the docks and climbed to the upper deck of the ferryboat where Johnson sat waiting, presumably to carry out her plan to travel to Manhattan and escape, this multitude of meanings erupted into a cacophony of voices as to what, exactly, her legal status was. Williamson and Still, for example, began by asserting that the act of crossing the border into Pennsylvania had created an offer of freedom on the part of the state of Pennsylvania. Enlisting the language of contract, they explained that the offer was one that Johnson was at liberty to accept or decline. "You are entitled to your freedom according to the laws of Pennsylvania, having been brought into the State by your owner," they lectured.[53] "If you prefer freedom to slavery . . . you have the chance to accept it now," they concluded.[54] This was an offer of freedom, they warned, that was time-bound: "*Remember, if you lose this chance, you may never get such another.*"[55]

Others who were on the upper deck were quick to offer their own assessment of the situation. One elderly gentleman who had taken an interest in the matter reminded everyone that Pennsylvania was hardly the only state that could extend such an offer. Speaking of Johnson and her children, he "remarked that they would have the same chance for their freedom in New-Jersey and New-York as they had then."[56] Others rejected the idea that the act of crossing across the state line had had any effect at all. "Let them alone; they are his *property*," roared one man who had risen to offer his assistance.[57] "Would you rob a man of his property?" another asked.[58] "*My woman* knows her rights," boomed the colonel.[59]

We cannot know how Johnson interpreted this multitude of statements. But we can speculate that as she watched the circle of men descended around her and her boys, she may well have decided that however much she wanted to seek her freedom in New York, the men now debating her status had compromised her plan. Perhaps with the realization that the colonel would never again let her out of his sight, perhaps with the realization that this was indeed the last moment to accept whatever offer Pennsylvania had extended, Johnson decided to act. She rose from her seat, and then, taking her oldest child by the hand, made her way down the stairs, as one of the people on board carried her youngest child.[60] The crowd that had assembled watched as Johnson climbed into a carriage with her children.[61] It was only later, only after the

[51] Ibid.
[52] Ibid.
[53] William Still to the Editor, July 30, 1855, ["Philadelphia Slave Case"], *New York Semi-Weekly Tribune*, Aug. 3, 1855.
[54] Ibid.
[55] Ibid.
[56] Ibid.
[57] Ibid.
[58] "The Wheeler Slave Case," *New York Semi-Weekly Tribune*, Sept. 4, 1855.
[59] *Narrative of Facts*, 15 (emphasis added).
[60] Ibid.
[61] Ibid.

carriage had carried them down the road towards Tenth Street, that she could "look upon herself and her children and *feel* free."[62]

In the space of a single July day in 1855, then, the legal significance of crossing from one jurisdiction to another had generated a multitude of meanings. There was those who believed that the act of crossing onto the free soil of Pennsylvania had meant nothing at all for the question of who owned Johnson's body. There were those who insisted that the act had freed her and her children at once. Then there were those who insisted that the act of crossing into Pennsylvania had created a contractual offer awaiting acceptance, and those who countered that, be that as it may, there were still offers to be had from the states of New Jersey and New York, just across the river. It was in this context of multiple competing visions as to the precise legal status of Johnson's body that a federal judge would turn to the chain and the rope to punt the question of title, and in doing so, secure a jurisdictional foothold with which to protect a master's claim to his movable household.

## II. The Chain & The Rope

Not long after the colonel watched as Johnson and her children disappeared into the July evening, he made his way to the place where he believed he would find assistance: the federal courts. To some, this choice of venue was not altogether surprising. As one commentator put it, "Where shall the bereaved bankrupt Wheeler seek redress? *Experience has taught him to hasten to the federal tribunals.* He knows this General Government has been organized and is sustained solely to mitigate the woe, to redress the injury and to sooth the souls of such as he."[63] The judge whom the colonel approached that evening may have seemed a particularly likely candidate to provide assistance. To begin with, Judge Kane was a personal friend of the colonel's father-in-law.[64] The two men were founding members of the Musical Fund Society, a group whose members had spent their Saturday nights playing Haydn, Mozart, and Beethoven, while eating crackers and cheese and drinking hot punch.[65]

Perhaps of equal importance, both the colonel and the judge descended from merchant families whose wealth depended on the settled expectation that their property would be able to move along the bordered jurisdictions of the Atlantic coast without obstruction.[66] Although the colonel introduced himself as a "farmer,"[67] his family hailed from a small river town in North Carolina known for the ships and cargos it dispatched down to the Atlantic coast.[68] Shortly after the Revolution, the colonel's

[62] William Still to the Editor, July 30, 1855, ["Philadelphia Slave Case"], *New York Semi-Weekly Tribune*, Aug. 3, 1855 (emphasis added).

[63] "Judicial Usurpation," *National Anti-Slavery Standard*, Aug. 4, 1855 (emphasis added).

[64] On Judge Kane and Thomas Sully's membership in the Musical Fund Society, see Dorothy T. Potter, *"Food for Apollo": Cultivated Music in Antebellum Philadelphia* (Lehigh: Lehigh University Press, 2011), 57.

[65] Ibid.

[66] On the centrality of the coastal trade in antebellum America, see Maeve Glass, "Citizens of the State," *University of Chicago Law Review* 85.4 (2018): 886–87.

[67] "The Wheeler Slave Case," *New York Semi-Weekly Tribune*, Sept. 4, 1855.

[68] On the early history of trade and shipbuilding in Murfreesboro, North Carolina, see William N. Still Jr. & Richard A. Stephenson, *Shipbuilding in North Carolina, 1688–1918* (Chapel Hill: University of North

father had moved to the river town from New Jersey and established himself as a prominent merchant and shipper.[69]

The judge, meanwhile, also hailed from a merchant family. His father, Elisha Kane, had moved to Philadelphia in 1801 to establish a branch of a New York–based firm that imported various goods, including rum, molassess, and sugar, from the West Indies and New Orleans.[70] Indeed, the Philadelphia wharves where the colonel had watched his claimed property disappear were likely near to where the judge's father had collected his shipments.[71] Continuing this tradition of moving property across jurisdictional borders, the colonel was that very summer of 1855 in communication with Charles Morgan, a New York shipping magnate who was seeking to open a route through South America that would connect the ports of the Atlantic coast to the Pacific coast.[72]

Although there is no record of the conversation between these two men that summer evening, we can speculate that there may have been some discussion as to the uncertainty surrounding the colonel's legal claim to Johnson and her children as property. He had, after all, voluntarily crossed over into a free state, raising the possibility that, in doing so, he had extinguished his claim to title. There may also have been a discussion as to the legal basis upon which the judge could intervene. As lawyers would later emphasize, federal courts were courts of limited jurisdiction, authorized to intervene only in the specific disputes enumerated in the federal Judiciary Act of 1789—and assisting travelers in recovering their claimed lost property down at the Philadelphia wharves was not one of them.[73]

The solution that the colonel and the judge landed upon that evening came in the form of the common law, and in particular, the writ of habeas corpus. Although the writ of habeas is often thought of as an emancipatory device by which people—including people imprisoned as fugitive slaves—could come before a court and challenge the terms of their confinement,[74] in this instance, the writ offered the colonel

Carolina, 2021), 23; 55; see also Thomas Parramore, "The Merchants Foote," *North Carolina Historical Review* 46.4 (1969): 368.

[69] Joseph S. Fowler, "Memoir of the Author, Colonel John Hill Wheeler, of Hertford County, North Carolina," in John Hill Wheeler, *Reminiscences and Memoirs of North Carolina and Eminent North Carolinians* (Columbus: Columbus Printing Works, 1884), i–ii.

[70] See "Co-partnership," *Philadelphia Gazette*, Oct. 14, 1801 (announcing the commercial partnership of John Kane and Elisha Kane "in the Grocery and Commission business"). For examples of commodities that Kane's father sold, see Advertisement, *Philadelphia Gazette*, Oct. 26, 1801 (announcing the sale of St. Kitts rum); Advertisement, *Philadelphia Gazette*, May 10, 1803 (announcing the sale of Havana molasses); Advertisement, *Philadelphia Gazette*, July 7, 1806 (announcing the sale of New Orleans and Martinique sugars).

[71] See Advertisement, *Gazette of the United States*, Feb. 13, 1802 (announcing the landing of a shipment of Jamaica rum on Chestnut Street Wharf to be sold by Elisha Kane).

[72] Wheeler maintained a correspondence with Charles Morgan, as evidenced by Wheeler's request that his mail be forwarded either to Central America or Charles Morgan. See John H. Wheeler to Governor Thomas Bragg, Aug. 5, 1855, in *The Wheeler Slave Case* (Raleigh: Holden & Wilson, 1857), 3. On Morgan's ventures in Nicaragua, see Calvin Schermerhorn, *The Business of Slavery and the Rise of American Capitalism, 1815–1860* (New Haven: Yale University Press, 2015), 229–31 .

[73] See supra note 8. For a different conclusion finding that the Judiciary Act conferred jurisdiction and that Judge Kane's grant of the writ was "sound law," see Ex parte Des Rochers, 7 F. Cas. 537, 539–40 (C.C.D. Cal. 1856).

[74] For examples of how enslaved people used the writ, see Kelly M. Kennington, *In the Shadow of Dred Scott: St. Louis Freedom Suits and the Legal Culture of Slavery in Antebellum America* (Athens: University

a potential means of reclaiming Johnson from the abolitionists who had helped her escape—without having to establish that he had a valid claim of title to her as property. To understand why, recall that under the rules of pleading at the time, civil litigants seeking a court's assistance had to plead their case using one of the existing forms of actions.[75] Ordinarily, masters like the colonel who were seeking to recover the people whom they claimed as slaves would have had to choose a form of action that required them to establish proof of title.[76] In contrast, the writ of habeas corpus had no similar requirement.[77] Instead, since the 1700s, the writ had been used by men to retrieve dependent members of their households, including wives, children, servants, and apprentices—all without having to establish proof of title.[78]

As one court had summarized, "A husband is entitled to this writ in favor of his wife, a guardian in favor of his ward, and, of course, a father for his infant son."[79] In 1836, for example, a father in Georgia applied for a writ of habeas corpus to recover his child from his in-laws,[80] while in New York in 1853, a court summarized that the writ could be used to "compel a reluctant wife to return to the house and submit to the authority of her husband."[81] Of particular relevance to the colonel, the famed jurist Joseph Story had issued the writ in an 1824 federal case involving a father's effort to retrieve his daughter—a case with which Judge Kane, by his own admission, was "very familiar."[82]

As this earlier case by Judge Story suggested, in addition to allowing the colonel to punt the question of title, the writ also offered at least the beginnings of a solution to the question of federal jurisdiction. Unlike the writs to recover property, the writ of habeas appeared in Section Fourteen of the Judiciary Act of 1789, which, at least on one reading, gave Judge Kane power to issue the writ.[83] In particular, by reading Section Fourteen not as an express limitation, but rather, as a broad grant of authority to intervene if and when the judge deemed it necessary to exercise another ground of

of Georgia Press, 2009), 48; Lea VanderVelde, *Redemption Songs: Suing for Freedom Before Dred Scott* (New York: Oxford University Press, 2014), 18.

[75] On the rules of pleading and importance of the forms of action, see William E. Nelson, *The Common Law in Colonial America: Vol. IV: Law and the Constitution on the Eve of Independence, 1735–1776* (New York: Oxford University Press, 2018), 7–9.

[76] For examples of the various writs that slaveholders used to recover people, see Dark v. Marsh, 2 Car. L. Rep. 249 (N.C. 1815) (writ of detinue); Vaiden v. Bell, 3 Va. 448 (Va. Ct. App. 1825) (writ of replevin); Scidmore v. Smith, 13 Johns. 322 (N.Y. 1816) (action of trespass); Foreman v. Neilson, 19 S.C. Eq. 287 (S.C. Ct. App. 1845) (trover).

[77] On the use of habeas corpus amidst a broader change in the laws of custody, see Michael Grossberg, "Who Gets the Child? Custody, Guardianship, and the Rise of a Judicial Patriarchy in Nineteenth-Century America," *Feminist Studies* 9.2 (1983): 235–60.

[78] See, for example, Rex v. Clarkson, 93 Eng. Rep. 625 (K.B. 1722).

[79] United States v. Anderson, 24 F. Cas. 813 (C.C.D. Tenn. 1812).

[80] *In re* Toulmin, 1 Charlt. 489 (Ga. 1836).

[81] People *ex rel.* Tappan v. Porter, 8 N.Y. Super. Ct. 709 (1853).

[82] United States v. Green, 26 F. Cas. 30 (C.C.D. R.I. 1824). By Judge Kane's own account, he was "very familiar" with the *Green* case. *Wheeler*, in *Case of Williamson*, 128.

[83] An Act to Establish the Judicial Courts of the United States, 1 Stat. 73 (1789). For the view that this statute gave Judge Kane authority to issue the writ under the theory that the writ was necessary to the district court's exercise of its jurisdiction in "restoring fugitive slaves," see *Hortz*, in *Case of Williamson*, 16.

federal jurisdiction—presumably here, the district court's jurisdiction in restoring fugitive slaves—the writ offered at least the façade of a jurisdictional hook.

And indeed, once the paperwork had been completed and the writ was signed and sealed, things moved quickly. That very same night, shortly before the eleven o'clock steam-whistle sounded on the west side of Schuylkill, a group of federal officers climbed the stairs to the front door of a quiet townhouse on Chestnut Street listed as the residence of the abolitionist Passmore Williamson.[84] Clanging the doorbell, the officers presented the abolitionist's dazed father who opened the door with an order bearing the official seal of the president of the United States. Under its terms, Williamson was directed to deliver up the three people whom he had ostensibly taken from the colonel and bring them to court where the judge would determine their fate.[85]

While this writ allowed the judge at least enough of a jurisdictional foothold to dispatch federal officers to a private residence in the middle of the night, proceedings soon took an unexpected turn. When the judge arrived at his courtroom two days later, he found Williamson waiting not with Johnson and her children at his side, but with a single piece of paper, known in legal terms as a "return." Drafted by Williamson at the dictation of his lawyer, this return appeared at first to be a standard, boilerplate defense to the writ's command. Written in the common law's traditional script, it declared that Williamson could not comply with the writ for the simple reason that Johnson and her children were not in his possession, custody, or control at the time he received the writ.[86] And yet, rather than remain confined to this boilerplate language, Williamson—encouraged by his father to assert the "truth and only truth"—had added a phrase that went beyond the standard script: Johnson and her children, he declared, had never "*at any other time*" been within his possession, custody, or control.[87]

This denial of possession should have been enough to end the matter. At common law, a return declaring "no custody" was a conclusive break in the link of the chain that made up the writ.[88] Instead of concluding the proceedings, however, the judge made a crucial move. Seizing upon Williamson's modification to the standard language of the return, the judge set down the chain and picked up the rope, or equity. As compared to the common law forms that required pleading and proving each link of binary choices that made up the writ, equity offered judges the latitude to weave together strands of detailed facts gleaned from extensive interrogatories in order to satisfy the judge's "conscience" and thus arrive at extraordinary remedies.[89]

The lawyers who were in the courtroom would have understood immediately what was happening. Citing the "evasive" language of Williamson's return, the judge announced that he would allow the colonel and his witnesses to testify as to what had happened down at the Philadelphia docks. As Judge Kane later explained, "[T]he

84 "The Case of Passmore Williamson, Statement by his Father," *Frederick Douglass' Paper*, Sept. 28, 1855.
85 Ibid.
86 *Wheeler*, in *Case of Williamson*, 6. On the drafting of the return, see "The Case of Passmore Williamson, Statement by his Father," *Frederick Douglass' Paper*, Sept. 28, 1855.
87 *Wheeler*, in *Case of Williamson*, 5 (emphasis added).
88 Ibid., 23.
89 Funk, "Equity's Federalism," 2061–64.

Court thought it its duty to ascertain and *satisfy its conscience*, whether, if a different state of facts were established, it was not matter for the judicial notice of the court . . . to bind the defendant over to answer on a charge of perjury."[90] By invoking this language of the court's "conscience," the judge thus used the well-known vocabulary of equity to create a space in the official record for the colonel to construct his own preferred narrative.

Listen, for example, to how the colonel seized upon this invitation to describe his relationship to Johnson and her sons. Instead of using the language of "slaves"—language that would immediately raise the thorny issue of title under state law—the colonel spoke in a language more akin to wardship, a traditional dominion of equity. "I am the owner of three colored *persons*, named Jane, Dan, and Isaiah," he began, and one could hear a subtle shift from the language of owning "slaves" to owning "persons" who were known to the colonel by their first names.[91] "I hold them to *labor* under the laws of the State of N. Carolina, and of my country," he continued, and one could hear again the subtle shift from holding "slaves" to holding "labor."[92] "I was upon my return to take passage from New York, in company with my three *servants*, whom I was taking to their mistress, who is now in Nicaragua," he continued, shifting the geography of the case from the territory of the free state of Pennsylvania to the fluid highways of the Americas, while using the language of "servants" that continued to conjure the idea of wardship.[93] Indeed, the only time the colonel spoke of "property" was when he quoted his own retort to Williamson on the ferry: "I told him that I was in a country of laws, and that it could protect me in *my person* and property."[94]

This way of framing the events that had transpired along the Philadelphia wharves echoed in the testimonies of the four white men whom the colonel's lawyers brought in as witnesses.[95] Using the language of a "woman" and her "children," these testimonies depicted Johnson and her family as the helpless victims of a violent, racialized crowd who, working under Williamson's direction, had ostensibly descended upon the ferry and shattered the peace of the colonel's household.[96]

By allowing these interrogatories, the judge had thus expanded the narrative universe of the case. In doing so, he had allowed the colonel to frame the issue not as that of a master and his (uncertain) claim to his slaves, but instead as that of a head of a household whose wards had been wrongfully seized.[97] To be sure, the risk of allowing such testimonies meant that competing voices might be heard in the courtroom as well. When, for example, Williamson rose to testify, he endeavored to recenter the language of property and emancipation. In Williamson's telling, Johnson and her sons were indeed "slaves," who had been purchased and held by the colonel against their will.[98] Johnson had not been kidnapped by a crowd of violent criminals; to the

[90] *Wheeler*, in *Case of Williamson*, 6 (emphasis added).
[91] Ibid. (emphasis added).
[92] Ibid. (emphasis added).
[93] Ibid., 7 (emphasis added).
[94] Ibid. (emphasis added).
[95] Ibid., 7–8 (quoting the testimony of Thomas Wallace, Robert T. Tumbleston, a "Mr. Edwards," and Andrew Heath).
[96] Ibid.
[97] Ibid.
[98] Ibid., 9.

contrary, she had asserted a legal right to freedom with the welcome help of members of the local Black community, who had "proceed[ed] peacefully and quietly."[99]

Here too, equity could provide a solution. When confronted with this unwanted version of events, Judge Kane simply turned to the equitable remedy of contempt to commit Williamson to custody.[100] "The Court," he wrote, quoting the 1824 habeas decision by Judge Story, "will not discharge the defendant ... if the conscience of the Court is not satisfied that all the material facts are fully disclosed. *That would be to listen to mere forms, against the claims of substantial justice.*"[101] By citing this earlier precedent involving a father seeking to reclaim his daughter—a precedent Judge Kane declared to be "singularly analogous" to that of the colonel seeking to reclaim Johnson[102]—the judge once again punted the question of property in persons. As he put it, "it seems to me altogether unimportant whether they were slaves or not."[103]

This embrace of the courtroom's procedural legal pluralism—one that first exploited the links of the common law chain that made up the writ and then, using the language of equity, opened the courtroom door to narrative strands that could be selectively braided together to silence competing accounts—soon received the endorsement of the highest court in the state. Not long after Williamson found himself in a cell in Moyamensing Prison for contempt, his lawyers appealed to the Chief Justice of the Pennsylvania Supreme Court for a writ of habeas corpus.[104] Evidently unimpressed by the lawyer's arguments that the federal court lacked jurisdiction, Chief Justice Ellis Lewis accepted the narrative made possible by the judge's use of the chain and the rope and left the contempt order intact.

True, Justice Ellis Lewis observed, the federal judge had chosen a form of action that was not technically intended to decide rights of property. "[B]ut," he noted, "the writ at *common law* may be issued to deliver an infant to a parent, or an apprentice to a master," effectively accepting the judge's invitation to see the case as something other than property.[105] True, Justice Lewis continued, the federal judge may have lacked jurisdiction to assist this particular head of the household in reclaiming his wards. But when, as here, "jurisdiction ... depends upon the existence of certain facts, and no objection to its authority are made on the hearing, the jurisdiction ought to be presumed."[106]

Indeed, when the other justices on the Pennsylvania Supreme Court considered the question, they too accepted the judge's use of the chain and the rope by simply disclaiming altogether any role for the state courts in the matter.[107] As one justice explained, "The jurisdiction of the Court ... and everything else which preceeded the conviction, are out of our reach; they are not examinable by us."[108] Even Justice Walter H. Lowrie, who found the "application of the habeas corpus seriously startling,"

[99] Ibid., 10.
[100] United States *ex rel.* Wheeler v. Williamson, No. 16-725, 28 F. Cas. 682, 686 (E.D. Pa. 1855).
[101] *Wheeler*, No. 16-726, 28 F. Cas. at 690 (emphasis added).
[102] Ibid.
[103] *Wheeler*, No. 16-725, 28 F. Cas. at 686.
[104] Commonwealth *ex rel.* Williamson v. *Wynkoop* (Pa. 1855), in *Case of Williamson*, 16.
[105] Ibid., 18.
[106] Ibid.
[107] *Hortz*, in *Case of Williamson*, 72.
[108] Ibid.

refused to intervene, citing his concerns for the spectre of a state court usurping the power of the federal judiciary.[109]

By the end of the summer, having lost their appeal to the Pennsylvania Supreme Court to secure Williamson's release, Williamson's lawyers switched strategy. Rather than continuing to focus on the arguments that the district court had no jurisdiction and the colonel had no title,[110] the lawyers honed in on the logic of the common law chain. This time, they would seek to explode a crucial link in the writ—that of involuntary detention—by inviting Johnson to recount her account of self-emancipation, one that would leave a flustered judge to invoke a constitutional tradition of exclusion said to be older than the republic itself.

## III. Of Testimony & Illumination

Nearly three months after federal officers set out in the middle of the night in search of her body, Johnson's words arrived in the judge's courtroom on a certified piece of paper.[111] Even before he began reading, Judge Kane likely had a sense of what they said. In one of the most noteworthy events of the year, Johnson had returned to Philadelphia in August to testify as a defense witness for the Black men who had assisted her off the ferry and who, at the colonel's urging, the state authorities of Pennsylvania had charged with riot and assault and battery.[112]

Johnson did not explain why she decided to return to Philadelphia and testify in the state trial, much less why she decided to submit a petition to the federal court. But the effect of her decision was clear. When, on August 29, 1855, Johnson made her way down to the witness stand in the state proceedings, she delivered a testimony that directly contravened the narrative of abduction that the colonel had so carefully crafted, prompting the colonel to turn the color of a "boiled lobster," rise from his seat, and walk out of the courtroom.[113]

After introducing herself as someone who did not have the luxury of knowing the year of her birth but who could speak without evident hesistation of her possible imminent death, Johnson described her act of self-emancipation with the force of repetition anchored in the word "I."[114] Piercing the myth that she had been kidnapped, Johnson described her departure from the ferry as her own volition. "I wanted to get off the boat," she said.[115] "[I] didn't listen to what he had to say," she continued.[116] "I

[109] Ibid., 90; 93–95.

[110] For an example of this line of argument that insisted Pennsylvania's statutes of 1780 and 1847 deprived the colonel of title, see ibid., 53.

[111] *Wheeler*, No. 16-726, 28 F. Cas. at 687.

[112] "The Wheeler Slave Case," *Trenton State Gazette*, Aug. 10, 1855.

[113] For the comparison of the colonel to a "boiled lobster," see "The Wheeler Slave Case," *National Era*, Sept. 6, 1855.

[114] As Johnson stated: "I can't tell my exact age; I guess I am about 25; I was born in Washington City; lived there this New Year's, if I shall live to see it, two years." See "The Wheeler Slave Case," *New York Semi-Weekly Tribune*, Sept. 4, 1855. For an analysis of this statement and the significance of Johnson's habit of starting her sentences with "I," see Barter, "Encrypted Citations," 62–63.

[115] "The Wheeler Slave Case," *New York Semi-Weekly Tribune*, Sept. 4, 1855.

[116] Ibid.

did not say I did not want my freedom," she declared.[117] "I have always wanted it."[118] And again: "I did not say I wanted to go with my master; I . . . was very glad to go."[119] Johnson closed her testimony with a comment some would later read as a warning: although she did not know the year of her birth, she had come into the world when the British had burnt down the Capitol, a reminder that even the legislative heart of their beloved republic could be reduced to ashes.[120]

Not long after this explosive testimony resulted in the jury's decision to acquit all of the defendants of riot, and all but two of the defendants of assault and battery,[121] lawyers for Williamson may well have realized its significance for liberating their own client. Most consequentially, Johnson's electrifying assertion that she had voluntarily left the colonel could break the first link in the chain in the writ of habeas corpus. As lawyers representing Johnson in her subsequent petition to Judge Kane explained, at common law, the person seeking the writ had to show that the party to be delivered up to the courts had been detained against their will.[122]

It followed, they argued, that because Johnson had left of her own volition, this requisite link in the writ was broken, and hence, the writ could not be maintained.[123] "It seems to me," the lawyer J. B. Townsend argued when submitting Johnson's petition, "that if any party to the proceeding can be heard, my colleague and myself represent the very party, *the sole question being whether there is any detention or restraint of this woman against her will.* Surely no one is so competent to satisfy the Court upon that point as the woman herself."[124] In making this argument that honed in on the link of involuntary detention, the lawyers recast Johnson from a helpless ward seeking to be returned to her master's household into an equal—even leading—party in the proceedings. "[I]t is the rights and liberties of Jane Johnson and her children that this Court is charged with protecting in this proceeding, and not the rights of Mr. Wheeler," the lawyers argued.[125] Indeed, the fate of the entire proceeding, they continued, belonged not to the colonel nor the judge, but to Johnson, who alone had the power to end it: "It being therefore *virtually her proceeding*, why cannot she terminate it?"[126]

Faced with the realization that his choice of the writ of habeas corpus had inadvertently opened the door to allowing a Black woman to "declare her knowledge" in his courtroom,[127] Judge Kane responded by setting aside the chain and the rope that he had used to try and bring her there. Rather than reciting the treatises of the laws of slavery that had already appeared in the newspapers justifying his decision,[128] the

117 Ibid.
118 Ibid.
119 Ibid.
120 Ibid. For an analysis of Johnson's characterization of the capital "as a contested zone of power," see Barter, "Encrypted Citations," 64.
121 Still, "Trial of the Emancipators," in *Underground Railroad*, 96.
122 *Wheeler*, in *Case of Williamson*, 168.
123 Ibid.
124 Ibid., 169 (emphasis added).
125 Ibid., 169.
126 Ibid. (emphasis added).
127 Ibid., 167.
128 For an example of one such essay that justified the judge's decision by citing treatises of the law of slavery, see "The Wheeler Slave Case," *Weekly Union*, Aug. 9, 1855.

judge looked beyond the formalities of common law and the latitude afforded him by equity and instead invoked the language of ancient custom. In doing so, he illuminated what he described as a geographically borderless, timeless tradition of republican citizenship: one that promised that the sovereigns of the nation would always protect the (white, male) property-owning citizens.

To see how Judge Kane invoked this tradition to exclude Johnson's voice from the courtroom, consider the rhetoric at work in the remarkable opinion that he authored in October 1855 refusing to admit Johnson's petition. Consider first how the judge constructed the relevant units of time and space. Instead of simply rehashing the events that began down at the Philadelphia wharves on the afternoon of July 18, 1855, the judge began his opinion with a sweeping history of the writ, guiding his readers across the centuries and the Atlantic Ocean to land in the ancient Roman Republic. It was there in the deep past that the intensely patriarchal logic of the writ—the chain that Johnson had dared to claim as her own—had first materialized. At common law, the judge explained, the writ had issued "from the courts of the sovereign, and in *his* name," whenever "a citizen had been deprived of *his* rightful control over any member of *his* household, *his* wife, *his* child, *his* ward or *his* servant."[129]

This ancient writ that promised the assistance of the courts in preserving a man's control over his household had travelled from England across the Atlantic to America, where it had flourished in the text of the Constitution and the subsequent words of Congress. Immune to the whims of the people and their legislatures, it had become "the birthright of *every man* within the borders of the states; like the right to air, and water, and motion and thought, rights imprescriptible, and above all legislative discretion or caprice."[130] It was this vital birthright, the judge concluded, that Williamson had betrayed when he entered his evasive and untrue return, earning the court's order of contempt.

Having invoked this narrative to justify the exercise of federal jurisdiction, the judge then used the same rhetorical strategy to justify the court's protection of a second right at stake: "the right of a citizen of one state to pass freely with *his* slaves through the territory of another state."[131] Here, the judge once again looked beyond the temporal and geographic boundaries of the nation, tracing the roots of this "right of transit" back to the "great moral code" and practices of "liberal commerce" that predated the union.[132] "Everything in and about the Constitution implies it," he declared of this right of transit.[133] It was, as one commentator had put it, part of the "*customary law of the colonies*."[134] Returning once more to the language of patriarchy, the judge then paired this right of trainsit with the right of a master to arrest his fugitive slaves, before once again analogizing it to the rights of "a husband, or father, or guardian, whose wife, or child, or ward, has run away."[135]

129 *Wheeler*, No. 16-726, 28 F. Cas. at 688 (emphasis added).
130 Ibid., at 689 (emphasis added).
131 Ibid., at 692 (emphasis added).
132 Ibid.
133 Ibid.
134 "Slaves in Transit," *Weekly Day Book*, Aug. 11, 1855 (emphasis added).
135 *Wheeler*, No. 16-726, 28 F. Cas. at 693.

In tracing this right of transit along the commercial highways of America, the judge paused to illuminate the political economy that this tradition of republican citizenship kept afloat.[136] This was an America, he reminded his readers, that was never simply a land of thirteen isolated colonies giving way to two feuding sections of North and South. This was an America built out of the movement of property across these jurisdictional and sectional borders. Allow one state to arrest that movement, he argued, and the wheels of commerce would come to a halt. "If the laws of a State can control the rights of property of strangers passing through its territory," he observed, "then the sugar of New Orleans, the cotton of Carolina, the wines of Ohio, and the rum of New England may have their markets bounded by the States in which they are produced."[137] In this America of commerce, the judge concluded—an America that he declared to be a "brotherhood of interest"[138]—the voice of a woman who had dared to claim authority over the use of the chain simply had no place in his courtroom. It followed, the judge concluded, that her application to speak in the official records of the court was refused, her body preserved instead as the object of a writ swaddled in an ancient tradition of judicial protection for those who claimed membership in America's brotherhood of men.

In the end, all that remained was to discipline, once more, the abolitionist who had joined Johnson in this affront to America's patriarchy. When, in mid-October, Williamson's lawyers submitted a petition that again protested the court's jurisdiction, Judge Kane at first refused to admit it, declaring that the only words that he could hear "as a judge" were those supplied by the forms of common law, namely, a statement that purged the defendant of contempt.[139] It was only after Williamson had agreed to the words that the court proposed—words that abandoned all earlier protests of the court's authority—that the judge at last granted Williamson his liberty.[140] In doing so, the judge brought the proceedings to a close, having performed for all to see a tradition by which the courts of the sovereign would offer their protection to the masters of America.

## IV. Conclusion

The land through which Jane Johnson traveled that summer day of 1855 is one that still often appears in collective memory as a land of fragments: fragments that ask us to decide who, as between North and South, freedom and slavery, nation and state, prevailed in the linear march of the nation from the Founding to the Second Founding. By peering beyond these fragments, we can begin to see a more complicated landscape. It was there, in the weeds of legal pluralism with multiple substantive rules at play, that a federal judge who was determined to extend the protection of the law over the master's movable household turned to the opportunities afforded by

136 Ibid., at 692.
137 Ibid.
138 Ibid.
139 *Wheeler*, in *Case of Williamson*, 96–97; 101.
140 Ibid., 160–63.

the procedural legal pluralism of the courtroom, welding an ancient writ of common law with the narrative latitude of equity, before at last landing upon the language of custom that existed back of the Constitution.

By attending to these intricate mechanisms of legal procedure, we can see the case as something more than a stepping stone on the nation's path to constitutional transformation. Instead, we can observe how, when faced with a challenge to his authority, a federal judge helped rework a dubious question of property into one of patriarchy, while celebrating in print a tradition that promised that the courts of the sovereign would come to the aid of men who claimed dominon over a woman's body. This was an exercise of judicial power that ignored the formalism of the common law links in the chain that might have liberated Johnson's abolitionist ally, justified instead by the pursuit of the judge's conscience to uphold a tradition of exclusion, one that would continue to sound long after the soldiers had returned from the battlefield and the formal laws of slavery had fallen.

# 8
# South Asians at the Inns of Court
## Empire, Expulsion, and Redemption circa 1900

*Mitra Sharafi**

Between the 1860s and 1940s, thousands of non-European students from across the British Empire studied at the Inns of Court in London to become barristers. In numbers, South Asians led the way. By the late 1920s, between a third and a half of admitted students at Middle Temple and Lincoln's Inn hailed from the Indian subcontinent.[1] The prospect of becoming a barrister in London "pleased and glittered," in the words of one Indian lawyer.[2] Being one of the "England-returned" in South Asia meant professional success and social status. But it was also ripe with hazard. Many South Asian families worried about deracination—that students would lose their sense of cultural and religious identity in London. Smoking, drinking alcohol, eating meat, being romantically involved with Europeans, gambling, and debt could derail one's studies and prospects back home, by this thinking.[3] Crossing the *kālā pāṇī* (black water) via long-distance sea travel caused Hindus like Gandhi to lose caste.[4] Some colonial students found that they fit in nowhere—neither the metropole nor the colony—after being educated in Britain.[5] There was also the cold, both the weather and the chilliness of elite British circles, particularly for people of color. Newspapers noted the "appalling loneliness" and even suicide of some Indian students in London.[6]

From the colonial state's perspective, the aim of Anglicized legal education for colonial populations was to create a group of collaborators who would prop up British

* For their feedback, I thank George Aumoithe, Mary Sarah Bilder, Erin Braatz, Tonya Brito, Christian Burset, Daniel R. Coquillette, Angela Creager, Cynthia Farid, Trina Hogg, Tom Johnson, Gwendolyn Leachman, Nikhil Menon, Quentin (Trais) Pearson, Linda Przybyszewski, Elizabeth Thornberry, Jesse Tumblin, Marjan Wardaki, Barbara Welke, and Natasha Wheatley, along with the editors of this volume, Kenneth Mack and Jacob Cogan. I am also grateful to research assistants Bennett Cross and Renu Paul; the UW-Madison Graduate School; the UW Law librarians; the Shelby Cullom Davis Center at Princeton's history department; and Celia Pilkington, archivist at the Honourable Society of the Inner Temple. In 2004, I was a "Paying Guest" at the home of R. P. Vachha of Mumbai (now deceased). He shared his experiences as a student at Lincoln's Inn, 1939–45. These stories inform this chapter in general ways. The views expressed here remain my own.

[1] Mitra Sharafi, *Law and Identity in Colonial South Asia: Parsi Legal Culture, 1772–1947* (New York: Cambridge University Press, 2014), 104.

[2] Anonymous, "The Reminiscences of a Solicitor," *Bombay Law Review* 13 (1935–6): 19.

[3] For example, see M. K. Gandhi, *An Autobiography, or The Story of My Experiments with Truth*, trans. Mahadev Desai (Ahmedabad: Navajivan Publishing House, 1927), 54–8.

[4] See Gandhi, *Autobiography*, 57–9; and Sumita Mukherjee, *Nationalism, Education, and Migrant Identities: The England-Returned* (London: Routledge, 2010), 31–4.

[5] On Nehru, see S. Mukherjee, *Nationalism, Education, and Migrant Identities*, 94.

[6] "Indian Affairs. Indians in England," *TL*, 19 Nov. 1906, 5. Similarly, see untitled editorial, *TI*, 16 Nov. 1876, 2.

Mitra Sharafi, *South Asians at the Inns of Court* In: *In Between and Across*. Edited by: Kenneth W. Mack and Jacob Katz Cogan, Oxford University Press. © Oxford University Press 2024. DOI: 10.1093/oso/9780197680995.003.0009

rule—in the case of the Inns, through the administration of the legal system. The point of English-style education for Indians, in the famous words of Thomas Babington Macaulay, was to create a class South Asian "in blood and color, but English in taste, in opinions, in morals, and in intellect."[7] As examples from M. K. Gandhi to V. D. Savarkar revealed, though, this model of colonial education did not always work as planned.[8] Among the "temptations" of London was the possibility of coming into contact with nationalist movements, pan-Asianism, anarchism, socialism, communism, Irish republicanism, positivism, and other anti-imperial influences.[9]

This chapter explores the disciplinary files of the Honourable Society of the Inner Temple, focusing on two previously unexplored cases of South Asian students or members around the turn of the twentieth century. Being disbarred or expelled from an Inn meant the death of one's legal career, with ripple effects on social status and family reputation. From the British perspective, expulsion could also mean the "failure" of colonial legal education, which had not replaced "native mendacity" with "good character" through Anglicization. Although the most common pattern in the Inner Temple archive was disbarment following a criminal conviction, neither case featured here was representative in this way. Even so, these cases deserve our attention for other reasons. One case shows us what giving someone a second chance looked like in an imperial profession suffused with Christian and capitalist values. The other tells the long story of a political U-turn—how an Inn shifted from defending imperialism to implicitly rejecting it a century later. This case demonstrates how to decolonize a historical disbarment.

In the first case, an Indian student named Akshaya Kumara Ghose withdrew then later applied for readmission to the Inn (1899–1902). Ghose had written fraudulent "spirit letters" to Miss Frances Henrietta Müller, a well-known figure in the Theosophist and women's movements who informally adopted him. This case was about nonromantic interracial intimacy, fictive or social kinship, and acculturation flowing in two directions. While Ghose's education in England was intended to Anglicize him, Müller adopted a Hindu ascetic lifestyle as a follower of an Indian-inspired spiritual movement. The second and more high-profile case involved the revolutionary editor of *The Indian Sociologist*, Shyamji Krishnavarma, who was disbarred for advocating the violent overthrow of British rule in India (1909). This case revealed the workings of global anti-imperial networks.[10]

[7] T. B. Macaulay, "Minute on Indian Education" (1835), in Mia Carter with Barbara Harlow, eds., *Archives of Empire. Vol. I: From the East India Company to the Suez Canal* (Durham: Duke University Press, 2003), 237.

[8] See Judith Brown, *Gandhi: Prisoner of Hope* (New Haven: Yale University Press, 1989); Ramachandra Guha, *Gandhi before India* (New York: Knopf, 2014); and *Gandhi: The Years That Changed the World, 1914–1948* (New York: Knopf, 2018). On Savarkar, see Harald Fischer-Tiné, *Shyamji Krishnavarma: Sanskrit, Sociology, and Anti-Imperialism* (London: Routledge, 2014), 65, 119–20; and "Making Britain" entry, *The Open University*, accessed on 22 May 2024, http://www.open.ac.uk/researchprojects/makingbritain/content/vinayak-damodar-savarkar.

[9] See S. Mukherjee, *Nationalism, Education, and Migrant* Identities, 81–112; Michael H. Fisher, Shompa Lahiri, and Shinder S. Thandi, eds., *A South Asian History of Britain: Four Centuries of Peoples from the Indian Sub-Continent* (Oxford: Greenwood World Publishing, 2007), 128–30; Rozina Visram, *Asians in Britain: 400 Years of History* (London: Sterling, 2002), 300–40; Kate O'Malley, *Ireland, India, and Empire: Indo-Irish Radical Connections, 1919–64* (Manchester: Manchester University Press); and Fischer-Tiné, *Shyamji Krishnavarma*, xxxii at note 24, 61, 68–70, and 74–83.

[10] The files are A. K. Ghose (DIS/1/G1) and S. Krishnavarma (DIS/1/K2).

Although the Inns were nonstate bodies, empire was more than just the backdrop to these cases.[11] The cases of Ghose and Krishnavarma allow us to reflect on what imperial lawyering meant at the turn of the twentieth century.[12] Imperial lawyering required the acceptance of empire as a political system and the rejection of the use of extralegal methods of resistance. Imperial lawyers could stumble ethically, but only early on. Ideally, the misstep would be followed by expressions of fault or sin, apology or confession, and the acceptance of personal responsibility that were consistent with Christian and capitalist value systems. It also helped if one's accuser was deemed an unreliable narrator due to her sex and unorthodox spiritual values. By contrast, a barrister could also achieve redemption by another route: through regret and renunciation *by the institution itself.* A century after the initial disbarment, an anticolonial revolutionary once expelled from the Inn could be readmitted posthumously. Now that the British Empire had ended, he was no longer *persona non grata* for advocating anti-imperial violence in print.

These two cases occurred in the relatively early days of the flow of South Asian students to the Inns. South Asians at the Inns were still a small group in the decades flanking 1900, a period that predated the establishment of many colonial student organizations and full-blown mass movements for independence.[13] These disciplinary cases revealed the working out of limits that would set the tone for the high era of South Asian students at the Inns during the 1920s through 1940s.

## I. South Asians at the Inns

The first South Asian students came to the Inns in the early 1860s.[14] A cluster of students from West Africa also appeared in the 1860s–1870s.[15] This was comparatively

[11] On the Inns being self-constituted and -governed voluntary societies, see Lindsay Russell, "The Bar of England," *The American Lawyer*, 11 (Nov. 1903): 481.

[12] By "imperial lawyering" and the "imperial legal profession," I refer to European and non-European law students, lawyers, and judges with a connection to the British Empire who were based or connected to Britain through education and continuing ties to Inns, universities, or courts there.

[13] On this later period, see S. Mukherjee, *Nationalism, Education, and Migrant* Identities, 81–112.

[14] The Middle Temple admissions register includes this entry for 27 April 1863: "Budroodeen Tyabjee, of Highbury New Park College, Middx., (17), fifth son of Tyabjee Bhoymeah of Bombay, Empire of India, gent. Called 30 April 1867." The future Bombay High Court judge Badruddin Tyabji is often identified as the first South Asian student at the Inns. See his admissions entry in H. A. C. Sturgess, ed., *Register of Admissions to the Honourable Society of the Middle Temple. From the Fifteenth Century to the Year 1944* (London: Butterworth, 1949), II, 539. However, Johannes Herapiet Wise Arathoon, an Armenian student from Calcutta, in fact predated Tyabji. Arathoon was admitted to Inner Temple on 22 October 1861 and called to the bar on 6 June 1864 (Inner Temple Admissions Database, accessed on 22 May 2024, https://archives.innertemple.org.uk/names/a24bf9f2-e804-4499-8acc-f6d3d7b8f330 ). There was also a Telugu-speaking South Indian Christian named Kasturi Venkataramayya who wrote to his brother in 1860 that he had "entered my name at Lincoln's Inn, where I am to attend the lectures." [Carl Towers and Alex Miller, eds., *The Diary of Kasturi Venkataramayya: An Indian in Victorian England* (Wigan, UK: Wigan Archives Service, 2012), 142, 155.]

[15] The earliest West African at the Inns was probably John Thorpe, from Sierra Leone and of Maroon Caribbean heritage. He was called to the bar in 1850 [Arthur T. Porter, *Creoledom: A Study of the Development of Freetown Society* (London: Oxford University Press, 1963), 14]. The next West Africans came in the 1860s and 1870s, led by Samuel Lewis (also from Sierra Leone) who was admitted to Middle Temple in January 1867. See John D. Hargreaves, "Lewis, Sir Samuel" in *Oxford Dictionary of National Biography*, online version of 3 Jan. 2008, accessed on 22 May 2024, https://doi-org.ezproxy.library.wisc.

early. Nonwhite individuals from the white settler colonies of Canada, Australia, New Zealand, and the aspiring settler colonies of southern and eastern Africa did not become lawyers until well into the twentieth century.[16] A search of admissions records for non-European students at the Inns between 1861 and 1948 yielded more than five thousand names.[17] Most of these students were coming from British colonies.[18] These records contain gaps, most notably the absence of any records from Gray's Inn, so it is likely that there were several thousand more nonwhite students from the empire during this period.[19] The highest concentrations of students came from South Asia, namely British India (including Burma) and Ceylon; and from West Africa, particularly Sierra Leone, Gold Coast, and Nigeria.[20] Only a tiny handful of these students were female, but there were probably several dozen women (mostly Indian) who studied at the bar during the century in question.[21]

The four Inns of Court—Inner Temple, Middle Temple, Lincoln's Inn, and Gray's Inn—were institutions dating from the medieval period that trained the litigators known as barristers in England's split legal profession.[22] Physically, the Inns consisted of Oxbridge college-like quadrangles of barristers' chambers and some lodgings, along with a dining hall, chapel, and library. The Inns were architecturally grand and historic, but also easy to miss. Then as now, they were tucked away behind the bustling

edu/10.1093/ref:odnb/72676. Most students from West African colonies were of African descent, including those with Christian names who were often of mixed-race background. I thank Erin Braatz for confirming this point.

[16] The racialized barriers to entry into the legal profession were less pronounced in colonies with very small white populations. See Mitra Sharafi, "A New History of Colonial Lawyering: Likhovski and Legal Identities in the British Empire," *Law & Social Inquiry* 32.4 (2007): 1079; and *Law and Identity*, 103–4.

[17] I thank Bennett Cross for compiling much of this database for me. It contains 5,327 entries for the period 1861–1948 (on file with author). In addition to using the Inner Temple Admissions Database, it draws on the published or printed admissions records of Inner Temple, Middle Temple, and Lincoln's Inn, namely: Baker; *Inner Temple Archives: Alphabetical Index of Members (1851–1929), Showing Dates of Admission and Call)* (London: n.p., 1997); *The Records of the Honourable Society of Lincoln's Inn* (London: Lincoln's Inn, 1896), II (1800–1893) and III (1894–1956); and Sturgess, II (1782–1909) and III (1910–44). For lists of South Asian students at the Inns, 1864–1947 (not including Gray's Inn and including Inner Temple entries only up to 1929), see my South Asian Legal History Resources website, accessed on 22 May 2024, https://salh.law.wisc.edu/south-asian-law-students-at-the-inns-of-court/. For a searchable database of all students at Inner Temple, 1547–1940, see the Inner Temple Admissions Database, accessed on 22 May 2024, https://archives.innertemple.org.uk/names/browse/admissions.

[18] See generally Daniel Duman, *The English and Colonial Bars in the Nineteenth Century* (London: Croom Helm, [1983]), 121–42. ch. 4.

[19] This estimate may be conservative in light of Gower's claim that after World War II, there were approximately two thousand African law students in London at any one time. [L. C. B. Gower, *Independent Africa: The Challenge to the Legal Profession* (Cambridge: Harvard University Press, 1967), 110.]

[20] On South Asian students, see Shompa Lahiri, *Indians in Britain: Anglo-Indian Encounters, Race and Identity, 1880–1930* (London: Routledge, 2013), 7–8.

[21] Of the 14 readily identifiable women in my database (see note 17), there were nine from South Asia, two from West Africa, and one from Penang. On Parsi female students at the Inns, see Sharafi, *Law and Identity*, 108 at note 140 and accompanying text.

[22] Inner Temple and Middle Temple were built on the site formerly occupied by the medieval Knights Templar, hence their names. See Russell, "The Bar of England," 481; C. E. A. Bedwell, *A Brief History of the Middle Temple* (London: Butterworth, 1909); Richard O. Havery, ed., *History of the Middle Temple* (Oxford: Hart, 2011); Angela Holdsworth, ed., *A Portrait of Lincoln's Inn* (London: Third Millennium, 2007); and Clare Rider and Val Horsler, eds., *The Inner Temple: A Community of Communities* (London: Third Millennium, 2007).

London shopfronts below Chancery Lane and the Royal Courts of Justice. A series of unassuming doorways led into the inner world of the imperial legal profession.

The legal profession in England consisted of barristers and solicitors. The latter were akin to general practitioners in medicine. A potential client would hire a solicitor. That solicitor would then engage a barrister for any court appearances. The client was "lathered in one shop and shaved in another."[23] The solicitor, who worked in a law firm with extensive office infrastructure, handled all aspects of the case before and after court appearances and provided support (like document retrieval) to the barrister in court. Barristers were self-employed, although they rented out office space known as "chambers" in clusters at an Inn of Court.[24] In most parts of the empire, the legal profession was not split between barristers and solicitors.[25] But most elite members of the legal profession in British India, for instance, were barristers. As Yves Dezalay and Bryant Garth have observed, elites justified their position back in the colony in part through their acquisition of "prestigious learned capital acquired abroad," including at the Inns.[26] Barrister status allowed them to appear in court across the British Empire.[27]

What did it take to be called to the bar? One first had to apply and be admitted to an Inn. By the late nineteenth century, this process required passing preliminary entrance examinations (on the English language, Latin, and English history) and submitting two certificates of "good character" from barristers of at least five years' standing.[28] Colonial students could gain exemption from the requirement that they pass the preliminary Latin exam, although not all did.[29] From the early twentieth century, candidates had to obtain a BA before joining the Inns.[30] It was also common practice to do a pupillage (apprenticeship) for at least one year with a barrister of minimum ten years' experience.[31] There was also the matter of funding. The club-like benefits of

[23] Russell, "The Bar of England," 482.

[24] For histories of the English Bar, see "Barristers" in the Earl of Halsbury, *The Laws of England Being a Complete Statement of the Whole Law of England* (London: Butterworth, 1908), II, 357–423; Raymond Cocks, *Foundations of the Modern Bar* (London: Sweet and Maxwell, 1983); David Lemmings, *Professors of the Law: Barristers and English Legal Culture in the Eighteenth Century* (Oxford: Oxford University Press, 2000); and Allyson May, *The Bar and the Old Bailey, 1750–1850* (Chapel Hill: University of North Carolina Press, 2003).

[25] Exceptions were Bombay, Ceylon, the Cape Colony, and New South Wales, which had split legal professions. [Bedwell, *A Brief History* (part 1), 210; Sharafi, *Law and Identity*, 109–11.]

[26] Yves Dezalay and Bryant G. Garth, *Asian Legal Revivals: Lawyers in the Shadow of Empire* (Chicago: University of Chicago Press, 2010), 4–5.

[27] By C. E. A. Bedwell in the *Journal of the Society of Comparative Legislation* (new series), see "Conditions of Admission to the Legal Profession throughout the British Empire" (part 1), 12.2 (1912): 209–32; and (part 2): 13.1 (1912), 130–44.

[28] Halsbury, *The Laws of England*, 363–4; Russell, "The Bar of England," 482; and Charles R. DiSalvo, *M. K. Gandhi, Attorney at Law: The Man before the Mahatma* (Berkeley: University of California Press, 2013), 8. See ADM/6: Admission Papers (1805–1927), ITA.

[29] For example, "J. E. Biney, a native of the Gold Coast, to be excused Latin in the Preliminary Examination" (11 Jan. 1901) in BTO (12 Jan. 1897–17 Dec. 1902)(BEN/1/31). Gandhi, however, learned Latin in order to pass the Latin exam [M. K. Gandhi, *The Law and the Lawyers* (Ahmedabad: Navajivan, 1962), 9.]

[30] A. J. C. Mistry, *Forty Years' Reminiscences of the High Court of Judicature at Bombay* (Bombay: Author, 1925), 42. Having passed "a public examination at any university within the British dominions" led to exemption from the entrance exams at the Inns (Russell, "The Bar of England," 482).

[31] Mistry, *Forty Years' Reminiscences*, 42. Gandhi did not do a pupillage (DiSalvo, *M. K. Gandhi*, 7–8).

being an imperial barrister did not come cheap. An Inns education was usually privately funded by the student's own family or sometimes through community-specific philanthropy.[32]

Admitted students usually spent about three years at an Inn, keeping 12 terms. Candidates had to be at least 21 years old.[33] There was an academic component: students had to pass exams in particular fields, but attendance at lectures was optional, and exams could be retaken.[34] Courses included Constitutional Law and Legal History, Criminal Law and Procedure, Real Property and Conveyances, and Roman Law. Taken almost exclusively by a small number of colonial students were Hindu and Mahomedan Law, along with Roman-Dutch law.[35] "The curriculum of study was easy," reported Gandhi in his autobiography. "Everyone knew that the examinations had practically no value."[36]

Just as important as the exams were the dinners. "Eating dinners" was in fact shorthand for studying at the Inns.[37] Students had to attend a minimum number of formal dinners (usually six per term) at their Inn.[38] A 1904 American account of the Inns described the meals thus:

> Four long oak tables, with primitive, backless benches, each accommodating about one hundred, and a shorter table in a dais for the Benchers, are arranged for lunch, and again at 6 o'clock, when many Benchers, barristers, and students, in their white wigs and black robes, assemble for dinner—[the African], the Hindoo, the Mohammedan, the West Indian, the Egyptian, the Boer—children of the Empire, who congregate in London, "the stony hearted stepmother," imbibe a little legal and perhaps other knowledge, and scatter to the four quarters of the globe.[39]

These dinners were as culturally distinctive as "formal hall" at an Oxbridge college. Each Inn's rules of etiquette had to be internalized.

The food could also be a challenge for South Asian students. As Gandhi described them in his autobiography, vegetarian meals usually meant "bread, boiled potato and cabbage." He often ate nothing at the dinners, but had to attend in order to fulfill the six-dinner requirement. Gandhi did not drink alcohol either. As a result, he was

[32] The cost of Gandhi's London studies was significant, given "the poverty of [his] family." Ultimately, his older brother raised the money (Gandhi, *Autobiography*, 52–6). On scholarships funded by Parsi philanthropists for Parsi students at the Inns, see Sharafi, *Law and Identity*, 109.

[33] Bedwell, "Conditions of Admission to the Legal Profession" (part 1), 210.

[34] See DiSalvo, *M. K. Gandhi*, 1–16.

[35] A set of 1893 figures for "Hindu and Mahommedan Law" and "Roman-Dutch Law" respectively reported particularly low attendance rates. ["Report by the Council of Legal Education to the Inns of Court," 3 in BTO (12 Jan. 1892–24 Nov. 1896) (BEN/1/30).] See also exam results in "Law Examination Results," *India*, 23 April 1909, 236–7; and "Council of Legal Education," *TL* (9 June 1909), 3.

[36] Gandhi, *Autobiography*, 67.

[37] For example, see Nari Rustomji, *Enchanted Frontiers: Sikkim, Bhutan, and India's North-Eastern Borderlands* (Bombay: Oxford University Press, 1971), 8.

[38] Bedwell, "Conditions of Admission to the Legal Profession" (part 1), 210.

[39] Russell, "The Bar of England," 481, quoted in "Gleanings. The Bar of England," *Bombay Law Reporter* 6 (1904) (journal section): 24. A term from the title of a Rudyard Kipling poem about the Soudan Expeditionary Force (1892) has been edited out [Rudyard Kipling, *Barrack Room Ballads and Other Poems* (London: Methuen, 1892), 10–12].

particularly in demand at special "grand night" dinners when the allotment of alcohol per four-person group was larger than usual.[40] Observant Muslim students had to avoid pork and alcohol.[41] Smoking after dinner was also a custom that forced some students to choose between violating religious norms and feeling socially excluded.[42] The Inns were as much Anglicizing finishing schools for colonials as they were inculcators of technical legal knowledge.

The Inns of Court had some lodgings available, but by the turn of the twentieth century, most students lived outside of the Inns in private accommodation. South Asian students were often lodgers or boarders known as "Paying Guests" (PGs) in British homes in London neighborhoods like Bloomsbury, Holborn, and Kensington.[43] Bayswater was known as "Asia Minor."[44] For many colonial students, socializing with elite Britons—particularly in the latters' homes—was an unusual event. Their British PG hosts were generally working-class.[45] Many of these hosts provided rented accommodation to a string of colonial law students over the years. In some cases, the law students or their relatives married the daughters of their landladies.[46] But by the 1920s with the rise of Indian student organizations and the independence movement, the criticism that colonial students only mixed with each other seemed to overshadow the social interaction with Britons in these homestays.[47]

Law courses and exams at the Inns were overseen by the Council for Legal Education.[48] All other aspects of life at the Inns were the domain of the Masters of the Bench (known as benchers) of each Inn. The benchers were a group of senior barristers (including some judges) in charge of Inn governance. They exercised a disciplinary power over all of the Inn's members, and could expel any student, disbar a barrister, or disbench one of their own group for conduct "unbecoming" of their profession.[49] In the words of an American observer in 1903:

> They may bar or disbar a member, and have the fullest control of and supervision over the morals and conduct of their members, so far as their professional etiquette

[40] Gandhi, *Autobiography*, 67; Guha, *Gandhi before India*, 36–54.

[41] Intoxicating substances were central to life at the Inns. Inner Temple had "Wine" and "Cigar" committees, for instance. See BTO 1908–11 (16 Nov. 1909) (BEN/1/33).

[42] Smoking violated the purity laws of the Zoroastrian religion, although many Parsis chose to be part of imperial smoking culture. See Sharafi, *Law and Identity*, 311.

[43] Even before the rise of online platforms like Airbnb, the term PG and the practice of taking in lodgers continued in India. For a fictional depiction of what could go wrong, see Rohinton Mistry's short story, "The Paying Guests" in his collection, *Swimming Lessons, and Other Stories from Firozsha Baag* (Boston: Houghton Mifflin, 1989), 123–42.

[44] Fischer-Tiné, *Shyamji Krishnavarma*, 54.

[45] S. Mukherjee, *Nationalism, Education, and Migrant* Identities, 57-8.

[46] For example, R. P. Vachha's cousin married the daughter of Vachha's English host, Mrs. Appleby. (Conversations with R. P. Vachha, Mumbai, 24 February–8 March 2004.) For Vachha's admission and call records, see *Records of Hon. Society of Lincoln's Inn*, III, 328; and P. V. Baker, ed., *The Records of the Honourable Society of Lincolns Inn. The Black Books. Vol.VI. AD 1914–AD 1965* (London: Lincolns' Inn, 2001), 770. See also Lahiri, *Indians in Britain*, 94, 140, 196–7.

[47] S. Mukherjee, *Nationalism, Education, and Migrant* Identities, 78, 82–89. For an early version of this critique (1909), see Lahiri, *Indians in Britain*, 119.

[48] Halsbury, *The Laws of England*, 361, 364.

[49] Halsbury, *The Laws of England*, 361–2.

and mere social decency is concerned, and in former days regulated dress, manners, morals, and religious observances of students.[50]

Most disbarments at Inner Temple followed criminal convictions.[51] Some had an imperial element.[52] Among the 47 files of disciplinary proceedings at Inner Temple (1821–1938) were cases of barristers convicted of fraud in Canada, perjury in British Honduras, and forgery in England leading to transportation for life (probably to Australia).[53] More unusual were cases involving fistfights in the courtroom, the indecency and insanity of a barrister, the impersonation of a Ministry of Munitions employee during World War I, and a seditious libel conviction for socialist publications in the *Workers' Weekly*.[54] The decision of an Inn's Benchers could be appealed to a Committee of Judges sitting under the Lord Chancellor in the House of Lords.[55]

There were at least five disbarments of South Asians from Inner Temple, plus Ghose's case of withdrawal followed by readmission. In addition to the case of Krishnavarma, Nasarwanji Framji Bhandara was disbarred in 1901 for "unprofessional conduct," Shapurji Kavasji Sanjana in 1903 for forging a will, and Syed Khelafat Husain in 1915 following a criminal conviction in India for "cheating."[56] And of course, there was the 1922 disbarment of M. K. Gandhi following his conviction for sedition in India.[57] He was readmitted posthumously in 1988, 40 years after his assassination and 100 years after his admission as a student.[58]

[50] Russell, "The Bar of England," 481.

[51] For a study of disbarments of British barristers at the Inns, see W. Wesley Pue, "The End of Free Trade in Law: Discipline at the Inns in the 1860s" in his book, *Lawyers' Empire: Legal Professions and Cultural Authority, 1780–1950* (Vancouver: University of British Columbia Press, 2016), 268–332.

[52] On West African barristers disbarred after criminal convictions, see the cases of O. Rotimi Aladé (1909, DIS/1/A1) and Isaac John Roberts (1893-6, DIS/1/R2).

[53] See the cases of A. C. J. Boulton (1895, DIS/1/B2), Abraham Malory Dillet ([1885], DIS/1/D2), and James Townshend Saward (1857, DIS/1/S7). In the 1885 case, Dillet (who was allegedly drunk) brought a whip to court and threatened to thrash the Attorney General of British Honduras for being an "impertinent fellow." See the Privy Council case of *In re Abraham Mallory Dillet* (1887) Law Reports Appeal Cases XII, 459–70.

[54] See the cases of John K. C. Roskill (1898, DIS/1/R1), John Horatio Lloyd (1849, DIS/1/L2/1–2), William Strafford Levinson (1921–23, DIS/1/L1), and T. H. Wintringham (1925–26, DIS/1/W4).

[55] Untitled, *India*, 14 May 1909, 287.

[56] There are no files on Bhandara, Sanjana, or Husain in the Inner Temple Disbarment Proceedings. This omission is probably due to the fact that historical records were not systematically collected and stored until the creation of the ITA in the late twentieth century. However, there are references elsewhere in the Inner Temple records to the disbarments of these three individuals. See entry of 22 Nov. 1901 (Bhandara) in BTO (1897–1902) (BEN/1/31); entry of 21 April 1903 (Sanjana) in BTO (13 Jan. 1903–22 Nov. 1907) (BEN/1/32); and entry of 18 June 1926 (Husain spelled Hussain in this instance) in BTO (12 Jan. 1926–25 Nov. 1930) (BEN/1/38). On Sanjana's trial, see "Bombay Criminal Sessions. Alleged Will Forgery," *TI* (17 Feb. 1905), 4. Sanjana and Bhandara were members of the Parsi community, which had extensive involvement in the colonial legal system. See Sharafi, *Law and Identity*.

[57] Gandhi pleaded guilty and was convicted of sedition for his writings under s.24A of the Indian Penal Code. See Gandhi, *Law*, 104–22; and Thomas Strangman, *Indian Courts and Characters* (London: William Heinemann, 1931), 127–43, 209–13.

[58] See Master Sedley, "Mahatma Gandhi and the Inner Temple: Disbarment and Reinstatement" in Rider and Horsler, *Inner Temple*, 52.

## II. The Spirit Letters of A. K. Ghose

The case of A. K. Ghose revolved around his relationship with Miss Frances Henrietta Müller, a Chilean-British figure who was well known for her work in the women's movement.[59] Müller and Ghose met in India in 1893. He was 21. She was about 45. Müller was then a Theosophist, part of a spiritual movement that borrowed heavily from Hindu and Buddhist mysticism and that counted elite Britons, Hindus, and Parsis in Eurasia and North America among its members.[60] Theosophy was a version of what we might call "New Age" religion today.[61] By Ghose's description, Theosophists believed that through "'yoga' meditation," they could be "in direct communion with invisible spirits called Mahatmas—invisible beings who are from the point of view of the Theosophists masters of the world." They also believed in reincarnation.[62] The Theosophists implicitly rejected the racial prejudice of most Britons in India, and one of the movement's leaders, Annie Besant, was elected president of the Indian National Congress in 1917–18.[63] Theosophists believed "in relationships between existing people in a past state of existence and in communication with the spirit world." In 1893–6, they were also "in the habit of imposing on one another with communications and letters purporting to come from the spirit world."[64] Müller started receiving letters from one Ram Linga Deb, a "Mahatma" existing in "another plane." These "spirit letters" were in fact written by Ghose. His aim was to convince her that they had been related in a former life and so "to endear myself to her the more."[65]

Müller was already on her way toward the ascetic life. When Ghose met her, she wore the robes of a sannyasin or female Hindu ascetic and was "living upon fruits."[66] She "took a great liking for Mr. Ghose" and decided that he had been her son in an earlier life.[67] Müller adopted Ghose, publishing announcements in the press in India and in the *Women's Herald* in England.[68] He took the surname Ghose-Müller, and together the new mother and son criss-crossed India and Britain.

[59] See entries for "(Frances) Henrietta Müller" in Elizabeth Crawford, *The Women's Suffrage Movement: A Reference Guide 1866–1928* (London: UCL Press, 1999), 428–30 and by Rosemary Auchmuty in *Oxford Dictionary of National Biography* (online version of 8 Oct. 2009). See also Gwilym Beckerlegge, *The Ramakrishna Mission: The Making of a Modern Hindu Movement* (Delhi: Oxford University Press, 2000), 180–201.

[60] See "Appendix: Theosophy: A Summary and A Criticism" in Geoffrey West, *The Life of Annie Besant* (London: Gerald Howe, 1933), 265–81; Joy Dixon, *Divine Feminine: Theosophy and Feminism in England* (Baltimore: Johns Hopkins University Press, 2001); and anonymous, *The Theosophical Movement, 1875–1925: A History and a Survey* (New York: Dutton, 1925). On white female Theosophists in colonial India, see Kumari Jayawardena, *The White Woman's Other Burden: Western Women and South Asia during British Rule* (New York: Routledge, 1995).

[61] Dixon, *Divine Feminine*, 3, 227–33.

[62] Emphasis original in quotation. Letter from A. K. Ghose to the Treasurer and Masters of the Bench of the Honourable Society of the Inner Temple, 21 Oct. 1901, 2 in Ghose file.

[63] Annie Besant was a leader of the Theosophical movement from the 1890s until her death in 1933.

[64] "Report of the Committee Appointed to Consider and Report on the Application of Mr. A. K. Ghose to be Readmitted as a Student of the Society, and to Have His Former Terms and Standing Allowed," 13 January 1902, 1 in Ghose file.

[65] Letter from Ghose to Inner Temple, 21 Oct. 1901, 2.

[66] Letter from Ghose to Inner Temple, 2.

[67] "Report of the Committee," 1.

[68] Letter from Ghose to Inner Temple, 3-4. It is not clear that this was an adoption recognized by law, as adoption did not yet exist as a legal device in many Anglophone jurisdictions during the late nineteenth century. See Sharafi, *Law and Identity*, 285 at note 60.

Ghose's spirit letters encouraged Müller on her path toward enlightenment. They also urged her to educate her new son in England. Ghose had been studying to become a pleader or vakil in India when he met Müller. Their connection made it possible for him to think of the Inns. Müller first sent him to Trinity Hall College in Cambridge in 1895, where he pursued undergraduate study. It was during his Cambridge days that he wrote many of the letters. At this point, Müller had shifted away from Theosophy and become a devotee of Swami Vivekananda, a Hindu mystic who promoted yoga and other Hindu traditions in the western world.[69] The most audacious spirit letter (written in 1896) encouraged Müller to become an ascetic and leave all her property to Ghose:

> Your best course would be to go to India with Swami [Vivekananda] and establish the Math (*Monastery*) with him, purely from contributions and collections gathered in India from rich people and princes. . . .Your son should either be your sole successor, or he and the property be left in the hands of trustees composed of the McLarens [Müller's sister and brother-in-law], and they be instructed to defray his and your expenses there . . . and re-transfer it to him when he finishes his education there.[70]

However, Ghose soon started to feel guilty. He confessed to his adoptive mother, "being seized with remorse for having fooled his benefactress and committed a great wrong."[71] Müller was "very much annoyed," but later forgave Ghose, writing that "you have my entire forgiveness and I have no bitterness in my heart against you."[72] She had cancelled the adoption and he dropped the name Müller. But after pulling him out of his Cambridge college, she then sent him to Inner Temple, still paying all of his expenses.[73] In a letter dated 1897, Ghose wrote:

> I am deeply touched by your ready forgiveness of my diabolical treachery. My conduct has been . . . a long series of treachery and wicked plans. . . . Before forming the plans I ascertained from Roi Loliere (*a Hindu residing at Ludhiana*) first in a casual way all about the Theosophists, about their credulity in believing everything. I had at this time no idea of forming the plan. It developed in me since then. . . . In the beginning I had no desire to be the sole possessor of all your property. This desire grew in me subsequently. I will no more make any concealments or hesitations, so tell you

[69] See Gwilym Beckerlegge, "Swami Vivekananda (1863–1902) 150 Years On: Critical Studies of an Influential Hindu Guru," *Religious Compass* 7/10 (2013): 444–53. For accounts from within Vivekananda's movement, see Swami Nikhilananda, *Vivekananda: A Biography* (New York: Ramakrishna-Vivekananda Center, 1953); and Swami Narasimhananda, ed., *Vivekananda Reader* (Kolkata: Avaita Ashrama, 2012).

[70] Extract from letter signed "Rama Singa Deb," 30 Sept. 1896 in Appendix II to "Report of the Committee," 19.

[71] "Report of the Committee," 2. Vivekananda did in fact create this monastery (the Belur Math), but largely through the financial contribution of Henrietta Müller. The Belur Math remains the present-day headquarters of Vivekananda's movement: the Ramakrishna Math and Mission in Howrah, West Bengal. See Gwilym Beckerlegge, "Ramakrishna Math and Mission" in Knut A. Jacobsen, Helene Basu, Angelika Malinar, Vasudha Narayanan, eds., *Brill's Encyclopedia of Hinduism Online* (Leiden: Brill, 2018), n.p.

[72] Letter from Ghose to Inner Temple, 5.

[73] Letter from Ghose to Inner Temple, 5.

> everything. I will say nothing but frank and honest truth, no quibble, no evasion. Believe once more. Give me one more chance, the last chance.[74]

Müller said she forgave Ghose. But a few years later—when Ghose was just one term away from being called to the bar in 1899—she changed her mind. She pulled all support and ordered Ghose to return to India within 24 hours on the next available steamer. It was not entirely clear what brought about this change. Ghose had to abandon his chances of becoming a barrister when he had almost completed his program at Inner Temple. He withdrew from the Inn, probably fearing disbarment if he did not.[75] Müller had written to Inner Temple with a detailed account of Ghose's actions. She called him "an extremely slippery person."[76] But as soon as he had returned to India, she wrote again asking the Inn to drop the matter.

After abandoning his London studies, Ghose took up a position in Baroda, a princely state in western India, and rose to the post of Superintendent of Opium Customs and Abkari, "a position of considerable trust and responsibility."[77] He married the daughter of a barrister. Then in 1901, he asked Müller to withdraw her original complaint to Inner Temple. She did so (again), but before Ghose could be readmitted, the Inn had to reinvestigate the charges made earlier. Out of this came a majority report by three members and a dissenting report by two.

According to Müller's initial allegations, a police inspector had recognized Ghose on the ship they were all traveling on from India to Britain. She claimed that Ghose was "known" to police in Calcutta and Simla as a forger. Inner Temple's committee found this claim to be unsubstantiated. The case against Ghose thus came down to the spirit letters. The minority report took a harsh view. Ghose deliberately deceived Müller "with the view and intent that she should adopt him as her son, that she should pay for his education and support and that she should make over certain property to him." These benchers considered his conduct to have been "fraudulent and criminal," although he was never convicted. Despite Ghose's good conduct since and the many character references he provided, these two benchers considered him to be unfit for readmission.[78]

Things looked different to the majority of the committee. From this group's perspective, *Müller* had suggested that Ghose was her son in a past life. The adoption had been her idea, too. She had offered to give Ghose her house at Maidenhead as a gift so he could have the rental income, but he had declined. He only wanted "a good

[74] Letter from Ghose to Müller (1897) in Appendix II to "Report of the Committee," 19–20.

[75] At this point, there was an Inner Temple committee that investigated Müller's accusation that Ghose had "written letters to obtain money by false pretenses." It concluded that Ghose should be permitted to withdraw, but left to some future committee the question of whether to issue him with any kind of certificate for the terms he had kept. Ghose wanted a certificate so he could migrate to another Inn, probably Gray's. Migration to another Inn was prohibited if one had been disbarred from one Inn. ["Report by Masters Poland and Cooper Willis, Members of the Committee Appointed to Consider and Report on the Application of Mr. A. K. Ghose to Be Readmitted as a Student of the Society, and to Have His Former Terms and Standing Allowed," 13 Jan. 1902, 5, 7 in Ghose file.]

[76] Letter from F. H. Müller to Sir Henry Lawrence, 1 or 2 May 1899, 1 in packet of letters (1899–1901), Ghose file.

[77] "Report of the Committee," 4.

[78] "Report by Poland and Cooper Willis," 8–9.

education." And although Ghose's 1896 letter was "very bad," Müller had already decided to lead an ascetic life and give her property to some monastic institution when Ghose wrote it. Even the passage about handing over her estate to Ghose (quoted above) had included a provision for a trust, and the trustees would have been Müller's relatives, who would have managed it with good sense. Ghose had confessed to his letter-writing ruse voluntarily and of his own accord, not long after the Maidenhead house offer, in fact. And he had expressed remorse and regret many times for acting with youthful foolishness.[79] He had reformed since then, and provided the committee with 15 letters of reference from Britons like his former Cambridge tutors and Müller's accountant (one Miss Gradwell), South Asian barristers in India, and high-up members of the Baroda government. These letters characterized Ghose as honest, trustworthy, and responsible.[80] The majority also realized that the future of Ghose and his family were at stake. He was the eldest child in his family. He had to support an elderly father and three sisters, and to educate two brothers. "My whole future depends upon the decision of the Masters of the Bench," pleaded Ghose, "and I hope they will not think it necessary to inflict a lifelong punishment upon me for the foolish wrongdoing of my youth."[81] Ghose was readmitted, but only by one vote.

The committee's decision could be understood in several ways. Ghose may have succeeded because his narrative meshed well with the imperial "civilizing mission" agenda, along with Christian and capitalist values. His was a story of sin followed by a guilty conscience, confession, forgiveness, redemption, and reform through hard work and the taking of personal responsibility. Other parts of the file noted that Ghose made "expressions of penitence and regret."[82] The fact that he voluntarily told Müller the truth would have struck the benchers as a good sign. Anglo education of colonial subjects aimed to replace "native mendacity" and dissimulation with honesty and directness, values most Britons of this era believed were not prioritized in South Asian culture.[83] The majority report and letters used words like honest, truthful, straightforward and trustworthy to describe Ghose.[84] Perhaps the benchers thought that the acculturative aims of an English education were being realized in Ghose's case despite the trickery and dishonesty of the original offense. Ghose said that he had written the spirit letters not out of greed for Müller's wealth, but out of hunger for "a good

[79] "Report of the Committee," 1–2.

[80] "Appendix III: Testimonials" in "Report of the Committee" booklet, 23–27.

[81] Letter from Ghose to Inner Temple, 8.

[82] For instance, "Report by Poland and Cooper Willis," 9.

[83] See Elizabeth Kolsky, *Colonial Justice in British India: White Violence and the Rule of Law* (Cambridge: Cambridge University Press, 2010), 108–19, 217–18; Bhavani Raman, *Document Raj: Writing and Scribes in Early Colonial South India* (Chicago: University of Chicago Press, 2012), 137–60; Wendie Ellen Schneider, *Engines of Truth: Producing Veracity in the Victorian Courtroom* (New Haven: Yale University Press, 2015), 103–42; Mitra Sharafi, "Abortion in South Asia, 1860–1947: A Medico-legal History," *Modern Asian Studies* 55.2 (2021), 396–400; and "The Imperial Serologist and Punitive Self-Harm: Bloodstains and Legal Pluralism in British India" in Ian Burney and Christopher Hamlin, eds., *Global Forensic Cultures: Making Fact and Justice in the Modern Era* (Baltimore: Johns Hopkins University Press, 2019), 60–85.

[84] For example, see "Report of the Committee," 3, 8; letter from S. M. Moses of Bombay, 5 July 1901, 26; and letter from Justice M. G. Ranade, Bombay High Court, 16 Feb. 1900, 27; all in "Report of the Committee" booklet.

education," which meant an English one.[85] To the committee's mind, Anglo education may have been both a source of temptation *and* of redemption.

Racial difference played a role in the case, too. As a Theosophist, Müller began her interactions with Ghose with an unusual openness to social mixing between South Asians and Europeans. Most Britons in India socialized in racially restricted zones like the club.[86] "England-returned" Indian students noted that the rare friendship they made with Britons in England cooled "after Suez," a reference to the point when an India-bound ship reached the Middle East on its route from Europe.[87] One British couple who met Müller socially in Calcutta learned that she had adopted "a young native" who had then "dropped her name when she stopped supplies." That "it should have ended thus" was no surprise to them.[88] This would have been a common attitude among Britons residing in India circa 1900. What was less expected was that Müller's sudden reversal, which forced Ghose to leave Inner Temple, was also racially motivated. The Inner Temple majority report was convinced that racial animus accounted for her change of heart. Müller seems to have taken "this cruel and arbitrary action" of reporting Ghose to Inner Temple several years after forgiving him "not by any dislike to Mr. Ghose personally, but because she had at that time *changed her mind as to India and Indians generally, and had taken a dislike to the country and the race*."[89] In readmitting Ghose, the benchers were thus counteracting the newly discovered racism of his once-adoptive mother.

Finally, while the benchers may have found Ghose's spirit letters troubling, they may also have had doubts about the mystical movements involved. The Inner Temple report referred to Theosophical communications with spirits as "absurdities" that had been exposed as a sham in the British press.[90] A British woman who met Müller socially in Calcutta thought her "a good & interesting person only rather cracked about her Deism or Theosophy."[91] Ghose's letter to the Inn also mentioned details that highlighted the movement's eccentricities. When he started at Cambridge, for instance, Müller told him she had reached the highest level of Theosophical meditation (the fourth plane of the "Raja-yoga") in which a person could see the future and "make events happen according to [her] will."[92] Theosophy's dubiousness may have helped tip the balance in Ghose's favor. Equally, the fact that Müller was female—and a strong-willed female who changed her mind—may have fed into gendered stereotypes of the era that characterized women as erratic, impulsive, emotional, and irrational, and assertive women as troublesome and difficult. Among Vivekananda and his disciplines, Müller was known for her "violent temper and overbearing conduct,

[85] Letter from Ghose to Inner Temple, 8.

[86] See Benjamin B. Cohen, *In the Club: Associational Life in Colonial South Asia* (Manchester: Manchester University Press, 2015).

[87] S. Mukherjee, *Nationalism, Education, and Migrant Identities*, 56.

[88] Typed version of letter from C. A. Elliott to Sir Henry Lawrence, 28 April 1899, in "Report of the Committee" booklet, 16.

[89] Emphasis added. "Report of the Committee," 3.

[90] Reference to "Isis very much unveiled," *Westminster Gazette*, in "Report of the Committee," 1.

[91] Emphasis probably added by Inner Temple reader. Handwritten version of letter from C. A. Elliott to Sir Henry Lawrence, 28 April 1899, in packet of letters (1899–1901), Ghose file.

[92] Letter from Ghose to Inner Temple, 4.

and her awfully vacillating mind."[93] It is hard to know how to interpret such descriptions of Henrietta Müller. But we may speculate that the convergence of her gender, confidence, spiritual associations, and newfound racism may have made Miss Müller seem to the benchers like an unreliable narrator.

## III. "Barrister-Outlaw" Shyamji Krishnavarma

The second case also featured a social movement, but of a very different kind from Theosophy and Vivekananda's following. Shyamji Krishnavarma was an Indian revolutionary branded a terrorist for his advocacy of the violent overthrow of British rule.[94] His strain of the anticolonial movement contrasted with the constitutionalists who led the Indian National Congress in 1885–1919 and the Gandhian advocates of nonviolence who came to dominate the movement from 1920 until Indian independence in 1947.[95] Both Krishnavarma and Gandhi were trained as barristers at Inner Temple.[96] Both advocated extralegal methods to combat colonial rule in India. And both would be disbarred for endorsing these methods, namely nonviolent mass protest, boycott, and hunger strikes for Gandhi and targeted violence for Krishnavarma.[97] Unlike Krishnavarma, Gandhi was disbarred following a criminal conviction.

Krishnavarma was originally from the western Indian princely state of Kutch, a fact he emphasized to stress that technically he owed no allegiance to Britain. He studied at Balliol College Oxford, having first arrived in Oxford as a Sanskrit scholar and assistant to Professor Monier Williams, one of the leading Orientalist scholars of the time. Krishnavarma was called to the bar at Inner Temple in 1884. He returned to India and practiced briefly at the Bombay High Court, before taking up the more prestigious position of diwan or prime minister in the small princely state of Rutlam in central India. Before studying in England, Krishnavarma had married into a family whose wealth, along with the products of his own shrewd investments, helped fund many of

[93] Letter from Vivekananda to Margaret Noble (Sister Nivedita), July 1897, in Beckerlegge, *The Ramakrishna Mission*, 194.

[94] See Fischer-Tiné *Shyamji Krishnavarma*; Indulal Yajnik, *Shyamji Krishnavarma: Life and Times of an Indian Revolutionary* (Bombay: Lakshmi, 1950); Alex Tickell, *Terrorism, Insurgency and Indian-English Literature, 1830–1947* (New York: Routledge, 2012), 135–54; Lahiri, *Indians in Britain*, 123–30; and the "Making Britain" entry, accessed on 22 May 2024, http://www.open.ac.uk/researchprojects/makingbritain/content/shyamaji-krishnavarma.

[95] On the constitutionalists, see Mitra Sharafi, "Indian constitutionalism, the rule of law, and Parsi legal culture," *Indian Law Review* 7.3 (2023): 259–80.. On the continuing work of the constitutionalists leading to the Government of India Act 1935, see Cynthia Farid, "Imperial Constitutionalism: Judicial Politics and Separation of Powers in Colonial India (1861–1935)," (SJD dissertation, University of Wisconsin Law School, 2020). On the Gandhians, see Judith Brown, *Gandhi's Rise to Power: Indian politics 1915–1922* (Cambridge: Cambridge University Press, 1972) and Guha, *Gandhi*. On debates over the use of violence between revolutionaries and Gandhians, see Durba Ghosh, "Gandhi and the Terrorists: Revolutionary Challenges from Bengal and Engagements with Non-Violent Political Protest," *South Asia: Journal of South Asian Studies* 39.3 (2016): 560–76; and Kama Maclean, *A Revolutionary History of Interwar India: Violence, Image, Voice and Text* (Oxford: Oxford University Press, 2015).

[96] On Gandhi's career and writings on law, see DiSalvo, *M. K. Gandhi*; and Gandhi, *Law*.

[97] On Gandhi's posthumous readmission, see note 58. On that of Krishnavarma, see p. 200.

his future political activities.[98] He and his wife returned to London in 1897. In 1905, he established India House in the Highgate neighborhood—what one British newspaper would call "the temple of treason."[99] India House provided lodging for Indian students. It soon became a gathering place for Indian revolutionaries, and was linked to bomb-making and the assassination of a British official named Sir William Curzon Wyllie in 1909.[100] Krishnavarma also published the revolutionary "penny monthly," *The Indian Sociologist,* and fled to Paris in 1907 to avoid arrest for his articles.[101] These writings were at the heart of his disbarment proceedings in 1909, when he was at the peak of his global fame and influence.

Shyamji Krishnavarma's disciplinary process was a reply to a two-sentence anonymous letter published in the *Times* (London). The author asked whether Inner Temple benchers were prepared to take any action against Krishnavarma.[102] In response, Krishnavarma was called to appear in person or put in a written statement at Inner Temple to show why he should not be disbarred.[103] Now living in exile in Paris to avoid arrest in Britain for his political activity, he submitted a long letter to Inner Temple along with a generous sample of *Indian Sociologist* issues containing some of his most scathing critiques of British imperialism.

Krishnavarma's writings inverted the standard colonial narrative about truth-telling and corruption among "natives." The fact that A. K. Ghose had decided to tell Müller the truth about his spirit letters worked in his favor; his was a story about the dissimulating colonial who did the difficult thing and chose honesty. Another colonial stereotype intertwined with the idea that "natives" lied was the assumption that they were corrupt. Krishnavarma took both ideas and turned them on their heads. It was not Indians who lied and dissimulated. British imperialists like the secretary of state for India, Lord Morley, were in fact the liars and hypocrites for pretending to be champions of press freedom and the parliamentary system while strangling both in India.[104] Krishnavarma would surely have regarded "corrupt" Indians working for the colonial state as subverting an illegitimate regime from within. He argued that all laws in British India were void for Indians, "they not being made by the Indian people."[105]

To counteract all of the incentives for colonial collaboration, Krishnavarma created scholarships for young Indians to study in England while staying at India House. Recipients were prohibited from working for the colonial state upon returning

[98] Fischer-Tiné, *Shyamji Krishnavarma*, 57. On Krishnavarma's teenaged marriage to "a millionaire's daughter," see Yajnik, *Shyamji Krishnavarma: Life and Times*, 12–13; and Fischer-Tiné, *Shyamji Krishnavarma*, 7.

[99] "The Educational Adviser of Indian Students," *TL*, 21 April 1909, 6 in Krishnavarma file. See also Fischer-Tiné, *Shyamji Krishnavarma*, 61–5.

[100] On the assassination known as the "London outrage," see Fischer-Tiné, *Shyamji Krishnavarma*, 154–61; and Ghosh, "Gandhi," 563–4.

[101] On *IS*, see Fischer Tiné, *Shyamji Krishnavarma*, 58–60.

[102] "Indian Anarchism in England," *TL*, 25 Feb. 1909, 9.

[103] Letter from Walter G. Wrangham, Sub-treasurer, Inner Temple to Shyamji Krishnavarma, 26 March 1909, Appendix I to letter from Shyamji Krishnavarma to the Masters of the Bench of the Honourable Society of the Inner Temple, 21 April 1909, in Krishnavarma file.

[104] "British Policy of Reform as an Outcome of Nationalist Agitation and Action. Tables Turned—Charge of Dishonesty Brought Home to the Secretary of State for India," *IS*, V.2 (February 1909): 1 in Krishnavarma file.

[105] "The Educational Adviser of Indian Students."

to India. The barrister also created positions for several "political missionaries" who would propagate the anti-imperial message in England. Beyond Britain, Krishnavarma helped forge a global diaspora of student revolutionaries: "my young countrymen now sojourning for study in Europe, America, Japan, and elsewhere are the rising hopes of the Indian nation."[106] He covered the postage "to all parts of the world" for *Indian Sociologist* subscribers.[107]

Similarly, Krishnavarma inverted colonial characterizations of good character. In 1908, a planned assassination of a British magistrate in Muzaffarpur, India, went wrong. Two British women (the wife and daughter of a British barrister) were killed when a bomb landed in their carriage by mistake. The murders of Mrs. and Miss Kennedy were held up in the British press as evidence of the cruelty of extremist radicals, who commemorated with monuments and scholarships "even the murder of defenseless Englishwomen."[108] Krishnavarma countered that while their killing had been "quite accidental and incidental," all Europeans who chose to live in British India were risking their lives. Krishnavarma warned his British friends and acquaintances "against the risks they run of losing their kith and kin by allowing them to go to India in these troubled times, since every Englishman who goes there for exploiting that country directly or indirectly is regarded as a potential enemy" by Indian nationalists.[109]

London newspapers described the Muzaffarpur bombers as cold-blooded killers and *The Indian Sociologist* as "largely devoted to the glorification of murder."[110] By contrast, Krishnavarma celebrated these men as brave individuals who sacrificed themselves for the good of the Indian people. Once detained and executed by the colonial state, they became martyrs. Three young Indians were executed for the Kennedy killings, while the fourth died by suicide before he could be taken into police custody. In honor of the men, Krishnavarma proposed additional scholarships, a memorial plaque at India House, and payments ("tokens of gratitude") to the men's relatives.[111]

Durba Ghosh has shown how powerful the language of martyrdom became with reference to Bengali nationalist "gentlemen terrorists" who died for the cause.[112] Krishnavarma turned his own disbarment into a kind of martyrdom. He relished the attention and reveled in the rejection: "[I]t would be a signal and unique honor conferred on a humble Indian like myself if the Benchers of the Inner Temple decide to

106 "The Educational Adviser of Indian Students." On California, see Maia Ramnath, *Haj to Utopia: How the Ghadar Movement Charted Global Radicalism and Attempted to Overthrow the British Empire* (Berkeley: University of California Press, 2011); S. Mukherjee, *Nationalism, Education, and Migrant* Identities, 98; and Fischer-Tiné, *Shyamji Krishnavarma*, 100 at note 114. On New York and Tokyo, see Fischer-Tiné, *Shyamji Krishnavarma*, 68–72.

107 See *IS*, V.2 (Feb. 1909): 1.

108 "Indian Anarchism in England" (letter to the editor by "Corruptio Optimi Pessima"), *TL*, 13 Feb. 1909, 10 in Krishnavarma file.

109 Untitled excerpt from *IS*, V.3 (March 1909): 11 in Krishnavarma file.

110 For example, see "Indian Anarchism in England," *TL* (13 Feb. 1909), 10.

111 The men were Prafulla Chaki, Khudiram Bose, Kanailal Dutt, and Satyendra Nath Bose. ["Indian Anarchism in England" (letter by "Corruptio Optimi Pessima"), *TL* (13 Feb. 1909), 10 in Krishnavarma file.] For a 1940s depiction of the hanging of Khudiram Bose, see Durba Ghosh, *Gentlemanly Terrorists: Political Violence and the Colonial State in India, 1919–1947* (Cambridge: Cambridge University Press, 2017), 25 and cover image.

112 Ghosh, *Gentlemanly Terrorists*, 84–86.

disbar me for the expression of my political opinions." It was no punishment for him to be disbarred, Krishnavarma continued, as he had stopped practicing law 16 years earlier and would not practice in India until and unless it became independent.[113] He rejoiced "at the prospect of persecution in England." Nothing would help his cause more than "Englishmen's open hostility to freedom of speech and writing."[114]

Krishnavarma rejected legal methods for defeating colonial rule, but he framed his case in a rule-of-law manner when speaking to lawyers at the Inns. He requested to know the precise charges made against him. Specifically, he asked the benchers to identify particular passages of his writings and explain why they were objectionable. The benchers did not comply with this request, and the general vagueness of their response suggested discomfort in articulating their position explicitly.[115] The legal profession was supposed to be apolitical. Indeed, Afrikaaner students at Inner Temple *fought against Britain* in the Second Boer War (1899–1902) and were permitted to return to the Inn afterwards. As Krishnavarma noted pointedly, *they were not disbarred.*[116] Yet somehow criticizing British rule in India was different—even though Krishnavarma argued that he hailed from an independent state just as Afrikaaner students did in the run-up to the Boer War.[117] Or perhaps the problem was being critical while Indian. In an eerie foreshadowing of WWII possibilities, Krishnavarma asked "whether an Indian is not entitled to plead for the independence of his own country just like an Englishman, supposing Germany or France conquers England and governs it despotically."[118] Had he lived to see the Blitz, Krishnavarma might have asked: Was Hitler not trying to colonize Britain? And were not all colonized or potentially colonized people (Britons included) justified in defending themselves?

Krishnavarma also marshalled the language of rights and freedoms. He asserted that he had a right to express his political views in "England, which is a free country as opposed to British India."[119] Krishnavarma's newspaper was banned in India, but not in Britain, for instance.[120] Indian students often commented on the liberty they observed in the imperial metropole, in stark contrast to the despotic rule they knew in British India.[121] The Macaulayan project of creating loyal colonized elites through education in Britain backfired in this way. Here again Krishnavarma pointed out that it was Britons, not colonized subjects, who were the liars and hypocrites: they

[113] "The English Press and Ourselves," *IS*, V.4 (April 1909): 1 in Krishnavarma file. For an abbreviated version, see letter from Krishnavarma to Inner Temple (21 April 1909), 9.

[114] Untitled excerpt in *IS*, V.4 (April 1909): 14 in Krishnavarma file.

[115] "Indian Anarchism and the Inner Temple" (letter by Krishnavarma), *TL*, 7 May 1909, 4 in Krishnavarma file.

[116] "Indian Anarchism and the Inner Temple." On the return of Boers as well as Americans who had fought in the American Revolution, see Lahiri, *Indians in Britain*, 127.

[117] Although Kutch was arguably only semi-independent from Britain, the same could be said of the South African Boer republics at the outbreak of the Boer War. On princely state sovereignty, see Priyasha Saksena, "Jousting over Jurisdiction: Sovereignty and International Law in Late Nineteenth-Century South Asia," *Law and History Review* 38.2 (2020), 409–57.

[118] Letter from Krishnavarma to Inner Temple (21 April 1909), 2. For related discussion, see M. K. Gandhi's remarkable letter to Adolf Hitler (24 Dec. 1940) in *The Collected Works of Mahatma Gandhi* (Delhi: Government of India, 2000–1), 454–6.

[119] "The Educational Adviser of Indian Students"; and "The English Press and Ourselves," 1.

[120] Untitled excerpt in *IS*, V.4 (April 1909): 14.

[121] S. Mukherjee, *Nationalism, Education, and Migrant* Identities, 90–2, 97.

celebrated liberty as an inherent feature of Britishness and provided it to the population in Britain, but denied it to their subjects in India. Like political "children" stuck in the "waiting room of history," colonized peoples were perpetually told "not yet" when they pressed for representative democracy.[122] Here was imperial mendacity in full bloom.

After setting up the right to express controversial political views, *The Indian Sociologist* gave voice to these opinions. The most subversive was the defense of violent methods, Krishnavarma's position between 1908 and 1918. His "ethics of dynamite" fetishized the use of explosives, in particular.[123] Krishnavarma reminded his readers that polities had been founded in Britain and America through violence. The American revolutionary George Washington—"the archenemy of England"—had created the United States of America through violence. Washington was now celebrated even by British ambassadors:

> Let it always be remembered that it was George Washington who, in 1769 . . . made the emphatic declaration that "no man should scruple or hesitate a moment to use arms in defense of freedom" . . . and [that] the representative of the British Government in America now openly holds up this successful arch-rebel—the first President of the United States—as a model man![124]

In England, the "arch-traitor" Oliver Cromwell and his puritans, including the "regicide John Milton," killed the king to establish their government in the mid-seventeenth century. Cromwell and Milton were now honored with tombs in Westminster Abbey, and Milton was celebrated as "a pioneer of democracy" to whom "the English race [largely owed] constitutional government."[125] Even the barons who extracted the Magna Carta of 1215 from King John did so not "by peaceful argument, but by an array of armed barons who imposed it on [King John] by threats of force."[126] The British claim that the use of violence was an unacceptable form of political action was thus belied by Britain's own history. Krishnavarma implied that the use of violence was wrong *only if one lost.*

Krishnavarma had Indian opponents as well as British ones for his "violence if necessary" stance. A number of South Asian critics had previously been his allies or followers.[127] They broke with him over his endorsement of violence, and published letters in the *Times* (London) insisting that Krishnavarma was a marginal figure who was out of touch with India, having lived abroad for years. He did not represent

[122] Uday Singh Mehta, *Liberalism and Empire: A Study in Nineteenth-Century British Liberal Thought* (Chicago: Chicago University Press, 1999), 31–3; and Dipesh Chakrabarty, *Provincializing Europe: Postcolonial Thought and Historical Difference* (Princeton: Princeton University Press, 2002), 8–10.

[123] See Fischer-Tiné, *Shyamji Krishnavarma*, 110–82.

[124] Letter to the editor of the *TL* by Krishnavarma, reprinted in *IS*, V.3 (March 1909): 10–11, in Krishnavarma file. Three decades later in the Indian National Army treason trial of 1945, a similar reference was made to the American revolution as justification for armed revolt against British rule. See Mithi Mukherjee, "The 'Right to Wage War' against Empire: Anticolonialism and the Challenge to International Law in the Indian National Army Trial of 1945," *Law & Social Inquiry* 44.2 (2019): 430–1.

[125] Letter to the editor by Krishnavarma in *IS*, V.3 (March 1909): 10.

[126] "India must use force. Advice to Indian Flunkeys" *IS*, V.2 (Feb.1909): 8 in Krishnavarma file.

[127] On Bipin Chandra Pal's break with Krishnavarma, see Fischer-Tiné, *Shyamji Krishnavarma*, 134.

Indian nationalists.[128] "Secret assassinations have no sanction in our political philosophy," wrote Bipin Chandra Pal, "and are repugnant to the moral instincts of our race." Krishnavarma countered that violence was hardly antithetical to Indian tradition. In Hindu scripture, Rama and Krishna were best known for killing the tyrants Ravana and Kansa, and Manu, the author of the classical Hindu law text, included a "long list of tyrannical rulers who were extirpated."[129]

Krishnavarma's case was an easy one for the Inner Temple benchers. Unlike in Ghose's case, the benchers were not divided amongst themselves. Krishnavarma showed no regret or remorse for his writings. He continued to propagate his views. His institutional work and writings threatened to spread his violent opposition to British rule like a contagion. The "barrister-outlaw" (Krishnavarma's own term) could be no barrister at all.[130] He was disbarred on 30 April 1909, trailing others in his wake. In the months that followed, two Indian students were investigated by Gray's Inn for their ties to Krishnavarma and India House. The Inn refused to call to the bar at least one: the future revolutionary leader, V. D. Savarkar.[131]

Krishnavarma's case had institutional consequences for other Indian students in England, too. In 1903, a Parsi barrister named S. A. Kapadia had written to Inner Temple proposing that Indian students have some kind of advisor to help them meet the considerable bureaucratic requirements of English institutions, including the Inns. This figure would also work to prevent the use of fraudulent references. The benchers rejected the idea because of its potential to be used in an inquisitorial and oppressive manner.[132] Six years later, after Krishnavarma's disbarment, the educational advisor to Indian students suddenly became viable, as did a new Bureau of Information for Indian Students. Both would be created by the secretary of state for India. Gone were concerns about alienating South Asian students. The advisor would help Indian students gather their documents. More important, though, he would watch for radicalization.[133] Krishnavarma's disbarment was thus a catalyst for the creation of a surveillance machinery that would monitor Indian students and create

[128] See letter from Virendranath Chattopadhyaya to the editor, "Indian Anarchism in England," *TL* (1 March 1909), 6 noted in "Ethics of Indian Nationalism," *IS*, V.4 (April 1909): 14 in Krishnavarma file. On the conflict between "Chatto" and Krishnavarma, see Fischer-Tiné, *Shyamji Krishnavarma*, 117.

[129] "Ethics of Indian Nationalism," 15–16. Bipin Chandra Pal was an early leader of the nationalist movement, moving between the Indian National Congress and more revolutionary circles. See Bipin Chandra Pal, *Memories of My Life and Times* (Calcutta: Modern Book Agency, 1932).

[130] In Krishnavarma's words, "it is a distinction by itself to be a Barrister-outlaw instead of Barrister-at-Law . . . " ["The English Press and Ourselves," 1.]

[131] Two untitled articles, *India*, 14 May 1909, 287; "Gray's Inn Indian Student," *The Westminster Gazette*, 15 July 1909, 10; and "Our London Letter," *The Devon and Exeter Gazette*, 9 Feb. 1910), 3. Savarkar continues to have influence in India today as the "father of Hindutva."

[132] Letter from S. A. Kapadia to Inner Temple Treasurer, 13 Jan. 1902, and Committee recommendation against Kapadia proposal (Ralph Neville, chairman), 16 July 1903, both reproduced in BTO (4 Aug. 1903) in BTO 1903-7 (BEN/1/32). Relatedly, see S. Mukherjee, *Nationalism, Education, and Migrant Identities*, 15–17.

[133] "By means of this agency it is hoped that the Educational Adviser will be able to obtain all information regarding individual students which may be desired by the University and other authorities in this country, and thus to meet what is understood to be a need which has made itself felt for detailed and trustworthy information as to the position, means, and character of Indian applicants." [Letter from [Colin] Campbell, India Office, Whitehall to Inner Temple benchers, 2 July 1909, reproduced in BTO (27 July 1909) in BTO 1908–11 (BEN/1/33). See also Lahiri, *Indians in Britain*, 127–37.

an atmosphere of mutual distrust in the decades to come.[134] This apparatus included spies posing as Indian law students and European landladies.[135]

## IV. Education, Race, and Sex at the Imperial Bar

These cases spoke to the role of education, race, and sex in setting the boundaries of membership at the imperial bar. One aim of Anglo education across the British empire was to replace "native deceptiveness" with "good character." Ghose's case was a successful redemption story in this way: an early fall from grace led to truth-telling and acceptance of fault, following by personal reform through hard work. By contrast, Krishnavarma's story was surely regarded by many Britons as a failure of Anglo education, evidencing what some would have considered "the practical impossibility of civilizing a savage."[136] Despite his time at Oxford and Inner Temple (or perhaps because of it), Krishnavarma had become an anti-imperial radical. The dinners had not worked. Here lurked the Frankenstein-like potential of educating colonial students in Britain: it could be excessively liberating. In the revolutionary's own words, "[T]his sort of education cannot avoid producing men with views hostile to a foreign yoke. . . ."[137]

The role of racial difference was another key theme in these cases. Krishnavarma implied that he was disciplined, unlike the Boer students returning from war, because he was not white. He considered British rule in India an "albinocracy"—a regime grounded in white supremacy.[138] At the same time, he claimed to have "thousands" of British friends and acquaintances, after living in Britain for years.[139] Like Gandhi, Krishnavarma recognized the strategic value of opposing a racist colonial regime without condemning all white people. The enemy was British rule, not all Britons. And yet he drew the line at sexual intermixing between the races. Krishnavarma felt that such relationships put revolutionary cells at risk.[140] More broadly, he adopted Spencer's antimiscegenation views, claiming that the result of intermixing between human races was "*inevitably a bad one in the long run*."[141] Relationships between non-European men and European women (usually working-class) were not uncommon in

[134] See S. Mukherjee, *Nationalism, Education, and Migrant* Identities, 25–6, 87, 95, 97, 102, 104, 110.

[135] For example, see Lahiri, *Indians in Britain*, 128–9; and "Employment and expenses of Indian informant, Sajani Ranjan Banerjea, alias Sukasagar Dutt, to watch Indian students in London" (Sept.1909–Sept. 1913) (IOR/L/PS/8/67). I owe the latter reference to Jesse Tumblin. See generally Richard Popplewell, "The Surveillance of Indian Revolutionaries in Great Britain and on the Continent," *Intelligence and National Security* 3 (1988).1, 56–76.

[136] This line was in fact used to describe India House resident Madan Lal Dhingra, the engineering student who assassinated Curzon Wyllie in 1909 [*Penny Illustrated Paper* (1909), cited in Fischer-Tiné, *Shyamji Krishnavarma*, 158 and 180 at note 273].

[137] Krishnavarma in Fischer-Tiné, *Shyamji Krishnavarma*, 130.

[138] Krishnavarma borrowed this term from Benoy Kumar Sarkar's 1939 book, *The Sociology of Races and Cultures and Human Progress: Studies in the Relations between Asia and Euro-America* (Fischer-Tiné, *Shyamji Krishnavarma*, 110, 164 at note 2).

[139] "The London 'Times' and Ourselves," *IS* (March 1909): 11.

[140] Fischer-Tiné, *Shyamji Krishnavarma*, 87.

[141] Krishnavarma quoting Spencer (italics in original), cited in Fischer-Tiné, *Shyamji Krishnavarma*, 87.

revolutionary circles in Europe.[142] Krishnavarma in fact fell out with fellow Gujarati and former law student S. R. Rana, a key revolutionary in Paris, because he disapproved of Rana's romantic involvement with a German woman, Therese Liszt.[143] This conflict between the two men, who had been close for years, contributed to Krishnavarma's alienation from other revolutionaries in Paris and his eventual flight to Geneva.

The Ghose case was also complex on race. The earlier relationship between Ghose and Müller reflected "affective community" and intimacy across the racial divide.[144] Ghose and Müller were fictive kin for a time. And yet, some of these ties may have been built on racialized stereotypes. Was Müller partly drawn to the young Ghose because she believed him to have a certain "spiritual capital" as a brown man from "the East"? Did Ghose fail to dispel this myth, which may have boosted his status and influence in Theosophical and other mystical circles of the day?

It is also worth noting how ideas about race and sex intersected in the Ghose case. Müller's turn against India and Indians may have been grounded in her feminism. Her withdrawal of support for Ghose and for the spiritual leader Vivekananda both happened around the same time—in 1898–9. By some accounts, she became disillusioned with Vivekananda because she disapproved of the way female followers worshipped at his feet. Some in the guru's inner circle disliked her for being "strong-minded," instead of "basking" in Vivekananda's presence.[145] In turn, the Inner Temple benchers readmitted Ghose in part to reject Müller's turn to racism.

What do these two cases tell us about the limits of acceptable behavior for imperial lawyers? One could fall but then redeem oneself (as did Ghose), especially if it happened early on. A fallen but penitent colonial male student (Ghose) might triumph over a spiritually questionable and indecisive European female accuser (Müller), particularly in a case where the accuser had become overtly racist. An advocate of anticolonial violent resistance was unredeemable (Krishnavarma), at least while the empire lasted. Seven decades after the end of empire, a figure branded a terrorist during his lifetime could be recharacterized as an Inn member exercising his right to free speech. Here the redemption (described shortly) was grounded in geopolitical and institutional change, not that of the individual. The boundaries of acceptable behavior inched outward and the "barrister-outlaw" could be absorbed once again—a surprise perhaps given the force of continuity and consistency in institutional culture.

## V. Conclusion: After the Inns, After Empire

What happened to these two figures, both in life and after death, following their Inner Temple cases? A. K. Ghose had a successful legal career in India after his readmission.

[142] For example, see Michael Goebel, *Anti-Imperial Metropolis: Interwar Paris and the Seeds of Third World Nationalism* (New York: Cambridge University Press, 2015), 89–115.

[143] Fischer-Tiné, *Shyamji Krishnavarma*, 56, 95 at note 18, 114–15, and 120.

[144] See Leela Gandhi, *Affective Communities: Anticolonial Thought, Fin-de-siècle Radicalism, and the Politics of Friendship* (Durham: Duke University Press, 2006).

[145] By Gwilym Beckerlegge, see "The Early Spread of Vedanta Societies: An Example of 'Imported Localism,'" *Numen* 51.3 (2004): 305, 311; and *The Ramakrishna Mission*, 180–201, especially at 193, 195–7.

In 1904, already with "considerable experience" with small causes work, he was appointed registrar of the Court of Small Causes in Calcutta.[146] By 1907, he was a faculty member (probably at Calcutta University) and a member of the National Council of Education for Bengal.[147] His cases were occasionally reported in the press, including a 1906 case in which he represented railway strikers and one in 1914, when he defended a man accused of murdering an Indian magistrate.[148] Frances Henrietta Müller died in 1906 at the age of about 60, in Washington D.C. Her will left an estate of considerable value, £12,750, to her sister, Eva McLaren. It made no mention of her former adoptee.[149]

Shyamji Krishnavarma continued to further the anti-imperial cause from Paris. He published *The Indian Sociologist* from 1905 until 1914, and then revived it between 1920 and 1922, this time from exile in Geneva. Krishnavarma died a natural death in 1930. By the time he moved to Geneva, he had lost the support of other Indian revolutionaries in Paris. They criticized his rigid and hierarchical leadership style and accused him of hypocrisy for living in safety while pushing young Indians to die for the cause.[150] Krishnavarma died in obscurity and did not become part of the official narrative of the Indian freedom struggle that crystallized in the 1950s.

In the twenty-first century, though, Krishnavarma's story has been rediscovered. His memory has undergone "saffronization": despite his espousal of a secular model of revolutionary nationalism that was open to Muslims as much as Hindus, Krishnavarma has been reconstituted as a hero of the Hindu Right in India. In 2003, the future prime minister Narendra Modi (then chief minister of Gujarat) brought Krishnavarma's ashes from Switzerland to India. In 2010, Krishnavarma's ashes were escorted across western India with great fanfare and deposited in a 52-acre memorial site created in his honor at his birthplace of Mandvi, Kutch. It includes a replica of India House and a statue of Krishnavarma and his wife.[151] And in 2015, the Inner Temple benchers readmitted the Indian revolutionary to the Inn, stating that "by modern standards," he had not received "an entirely fair hearing," that free speech deserved protection, and that Krishnavarma "may have been a nationalist but he was not a terrorist."[152] In line with popular Indian narratives about the independence struggle, the Inn downplayed the distinction between violent and nonviolent freedom fighters. Given the pride Krishnavarma took in his disbarment, it is not clear that he would have wanted to be readmitted.

These cases revealed how race and sex intersected with notions of truthfulness, deception, and good character (Ghose). They involved social movements,

146 Untitled article, *Calcutta Weekly Notes* 8.19, 28 March 1904, 149.

147 National Council of Education, Bengal, *Calendar 1906–1908* (Calcutta: National Council of Education, Bengal, 1908), 9, 26, 29, 36b.

148 See in *TI*: "The Asansol Strike. Prosecution of Clerks," 13 Sept. 1906, 8; and "Calcutta Outrage. The Accused Confesses," 23 Jan. 1914, 10.

149 "(Frances) Henrietta Müller."

150 See Fischer-Tiné, *Shyamji Krishnavarma*, 115–18.

151 Fischer-Tiné, *Shyamji Krishnavarma*, particularly at 187–90; "Modi dedicates 'Kranti Teerth' memorial to Shyamji Krishna Verma," *TI*, 13 Dec. 2010.

152 "Indian Lawyer Disbarred from Inner Temple a Century Ago Is Reinstated," *Guardian*, 11 Nov. 2015. There was at least one request to readmit Krishnavarma. See letter from Bombay High Court advocate Ankit L. Shah to Inner Temple, 1 January 2015, in Krishnavarma file.

particularly Theosophy and Indian spiritual movements that attracted European followers (Ghose), as well as the violent non-Gandhian branch of the Indian independence movement (Krishnavarma). They shed light on conflicts over the definition of terrorism and the legitimacy of using violence to resist colonial authoritarianism (Krishnavarma). And they reflected narratives of redemption, offering two models of how to regret and renounce earlier behavior in ways acceptable to the profession. One redemption narrative was delivered by a colonial subject mirroring Christian and capitalist models of the good recovery or upward trajectory (Ghose). In the other, it was the institution that acknowledged implicitly that it had been wrong a century earlier (Krishnavarma). In one case, the individual shifted, enabling re-entry. In the other, it was the institution that changed. Across a century that included South Asian decolonization, a new kind of redemption narrative became viable. It smoothed the path for an imperial legal profession to reimagine itself as a globalized one.

It is easy to assume that the pursuit of British and North American law degrees (like LLMs and SJDs) by students from the Global South is a relatively recent phenomenon.[153] But there is nothing new or simple about transcontinental migration for legal education. Like the blue English Heritage plaques that dot London's streets, this chapter reminds us of England's experiment in global legal education circa 1900 and how it helped constitute an imperial legal profession through narratives of fault and redemption that were inseparable from ideas about race, sex, education, and colonialism.[154] Disciplinary cases like the two examined here revealed the contours of the imperial legal profession, confirming the words of chronicler C. E. A. Bedwell in 1912 that "the [b]ar is a bond of empire."[155]

[153] On these students, see Swethaa Ballakrishnen, "Homeward Bound: What Does a Global Legal Education Offer the Indian Returnees?" *Fordham Law Review* 80 (2011–12): 2441–80.

[154] For instance, a blue plaque at 20 Baron's Court Road, London reads "Mahatma Gandhi 1869–1948 lived here as a law student."

[155] Bedwell, *A Brief History* (part 1), 209.

# PART III
# RETHINKING METHOD
*Law and Everything Else*

# 9

# "Our Experiences Make Us Who We Are"

## Lessons from Thomas Ruffin and Dirk Hartog

*Jessica K. Lowe**

It was spring of 1804, and Thomas Ruffin had a problem. The sixteen-year-old College of New Jersey student—who would one day become the chief justice of the North Carolina Supreme Court—was beginning to have concerns about slavery.[1] As a native of southern Virginia and descendant of two powerful planter families, slavery formed the essence of young Ruffin's world.[2] It shaped his days and nights, his very identity, and was the backbone of the only culture he knew. But now, as a student in Princeton, New Jersey, he had seen other possibilities.

It wasn't, of course, that slavery didn't exist in New Jersey, as Dirk Hartog's work has recently reminded us, or that it didn't exist at Princeton for that matter—it certainly did, in ways that are being increasingly documented by the work of the Princeton and Slavery Project.[3] Instead, it was that slavery in Princeton looked somewhat different from slavery in Ruffin's southern Virginia home; plus, New Jersey had only months ago passed a gradual emancipation plan.[4] This meant that Ruffin was surrounded by

* A version of this essay was first composed for Dirk Hartog's retirement conference in 2018, although illness prevented me from participating in that event. Many thanks to the Center of Theological Inquiry and Princeton University Program in Law and Public Affairs for their support this project as part of a 2014–15 Templeton Grant, and to the University of Virginia Law Library's Ben Doherty, Kent Olson, and Daniel Radthorne for assistance in obtaining much of the source material used herein. Additional thanks to Joseph Stuart for superb editing and formatting assistance; to volume editors Jacob Cogan and Kenneth Mack for their feedback; to Dean Risa Goluboff, Josh Bowers, Al Brophy, Mary Anne Case, Malick Ghachem, Sally Greene, William Chester Jordan, Cynthia Nicoletti, Peter Onuf, Rich Schragger, Heather Warren, and Barbara Welke for comments/conversations on this essay; and to Dirk Hartog himself for generously reading an early draft. Many distinguished historians have delved into *State v. Mann*, with significant insight; this essay, part of a larger examination of proslavery Christianity and jurisprudence in American history, is deeply indebted to their work and intends to merely explore one aspect of this famous case. It also attempts to reflect the influence of my undergraduate mentor William Lee Miller, and his work integrating Christian ethics and American history.

[1] The College of New Jersey would, of course, later become known as Princeton University. See April Armstrong, "When Did the College of New Jersey Change to Princeton University?" *Mudd Manuscript Library Blog*, accessed September 29, 2022, https://blogs.princeton.edu/mudd/2015/07/when-did-the-college-of-new-jersey-change-to-princeton-university/.

[2] Thomas Ruffin's mother was Alice Roane. Virginia jurist Spencer Roane was her first cousin. *The Papers of Thomas Ruffin*, edited by J. G. De Roulhac Hamilton, 4 vols. (Raleigh: Edwards & Broughton Printers, 1918) (hereafter "Ruffin Papers") 1:19. On the Ruffin side, proslavery advocate Edmund Ruffin was his distant cousin and friend, and a later correspondent. "Ruffin Family," *William and Mary Quarterly* 18.4 (April 1910): 253.

[3] Hendrik Hartog, *The Trouble with Minna: A Case of Slavery and Emancipation in the Antebellum North* (Chapel Hill: University of North Carolina Press, 2018); "The Princeton & Slavery Project," *Princeton and Slavery*, accessed May 25, 2022, https://slavery.princeton.edu/.

[4] On New Jersey's gradual emancipation and the nature of slavery in the state, see Hartog, *The Trouble with Minna*, 1–11, 16–7, 47–62.

Jessica K. Lowe, *"Our Experiences Make Us Who We Are"* In: *In Between and Across*. Edited by: Kenneth W. Mack and Jacob Katz Cogan, Oxford University Press. © Oxford University Press 2024. DOI: 10.1093/oso/9780197680995.003.0010

a fierce debate about the institution—including by his friends, some of whom, though Southerners, were antislavery.[5]

So young Tom Ruffin (as his family called him) did what teenagers who trust their parents sometimes do: he shared his doubts with his father. Sterling Ruffin was a Virginia planter, to be sure, but not only that—he was also a convert to Methodism, one of the great antislavery religious movements of the eighteenth century.[6] In his young adulthood, likely during the 1780s, the elder Ruffin had stumbled into a Methodist camp meeting on his way to a Richmond horse race in which he was heavily invested.[7] According to his son's eulogizer, "A Methodist camp meeting was in progress at a place where [Sterling] stopped for the night. He attended it, was converted, went on to Richmond, withdrew his horses from the races, paying the forfeit, and sold them all at a sacrifice, and ever afterward was an ardent Methodist, becoming a preacher of that denomination late in life."[8] Sterling's brother also converted, and as Sterling's great-nephew would recall, "[T]hey had both been gay men, but they became very devout and gave up as many of this world's vanities as most persons of their persuasion; though neither could surrender blooded horses entirely." Sterling Ruffin, according to the nephew, would "exhort, with the usual gesticulations of his sect, until he would sit down thoroughly exhausted, panting and wet with perspiration."[9]

Sterling Ruffin took his Methodism seriously, and in the late eighteenth and early nineteenth centuries, Methodism had serious concerns about slavery. Methodism had begun as a reform movement in the Church of England that emphasized personal piety, spiritual growth, and radical community and kinship in Christ, and had nearly from its inception involved ministry to and inclusion of Blacks as well as whites. John Wesley, Methodism's English founder, had spent time in the 1730s as a missionary in Georgia and, in the words of one scholar, believed that "slavery (in all its forms)" was "irreconcilable with any 'degree of either justice or mercy.'"[10] Methodists, as a historian of the movement has put it, "symbolized the radical, world-transforming character of new kinship and new community by including slaves."[11] By the late 1790s, the great majority of enslaved Virginians were Christians, often engaged and fervent ones, with Blacks making up approximately one-quarter of the

[5] For Ruffin at Princeton and his antislavery friends, which included Virginian William Garnett, see Sally Hadden, "Judging Slavery: Thomas Ruffin and *State v. Mann*," in *Local Matters: Race, Crime, and Justice in the Nineteenth-Century South*, eds. Christopher Waldrep and Donald G. Nieman (Athens: University of Georgia Press, 2001), 2 n. 8. The Ruffin family relocated to North Carolina in 1807, after Sterling Ruffin's "fortune [became] impaired." *Ruffin Papers*, 1:36.

[6] See *Ruffin Papers*, 1:36.

[7] Methodist camp meetings were frequent in Virginia in the 1780s. See*The Journal of the Rev. Francis Asbury, Bishop of the Methodist Episcopal Church from August 7, 1771 to December 7, 1815....*, vol. 1 (New York: N. Bangs and T. Mason, 1821); John Wigger, *American Saint: Francis Asbury and the Methodists* (New York: Oxford University Press, 2009), e.g. 115–28; Rhys Isaac, *The Transformation of Virginia: 1740–1790* (Chapel Hill: University of North Carolina Press, for the Omohundro Institute of Early American History and Culture, 1982).

[8] *Ruffin Papers*, 1:36.

[9] Recollections of Col. Frank G. Ruffin, in "Ruffin Family," 256.

[10] Daniel J. Pratt Morris-Chapman, "John Wesley and Methodist Responses to Slavery in America," *Holiness, The Journal of Wesley House Cambridge*, 5.1 (2019): 39. For more on Methodists and slavery, see also Frederick A. Norwood, *The Story of American Methodism* (Nashville: Abingdon Press, 1974), 80, 93; Russell Richey, *Early American Methodism* (Bloomington: Indiana University Press, 1991); and Jason Vickers ed., *The Cambridge Companion to American Methodism* (New York: Cambridge University Press, 2013) and essays therein.

[11] Richey, *Early American Methodism*, 5.

Methodist membership in Maryland, Virginia, and North Carolina; at the same time, Methodism's antislavery egalitarianism was "laced with racism."[12] For instance, although there might be Black as well as white preachers and members at a gathering, there were often two sets of "exhortations," one inside, for white participants, and one outside for Black ones.[13] Nonetheless, one Methodist observed, "In general the dear black people, that profess Religion, are much more engaged than the whites."[14] And an itinerant Methodist preacher recorded in his journal that he hoped to see enslaved people in Heaven and "their cruel, bloody oppressive masters ... burn in Hell fire forever & ever."[15] Convicted by their newfound faith and perhaps by their encounters with their fellow worshippers, by the late eighteenth and early nineteenth centuries some white Virginia Methodists were freeing their enslaved laborers and migrating to the free territories of the upper Midwest.[16]

But despite his Methodism, Sterling Ruffin remained a slaveholder and planter, so as he pondered his son's letter in 1804, he had some thinking to do.[17] Sterling let the letter sit and, after waiting a month, finally put pen to paper. His response to his son both strongly affirmed the moral praiseworthiness of Tom's doubts and proceeded to provide a dose of "real-world" advice: in the world as it actually existed, enslaved people could only be governed "as fear, servile fear operates upon them."[18] He tempered this brutal rendition of reality with an eschatological hope—hope that someday, God would intervene to change men's hearts.

Twenty years later, Sterling's admonitions to young Tom, transformed from an explanation into a mandate, would show up almost verbatim in his son's notorious opinion for the North Carolina Supreme Court in *State v. Mann*. Considered by many both then and now to be the paradigmatic statement of the law of slavery, Harriet Beecher Stowe would conclude, based on the opinion, that Ruffin was among "men of honor, men of humanity, men of kindest and gentlest feelings" nonetheless "*obliged* to interpret these severe laws with inflexible severity."[19] But a close comparison of Ruffin's exchange with his father and his opinion in *Mann* reveals something more complicated: the extent to which the case threatened his youthful settlement on the slavery question, provoking a visceral response in which he forcefully reiterated that settlement while simultaneously foreclosing other real options that lay before the court. And instead of that reasoning being merely a private grappling with the moral conundrum of slavery, Judge Ruffin's blunt and brutal opinion would carry with it the force of law—not just justifying horrific dominance but amplifying it, in North Carolina and in states that followed its lead.

[12] Richey, *Early American Methodism*, 58–60; Alan Taylor, *The Internal Enemy: Slavery and War in Virginia, 1772–1832* (New York: Norton, 2013), 36.

[13] Richey, *Early American Methodism*, 58–60.

[14] Taylor, *The Internal Enemy*, 36.

[15] Richey, *Early American Methodism*, 58.

[16] See Richey, *Early American Methodism*, 52–3; Taylor, *The Internal Enemy*, 37; for examples, see Jessica Lowe, *Murder in the Shenandoah: Making Law Sovereign in Revolutionary Virginia* (New York: Cambridge University Press, 2019), 186.

[17] See entry for "Colo. Sterling Ruffin," 1820 U S Census; Census Place: Caswell, North Carolina; Page: 84; NARA Roll: M33_81; Image: 59.

[18] Sterling Ruffin to Thomas Ruffin, Brunswick, VA, June 1804, in *Ruffin Papers*, 1:55.

[19] Stowe is quoted in Mark Tushnet, *Slave Law in the American South:* State v. Mann *in History and Literature* (Lawrence: University Press of Kansas, 2003), 2.

## I. A Tale of Two Crises

Tom Ruffin's student crisis about slavery was in 1804; two hundred years later, I was a Princeton student myself, undergoing my own, very different crisis. I had applied to Princeton's history department in the fall of 2004; I was a law school graduate and knew I wanted to return for a Ph.D. in history but was inclined to look at schools with which I already had a connection—and at schools that had law schools, for that matter. But everywhere I turned, people I respected gave the same advice: the thing to do for legal history was to work with Dirk Hartog. So, I submitted my application and in spring 2005 received Dirk's offer of admission, kindly conveyed with a personal voicemail message on my small, top-of-the-line "flip" cellular phone. I remember the moment vividly because I was just returning to chambers in Charleston, West Virginia, where I was a clerk on the U.S. Court of Appeals for the Fourth Circuit, after a busy week of oral arguments with the full court in Richmond, Virginia. At that moment, graduate school seemed far off, but the decision was pressing. A college friend put me in touch with a senior legal historian she knew, who was helpfully frank: "No one turns down Dirk Hartog." So, I accepted Princeton's offer and, with the weight of the application season off my shoulders, settled in to enjoy the next few months.

But tragedy intervened. Shortly thereafter, while still in West Virginia, I received another phone call on that same tiny phone: my healthy younger brother, only twenty-four, had died suddenly while playing pick-up basketball with friends at Ohio University, his alma mater, where he was working in the athletic department. On that dark Friday night in June 2005, a call from an emergency room doctor in rural Ohio transformed my life—in the five minutes or so that our conversation lasted—from one with no big hurts or losses, into one of profound suffering.

In the throes of dealing with the blindsidingly unexpected, I emailed this new "Professor Hartog," whom I had met only briefly during Princeton's admitted students weekend. I told him what had happened and that my plans for the fall semester might be up in the air. Dirk replied quickly, with the expected words of sympathy, and then concluded with a sentence that caught my attention, something that I didn't quite know what to do with: "Our experiences make us who we are, as people and as scholars."

I pushed the email aside, submerged in shock and grief and the mountain of tasks that came with it, not to mention packing up an apartment, finishing a job, and moving to a new state and life stage. In August 2005, approximately eight weeks later, I arrived in Princeton, still disoriented and in shock, too dazed—I now realize—for it to register that during those first weeks in a new place, Dirk was the only person on campus who knew what had just happened to my family. I had long dreamed of earning a Ph.D. and I loved Princeton—the exhilaration of being paid to do something I deeply enjoyed, my fascinating new classes, and equally engaging classmates. I coped by throwing myself into campus life, department socializing, and spending 12 to 14 hours per day in the library, all while carrying around a small travel mug of my brother's, emblazoned with his college logo and filled with the rounds of coffee that kept me going. In my grief, I was Jessica, but more so—extra blunt and a bit frenetic, by turns jittery, snappy, devastated, and exuberant.

Through it all, Dirk was incredibly gracious. During one of our first meetings, he told me about a challenging experience in his own life and that it had taken him an extended time to write again in its wake; if I too had trouble writing for a while, he assured me, it was OK, normal even. I appreciated his kindness but thought to myself cockily (after all, I had not been *totally* submerged by grief) that that wouldn't be the case for *me*. Then the end of the semester came, and the due dates for my two required seminar papers, and I discovered that extracting each phrase, each paragraph took excruciating effort—realizing that this was what Dirk had been talking about.

In those years, Dirk was doing the ordinary (but also extraordinary) work of mentoring—and how grateful I am every day that the universe had set up that arrangement before I knew I would need it. But he was also, through his own "everyday life," to use a key Hartogian phrase, teaching something profound about history and scholarship. After all, Dirk's approach to legal history intertwines lived experience and the ideas we produce, links law and the lives of its people. And, in that vein, during one of our early advising meetings, he suggested something else: that I might want to look into Thomas Ruffin, nineteenth-century Southern jurist and devout Episcopalian (like me), who had once been a Princeton student.

Dirk had offered me wise and kind advice during a difficult time, and in 1804, young Tom Ruffin got advice as well—from his father, advice that would follow him into adulthood, profoundly shaping how the primary moral conflict of his young life would unfold in the years that followed. What might it have been like for young Ruffin, the teenager from Virginia's slaveholding gentry, to be at Princeton during the throes of New Jersey's debates over gradual emancipation? It is easy in retrospect to dismiss the expressed concerns of Southern slaveholders like Thomas Ruffin, who later made horrific decisions, both private and public, that fell with their full weight on hundreds of thousands of oppressed people. But while attending Princeton as a teenager, Tom Ruffin was in fact confronting the greatest moral question of the United States. After all, 1804 was a year in which slavery was receiving new scrutiny—and was under new pressure. There were the movements toward some form of emancipation, however drawn out, in the North; the Haitian Revolution to the south; and Gabriel Prosser's thwarted rebellion in Ruffin's own home state of Virginia in 1800, only four years earlier.[20] On top of that, Ruffin had surely experienced, at least vicariously, some of the Methodist movement's theology. His father's frequent letters unceasingly stressed the importance of faith and character, all while Tom was immersed in a world where the community around him was considering adopting gradual emancipation, debating the very system upon which Ruffin's white Virginian planter class had built its wealth and identity. What might that have sparked in him to wonder if his entire way of life might be fundamentally wrong, even immoral? To be confronted with alternatives to his social world? Tom's distress struck deep enough that he wrote home about it, to express his new "sentiments"—sentiments that, whatever exactly they were (the letter does not survive), his father summarized in his reply as "feel[ing] most sensibly" for the "miserable situation of these unhappy beings."[21]

[20] See, e.g. Hartog, *The Trouble with Minna*, 38–86; and Joanne Pope Melish, *Disowning Slavery: Gradual Emancipation and Race in New England, 1780–1860* (Ithaca: Cornell University Press, 2000) (on emancipation in New England); James Alexander Dun, *Dangerous Neighbors: Making the Haitian Revolution in Early America* (Philadelphia: University of Pennsylvania Press, 2016) (on the impact of the Haitian Revolution in America); Douglas Egerton, *Gabriel's Rebellion: The Virginia Slave Conspiracies of 1800 and 1802* (Chapel Hill: University of North Carolina Press, 1993) (on Gabriel's Rebellion and its effect on Virginia politics).

[21] Sterling Ruffin to Thomas Ruffin, Brunswick, VA, November 1804, *Ruffin Papers*, 1:54.

Others from similar backgrounds would face Tom Ruffin's doubts and go on to find different, more courageous answers. There were, for instance, the Grimke sisters of South Carolina, who abandoned their prominent slaveholding family and became aggressive, committed antislavery activists.[22] There were southerners like Robert Carter III, Edward Coles, and Cassius Clay, who freed their enslaved laborers and/or became vocal critics of the institution, not to mention those of Sterling Ruffin's Virginia Methodist brethren who did the same, a number that included two future governors of Ohio.[23] There were, less courageously, advocates of colonization, like so many of the new nation's founders and early statesmen, who found in that effort a way to appease their racism while nominally opposing slavery, and the self-righteous ameliorationists and paternalists, who opted for an ideology of improving slavery's conditions, soothing their consciences without disturbing their racial or economic realities.[24] These, too, were options.

But in his confusion and crisis, young Tom Ruffin turned to his father, who offered him a different compromise. The elder Ruffin's response was a jarringly heartfelt affirmation (on the one hand) of his son's revulsion at slavery's horrors and a jarringly honest justification (on the other) of those same horrors. First, Sterling told Tom that Tom's new misgivings testified to his son's good character. "I was not surpris'd," he began, "at reading your sentiments on Slavery, as I was well aware of the impressions which a different mode of treatment than that pursued in Virginia, would make on a Heart, which I hop'd was capable at all times of sympathizing in the misfortunes of a fellow mortal." He had hoped, he shared, that "as the mind matured, and contemplated the miserable situation of these unhappy beings," that Tom would "feel most sensibly for them."[25]

But that said, the elder Ruffin moved immediately—in a single drawn-out sentence, without so much as a period that would allow his condemnation of slavery to stand alone—on to the intractability of the slavery problem: "but alas! like all others who are not entirely void of every spark of sensibility you feel for them, lament, greatly lament, their uncommon hard fate, without being able to devise any means by which it may be ameliorated!" Then he became blunt: "That they are a great civil, political, and moral evil no Person will deny, but how to get rid of them, is a question which had imploy'd many much more expansive minds than mine." Despite those efforts, Sterling suggested, no one had yet found "any rational, or probable, means to make their situations more comfortable, without endangering the political safety of the State, and perhaps Jeopardizing the lives, property, and everything sacred and dear of the Whites."

[22] See, e.g. Gerda Lerner, *The Grimke Sisters from South Carolina: Pioneers for Women's Rights and Abolition* (New York: Schocken Books, 1971; reprinted New York: Oxford University Press, 1998).

[23] On Carter, see "Robert Carter (1728–1804)," *Encyclopedia Virginia*, https://encyclopediavirginia.org/entries/carter-robert-1728-1804/ accessed on May 31, 2022; and Taylor, *The Internal Enemy*, 38. On Coles, see "Edward Coles," *Thomas Jefferson's Monticello*, http://monticello.org/research-education/thomas-jefferson-encyclopedia/Edward-Coles, accessed on May 31, 2022. On Clay, see Michael Medved, "Americans Should Know the Story of Abolitionist Cassius Clay," *Wall Street Journal* (New York), June 18, 2021, https://www.wsj.com/articles/americans-should-know-the-story-of-abolitionist-cassius-clay-11624053172; and Cassius M. Clay, *Memoirs, Writings, Speeches* (Cincinnati: J. Fletcher Brennan, 1886), especially 25–30. On Methodists, see Lowe, *Murder in the Shenandoah*, 186.

[24] See Egerton, *Gabriel's Rebellion* (on the beginnings of colonization); Charles Irons, *The Origins of Proslavery Christianity: White and Black Evangelicals in Colonial and Antebellum Virginia* (Chapel Hill: University of North Carolina Press, 2008) (on ameliorationism).

[25] Sterling Ruffin to Thomas Ruffin, June 1804, *Ruffin Papers*, 1:54.

In articulating an intractable situation, Sterling Ruffin echoed many of his contemporaries, including his famous Virginia countryman Thomas Jefferson, who later phrased the dilemma as "justice is in one scale, and self-preservation in the other."[26] And like other southerners of his time, Sterling Ruffin disclaimed white Americans' culpability for slavery. It was a difficult situation to contend with, he admitted, but it wasn't their fault: "You will not pretend," Sterling wrote, "to throw blame on the present generation, for the situation of these unhappy domestics," he wrote, "for as they are impos'd on us, and not with our consent, the thing is unavoidable."[27]

But then his searing assessment took another step. "You will perhaps ask," he anticipated of his son, "why we do not treat them with more humanity?" The answer was "obvious: the fewer there are of this discription intermix'd with the Whites, the more they are under our immediate eye, and the more they partake of the manners and habits of the whites." Fewer enslaved people in a region—as in, say, New Jersey—meant they "require[d] less rigidness of treatment to get from them, those services which are absolutely necessary for their support and very existence."[28] There was no way in Virginia to find a means "to make their situations more comfortable"—without endangering "the political safety of the state" and the lives and property "of the Whites."[29] Instead, "Unhappily for us and for them," Sterling Ruffin wrote, "there are too many with us to render a tolerably free intercourse of sentiment possible," and "of course their minds have degenerated into as abject slavery as their persons." And since "there is no tye of gratitude or affection on their parts towards their masters, nothing is to be expected from them, but as fear, servile fear operates on them." This "servile fear produces a sluggishness of action, which must be increased momentarily by a greater degree of fear, with a greater degree of personal attention on our parts."[30] Virginia slavery, according to Sterling, only worked through fear, escalating in some unending spiral of brutality.

Although Sterling's words might seem like something any white southerner might say—and not even just white southerners, but many white northerners as well, since slavery existed in many places in the United States—it is worth pausing at this point in the letter to consider the full horror of his proposition. Sterling was not merely telling his teenage son that there was no remedy for slavery at this time, something many Virginians might have said in 1804 (although proposals were being advanced for gradual emancipation in Virginia at this time as well).[31] He was not just saying that the

[26] Thomas Jefferson to John Holmes, Monticello, April 22, 1820, in J. Jefferson Looney et al., eds., *The Papers of Thomas Jefferson, Retirement Series*, Volume 15 (Princeton: Princeton University Press, 2018):550.

[27] Sterling Ruffin to Thomas Ruffin, Brunswick, VA, June 1804, *Ruffin Papers*, 1:54.

[28] *Ruffin Papers*, 1:54–5.

[29] Ibid.

[30] Ibid.

[31] By the time Sterling Ruffin wrote in 1804, both Thomas Jefferson and Judge St. George Tucker had suggested proposals for gradual emancipation in Virginia. It is not clear how widely Jefferson's proposal, which was to be part of the Virginia's post-independence revisal of the laws, was circulated, although he later wrote that the principle of gradual emancipation had been presented to the committee of revisors and "the principles of the amendment . . . were agreed on, that is to say, the freedom of all born after a certain day, and deportation at a proper age. But it was found that the public mind would not yet bear the proposition." See note accompanying "51. A Bill concerning Slaves, 18 June 1779," *Founders Online*, National Archives, https://founders.archives.gov/documents/Jefferson/01-02-02-0132-0004-0051; Original source: Julian P. Boyd ed., *The Papers of Thomas Jefferson, Volume 2: 1777–18 June 1779*, (Princeton: Princeton University

institution was wrong but that he and his fellow Virginia enslavers, like young Tom, were stuck with it for safety's sake, in the same vein as Thomas Jefferson's famous 1820 remark about slavery: "But, as it is, we have the wolf by the ear, and we can neither hold him, nor safely let him go."[32] Nor was Sterling saying that because emancipation was untenable in Virginia, he and others were forced, in his view, to continue to keep their "fellow mortals," or even fellow brothers and sisters in Christ, in bondage, while doing what they could to ameliorate the institution.[33] Others would take that perspective, publicly or privately, including Jefferson who was, at the time Sterling Ruffin wrote, Virginia's most famous living citizen and the current president of the United States. Indeed, only a few months later in June 1805, Jefferson would write his own letter about slavery to the agent back in Virginia tasked with hiring a new plantation manager for Monticello; Jefferson advised that the new manager's style should be in line with Jefferson's own views: "I love industry and abhor severity."[34] Ten years later, Jefferson would expound on this in a letter to Edward Coles: "[M]y opinion has ever been that, until more can be done for them, we should endeavor, with those whom fortune has thrown on our hands, to feed & clothe them well, protect them from ill usage, [and] require such reasonable labor only as is performed voluntarily by freemen."[35] While those words did not always reflect reality for the people Jefferson enslaved, and that aim, even if practiced, would not have negated the inherent violence of the institution of slavery, it is important to note that Sterling Ruffin was saying something very different. Slavery, Sterling was telling his son, had to be animated by "servile fear"; even to "make their situations more comfortable" would court danger.[36] In other words, although some of Sterling's his Methodist brethren might hope to see

Press, 1950), 470–73. Tucker's proposal was published in 1796 and generated much controversy. St. George Tucker, *A Dissertation on Slavery with a Proposal for the Gradual Abolition of It, in the State of Virginia*, (Philadelphia: Matthew Carey, 1796).

[32] Thomas Jefferson to John Holmes, April 22, 1820, *Papers of Thomas Jefferson*, 15:550.

[33] For Sterling Ruffin's words, see *Ruffin Papers*, 1:54, 55. Particularly after the Virginia Assembly clamped down on emancipation in 1806 by requiring that all newly freed people leave the state within a month or be reenslaved, moving from enslaver to not, from enslaved to free would become more complicated. Compare "An Act to Authorize the Manumission of Slaves," 1782 Va. Acts 159, *reprinted in* 11 *The Statutes at Large: Being a Collection of the Law of Virginia since the First Session of the Legislature in the Year 1619*, at 39 (William Waller Hening ed., 1823), with "An Act to Amend the Several Laws Concerning Slaves," § 10, 1805 Va. Acts 35, 36 (1806), reprinted in 3 *The Statutes at Large of Virginia: From October Session 1792, to December Session 1806, Inclusive, in Three Volumes (New Series) Being a Continuation of Hening 251, 252* (Samuel Shepherd ed., 1836). For a dated but focused account of the history and progression of Virginia manumission laws, see Theodore Stoddard Babcock, "Manumission in Virginia 1782–1806," (M.A. Thesis, University of Virginia, 1974), available at the University of Virginia Library, https://doi.org/10.18130/V3FS89. Virginia's changing laws are also discussed in Taylor, *The Internal Enemy*, especially 35–9.

[34] See "From Thomas Jefferson to John Strode, 5 June 1805," *Founders Online*, National Archives, https://founders.archives.gov/documents/Jefferson/99-01-02-1851 (early access version, retrieved August 8, 2022). For deeper discussion of the reality of slavery at Monticello and Jefferson's views, including the impact of changing Virginia laws regarding emancipation, see Annette Gordon-Reed, *The Hemingses of Monticello: An American Family* (New York: Norton, 2008) and Lucia Stanton, *Those Who Labor for My Happiness* (Charlottesville: University of Virginia Press, 2012).

[35] "Thomas Jefferson to Edward Coles, 25 August 1814," *Founders Online*, National Archives, https://founders.archives.gov/documents/Jefferson/03-07-02-0439; Original source: *The Papers of Thomas Jefferson, Retirement Series, Volume 7: 28 November 1813 to 30 September 1814*, ed. J. Jefferson Looney. (Princeton: Princeton University Press, 2010), 603–5.

[36] *Ruffin Papers*, 1:54–5.

the "cruel, bloody oppressive masters ... burn in Hell fire forever & ever," for Sterling Ruffin that cruelty, that oppression, was a necessity.[37]

However, Sterling was also still a Methodist, so after this blunt assessment of enslaved people's trauma and advocating the necessity of perpetuating that trauma, his letter pivoted abruptly to hope. He told Tom, "[I]t has been one of the many benefits which has resulted to Society from the Christian Religion to expose the impropriety of keeping our Brothers in bondage," and cautioned that "however *we may* at present justify ourselves from the peculiar situation of our Country consider'd politically; I cannot but look forward with pleasure to the time, when an Alwise, and Mercifull Creator will by a more universal revival of his blessed Religion prepare the Hearts of all men to consider each other as Brothers." Significantly, Sterling thought such a future change would not only prompt a spirit of brotherhood but also "put us more on an equallity [sic] even in temporal things." When this would happen, or "what will be the means adopted for a general emancipation, I do not pretend to divine; but that such a time will be, I have little doubt."[38] This was hope, but an eschatological one—hope that fused the spirit of evangelical commitment and the Methodists' ramshackle, multiracial community, but also pushed that reckoning into a future, divinely appointed time.

It was an ill-suited pairing, Sterling's profession of egalitarian brotherhood with his exhortation to racial dominance, but in the wake of recent events, it may have seemed to him necessary. So, in response to his son's doubts, the father offered a tenuous juxtaposition of his Methodism and his Virginia "self-preservation" (as Jefferson would term it): sympathizing with the enslaved was the mark of a good heart, but good politics—at least for now—required keeping them in "servile fear."[39]

## II. The Student Becomes the Judge

Sterling Ruffin's letter might have been any letter from father to son at the turn of the nineteenth century—except for the fact that the son would become one of the most influential jurists of the nineteenth-century United States and the author of the most notorious decision on slave law in American history. In his opinion in *State v. Mann*, Judge Ruffin would recapitulate almost precisely the lesson he had learned from his father's letter twenty years earlier. But in the process, Judge Ruffin would transform his father's words from a mere private admonition into the law of North Carolina.

The facts of this infamous case are generally familiar to legal historians, American historians, and legal scholars. John Mann was indicted for battery on Lydia, an enslaved woman owned by Elizabeth Jones, an orphaned minor. At the trial, it "appeared," as the court reporter's preface to the opinion explained, "that the Defendant had hired the slave for a year," and while in his possession, she had "committed some small

[37] Richey, *Early American Methodism*, 58.

[38] *Ruffin Papers*, 1:55.

[39] For "self-preservation," see Thomas Jefferson to John Holmes, April 22, 1820, *Papers of Thomas Jefferson*, 15:550.

offence, for which the Defendant undertook to chastise her."[40] During this "chastisement" — which, given Mann's subsequent behavior, was likely pretty brutal—Lydia "ran off, whereupon the Defendant called upon her to stop." He "shot at and wounded her when she did not stop, shooting her in the back but not killing her.[41]

Mann was indicted for assault and battery in the Chowan County Superior Court and convicted at trial. The trial judge instructed the jury that Mann (as Lydia's hirer, not her owner) had only a "special property" in Lydia, and that if the jury "believed the punishment inflicted by the Defendant was cruel and unwarrantable, and disproportionate to the offence committed by the slave," then "in law the defendant was guilty."[42] Mann appealed his conviction to the North Carolina Supreme Court, which had just gained a new judge: Thomas Ruffin.[43]

In the 25 years since he had questioned slavery's rightness as a young Princeton student, Tom Ruffin had morphed into a plantation-running slaveholder and a formidable lawyer. His parents had relocated to North Carolina in 1807 after Sterling Ruffin's finances began to fail, and Tom had followed them there, studying law and then joining the North Carolina Bar in 1808.[44] That same year, his friend Benjamin Tappan (Democratic politician and older brother of later abolitionists Arthur and Lewis Tappan), wrote to him from the city Tappan had founded in Ohio, and attempted in a series of letters to convince Tom to join him and open a law practice there.[45] "In the whole extent of the new county there is but one lawyer," Tappan wrote, referring to himself and his home in the area of Portage County, Ohio (near modern-day Akron).[46] It is not clear how the two men knew each other, but Ruffin was apparently somewhat interested or at least being polite, because Tappan wrote again, summarizing his friend's previous letter as saying, "you wish you had funds to live in Ohio."[47] Tappan attempted to assuage this concern, writing, "I assure you that you have ample funds our citizens are neither so honest or discreet as to live without lawsuits, so that you would have some fees, a property of ten thousand dollars in Virginia is no nearer riches than one thousand here." Knowing Tom was reluctant to leave his family, Tappan also offered that maybe Sterling would be willing to move with him: "[S]uppose I could give your Father an opportunity to *double* his property by a purchase here would he forego slavery?"[48] By February 1808, however, Tappan was

[40] State v. Mann, 13 N.C. 263 (1829). For more on the case and its local background, including Jones as an orphan, see the excellent treatment of Sally Greene, "State v. Mann Exhumed," 87 *North Carolina Law Review* 701, 722 (2009), and Eric L. Muller, "Judging Thomas Ruffin and the Hindsight Defense," 87 *North Carolina Law Review* 757 (2009).

[41] *Mann*, 13 N.C. at 263.

[42] Id. at 263; Sally Greene speculates that Lydia's guardian, Josiah Small, pursued a criminal indictment because Mann was too poor to make a civil suit worth the while. Greene, "State v. Mann Exhumed," 722; Sally Greene, "More from Greene: State v. Mann: The Archives Deliver," *Legal History Blog*, accessed April 26, 2020, http://legalhistoryblog.blogspot.com/2009/06/more-from-greene-state-v-mann-archives.html.

[43] Hadden explains that Mann was the last case of the 1829 term, heard on February 15, 1830, after Ruffin had joined the court. Hadden, "Judging Slavery," 8.

[44] *Ruffin Papers*, 1:36–7.

[45] For more on the Tappans, see Daniel Feller, "A Brother in Arms: Benjamin Tappan and the Antislavery Democracy," *The Journal of American History*, 88.1 (Jun. 2001): 48–74.

[46] Benjamin Tappan to Thomas Ruffin, Ravenna, [Ohio], Feb. 16, 1808, in *Ruffin Papers* 1:117.

[47] Benjamin Tappan to Thomas Ruffin, Ravenna, [Ohio], Jan. 5, 1808, in *Ruffin Papers*, 1:115–6.

[48] Benjamin Tappan to Thomas Ruffin, Jan. 5, 1808, *Ruffin Papers*, 1:116.

beginning to suspect that Ruffin had already made up his mind to stay put in North Carolina.[49]

Indeed, both Ruffins did stay in North Carolina, and Tom married Annie Kirkland there in 1809.[50] Now personally and professionally settled, Ruffin next went on to achieve a series of professional recognitions: terms in the legislature; a brief appointment to the circuit court bench, which he resigned in favor of more lucrative pursuits; a stint as president of the Bank of North Carolina, appointed to straighten out its finances; and another appointment to the circuit court. Then, in 1829, upon the death of Chief Justice John Louis Taylor, he was appointed a North Carolina Supreme Court justice.[51]

In adulthood, Tom Ruffin had earned a reputation—responsible, conservative, and pious, although, unlike his father, he had opted for the Episcopal Church of his Virginia gentry ancestors, which was both more attuned to the gentry and more comfortable with slavery.[52] But Ruffin's contemporaries also noted a severe side—a hardness and fury in the man whose father had once lauded his "Heart, which I hop'd was capable at all times of sympathising in the misfortune of a fellow mortal."[53] As historian Timothy Huebner relates, "Ruffin's reputation rested [not on oratory but] on his brash but effective courtroom demeanor." Huebner recounts that one Ruffin contemporary described his behavior as a lawyer this way: "His manner at the bar towards opposing litigants and opposing witnesses was rough and often offensive, hardly ever courteous and not always respectful and frequently abusive."[54] As legal scholar Mark Tushnet puts it, quoting one of Ruffin's contemporaries, Ruffin was "unpopular with the common people and with many who were not very common."[55] Historian Sally Hadden reports a similar reputation: "Even to men who knew him well, Ruffin was remote, distant, and less than humane–and these were opinions about how he dealt with whites."[56] At his death in 1870, his eulogizer described him as a judge who, in his discretion, gave out "sentences ... such as to inspire evil doers with terror, but eminently tended to give protection to society and confidence to honest and law-abiding men."[57] His "temperament was mercurial," the eulogizer explained, "his actions quick and energetic, and his whole bearing in the farthest possible degree removed from sloth, inertness, and despondency."[58] Another described him as a "great but rugged personality." In comparing him to Chief Justice John Marshall, the second eulogizer noted that they shared many characteristics, including a brilliant "legal mind," great courage, strength of will, ambition, hard work, and vigor, but "Marshall, however, had a calm evenness of temper, a sweetness of disposition, a thorough control over his

[49] Benjamin Tappan to Thomas Ruffin, Feb. 16, 1808, *Ruffin Papers*, 1:117.
[50] *Ruffin Papers*, 1:36–7; "Thomas Ruffin (1787–1870)," *North Carolina History Project*, https://northcarolinahistory.org/encyclopedia/thomas-ruffin-1787-1870/ accessed June 6, 2022.
[51] *Ruffin Papers*, 1:19–25.
[52] *Ruffin Papers*, 1:34.
[53] Sterling Ruffin to Thomas Ruffin, Brunswick, VA, November 1804, in *Ruffin Papers*, 1:54.
[54] Timothy Huebner, *The Southern Judicial Tradition: State Judges and Sectional Distinctiveness, 1790–1890* (Athens: University of Georgia Press, 1999), 1334.
[55] Tushnet, *Slave Law in the American South*, 87.
[56] Hadden, "Judging Slavery," 4.
[57] *Ruffin Papers*, 1:27.
[58] *Ruffin Papers*, 1:32.

prejudices that Ruffin never had, nor could ever acquire." Ruffin, the eulogizer intimated, had been held back from true greatness by "the ardor of his temperament."[59]

Recent historical work has further highlighted the severity and harshness of Thomas Ruffin's private life, particularly concerning slavery. As two scholars of Ruffin, Eric Muller and Sally Greene, have succinctly put it, Ruffin "behaved viciously even within his context." At his plantation, he "ran a brutal operation.... His overseers burned his slaves, rubbing salt and pepper into their wounds. He sold husbands away from wives and children away from parents."[60] Ruffin was well aware of the abuse on his plantation, described by scholar Mark Tushnet as "grotesque"; friends and his wife informed him of their concerns about the "evil and barbarous Treatment of your Negroes by your overseer" and that "some of the atrocities were 'too revolting to be put on paper.' "[61]

Moreover, as Eric Muller has comprehensively detailed, shortly after *Mann*, Ruffin himself told in a letter of caning a slave woman who belonged to a friend because she "gave [him] a look of insolent audacity" and the overseer refused to whip her.[62] Beyond this, Ruffin was also a "silent partner in a slave-trading business that bought people in the border states and sold them at profit in the deep south" from 1821 to 1826, when "that business was uncommon among men of his station."[63] By 1830, the young man who had found himself shaken during New Jersey's debates on gradual emancipation had, by these accounts, become a willingly brutal practitioner of the institution of slavery.

Now, in one of Ruffin's first cases on the bench, he confronted a critical question for law in the American South: When could a white person be held criminally liable for an assault on an enslaved person? North Carolina's Attorney General said there could be such liability in Mann's case and urged the court to uphold the jury's conviction of Mann for assault and battery.

The threshold issue was whether any white person could ever be held so liable, and that had already been decided by the North Carolina Supreme Court in the affirmative six years earlier, in a case called *State v. Hale*.[64] *Hale* had involved an assault by a white person on an enslaved person with whom he had no property relationship (a "stranger"), and the jury in *Hale* had rendered a special verdict, finding that the defendant had struck the enslaved person in question but leaving it to the court to decide "whether a battery committed on a slave, no justification or circumstances attending it, being shewn, is an indictable offence."[65] In a long and thoughtful opinion, Chief

[59] *Ruffin Papers*, 1:38, 40.

[60] Eric Muller and Sally Greene, "His Pro-slavery Rhetoric Was Extreme. And His Portrait Dominates Our Top NC Courtroom," *The News and Observer* (Raleigh, NC), October 25, 2018, https://www.newsobserver.com/opinion/article220326985.html. Muller, "Judging Thomas Ruffin and the Hindsight Defense," 766.

[61] Hadden, "Judging Slavery," 5–6. "Grotesque" is from Tushnet, *Slave Law in the American South*, 90.

[62] Muller, "Judging Thomas Ruffin and the Hindsight Defense," 783.

[63] Muller and Greene, "His Pro-slavery Rhetoric Was Extreme"; on slave-trading and dates, see Hadden, "Judging Slavery," 7; on it being uncommon, see Muller, "Judging Thomas Ruffin and the Hindsight Defense," 791. Muller makes a convincing case that Ruffin "got into the slave-trading business as a speculator, plain and simple," not under financial duress.

[64] State v. Hale, 9 N.C. 582 (1823).

[65] *Hale*, 9 N.C. at 582. Although this essay uses the more appropriate term of *enslaved* in its own text, the word *slave* has been preserved where it appears in the original source.

Justice Taylor (whose recent death had opened the North Carolina Supreme Court seat in which Ruffin now sat) had explained that since there was no positive/statutory law on the subject, the court would turn to the "common law, adapted to the existing condition and circumstances of our society."[66] Although the defense objected that the offense was not covered by the state's criminal code, Chief Justice Taylor brushed aside that concern. "Neither the common law, nor any other code yet devised by man, could foresee and specify every case," but, he explained, "[the common law] furnishes the principles of justice adapted to every state and condition of society."[67] Since the common law had long been used for this type of offense, he reasoned, the legislature was clearly aware of this usage and had not intervened; moreover, sanctioning such behavior was in keeping with existing legislative acts which, according to Taylor, had worked to "secur[e] to this class of persons milder treatment and more attention to their safety."[68] Bringing the law to bear on abuse of enslaved people was important, Taylor emphasized, because "the very circumstance of [enslaved people] being brought within the pale of legal protections, has had a corresponding influence upon the tone of public feeling towards them … and suppressed many outrages, which were, before, but too frequent."[69]

To the objection that the owner of an enslaved person could always sue an assailant to recover monetary damages, Justice Taylor asserted that the existence of a private civil action for damages was not sufficient because an assault on an enslaved person in such circumstances was also a breach of the peace, one with potentially serious consequences. It was "injurious to the citizens at large … by the terror and alarm it excites, by the disturbance of that social order which it is the primary object of the law to maintain, and by the contagious example of crimes."[70] Moreover, it created a particularly perilous situation for an enslaved person, whose natural instincts for defense and survival would assert themselves; while an enslaved person might be resigned to "chastisement, whether it be merited or not" from an owner, "when the same authority is wantonly usurped by a stranger, nature is disposed to assert her rights, and prompt the slave to a resistance, often, momentarily successful, sometimes fatally so."[71] As a result, in such situations "the public peace is thus broken, as much as if a free man had been beaten," with such situations ultimately ending "by overpowering the slave and inflicting on him a severe chastisement," and possibly by provoking the enslaved person's owner as well.[72] As a result, Taylor concluded, there was much reason to make such assaults indictable and to attempt to deter them. This was, he emphasized, a long-standing use of the common law: "[t]he common law has often been called into efficient operation, for the punishment of public cruelty inflicted upon animals, for needless and wanton barbarity exercised even by masters upon their slaves, and for various violations of decency, morals, and comfort."[73] After all, "[r]eason and analogy

66 Ibid. at 582–583.
67 Ibid. at 583.
68 Ibid.
69 Ibid.
70 Ibid. at 583–4.
71 Ibid. at 584.
72 Ibid. at 584.
73 Ibid. at 585.

seem to require that a human being, although the subject of property, should be so far protected as the public might be injured through him."[74] Such protections, Chief Justice Taylor noted, also had the benefit of serving as a "more effectual guarantee" of the master's "right of property."[75] Most southern courts agreed.[76]

*Hale* had involved a "stranger," but Mann was a hirer—what then? North Carolina's Supreme Court had not yet faced this question, but the appellate courts of Ruffin's home state, neighboring Virginia, had already encountered the issue: Could a hirer be indicted for an excessive assault on an enslaved person they had hired?[77] The case was *Commonwealth v. Booth*, and defendant Booth had been indicted in the lower court for an assault on "*Bob*, the property of *Robert Fenn*"; however, the indictment had failed to mention the critical fact that Booth had hired Bob from Fenn for a month.[78] In an era where Virginia's courts frequently overturned criminal convictions based on technicalities within indictments and used special verdicts to isolate such issues, Booth's jury rendered a special verdict, posing two questions to the court.[79] First, on the merits, the jury had asked, "Can the Defendant be indicted and punished for the excessive, cruel and inhuman infliction of stripes on the slave *Bob*, while in his possession, and under his control as a hired slave, for the space of one month, no permanent injury having resulted to the said slave from such infliction?" Second: "Can the Defendant be punished under the Indictment found in this Case?"[80]

Virginia's General Court opted to answer the second, technical question—whether the indictment was fatally flawed—and determined that it was. The court explained that because Booth was a hirer, his assault on Bob was not "unlawful *per se*," as it would have been if he were a stranger, but instead, where the defendant had hired the enslaved person, "the original assault is justified by the relation of master and slave, and the *gravamen* of the charge is the *want of moderation* in the subsequent chastisement."[81] Because Booth needed to defend against this latter question—want of moderation—the court decided that the "indictment should be more special" to give him notice of the specifics of the charge.[82] By way of instruction to the court below, the General Court suggested as a model using the indictments of masters for mistreating their apprentices: "In looking into the forms of Indictment against masters for ill-treating their apprentices, we find that these circumstances are set out, and we are not disposed to depart from those forms, especially where they seem to have reason on their side."[83] The court reiterated that the "offence of making an unlawful assault

[74] Ibid.

[75] Ibid. at 585-586.

[76] Tushnet reports, "Most Southern courts drew the natural conclusion that a 'stranger,' that is, someone other than the slave's owner, could indeed be convicted for killing or assaulting a slave." *Slave Law in the American South*, 14.

[77] Commonwealth v. Booth, 4 Va. 394 (1824). On Brockenbrough-Ruffin relationship see Hadden, "Judging Slavery," 15–16; on *Booth*, see Muller, "Judging Thomas Ruffin and the Hindsight Defense," 774.

[78] *Booth*, 4 Va. at 395.

[79] For more on special verdicts in the early republic, see Lowe, *Murder in the Shenandoah*, 142–62.

[80] *Booth*, 4 Va. at 394.

[81] Ibid. at 395.

[82] Ibid. at 396.

[83] Moreover, forty years earlier a majority of Virginia General Court judges had agreed that a hirer should be treated differently from an owner on a related issue: for the purposes of construing a statute limiting the criminal liability of owners in cases involving the death of enslaved people they owned. More recently, *Booth* had also suggested that the situations of owner and hirer were, on this question, analytically

upon the slave of another person, however cruel and severe the subsequent battery, is, certainly, not the same offence with making an assault upon one's own slave, which, in general, becomes unlawful by subsequent excess and inhumanity."[84] The court thus entered judgment for Booth on the special verdict's second question, and reserved judgment on the first and "more interesting" question of the specifics of hirer criminal liability, which would require a "delicate enquiry."[85]

Ruffin was undoubtedly aware of the case—after all, his first cousin and correspondent, William Brockenbrough, was a judge on the Virginia General Court. And he was also undoubtedly aware of another Virginia case that came a couple of years later, in 1827: *Commonwealth v. Turner*.[86] *Turner* addressed the question of an enslaver's criminal liability for violence against an enslaved person they owned. Here, the General Court majority had gone a different way from *Booth*: it had determined that an owner could not be indicted for cruelly beating their own enslaved laborer, beginning the opinion with the striking statement that the "Court has considered it to be its duty to ascertain, not what may be expedient, or morally, or politically right in relation to this matter, but what *is the law*."[87] Here, the General Court had asserted that, unlike what it had suggested in *Booth* and what North Carolina's court had ruled in *Hale*, that the common law could not cover slavery because slavery had been a new introduction to the colonies, unknown to English history. "When great changes take place in the social order," the *Turner* court decided, "a stronger hand, that of the Legislature, must be applied."[88]

Ruffin not only would have known about *Turner* but also that his cousin Judge Brockenbrough had filed a vehement dissent. Brockenbrough had invoked a long line of learned sources to insist that the common law did apply and that the enslaved person's body "was protected from all unnecessary, cruel, and inhuman punishments."[89] Although slavery was unknown to the common law, Brockenbrough argued that the common law adapted to the power relations given to it. An enslaver was entitled to all power necessary for the enjoyment of his property, but no further: "[h]e might correct him for disobedience; he might sell him to another master; and he would be liable for the payment of his debts. If he were merely property, and nothing else, he might be destroyed by his master."[90] But "to this extent the common law would not allow his power to reach, because it was unnecessary for full enjoyment of the right of property."[91]

distinct. "Thomas Sorrel's Case," April 6, 1786, in *St. George Tucker's Law Reports and Selected Papers*, ed. Charles F. Hobson 4 vols (Chapel Hill: University of North Carolina Press for the Omohundro Institute of Early American History and Culture, 2013), 1:117–9.

84 *Booth*, 4 Va. at 395.

85 Ibid. at 396.

86 Commonwealth v. Turner, 26 Va. 678 (1827).

87 Ibid. at 678.

88 Ibid. at 680. This, of course, was sleight of hand; Virginia's courts had been applying the common law to matters of slavery, particularly in property matters, for hundreds of years. See, e.g., the discussion of Spotswood v. Claiborne's Executors, 25 Sept. 1792, in *St. George Tucker's Law Reports and Selected Papers*, 1:41.

89 *Turner*, 26 Va. at 689 (Brokenbrough, J. dissenting).

90 Ibid. at 688.

91 Ibid.

Into this muddle came *State v. Mann*. Protection of the owner's interest and the public peace favored a hirer's liability, as in the case of an assault on an enslaved person by a white stranger. In contrast, protection of the enslaver's prerogative favored no liability as in *Turner* or the limited liability advocated by Brockenbrough's dissent, as in the case of assault by an owner. And in 1830, *Mann* placed the issue squarely before the North Carolina Supreme Court.

## III. Advice Becomes Mandate

"Our experiences make us who we are," Dirk had said to me, and as Judge Ruffin climbed to the bench on February 15, 1830, he might have agreed. After all, Ruffin was what historian Timothy Huebner has described as a "pragmatic" judge whose "judicial philosophy and substantive record were shaped by an acute awareness of the larger implications of his opinions."[92] But as he heard Mann's case, Ruffin's experiences would have pointed in different directions. He was an enslaver to be sure—a slave-trader even—but he was also the person who had lived in New Jersey during that state's emancipation debate, who had questioned slavery, and whose father had looked forward to a world, however distant, where "an Alwise, and Mercifull Creator will … prepare the Hearts of all men to consider each other as Brothers" and "put us more on an equallity [sic] even in temporal things."[93] Now, in his first year on the bench, such a case was before him. What would Judge Ruffin—and Tom Ruffin, former Princeton student—say to the Chowan County judge and jury who had convicted John Mann?

As Ruffin faced the case, there were several possible outcomes. First, the North Carolina attorney general urged the court to uphold Mann's conviction, relying on former Chief Justice Taylor's *Hale* opinion—the governing law in the state—and arguing that "no difference existed" between them. In both cases, he emphasized, the assailant had used a weapon meant to cause death. Using *Hale's* logic and reliance on the common law, the attorney general compared the master-slave relationship to other power relationships like "parents and children, masters and apprentices, and tutors and scholars, and upon the limitations to the right of the superiors in those relations," contending that even where the batterer had hired the enslaved person in question, he was still subject to common law restraints.[94]

Second, the case presented itself to the court in the exact same posture as *Booth* had in Virginia—with a faulty indictment—which offered another opportunity. As in *Booth*, Mann had been indicted for battery on "Lydia, the slave of one Elizabeth Jones," even though he was Lydia's hirer.[95] In a similar situation, the Virginia court had opted to find the indictment flawed and dodge the larger question of hirer liability.[96]

[92] For date, see Hadden, "Judging Slavery," 8; Huebner, *The Southern Judicial Tradition*, 131. See also Tushnet, *Slave Law in the American South*, 84.
[93] Sterling Ruffin to Thomas Ruffin, Brunswick Va., November 1804, *Ruffin Papers*, 1:54.
[94] *Mann*, 13 N.C. at 263–4.
[95] Ibid. at 263.
[96] *Booth*, 4 Va. at 395.

Ruffin, however, brand new to the North Carolina Supreme Court, did the opposite: he leaped over the flaw in the indictment and even the more nuanced question of a hirer's liability to opine directly on a master's liability for assault and battery on an enslaved person whom he owned.[97] Ultimately, he reached a chilling conclusion: that a hirer was the same as an owner and that the owner could not be liable for an assault on an enslaved person. Faced with the lower court's indictment and conviction of Mann, Ruffin responded to them (and to others who might be tempted to follow their lead) in the way that his father had once answered him: with an admonition that gestured toward humanity but explained that the only way to control a slave society was unchecked domination and fear. That conclusion would mark the case as one of the most infamous in the history of American law—and it echoed Sterling Ruffin's 1804 letter almost to the phrase.[98]

Ruffin began his opinion by feigning reluctance. "A Judge cannot but lament," he wrote, "when such cases as the present are brought into judgment." After all, "[i]t is impossible that the reasons on which they go can be appreciated, but where institutions similar to our own, exist and are thoroughly understood." Here, Ruffin was preemptively deflecting criticism and articulating what his father had once said: things might seem one way in states like New Jersey, but the South was different. He then paid lip service to his own concern about the case; after all, a "good heart," his father had taught him, could sympathize with the enslaved. "The struggle, too in the Judge's own breast between the feelings of the man, and the duty of the magistrate is a severe one," he wrote, "presenting strong temptation to put aside such questions, if it be possible."[99] He was, he emphasized, a good man with a good heart stuck in a terrible situation—not unlike his father had lamented, "You will not pretend to throw blame on the present generation, for the situation of these unhappy domestics, for as they are impos'd on us, and not with our consent, the thing is unavoidable."[100]

Ruffin then waived a resigned hand at any moral conflict, as he had in his own life. "It is useless however," he continued, "to complain of things inherent in our political state." More than that, it would be "criminal in a Court to avoid any responsibility which the laws impose."[101] The rhetorical criminality was now not on Mann and his brutal conduct, which had, it must be stressed, been found criminal by a jury in the court below, but on the court (or person) that dared to interfere with Mann's brutality.

[97] Tushnet notes that Ruffin's first draft did not make the point of the indictment at all; perhaps he learned of *Booth* later and added it or did so in response to pressure from others on the court. Tushnet, *Slave Law in the American South*, 22.

[98] We can't know for sure if Ruffin directly consulted the letter while writing *Mann*, but we know he had saved it, with a handful of other documents – his papers, "preserved by Judge Ruffin himself," were passed to his son and then his grandson, who had them published in 1918. See "Preface," *Ruffin Papers*, 1:3. And although this essay had taken shape before I encountered these discussions, Eric Muller and Mark Tushnet also note similarities between Sterling Ruffin's letter and the opinion in *Mann*. Muller focuses primarily on Ruffin's assertion in *Mann* that the best way to end slavery was population decline/dispersal, and Tushnet generally acknowledges an "uncanny resemblance" between the letter and opinion but hypothesizes that it might be attributable to the general common characteristics of Southern defenses of slavery. Muller, "Judging Thomas Ruffin and the Hindsight Defense," 776, and Tushnet, *Slave Law in the American South*, 92.

[99] *Mann*, 13 N.C. at 264.

[100] Sterling Ruffin to Thomas Ruffin, Brunswick, VA, November 1804, *Ruffin Papers*, 1:54–5.

[101] *Mann*, 13 N.C. at 264.

That was where Ruffin was going: "With whatever reluctance therefore it is done, the Court is compelled," he explained, "to express an opinion upon the extent of the dominion of the master over the slave in North Carolina."[102]

The law, of course, nowhere "compelled" Ruffin into the severe opinion he was about to issue; thorough jurist that he was, he briefly acknowledged this, first distinguishing *Hale* and then noting that the hirer should be considered as the master, disagreeing with the lower court's assessment that a hirer had only a "special property."[103] He then conceded: "This opinion would, perhaps dispose of this particular case; because the indictment, which charges a battery upon the slave of *Elizabeth Jones*, is not supported by proof of a battery upon Defendant's own slave; since different justifications may be applicable to the two cases."[104] The Virginia court in *Booth* had stopped there, certifying to the court below on a similar indictment that judgment should be entered on behalf of the defendant, because the indictment had charged the battery of someone else's slave, when in fact the enslaved victim belonged temporarily to the defendant.[105]

However, Ruffin now plowed ahead into an opinion on the criminal liability of a master who had battered his own enslaved worker. First, Ruffin claimed that "the established habits and uniform practice of the country" supported his assessment that a master could not be so liable. Of course, the truth was that the lower court, the attorney general, and the jury of Chowan County had all disagreed with that statement, and even further, the court's own precedent in *Hale* had suggested that an enslaver might face limits to his power.[106] But with this fiction in place, Ruffin absolved himself: "If we thought differently, we could not set our notions in array against the judgment of every body else, and say that this, or that authority, may be safely lopped off."[107] The use of authority is odd, given that here, Ruffin *was* the authority; was he in some sense referring to the other judges on the court, who joined his opinion and issued it *per curiam*? If so, the statement was still untrue; he could have written a narrower concurrence or dissented. Was this also how he had rationalized rejecting his teenage convictions—that even if he thought differently, he could not set his notions against everyone else, including his father?

Ruffin next aimed at the attorney general's claim that common law could govern the case. He did this by highlighting, as his father once had, the necessity of the master's complete domination and the distance of slavery from power relations like master and apprentice. Years earlier, Sterling had written that Virginia slavery had to be harsh, unlike (his view of) New Jersey slavery, because in Virginia there were so many enslaved people compared to the number of whites. In Virginia, he claimed, enslaved

[102] Ibid. at 263.
[103] Ibid. at 264–5.
[104] Ibid. at 265. There was also another way to dispose of the case, Sally Greene argues: Lydia's lease had expired, making Mann her possessor but not necessarily her hirer. Greene suggests that it was this fact that led Ruffin to embrace such broad language attributing a master's power even to a "possessor." Greene, "State v. Mann Exhumed," 719 n.88.
[105] *Booth*, 4 Va. at 395.
[106] See *Hale*, 9 N.C. at 585. Greene makes a convincing case that Ruffin was in fact doing exactly what he claimed he shouldn't: overturning the consensus of the Chowan County community. Greene, "State v. Mann Exhumed," 722–7.
[107] *Mann*, 13 N.C. at 265.

people's minds had "degenerated into as abject slavery as their persons; and as there is no tye of gratitude or affection on their parts towards their masters."[108] In 1830, Judge Ruffin likewise insisted that common law rules and limits applicable to other status relationships could never apply to enslavers and the enslaved because "[t]here is no likeness between the cases." He wrote, "The difference is that which exists between freedom and slavery—and a greater cannot be imagined. In the one, the end in view is the happiness of the youth, born to equal rights with that governor, on whom the duty devolves of training the young to usefulness, in a station which he is afterwards to assume among freemen." But "with slavery it is far otherwise."[109]

The fact that slavery was different had consequences. Sterling had written that given their lack of hope and (in his opinion) lack of affinity for those around them, enslaved people could only be governed as "servile fear" worked upon them, and that that fear in turn "produces a sluggishness of action, which must be increased momentarily by a greater degree of fear, with a greater degree of personal attention on our parts."[110] Now Judge Ruffin said something similar: "The end [of slavery] is the profit of the master, his security and the public safety; the subject, one doomed in his own person, and his posterity, to live without knowledge, and without the capacity to make any thing his own, and to toil that another may reap the fruits." In these circumstances, "[w]hat moral considerations shall be addressed to such a being, to convince him what, it is impossible but that the most stupid must feel and know can never be true—that he is thus to labour upon a principle of natural duty, or for the sake of his own personal happiness[?]" Ruffin reasoned, "[S]uch services can only be expected from one who has no will of his own, who surrenders his will in implicit obedience to that of another. Such obedience is the consequence only of uncontrolled authority over the body. There is nothing else which can operate to produce the effect."[111] Then, to ensure his meaning was clear, he reiterated: "The power of the master must be absolute, to render the submission of the slave perfect."[112]

Having recapitulated the lesson he had learned in 1804—that slavery required domination and fear—Ruffin now offered his thoughts on it. "I most freely confess," he said, "my sense of the harshness of this proposition, I feel it as deeply as any man can. And as a principle of moral right, every person in his retirement must repudiate it. But in the actual condition of things, it must be so. There is no remedy."[113] How was there no remedy when the court and jury below had found one? Here, Ruffin defended his conclusion as realism. Sterling Ruffin had insisted that even amelioration was dangerous and unwise—was incompatible, even, with Southern slavery—and Judge Ruffin now agreed: "This discipline belongs to the state of slavery. They cannot be disunited, without abrogating at once the rights of the master, and absolving the slave from his subjection. It constitutes the curse of slavery to both the bond and free portions of our population. But it is inherent in the relation of master and slave." Ruffin then added this truth to the "self-evident truths" of the American pantheon: "The

[108] Sterling Ruffin to Thomas Ruffin, Brunswick, VA, November 1804, *Ruffin Papers*, 1:55.
[109] *Mann*, 13 N.C. at 265–6.
[110] Sterling Ruffin to Thomas Ruffin, Brunswick, VA, November 1804, *Ruffin Papers*, 1:55.
[111] Ibid. at 266.
[112] *Mann*, 13 N.C. at 266.
[113] Ibid.

truth is," he continued, "that we are forbidden to enter upon a train of general reasoning on the subject."[114] After all, where might such reasoning—professional or, one wonders, personal—lead if it were allowed to begin?

As if to make the point unassailable by repeating it, Ruffin circled back yet again to the necessity of total power of enslaver over the enslaved, evincing a rigidity and barely suppressed fear so different from Chief Justice Taylor or Ruffin's cousin, Judge Brockenbrough. He insisted as his father had that the relationship could not sustain even the slightest amelioration or tiniest bit of humanity so that even to question or ameliorate was forbidden. Offering a convoluted argument that if enslaved people thought they had any hope of outside protection, they would be less submissive, and masters would be more brutal, Ruffin then argued that courts would also enter onto a slippery slope of adjudicating master brutality. This would not do. "We cannot allow the right of the master," he wrote, in what became one of the opinion's most infamous passages, "to be brought into discussion in the Courts of Justice. The slave, to remain a slave, must be made sensible, that there is no appeal from his master; that his power is in no instance, usurped; but is conferred by the laws of man at least, if not by the law of God."[115] He insisted that courts were not competent to weigh in on such a relationship, and "The Court therefore disclaims the power of changing the relation in which these parts of our people stand to each other."[116]

Next, Ruffin pivoted to oddly celebrating the fact that public opinion was, in his view, changing in such a way as to protect the enslaved person—much as his father had looked confidently to God's future intervention that would bring men to see each other as brothers. He did this even though his opinion was, in fact, reversing the community's conviction in the court below and abrogating—without admitting it—the court's own precedent, which had applied the common law to slavery. "We are happy to see," he sunnily concluded, "that there is daily less and less occasion for the interposition of the Courts." Why? "The protection already afforded by several statutes, that all powerful motive, the private interest of the owner, the benevolences towards each other, seated in the hearts of those who have been born and bred together, the frowns and deep execrations of the community upon the barbarian, who is guilty of excessive and brutal cruelty to his unprotected slave."[117] This was operating to produce a "mildness of treatment, and attention to the comforts of the unfortunate class of slaves, greatly mitigating the rigors of servitude, and ameliorating the condition of the slaves."[118] Of course, since he was overturning the Chowan County jury's attempt to do just that, Ruffin was implicitly saying that communities could censure, but they needed to use social disapproval and pressure – "frowns"—not their courts.

Ruffin then offered a somewhat delusional hope that again echoed his father's letter. Amelioration would happen in the only way that (as he had been taught) was acceptable: North Carolina must become demographically more like, say, New Jersey.[119] "The same causes are operating, and will continue to operate with increased

[114] Ibid. at 267.
[115] Ibid.
[116] Ibid.
[117] Ibid. at 267–8.
[118] Ibid. at 268
[119] Muller also makes this point. Muller, "Judging Thomas Ruffin and the Hindsight Defense," 776.

action," he wrote, "until the disparity in numbers between the whites and blacks, shall have rendered the latter in no degree dangerous to the former, when the police now existing may be further relaxed."[120] Was this how he had justified his slave-trading? Letting nature, demographics, slave-trading, God, or any other cause, make North Carolina demographically suitable for a "New Jersey" type of slavery was the right way to go about it, Ruffin insisted, and was "now in progress." He believed this would produce a better outcome than "any rash expositions of abstract truths, by a Judiciary tainted with a false and fanatical philanthropy, seeking to redress an acknowledged evil, by means still more wicked and appalling than even that evil."[121] Here, Ruffin juxtaposed the exact dilemma he had faced in 1804: the bourgeoning antislavery sentiment of his friends and surroundings versus his father's admonition that a different way could only exist in states where enslaved people were dispersed and fewer in numbers. And he directed his harshest criticism at the path he had personally considered and rejected—the "false and fanatical philanthropy" that would seek to make a change.[122] Thomas Ruffin would not be a Grimke, or a Cassius Clay, or an Edward Coles, or a Robert Carter III, and he would not be joining Benjamin Tappan in Ohio to start over. He had passed on the possibility of a different life long ago, and now he buckled down.

Ruffin's framework on slavery had been powerfully shaped as a teenager, and as he poured out those lessons in his first slavery-related opinion on the bench, the judge ended with his own version of his father's religious hope. He announced his commitment to upholding this severe state of affairs "while slavery exists amongst us in its present state, or until it shall seem fit to the Legislature to interpose express enactments to the contrary. . . ."[123] As Ruffin scholar Sally Greene has noted, here the legislature took on the role that southern writings on slavery often reserved for God—the role that Sterling Ruffin had explicitly invoked—as the outside force that would at some future, undetermined day fix the injustices that the current speaker claimed it was untenable to address.[124] But until that day, "it will be the imperative duty of the Judges to recognize the full dominion of the owner over the slave."[125] Judge Ruffin had imparted to the Chowan County judge and jury—and the world—the lesson his father had in 1804 taught him.

Of course, Ruffin's ruling did not occur in a vacuum. As other scholars have noted, various political and functional considerations impacted the court's decision to reverse Mann's conviction. There were, for instance, threats to the independence of the courts from the North Carolina legislature; Ruffin's pragmatic style of jurisprudence; and concerns about rising abolitionism and possible slave revolts, especially after the recent publication of David Walker's *Appeal*.[126] More personally, there were Ruffin's

[120] Ibid.
[121] Ibid.
[122] Ibid.
[123] Ibid.
[124] Greene, "*State v. Mann* Exhumed," 753 n.267.
[125] *Mann*, 13 N.C. at 268.
[126] On the legislative-judiciary battle and Ruffin's pragmatism, see Huebner, *The Southern Judicial Tradition*, chapter 5; on concerns about slave revolts, see Hadden, "Judging Slavery," at 12–5. Tushnet adds the dimension of honor, noting that the language of *Mann*, one of Ruffin's first cases, may have been "part of his attempt to construct an honorable character in his capacity as judge." Tushnet, *Slave Law in the American South*, 86.

own "autocratic tendencies," his history of renting the labor of enslaved people, his slave-trading ventures, and the fact that whether a hirer could be indicted under the common law for battery on an enslaved person was "hotly debated" in the South.[127] Sterling Ruffin's letter was not—all by itself—the *cause* of *State v. Mann.*

But it does seem to have shaped what the ruling ultimately looked like. Most important, Sterling's letter had emphasized that slavery required brutality, that it would not work otherwise, and that same proposition became the most striking, most gutting, assertion of Thomas Ruffin's opinion. Ruffin's rough drafts in *Mann* show his vacillation around this point. His final opinion was at least a third draft; two previous drafts survive in his papers and are instructive for revealing what was in Ruffin's mind as he wrote.[128] In all drafts, Ruffin rejected the analogy of enslaved people to apprentices, contrary to what his cousin Judge Brockenbrough had urged in his *Turner* dissent; that part was not, at least for Ruffin, up for grabs. In each draft, Ruffin also used the same explanation, seemingly borrowed from his father's letter, for rejecting that analogy: no enslaved person would voluntarily labor well for a master ("There is no tie of gratitude or affection," Sterling had said) as they had no interest or free future. This meant, for Ruffin, that the situation of enslaved people was wholly distinguishable from apprentices, who were preparing to one day be members of society.[129]

But a question for Ruffin remained: could slavery be improved, or did it need to be brutal? Here, his drafts wavered. In the first draft, he emphasized that because of the fundamental difference of slavery from other forms of servitude, "Restraint ... constant, vigilant, not infrequently severe and exemplary and painful punishments of the slave is the unwelcome, and necessary task of the Master."[130] With this startling statement, Thomas Ruffin put forth that such severity was not just—horribly enough—a background rule for the law in light of which individual actions could vary, but "necessary," a prescription which could not be diluted "without abrogating all the rights of the master and annulling the duties of the slave."[131] In his next draft, however, Ruffin took the opposite tack. Here, he argued that whatever the duty of the court to decide about the extent of the rights of the master, slavery had actually become lenient; the censure of the community writ large, he explained, had "produced a mildness of treatment and an attention to the comforts of that unfortunate class, greatly mitigating the rigors of slavery and ameliorating the condition of the slaves."[132] Could slavery be lenient, or was it required to be severe? Ruffin was still grappling with that question—or, at least, with what he wanted public perception of himself to be, since evidence suggests that he already favored brutality in his own life. His was, in a sense, the same dilemma his father had once faced: in Sterling's case, how to be a good, pious Methodist—and there seems to be no question of the depth of Sterling Ruffin's piety—in the world in which he inhabited. Sterling had deeply internalized the spiritual

[127] Hadden, "Judging Slavery," 8–9.

[128] *Ruffin Papers*, 4:249–57. Thank you to Sally Greene for reminding me about these drafts.

[129] Sterling Ruffin to Thomas Ruffin, Brunswick, VA, November 1804, *Ruffin Papers*, 1:55.

[130] *Ruffin Papers*, 4:250–1.

[131] *Ruffin Papers*, 4:251.

[132] *Ruffin Papers*, 4:253. In that draft, he also sent the case back for a new trial, despite having specified that the owner could not be held liable for the battery of his own slave and that the hirer was "for the time being, the owner" (250).

lessons of his Methodism—conversion, faith—but just as his nephew remembered that he had been "unable to give up blooded horses entirely," the Ruffins had also been unable to give up that other marker of gentry identity, slavery, even when opportunities were available for them to do so. Now Thomas also sought to defend two memberships: his membership in the fraternity of people and correspondents he knew from his time at Princeton, people who he knew opposed slavery, and his identity as a Southern gentry enslaver.

Ruffin's final draft married both statements, generalizing some of the language about the necessity of violence from draft one, and retaining some of the suggestion that slavery was improving from draft two. But in the end, Ruffin's opinion in *Mann* still went to a place that even the *Turner* court in Virginia had not dared to go, the same place Sterling's letter had once gone: the assertion that violence, in a slave society, was in a way a good, even if morally repulsive when reflected upon "in retirement." The *Turner* court, after all, had said that the offense in question was odious but should be corrected by the legislature. Ruffin went further; he also suggested that the legislature might intervene but at the same time affirmed that violence was necessary, implicit, not deviant: "There is no remedy."[133] The Chowan County judge and jury and North Carolina's attorney general, building on the logic of *Hale*, had put forward a premise: that slavery could be restrained by a community acting through the common law, and analogized to other states of unfreedom in history and in the world, but that proposition challenged the logic on which Ruffin had built his life. Slavery, Ruffin had already decided in his private life, was not like those other relationships, and it could not and should not be made better. As he now put it, "The power of the master must be absolute, to render the submission of the slave perfect."[134]

Ruffin learned an important lesson in 1804, and he had submitted himself to it. Now, in 1830, he imposed those lessons on the state of North Carolina—including the judge and jury who had convicted John Mann.

## IV. "Our Experiences Make Us Who We Are"

What Dirk had been telling me in 2005, when I shared my awful news, was that experiences shape us, change us, "make us who we are." I didn't fully understand that at the time, partly because I'd never before been through a life-altering tragedy. Of course, as any good historian will tell you, our quotidian experiences shape us too—where we're born, what kind of a family or town we grow up in, our privileges or lack thereof, oppression and deprivation experienced, advantages gained. But what I learned in 2005, and in the years that followed, was about what it is like to have your world as you've known it collapse, and to have to—to have no choice but to—face the rubble.

Tragedies—true tragedies—rearrange, and grief is a rolling tide, first the initial shattering of reality in one fell swoop and then a continual battering, an erosion, with wave after wave after long wave that comes in its wake. It was also, for me, something of a purging, a clearing out, if a slow and painful one, that ultimately opened me to

133 *Mann*, 13 N.C. at 267.
134 *Mann*, 13 N.C. at 266.

dimensions of myself and other people, of suffering and the world's pain, that I hadn't been aware of before. A counselor I saw in the months after Dan died described it as the "fellowship of the bereaved," the depth of suffering shared by those who have lost loved ones, especially in difficult circumstances. What I came to understand over time is that that fellowship is not confined to losing loved ones, but to other deep losses as well—loss of autonomy to illness, loss of employment, loss of dreams to some unexpected development, any type of sustained suffering that brings powerlessness in its wake. And what I also learned, through my own suffering and the reaction of others to it, is that having the world change can be experienced as a tremendous threat—witness the rallying cry of the COVID-19 pandemic, the desperate yearning of "Back to normal!" even when true normal was nowhere to be found. Sometimes it is much easier to cling to what we had, instead of to recognize the potential in what might be. And that was the other thing I learned: that change also brings with it truth, and with that truth, wisdom and opportunity.

In 1804, Ruffin was facing something different, of course, and that difference cannot be overstated. His was not the threat of grief over loss of a loved one, but the dawning realization that the brutal institution on which his family and his society had unjustly built their lives, their fortunes, and their very selves, might be wrong, immoral, unfitting for a republic, or even a sin, as abolitionists would increasingly term it. But the problem Ruffin faced in 1804 was also one of whether he would be willing to confront that reality and change, to learn, to incorporate its lessons, or if he would buckle down to a desperate defense of his own normal. It was something that other white Americans confronted and to which at least a few responded differently, and a reality with which the enslaved people of both the North and South lived every day. But Thomas Ruffin had been reared in a society that promised him immense privilege through dominance over others and letting go of that was ultimately too much to bear. Instead of following the lead of Justice Taylor in *Hale*, lauding the halting steps toward men coming to see each other (however imperfectly) as "brothers," as Sterling Ruffin had once claimed to hope, or taking the position that his cousin had in *Turner*, that the common law imposed limits as to what an owner could do to an enslaved person, Ruffin went another direction. He repeated the lessons he had learned from his father in 1804, lessons he had internalized to quell his roiling doubt. But while the father had looked forward (at least) to a change in hearts and minds, the son encountered such sentiments in Chowan County's conviction of John Mann—and used his father's reasoning to roll them back.

Ruffin had written a critical and notorious opinion for the North Carolina Supreme Court, but *Mann* appears to have also catapulted him back into the steely settlement he had made with himself and his world back in 1804 — the pull between the conscience of a young college student, and the Virginian (later North Carolinian) planter on-the-make. Mark Tushnet, recognizing the similarity, has suggested that Sterling Ruffin's 1804 letter drew on familiar tropes, thus accounting for the bulk of the parallels between that letter and his son's infamous opinion.[135] Although that is to some degree undoubtedly true, Sterling's letter had also, as discussed above, taken the analysis

[135] See Tushnet, *Slave Law in the American South*, 92.

in a particularly stark direction for 1804, emphasizing that slavery in its essence relied on the absolute domination of enslaved people to such a degree that even amelioration was unwise; this same proposition in *Mann* is what made and continues to make Ruffin's opinion stand out.[136]

Of course, Methodism had never been perfect on this issue, and by 1830 the church was experiencing intense conflict over slavery. By the 1840s, the denomination would split along regional lines as an affirmatively proslavery version of Christian faith began to dominate the South.[137] In *Mann*, at least, Ruffin had continued to express an understanding of the older attitude of the Revolutionary era, affirmed by his father, that slavery was on some level morally wrong "in retirement," if appending to that view an equally strong conviction that its brutality and continued existence was necessary and in that sense morally right. Eventually, Ruffin himself would follow his Southern proslavery brethren and come to embrace slavery as an affirmative good.[138]

But in 1830, with the world quickly shifting around him, Thomas Ruffin made a decisive choice. Departing from the groundwork laid by his predecessor, Ruffin inserted in its place the brutal and conflicted settlement he had learned twenty years earlier. Just as his father, now several years deceased, had once admonished him, this time Thomas Ruffin did the writing himself—admonishing the wavering judge and jury of Chowan County, who had dared to convict John Mann.

"Our experiences make us who we are," Dirk had said to me, but how we respond to those experiences also makes us. Experiences can create practical detours and obstacles, as my grief did, and can also open new ways of thinking and knowing, as it also did. They can give us knowledge we might not have otherwise had, as when Dirk had imparted his own hard-won wisdom in my time of need. Experiences can also shape us in other ways, giving us limits, fears, blind spots, and desperate ways of being that we cling to, attempts to structure or restructure our worlds in the chaos that follows.[139] In 1830, Ruffin had various options on his judicial table and various ways he could have learned from his youthful experiences. Instead, the boy who had begun the nineteenth-century questioning slavery now used his power to cement its brutality in American law.[140] In this trajectory, Thomas Ruffin mirrored many of his contemporaries and his region. However, in Ruffin's case—a man lauded by contemporaries for his vigor—passive acceptance of the status quo took an enforcing form. As he penned *State v. Mann*, Ruffin reiterated to himself the rightness of his own resolute resignation—his "perfect submission" to slavery—as he seized the opportunity to act it out on thousands of enslaved people in North Carolina, not to mention in

[136] Perhaps this characterization in Ruffin's opinion struck a perverse chord and seemed peculiarly honest, if despicable, to his abolitionist contemporaries because the argument had first been shaped by Sterling, who was steeped in Methodist concerns about slavery even if he did not fully adopt them for himself.

[137] See, e.g., Irons, *Origins of Proslavery Christianity*, 197–201.

[138] See, e.g., Muller, "Judging Thomas Ruffin," 777–8. Muller also suggests that Ruffin invoked his father's lesson not in good faith, but as a cover for a harsh opinion.

[139] Thanks to Rev. Mark Wastler for a November 17, 2019, sermon at St. Paul's Memorial Church, Charlottesville, Virginia, that helped to solidify these thoughts. Fr. Richard Rohr explores similar ideas in much of his work, including *Falling Upward, A Spirituality for the Two Halves of Life* (San Francisco: Jossey-Bass, 2011).

[140] Huebner, *The Southern Judicial Tradition*, 155–9.

whatever states would later follow his lead. Protesting that he was powerless while exercising great power, he aggressively made his own personal settlement into the law of North Carolina.

In the end, Thomas Ruffin provides a cautionary tale: experiences matter, but so does what we decide to do with them.

# 10
# Debtor Constitutionalism

*Farah Peterson*[*]

## I. Introduction

What every schoolchild learns about the Boston Tea Party is that a group of men dressed themselves as Indians and dumped tea into Boston Harbor. If the social studies teacher is good and the child is paying attention, the lesson will also connect those actions to the proto-Revolutionary slogan, "No taxation without representation." But why do we teach the Boston Tea Party this way? We do not remember what other men were wearing when they did other historically significant things. For this event, however, the choice of costume has always been an integral element of the story. In the 1830s, an old shoemaker looking back on his role in the Tea Party began his recollections of that night this way:

> It was now evening, and I immediately dressed myself in the costume of an Indian, equipped with a small hatchet, which I and my associates denominated the tomahawk, with which, and a club, after having painted my face and hands with coal dust in the shop of a blacksmith, I repaired to Griffin's wharf, where the ships lay that contained the tea. When I first appeared in the street after being thus disguised, I fell in with many who were dressed, equipped, and painted as I was, and who fell in with me, and marched in order to the place of our destination.[1]

A legal scholar reading this should immediately have a few questions. He dressed as an Indian, complete with a symbolic weapon that was not a tomahawk but that he decided to *call* a tomahawk. He painted his skin, and not just his face in order to disguise himself, but his hands, too. This was a performance meant to express something. If the shoemaker's recollection is accurate, then the blacksmith from whom he borrowed coal dust would have understood its message and so would all of the men out that night in the streets of Boston. And whether accurate in every detail or not, there is significance in his choice to remember it that way. Those mechanics, artisans, and labor organizers who discovered and elevated this shoemaker in the 1830s as one of the last surviving members of a heroic generation, and who promoted his memoir as part of an elaborate Independence Day commemoration, must have understood

* I am grateful to Gabrielle Candes, Maya Lorey, and Gabrielle Siewert for their assistance preparing this draft. A longer version of this article first appeared as "Constitutionalism in Unexpected Places," *Virginia Law Review* 106.3 (May 2020): 559–609.

1 James Hawkes, *A Retrospect of the Boston Tea Party, with a Memoir of George R. T. Hewes*, by a Citizen of New York (New York: S.S. Bliss Printer, 1834), 38.

Farah Peterson, *Debtor Constitutionalism* In: *In Between and Across.* Edited by: Kenneth W. Mack and Jacob Katz Cogan, Oxford University Press. © Oxford University Press 2024. DOI: 10.1093/oso/9780197680995.003.0011

the message he conveyed by making Indian costume so central to the story.[2] They must, in fact, have meant to amplify it. But from this distance of time, *we* no longer understand it.

Scholars know (or should know) the Boston Tea Party as a legal event. The Tea Party protestors asserted that their constitutional rights had been violated and demanded redress. But what we have failed to appreciate is that the Bostonians believed that their costumes added something to that claim.[3] It is important that Americans dressed up to assert their rights, and it is just as important that Americans remembered the costume as integral, although we may not understand why. And the mystery of it grows in importance when we realize that the costume element of the Boston Tea Party demonstration was far from unique to that event. From the 1760s through at least the 1840s, this was a common element in many protests against sheriffs bearing eviction notices or threatening action from a creditor. White Americans would dress up in Indian costume, make up their faces with their idea of Indian war paint, and participate in destructive and sometimes violent demonstrations.

This is a strange fact about the past, and difficult to square with our lionization of that group of ordinary men now ennobled by the title, "the Founding generation." But this oddity, and others like it, are critical evidence if we are to understand the constitutional ideas and legal imaginations of men of that generation and those that followed. The Boston Tea Party participants thought they were making a constitutional argument and so did all of the protesters dressing in costume to assert their claims in the decades that followed. But what did "constitution" mean? We are accustomed to using that word in one way before the Founding-era, and in a completely different sense as soon as Americans began writing their plans of government down. But the longevity and apparent power of this protest symbol attests to the endurance of a British North American form of constitutional expression that did not die out at the Founding and that was not successfully replaced by written constitutions for several generations.

Before, during, and after the ratification of the federal Constitution of 1787, Americans believed that they were governed under an unwritten constitution, a constitution that confirmed ancient rights and that restricted government action. In discussing an "unwritten constitution," this article is not drawing the distinction that some scholars have between the text of the written Constitution and the policies and principles that underlie it. Nor does it mean to invoke the distinction between the text of the Constitution and the penumbra that has developed around it since. To Americans of the Founding generation, the unwritten constitution was simply the fundamental law: the law of their forefathers, the law justifying their pride in their English heritage, the law that they fought to defend in the Revolution.

[2] See Alfred F. Young, "George Robert Twelve Hewes (1742–1840): A Boston Shoemaker and the Memory of the American Revolution," *William and Mary Quarterly* 38.4 (Oct. 1981): 619–20.

[3] For another consideration of the importance and legal significance of clothing in early America, see Laura F. Edwards, "James and His Striped Velvet Pantaloons: Textiles, Commerce, and the Law in the New Republic," *Journal of American History* 107.2 (Sep. 2020): 338 (arguing that "[t]extiles . . . mattered" and that "[w]hen draped in this form of property, people of marginal status assumed distinct legal forms that were difficult to ignore").

The existence of this unwritten constitution, and particularly its continuity, is something legal scholars have not adequately understood.[4] Originalists have missed its importance because of their focus on the meaning of ratified constitutional text. They believe that the moment of ratification "fixed" constitutional rights and obligations, and that these may be found in the Constitution's words. The main branches of originalist debate concern where to find the meaning of those words, whether in convention debates or in the ratification debates or elsewhere.[5] A premise underlying this view is that Founding-era Americans would have agreed that the written Constitution was the be-all-end-all, at least as far as constitutions go.[6]

Nonoriginalist scholars, on the other hand, have sought to identify values that have come into the Constitution over its two-hundred year "life."[7] Building on the concept of a "penumbra" around constitutional terms, these scholars observe that the Constitution's words have thickened with meaning over time and through their use by an evolving society. But even those scholars start from the premise that all of this development *began* in 1787.

In short, originalist and nonoriginalist scholars share a perspective on the written Constitution: that it operated as a hard break.[8] Even when scholars and jurists look back further than the 1780s, they do so largely to learn whether certain terms contained in constitutional text incorporated a preexisting common law meaning. They do not look back to a constitution that exists separately from our written one. They share a view that whatever American colonial subjects believed a "constitution" was before the Revolution, Americans altered that idea completely once the property-holding gentlemen among them met and decided to write something down.

[4] In discussing the existence of an unwritten constitution at the Founding, I do not take sides in debates over "popular constitutionalism," the idea that "the public generally should participate in shaping constitutional law more directly ...." Mark Tushnet, *Taking the Constitution Away from the Courts* (Princeton: Princeton University Press, 1999), 194. Those debates focus on how the written Constitution is implemented—and specifically on the role of the "the people," in ensuring it is "properly interpreted." Larry D. Kramer, *The People Themselves: Popular Constitutionalism and Judicial Review* (New York: Oxford University Press, 2004), 5–7. This article, by contrast, focuses on a separate source of law entirely, an unwritten constitution, and how citizens both understood and enforced it during the Founding period.

[5] I cannot convey the nuances of this literature here, but for an overview, see, e.g., Robert W. Bennett & Lawrence B. Solum, *Constitutional Originalism: A Debate* (Ithaca: Cornell University Press, 2011).

[6] See generally Antonin Scalia, "Judicial Adherence to the Text of Our Basic Law: A Theory of Constitutional Interpretation," Address at the Catholic University of America, Oct. 18, 1996, transcript https://www.proconservative.net/PCVol5Is225ScaliaTheoryConstlInterpretation.shtml ConstlInterpretation.shtml.

[7] See, e.g., Bruce Ackerman, "The Living Constitution," *Harvard Law Review* 120.7 (May 2007): 1737–812; Ernest A. Young, "The Constitution outside the Constitution," *Yale Law Journal* 117.3 (Dec. 2007): 413–4 (defining the "functional" constitution to include formal practices, norms, and structures of government). This article is not about a written constitution that evolves because it is "alive," but about a separate and supplementary unwritten constitution that existed before and persisted through the social and legal changes of the 1780s.

[8] See, e.g., Lawrence B. Solum, "The Fixation Thesis: The Role of Historical Fact in Original Meaning," *Notre Dame Law Review* 91.1 (Nov. 2015): 6–7 (explaining that a "core idea[]" of originalist constitutional theory is that "the original meaning ... of the constitutional text is fixed at the time each provision is framed and ratified"). The originalist shares this focus on that one moment with, for instance, Akhil Amar, whose critical question is, "How can Americans be faithful to a written Constitution"? Akhil Reed Amar, *America's Unwritten Constitution: The Precedents and Principles We Live By* (New York: Basic Books, 2012), x.

This article starts from a different premise: that Americans of the Founding generation did not share our view that the only "constitution" that mattered was the one the framers designed. Instead, having grown up as Britons, and having lost friends and family in a war to defend their rights as such, they still thought of themselves as the beneficiaries of a constitution of customary right. This is not to deny the importance of the written Constitution, or to dispute that it was significant that the Founders decided to write something down.[9] It is only to assert, as does the written Constitution itself, that the Founders did not intend that "[t]he enumeration in the Constitution[] of certain rights" would "be construed to deny or disparage others retained by the people."[10]

The way legal scholars ask historical questions has hindered our ability to appreciate the endurance and the continuity of unwritten constitutionalism. It is common for a legal scholar to plumb the historical record to either confirm or deny a theory about what the Constitution means for us right now. But the archive does not function well as a Magic 8 Ball. The yes/no/maybe/ask again approach to historical research, by fixating on narrow questions about constitutional text, forecloses really interesting questions about *what a constitution is.*

What one finds in a historical record provides a small window onto the past, through which we can dimly perceive only a part of the action. When a legal scholar goes into the archive with a fixed question in mind, she must dismiss as irrelevant anything that is not responsive, along with anything that she does not understand. But given the very limited view the historical record provides, dismissing any evidence at all risks missing important truths. The puzzles one encounters during primary research are actually the archives' greatest prizes. Instead of skipping over these to chase after hints in the records that might confirm a favorite hunch or cherished thesis, it is worthwhile to linger on the oddities. Exploring these reveals the past on its own terms, allowing the record to propose its own questions, and suggest its own answers.

This paper is about a protester that I will call the "white Indian," because that is what this man would have called himself. He emerged again and again from archival research while I was hunting for something else. Wherever conflicts arose over the fairness of a law pitting owners or creditors against renters and debtors, whether in staid newspaper debates or in all-too-frequent armed insurrections, this white man in moccasins, or with a blanket around his shoulders, or with a painted face, or wielding a tomahawk, appeared as the avatar of the honest debtor or the dispossessed squatter. I was so puzzled by him that I stopped what I was doing and gave this recurring figure a closer look. I found that at least two scholarly works had already lingered over white Indians: an elegant short essay by Alan Taylor, written when he was still a graduate student, and a thoughtful full-length intellectual history by Philip Deloria.[11] But given my preoccupations as a legal historian, I read these figures in a different light. I came to understand that they represented a series of interconnected ideas about authentic

[9] See Nikolas Bowie, "Why the Constitution Was Written Down," *Stanford Law Review* 71.6 (June 2019): 1400.

[10] U.S. Const. amend. IX.

[11] Philip J. Deloria, *Playing Indian* (Chelsea: BookCrafters, Inc., 1998); Alan Taylor, "'Stopping the Progress of Rogues and Deceivers': A White Indian Recruiting Notice of 1808," *William and Mary Quarterly* 42.1 (Jan. 1985).

American identity and virtue.[12] And more than this, the Indian dress was a potent *legal* symbol, both for the people who wore the costume and the people who saw it.

I came to see the white man in Indian dress as an assertion of rights under America's unwritten constitution. This article will explain why, and in the process, model an alternative way of bringing history into legal scholarship. To take Americans' unwritten constitution seriously, one has to see behaviors, norms, and cultural practices as relevant that are typically invisible to the legal scholar. Scholars parsing and reparsing text, opinions, dictionaries, and the like have missed the unwritten constitution because its defenders often made their claims out of court. My goal is not to resolve the relationship between the unwritten constitution and the written one. My goal is simply to show that it exists, to suggest that the relationship between it and the written Constitution is important, and to begin looking for this constitutionalism, which appears more often than not in unexpected places.

## II. The Constitutionalism of Crowd Actions

The men engaged in the civil unrest that led to the new American republic were asserting their entitlement to the "essential privileges of the British constitution."[13] It was the constitution whose principles, John Adams asserted, were "intimately known, they are sensibly felt by every Briton[, and] it is scarcely extravagant to say, they are drawn in and imbibed with the Nurses Milk and first Air."[14] But their constitution was not written, had not been deliberated upon, had no specific origin point. As Bernard Bailyn described it, what they meant by the term *constitution* was "the constituted—that is, existing—arrangement of governmental institutions, laws, and customs together with the principles and goals that animated them."[15]

John Adams would compare the British constitution to "the constitution of the human body," which included "certain Contextures of the Nerves, fibres, and Muscles, or certain Qualities of the Blood and Juices" whose end was life and health, and to the constitution of a watch, which had "a certain Combination of Weights, Springs, Wheels and Levers" whose "Use and End is the Mensuration of Time."[16] Government was "a Frame, a scheme, a system, a Combination of Powers," including those of "the King, the Lords, the Commons, and the People."[17] What was special about the British

[12] This article does not fully explore import of this custom to the history of American racism, or its connections, such as they are, to the blackface tradition. For a cultural history starting point, see S. Elizabeth Bird, ed., *Dressing in Feathers: The Construction of the Indian in American Popular Culture* (Nashville: Westview Press, 1996), 2–3 and Deloria, *Playing Indian*, 5.

[13] Thomas Fitch et al., "Reasons Why the British Colonies in America Should Not Be Charged with Internal Taxes" (New Haven, 1764), in vol. 1 of *Pamphlets of the American Revolution, 1750–1776*, ed. Bernard Bailyn (Cambridge: The Belknap Press of Harvard University Press, 1965), 378, 389.

[14] John Adams, "Adams' Diary Notes on the Right of Juries," vol. 1 of *Legal Papers of John Adams*, ed. L. Kinvin Wroth & Hiller B. Zobel (Cambridge: The Belknap Press of Harvard University Press, 1965), 228, 230.

[15] Bailyn, *Pamphlets of the American Revolution*, 45.

[16] Vol. 1 of *Diary and Autobiography of John Adams*, ed. L. H. Butterfield (Cambridge: The Belknap Press of Harvard University Press, 1961), 296–7.

[17] Butterfield, *Diary and Autobiography of John Adams*, 297–8.

Constitution, Adams wrote, was that "the preservation of Liberty is its End."[18] The founders conceived of rights under this constitution, not as a list of agreed-upon immunities from the power of normal legislation or executive command, but rather, as any of the "essentials and Fundamentals" that guaranteed the efficacy of this constitution for its grand purpose.[19]

British North Americans shared with fellow Britons a legal culture of self-congratulation, a belief that the way power had traditionally been arranged in British government, as between the Lords and People, King and Commons, landowner and tenant, defendant and jury, colony and metropole, was sufficient, without amendment, to guarantee the most perfect liberty to which they could aspire. The legal case Americans made in the Declaration of Independence was simply that their settled expectations had been disappointed. The word *constitution,* therefore, designated a status quo under a system of law that Dirk Hartog has described "not as an instrument of state policy but as … a reflection and a defender of community, customary authority."[20] One found this constitution, like other law, in "custom and community consensus,"[21] to use J. R. Pole's formulation, in prerogatives continuously asserted and continuously accepted.

A mob in the streets represented a rupture in that community consensus. Such a rupture provided both the irrefutable proof of constitutional disorder and its remedy. And indeed, historians have accumulated a substantial record of the vindication of custom in eighteenth-century crowd actions, and of mobs gathering to conserve existing power arrangements. Pauline Maier has written about mobs sometimes using "extralegal means to implement official demands or to enforce laws not otherwise enforceable" or to "extend[] the law in urgent situations beyond its technical limits."[22] These "uprisings," she wrote, complemented existing law and power structures, proving "*extra-institutional* in character more often than they were anti-institutional."[23] Likewise, John Phillip Reid has offered one anecdote after another showing eighteenth-century American mobs' restrained application of lawlike discretion: an incident in which a mob avoided destroying the wrong victim's property; engaged in parlay with a sheriff and agreed to temporary forbearance; or gave legal justifications for its actions and notice that the violence would escalate if certain conditions weren't met, among other examples.[24]

The Revolutionary Whig understanding was that these mobs were not apolitical but rather were the work of "groups who could find no alternative institutional

[18] Butterfield, *Diary and Autobiography of John Adams*, 298.

[19] Butterfield, *Diary and Autobiography of John Adams*, 297.

[20] Hendrik Hartog, "Distancing Oneself from the Eighteenth Century: A Commentary on Changing Pictures of American Legal History," in *Law in the American Revolution and the Revolution in the Law*, ed. Hendrik Hartog (New York: New York University Press, 1981), 229, 241.

[21] Jack P. Greene, "Law and the Origins of the American Revolution," in vol. 1 *The Cambridge History of Law in America*, eds. Michael Grossberg and Christopher Tomlins (New York: Cambridge University Press, 2008), 447, 470.

[22] Pauline Maier, "Popular Uprisings and Civil Authority in Eighteenth-Century America," *William and Mary Quarterly* 27.1 (Jan. 1970): 4.

[23] Maier, "Popular Uprisings and Civil Authority," 7–8.

[24] John Phillip Reid, "In a Defensive Rage: The Uses of the Mob, the Justification in Law, and the Coming of the American Revolution," *New York University Law Review* 49.6 (Dec. 1974): 1055–7.

expression for their demands and grievances, which were more often than not political."[25] A political grievance shared by a sufficient number of "the people" to result in a mass demonstration is, in the context of the constitution we've been discussing, a demand for constitutional redress. Indeed, "Good Whigs," Gordon Wood tells us, sometimes were "willing to grant a measure of legitimacy to" mob actions because they "recognized and appreciated the political existence of the people 'out-of-doors,' that is, outside of the legal representative institutions."[26]

Initially, the scholarship on American colonial mobs contrasted these features with the horrors of popular uprisings in Europe, including the bread riots of England and crowd actions in Revolutionary France. Richard Hofstadter once summarized the observations of so-called "consensus" historians when he wrote of eighteenth-century American riots that they were "low-key and almost charmingly benign."[27] But a 1974 masterwork on the European crowd by George Rudé rejected earlier European scholars' descriptions of crowd actions as animalistic responses to provocation, "the instinctive reaction of virility to hunger."[28] Instead, Rudé painted them too as purposeful, restrained, and nonviolent.[29] The eighteenth-century American asserting his legal rights by rallying out-of-doors was hardly unique; he shared a culture of political engagement with European cultural cousins like the French and, of course, with his fellow Briton.

In fact, American mobs demonstrated the qualities E. P. Thompson described as hallmarks of late eighteenth-century crowd actions in England, especially their "counter-theatre."[30] Like their contemporaries in England, Americans employed a "language of crowd symbolism" using violence against property with "an almost ritualistic significance," in order to perform a "theatre of threat and sedition."[31] They also displayed the other two characteristics Thompson noted as typical: a remarkable "capacity for swift direct action," which involved responding on the spot and with decisive force to perceived invasions of customary rights or privileges, and, key for our analysis, a version of "the anonymous tradition," that is, covering their faces and acting under cover of night.[32] Masks, in other words, were a characteristic element of

[25] Gordon S. Wood, *The Creation of the American Republic, 1776–1787*, 2nd ed. (Chapel Hill: University of North Carolina Press, 1998), 320.

[26] Wood, *Creation of the American Republic*, 320–1.

[27] Richard Hofstadter, "Reflections on Violence in the United States," in *American Violence: A Documentary History*, ed. Richard Hofstadter and Michael Wallace (New York: Knopf, 1970), 3, 10. Later New Left historians challenged this thesis by showing that the eighteenth century saw its share of violent and uncontrolled mob actions instigated by economic complaints against the rich. See, e.g., Jesse Lemisch, "Jack Tar in the Streets: Merchant Seamen in the Politics of Revolutionary America," *William and Mary Quarterly* 25.3 (July 1968): 406. See also Alfred F. Young, "American Historians Confront the Transforming Hand of Revolution: Reconsidering the American Revolution as a Social Movement," in *The Transforming Hand of Revolution*, ed. Ronald Hoffman and Peter J. Albert (Charlottesville: University of Virginia Press, 1995), 346–93 (discussing these New Left historians with comprehensive bibliographical references).

[28] Thomas Southcliffe Ashton and Joseph Sykes, *The Coal Industry of the Eighteenth Century* (Manchester: Manchester University Press, 1929), 131.

[29] George Rudé, The Crowd in History: A Study of Popular Disturbances in France and England, 1730–1848 (London: Lawrence & Wishart Ltd., 1981), 254.

[30] E. P. Thompson, Customs in Common: Studies in Traditional Popular Culture (New York: The New Press, 1993), 57.

[31] Thompson, *Customs in Common*, 67.

[32] Thompson, *Customs in Common*, 66, 69.

the mob actions through which subjects prosecuted constitutional grievances on both sides of the Atlantic.

But there was more to the white Indian than E. P. Thompson's descriptions of British crowd actions capture. Thompson describes his crowds' tendency to operate under cover of darkness as a symptom of "a society of total clientage and dependency," in which "any open, identified resistance to the ruling power may result in instant retaliation—loss of home, employment, tenancy, if not victimization at law ...."[33] By contrast, the costume of the American Indian, at once noble and terrifying, was not about concealment. It contained within it what the Russian theorist Mikhail Bakhtin has described as the carnivalesque tradition, a boisterous throwing-off of social hierarchy and mores, a world "upside-down."[34] It is fitting that Ebenezer Macintosh, the tradesman who led the mob in Boston protesting the Stamp Act and claimed a role in the Boston Tea Party, got his training, as it were, as an organizer of Boston's annual Pope's Day celebration, with its ritual costuming, effigies, crownings, and debasements.[35]

Indian costume was a critical part of how the "people out-of-doors" made known their constitutional claims: not just with violence, but with theater.[36] While the Boston Tea Party is the most well-remembered instance of mob action in Indian dress, another episode in nearby Weston, Massachusetts, in which a mob destroyed the home and business of an innkeeper selling tea, more clearly demonstrates that disguise alone was not the goal of the costume. First, a crowd gathered in front of the Inn and issued "a loud Indian WHOOP, and immediately went off without speaking."[37] They returned that night, "disguised with Paints, Paper Visages, &c" and methodically "ransacked" the building.[38] They did not call attention to themselves, leave, and then return with different clothes in a cartoonish attempt to avoid recognition. In fact, a newspaper report mentions that as mob participants destroyed the inn's contents, "Several of them were known by the [p]eople in the [h]ouse and called to by [n] ame."[39] The Indian costume was not a bid for anonymity so much as a claim to universality; it was not a self-protective gesture but rather a self-assertive one.

[33] Thompson, *Customs in Common*, 66.

[34] Mikhail Bakhtin, *Rabelais and His World*, trans. Helene Iswolsky (Cambridge: The MIT Press, 1968), 426.

[35] See Brendan McConville, *The King's Three Faces* (Chapel Hill: University of North Carolina Press, 2006), 56–63, 69; William Pencak, "Play as Prelude to Revolution," in *Riot and Revelry in Early America*, eds. William Pencak, Matthew Dennis, and Simon P. Newman (University Park: Pennsylvania State University Press, 2002), 125, 133–4; Simon P. Newman, *Parades and the Politics of the Streets: Festive Culture in the Early American Republic* (Philadelphia: University of Pennsylvania Press, 1997), 21–2.

[36] The Indian dress tradition also shared something in common with "rough music," also called "skimmington" or "shivaree," the American custom of enforcing social and sexual mores through loud and boisterous rituals meant to publicly embarrass transgressors. See, e.g., Steven J. Stewart, "Skimmington in the Middle and New England Colonies" in Pencak, *Riot and Revelry*; Brendan McConville, "The Rise of Rough Music: Reflections on an Ancient New Custom in Eighteenth-Century New Jersey" in Pencak, *Riot and Revelry*; Thomas J. Humphrey, "Crowd and Court: Rough Music and Popular Justice in Colonial New York," in Pencak, *Riot and Revelry*.

[37] The Massachusetts Gazette: and the Boston Weekly News-Letter, Mar. 31, 1774, 3.

[38] Ibid..

[39] Ibid.

## III. The Meaning of Indian Dress

To the Founding generation, the word *constitution* described the constituted arrangement of their community as it had developed over time. The word embraced the arrangement of institutions, the practices of political engagement, the doctrines of legal restraint on power, and the formal relations between the orders of society. Its aim was the preservation of all the accreted immunities and privileges contributing to their sense, specific culturally and specific in historical time, of what "liberty" entailed. The claim American revolutionaries made in the Declaration of Independence and elsewhere, that parliament and king had violated this unwritten constitution, was not just a negative. It also required Americans to engage in the collective project of asserting where Britain had gone wrong and what a constitution aimed at liberty really required. One consequence of the Revolution—and one that American elites would come to regret—was that it added ideas about economic justice to the American understanding of constitutional liberty.

The rhetorical association of burdensome debt and rapacious creditors with tyranny became a key theme in American justifications for the rebellion. But while other themes in the legal and intellectual case for independence, including those concerning standing armies, taxes, representation, jury trial, and legislative privilege, took their power from their connection to the past century and more of English political history, this economic theme was distinctly an outgrowth of the colonial relationship.

During the eighteenth century, British North America experienced what some historians have called a "consumer revolution," a maturation of the market resulting in the proliferation of choice for all kinds of goods.[40] North American demand for manufactured goods created a trade imbalance, which drained the colonies of hard currency and kept Americans chained to British credit. Out of a belief that this market dynamic strengthened imperial control, Britain worked to maintain this imbalance through policies requiring British North Americans to trade only with the mother country and discouraging domestic manufacturing.[41]

But this bond of empire was tenuous. British political observers continually fretted that if the colonies started manufacturing finished goods, they might "set up for themselves, and cast off the *English* Government."[42] And Americans chafed at the restrictions. As Richard Henry Lee explained, Britain's trade policies meant that she "not only received the entire produce of the lands ... but has besides involved the people here in a heavy debt, which agriculture ... will probably never pay."[43]

[40] See Neil McKendrick, John Brewer, and J. H. Plumb, *The Birth of a Consumer Society: The Commercialization of Eighteenth-Century England* (Bloomington: Indiana University Press, 1982), 1. See also T. H. Breen, "'Baubles of Britain': The American and Consumer Revolutions of the Eighteenth Century," *Past & Present* 119.1 (1988): 74–75.

[41] Daniel Defoe, *A Plan of the English Commerce* (London: C. Rivington, 1728), 361.

[42] Joshua Gee, *The Trade and Navigation of Great-Britain Considered* (London: Amen-Corner, 1730), 71; see also J. M. Bumsted, "'Things in the Womb of Time': Ideas of American Independence, 1633 to 1763," *William and Mary Quarterly* 31.4 (1974): 534 (discussing arguments for separation).

[43] Richard Henry Lee, *The Farmer's and Monitor's Letters to the Inhabitants of the British Colonies* (Williamsburg: William Rind, 1769), i, iii.

Mid-eighteenth-century colonial commentary on the trade imbalance already hinted at the connection the American revolutionaries would make, increasingly directly, between constitutional liberty and freedom from coercive debt. New York grandee Archibald Kennedy complained, "In Debt we are, and in Debt we must be, for those vast Importations from *Europe*."[44] British North Americans, he warned, would not put up with these policies indefinitely. "[W]here People in such Circumstances are numerous and free, they will push what they think is for their Interest," opposing the "Oppression" of laws that "they have no Hand in the contriving or making" and that therefore failed to accord with "the Conceptions we have of *English Liberty*."[45]

Resentment over the trade laws grew in the 1760s in the aftermath of the French and Indian War. New York and Philadelphia experienced an unprecedented number of foreclosures and actions for debt during that period.[46] At the same time, taxes to repay the war debt helped push record numbers onto the poor rolls in both cities.[47] The end of the war brought economic challenges in the South as well. Planters had used the easy credit in the lead-up to war to mortgage unplanted crops to pay for luxury imports from Europe. In 1762, British merchants suddenly tightened credit when the value of local money fell against the British pound.[48] By the time Parliament imposed the Stamp Act on the colonies, it was received as a calculated attempt, John Dickenson would write, to "draw[] off, as it were, the last drops of their blood."[49]

Americans began to think of their indebtedness, and all the tricks and policies that created and maintained it, as another manifestation of imperial oppression. Looking back on this period, Thomas Jefferson accused British merchants of intentionally undermining their American trading partners. Having given "good prices and credit to the planter, till they got him more immersed in debt than he could pay without selling his lands or slaves" he explained, "[t]hey then reduced the prices given for his tobacco so that let his shipments be ever so great, and his demand of necessaries ever so economical, they never permitted him to clear off his debt."[50] The result was that heavy debts became "hereditary from father to son for many generations, so that the planters were a species of property annexed to certain mercantile houses in London."[51] The Currency Act and other measures placed the British government in cahoots with the merchant, whose very profession, Landon Carter said, "kick[ed] Conscience out of doors like a fawning Puppy,"[52] and with the broker, "a villain in the

[44] Lee, *The Farmer's and Monitor's Letters*, 9–10.

[45] Lee, *The Farmer's and Monitor's Letters*, 10.

[46] Gary B. Nash, *The Urban Crucible: Social Change, Political Consciousness, and the Origins of the American Revolution* (Cambridge: Harvard University Press, 1979), 250 (describing an unprecedented number of actions for debt in New York).

[47] See Fred Anderson, *Crucible of War: The Seven Years' War and the Fate of Empire in British North America 1754–1766* (New York: Vintage Books, 2000), 589.

[48] See, e.g., Anderson, *Crucible of War*, 592.

[49] John Dickinson, "The Late Regulations" in *The Writings of John Dickinson: Political Writings 1764–1774*, ed. Paul Leicester Ford (Philadelphia: The Historical Society of Pennsylvania, 1895), 228.

[50] Thomas Jefferson, "The Article on the United States in the *Encyclopédie Méthodique*," in *The Papers of Thomas Jefferson*, ed. Julian P. Boyd (Princeton: Princeton University Press, 1954), 3, 27.

[51] Ibid.

[52] Landon Carter, *The Diary of Colonel Landon Carter of Sabine Hall, 1752–1778*, ed. Jack P. Greene, (Charlottesville: University Press of Virginia for the Virginia Historical Society, 1965), 813.

very engagements he enters into."[53] Resistance to these venal creditors became a central rationale for rebellion.[54]

The growing belief that economic coercion was antithetical to constitutional liberty fueled the nonimportation and nonconsumption movements. These movements were hugely important. It was becoming clear, warned a Bostonian, that Americans' "fondness" for imports was "the engine intended to be used to destroy the free constitution of [their] country."[55] T. H. Breen has argued that these organized efforts laid critical groundwork for the coming Revolution by knitting Americans of different social classes and in far-flung settlements together in a community of interest.[56] The boycott was "the distinguishing mark of colonial protest," its "signature."[57] Americans formed hundreds of organizations to ensure that local merchants complied with nonimportation resolutions and signed thousands of petitions agreeing with their neighbors to forego imported goods, urging each other that these agreements would "prove a means of restoring our liberty."[58]

Costume was these movements' dominant mode of expression. Proponents of nonimportation used the press to publicly shame neighbors who might "value liberty at so small a price as a ribbon ... or a silk neckcloth."[59] "[C]an he be a true lover of his country," asked another writer, "who would sooner be seen strutting about the streets, clad in foreign fripperies, than to be nobly independent in the russet grey[]"?[60] By 1774, one Virginian observed, "People ... will go naked rather than have any commerce or connection with Great Brittain ... I never expected to see such a spirit of opposition and resistance."[61]

Before long, Indian dress became a signal of the patriot cause. Newspapers carrying the story of the Boston Tea Party made the initial intercolony connection between the imagery of Indian dress and constitutional protest. The nonconsumption movement built on that theme. "Who that has the spirit of a man but would rather forego ... the luxuries of life," one pamphleteer asked, when those luxuries risked "enervating our constitutions and shrinking the human race into pigmies," when the cost of those luxuries "entail[s] slavery on his unborn posterity to the end of time?"[62]

[53] Carter, *The Diary*, 373.

[54] Jefferson was so convinced that indebtedness reduced freedom that he was ready to turn it as a weapon to use on others. As president he planned to promote measures to turn Indians to farming. When they "perceive how useless to them are their extensive forests" he expected they would "be willing to pare them off from time to time in exchange for necessaries for their farms & families." Then, "[t]o promote this disposition to exchange lands which they have to spare & we want, for necessaries, which we have to spare & they want, we shall push our trading houses, and be glad to see the good & influential individuals among them run in debt, because we observe that when these debts get beyond what the individuals can pay, they become willing to lop th[em off] by a cession of lands." President Thomas Jefferson to Governor William H. Harrison, February 27, 1803, in *The Papers of Thomas Jefferson*, ed. Barbara B. Oberg (Princeton: Princeton University Press, 2012), 589–92.

[55] Miles Standish, "To Every Freeholder in the Province of the Massachusetts-Bay, and All Other Persons Who Possess Any Kind of Property," *Boston Gazette & Country Journal*, February 19, 1770.

[56] T. H. Breen, The Marketplace of Revolution: How Consumer Politics Shaped American Independence (New York: Oxford University Press, 2004), xv–xvi.

[57] Breen, *The Marketplace of Revolution*, xv–xvi.

[58] Breen, *The Marketplace of Revolution*, 24, 254 (quoting "To the Inhabitants of the Province of South-Carolina, About to Assemble on the 6th of July, July 4, 1774," in *American Archives No. 4*, ed. Peter Force [Washington, D.C.: M. St. Claire and Peter Force, 1837], 508, 511).

[59] Farmer, "To the Printers," *Massachusetts Spy*, November 13, 1770.

[60] "To the Printers of the Providence Gazette," *Providence Gazette*, November 14, 1767.

[61] William Carr to James Russell, October 23, 1774, quoted in Emory G. Evans, "Planter Indebtedness and the Coming of the Revolution in Virginia," *William & Mary Quarterly* 19.4 (1962): 529.

[62] Force, "To the Inhabitants of the Province of South-Carolina," 508, 511.

He continued, "Nothing but custom makes the curl-pated beau a more agreeable sight with his powder and pomatum, than the tawny savage with his paint and bear's grease."[63] Another popular pamphleteer declared, "We engage to deprive ourselves of the comforts of life . . . and to live like savages, if the Parliament will not consent to give up its authority."[64]

In Virginia, frontiersman's clothes, incorporating elements of Indian costume, became the uniform of the moment. When Lord Dunmore dissolved the Virginia assembly in 1774, an observer reported that a group of 1,000 men assembled in protest, "among which was 600 good Rifle men . . . evry Man Rich and poor with their hunting shirts Belts and Tomahawke fixed of[f] in the best manner."[65] Lord Dunmore would not return to Williamsburg, complained a loyalist, until "these Shirt men" in "Virginia uniform," that is, men "dressed with an Oznab[urg] Shirt over their Cloaths, a belt round them with a Tommyhawk or Scalping knife," "are sent away."[66] An article announcing a 1775 patriotic assembly recommended that Virginia burgesses attend in "shirtsmen's" attire, "which best suits the times, as the cheapest, and the most martial."[67] Many burgesses complied with this instruction, attending the assembly wearing "Coarse linnen or Canvass over their Cloaths and a Tomahawk by their Sides."[68] By wearing these tomahawks to their first councils contemplating independence, Virginia's elite could signal a range of virtues with one stroke, including a superior grasp of the natural law that, they believed, underpinned the English constitution and any fair government.

There was an irony to all of this, the historian Woody Holton has pointed out, as Indians east of the Mississippi "had become highly dependent on European manufactured goods," and even their "famous hunting shirts and tomahawks were generally made in Europe."[69] One wonders how many of the shirts the "shirt men" wore actually complied with the boycott of European articles. It hardly mattered. What was important about the costume was the signal it sent to other Americans about solidarity in a cause and commitment to a set of shared values. And, of course, British North Americans were not dressing up as actual Indians but idealized ones.

Rhetorically, the nonimportation and nonconsumption movements were as much about moral purification as economics—the belief that popular virtue would prove critical if Americans hoped to restore their constitution to its first principles.[70] Revolutionaries explained that it was the "vigour of natural principles" that "drew them to resist the *unnatural* violence of a *Provincial* Government."[71] Enlightenment

63 Breen, *Marketplace of Revolution*, 99.

64 Samuel Galloway, *What Think Ye of Congress Now?* (New York: J. Rivington, 1775), 27.

65 Rhys Isaac, "Dramatizing the Ideology of Revolution: Popular Mobilization in Virginia, 1774 to 1776," *William and Mary Quarterly* 33.3 (1976): 380 (quoting Michael Brown Wallace to Gustavus Brown Wallace, May 14, 1775, in *Wallace Family Papers, 1750–1781*, [on file with the Alderman Library, University of Virginia]).

66 Isaac, "Dramatizing the Ideology of Revolution," 381 (quoting James Parker to Charles Steuart, Jun. 12, 1775, Letters from Va., 3 *Mag. Hist.* 151 [1906]: 159).

67 Isaac, 381–82 (quoting "An American," *Virginia Gazette*, May 19, 1775).

68 Isaac, 382 (quoting Lord Dunmore to Earl of Dartmouth, June 25, 1775, Dunmore Correspondence, Special Collections, John D. Rockefeller Jr. Library, Williamsburg, Virginia).

69 Woody Holton, *Forced Founders: Indians, Debtors, Slaves, and the Making of the American Revolution in Virginia* (Chapel Hill: University of North Carolina Press, 1999), 104n58.

70 Wood, *Creation of the American Republic*, 34.

71 T. Pownall, *A Memorial Addressed to the Sovereigns of America* (London: J. Debrett, 1783).

thinkers like John Locke gave these words meaning, and native life (or their idea of it) had long provided their standard for the ideal "natural" society.[72] In indigenous society, St. John Crèvecœur opined, "There must be something more congenial to our native dispositions, than the fictitious society in which we live."[73] Rousseau spoke of the "savages of America" as "those happy nations who did not even know the name of many vices which we find it difficult to suppress."[74]

The Enlightenment caricature of the noble savage was a fitting avatar for Americans' grievances against economic subjugation. Whereas credit and debt are time-bound, receiving now and remitting later, the imagined Indian lived a life free from time. The Indian's "soul, which nothing disturbs, is wholly wrapped up in the feeling of its present existence, without any idea of the future, however near at hand; while his projects, as limited as his views, hardly extend to the close of day."[75] The fantasy also provided a foil for European materialism.[76] To keep himself supplied with luxuries, a man would "danc[e] the vilest pantomime," Diderot said, echoing the sentiments of the nonimportation movement.[77] "Whom does the savage beg from? The earth, the animals and fishes, the trees and plants and roots and streams."[78] Rousseau added that the desire for unnecessary "things" created political dependence. By contrast, "The American savages, who go naked, and live entirely on the products of the chase, have been always impossible to subdue. What yoke, indeed, can be imposed on men who stand in need of nothing?"[79]

Indian costume also amounted to an assertion that colonial Americans were native here, and that they held a superior claim to the soil than their governors in London. But of course, many of the men dressing up in Indian costume had encountered actual Native Americans, had grown to adulthood during a generation of violent war with Indian nations along the frontier. Some of them would participate, during the "closing years of the Revolution," in "extraordinary anti-Indian violence."[80] Americans were dressing up as Indians even as, historian Peter Silver has demonstrated, a "horror and fear" of Indian attacks "became a vital means of forming public coalitions," knitting the various European groups of colonial society into a "new group" of interest: "the

[72] John Locke, *The Second Treatise of Government*, ed. Richard H. Cox (Hoboken: Wiley-Blackwell, 1982), 3–10. See Bernard Bailyn, *The Ideological Origins of the American Revolution* (Cambridge: The Belknap Press of Harvard University Press, 1967), 27. (The influence of "the European Enlightenment on eighteenth-century Americans ... remains, and is profusely illustrated in the political literature.... The ideas and writings of the leading secular thinkers of the European Enlightenment ... were quoted everywhere in the colonies, by everyone who claimed a broad awareness.")

[73] J. Hector St. John Crèvecœur, *Letters From an American Farmer* (New York: Fox, Duffield & Company, 1904), 306.

[74] Jean Jacques Rousseau, *The Social Contract and Discourses*, trans. G. D. H. Cole (New York: E. P. Dutton, 1950), 153n1.

[75] Rousseau, *Social Contract*, 211.

[76] Denis Diderot, *Rameau's Nephew and Other Works*, trans. Jacques Barzun and Ralph H. Bowen (Indianapolis: Hackett, 2001) xii, 186. Diderot wrote this book during the 1770s, but it was only published after his death, in 1805. See Jack Undack, "Diderot at the Crossroads of Speech," in *A New History of French Literature*, ed. Denis Hollier (Cambridge: Harvard University Press, 1989), 517, 519.

[77] Diderot, *Rameau's Nephew*, 84–85.

[78] Ibid., 84.

[79] Rousseau, *Social Contract*, 147n1.

[80] Peter Silver, *Our Savage Neighbors: How Indian War Transformed Early America* (New York: Norton, 2008), xxiii.

white people."[81] Silver argues that this new way of thinking of whites as a cohesive, aggrieved community contributed to "a democratic revolution," because part of the patriot's case against the British was that they "car[ed] too much for Indians" and that they were "indifferent to or even complicit in ordinary country people's sufferings at Indian hands."[82] A central aspect of their complaint was, in the language of the Declaration of Independence, that the King had "endeavoured to bring on the inhabitants of our frontiers, the merciless Indian Savages, whose known rule of warfare, is an undistinguished destruction of all ages, sexes and conditions."[83]

But the anti-Indian aspect of the Revolutionary cause was not in tension with the choice of Indian dress as the patriot's costume. Rather, it added to the costume's power. There was what the French theorist René Girard would call a "mimetic rivalry" inherent in the performance of Indian dress, amounting to a violent rejection of the claims of true natives.[84] The message of the costume to actual Native Americans who saw it would have been something like, "We will kill you and then dance around in your skin"—more menace, in other words, than praise. Michael Cresap, a frontiersman once reviled as barbaric for his role in a massacre of Indian women and children, would become a celebrated hero in the lead-up to Independence while wearing Indian clothing.[85] In 1775, Cresap paraded through the Northern colonies with "a formidable Company," all "painted like Indians, armed with Tomahawk's and Rifles, dressed in hunting Shirts and Mackasons."[86] His men could surely overawe Lord North's formal army, urged one newspaper account, because of their Indian-like qualities. "What would a regular army ... in the Forest of America do with 1,000 of these Men,"[87] it asked, "who want nothing to preserve their Health and Courage, but Water from the Spring, with a little parched Corn, and what they can easily procure in Hunting; and who, wrapped in their Blankets in the Damp of Night, would choose the shade of a Tree for their Covering, and the Earth for their Bed?"[88]

The former pariah became a champion of the cause as newspapers marked his progress through Pennsylvania and New York on his way to the front lines.

There is more to say about the white Indian as an expression of race and of racism, and to do those issues justice is beyond the scope of this Article. But I'll note just one point here: patriots' performance of Indian dress, which often including darkening their skin, likely contributed to the cultural transformations that preceded and help to explain the political Revolution. Again, Peter Silver has shown how, during the lead-up to the American Revolution, a very culturally diverse set of European peoples began

81 Ibid., xviii–xx.

82 Ibid., xviii, xxiii.

83 Declaration of Independence para. 29 (U.S. 1776).

84 René Girard, "Mimesis and Violence: Perspectives in Cultural Criticism," *Berkshire Review* 19, (1979): 9. ("If the appropriative gesture of an individual named A is rooted in the imitation of an individual named B, it means that A and B must reach together for one and the same object .... Violence is generated by this process."). Here, the "objects" are sovereignty over American soil, along with the claim to belonging or native status here, and authenticity as "Americans," rather than Britons.

85 See Robert G. Parkinson, "From Indian Killer to Worthy Citizen: The Revolutionary Transformation of Michael Cresap," *William and Mary Quarterly* 63.1 (2006): 97.

86 "Extract of a Letter from Frederick-Town, August 1," *New York Gazette and Weekly Mercury*, August 21, 1775.

87 Ibid.

88 Ibid.

to think of themselves as one aggrieved "white" people.[89] The invention of this new identity was hard work and it required imagination. Indians were no monolith, but there was a simplistic caricature of the Indian that denied their real differences, with which European-Americans were familiar. With Indian dress, patriots borrowed a monolithic racial identity from this caricature. Likewise, enslaved African Americans were no cultural monolith, but European-Americans also had a singular caricature in mind when speaking of them. American patriots constantly warned each other that submission to Britain would make them "in no respect different from the sooty *Africans*, whose persons and properties are subject to the disposal of their tyrannical masters," as Joseph Galloway put it.[90] Or, in George Washington's words, submission would "make us as tame, & abject Slaves, as the Blacks we Rule over with such arbitrary Sway."[91] In defining themselves both as comparators to an imagined monolith (the Indians) and against an imagined monolith (Black slaves), the Revolutionaries achieved a new monolithic self-identity as "whites."

Indeed, the power of Indian dress lay in its ability to express, all at once, high ideals about natural rights, a superior colonial claim to the soil, the violent fantasies of the white subaltern, ritual purification from European luxuries, and the colonies' pressing economic grievances, including their rejection of unfair debt. It is no wonder Americans recurred to this symbol so often during their movement for independence. And it is no surprise that such a useful symbol endured. Seventy years after Independence, Indian costume would remain a powerful element of American counter-theatre.

## IV. Three Generations of Debtor Constitutionalism

The Whig legal philosophy that acknowledged the constitutional role of the people out-of-doors was at its height during the revolt that founded the nation.[92] A mob assembling to protest a constitutional injury had the same claim to legitimacy, after all, as that of patriots of all social classes who dared take up arms against their king. After peace with Britain, many Americans continued to believe that they had created a society in which the people out-of-doors had a legitimate place in constitutional governance. They may not have had their own article in the federal Constitution—may, in fact, have been relegated to mentions in the subsequent Bill of Rights—but that did not spell the end of what Alexander Hamilton would call "tumultuary assemblies of the collective body of the people."[93] That is because not everyone understood or agreed that the advent of written constitutions meant the death of the unwritten one.

[89] Silver, *Our Savage Neighbors*, xxii–xxiii.

[90] F. Nwabueze Okoye, "Chattel Slavery as the Nightmare of the American Revolutionaries," *William and Mary Quarterly* 37.1 (Jan. 1980): 12 (quoting Joseph Galloway, A Letter to the People of Pennsylvania 38–39 [n.p., n.d.]).

[91] François Furstenberg, "Beyond Freedom and Slavery: Autonomy, Virtue, and Resistance in Early American Political Discourse," *Journal of American History* 89.4 (2003): 1301 (quoting George Washington to Bryan Fairfax, August 24, 1774, in *The Papers of George Washington: Colonial Series*, eds. W.W. Abbot & Dorothy Twohig [Charlottesville: University Press of Virginia, 1995]).

[92] Reid, "Defensive Rage," 1044.

[93] Alexander Hamilton, "The Continentalist No. 1, [12 July 1781]" (N.Y. Packet & Am. Advertiser, 1781). Reprint *The Papers of Alexander Hamilton* vol. 2, ed. Harold C. Syrett (1961), 651.

To repeat John Adams's formulation, the unwritten constitution was "a frame, a scheme, a system, a combination of powers," with "the preservation of liberty" as its "end."[94] But if this was so, Americans faced a dilemma: after all the revolutionary rhetoric portraying their cause as antimaterialistic, prodebtor, and connected to a fairness-based "natural law," they no longer agreed on what "liberty" entailed. The economic justifications for the war had always posed obvious risks to those who had enjoyed privileged positions in colonial society. In 1776, a loyalist responding to Paine's *Common Sense* had warned that separation from Britain would cause such market turmoil that "[a] war will ensue between the creditors and their debtors."[95] Although this warning may have been overblown, the patriots' emphasis on economic justice did affect some Americans' subsequent views on the content of the unwritten constitution they had bled to defend. For those who took the prodebtor aspect seriously, economic conditions after the Revolution left a lot to be desired, and amply justified continued armed protest.

Legislatures discarded the economic fairness agenda just as Americans were hit with a postwar economic slump. Unprecedented taxes and a scarcity of currency had figured high among the colonial complaints against Britain.[96] Furthermore, continental soldiers had accepted pay in the form of government bonds—essentially, promissory notes. When they returned home, soldiers who needed currency to pay their debts and buy food for their families began selling their bonds for whatever money they could get, always at prices far below their face value. Wealthier Americans bought up the bonds at discounted prices and then influenced the legislatures to levy taxes sufficient to redeem them at their full printed value. Many Americans faced taxes averaging three or four times those of the colonial era.[97] To make matters worse, the courts reopened after the war, exposing debtors to the claims of foreign and domestic private creditors.

Some saw this redistribution of wealth from the taxed and indebted masses to the wealthy few as a good outcome. As one commentator put it, it was important to enforce judgments against delinquent debtors in order to "put the property into the hands of those who would manage it better."[98] Others questioned this logic. To "lay the Burden on, and distress the Labourer," would only "lessen our Stock of Prosperty, and destroy that Fountain out of which it rises, and make good the Proverb, of killing the Hen that laid a golden Egg every Day."[99] A Pennsylvania pamphleteer argued that a policy enforcing creditors' claims against this "labouring Part," to the extent of auctioning off "their Implements of Labour, their Horses, Oxen, &c.," amounted to a decision "to stab ourselves to the very Heart."[100]

[94] Bailyn, *Ideological Origins*, 67–8 (quoting diary of John Adams, January 18, 1766, in Butterfield, *Diary and Autobiography of John Adams*, 296).

[95] James Chalmers, *Plain Truth: Addressed to the Inhabitants of America* (Philadelphia: R. Bell, 1776), 36.

[96] Terry Bouton, *Taming Democracy: "The People," the Founders, and the Troubled Ending of the American Revolution* (New York: Oxford University Press, 2007), 91.

[97] Woody Holton, "Did Democracy Cause the Recession That Led to the Constitution?," *Journal of American History* 92.2 (2005): 442, 445–7.

[98] "Amicus," Virginia Independent Chronicle, July 4, 1787.

[99] [Herman Husband], *Proposals to Amend and Perfect the Policy of the Government of the United States of America* (n.p., 1782), 21.

[100] Ibid.

Legislatures exacerbated the economic hardships ordinary Americans faced, leaving many feeling betrayed. For many, the prodebtor rhetoric of the Revolution had been about more than strategic pressure on a trading partner. Instead, it heralded a leveling of class distinctions and the radical promise of economic equality. It had meant, at the very least, that compassion for one's fellow man must take precedence over timely remission of debts. After all, credit was an inescapable part of the economic cycle, and an inability to satisfy one's obligations was often the result of a bad storm or a harvest-eating pest rather than profligacy. Everyone borrowed, and, in hard times, everyone defaulted.

It was not naïve to have expected a legal reorientation in favor of debtors after the Revolution. In other areas of the law, the historian Holly Brewer has argued, this period saw a meaningful shift in how Americans thought about culpability and assigned punishment. Before the Revolution, she shows, "[t]he question was less whether one meant to do something than whether one actually had done it," reflecting a sixteenth-century framework in which "guilt depended only partly on intention but more on direct causation and on status."[101] In the decades after the Revolution, "[p]roof of criminal intent . . . was the general requirement," including in "crimes against property or involving business dealings."[102] But as other areas of law changed, imprisonment of the honest debtor, often to the utter ruination of his health and the destruction of his family, remained the norm.

The failure of the economically radical promises of the revolutionary movement inspired many mob actions over the following decades. Shays's Rebellion, the 1786 armed insurrection in Massachusetts, is only the most well-known of many conflagrations.[103] These conflicts represented a clash between those who expected continuity with the radical constitutional values of the Revolutionary era, along with that era's mode of discerning and defending the constitution, and those who believed that the time for all that had passed. Some, even more conservative local leaders such as future treasury secretary Albert Gallatin, agreed that armed resistance might at some point become necessary. He counseled caution and compliance with the law simply because he did not think that the imposition of taxes alone was a sufficient threat to liberty to justify armed resistance *yet.*[104]

To men like George Washington, on the other hand, the rebels were a "treason[ous] opposition ... propogating [*sic*] principles of anarchy ... [and] acts of insurrection."[105] In the proclamation Washington issued as he marched out at the head of a 13,000-man army to subdue the Pennsylvania Whiskey rebels, he explained that the Revolution had eliminated any moral justification for armed insurrection.[106] If the rallying cry had once been "No taxation without representation," then the right to

[101] Holly Brewer, *By Birth or Consent: Children, Law, and the Anglo-American Revolution in Authority* (Chapel Hill: University of North Carolina Press, 2005), 226.

[102] James Willard Hurst, *Law and the Conditions of Freedom in the Nineteenth-Century United States* (Madison: University of Wisconsin Press, 1956), 18.

[103] David P. Szatmary, *Shays' Rebellion: The Making of an Agrarian Insurrection* (Amhurst: University of Massachusetts Press, 1980), 124.

[104] See "Declaration of the Committees of Fayette County, September 1794," in *The Writings of Albert Gallatin* vol. 1, ed. Henry Adams (Philadelphia: Lippincott, 1879), 4, 6–7.

[105] Proclamation of September 25, 1794, 43 Annals of Cong. 1413, 1414 (1793).

[106] Ibid., 1415.

elect representatives had succeeded the right to take up arms. Even Samuel Adams, a great supporter of the mob in pre-Revolutionary Massachusetts, called for the leaders of Shays's Rebellion to be hanged, explaining, "In monarchies the crime of treason and rebellion may admit of being pardoned or lightly punished, but the man who dares rebel against the laws of a republic ought to suffer death."[107]

It is tempting to see Washington's and Adams's as the winning argument simply because it is familiar. But as a practical matter, it is not clear that the vote resolved any of the issues rebels throughout the new states were complaining about. Many justly complained that voting was not worth much. The western Pennsylvanians could vote, but they found themselves effectively shut out of Pennsylvania politics since "eastern speculators in western lands … packed more clout in the assembly than frontiersmen."[108] Pennsylvania was not the only state in which indifference to the unique grievances of frontiersmen led to interregional battles between the well-settled capital and shoreline regions and more sparsely settled frontiers.[109] And in other states, rebels may not have met the property qualifications to vote. Indeed, in North Carolina, the angry frontiersmen were not represented in their state legislature at all.[110] In the convention that would ultimately found the short-lived independent state of Franklin on North Carolina's western border, "One man rose, took from his pocket a copy of the Declaration of Independence, and angrily recounted the unfulfilled promises of the drafters. He then described parallels between the principles and grievances of the Declaration and those of frontiersmen."[111]

In the context of this argument over the Revolution's legacy, Indian costume took on new significance. Imbued with the rich associations it had gathered during the war, Indian dress now announced the wearers as the true defenders of the "Spirit of '76." It stood for the idea that, so long as economic abuses continued, so long as a distant government continued to exact oppressive taxes, the work of the Revolution was not finished. And it recurred again and again. In October 1791, a mob scared off an Albany sheriff's lieutenant when he tried to auction a local debtor's possessions. The sheriff and his brother rode to the site of the auction the next day to support the lieutenant, but the lieutenant never appeared with the writ of execution and the auction could not take place. An ambush prevented them from leaving town. As they rode away, the insolvent debtor "fired a pistol, at which signal seventeen men, painted and in Indian dress, sallied forth from the barn, fired and marched after them."[112] The unlucky sheriff did not survive the encounter.[113]

During the Whisky Rebellion of 1794, an eyewitness described "[l]iberty poles … raised every where," bearing messages like "an equal tax, and no excise," and "devices, such as a snake divided, with this motto, 'united we stand, divided we

[107] William Pencak, "Introduction: A Historical Perspective," in Pencak, *Riot and Revelry*.
[108] Thomas P. Slaughter, *The Whiskey Rebellion: Frontier Epilogue to the American Revolution* (New York: Oxford University Press, 1986), 37.
[109] Ibid.
[110] Ibid.
[111] Ibid.
[112] "American Intelligence: Albany, October 31, 1791," *Western Star*, November 8, 1791, 3.
[113] Ibid.

fall.' "[114] "[T]he people acted and spoke" said the witness, "as if we were in a state of revolution."[115] Of course, the whiskey rebels also took their Indian costumes out of chests and shook out the creases. An eyewitness described how protesters "were dressed in what we call hunting shirts," and that some of them "painted themselves black, as the warriors amongst the Indians do, when they go to war."[116] With familiar bombast, the rebels bragged to the Pennsylvanian authorities, "It is a common thing for Indians to fight your best armies at the proportion of one to five; therefore we would not hesitate a moment to attack this army at the rate of one to ten &c."[117] These men urged the cause of the hounded debtor, the squatter asserting a superior claim to the soil than the titular owner, and the beleaguered victims of what they saw as an exorbitant tax. Like the western patriots of the Revolution, "[t]o them, the link between Indian depredations and federal taxes seemed obvious." As "whites" who "lived in fear" because of their direct conflict with Indian nations along the frontier, they believed they were owed "an exemption from additional burdens."[118] The connection between these claims and the constitutional grievances that had justified the American Revolution could not be clearer.

Men continued to mob in Indian costume to defend the debtor's right to fair treatment or the squatter's higher claim to the soil—claims hallowed in the Revolutionary struggle—for decades after Independence. In 1808 and 1809, a town in what is now central Maine experienced a civil war. The "Malta War," as residents remembered it, was a conflict over land titles that turned into an armed insurrection.[119] Farmers squatting on land owned by the absentee Plymouth Company began to clear parcels of timber, resulting in confrontations, court cases, and eviction notices. When sheriffs presented the squatters with writs enforcing the Plymouth Company's rights, those who resisted were jailed. This led to further escalation.

In March 1808, local papers reported that "Indians, otherwise [known as] squatters, were coming down in great force ... to liberate the prisoners, to seize and destroy the gaoler's papers, together with the records of the court, and set fire to the court-house and gaol."[120] In 1809, a Maine citizen wrote that again, "[t]he inhabitants of this town for about a week past have been kept in a continual state of requisition and alarm, by bodies of armed men skulking in the neighboring woods, disguised as Indians, and threatening to liberate the prisoners in our goal [*sic*]."[121] This "body of between 5 or 600 men, in Indian guise, called squatters," said another report, was "determined to rescue" their jailed confederates "or perish in the attempt."[122] Over

114 Hugh H. Brackenridge, *Incidents of the Insurrection in the Western Parts of Pennsylvania, in the Year 1794* (Philadelphia, 1795), 76.
115 Ibid.
116 Ibid., 52, 54.
117 William Findley, *History of the Insurrection, in the Four Western Counties of Pennsylvania* (Philadelphia: Samuel Harrison Smith, 1796), 163.
118 Slaughter, *Whiskey Rebellion*, 93.
119 George J. Varney, "The Malta War in Court," *Green Bag* 7 (1895): 477–78.
120 "Maine, Augusta, March 18," *New-Bedford Mercury*, April 8, 1808, 4.
121 "Insurrection," *Merrimack Intelligencer*, October 14, 1809, 3.
122 "Extract of a Letter from a Gentleman in Hallowell, to his Friend in Portland, Dated Oct. 5, 1809," *Pennsylvania Herald, and Easton Intelligencer*, October 25, 1809, 2.

the course of these confrontations, the protesters murdered the man the Plymouth Company had employed to make a land survey and damaged the local jail.[123]

The disguises were elaborate. These costumes, said one witness, "were decorated with the most uncouth images imaginable. The masks were some of bearskin, some sheepskin, some stuck over with hog's bristles &c.... The frantic imagination of a lunatic in the depth of desperation could not conceive of more horrid or ghastly spectres."[124] The father of a Maine sheriff reported a personal encounter with the "squatters" when they came to his house at midnight intending to destroy writs of execution: "[S]ome body knocked at the kitchen door ... on opening the door, four persons rushed into the room, in Indian garb. One of them presented a musket at my breast. I inquired to know the cause of all this—They demanded my papers—(I imagined they mistook me for my son)."[125]

When a member of the household tried to light a candle, the intruders protested with "Indians no have light!"[126] When another tried to light the hearth, the intruders prevented him too, saying "Indians have no fire."[127] The patriarch told them that he didn't have the papers and that his son was out for the evening.[128] The "Indians" accordingly changed their demand, and then wanted the "Plan" (perhaps the surveyor's map of the disputed territory), threatening that "'Indian do much damage—Indian burn um house—Indian burn um barn,' &c."[129] Their costume was both visual and oral. Alan Taylor, who wrote an article about this episode, found that some of the protesters actually "affected a guttural, broken English ... enhanced by placing a wood chip in [their] mouth[s]."[130]

But these men did not need spoken English to explain themselves. When they turned up in the home of the local sheriff, their costumes communicated their views. The white Indians in this Maine rebellion had been recruited through an advertisement calling on settlers to "aquipp thimselves with a Capp and blanket and a gun and tommahawk" and join the "indians" in the effort to secure their "right and privilidges and libertys."[131] The notice contained, in its unpunctuated, 570-word sentence, nearly a complete list of the legal grievances the Indian costume had come to represent.

It was a rare written exegesis of the white Indian position. In a "for us or against us" manifesto, the broadside warned settlers that anyone who didn't join in would reveal himself as an "English subject[]," "friend to poopery," and "supportr of the Devil and a brother to rogues."[132] It called on settlers to protest the Plymouth Company and its agents, explaining that the company was "trying to git away all that" the settlers "have

123 See "More of the Squatters," *Portland Gazette, and Maine Advertiser*, October, 23, 1809, 3 (reporting that men in Indian dress had shot a land surveyor); "Maine, Augusta, March 18," ("Indians ... set fire to the court-house and gaol.").

124 Pitt Dillingham to Arthur Lithgow, January 30, 1808, quoted in Taylor, "Stopping the Progress of Rogues and Deceivers," 94.

125 "Alarm!," *Portland Gazette, and Maine Advertiser*, December 19, 1808, 3.

126 Ibid.

127 Ibid.

128 Ibid.

129 Ibid. "Alarm!," 3.

130 Taylor, "Stopping the Progress of Rogues and Deceivers," 94.

131 Ibid., 102.

132 Ibid.

got and to turn them out of house and home by a pollitick Craft of roguery."[133] Specific grievances included that the owners of the Plymouth Company "pick up all the land and Call it theirn."[134] After "people settles on the land as they are Cultivators of soil and Dont git their living by making monney nor Drawing sallaries nor fees" these evildoers then "Come and Demand pay for the land [at] a price of their own and so gits all their monney back into their own hands again."[135] The result was that when taxes were levied, and when "all the debts of the Community that coms by trading must be paid and their must be monney" the settlers suffered because there was no hard currency in circulation—"their is none in the Countrey."[136] Lawyers and courts only made matters worse: "[T]hen Comes law Charges and fees and the honest Debt together in an execution and Vendues and demands monney and for want of it they take all a man has and give it to another for a third part of its Value and so robs him and turns him out of house and home for he gits no title to the land only a quit Claim or a teen year leeas."[137]

Here we have in one breath the debtors and squatters' lament, a rallying cry to join in "Defenc of Justice," rehearsing arguments about economic fairness that predated the Revolution.[138]

If elites rejected these claims, they could not deny their force. After the Malta War, the Massachusetts legislature passed a statute "making it a high crime for any person to disguise himself in the likeness of an Indian, or otherwise, with intent to molest a sheriff or surveyor in the discharge of his duties."[139] In a stark recognition of the symbol's power, the law included harsh penalties for militiamen who refused to help officials enforce it.[140]

Government attempts to abate white Indian protests were frequently followed by extensions of clemency and diplomatic engagement with protesters. Officials understood that written law was not hegemonic and that they could not simply crush the white Indian, punish him as a troublemaker, or dismiss his understanding of rights as lawless or incoherent. The written law instead competed and interacted with his unwritten understanding of fundamental law. In the 1790s, some of the Indian-costumed whiskey rebels were tried and sentenced to death for treason. But the following year, President Adams issued both a pardon for the convicted traitors and a general amnesty for anyone else who might have been involved.[141] Likewise, the leader of the Indian-costumed participants in the Anti-Rent War of the 1840s was

133 Ibid.
134 Ibid.
135 Ibid., 103.
136 Ibid.
137 Ibid.
138 Ibid., 102.
139 Varney, "The Malta War in Court," 476, 478.
140 See *An Act for the More Speedy and Effectual Suppression of Tumults and Insurrections in the Commonwealth*, ch. 122, § 4, 1810 Mass. Acts 218, 220–1.
141 See John Adams, Proclamation, "Granting Pardon to the Pennsylvania Insurgents" (May 21, 1800), in *The Works of John Adams, Second President of the United States*, vol. 9 ed. Charles Francis Adams (Boston: Little, Brown, 1854), 178.

tried and given a life sentence, but he also received a pardon shortly after from the governor of New York.[142]

All of this provides important context for the Tea Party shoemaker's recollections quoted at the start of this article. His memory of the Boston Tea Party and of his Indian costuming was amplified in the 1830s by working-class groups who felt that the economic justice ideals of the Revolution, and the common man's centrality to the Republic, were being forgotten.[143] The white Indian symbol marked an ongoing conflict between those who could vote and serve on juries and whose interests were represented in state and federal government in the new nation, and those who continued to feel shut out. The American who continued to put on Indian costume to express himself was not participating in a mere social movement. He was continuing a constitutional tradition of the pre-Revolutionary era—in part because the new era had failed to provide him an adequate institutional alternative.

In short, the legal claims of those who rallied in Indian dress, raised liberty poles, and prepared to throw off United States authority during the Whiskey Rebellion in 1791 were not different or more radical than those of the patriots who had won independence from Britain. The rebels saw themselves as asserting the *exact same* claims. By defending the government's power to tax under the status quo, and by marching at the head of an army to suppress the insurrection of men who had inadequate representation in their government, Washington stepped into the role of the British, asserting that virtual representation should satisfy the colonies.[144] If we accept that American patriots fighting the British were, as they claimed, defending their constitution, then we must also accept that many of the men dressing up as Indians in subsequent years to protest high taxes, unfair creditors, or distant landowners believed they were defending the same constitution.

The white man in Indian dress retained his power to evoke the constitutional grievances of the Revolutionary era because the symbol and its meanings never faded from public view. Natty Bumppo, the central character in James Fenimore Cooper's popular *Leatherstocking Tales*, is a figure in this mold. The politician Daniel Boone, whom John James Audubon described as "a stout, hale, and athletic man, dressed in a homespun hunting-shirt, bare-legged and moccasined," used the theme as well.[145]

Perhaps the most important nineteenth-century inheritor of the symbolism, however, was Andrew Jackson. Jackson first gained prominence as a representative to the Tennessee constitutional convention. A eulogist numbered him among frontiersmen whom he described as "sons of nature, … educated only by the spirit of freedom" who "longed to come together in organized society." Out of this desire, those "[d]wellers in

142 Charles W. McCurdy, *The Anti-Rent Era in New York Law and Politics 1839–1865* (Chapel Hill: University of North Carolina Press, 2001), 252, 270–1.

143 See Young, "Boston Shoemaker," 619.

144 Also like the British, Washington's philosophical views on political rights may have been helped along by self-interest. Washington was, in addition to the commander-in-chief, a speculator in Pennsylvania's western lands who nursed a long-held "disdain for its inhabitants." Slaughter, *Whiskey Rebellion*, 88. He maintained, as a result of his investments, a "'personal economic stake' in the outcome of the Whiskey Rebellion." Slaughter, *Whiskey Rebellion*, 89 (quoting James Thomas Flexner, *George Washington: Anguish and Farewell (1793–1799)* [Little, Brown, 1972], 163).

145 John James Audubon, *Delineations of American Scenery and Character* (New York: G. A. Baker, 1926), 61.

the forest, freest of the free ... came up by their representatives ... through the forest, along the streams, by the buffalo traces, by the Indian paths, ... to meet in convention." And "Andrew Jackson was there, the greatest man of them all."[146]

Jackson campaigners made use of this image throughout his public career. It was common for Jackson supporters to vow that they would never leave him "whilst 'woods grow and waters run,'" an "Indian" phrase suited to the character he played.[147] In lauding his virtues, admirers often compared him to his Indian adversaries. "The red braves of the wilderness confessed that in ... their highest virtues, General Jackson equalled the most celebrated of their Chiefs."[148] When he left office in 1837, his followers called him a man "straight as an Indian's arrow," who appealed to "the principles of the People," not their "pockets."[149] In keeping with the symbol's Revolutionary heritage, Jackson's Indian mystique did not suffer as a result of his crimes against the Creek and the Cherokee.

To Jackson and his supporters, this white Indian costuming signaled a suite of constitutional commitments that rejected unfair and "unnatural" credit relationships. Jackson's youthful experiences with insolvency fostered a life-long hatred of creditors' instruments and his political agenda centered on his "oppos[ition] to the U. States Bank, nay all Banks."[150] Banks, he charged, exercised a "corrupting influence" by encouraging people to get in over their heads to the benefit of the banking and creditor classes.[151] His bank veto message of 1832 accused bankers of oppressing the poor.[152] Laws benefitting the creditor class added "artificial distinctions" and "exclusive privileges" that would "make the rich richer and the potent more powerful," to the detriment of "the humble members of society—the farmers, mechanics, and laborers."[153] In another message to Congress, he inveighed against debtor's prison. "The personal liberty of the citizen seems too sacred," he said in that address, "to be held ... at the will of a creditor to whom he is willing to surrender all the means he has of discharging his debt."[154] As his followers triumphantly put it, Jackson's democracy was "a government of *men*, and not *property*."[155]

146 "Mr. Bancroft's Eulogy," *Georgia Telegraph & Republic*, July 15, 1845.

147 "The Elections in the West," *The Age*, September 19, 1832, 2.

148 "Funeral Obsequies in Philadelphia," *Sun*, June 28, 1845, 1. Even his critics found the Indian imagery inescapable. One opponent described Jackson as the creation of political visionaries, "who so assiduously labored to disguise his Indian Warrior in the trappings of a civilized patriot, and invest him with the robes of a perfect statesmen, the grossness of the error common to all his supporters." "On the Presidential Elections of 1824 and 1828," *Easton Gazette*, November 5, 1831, 1.

149 "Andrew Jackson," *Patriot & Democrat*, April 1, 1837.

150 Sean Wilentz, *The Rise of American Democracy: Jefferson to Lincoln* (New York: Norton, 2006), 361 (quoting Jackson to James K. Polk, December 23, 1833 in *Correspondence of Andrew Jackson, 1833–1838*, vol. 5, ed. John Spencer Bassett [Carnegie Institution of Washington, 1931], 235, 236.)

151 Wilentz, *American Democracy*, 361. This emphasizes the aspect of Jackson's position most relevant to this Article, but it should not be taken as a summary of his objections to the Bank of the US. Jackson's war against Biddle's bank was personal, political, and based on constitutional objections born of the bank's interference with presidential elections. It also involved the clash of two incompatible visions for the economic future of the United States. For a neat overview, see Wilentz, *American Democracy*, 360–74.

152 Andrew Jackson, "Veto Message" (July 10, 1832), in *A Compilation of the Messages and Papers of the Presidents* vol. 3, ed. James D. Richardson (New York: Bureau of National Literature, 1897), 1139, 1153 repr. Wilentz, *American Democracy*, 370.

153 Jackson, "Veto Message."

154 "President's Message," *Eastern Argus*, December 13, 1831, 2.

155 "The Sixtieth Anniversary of American Independence," *Eastern Argus*, July 12, 1836. Jackson's critic, Davy Crockett, also benefitted from the frontiersman's trope. His politics were concerned more with home

The longevity of the symbol of the white Indian and its enduring usefulness as a bearer of Revolutionary values is simply astonishing. Henry David Thoreau was able to rely on it as late as the 1850s. In *Walden*, he decried Americans' desire for luxuries and the dominion of creditors, and the moral burden of insolvency. "I have no doubt," Thoreau told his reader, "that some of you who read this book are unable to pay ... for the coats and shoes which are fast wearing or are already worn out, and have come to this page to spend borrowed or stolen time, robbing your creditors of an hour."[156]

Like proponents of nonimportation, Thoreau found a central symbol of the degradation of civilized man in his costume. "[T]here is more anxiety, commonly, to have fashionable ... clothes, than to have a sound conscience," and "It would be easier for [an American] to hobble to town with a broken leg than with a broken pantaloon."[157] But, he asked, "if the civilized man's pursuits are no worthier than the savage's, if he is employed the greater part of his life in obtaining gross necessaries and comforts merely, why should he have a better dwelling than the former?"[158] After identifying the main ailments of American culture, *Walden*'s prescription is the exchange of a house for a "wigwam."[159] To achieve moral independence, Thoreau advised, the white man must purge himself of European luxury and put on the trappings of Indian life.

The symbol's use and reuse in nineteenth-century American culture is undeniable. As we have seen, it became a fixture in politics, literature, and in the rhetorical toolkit of anyone arguing about economic justice in the public sphere. It also survived because it remained a potent tool of political engagement. Men continued to put on Indian dress and participate in mob actions to defend their constitutional rights generations after Independence.

It may seem bizarre to find this eighteenth-century style of political engagement, the mobbing of "groups who could find no alternative institutional expression for their demands and grievances, which were more often than not political," enduring into the 1840s.[160] We are used to celebrating, along with the Founders, the creation of a rational, participatory government in which law is based on the consent of the governed. The white Indian tradition is, by contrast, a carnivalesque spectacle, involving ritualistic demonstrations of the people's raw physical power, and it seems a relic of a legal regime characterized by hierarchy and inherited position. Its continued usefulness suggests that many Americans—even white, male Americans—did not experience the transition from status to contract, from hierarchy to equality, from the politics of deference to the politics of reasoned persuasion. If, indeed, this is part of the explanation, the symbol's late appearance in the context of the feudal estates of upstate New York makes perfect sense.

rule and squatter's rights than debtor freedom, however. See David Crockett, *A Narrative of the Life of David Crockett* (Philadelphia: E.L. Carey & A. Hart, 1834), 133–5.

156 Henry David Thoreau, *Walden and Civil Disobedience: Complete Texts with Introduction*, ed. Paul Lautner (Wadsworth Publishing, 2000), 41–2.

157 Ibid., 53.

158 Ibid., 62 (emphasis omitted).

159 Ibid., 59.

160 Wood, *Creation of the American Republic*, 320.

## V. Conclusion

The white Indian offers some insights about American constitutionalism, about the relationship between the unwritten constitution and the written, and about methods for future investigation in legal scholarship.

First, on constitutionalism. This paper necessarily provokes more questions than it resolves, but one thing is clear: the unwritten constitution of British North America endured, strengthened and enriched by the Revolution, to affect how American citizens interacted with their government and with each other for at least fifty years after the Founding. The endurance of unwritten constitutionalism, of British-style legal thinking, should not come as a surprise. While we are accustomed to thinking of 1787 as a hard break, that is an unreasonable and unhistorical expectation. The ancient does not become the modern overnight. Human beings reared in one culture tend not to experience "hard breaks" from that culture and willy-nilly adopt a completely different one.

It is equally clear that this unwritten constitutionalism interacted with what we think of as positive law. Andrew Jackson's embodiment of the white Indian's interconnected constitutional ideas could hardly be more complete. His political commitments included his sympathy for the honest debtor, suspicion of entrenched credit relationships, endorsement of the 1830 Preemption Act and successive legislation protecting squatter's rights, and, of course, his commitment to white supremacy—in particular, the white American's destiny as the Indian's replacement. It may seem that Jackson's orientation toward the Cherokee, for example, was lawless. But my research suggests another view: that Americans of the nineteenth century were able to keep an alternative vision of fundamental law alive, a constitutionalism so potent that it was able to re-enter positive law through the electoral process. Jackson's presidency represents, therefore, not so much a lawlessness, as the unwritten constitution reentering the weave of positive law. This thought is just a start, but there is more work to be done on the interaction between written and unwritten fundamental law during this period.

Attention to cultural trends, to behavior, to performances in public spaces, to the life an idea may have in literature and other art, requires a kind of historical investigation legal scholarship rarely attempts. That's a deficit that we should address. The problem with the way legal scholars typically plunder the historical record is not only that the methodology amounts to "looking over a crowd and picking out your friends."[161] To restrict one's focus to official texts, the published letters of great men, legal opinions, and the like, is to approach the legal world of the past as though it necessarily shares an anatomy with ours. The premise of such investigations is that the

[161] Patricia M. Wald, "Some Observations on the Use of Legislative History in the 1981 Supreme Court Term," *Iowa Law Review* 68.2 (Jan. 1983): 214 ("It sometimes seems that citing legislative history is still, as my late colleague [Judge] Harold Leventhal once observed, akin to 'looking over a crowd and picking out your friends.'").

differences between now and then are superficial—a matter of word choice. But the past, even our own, is a foreign country.[162] It is unfortunate that the Founders spoke English, because it tempts us to believe we share a language with them. We do not. Comprehending their words requires immersion. It is impossible otherwise to appreciate the immensity of our more than two centuries, or to grasp how dramatically our legal culture and institutions have transformed.

[162] See L. P. Hartley, *The Go-Between* (London: H. Hamilton, 1953), 9.

# 11
# Roosters and Resistance

*Christina D. Ponsa-Kraus**

In August 2018, the Board of Immigration Appeals (BIA) held that sponsoring or exhibiting a gamecock in a cockfight is a crime involving moral turpitude (CIMT).[1] The case concerned a man by the name of Agustín Ortega López, who came to the United States illegally from Mexico in 1992, has three U.S.-citizen children, and had no criminal record until he pled guilty to one misdemeanor count of cockfighting. At stake was whether Ortega López, who conceded that he was "removable" (that is, deportable), was eligible for "cancellation of removal": If the crime of which he had been convicted was a CIMT, he would not be.[2]

The BIA had already held once before that Ortega López was ineligible for cancellation of removal, and the case was at the BIA for a second time on remand from the Court of Appeals for the Ninth Circuit, which had decided an appeal from the original BIA decision.[3] The Ninth Circuit had explained that although "Congress has declared cockfighting is a scourge that warrants prosecution, and we have no quarrel with that," the court nevertheless could not conclude that cockfighting is a CIMT under the Ninth Circuit's definition of the term. That definition includes crimes that fall into two categories: (1) "those involving fraud" (not relevant here), and (2) "those involving grave acts of baseness or depravity," which, according to the Ninth Circuit, "almost always involve an intent to harm someone, the actual infliction of harm upon someone, or an action that affects a protected class of victim."[4] Whether gamecocks are a "protected class of victim" was the question the Ninth Circuit posed to the BIA on remand.[5]

But the BIA took a different tack. Rejecting what it described as the Ninth Circuit's unduly narrow definition of what constitutes a CIMT, the BIA instead explained its own broader and more flexible understanding: an offense that is "inherently vile,

* My thanks to Jacob Cogan, Erin Delaney, Jody Kraus, Kenneth Mack, Yael Sternhell, and the participants in the conference celebrating Dirk Hartog, especially commentator Rebecca Scott, for their feedback on earlier drafts. I am grateful also to Kyra DeTone, Valeria Flores-Morales, Julia Levitan, Mónica Pascual, and the reference librarians at Columbia Law School for their excellent research assistance on this essay, which nevertheless remains a very early set of musings on a project that may or may not come to be. The title (and, in many ways, the spirit) of this essay was inspired by Hendrik Hartog, "Pigs and Positivism," in *Wisconsin Law Review* (University of Wisconsin, 1985).

[1] *In re* Agustín Ortega López, 27 I&N Dec. 382 (BIA, 2018), *petition for review denied*, 978 F.3d 680 (9th Cir. 2020). The relevant statute, the Unlawful Animal Venture Prohibition, 7 U.S.C. § 2156(a)(1), provides that "[i]t shall be unlawful for any person to knowingly sponsor or exhibit an animal in an animal fighting venture," and the facts of the case concerned cockfighting.

[2] See 8 U.S.C. § 1229b(b)(1)(C).

[3] Ortega v. Lynch, 834 F.3d 1015 (9th Cir. 2016).

[4] Ibid. at 1018.

[5] Ibid.

Christina D. Ponsa-Kraus, *Roosters and Resistance* In: *In Between and Across*. Edited by: Kenneth W. Mack and Jacob Katz Cogan, Oxford University Press. © Oxford University Press 2024. DOI: 10.1093/oso/9780197680995.003.0012

base, or depraved, and contrary to the accepted rules of morality and the duties owed between persons or to society in general," or that involves behavior "so contrary to the standards of a civilized society as to be morally reprehensible," regardless of whether it affects a "protected class of victim."[6] Given the broader definition, it was not necessary for the BIA to decide whether the "victim" could be a gamecock. The BIA then once again held that sponsoring or exhibiting a gamecock at a cockfight is a CIMT, and that as a result, Ortega López was ineligible for cancellation of removal.[7]

Both the Ninth Circuit and the BIA raised, only then to avoid, an uncomfortable qualification to their observations about the moral turpitude of cockfighting. After endorsing Congress's declaration that cockfighting is a "scourge," the Ninth Circuit added in a footnote that, "[u]nlike dogfighting, which is illegal everywhere in the United States, cockfighting remains legal in Guam, the Northern Marianas, Puerto Rico, and the U.S. Virgin Islands."[8] Neither the footnote nor the rest of the opinion elaborated any further on the implications of that fact for the conclusion that cockfighting is a CIMT.[9] The BIA, too, noted this troubling exception, but then summarily dismissed any concerns it might raise. "We recognize ..." they wrote:

> that cockfighting is not criminalized in all jurisdictions throughout the United States. However, the fact that some territories of the United States have not updated their laws to ban some forms of animal fighting does not change our conclusion regarding the profoundly degrading nature of such conduct. The clear consensus in American society, as embodied by the laws of all fifty states and the District of Columbia and Federal law, is that sponsoring or exhibiting the spectacle of animal suffering is morally reprehensible.[10]

And that was that.[11]

[6] 27 I&N Dec. at 386.

[7] 27 Ibid. at 386–91, 398. As for merely paying a fee to watch a cockfight— and there was some indication that was all Ortega López had done—the BIA noted that, since Ortega López had been convicted, Congress had outlawed this as well. See 7 U.S.C. § 2156(a)(2). (At this point, I want to write about why our laws don't consider the deportation of a man who has lived in this country for nearly thirty years, has children here, and has no criminal record except for a misdemeanor, a practice at least as barbaric as that of cockfighting. Maybe I will, someday.)

[8] 834 F.3d at 1018 n.1. As discussed below, it no longer does, as a result of a 2016 amendment to 7 U.S.C. § 2156.

[9] The footnote did cite a case, White v. United States, 601 F.3d 545 (6th Cir. 2010), which itself mentioned the exception several times, but also did not discuss it.

[10] 27 I&N Dec. at 390.

[11] One of the BIA judges struggled considerably more with the question at oral argument, repeatedly asking the government's lawyer how it could be said that cockfighting is a CIMT if it remains legal in several U.S. jurisdictions. Despite his persistent questioning, apparently he was ultimately convinced by the government's argument. (The judge also raised the question of why the government wouldn't exercise its discretion to decline to pursue this particular case, but he didn't make any progress there either.) In its opinion, the BIA did note that other activities raise a similar, though not identical, problem. For example, prostitution, too, is a CIMT for immigration purposes, yet it is not illegal in every jurisdiction of every state. But for precisely that reason—that there are states where prostitution remains legal—the court could not have said about it what it said about cockfighting: namely, that the "clear consensus of American society, as embodied by the laws of all fifty states and the District of Columbia and Federal law," is that prostitution is morally reprehensible.

If we were to spend some time unpacking these statements, we would notice several things worth thinking about. We would notice the ambiguity with respect to what the United States is. This ambiguity is entirely familiar and unsurprising in a discussion concerning the U.S. territories, those liminal places that the U.S. Supreme Court has described as "belonging to the United States, but not a part of the United States."[12] Both courts in Ortega López's case assumed that "everywhere in the United States" and "throughout the United States" includes the territories, but by the time the BIA described the contrast between the territories and "American society," locating the latter in the "fifty states and the District of Columbia and Federal law," it was no longer clear just what the United States is, or where exactly its territories are.

We would notice as well that, at the time the BIA noted that federal law embodied a purported American consensus that cockfighting is morally reprehensible, it was due to federal law that cockfighting remained legal in the territories: that is, the same federal law banning it in the fifty states and the District of Columbia exempted the U.S. territories from its ban.[13] So, which is it? Is there a clear consensus reflected in federal law or isn't there?

That said, a little over a year after the second BIA decision, Congress eliminated the exemption—over the objection of every representative in Congress from the territories, none of whom has the power to vote on any federal legislation, this amendment included.[14] The sponsors of the amendment referred to it as an effort to achieve "parity" among all U.S. jurisdictions with respect to banning cockfighting, undeterred by the hypocrisy of insisting on parity with respect to cockfighting while simultaneously denying the territories parity with respect to voting rights (and much else besides). Quite literally, these holier-than-thou members of Congress lectured their colonial subjects on the importance of equality before proceeding to impose upon them a rule they opposed but could not vote against. It remains questionable whether this federal law reflects a "clear consensus" on the morality of cockfighting, but it undoubtedly reflects a clear consensus among voting members of Congress that the United States remains quite content to have colonies, still.

## I. Cockfighting and Colonialism

Cockfighting has been a popular sport in the colony of Puerto Rico since before it was a colony of the United States: from when there were no laws about it on the books, through when the Spanish government began regulating it in 1770, through when Spanish governor Miguel de la Torre issued a detailed decree on the subject in 1823, through when the United States annexed Puerto Rico in 1898 and immediately banned it, through when that ban was lifted in 1933 with the blessing of U.S.-appointed governor Robert Hayes Gore (who remarked on the occasion that he'd enjoyed cockfighting in his native Kentucky), and through the enactment of Puerto

[12] Downes v. Bidwell, 182 U.S. 244, 287 (1901).
[13] 7 U.S.C. § 2156(b).
[14] Petition for Writ of Certiorari, Ortiz-Díaz v. United States, cert. denied, 142 S.Ct. 336, 3 (2021) (No. 20-1735).

Rico's *Ley de Gallos*, which was in force at the time the federal ban was enacted, and which begins by declaring cockfighting a "Cultural Right of Puerto Ricans."[15] Surely Puerto Rico and any other U.S. territory where cockfighting is popular would be no different in this respect from states where cockfighting is popular. But the territories would have an even more robust democratic theory underlying their arguments for the continuing legitimacy—let's just say legality—of cockfighting despite a federal ban, insofar as the federal ban was imposed upon them by a legislative body in which they have no voting representation, while the legislative bodies in which they do have voting representation allowed it.

The idea that extending the federal ban to the territories would result in parity was also misleading, insofar as "parity" implies equal treatment for the similarly situated, because Congress did not ban cockfighting in jurisdictions where it was legal until every state had made cockfighting illegal. Only then did it extend the federal ban even to jurisdictions where cockfighting remained legal—by then, only the territories.[16] In other words, the ban supplemented state law, but contradicted territorial law. According to the BIA, the territories had yet to "update" their laws, but this statement just gives us something else to unpack, for it implies that the territories are living in the past, and in need of catching up with the mainland, whereas arguably it's the judges who are living in the past when they suggest that the territories are backward and in need of the United States's civilizing influence.

On the other hand, one might interpret the court's remark about the territories' failure to "update" their laws as an effort to be flattering, or at least to avoid insult. That is, one could interpret the court as saying, essentially, "Of course the territories agree with us that cockfighting is a vile, base, and depraved activity; they just haven't had the time to make it official." That would be wrong, though, at least judging from the opposition to the extension of the federal ban voiced by the territories' nonvoting representatives in Congress. More important, it would be a failure to grapple with the thorny problem of cultural difference and national sameness pressed by the question of whether the federal ban should extend to the territories.

There's relatively little out there by way of scholarly work on cockfighting in Puerto Rico. The brief histories of cockfighting I've found identify three epochs or eras: *época antigua* (from its origins to the U.S.-imposed ban in 1898), *época romántica* (from 1898 to the lifting of the ban in 1933), and *época moderna* (from 1933 to the present).[17] So far, I've found almost nothing at all about that first era, and I haven't yet explored the third. As for the second, in scholarly discussions cockfighting immediately—seemingly automatically—becomes a metaphor for colonial resistance

[15] Juan Llanes Santos, "Beaks and Spurs: Cockfighting in Puerto Rico," National Register of Historic Places Multiple Property Documentation Form (Washington, DC: U.S. Department of the Interior, National Park Service, 2014), Section E; "Reglamento de Galleras, Puerto Rico, Marzo 14 de 1823," in *Boletín Histórico*, ed. Cayetano Coll y Toste (San Juan: Ateneo Puertorriqueño, Editorial LEA), 3:296; Janet M. Davis, *The Gospel of Kindness: Animal Welfare and the Making of Modern America* (New York: Oxford University Press, 2016): 139–41; and 2007 P.R. Laws 98 (referencing preamble "Para... establecer como Derecho Cultural de los Puertorriqueños las peleas de gallos").

[16] Petition for Writ of Certiorari, Ortiz-Díaz, 142 S.Ct. at 2–3.

[17] Eduardo Piña Méndez, "Las Peleas de Gallo en Puerto Rico," *Isla Literaria* (San Juan: June–July 1970), 21; Lorence Morell Vega, "Las Peleas de Gallo como Prácticas Culturales en Puerto Rico" (una revisión de literatura y notas preliminares), *Revista (In)genios* (Río Piedras: Universidad de Puerto Rico, 2006), 3:8.

to imperial imposition. One work puts it this way: "After 1898, the sport was prohibited by the new United States' administrators. For the next forty years, the illegal-countryside-hidden *galleras* became a dissident space, a pit of cultural resistance, opposed to the new colonial metropolis's policies. Puerto Rico's *galleras* are legitimate heirs of this significant past."[18] Another puts it like this: "It is important to add that, for many Puerto Ricans, maintaining this tradition means maintaining alive a national identity that represents an extensive group of people, due to which to prohibit this practice means to condemn the cultural expression of a specific community."[19] And another: "The fighting cock, however, remained a political and cultural minefield whose fate was tied to competing visions of cultural identity, citizenship, civilization, and self-determination."[20]

Why do I resist these statements? Surely there's some truth to them. But they feel too easy, too automatic, too instinctive. How much would I really have to learn about cockfighting to reach the conclusion that, in Puerto Rico, cockfighting symbolizes colonial resistance? Couldn't I have told you that before I read a word? I want to catch myself before I settle comfortably into a recognizable understanding. I want to find a space in which I can *see* something, before all I can see is empire.

## II. Resisting Resistance

Perhaps cockfighting was not the best way to get there. The subject led, instantly and seemingly inevitably, to empire. Once I started learning about cockfighting (and empire) in Puerto Rico, it wasn't long before I was facing the familiar comparison between Puerto Rico and Cuba. As one commentator pithily puts it, why is Cuba sexy, and Puerto Rico not?[21] After annexation, the United States banned cockfighting in both Cuba and Puerto Rico. Sure enough, Cubans vociferously resisted; Puerto Ricans, not so vociferously. In Cuba, the defenders of cockfighting responded to the ban by organizing "huge parades, rallies, and petitions across Cuba. Each petition defended cockfighting with the same language of virtuous citizenship and cultural nationalism that President [Tomás Estrada] Palma used to justify the ban."[22] And Puerto Rico? Well, they did organize petitions too.[23] But if there were huge parades or rallies or marches on the governor's mansion to defend cockfighting, they seem to have disappeared from the historical record.

Could it be that I'm overstating the contrast, because of my own preoccupations? Could it be that Puerto Ricans did march on the governor's mansion to defend cockfighting, and somehow, no one remembers it, or they did and they do, and

18 Llanes Santos, "Beaks and Spurs," 2.

19 Morell Vega, "Las Peleas de Gallos," 2 (my translation).

20 Davis, *The Gospel of Kindness*, 141.

21 Frances Negrón Muntaner, "Why Do Americans Find Cuba Sexy, and Not Puerto Rico?" *Pacific Standard*, Sept. 9, 2016, https://psmag.com/news/why-do-americans-find-cuba-sexy-but-not-puerto-rico.

22 Davis, *The Gospel of Kindness*, 135.

23 See, e.g., references to various petitions to the Puerto Rico legislature for the repeal of the ban on cockfighting in the Actas de la Cámara de Delegados (minutes) in the years following the annexation of Puerto Rico by the United States, available at https://www.academiajurisprudenciapr.org/actas-de-la-camara-de-delegados-de-puerto-rico/.

I just haven't found references to it yet? Puerto Ricans march sometimes. And there was plenty of politically motivated mob violence during the transition from Spanish to American rule, even if there wasn't an uprising against the United States, as in the Philippines, just as there wasn't an uprising against Spain, as in Cuba and the Philippines. But the contrast casts a shadow over the period surrounding 1898, when one sees Puerto Ricans proclaiming their loyalty to Spain (and asking to be rewarded with "autonomy"), and then, essentially overnight, proclaiming their loyalty to the United States (and asking to be rewarded with "autonomy").[24] So when I decide I'm going to explore cockfighting, my heart sinks as I realize that even here, the contrast—why Cubans fight and Puerto Ricans don't—must once again be reckoned with.

The contrast may well have inspired the wistful remark of a Puerto Rican legislator during a debate in Puerto Rico's Cámara de Delegados on an amendment to the ban on cockfighting in March 1910: "If only in this country, every man were a gamecock."[25] Or one could bring a more lighthearted attitude to the situation, as Puerto Ricans often do, in this case with a witty saying about how they deal with the imperial imposition of laws they don't like. As the saying goes, "Americans make laws; Puerto Ricans interpret them."[26]

Pushing past the ban to find descriptions of cockfighting itself, I stumble upon a book by William Dinwiddie, an American who traveled to Puerto Rico immediately after its annexation—which is to say, I haven't pushed past anything at all, really.[27] Dinwiddie spent two months touring the island at the direction of his publishers, Harper & Brothers, and the resulting book included a chapter on cockfighting, which Dinwiddie introduces as "[t]he only real recreation of the rural Puertoriqueños [*sic*]." Bullfighting, he explains, has never taken hold on the island because Puerto Ricans cannot afford "the expensive luxury of importing any of the distinguished matadors from home," without whom bullfighting becomes "mere brutality." "As a matter of fact," he continues, "cock-mains are more reprehensible, morally, than bull-rings, since the former is displayed in a brutal fight to the death between untrained but plucky birds, while the latter call for an exhibition of skill of hand and nerves of iron on the part of the human participants."[28] I keep pushing past—past the moral opprobrium; past the line-drawing between superior Europeans and inferior islanders—to get to whatever description of cockfighting itself may be found here. We learn that every town had at least one cockpit and what the cockpits looked like; that throughout the countryside, Puerto Rican peasants spent their Sunday afternoons—"after a hasty visit to the church in the morning"—engaged in their favorite pastime of cockfighting

24 See Christina D. Ponsa-Kraus, "When Statehood Was Autonomy," in *Reconsidering the Insular Cases: The Past and Future of American Empire,* eds. Gerald Neuman & Tomiko Brown-Nagin (Cambridge: Harvard University Press, 2015).

25 "La Sesión del Jueves," *La Correspondencia* (Puerto Rico), March 7, 1910. "Ojalá que en este país, cada hombre resultara un gallo." The translation of "gallo" could be "rooster," not gamecock, but this being a debate about the ban on cockfighting, "gamecock" is the better translation. Something else that came up in that debate that would be worth exploring further was the argument that the ban on cockfighting was merely an excuse to violate the privacy of the home, on the pretext of looking for cockfights.

26 "*Los americanos hacen las leyes; los puertorriqueños las interpretan.*" Or in any event, it's what my mother and her friends used to say.

27 William Dinwiddie, *Puerto Rico: Its Conditions and Possibilities* (New York: Harper & Bros., 1899).

28 Ibid., 175. And apropos of that "*sic*," at least he didn't say "Porto Ricans."

(though I suspect from other descriptions that he must mean Puerto Rican *men*); that it was even more popular on holidays; that members of the "wealthier and commercial classes" watched, too, now and again, but that its devotees consist mainly of "the poorer element"; and that these were "quiet, hardworking people, when work is to be had, who enjoy intensely their few simple pleasures, and go into ecstasies over their great sport of cock-maiming."[29]

I have yet to see a cockfight in person, but to judge from the descriptions I've read, "ecstasy" is an apt term to describe the experience of those involved—except, probably, the roosters. Dinwiddie's description captures some of that ecstasy:

> The birds are teased into fighting humor while held in the hand, and viciously pluck at each other's heads; now they are dropped on the ground with a quick movement, and at the order of the referee they are at it. High up in the air they strike the first few plunges, and one dodges under, while the uppermost bird lands over his enemy with a surprised look, but whirls and grabs his opponent on the red comb with a strong beak, and plants his gaff fairly on the side of the other's head. A roar of approval goes up from the crowd who have backed this bird, and a counter set of *hi*'s [*sic*][30] of fear rise from those wishing for the success of the other favorite. The fight is fast and furious.
>
> At last the red cock sinks his head with blinded eyes, and the blood drips off upon the ground. His panting antagonist watches him a moment, as if not willing to take advantage of his desperate condition, and, at the lull, each owner rushes forward and grabs his bird. One takes the bloody head and neck of his pet into his mouth and sucks the congealing blood, and then breathes new life into the sinking cock from his own lungs; the other resorts to a water-bottle from which he fills his mouth and blows it on the head and neck, and under the wings of his bird until the closing eyes brighten from the refreshing spray.
>
> Time is called! In the center of the ring lies a small square, outlined with sunken wooden sticks, and on its opposite edges the birds are set. The mongrel-spotted bird goes for his game-colored enemy immediately, and strikes him three times to the other's once. Poor fellow! The fight is over! he [*sic*] turns and runs away, followed by his fierce tantalizer. Once more they are rubbed into shape. One vicious gaff, as they come together, and the red bird sinks dead, the bone lance going deep into his eye and brain.[31]

I'm not just reading this description, but staring at it. I'm staring at the gamecocks, the fight, the blood, the handlers sucking the congealed blood off the roosters, the half-dead animal being put back in to fight some more. I'm staring at the participants in the cockfight. For just a moment, I forget all about Dinwiddie. But then I remember him again, and I tell myself it's a good thing, because one would not want to be lulled

[29] Ibid., 176.

[30] Doubtless what he was hearing was "*¡ay!*" which roughly translates as "oh, no!" or "oh my goodness" or "poor thing!"

[31] Dinwiddie, *Puerto Rico*, 177–8.

into a sense of complacency about where the boot of empire went. It's still there—right there, on my neck.

Dinwiddie's narrative continues. We learn that immediately after the end of each fight, all bets were paid; that the entire event lasted for hours, "until the hundred contestants have been reduced by half"; that "[t]here was no drinking, no carousing among the spectators; no ugly swearing; no bad feeling engendered, and no taint of rowdyism such as we see in our own country at such gatherings." As he concludes, Dinwiddie endeavors to give his reader deeper insight into these people: "That the amusement was brutal and of low order seemed not to occur to anyone. They had been taught this form of pastime, and conscience did not trouble them."[32] The chapter concludes with a description of "a little black youngster," wearing a soldier's discarded hat, a coat but no shirt, and happily carrying a few "*centavos*" that he won in a cockfighting bet that day, pausing in awe as a priest walks by. "Verily," concludes Dinwiddie, "only such a mercurial race could have stood the blighting abuses of a despotic government with complacence." Still there.

To Dinwiddie, Puerto Ricans are pliant, passive, and unreflective. They fight cocks because they always have, they enjoy their simple pleasures, and they don't even think about the morality—the implication seems to be, because they can't. The sense of superiority, the condescension, the othering is so transparent, there's almost nothing left to interpret.

This passage is at least as much about Dinwiddie and the condescending imperial lens he's looking through as it is about anything he describes. So where would I find a description of cockfighting in Puerto Rico that wasn't about Puerto Rico being a colony? After all, there never has been a cockfight in Puerto Rico that wasn't a fight in a colony. But perhaps Manuel A. Alonso's mid-nineteenth-century description of a cockfight in Puerto Rico comes closer—or at any rate, here is a description by a native Puerto Rican. A writer and a poet who studied medicine in Barcelona in the 1840s, Alonso published a book called *El gíbaro* in 1849.[33] *El gíbaro* is a book of essays and poems about Puerto Rican peasants and rural life on the island, and it includes two chapters on cockfighting. Alonso's detailed description focuses more directly than Dinwiddie's on the activity itself: the cockpit, the handlers, their gamecocks, the details of their care and training (contrary to Dinwiddie's claim, there is training involved). And the fight:

> There are no words to describe the fierceness of those animals: at the beginning they don't peck at each other, but rather they injure each other during flight: these first blows are known as *flying blows*;[34] but they do not delay in commencing, and every *peck* is followed by a *stab*, which the opponent avoids with dexterity, and receives

[32] Ibid., 179.

[33] Manuel A. Alonso, *El jíbaro* (San Juan: Ediciones Huracán, 2001). I'm working from a recent edition, itself based on the second edition, published in 1882; the first edition was published in 1849. The original used the nineteenth-century spelling of the word in its title, *gíbaro* (Puerto Rican peasant). The recent edition uses the modern spelling, *jíbaro*.

[34] Ibid., 119. My translation. All italics in the original Spanish. "Flying blows" is "*tiros bolaos*." "*Tiros bolaos*" would be a colloquially casual pronunciation of "*tiros volados*," which is, literally, "flown blows," but better translated as "flying blows," as in, "blows while flying."

> with heroic valor; their bodies are covered in blood and dust, they lose sight, and they can barely hold themselves up; becoming fatigued many times during several hours without either of the two emerging victorious:[35] this is called *settling the fight*: other times one flees, dies, or is spent, rendering the other the winner.[36]
>
> There are roosters that have favorite blows; such as pecking at the head of the wing, nailing the spur beneath it, hitting in the *yunque*, which is the name for the nape of the neck, etc....
>
> When the combatants pause their fighting for a moment, it is time for a *break*, their *handlers* pick them up, clean them by sucking the blood off their necks, and examine them;[37] and with this care they regain sight, and they are reanimated to return to the fray. After a determined number of breaks, if neither combatant defeats the other, the fight is settled.[38]

There's much more in Alonso to discuss, but for now I'll pause to note something that captures, as far as I can tell, several themes in the discussions of cockfighting I've read. About the handler, Alonso writes:

> [T]his is a man, white, black, or mulatto, fat or skinny, tall or short, usually of some age or another, who is capable, because of his extensive knowledge of the matter and because of his tried and tested patience, of teaching a gamecock, getting every advantage possible based on the dispositions he shows, unknown to those profane in the art; but which for him are the object of continuous study. He must also be *vir probus* in every respect, for on his word great sums are wagered, as we will see later.[39]

The themes here include the (apparently) radically democratic nature of cockfighting; the knowledge and skill a handler must have to train a gamecock; the importance as well of his honor and probity. Is it naive to think that the weight of that boot might lift, just a bit, if I keep going?

Elaborate unwritten norms govern the cockpit. Written norms do too, and I don't just mean the U.S.-imposed ban (there it is again). As noted above, in 1823 Governor Miguel de la Torre issued a decree with rules on cockfighting, consisting of six chapters spanning over ten single-spaced pages, along with another page-and-a-half of addenda. From this detailed *Reglamento de Galleras* we learn a great deal: among other things, that cockfighting was not quite democratic enough to allow the participation of enslaved persons.[40] (Or rather, that it was, and that's precisely why the governor tried to outlaw their participation. I did see a reference in a newspaper to a conviction for engaging in cockfighting with an enslaved person, and several

[35] Ibid. There's something strange here: Everything else I've read tells me cockfights don't last hours; they last minutes. But that's what the passage says: "*llegando muchas veces a quedar después de algunas horas rendidos de fatiga.*"

[36] Ibid. "Settling the fight": "*entablar la pelea.*" "Spent": "*queda fuera de combate*" (as in, "has no fight left in him").

[37] Ibid. "Examine them": "*examinan sus miembros.*" I've settled on this as the most accurate translation, understanding "*miembros*," that is, "members," to refer to "parts," as in "body parts."

[38] Ibid., 119–20. "Settled": "*entablada.*"

[39] Ibid., 120.

[40] *Reglamento de Galleras*, ch. 2, art. 5.

references in secondary literature to the cockpit as a space in which even enslaved persons participated on equal terms, so I don't yet know exactly what to believe.)

Democracy, equality, honor, simplicity, colonialism, nationalism, defiance, empire, law. Why do I still feel like all of this will eclipse the thing I should see before I can see it? Clifford Geertz's famous essay on cockfighting isn't going to solve my problem, but it does keep coming to mind—specifically, for its description of a cockfight as the instantiation of "Platonic hate."[41] Does Geertz mean the roosters? Or the human participants? Is "hate" the place where I will see something, before all I can see is empire?

I'm not sure. What I know is, the notion that cockfighting embodies pure hate is a metaphor too, and yet, somehow, it's a metaphor for the absence of metaphor. Meanwhile, all I'm trying to do is get out from under that boot—as was, I bet, the person who published the following in an article titled "The Cockfight" in one of Puerto Rico's leading newspapers in March 1909: "These two animals do not confront danger for the idea of country, nor for the gods of their fathers, nor to defend the honor of their ancestors. Nor do they think of glory, or the liberty of their children. Each of these gamecocks fights, solely, in order not to be defeated; they do not want to know the shame of defeat."[42]

The passage purports to be from a speech given by the Athenian general Themistocles to his soldiers to prepare them for battle. It was published in the wake of events known as the Crisis of 1909, when the Puerto Rican legislature stood up to the U.S.-controlled Executive Council by refusing to pass a budget, upon which President William Howard Taft made a speech berating Puerto Ricans for their ingratitude and calling on Congress to pass legislation pursuant to which, if the legislature failed to pass a budget, the previous year's budget would automatically be repassed, which Congress then did.[43] Right. The boot.

## III. Looking for Puerto Rico

Speaking of which, why didn't the federal government impose a ban on cockfighting in Hawaii? The United States annexed Hawaii shortly before it annexed Puerto Rico, Cuba, the Philippines, and Guam. Hawaii's circumstances, and its fate, were different, yes, but Hawaii was also noncontiguous territory, and it also had a native population with its own culture and traditions. Although it had already been subject to the assimilationist efforts of American missionaries, cockfighting was also popular there—popular enough to ban, that is, and the answer to why the federal government did

[41] Clifford Geertz, "Deep Play: Notes on the Balinese Cockfight," *Daedalus* (Cambridge: The MIT Press, 1972), 101:9.

[42] "La riña de gallos," *La Correspondencia* (Puerto Rico), March 13, 1909. "Estos dos animales no confrontan el peligro por la idea de la patria, ni por los dioses de sus padres, ni por defender la memoria de sus antecesores. Tampoco piensan en la gloria, ni en la libertad de sus hijos. Cada uno de esos gallos combate, únicamente, para no ser vencido; no quieren conocer la vergüenza de la derrota."

[43] José Trías Monge, *Historia Constitucional de Puerto Rico* (Puerto Rico: La Editorial Universidad de Puerto Rico, 1981): 2: 21–25; Christina D. Ponsa-Kraus, "The Crisis of 1909, and the Other Crisis of 1909," *Revista de la Academia Puertorriqueña de Jurisprudencia y Legislación*, XIII (2016), https://www.academiajurisprudenciapr.org/the-crisis-of-1909-and-the-other-crisis-of-1909/.

not impose a ban on Hawaii looks like it might turn out to be rather simple: Hawaii already had a ban, dating from 1884.[44]

And I, out of ideas for how to get out from under the boot of empire, suddenly find myself wondering what I would find if I looked for Puerto Ricans cockfighting in Hawaii. Which, if one's goal is to get out from under the boot of empire, is perverse. I know.

There is reason to believe one would find Puerto Ricans cockfighting in Hawaii. Several months after Puerto Rico's annexation by the United States, the San Ciriaco hurricane hit the island. One of the worst hurricanes ever to make landfall there, it devastated the place, leaving many Puerto Ricans out of work and in dire conditions. At around the same time, a number of Hawaiian plantation owners found themselves desirous of a more pliable workforce, as labor unrest began to stir among Japanese workers in Hawaii. Soon enough, agents from Hawaiian plantations were in Puerto Rico recruiting workers, and on November 22, 1900, the first of several ships carrying scores of Puerto Rican workers and their families left for Hawaii.[45]

The ship, the *Arkadia*, took a route that one might describe, from a distance, as an ironic tour of the highlights of American westward expansion, given that the people on the ship were colonial subjects en route from one U.S. territory to another: They sailed from Puerto Rico to New Orleans (the Louisiana Purchase!), where they disembarked and transferred onto a train. They stopped in Texas (the annexation of Texas!) and again somewhere near an Indian reservation (Indian "removal"!), before continuing onto California (the war with Mexico!). About forty Puerto Ricans stayed in San Francisco, while the rest continued to Honolulu (1898!).[46]

Although there is, unquestionably, more looking to be done, I could not find any reference anywhere to any Puerto Rican cockfighting in Hawaii. The closest I came were some references to arrests of Puerto Ricans in documents relating to what happened to Puerto Rican workers who left the plantations where they had originally been brought to work. These arrests included arrests for vagrancy and gambling, and my guess is, those might be arrests for cockfighting. But I could find nothing explicit about cockfighting itself.

These Puerto Ricans in Hawaii, who used to spend every Sunday at the cockpit (after a quick visit to the church), could not possibly have abandoned cockfighting once they arrived in Hawaii, could they? But I couldn't find them anywhere. And yet what I find myself thinking is that *not* finding them feels like the closest I'm ever going

[44] 1884 Haw. Sess. Laws ch. 51, § 2 ("Any person who shall keep or use, or in any way be connected with or interested in the management of, or shall receive money for the admission of any person to, any place kept or used for the purpose of fighting or baiting any bull, bear, dog, cock, or other creature, and any person who shall encourage, aid, or assist therein, or who shall permit or suffer any place to be so kept or used, shall, upon conviction thereof, be adjudged guilty of a misdemeanor."). I understand this provision, like others criminalizing an activity, as a "ban" on that activity.

[45] Norma Carr, "The Puerto Ricans in Hawaii: 1900–1958," (Ph.D. diss., University of Hawaii, 1989), 92; Carmelo Rosario Natal, *Exodo puertorriqueño: (las emigraciones al Caribe y Hawaii, 1900–1915)* (San Juan, P.R.: C. Rosario Natal, 1983). Both of these works describe Puerto Ricans' work and leisure in Hawaii, but neither discusses cockfighting. Chapter 6 of Rosario Natal's book mentions dance, music, baseball, and boxing in particular among Puerto Ricans' entertainments, but not cockfighting (see p. 108).

[46] For a description of the migration of several groups from 1900–1901, see Carr, "The Puerto Ricans in Hawaii," 85–169.

to get, out from under the boot of empire. Surely that would be cheating, not to mention deceiving myself. Moreover, even if I never find anything at all, that won't change the fact that the people I'm talking about were themselves caught under the boot of empire, federal cockfighting ban or no federal cockfighting ban. Still, at the moment I'm just trying to find my way—trying to find my way to a Puerto Rico I could write about that wouldn't be defined by its colonial condition. Right now, I can't help but think that that place is *nowhere.*

# 12

# Law, History, and the Interwar ACLU's Jewish Lawyers

*Laura Weinrib*[*]

"Go home to Russia you dirty swine," an anonymous correspondent wrote in June 1938 to Morris Ernst, an ACLU lawyer who was born in 1881 in Uniontown, Alabama, and spent most of his childhood in New York City. "Every dirty Jew bites the hand that feeds him."[1]

The letter arrived just three months after the annexation of Austria into Nazi Germany, and one year after the United States Supreme Court astounded court-watchers by upholding the National Labor Relations Act.[2] Ernst, its recipient, was a graduate of Williams College who attended New York Law School's night program while working in his family's shirt business and managing a furniture store. In his private law practice, Ernst defended publishing houses against obscenity charges, and he was an outspoken critic of censorship laws. In 1926, he declined the ACLU's invitation to become chief counsel for the organization. Four years later, he agreed to sign on as a co–general counsel, a role he retained for the next quarter-century.[3]

Ernst was accustomed to antisemitism, and he claimed to be unshaken by the many hostile missives he received.[4] Still, the threats were becoming more credible in the new global environment, and the linkage between Jewishness and foreignness more disturbing. "[I]f you damned Jews don't cease your un-American, un-Christian agitation, you'll get the same medicine you are getting in Germany and other parts of the world," an unnamed "loyal patriotic American" wrote to Ernst.[5] According to Ernst's

* Many thanks to Jacob Cogan, Kenneth Mack, William Forbath, Beck Boorstein, Isaac May, and Daniel Rauch for helpful comments on this draft. This chapter, like this volume, is dedicated to Dirk Hartog, whose extraordinary generosity, insight, and friendship have immeasurably improved my scholarship and profoundly enriched my life.

1 Anonymous to Morris Ernst, 16 June 1938, Morris Leopold Ernst Papers, Harry Ransom Center, University of Texas at Austin [hereinafter Ernst Papers], box 39, folder 2. Ernst's father, who was raised in a German-speaking Jewish family, immigrated from Pilsen, Bohemia (now in the Czech Republic), following his older brother; his mother grew up in the United States. Samantha Barbas, *The Rise and Fall of Morris Ernst, Free Speech Renegade* (Chicago: Chicago University Press, 2021), 8.

2 NLRB v. Jones and Laughlin Steel, 301 U.S. 1 (1937).

3 On Ernst's role in the early ACLU, see Laura Weinrib, *The Taming of Free Speech: America's Civil Liberties Compromise* (Cambridge: Harvard University Press, 2016); Laura M. Weinrib, "The Sex Side of Civil Liberties: *United States v. Dennett* and the Changing Face of Free Speech," *Law and History Review* 30 (2012): 325–86.

4 Ernst recalled being told in his youth that he was inferior because he was Jewish. Brett Gary, *Dirty Works: Obscenity on Trial in America's First Sexual Revolution* (Stanford: Stanford University Press, 2021), 20.

5 "A Loyal Patriotic American" to Morris Ernst, 21 June 1938, Ernst Papers, box 39, folder 2.

Laura Weinrib, *Law, History, and the Interwar ACLU's Jewish Lawyers* In: *In Between and Across.* Edited by: Kenneth W. Mack and Jacob Katz Cogan, Oxford University Press. © Oxford University Press 2024. DOI: 10.1093/oso/9780197680995.003.0013

aggressors, Jewish efforts to transform American law and politics were part of a larger plot to infiltrate and undermine American institutions and values.

The immediate impetus for the attacks on Ernst was the ACLU's publicity campaign against Jersey City's autocratic mayor Frank Hague, which Ernst had helped to orchestrate. The ACLU's objective was to open Jersey City up to labor organizers affiliated with the Committee for Industrial Organization of the American Federation of Labor (AFL), which reorganized in 1938 as the independent Congress of Industrial Organizations (CIO). Early in his political career, Hague had voiced support for the AFL and had attracted union endorsements. After the Depression eviscerated Jersey City industry, however, Hague had vilified unions for eroding corporate profits and had barred labor organizers from parks and street corners.[6]

For the ACLU, the issues involved were easy ones. The organization's leadership broke over many questions during the late 1930s, from the scope of speech rights on private property to the appropriate role of government in amplifying disfavored views. What Hague was doing in Jersey City, however, intruded squarely on the First Amendment as the ACLU had worked to define it—in the courts and in public opinion—over the prior two decades. The organization and its allies tarred Hague as the "Hudson Hitler," an authoritarian worthy of popular ire.[7] The enthusiastic reception for the ACLU's position in the mainstream press was a testament to the success of its decades-long campaign to equate American democracy with the vigorous enforcement of the First Amendment.[8]

Nonetheless, the ACLU's approach had its holdouts. Many Jersey City residents regarded Hague as a committed patriot, even a working-class hero, who was defending American values against radical insurgents. Of this contingent, some voiced familiar antisemitic tropes. "As a resident of Jersey City, I want you to know that the people of our city are 100% behind Mayor Hague in this fight [to preserve] one of the few American cities in the East," one such letter expounded. Its anonymous author addressed Ernst as a "sawed-off runt" and a "dirty little kike" and accused him of "trying to bore from within."[9]

That the ACLU's presence in Jersey City was unleashing an antisemitic backlash provoked considerable dissension within the Jewish community. Many of Ernst's Jewish correspondents worried that his public profile would draw unwelcome

[6] On the ACLU's conflict with Frank Hague, see Weinrib, *Taming of Free Speech*, ch. 7; Donald W. Rodgers, *Workers against the City: The Fight for Free Speech in Hague v. CIO* (Champaign: University of Illinois Press, 2020); John J. Gibbons, "Hague v. CIO: A Retrospective," *New York University Law Review* 52 (1977): 731–809. On Frank Hague, see Richard Connors, *A Cycle of Power: The Career of Jersey City Mayor Frank Hague* (Metuchen, NJ: Scarecrow Press, 1971); James Fischer, *On the Irish Waterfront: The Crusader, the Movie, and the Soul of the Port of New York* (Ithaca: Cornell University Press, 2009); Matthew Raffety, "Political Ethics and Public Style in the Early Career of Jersey City's Frank Hague," *New Jersey History* 124 (2009): 29–56.

[7] Clipping, *New York Evening Post*, January 12, 1938, American Civil Liberties Union Records, The Roger Baldwin Years, 1917–1950, Princeton University Seeley G. Mudd Manuscript Library [hereinafter ACLU Papers], vol. 2020.

[8] On the interwar ACLU, see Weinrib, *Taming of Free Speech*; Samuel Walker, *In Defense of American Liberties: A History of the ACLU* (New York: Oxford University Press, 1990); Judy Kutulas, *The American Civil Liberties Union and the Making of Modern Liberalism, 1930–1960* (Chapel Hill: University of North Carolina Press, 2006).

[9] "A Loyal Patriotic American" to Morris Ernst, 21 June 1938, Ernst Papers, box 39, folder 2.

attention to American Jewry and embolden antisemites—that 1938 was "no time for Jews to be the center of newspaper publicity," let alone advocating radical causes.[10] To Ernst, criticism of this kind was more troubling than the antisemitic attacks themselves.

In grappling with these unsettling exchanges, Ernst turned for advice, as he often did, to his friend and mentor Louis Brandeis. A progressive icon and the first Jewish justice of the United States Supreme Court, Brandeis was thirty years Ernst's senior. His parents, like Ernst's father, were Bohemian immigrants who acculturated relatively quickly to life in the United States.[11] Ernst deeply valued Brandeis's opinion; in fact, he described himself as a "Brandeis disciple," and a portrait of the justice hung on his office wall.[12] Yet Jewishness, for Brandeis, had assumed a centrality that Ernst (who mailed out "Christmas" cards in the 1920s before shifting to "Holidays" or "New Year"[13]) was slower to embrace.[14]

In June 1938, Ernst wrote to Brandeis that he was receiving a flood of letters from "rich Jewish people begging [him] to withdraw" from his activities in Jersey City.[15] Characteristic of these communications was a letter from a prominent New York stockbroker, Otto Abraham, which he enclosed. Abraham told Ernst that he had "warned [his] German Jewish friends repeatedly" to avoid publicity; had they been more cautious, he suggested, they might have averted the worst antisemitism. The dire turn of events in Germany had put American Jews on notice: it was against "the interest of their co-religionists" to lead movements that the majority of Americans regarded as inimical to the public good. "If there is a necessity to defend certain groups, or what is considered by some people as the 'rights' of minorities," Abraham advised Ernst, "then it should be possible to find enough able, non-Jews to do so."[16] Ernst was unconvinced. "I think that members of all religious groups should act like Americans," he responded. "As soon as the Jews or the Catholics or the Protestants start to act as if they were not Americans first but Jews, Protestants, or Catholics first, they are conceding the concept of a divided America."[17]

Brandeis apparently considered the issues involved too cumbersome or complicated to resolve by post, and he invited Ernst to Washington to discuss the matter.[18]

[10] Maurice Tishman to Morris Ernst, 23 June 1938, Ernst Papers, box 39, folder 2.

[11] On Brandeis, see Jeffrey Rosen, *Louis D. Brandeis, American Prophet* (New Haven: Yale University Press, 2016); Melvin I. Urofsky, *Louis D. Brandeis: A Life* (New York: Pantheon, 2009).

[12] Alden Whitman, "Morris Ernst, 'Ulysses' Case Lawyer, Dies," *New York Times*, May 23, 1976; Morris Ernst to Louis D. Brandeis, 29 April 1938, Ernst Papers, box 39, folder 2.

[13] For example, the Ernst family holiday card in 1927 was titled "Christmas 1927." Ernst Papers, box 238.

[14] On the relationship between Brandeis's Jewishness and his identity as a lawyer, see William E. Forbath, "Jews, Law, and Identity Politics," draft, available at https://law.utexas.edu/conferences/constitutional/papers/forbath_jews_law_identity_politics.pdf; William E. Forbath, "The Jewish Constitutional Moment," draft, available at https://law.utexas.edu/faculty/william-e-forbath/activityfile/3161; Robert A. Burt, *Two Jewish Justices: Outcasts in the Promised Land* (Berkeley; University of California Press, 1988).

[15] Morris Ernst to Hon. Louis Brandeis, 22 June 1938, Ernst Papers, box 39, folder 2.

[16] Otto Abraham to Morris Ernst, 18 June 1938, Ernst Papers, box 39, folder 2.

[17] Morris Ernst to Otto Abraham, 21 June 1938, Ernst Papers, box 39, folder 2.

[18] Decades later, Ernst described Brandeis's return advice, while omitting discussion of Jewish identity. He wrote: "'Morris,' the wise judge said, 'if you ever decide to accept a brief or decline one because of the popularity of the client, I suggest you first resign from the bar.' He paused for a long moment; then he added slowly, 'Maybe, if that happens, you should even resign from the human race.'" Morris L. Ernst, *A Love Affair with The Law* (New York: Macmillan, 1968), 41.

For the time being, out of a conciliatory impulse or from genuine conviction, the erstwhile champion of "hyphenated" Jewry supplied a one-sentence assessment of Ernst's approach: "Your answer was a good one."[19] Whether or not it was apparent to Brandeis, Abraham had misconceived Ernst's objectives in Jersey City. It was not Ernst's goal to "defend certain groups." In declaring a right of radicals and labor organizers to congregate in Jersey City, Ernst was valorizing individual freedom, not group rights. For Ernst, that was precisely what it meant to be an "American[] first."[20]

## I. The Stakes of Civil Liberties Lawyering

Through the lens of Morris Ernst and his contemporaries, this chapter explores the organizing assumption of this volume: that legal history today blurs and permeates boundaries. It takes as its starting point a vision of law articulated by the legal historian Hendrik Hartog, which has shaped the discipline for more than three decades: that law is an "arena of conflict within which alternative social visions contended, bargained, and survived."[21] It pairs that premise with a lesser known and seemingly unconnected aspect of Hartog's approach to legal history, in the form of a puzzling concession to fellow historian Joyce Appleby. "You Baby Boomers," Appleby told him, "you just want to write about your own lives." Hartog acquiesced to the charge.[22] He did so notwithstanding his steadfast insistence on understanding the past in its present tense, as a "now,"[23] rather than a step along a forward journey or a manual for navigating our twenty-first century predicaments.[24] If legal history is a repository of contending normative orders, removed from the tussles of today, what might writing about our own lives entail?

To be sure, neither temporal nor geographic boundaries are entirely expendable; the goal of legal history is not to "obliterate distance or time."[25] Yet there is something

[19] Louis Brandeis to Morris Ernst, 24 June 1938, Ernst Papers, box 39, folder 2.

[20] Notably, Ernst wrote that despite their close relationship, "Many areas of his life never entered into my talks with Louis Dembitz Brandeis. One such was Zionism, for soon after we first met the judge was aware of my rejection of joinder of any state and any religion." Ernst, *Love Affair*, 41.

[21] Hendrik Hartog, "Pigs and Positivism," *Wisconsin Law Review* (1985): 899–935, 934–5. For Hartog, law is neither an authoritative distillation of shared commitments nor the "command of the sovereign." Hartog, "Pigs and Positivism," 934. If it were either, then to focus on its ordinary operation would tell us little about the struggles and aspirations of the people to whom it applied.

[22] Barbara Young Welke and Hendrik Hartog, "'Glimmers of Life': A Conversation with Hendrik Hartog," *Law & History Review* 27 (2009): 629–55, 643. Hartog's first book was tied to his work for the city of New York. Hendrik Hartog, *Public Property and Private Power: The Corporation of the City of New York in American Law, 1730–1870* (Chapel Hill: University of North Carolina Press, 1983). The second connected to his life as a long-time married person. Hendrik Hartog, *Man and Wife in America: A History* (Cambridge: Harvard University Press, 2000). His third, written as he arranged care for his aging parents, was about inheritance and old age. Hendrik Hartog, *Someday All This Will Be Yours: A History of Inheritance and Old Age* (Cambridge: Harvard University Press, 2012). Even the canonical article "Pigs and Positivism" channeled his family roots in the Dutch pork industry.

[23] Hendrik Hartog, *The Trouble with Minna: A Case of Slavery and Emancipation in the Antebellum North* (Chapel Hill: University of North Carolina Press, 2018), 9.

[24] Hendrik Hartog, "A Muddle in the Middle," *Law & Social Inquiry* 44 (2019): 534–47, 543 ("I am congenitally disinterested in beginnings and endings. I think questions of origins are unanswerable, or at least unanswerable with the tools at my disposal.").

[25] Hendrik Hartog, "Four Fragments on Doing Legal History, or Thinking with and against Willard Hurst," *Law & History* Review 39 (2021): 835–65, 841.

that, if not precisely transhistorical, at least is recognizable about the figures that populate the past. Rendered compassionately, their struggles seem deeply relevant; exploring the echoes of their experiences cultivates empathy and nurtures human understanding.[26] On this view, the study of law's past is productive not because it yields the provenance of doctrinal categories, or because it furnishes forgotten sources of resistance, or even because it defamiliarizes conventional wisdoms about our own legal order.[27] What legal history illuminates is nothing less than the "bedrocks of the human condition."[28]

In short, historians mediate and translate. They "present sympathetically perspectives and points of view" that seem to others to be "unattractive."[29] They bridge contending legal and normative orders and reframe demands and desires in a register that is legible across the divide, in a manner that inevitably both shapes and reflects their own lives. And in so doing, historians act very much like lawyers. Trial transcripts and court filings may not reveal how litigants lived their lives, but they do tell us how lawyers communicated their clients' experiences in ways that would be most persuasive to judges and juries and therefore most amenable to legal redress—even, or especially, when formal law was stacked against them. Litigants have laid claim to rights, perennially resisting and reinterpreting, but it is the lawyers who have framed the claiming. Occasionally, perhaps often, those lawyers have also introduced claims of their own. That is, they have litigated about their own lives.

To write historically about lawyering, then, is to perform an act of double-translation. And, taking my cue from Hartog, that is the task I undertake in this chapter. I do so by focusing on Jewish lawyers within the interwar ACLU. Elsewhere, I have explored the solutions they introduced and eventually inscribed into constitutional law.[30] Here, however, I set their legal successes aside and ask instead how their Jewishness infused their advocacy and ideas. Notably, the lawyers I consider here were acting not only as agents for clients, but also (à la Brandeis) as their people's lawyers.[31] They were working to make the concerns and aspirations of American Jewry accessible to law.

I have argued in previous work that the leaders of the ACLU promoted a strong version of free speech—one that drew the line at physical violence, and that deliberately

[26] As Hartog puts it, "We will understand our parents and grandparents better, and we will understand ourselves better in relation to them, if we explore their legal world as the terrain on which they lived their ... lives, paying less attention to the legal world they helped bring into being and more to the circumstances they confronted." Hartog, *Man and Wife*, 5.

[27] Presumably the availability of law as an arena of conflict is itself a historically contingent development. There may be moments—perhaps Nazi Germany was one of them—when law is imposed from above and becomes, for some, an "external, objective social fact ... outside of the control of the law and client." Hartog, "Pigs and Positivism," 931.

[28] Hartog, *Someday All This Will Be Yours* (jacket copy).

[29] Hartog, *Man and Wife*, 5. More recently, Hartog has alluded to the "widening of sympathy that history may offer." Hartog, "Four Fragments," 838.

[30] See generally Weinrib, *Taming*; Weinrib, "Sex Side of Civil Liberties"; Laura M. Weinrib, "From Left to Rights: Civil Liberties Lawyering between the World Wars," *Law, Culture, and the Humanities* (2016).

[31] On Brandeis as "people's lawyer," see, for example, Clyde Spillinger, "Elusive Advocate: Reconsidering Brandeis as People's Lawyer," *Yale Law Journal* 105 (1996): 1445–1535; Philippa Strum, "The Legacy of Louis Dembitz Brandeis, 'People's Attorney,'" *American Jewish History* 81 (1994): 406–27. In this, they bore a resemblance to the Black lawyers explored by Kenneth Mack, who struggled with the problem of "representing the race." Kenneth W. Mack, *Representing the Race* (Cambridge: Harvard University Press, 2012).

excluded the power differentials that words themselves produce—because they believed that workers could bring about revolutionary economic change only if they were permitted to engage in concerted labor activity without interference by the state.[32] That vision informed every aspect of their civil liberties program. Indeed, they defended Nazi speech in service of the organization's broader project of constitutionalizing the right of mass picketing, which judges deemed equivalently dangerous and disruptive.[33]

Yet that story, told from a temporal and personal distance, is incomplete. In returning to the ACLU's Jewish lawyers with an eye toward their identity, it is evident that for the Jewish lawyers on the front lines of the free speech fights, something more than labor picketing was at stake. Their experiences as Jewish lawyers living through the 1930s influenced the decisions they made within and outside the ACLU and shaped their attitudes toward legal advocacy and individual rights. I do not believe these accounts are mutually exclusive. It may be an accident of the moment I am studying, or of the moment in which I am writing, that understanding how they maneuvered in their moment also yields valuable insights into the legal world they helped to create. Still, in entering into "imagined dialogue with those who came before us,"[34] some of the structure falls away, and something more granular comes into view.

I make no attempt here to catalog or classify the ACLU's Jewish lawyers during the interwar period, let alone to offer a robust psychological or sociological account of their goals. Nor do I speculate about a larger question to which my inquiry here is related: why American Jews gravitated disproportionately to the practice of law, and to constitutional law in particular, during the early twentieth century and after.[35]

Instead, I highlight a few episodes in the ACLU's interwar trajectory to which questions of Jewish identity were surely relevant, but from which I excised the significance of Jewishness in my own prior work. In so doing, I want to gesture in a potentially fruitful direction for future study, asking where and why the ACLU's Jewish lawyers may have diverged in their motivations and preferences from their non-Jewish contemporaries.[36] The ACLU's Jewish lawyers advanced an audacious vision of civil

[32] Laura M. Weinrib, "Civil Liberties outside the Courts," *Supreme Court Review* 2014 (2015): 297–362.

[33] Laura Weinrib, "Untangling the Radical Roots of America's Civil Liberties Settlement: Causation, Compromise, and the Taming of Free Speech," *Jerusalem Review of Legal Studies* 88 (2019): 88–107.

[34] Hartog, *Man and Wife*, 5.

[35] I am enormously indebted here to William Forbath's emerging work, and in particular, one published essay and three works in progress: William Forbath, "Constitutionalism, Human Rights, and the Genealogy of Jewish American Liberalism," in James Loeffler & Moria Paz, eds., *The Law of Strangers: Jewish Lawyers and International Law in the Twentieth Century*, 118–40 (Cambridge: Cambridge University Press, 2019); Forbath, "Jewish Constitutional Moment"; Forbath, "Jews, Law, and Identity Politics"; and Forbath, "Class Struggle, Group Rights, and Socialist Pluralism on the Lower East Side – Radical Lawyering and Constitutional Imagination in the Early Twentieth Century," draft (available at SSRN: https://ssrn.com/abstract=3485241). The high prevalence of Jewish lawyers has been explored widely in the literature. It is clearly relevant that legal education was open and accessible during the early twentieth century, which made law practice an appealing point of entry to the middle class; elite law firms were not, which made government and cause lawyering comparatively attractive. Other explanations explore Jewish values, education, and religious principles. See, for example, Jerold Auerbach, *Rabbis and Lawyers: the Journey from Torah to Constitution* (Bloomington: Indiana University Press, 1990); Jerold S. Auerbach, *Unequal Justice: Lawyers and Social Change in Modern America* (New York: Oxford University Press, 1976).

[36] Notably, the ACLU's leaders during this period included Unitarian minister John Haynes Holmes, Presbyterian minister Norman Thomas, and Methodist minister Harry F. Ward. The relevance of Christian identity to their civil liberties advocacy also warrants study. See, for example, Louisa

liberties in part to accomplish specific substantive ends: to protect their clients, who quite reasonably preferred to avoid fines and prison, and to clear space for political and economic agitation. But in so doing, whether intentionally or unconsciously, they also participated in a second task. They helped to construct a vision of American liberalism that was expansive enough to accommodate them.

In what follows, I focus primarily on two lawyers—Morris Ernst, and his ACLU co-counsel Arthur Garfield Hays—and offer some initial thoughts on how their Jewishness informed their thinking and advocacy. I have chosen these lawyers because they played a formative role within the interwar ACLU, and over the years I have gotten to know them well—though regrettably, I know much more from their files and correspondence about their career aspirations and their politics than I do about their Jewish identity or religious practices.[37] I emphasize them also because they reflect a particular and familiar way of being Jewish in the United States in the early twentieth century and after. In other words, through their connections to the ACLU, Ernst and Hays may have been exceptional in their access to the levers of legal change. The civil liberties vision they espoused, however, was already recognizable in Jewish circles. It is telling that the September 1925 issue of the *American Hebrew* was devoted to "Liberalism: The Gospel of the Open Mind."[38]

For the ACLU's Jewish lawyers, staking out a strong claim to civil liberties, and to constitutional liberalism more broadly, served many overlapping functions. Legally, it created a framework for protecting people and practices that were susceptible to majoritarian suppression. By defending the disenfranchised, Jewish lawyers habituated the courts to the protection of minority rights and expanded legislative and administrative accommodations of minority groups, even as they facilitated the extension of federal power to new domains.[39] In so doing, they identified with the people they represented, drawing connections to a shared legacy of oppression. At the same time, they hoped that advocacy on behalf of "others" would preserve the Jewish people's legal "invisibility" while helping to secure their rights.[40] In all this, they were

Thomas, *Conscience: Two Soldiers, Two Pacifists, One Family: A Test of Will and Faith in World War I* (New York: Penguin, 2011) (on Norman Thomas).

37 Three recent book-length accounts of Ernst's life and work help to flesh out his motivations: Barbas, *Rise and Fall*; Gary, *Dirty Works*; Joel Silverman, *The Legal Exhibitionist: Morris Ernst, Jewish Identity, and the Modern Celebrity Lawyer* (Lanham: Fairleigh Dickinson University Press, 2022).

38 "Liberalism: The Gospel of the Open Mind," *American Hebrew*, Sept. 18, 1925, 535. For a discussion of the symposium in the *American Hebrew*, see Weinrib, "Against Intolerance," 8–9, 23–4.

39 For example, they were acutely aware of the frequency of horrific acts of racial violence against Black Americans, and they strongly advocated for federal antilynching legislation. In doing so, they drew attention to the deep connections between state policy and putatively private violence, even as they sought to differentiate between "legal discriminations" and "lawless mobs." ACLU, *Black Justice* 3 (1931). See also "Ernst, Hays, Morris on NAACP Committee," *Afro American*, November 28, 1931, 10; Walter White to Roger Baldwin, 7 January 1935, ACLU Papers, vol. 785; "Memorandum of Bills Proposed for Discussion, Conference on Civil Liberties under the New Deal," ACLU Papers, vol. 719; Walter White to Roger Baldwin, 7 January 1935, ACLU Papers, vol. 785. On antilynching legislation during the interwar period, see Megan Ming Francis, *Civil Rights and the Making of the Modern American State* (New York: Cambridge University Press, 2014).

40 David Levering Lewis, "Parallels and Divergences: Assimilationist Strategies of Afro-American and Jewish Elites from 1910 to the Early 1930s," *Journal of American History* 71 (1984): 543–64; James Loeffler, "Nationalism without a Nation: On the Invisibility of American Jewish Politics," *Jewish Quarterly Review* 105 (2015): 367–98.

articulating and enacting a strain of Jewish identity expressly premised on universalism (whether liberal or class-based) in justice-seeking.[41] Their evolving vision swept in the defense of marginalized ideas as well as persecuted peoples. In comparison with civil rights and racial justice work, their efforts on behalf of labor agitators and political dissidents were less clearly linked to their particular interests as Jews. Like their non-Jewish allies, they were motivated in large part by concerns about economic equality and democratic legitimacy. But they also believed that defending unpopular views would promote pluralism and cultivate tolerance—goals they valued as Jews as well as labor advocates.

Above all, for the ACLU's Jewish lawyers, casting civil liberties as core to American democracy served to deflect accusations of foreignness and to construct a shared, if imagined, cultural heritage. No doubt, invoking a time-honored American commitment to free speech made their rights claims more plausible and improved their traction in the courts.[42] As I explain elsewhere, the formal legal recognition of a constitutional right to free speech reflected a convergence of ideological commitments as well as material interests.[43] Yet the appeal to common norms was also, fundamentally, about asserting Americanness. Its champions laid claim not only to rights, but to a cherished national tradition—one that their own experiences and values made them competent, indeed especially well suited, to expound. Free speech, in and through their hands, became a weapon in a contest over American identity.

## II. Liberal Constitutionalism and the ACLU's Jewish Lawyers

Morris Ernst was not the only ACLU lawyer whose visibility in Jersey City attracted Jewish apprehension and antisemitic ire. On the contrary, onlookers were acutely aware of the disproportionate Jewish representation among civil liberties advocates within and outside the ACLU. During the 1930s, the organization hired a string of lawyers and worked with distinguished Supreme Court litigators on its high-profile cases. Very often, those lawyers were Jewish. Among others, attorneys Osmond Fraenkel (Ernst's high school classmate[44]), Walter Frank, Abraham Isserman, Walter Pollak, and Harriet Pilpel helped to shape the ACLU's litigation program as well as its policy priorities.

Their prominence was notable in part because of its novelty. When the ACLU was founded in 1920, its leadership was overwhelmingly Protestant.[45] Among the

[41] Forbath, "Jews, Laws, and Identity Politics," 37.

[42] Despite a widely shared stated commitment to free speech, speech rights were fiercely contested and sharply limited in practice. See, e.g., "Peace-Time Sedition Law," *Cincinnati Tribune*, August 18, 1919 ("Everybody says they are in favor of free speech, but not everyone agrees as to how free 'free speech' should be."). Before the interwar period, the right to speak freely was generally conditioned on the speaker's compliance with social norms. Weinrib, *Taming of Free Speech*, 3–5.

[43] See generally ibid.

[44] Ernst and Fraenkel graduated from Horace Mann High School in 1905. Barbas, *Rise and Fall*, 16.

[45] Walker, *In Defense of American Liberties*, 29. In the prewar period, too, most free speech advocates were Protestant, with several prominent exceptions, including Emma Goldman and Harry Weinberger. See generally David M. Rabban, *Free Speech in Its Forgotten Years, 1870–1920* (New York: Cambridge University

organization's supporters and advisors were a few important exceptions, including Harold Laski, Ernst Freund, and Felix Frankfurter, but they were decidedly in the minority.[46] Not coincidentally, the ACLU's vision of civil liberties in its early years was not a legal one. On the contrary, the ACLU's founders were generally hostile to litigation as a mechanism for pursuing free speech, and most deeply distrusted the courts. Only three of the ACLU's twenty executive committee members in 1920 were lawyers, and lawyers played a relatively marginal role in advancing the organization's agenda, which centered on labor's rights to picket, boycott, and strike.[47]

The next two decades witnessed dramatic change on both fronts. Increasingly, the ACLU's executive board and national committee filled up with Jewish names. At the same time, the ACLU gradually embraced a court-centered strategy for protecting civil liberties. The Jewish lawyers who led the ACLU during the late 1920s and 1930s helped to shape the modern civil liberties agenda. In fact, they institutionalized a fundamental constitutional commitment to individual rights of a new and distinctive kind. To be sure, correlation is not causation. Yet I suspect their Jewishness mattered. Certainly their contemporaries believed it did.[48]

Central to the transition within the ACLU was the appointment of Morris Ernst and Arthur Garfield Hays as the organization's general counsels. Like Ernst, Hays was Jewish—though one Jewish Minnesotan, who rejected the "task of reforming other peoples," accused him of "masquerading [by his name] as somebody who descended from a president of the United States."[49]

Hays was born in Rochester, New York, in 1881 to a prosperous family of German-Jewish descent. Both of his grandfathers were successful clothing manufacturers; one was a close friend of freethinker Robert Ingersoll.[50] After a stint at City College of New York, Hays graduated from Columbia College in 1902 and earned an LLB from the law school three years later. As an undergraduate, he was an early member of the primarily Jewish but nonsectarian fraternity Pi Lambda Phi, which promoted "open-mindedness, farsightedness, and a progressive, forward-looking attitude," and he considered that experience sufficiently foundational to serve as president of the

Press, 1997); Michael Willrich, *American Anarchy: The Epic Struggle between Immigrant Radicals and the US Government at the Dawn of the Twentieth Century* (New York: Basic Books, 2023).

[46] In 1917, Baldwin deflected a wartime charge that there were too many German names among the leadership of the internationalist and "radical peace" organizations by explaining that most were "not names of Germans as such, but of Jews, whose sympathies, as you know, are not nationalistic in any sense, but international," and who were a "strong factor in every such movement." Roger Baldwin to Lawrence Brooks, 24 September 1917, ACLU papers, vol. 32.

[47] Walker, *In Defense of American Liberties*, 69; cf. Weinrib, "From Left to Rights."

[48] See, for example, Edward D. Tittman to Roger Baldwin, 9 June 1937, ACLU papers, vol. 978 ("I have read the pamphlet by Mr. Fraenkel [and] it convinces me that the semitic view point is not in line with the viewpoint of America's traditions, and strongly suggests that a considerable portion of our troubles is traceable to the influence of radical jewish [*sic*] thought. Of course they have a right to exercise that influence but I cant [*sic*] see why an impartial organization should help them by spreading the Fraenkel gospel.").

[49] A. J. Lipsky to Morris L. Ernst, 4 September 1931, Ernst Papers, box 3, folder 3. Hays's paternal grandfather anglicized his name from Haas. "Arthur Garfield Hays Dies at 73; Counsel to Civil Liberties Union," *New York Times*, Dec. 15, 1954.

[50] Arthur Garfield Hays, *City Lawyer: The Autobiography of a Law Practice* (New York: Simon & Schuster, 1942), 18; Oswald Garrison Villard, "Review of City Lawyer by Arthur Garfield Hays," *Harvard Law Review* 56 (1942): 333–6.

organization in the 1930s.[51] Together with two of his classmates, he built a thriving law practice and "led a double life in the courts of law." As the "about the author" section of his autobiography explained: "Half the time he has represented big corporations and wealthy clients. The other half of the time he has pleaded for the insulted and injured, the scorned and rejected."[52]

Although he often identified himself as Jewish in public writing and engagements, Hays consistently described his allegiances in terms of principles and worldviews rather than racial or religious affiliations.[53] His "kind," as he put it, were all people who valorized the individual, eschewed labels, and were independent, unconventional, and tolerant.[54] Like Ernst—and in stark contrast to liberal pluralists like Louis Brandeis—he was also skeptical of Zionism. He believed (according to a Jewish Telegraphic Agency [JTA] bulletin) that "Zionism breeds anti-Semitism by contending that Jews are merely 'sojourners' in the U.S. and by encouraging differentiation between Jews and non-Jews."[55] In all of this, he resembled a subset of elite Reform Jews of a classical liberal mold, who collapsed their Jewishness into constitutional liberalism and the demand for equal rights.[56] Indeed, upon his death in 1954, an ACLU colleague lamented the "remov[al] from the American scene of one of the last links with a type of nineteenth century liberalism that is practically extinct today," by which he meant a persistent skepticism of state power and of "big paternalistic government."[57]

This posthumous assessment was, however, not quite right. In reality, Hays's liberalism evolved over time. After the First World War, he was a member of the "Committee of Forty-Eight," a fleeting political party of "middle class 'liberals'" who considered themselves too "radical" for the Republican or Democratic parties, and who urged the equalization of workers' bargaining power and the government ownership of public utilities and natural resources along with "equal rights irrespective of sex and color [and] the immediate and unqualified restoration of all civil liberties guaranteed by the Constitution."[58] Hays frequently found himself on the front lines

[51] "Arthur Hays to Speak on Forum Series Wednesday," *Jewish Press*, Jan. 11, 1935.

[52] Hays, *City Lawyer* (about the author).

[53] Richard F. Hamm, "Race and Relevance: Arthur Garfield Hays and the Integration of the American Bar Association," *American Journal of Legal History* 60 (2020): 284–310, 291. He married twice, both times to Jewish women (Blanche Marks and, after their divorce, Aline Fleisher). Ibid. Although racialized understandings of Jewishness were common during the late nineteenth and early twentieth centuries, American Jews had largely ceased to define themselves in racial terms by World War II. See Eric L. Goldstein, *The Price of Whiteness: Jews, Race, and American Identity* (Princeton: Princeton University Press, 2008).

[54] Hays, *City Lawyer* (about the author).

[55] JTA Daily News Bulletin, Oct. 28, 1949, available at https://www.jta.org/archive/arthur-garfield-hays-tells-judaism-council-meeting-zionism-breeds-anti-semitism. On the relationship between Reform Jewish universalism and Zionism, see Ofer Shiff, *Survival through Integration: American Reform Jewish Universalism and the Holocaust* (Leiden: Brill, 2004).

[56] See generally Shiff, *Survival through Integration*; Forbath, "Jews, Law, and Identity Politics"; James Loeffler, "'A Certain Type of Liberalism': Minority Rights in Jewish Liberal Discourse, 1848–1948," in Abigail Green & Simon Levis Sullam, eds., *Jews, Liberalism, Antisemitism: A Global History* (Cham, Switzerland: Palgrave Macmillan, 2020): 365–85.

[57] Clifford Forster, "Tribute to Mr. Hays," *New York Times*, Dec. 23, 1954.

[58] "Platforms for Progressives," *New Republic*, Dec. 31, 1919, 133–5. On the Committee of Forty-Eight, see Paul W. Glad, "Progressives and the Business Culture of the 1920s," *Journal of American History* 53 (1966): 75–89; Eugene M. Tobin, *Organize or Perish: America's Independent Progressives, 1913–1933* (New York, 1986), 101–24. Notably, Hays affiliated with "liberals" in a period when many contemporaries continued to call themselves "progressives."

of the labor struggle. When he courted his own arrest alongside striking workers, and when he risked his life in Harlan County to aid beleaguered miners, he spoke in terms of economic equality as well as expressive freedom, even if he tended to defend the collective exercise of labor power as an aggregation of individual rights. In the late 1930s, he personally favored the CIO. To be sure, he disavowed revolutionary class struggle; already in the 1920s, he championed "liberalism" over "radicalism" in a debate at the Ford Hall Forum.[59] Still, only decades later would he worry whether the Fair Employment Practices Committee might infringe on "employers' freedom to select help."[60]

As for Ernst, a 1944 feature in *Life Magazine* described him as "a civil-liberal and union lawyer with no qualms about taking on straight commercial or other law work for clients who can pay respectable fees."[61] Ernst enjoyed a comfortable childhood in Manhattan, where his father, Carl, was successful in the real estate business. His family socialized with assimilated German Jews, though they were always self-conscious about Carl's less privileged Austro-Hungarian roots.[62] On High Holidays, his family attended services at Temple Israel, a Reform congregation that was committed to modernizing Jewish observance and introducing English-language prayer. He participated in a Jewish education program for several years before concluding that religion was irrational.[63]

Ernst attended Horace Mann and then Williams College, where he was one of three Jews in his class.[64] He subsequently enrolled in New York Law School's night program; the *Life* profile attributed his dogged determination and prodigious ambition to the "knowledge that he did not attend .... a first-class law school, that he never made Phi Beta Kappa in college, that he was never much of a muchness until he was over 30."[65] Whatever the explanation, Ernst was practically unparalleled in his ability to "first-nam[e] the famous."[66] A staunch New Dealer, he attracted attention as Franklin Roosevelt's "fixer"[67] and later found notoriety as a regular correspondent of J. Edgar Hoover.[68]

In some ways, then, Ernst's trajectory as a Jewish lawyer differed from Hays's, and perhaps was more idiosyncratic. Like Hays, however, he was an outspoken proponent of individual autonomy throughout his career. Together with Edward and Lawrence Greenbaum and Herbert A. Wolff (all of Jewish heritage, though Wolff's family had

[59] Circular, "Is Liberalism a Menace," Mary Ware Dennett Papers, 1874–1947, MC 392, Schlesinger Library, Radcliffe Institute, Harvard University, Cambridge, MA, reel 22, file 477 (arguing that "the solution of our economic problems must be accomplished by education and law, not by revolution").

[60] Forster, "Tribute to Mr. Hays."

[61] Fred Rodell, "Morris Ernst: New York's Unlawyerlike Liberal Lawyer Is the Censor's Enemy, the President's Friend," *Life*, Feb. 21, 1944, 97–8.

[62] Barbas, *Rise and Fall*, 10–1.

[63] Ibid. According to Barbas, Ernst never again entered a temple.

[64] Ibid., 18. Silverman suggests that Ernst's awareness of his difference as a Jew dates back to his experience at a nudist summer camp for boys. Silverman, *Legal Exhibitionist*, 22.

[65] Rodell, "Morris Ernst," 107.

[66] Ibid., 97.

[67] Ibid., 98.

[68] Ernst became fiercely anticommunist and eventually collaborated with Hoover. For an account of that trajectory, see Brett Gary, "Morris Ernst's Troubled Legacy," *Reconstruction* 8 (2008).

long since decamped to the New York Society for Ethical Culture[69]), he founded a law firm in 1915. In doing so, he followed a path well-trodden by Jewish lawyers who were largely excluded from elite corporate firms.[70]

In his private law practice, Ernst defended publishing houses against obscenity charges and, like his clients, had strong financial incentives to distrust state censorship.[71] But he was equally uncomfortable with corporate consolidation and, building from Brandeis, he condemned excessive "bigness" in business as well as government for encroaching on individual rights.[72] Also like Brandeis, he imagined a role for the state in fracturing and counterbalancing corporate power, both in the economic realm and in the marketplace of ideas. He convinced President Roosevelt to introduce a discounted postage rate for books, an innovation that benefited his publisher clients but also facilitated "a flow into the market place of great additional diversity of points of view."[73] Although he staunchly opposed government-run newspapers and radio stations, he advocated for the mandatory allocation of radio airtime to the discussion of "important public questions" and controversial ideas.[74] He was also deeply committed to labor's right to organize. He joined the American Labor Party (albeit its anticommunist wing) and helped to found the CIO-affiliated American Newspaper Guild.[75]

Within the ACLU, Ernst and Hays were critical in moving the organization from its early, class-focused agenda into areas like academic freedom, sex education, artistic freedom, and even birth control. At first, they pitched the new frontier as primarily tactical, a means of attracting support from mainstream progressives for the civil liberties cause. As ACLU co-founder Roger Baldwin put the point in connection with the *Scopes* trial, "supporters of educational and scientific work" could endorse an issue like academic freedom without "fear[ing] contamination with the defense of reds."[76] But for Ernst and Hays, who resisted enforced conformity and cultural conservatism as much as or more than capitalist oppression, the expansion of the ACLU's agenda meant more than a broader donor base. Eventually, they were claiming free speech as a value-neutral right inhering in individuals—a private sphere isolated from the intervention of the state.

That Jewish lawyers led this charge was not lost on the ACLU's early leadership. In 1940, the Unitarian minister and ACLU chairman John Haynes Holmes, who

69 Walter H. Waggoner, "Herbert A. Wolff, 90; Lawyer Who Headed Ethical Culture Society," *New York Times*, Feb. 27, 1980.

70 Lawrence M. Friedman, *American Law in the Twentieth Century* (New Haven: Yale University Press, 2002), 40–1.

71 For a rich account of Ernst's antiobscenity work, see Gary, *Dirty Works*; Leigh Ann Wheeler, *How Sex Became a Civil Liberty* (New York: Oxford University Press, 2013). Barbas attributes Ernst's embrace of modernist literature to the influence of his mother, Sarah. Barbas, *Rise and Fall*, 12–3.

72 His 1940 book, *Too Big*, was an homage to his hero. Morris Ernst, *Too Big* (Boston: Little, Brown, 1940).

73 Rodell, "Morris Ernst"; ACLU, *Liberty on the Home Front: In the Fourth Year of War* (New York: The Union, 1945), 60.

74 ACLU, *Radio Programs in the Public Interest* (ACLU: New York, July 1946).

75 Weinrib, *Taming of Free Speech*, ch. 7.

76 Letter from Roger Baldwin, undated, ACLU Papers, vol. 274. On Baldwin, see generally Robert Cottrell, *Roger Nash Baldwin and the American Civil Liberties Union* (New York: Columbia University Press, 2000); Peggy Lamson, *Roger Baldwin, Founder of the American Civil Liberties Union: A Portrait* (Boston: Houghton Mifflin, 1976).

had been a founding member of the organization, acknowledged Ernst's initiative in introducing the ACLU to anticensorship work. Apologizing for his own reluctance on the issue, he attributed his "squeamishness in the field of censorship" to his "rigorous New England" upbringing and his "puritanical instinct."[77] Ernst and Hays had no such baggage to weigh them down.

It is one thing to highlight Ernst and Hays's Jewish background; it is another to elucidate precisely why they gravitated toward unorthodoxy and defended personal freedom. Historians who have examined Jews' involvement in liberal and civil rights causes have largely rejected the idea that religious principles drove their civic engagement.[78] To some extent, the linkage may be pragmatic. In the early twentieth century, Jews embraced liberal individualism and endorsed antidiscrimination norms partly to deflect antisemitism and facilitate entry into elite institutions. In this respect, the ACLU's Jewish lawyers were typical. For example, both Hays and Ernst were vocal opponents of the American Bar Association's exclusion of Black lawyers and refused (Ernst) or resigned (Hays) membership on that ground, and both served on the National Legal Committee of the NAACP.[79] Moreover, both regarded the courts as uniquely conducive to the enforcement of minority rights. During the first decades of the twentieth century, as the political branches succumbed to aggressive assimilationism and hostility to immigrant culture, legalism emerged as an appealing check on state-enforced conformity.[80]

Still, hard-headed accounts of this kind are incomplete. Recent scholarship on Progressive-era Jewish lawyers has instead emphasized the ways in which liberal constitutionalism served to channel Jewish identity. Writing about Jewish lawyers during the Progressive era, William Forbath describes a "double movement" comprising, on the one hand, a secularization of Jewish religious commitments as universal human rights, and on the other, the sacralization of liberal legal advocacy as a secular calling.[81] On this account, Jewish lawyers asserted their particularity as Jews by means of, rather than despite, the universalism of civil liberties lawyering.

Forbath demonstrates that at least until the 1920s, Jewish lawyers fell into competing camps. Some, like the American Jewish Committee's Louis Marshall, represented the Jewish elite and endorsed classical liberalism as a distillation of Jewish values.[82] Others, like Isaac Hourwich, spoke for the Eastern European immigrants

77 John Haynes Holmes to Morris Ernst, 16 January 1940, Ernst Papers, box 5, folder 1.

78 See, for example, Stuart Svonkin, *Jews against Prejudice: American Jews and the Fight for Civil Liberties* (New York: Columbia University Press, 1997), 20; Samuel Moyn, "Louis Henkin, Human Rights, and American Jewish Constitutional Patriotism," in James Loeffler & Moria Paz, eds., *The Law of Strangers: Jewish Lawyers and International Law in the Twentieth Century*, 93–113 (Cambridge: Cambridge University Press, 2019).

79 "The Bar Association Held Reactionary," *New York Times*, Dec. 23, 1936; Richard F. Hamm, "Race and Relevance: Arthur Garfield Hays and the Integration of the American Bar Association," *American Journal of Legal History* 60 (2020): 284–310, 284. See also Auerbach, *Unequal Justice*, 65–6.

80 See Weinrib, "Against Intolerance."

81 Forbath, "Jews, Law, and Identity Politics," 37.

82 Although Marshall initially opposed a group rights framework, his views shifted over time. According to Forbath, "Group rights had no more ardent classical liberal foe in the U.S. than Louis Marshall; ironically, he would become their most important and effective advocate in the international arena at Paris." Forbath, "Jews, Law and Identity Politics," 71; *cf.* James Loeffler, *Rooted Cosmopolitans: Jews and Human Rights in the Twentieth Century* (New Haven: Yale University Press, 2018), 11–6.

on New York's Lower East Side; under the auspices of the American Jewish Congress, they imagined both constitutional law and Jewish identity in terms of group rather than individual rights,[83] and they called for national self-determination in Palestine and the diaspora. Still others—most famously Louis Brandeis—split the difference, articulating a new strain of liberalism premised on cultural pluralism.[84] These groups differed on many issues, but they converged in their resistance to government orthodoxy and enforced conformity. Marshall opposed New York's speech-suppressive Lusk laws "as an infringement of constitutional rights"[85] and argued in an amicus brief that the Oregon compulsory school law at issue in *Pierce v. Society of Sisters* was unconstitutional.[86] Hourwich contributed to the ACLU from its inaugural year and assisted in the campaign for amnesty for imprisoned World War I dissenters.[87] Brandeis, of course, authored some of the Supreme Court's most influential First Amendment dissents, in addition to mentoring Morris Ernst.[88]

These variations on American Jewish identity map imperfectly onto the constituencies of the interwar civil liberties coalition, which comprised labor radicals, progressives, and eventually corporate lawyers. But they do help to illuminate the early involvement of Jewish lawyers like Ernst and Hays, as well as the warm reception for the ACLU's expanding agenda among leading Jewish figures, from Samuel Untermyer to Morris Hillquit, who agreed on little else.[89] Ernst and Hays's relationship to constitutional liberalism defies neat categorization. During the 1920s, when the ACLU and its allies were perennially on the defensive, it was unnecessary to commit to one of the various factions under the overarching civil liberties umbrella. The key point is that Ernst and Hays navigated deftly among them, appealing to core aspects of each.

In my past work, I have portrayed Ernst and Hays as outliers within the ACLU, whose commitment to unfettered speech and assembly—which overlapped with that of the core leadership, but for drastically different reasons—opened the door to their influence and eventually transformed the organization's mission from the service of labor to the service of liberalism. It was Ernst who overcame the ACLU's initial insistence that "personal liberties" were orthogonal to the "wider political question" the organization was then pursuing.[90] It was Hays who pushed the ACLU to seek anti-employer injunctions in the courts, at a time when labor lawyers dismissed judges as

[83] Forbath, "Jews, Law and Identity Politics," 71–4. On the competing liberalisms of the American Jewish Congress and the American Jewish Committee, see also Marc Dollinger, *Quest for Inclusion: Jews and Liberalism in Modern America* (Princeton: Princeton University Press, 2000).

[84] Forbath, "Constitutionalism, Human Rights, and Jewish American Liberalism," 135.

[85] "Five Speakers Demand Lusk Laws' Repeal," *New York Call*, 12 January 1921.

[86] The ACLU hoped to persuade him to argue *Whitney v. California* in the United States Supreme Court. ACLU Executive Committee Minutes, 6 October 1924, ACLU Papers, vol. 250.

[87] ACLU, *Fight for Free Speech*, 22; Along with Theodore Schroeder and Harry Weinberger, Hourwich served on the legal advisory board of the League for the Amnesty of Political Prisoners. M. E. Fitzgerald to Albert De Silver, 11 March 1919, ACLU Papers, vol. 84.

[88] For example, Schaefer v. United States, 251 U.S. 466 (1920) (Brandeis, J., dissenting); Pierce v. United States, 252 U.S. 239 (1920) (Brandeis, J., dissenting). Brandeis's concurring opinion in *Whitney v. California* was especially influential. Whitney v. California, 274 U.S. 357 (1927) (Brandeis, J., concurring). Ernst referred to Brandeis as his "legal dominie." Ernst, *Love Affair*, 43.

[89] In fact, Untermyer declared Hillquit's mayoral candidacy a "catastrophe to our race." "Urges the Jews to Oppose Hillquit," *New York Times*, Nov. 2, 1917.

[90] Roger Baldwin to Theodore Schroeder, 7 December 1917, ACLU Papers, vol. 3.

shills for big business.[91] When he defended the right of Tennessee public teachers to teach evolution in the Scopes Trial, Hays emphasized that "the majority of today may be a minority of tomorrow."[92] Whether tactical or heartfelt, his was a forceful articulation of a position that would soon command general agreement: "The court is the barrier which protects the minority from vicious, or even well-intended legislation, the effect of which is inimical to the State."[93]

Hays and Ernst helped to build the ACLU's network of respectable members and donors and to expand the organization's scope of activity into the field of personal rights. They were forward thinking—indeed, path-breaking—in their publicity and litigation strategies. And yet, taking their Jewishness into account, the principles they espoused seem less incongruous and easier to explain. They built on ideas already circulating within the established Jewish community—above all, that "[i]ntolerance is the handmaiden of illiberalism."[94]

It was not until the 1930s—when the ACLU's allies gained access to the levers of power—that the fault lines in the civil liberties coalition were exposed. Over the course of the decade, the movement fractured over everything from the status of economic rights in a constitutional democracy to the line between persuasion and coercion. Gradually, and with much friction, the ACLU moved from a class-based perspective toward a focus on individual rights. Ernst and Hays led the charge. Ernst worked to excise economic equality from the constellation of civil liberties, arguing that his own sympathy for organized labor had no place within the ACLU.[95] Hays, who was "ready to reform institutions but not so keen about reforming individuals," went further.[96] Although he celebrated the ascendance of the CIO, he worried that aggressive union tactics might undermine the "civil liberties" of employers, or the "right of non-union men to work."[97] By the early 1940s, even Ernst was somewhat dismissive of Hays for his steadfast "belief in laissez faire in the realm of thought."[98]

To be sure, the revised approach differed from its *Lochner*-era antecedents in that it elevated "personal rights" over property rights, rather than the other way around. This new formulation, with its broad deference to social and economic regulation subject to strong protections for democratic dissent and minority rights, became the blueprint for the post–New Deal constitutional order. It did not mark a return to classical liberalism. But in some if not all contexts, it did elevate individual autonomy over

[91] ACLU, *Sept. 1921 to Jan. 1923*, 27 (Hays's use of injunction against officials in mining town); ACLU Executive Committee Minutes, 26 October 1925 (describing Hays's proposed study of prolabor "affirmative legal action"); Arthur Garfield Hays, Clement Wood & McAlister Coleman, *Don't Tread on Me: A Study of Aggressive Legal Tactics for Labor* (New York: Vanguard Press, 1928). For a discussion of labor's use of injunctions, see William E. Forbath, *Law and the Shaping of the American Labor Movement* (Cambridge: Harvard University Press, 1991), 118–27.

[92] Argument of Arthur Garfield Hays in the Supreme Court of Tennessee, 31 May 1926, 12–14, 20, Arthur Garfield Hays Papers, Seeley G. Mudd Manuscript Library, Princeton University, Princeton, NJ, box 31, folder 7.

[93] Reply Brief and Argument for the State of Tennessee, Scopes v. State, 278 S.W. 57 (Tenn. 1925), 80.

[94] "Liberalism: The Gospel of the Open Mind," *American Hebrew*, Sept. 18, 1925, 535.

[95] Morris Ernst to Roger Baldwin, 16 March 1936, ACLU papers, vol. 970.

[96] R. L. Duffus, "Memoirs of a Liberal Lawyer," *New York Times Book Review*, Aug. 16, 1942, 4..

[97] Arthur Garfield Hays to ACLU, 19 March 1937, ACLU papers, vol. 970; Arthur Garfield Hays to ACLU, 13 March 1937, ACLU Papers, vol. 970.

[98] Morris Ernst to John Haynes Holmes, 14 April 1942, ACLU papers, vol. 2355.

the exercise of collective power. Like Ernst and Hays, many of the ACLU's new supporters during the 1930s embraced civil liberties because they believed that people's beliefs and behavior were best left to private control. They endorsed what a 1934 statement of the ACLU's National Council for Freedom from Censorship labeled "personal choice."[99]

The liberal legal project gained adherents over the course of the decade, and the ACLU's Jewish lawyers were instrumental in eliciting conversions. Its increasing appeal was a function in part of the rise of Nazism in Germany, an issue that profoundly troubled Ernst and Hays. In 1933, Hays was a member of the Legal Commission of Inquiry into the Reichstag fire.[100] That body, which met in London, cleared the communist leadership of setting fire to the German parliament building, which became the pretext for a Nazi decree suspending civil liberties. Hays subsequently traveled to Germany to assist in defending the accused communists during the trial. In reporting on his experiences, Hays contrasted commitment to rule of law and liberal values with fascism. In a widely publicized statement, he explained that there was "no law [in Germany] which the government [was] bound to respect."[101] Noting the propensity of unrestrained governments to "steal a citizen's liberty, and to take his property," Hays professed to return to the United States with a "fervent revival of appreciation of democracy."[102]

Given the positive attention generated by his activity abroad, Hays brought the same technique to American soil. Along with the American Jewish Congress, he helped to organize a widely publicized event at Madison Square Garden, a mock trial of the Nazi regime, which was billed as "The Case of Civilization against Hitler."[103] As he had in Europe, he cast the preservation of "civil liberties" as an antidote to fascism and a quintessential American value.

A similar insight shaped the ACLU's criticism of Boss Hague, the "Hudson Hitler."[104] Just as Hays treated the Nazis' attack on discrete minority groups as part of a larger attack on democracy and liberal tolerance, so too did Hays and Ernst reframe Hague's suppression of labor as a single component of a broader assault on American values. Hays, Ernst, and others quite self-consciously deflected charges that Jersey City's Jews were subversive and un-American by villainizing Hague instead. In their inverted account, the ACLU was fighting for American principles of tolerance and respect for individual rights; Hague was the real subversive, "the greatest radical of our day."[105] As Manhattan borough president Stanley Isaacs put it, "The Jew who gives aid

[99] Statement by the National Council on Freedom from Censorship, 16 July 1934, ACLU Papers, vol. 678.

[100] On the Reichstag fire, see Benjamin Carter Hett, *Burning the Reichstag: An Investigation into the Third Reich's Enduring Mystery* (New York: Oxford University Press, 2014).

[101] "Hays Clears Reds in Reich Fire Trial," *New York Times*, Nov. 2, 1933.

[102] Ibid. Hays noted that Germans countered criticism of their treatment of the Jews by "point[ing] out our treatment of Negroes," though he proceeded to distinguish between "governmental propaganda against a race, or discrimination by law and actions by and prejudices of individuals." Ibid. On the relationship between American and Nazi race law, see James Q. Whitman, *Hitler's American Model: The United States and the Making of Nazi Race Law* (Princeton: Princeton University Press, 2017).

[103] See generally Louis Anthes, "Publicly Deliberative Drama: The 1934 Mock Trial of Adolf Hitler for 'Crimes against Civilization,'" *American Journal of Legal History* 42 (1998): 391–410.

[104] Clipping, *New York Evening Post*, January 12, 1938, ACLU Papers, vol. 2020; Arthur Garfield Hays to Frank Hague, 10 December 1937, ACLU Papers, vol. 1051; Norman Thomas, *Hagueism Is Fascism* (Workers' Defense League: New York, 1938), 4.

[105] "CIO Seeks Writ to 'Stop' Hague," *New York World-Telegram*, 7 January 1938, ACLU Papers, vol. 2020.

to a man like Mayor Hague is a traitor to his race." He explained, "We must be on the side of those who are supporting democracy, for the forces that would destroy democracy would likewise destroy liberty and Judaism."[106]

Hays consistently argued that adherence to the American creed would blunt the force of antisemitism in the United States. He stated publicly that the extent of American antisemitism was overblown. At the same time, he argued that some degree of prejudice was inevitable as long as Jews failed to integrate into American life.[107] "The best way, the only way, to meet antisemitic prejudice is to fight intolerance in general," he insisted, "whether directed at Catholics, Jews or Protestants, Negroes or Japanese, the C.I.O. or the A.F. of L., the American Civil Liberties Union or the Liberty League, socialists, communists, democrats or republicans."[108] Others within the ACLU adopted the same line, even if they were suspicious of individual rights in the labor context. When Roger Baldwin fielded complaints from disgruntled ACLU members who resented Jewish involvement, he dismissed their concerns as antimodern. In his view, antisemitism, like racism, was simply a symptom of "economic reaction."[109] As he expressed the point in a statement, "Far too many Jews ... emphasize the very issue of racial separation which is the stock-in-trade of the Fascist-minded. The only solution [to antisemitism] in the long run for everybody, Jews and non-Jews alike, is to forget racial origins."[110] In that spirit (and also out of a long-standing concern that asserting Jewish identity would undermine class solidarity), he urged American Jews "to so completely identify themselves with the life of the country that they do not stand out as a separate racial group."[111] Confronted with the pernicious potential of strong group identification in the form of National Socialism, the ACLU and its lawyers emphasized universality and individual autonomy.

Certainly Baldwin's prescription had plenty of detractors, within and outside the ACLU. Rabbi Stephen Wise, who headed the American Jewish Congress, was a founding ACLU member. Like many New Dealers, he vocally criticized the individual rights rhetoric of the Lochner Era and preferred a group rights framework.[112] He was nonetheless quick to denounce Nazism for its dogmatism and its threat to democratic progress and human flourishing as much as its suppression of targeted groups. The "Jewish case against Hitlerism" was "but a single link in the chain of evidence against Hitlerism," he explained. The "indictment of Hitlerism" turned also on "its

[106] "Isaacs Denounces Jews Aiding Hague," *New York Times*, May 19, 1938.

[107] Arthur Garfield Hays, "On Free Speech," *Menorah Journal* 27 (1939): 343–45.

[108] Ibid.

[109] Roger Baldwin to A. Golden, 19 July 1934, ACLU Papers, vol. 700; for Baldwin's description of racism as a function of the class struggle, see Roger Baldwin, "Memorandum on the South as Observed in a Trip in May and June 1920," ACLU Papers, vol. 166. Osmond Fraenkel similarly blamed economic inequality for antisemitism. Osmond Fraenkel, "For Free Speech," *Menorah Journal* vol. 24 (1936) (reprinted by ACLU) ("Only through the long and difficult way of education will it ever be possible to prove to men that the insecurity which is the real prompter of the 'holy war' cannot be averted by measures of intolerance.").

[110] Roger Baldwin, Statement on "Anti-Semitism and the Law," December 1938, ACLU Papers, vol. 1079.

[111] Roger Baldwin to Roy Benjamin Jr., 11 April 1939, ACLU Papers, vol. 2147. He continued: "My general recipe for anti-Semitism or any other form of race prejudice is to 'forget it.' If people make issues of their differences they will find them aplenty." Ibid.

[112] Forbath, "Jews, Law, and Identity Politics," 67–75. A commitment to group rights survived well into the postwar period. James Loeffler, "An Abandoned Weapon in the Fight against Hate Speech," *Atlantic*, June 16, 2019.

threat to civil liberties and democracy; to science; to the arts; the liberal professions; the churches; the status of women."[113] Underlying this alternative assessment was the notion that American constitutionalism rested on pluralism—not just cultural pluralism, but also ideological pluralism. On this conception, a commitment to freedom was what made Jews model Americans.

## III. Group Rights and State Power

When Ernst, Hays and their interlocutors argued about their legal advocacy as "hyphenated Americans," they were arguing not only about their Jewish identity, but also about the power of law. For individualists like Hays, that power was limited. Hays repeatedly enjoined his contemporaries "not to rely too much upon the law, except to insist upon the legal right to express yourself."[114] Legal action would only invite public attention and exacerbate racial and religious tension.[115] "Given equal rights under the law, we Jews can take care of ourselves," he claimed. "We need no favoring laws."[116] Just as they had initially opposed the National Labor Relations Act (NLRA) for fear of strengthening and legitimating government coercion, many within the ACLU's inner circle favored persuasion over antidiscrimination law.[117] The way to fight antisemitism in America was by promoting tolerance and democratic values, not by invoking the repressive force of the state.

To the champions of group rights associated with the American Jewish Congress, the minimalist approach seemed both misguided and mistaken. It was an artifact of the (contingent) historical nature of organized antisemitism in the United States—which, in contrast to the state-structured racial apartheid of Jim Crow, operated primarily through private rather than government power.[118] Moreover, antisemitism—unlike the frank racial animus directed toward Black Americans and members of other openly marginalized groups—often simmered underground in unrespectable quarters. The result was that litigation by Jewish groups (with the exception of church-state litigation) tended to turn on questions of fact, with limited precedential value.[119]

[113] JTA Jewish Daily Bulletin, Jan. 30, 1934, available at https://www.jta.org/archive/to-present-case-against-hitler-at-madison-square.

[114] Hays, "On Free Speech," 343.

[115] Ibid.

[116] Ibid.

[117] Weinrib, *Taming of Free Speech*, ch. 6; Cf. Roger Baldwin to Roy Benjamin Jr., 11 April 1939, ACLU Papers, vol. 2147 ("I know no recipe for race intolerance except the ability of us all independently and collectively to rise above those differences.").

[118] See, for example, Will Maslow, "Anti-Semitism and the Law," *Congress Weekly*, Nov. 16, 1945; Will Maslow, "The Uses of Law in the Struggle for Equality" (1954), ACLU Papers, box 1104, folder 42. The regulation of immigration is an important exception. As William Forbath has demonstrated, the prospect of racial and national bars against Jewish immigration (some explicit and some by proxy) "fueled the politics of Jewish-American identity in the Progressive Era, and lawyers crafted the answers Jewish organizations gave to them." See Forbath, "Jews, Laws, and Identity Politics," 3. For a critique of the concept of "social anti-Semitism" and an argument that American antisemitism should be understood as legally enabled and sanctioned even in the nineteenth century, see Britt P. Tevis, "'Jews Not Admitted': Anti-Semitism, Civil Rights, and Public Accommodation Laws," *Journal of American History* 107 (March 2021): 847-70.

[119] Maslow, "Uses of Law."

For those reasons, among others, the American Jewish Committee (AJC) advocated education rather than legal coercion as the antidote to antisemitism.[120] Indeed, that organization's secretary made the point expressly in a letter to the ACLU. "The civil rights of Jews in America can only be defended by means of a long-range program of education against this deep-rooted, but not insoluble, prejudice," he wrote, "and not by means of laws which bring greater evils than they are intended to overcome."[121]

For many American Jews, however, Hitler's ascension prompted a reevaluation of the noninterventionist line. Alexander Pekelis, an Odessa-born émigré who had settled in Italy and served as a professor of jurisprudence at the University of Rome until the passage of the Italian racial laws barred him from practicing his profession, was acutely aware of law's capacity to mitigate or amplify antisemitism. After fleeing Paris in 1940, he eventually arrived with his family in the United States, where he accepted a professorship at the New School of Social Research while attending Columbia Law School.[122] On behalf of the American Jewish Congress, he pioneered new legal arguments against school segregation.[123] As an obituary in *Law and Social Action* reflected after Pekelis's death in a plane crash in 1946, Pekelis was convinced that in the effort to secure "democratic rights in a pluralistic and multicultural society like the United States," law would be an indispensable tool.[124] Others within the American Jewish Congress shared his view that the private nature of American antisemitism required more law to counter it, not less. "The Jews in America, unlike their European brethren, suffer not from decrees of the state, but from those employers, educators, landlords, and publicists, whose vast but long unregulated power is intent upon creating a second-class citizenship," observed Hays's one-time law firm associate Will Maslow, noting that law already structured racial subordination through the enforcement of restrictive real estate covenants and the conferral of tax exemptions on discriminatory institutions. Law "actively fosters discrimination and prejudice," he insisted, and that "power needs governmental control."[125] He therefore called on state and federal

[120] Until the 1920s, Louis Marshall and the AJC were more open to legal intervention and promoted the expansion of public accommodations laws. Evan P. Schultz, "Group Rights, American Jews, and the Failure of Group Libel Laws, 1913–1952," *Brooklyn Law Review* (Spring 2000): 71–145, 96–100.

[121] Morris D. Waldman (secretary, American Jewish Committee) to Florina Lasker, 20 February 1936, ACLU Papers, vol. 897. By the late 1940s, the AJC had modified this view. Although it continued to oppose hate speech regulation and regarded the "eradication of racial and religious prejudice [as] basically an educational process, and not a legal one," its statement to the president's Committee on Civil Rights stated, "We, at the American Jewish Committee, have learned through our studies and our activities that there are two approaches to the problem of how to protect and strengthen civil rights: one, the legal and legislative; the other, the educational. ... One is not the alternative for the other; each needs the other as its complement." It went on to explain: "We do not believe that prejudice can be eliminated by law. We believe that discriminatory practices may be, and that the attack upon discrimination is of itself an educational process which will, in turn, be a potent force in reducing prejudice." American Jewish Committee, "A National Program for Civil Liberties presented to the President's Committee on Civil Rights," 1 May 1947, ACLU Papers, Correspondence-Federal Departments, vol. 38.

[122] On Pekelis, see Loeffler, "Abandoned Weapon."

[123] See Will Maslow, Pauli Murray, Carey McWilliams, and Alexander Pekelis, Brief for the American Jewish Congress as Amicus Curiae, Westminster School District of Orange County, et al. v. Mendez, 161 F.2d 774 (9th Cir. 1947). The ACLU, with the National Lawyers Guild, also filed an amicus brief in the case. On *Mendez*, see Philippa Strum, *Mendez v. Westminster: School Desegregation and Mexican-American Rights* (Lawrence: University Press of Kansas, 2010).

[124] "Alexander H. Pekelis," *Law and Social Action* 2.10 (Jan. 1947): 45–6.

[125] Maslow, "Anti-Semitism and the Law."

governments to outlaw discriminatory practices and to "creat[e] administrative machinery to investigate and prosecute violations."[126]

The appeal to state intervention by the American Jewish Congress was avant-garde in some respects and already obsolete in others. In the 1940s, the ACLU eagerly backed Pekelis's campaign to secure a New York antidiscrimination law. In fact, the effort to "transform the law from a sword to a shield and to utilize it in combatting racism," as Maslow described the method, was of a piece with the ACLU's newfound deployment of law to combat employers' nongovernmental suppression of labor's rights to organize and strike—a program that most, if not all, of the ACLU's Jewish lawyers heartily endorsed.[127]

At the same time, there were simmering tensions between the ACLU's approach and the preference within the American Jewish Congress for the expansion of administrative power to enforce group rights. Increasingly, the ACLU was committed to blocking the exercise of state power where it arguably infringed on individual autonomy. Moreover, the organization was ever more partial toward the judiciary, an institution that remained strongly linked to individual rights.[128] Hays, for example, was sharply critical of what he perceived as administrative excess or unchecked executive power, and he was among the most important champions of legalism within the ACLU. In fact, he broke with other ACLU board members in his sympathy for something like the Administrative Procedure Act; he worried about a trend toward "trial by commissions" and accused administrators of censoring business, "which [was] just as bad as a censorship over literature."[129]

It bears emphasis that Jewish lawyers differed markedly in their attitudes toward the new liberal constitutionalism, and they often squared off on the airwaves and in congressional debate. Among the holdouts who continued to espouse direct action or preferred to insulate the political branches from judicial review—especially New Dealers and labor leaders, many of whom were themselves Jewish—there was a tendency to blame lawyers like Ernst and Hays for spearheading the shift.[130]

By the late 1930s, however, theirs was a losing battle. The linkage between civil liberties, court-centered constitutionalism, and individual rights had come to dominate not only the ACLU, but also the public imagination.[131] Indeed, the Court-packing

126 Ibid.

127 Ibid. See Weinrib, *Taming of Free Speech*, ch. 7; Risa Lauren Goluboff, *The Lost Promise of Civil Rights* (Cambridge: Harvard University Press, 2007), 136–8. The embrace of law by the American Jewish Congress coincided with increasingly vocal demands by the World Jewish Congress (founded in 1936 at the instigation of the former organization) for the punishment of Nazi war criminals. See Shlomo Shafir, *Ambiguous Relations: The American Jewish Community and Germany since 1945* (Detroit: Wayne State University Press, 1999), ch. 1.

128 Relatedly, the appointment of Jewish judges to the bench transformed legal ideology during this period, which presumably made litigation more appealing to some Jewish lawyers. See for example, William Edward Nelson, *The Legalist Reformation: Law, Politics, and Ideology in New York, 1920–1980* (Chapel Hill, 2001).

129 Arthur Garfield Hays to ACLU, 26 January 1939, ACLU Papers, vol. 2081.

130 See, for example, Weinrib, *Taming of Free Speech*, 299.

131 Notably, the ACLU's Roger Baldwin considered David Riesman's article "Civil Liberties in a Period of Transition," *Public Policy* 3 (1942): 33–96, which rested on a group-rights conception of democracy, to pose a fundamental challenge to the ACLU's commitments. He wrote to the National Committee and board that Riesman's "thesis ... that the break-down of a laissez-faire economy and the changed tactics of reaction require the protection and enlargement of social liberties rather than the defense of individual freedom against governmental interference ... deserves the attention of all of us, and in our own minds an adequate

plan was defeated in large part through a self-conscious strategy to identify judicial independence with the protection of members of minority groups. The new and promising approach is captured neatly by a radio broadcast by media mogul Frank Gannett (a Unitarian) on behalf of the National Committee to Uphold Constitutional Government. "The other day a barber was cutting my hair," Gannett recounts. "He said to me: 'You know, Mr. Gannett, I am deeply interested in preserving the Supreme Court.' I asked him why. He said: 'I am a Jew, and therefore one of a minority. I realize that if it were not for the Supreme Court, I might be treated here as they treat the Jews in Germany.'"[132] In the mid-1930s, the judicial protection of minorities was an ambition, not a fact. Notwithstanding their own ambivalence about judicial review, lawyers like Ernst and Hays may have helped to make it a reality.

For the ACLU's Jewish lawyers, the pernicious potential of ethnic nationalism prompted a cautious reevaluation of group rights in all of its manifestations, including labor unions and Jewish national identity. Going forward, they would trust in the courts to defend individual liberties against incursions by an overreaching state. Indeed, Hays believed that as an organization committed to judicial enforcement of the Bill of Rights, the ACLU "[did] more for Jews than any organization could do formed for the purpose of combatting anti-Semitic propaganda."[133]

## IV. Jewish Identity and the Hate Speech Debate

Perhaps the clearest example of both the dominance of the new liberalism and of its relationship to Jewishness is the debate within the ACLU over the constitutionality of regulating racist and antisemitic speech. At a fundamental level, it was the ACLU's Jewish lawyers who both pioneered and lent credibility to the notion that a mature and stable democracy would tolerate hateful speech. That is, they helped to frame the value-neutral concept of free speech that emerged as dominant by the late New Deal.

During the 1920s, the ACLU had defended the right of the Ku Klux Klan to speak and gather in Boston.[134] Many within the organization regarded the rights of the Nazi party to march in New Jersey and to hold rallies in New York as an extension of the same principles. Among others, the board consulted Felix Frankfurter, who replied (as he recounted at his Supreme Court confirmation hearing in 1939) that the ACLU had been right to defend the Klan and should not hesitate to represent Nazis in court.[135] Like many of the ACLU's members and supporters, Frankfurter, though a founding member of the American Jewish Congress, expressed his "hearty approval"

answer if we are to continue without modifying our present emphasis." Roger Baldwin to Members of the National Committee, Board and Correspondents, 27 August 1942, ACLU Papers, vol. 2356.

132 National Committee to Uphold Constitutional Government (Frank Gannett, Chairman), Report of Progress (statement broadcast on February 21, 1937, by CBS), ACLU papers, vol. 2100.

133 Arthur Garfield Hays to Jerome Count, 5 January 1939, ACLU Papers, vol. 2147.

134 Walker, *In Defense of American Liberties*, 60.

135 Nominations of Felix Frankfurter: Hearings before a Subcommittee of the Committee on the Judiciary, United States Senate, 76th Congress, 11–12 January 1939, 112.

for the principle that "civil liberty means liberty for those whom we do not like or even detest."[136]

But for some within and outside the ACLU, defending Nazis was a bridge too far. The organization's critics claimed that an excessive commitment to abstract pluralist principles had facilitated the Nazis' rise to power in Germany, and the ACLU was inadvertently condemning America to the same fate.[137] In defending against such accusations, the ACLU routinely emphasized that its Jewish lawyers were steering the organization toward its unpopular stance.[138] Other entities adopted the same line. When Madison Square Garden opened its facilities to the Nazi Party in the mid-1930s, it issued a statement explaining that the ACLU's Jewish lawyers, together with the American Jewish Committee, had advocated for that position.[139]

Morris Ernst and Arthur Garfield Hays led the speech-protective charge.[140] They offered multiple rationales for their position, many of which became mainstays in subsequent debates over hate-speech regulation. They argued that the surest way to fend off totalitarianism was to strengthen the Bill of Rights. They stressed the difficulty of line-drawing and the likelihood that restrictive laws would be deployed against political dissenters. They reasoned that prosecution produced martyrs, and they pointed to counterspeech and education as more effective means of reducing antisemitism.[141] They cautioned that prosecution and lawsuits would draw attention to rabble-rousers and exacerbate conflicts that would otherwise attract little sympathy.[142] They also predicted that coordinated suppression would unify factions that would otherwise devolve into infighting.[143] In all this, Hays considered it "a great thing for the Jews, or for any minority race, to be leaders in the fight for freedom of expression."[144]

Some arguments related more specifically to the interwar agenda of the ACLU. As Ernst, Hays, and others often emphasized, the same laws that were used to target antisemites could be turned against radicals and labor advocates. Defending antisemitic propaganda undermined allegations that they were invoking free speech as cover for their own subversive views. Protecting Nazi marches lent credibility to their

[136] Ibid., 111. Frankfurter would write the majority opinion upholding a group libel law in *Beauharnais v. Illinois*, 343 U.S. 250 (1952).

[137] Hays contested this claim. See, for example, Hays, "On Free Speech," 343 ("[F]ree speech was not the reason for Hitler's rise in Germany.").

[138] See, for example, Roger Baldwin, "Free Speech for Nazis?" *World Tomorrow* 16.26 (Nov. 9, 1933), 433 ("[T]wo lawyers representing the Union, both Jews, Morris L. Ernst and Harry Weinberger, arose at the Mayor's meeting and championed the rights even of their bitter enemies to the same liberties which as lawyers and libertarians they have so long demanded for all without discrimination").

[139] See also Stanton Griffis to Edna Ferber, 1 March 1939, Ernst Papers, box 40, folder 1 (noting that Madison Square Garden had consulted its Jewish directors, who "were firm in their belief that we should proceed with the meeting," as well as Morris Ernst and "various Jewish organizations," all of whom "felt that the meeting should proceed").

[140] For example, in 1933 the Brooklyn Jewish Examiner criticized Ernst for defending Robert P. Shuler, who was "notorious for his anti-Semitic views." "Civil Liberty," *Brooklyn Jewish Examiner*, Feb. 4, 1933. See also ACLU Press Release, 10 April 1935, ACLU Papers, vol. 846 (describing Hays's opposition to New Jersey anti-Nazi regulation).

[141] For example, "Shall We Defend Free Speech for Nazis in America," ACLU Papers, vol. 678.

[142] "Libels against Race and Religion: Memorandum of Law and Policy Prepared by the American Civil Liberties Union, April 1939," ACLU Papers, vol. 2111.

[143] Arthur Garfield Hays to William J. Robinson, 29 June 1934, ACLU Papers, vol. 700.

[144] Ibid.

claims that the intimidating nature of mass pickets did not warrant shutting them down. For example, when Hays organized a test case of a New Jersey labor picketing law, the city's attorney called him a communist. Hays responded that he had personally defended the right of the Nazi Party to march in Hudson County. The judge, accepting Hays's appeal to neutrality, interjected, "Certainly you cannot accuse Mr. Hays of being a Nazi."[145]

Other justifications, while still in some sense tactical, pertained more directly to the interest of the ACLU's lawyers as Jews. As an ACLU pamphlet put it, "In what position are Jews to protest against repression of their own minority in other lands when they become parties to repression in New York?"[146] Promoting free speech, even for Nazis, was the best means of ensuring that Jewish speakers, especially radical and unpopular Jewish speakers, were also protected. Moreover, Ernst and Hays believed that defending antisemitic propaganda would cultivate tolerance of minority groups. As Roger Baldwin explained the point, "For the sake of the cause of the Jews, a minority people, they urged even for Nazis that tolerance which the Jews are always demanding for themselves; and they did this not as a matter of principle but as a matter of strengthening the Jewish cause."[147]

Needless to say, Ernst and Hays's were not the only views. When the Anti-Defamation League (ADL) launched in 1913, its express goal was "to stop, by appeals to reason and conscience, and if necessary, by appeals to law, the defamation of the Jewish people."[148] Many Jews affiliated with the NAACP had advocated bans on the virulently racist film *Birth of a Nation*, among other interwar causes, and they turned to law to limit antisemitic expression as well.[149] To be sure, the ACLU's position found support within influential pockets of the Jewish community. While Louis Marshall had supported group libel legislation in the early 1920s, he eventually changed course, and in the 1930s, the American Jewish Committee opposed legislation criminalizing hate speech.[150] "As Americans and Jews," the organization insisted, "our first duty is to protect the Constitutional rights of free speech and free press, believing as we do that whenever and wherever these democratic principles are abridged or destroyed

145 ACLU v. Casey, 5 March 1937, before Hon. William Clark, Newark: Testimony of Arthur Garfield Hays, ACLU Papers, vol. 1051.

146 "Statement to Civil Liberties Union on the Advocacy by the Union's Attorneys of the Right of Nazi Propagandists to Speak in New York," ACLU Papers, vol. 601.

147 Baldwin, "Free Speech for Nazis," 433.

148 "Anti-Defamation League," *B'nai B'rith News*, October 1913. For a thoughtful analysis of American Jews' changing attitudes toward group libel laws, see Schultz, "Group Rights." On group libel more generally, see Joseph Tanenhaus, "Group Libel," *Cornell Law Quarterly* 35 (1950): 261–302; Harry Kalven, Jr., *The Negro and the First Amendment* (Columbus: Ohio State University Press, 1965); Samuel Walker, *Hate Speech: The History of an American Controversy* (Lincoln: University of Nebraska Press, 1994); Samantha Barbas, "The Rise and Fall of Group Libel: The Forgotten Campaign for Hate Speech Laws," *Loyola University Chicago Law Review* 54 (2022): 297–340.

149 In the late 1940s, Jewish organizations fractured over whether to oppose the exhibition of the film *Oliver Twist.* See Stephen H. Norwood, *Antisemitism and the American Far Left* (New York: Cambridge University Press, 2013), 89–91.

150 Schultz, "Group Rights," 96–104. Marshall also helped to draft an early law prohibiting advertisements excluding Jews from public accommodations. Ibid., 96. For an account of Marshall's evolving position and its relationship to litigation over Henry Ford's *Dearborn Independent*, see Victoria Saker Woeste, *Henry Ford's War on Jews and the Legal Battle against Hate Speech* (Stanford: Stanford University Press, 2012).

the security and safety of society are imperiled."[151] But other organizations were ambivalent. With ACLU prodding, the American Jewish Congress ultimately opposed a proposed New York bill authorizing criminal prosecution for antisemitic speech.[152] Although Stephen Wise initially endorsed legal measures to rein in Nazi propaganda, his organization's Commission on Law concluded that the legislation posed "a danger to the traditional liberal and democratic principles for which the Jewish people have always striven—particularly as such principles have been adhered to throughout the record of the American Jewish Congress in its defense of minority rights of all people in every land."[153] Nonetheless, the American Jewish Congress rejected the ACLU's absolutist position and "hope[d] to find some method by which these uncontrolled and irresponsible libels upon the Jewish people may be curbed."[154] Over the next decade, its leaders continued to endorse other means of regulating hateful expression, including disclosure requirements, right-of-reply provisions, and in some cases, closely drawn group libel laws targeting factual misrepresentations. Defending a proposed postal restriction on hate speech at a congressional hearing, the vice president of the American Jewish Congress reflected: "All this talk about providing education and then the truth will prevail ... is grand for Arthur Garfield Hays and Morris Ernst, who want no protection; but the masses have to be safeguarded and protected against false propaganda that makes their neighbors hate them."[155]

Throughout this period, the ACLU was under pressure to reconsider its blanket opposition to regulation. The organization received letters, resignations, and withdrawals of donations from individuals who were allies in other contexts. In 1933, one critic chided the ACLU for "invok[ing] Voltaire's dictum without realizing the historical forces which gave it birth."[156] Notably, Roger Baldwin defended the organization's position as the product of its own historical circumstance. "The only reason I am willing to fight for the rights of reactionaries is the present state of affairs in this country," he responded. "Practically speaking it is the only sound position to get the results you want—at least in this country and at this particular period."[157] This was no celebration of free speech as a timeless truth; changing circumstances might compel reevaluation. And as the scope of the Nazi atrocities in Europe became increasingly

151 Morris D. Waldman (secretary, American Jewish Committee) to Florina Lasker, 20 February 1936, ACLU Papers, vol. 897.

152 Charles Clift to Harvey M. Watts, 25 March 1936, ACLU Papers, vol. 897 (describing ACLU efforts to persuade Wise to withdraw support from the Schwartzwald Bill in New York).

153 Carl Sherman (chairman), Report of the Commission on Law, to Stephen S. Wise, 18 February 1936, ACLU Papers, vol 897. By November 1937, Horace Kallen stressed the "tremendous importance of equal rights for all views and opinions for the upkeep of democracy on which the Jewish position depends." Horace Kallen to Roger Baldwin, 5 November 1937, ACLU Papers, vol. 989. Similarly, Stephen Wise wrote that the commitment of the American Jewish Congress to the "principle of civil liberty" was as firm as the ACLU's," claiming that the organization "has ever rejected and will ever continue to reject as dishonorable the use against an opponent, of precisely those Nazi methods of suppression which, as a Jewish organization dedicated to the defense of democracy, it condemns." Stephen Wise to Roger Baldwin, 10 November 1937, ACLU Papers, vol. 989.

154 Sherman, Report of the Commission on Law.

155 Maslow, "Anti-Semitism and the Law"; Statement of Judge Nathan D. Perlman (vice president, American Jewish Congress), Hearings Before the Committee on The Post Office and Post Roads, House of Representatives, Seventy-Eighth Congress, March 16, 1944, 124 (testifying on behalf of the Lynch Bill).

156 Herman Marx to Roger Baldwin, 26 October 1933, ACLU Papers, vol. 601.

157 Roger Baldwin to Herman Marx, 30 October 1933, ACLU Papers, vol. 601.

apparent, many within the ACLU wondered whether reassessment of the organization's stance was in order. Even Ernst—emphasizing, like Baldwin, that constitutional principles must adapt to meet present exigencies—endorsed the compelled disclosure of the authors and funders of offensive materials.[158] Although he continued to oppose criminal sanctions, he also expressed openness to a group defamation model, that is, to an extension of existing libel law to prohibit the deliberate circulation of falsehoods concerning racial and religious groups.[159] As historian James Loeffler has shown, that was an approach that found significant purchase among Jewish leaders and thinkers affiliated with the American Jewish Congress who, like the ACLU's early leadership, had been conditioned by service to the labor movement to favor group rights.[160] As Will Maslow later put the point, "Jews who are defamed as a group should have the privilege of defending themselves as a group."[161]

There was enough support within the ACLU board for "a group defense against group libel"[162] that a subcommittee was appointed to consider the issue, consisting of Whitney North Seymour, Karl Llewellyn, and Hays. More than anyone else, it was Hays who clung to an absolutist position.[163] In March 1939, Roger Baldwin wrote to him to express dissatisfaction on the board with his inflexibility, noting a rising sense that "something can be done to stop the spreading of charges proved to be false," such as the Protocols of the Elders of Zion.[164] Hays was unmoved. As he wrote in a memorandum that was subsequently circulated by the board, he adhered to the view that "racial and religious intolerance cannot be cured by suppression." Although he did not discount the danger of Nazi propaganda, he believed that "laws passed with the intent of preventing anti-Semitism" were likely "to have just the opposite effect."[165]

158 Memorandum by Morris Ernst Prepared at the Request of the Board of Directors at the Special Meeting held Thursday, Oct. 9, 1941, ACLU papers, vol. 2268.

159 Ibid.

160 Loeffler, "Abandoned Weapon"; see also Norman L. Rosenberg, "Another History of Free Speech: The 1920s and the 1940s," *Law and Inequality: A Journal of Theory and Practice* 7 (1989): 333–66, 348–54. Maslow later repudiated his early support for group libel laws, deeming them likely to do more harm than good, though he maintained that "[i]f the day ever arises when anti-Semitic propaganda is disseminated in this country on such a scale and under such auspices that it is a menace rather than an irritation," it might be necessary to "run these risks." His later view sounded much like Hays's: "Jewish organizations are now beginning to recognize that the chief threat to their security in the United States comes from efforts that have the effect, if not always the purpose, of evading basic constitutional guarantees, the main bulwark not only of Jews but of all Americans." Maslow, "Uses of Law." David Riesman, whose 1942 article "Democracy and Defamation" was the most influential early scholarly defense of group libel, experienced a similar change of heart. David Riesman, "Democracy and Defamation: Control of Group Libel," *Columbia Law Review* 42 (1942): 727–80; Walker, *Hate Speech*, 99.

161 Maslow, "Anti-Semitism and the Law."

162 Ibid.

163 Llewellyn rejected Hays's position; Seymour joined Hays in opposition to group libel law.

164 Roger Baldwin to Arthur Garfield Hays, 29 March 1939, ACLU Papers, vol. 2111. Just two days later, he wrote to Norman Thomas (who expressed openness to a narrowly drawn group libel law) inviting comments on Hays's draft, noting that "I'm sure the inclination of the Board would be to go in your direction." Roger Baldwin to Norman Thomas, 31 March 1939, ACLU Papers, vol. 2111. In 1940, at least six members of the ACLU board thought it would be possible to draft a workable group libel law. As late as 1946, Baldwin told Alexander Pekelis that he would not object to mail fraud charges against a publication advertising the Protocols of the Elders of Zion as "a copy of the genuine document issued by Jews." Roger Baldwin to Alexander Pekelis, 7 May 1946, ACLU Papers, vol. 2719.

165 "Libels against Race and Religion: Memorandum of Law and Policy Prepared by the American Civil Liberties Union, April 1939," ACLU Papers, vol. 2111.

That Jews were on all sides of this debate, within the ACLU board and among its supporters, might suggest that their Jewishness was orthogonal to their views—that their economic inclinations or political allegiances or commitments to clients ultimately shaped their positions on hate speech. Certainly Jewishness did not produce a particular position on hate speech regulation in any deterministic sense. Even those whose general attitudes toward religious liberalism or cultural pluralism coincided often diverged when it came to whether and what kind of legal regulation of antisemitic expression was desirable.

Yet to discount the importance of Jewish identity because its effects were indeterminate would be shortsighted. The 1930s was not the first time that America's Jewish lawyers and activists encountered the problem of hate speech regulation. But never before had the issue assumed such urgency. Jewishness may not explain why some American Jews blamed Hitler's rise on government inaction while others pointed to the perils of empowering a strong state. Nor can it account for their differing prescriptions for countering Hitler's power in Europe or preventing its germination at home. To many, the judicial enforcement of individual liberty promised to constrain autocracy and reinforce rule of law; to many others, the emergency of organized antisemitism required a coordinated response from a strong and flexible administrative state. To all, however, the events in Europe conveyed with heart-wrenching clarity the stakes of the debate.

That the regulation of Nazi speech tore open the seams of the civil liberties coalition reflects the centrality of the participants' Jewishness, not its irrelevance. Here was an issue that penetrated to the core of their identity and beliefs, not to mention the prospect of personal safety and social belonging for their own and subsequent generations. It was one thing to bracket differences over scientific education in the schools or the censorship of sexually explicit art. It was another to suspend disagreement about how best to stanch a global wave of antisemitic violence—an eruption that threatened not just status and respectability or even deeply held views about social and economic justice, but their very survival.

That kind of peril had personal as well as professional consequences. Although Hays confessed (according to the *New York Times*) that he was not always eager to "stake all for principle," and he was "sometimes scared," he chose to participate in the Reichstag trial despite the risk. Publicly, perhaps strategically, he insisted that the threat of American antisemitism was overblown.[166] But it hardly seems a stretch to assume that it was his precarity as a Jew that compelled him "to do certain things that seem to need doing, though they may be difficult, unremunerative, and even dangerous."[167] For the ACLU's Jewish lawyers, the 1930s generated a depth of belief and willingness to sacrifice that verged, as Ernst put it, on a "religion of life."[168]

166 Duffus, "Memoirs of a Liberal Lawyer," 4; "Hays Sees Small Danger of Anti-Semitism in U.S.," *Jersey City Journal*, Apr. 16, 1936.

167 Duffus, "Memoirs of a Liberal Lawyer," 4.

168 Memorandum by Morris Ernst Prepared at the Request of the Board of Directors at the Special Meeting held Thursday, Oct. 9, 1941, ACLU papers, vol. 2268.

## V. Conclusion

The conflict over Nazi speech among Jewish lawyers and activists during the 1930s produced a flowering of theoretical insights and regulatory approaches that has shaped debates over hate speech regulation ever since. Those who have defended regulation have often echoed arguments made by interwar advocates—arguments that inspired a proliferation of group defamation laws and might well have produced national legislation, as the American Jewish Congress recommended to the President's Committee on Civil Rights, had the Cold War and competing Jewish groups not intervened.[169] Among advocates of racial justice during the Civil Rights era and after, discussion of regulation persisted.[170] But within the ACLU, openness to interventionist approaches receded with the totalitarian tide. Indeed, when the organization defended the right of Nazis to march in Skokie in the 1970s, its national leadership hewed more closely to Hays's arguments than Hays's own contemporaries had. The resulting settlement appeared adamantine until the twenty-first century, when a resurgence of racism, religious persecution, and demagoguery began to reveal new cracks.

In the fall of 2023, those incipient fractures unexpectedly ruptured, rattling the foundations of the modern free speech consensus. In responding to the brutal Hamas attack of October 7, 2023, and the tragic costs of the retaliatory war that has followed, American Jews have once again expressed sharp disagreement about the nature of Jewish identity, the pervasiveness of antisemitism in the United States, and the limits of free speech. The transformation in public discourse was as sweeping as it was sudden. Just a few months earlier, when I submitted an initial draft of this chapter to Oxford University Press, I wrote that the vision of civil liberties that the interwar ACLU championed had prevailed so completely that counterarguments were dismissed as marginal, radical, and inconsistent with "American values." Now, for the first time in decades, the future appears uncertain.

Although it is not yet possible to approach these developments with historical distance, I take seriously Hendrik Hartog's challenge to "present sympathetically perspectives and points of view" that others may consider "unattractive," attending to "the circumstances they [are] confront[ing]" with the goal of "understand[ing] ourselves better in relation to them."[171] With that framework in mind, I attempt here to paint, briefly and in broad strokes, the contours of the unfolding debate among Jewish lawyers, scholars, organizations, and individuals.

One camp, pointing to evidence that violent attacks on Jews, as well as Muslims, have surged across the globe, has demanded new measures to counteract bias and extremism. Foregrounding the fear and vulnerability that vocal and visibly Jewish people are experiencing, they argue not only that public officials and university

[169] Statement of the American Jewish Congress presented to the President's Committee on Civil Rights, May 1, 1947, ACLU Papers, Correspondence-Federal Departments, Volume 38 (Will Maslow, Director, Commission on Law & Social Action, American Jewish Congress). The AJC, ADL, and Jewish Labor Committee all opposed the bill. Schultz, "Group Rights," 129–30.

[170] Although the American Jewish Congress rescinded its earlier support for group libel legislation in 1960, new proponents of hate speech regulation emerged. Walker, *Hate Speech*, 100.

[171] Hartog, *Man and Wife*, 5.

administrators must deploy more resources to combat antisemitism and ensure the physical safety of Jewish communities and institutions, but that they must also, at least on college campuses, condemn and discipline speech that calls for the "genocide of Jews." They contend that to allow advocacy of Jewish genocide, whatever the "context," is to deny the equal worth of Jewish people and to ignore the catastrophic reality of past persecution.

The other side argues that their opponents have misconstrued the aspirations of pro-Palestinian protest, conflating criticism of Israel and its policies with antisemitism. Although many personally support Israel's right to exist, they defend even outright calls for the abolition of the Jewish state as political speech deserving of protection. Within this emerging coalition, some pushed for speech-protective rules long before October 7. Others have begun to question their own earlier openness to campus hate-speech policies and to adopt the line-drawing concerns of their one-time opponents (many of whom have also flipped sides), suggesting that the impulse to treat all pro-Palestinian protest as hate speech demonstrates how hard it is to disentangle expression that targets race, religion, and national origin from political agitation.

It is tempting to map these positions onto the debates of the 1930s. It was Ernst and Hays, after all, who coupled a vigorous defense of hate speech protections with skepticism toward Zionism, while the staunchly Zionist American Jewish Congress led the charge for group libel laws. As a historian, I both appreciate and resist comparisons of this kind. Certainly there is much that is recognizable in the agonized disputes within and among the ACLU and Jewish institutions in the 1930s. Notwithstanding some continuities, however, today's arguments are occurring on a landscape that has been vastly transformed politically, culturally, and institutionally. Among other factors, it is operating against a backdrop of far-ranging (though often underenforced) state and federal antidiscrimination law; strong judicial enforcement of civil liberties and civil rights; widespread (but incomplete) acceptance of cultural pluralism; and perhaps most saliently, the presence of a powerful, if embattled, Jewish state.

Given the magnitude of these and other shifts, efforts to navigate current predicaments by reference to history tell us more about the present than they do about the past. To take one revealing example, both Jewish defenders and Jewish critics of Israel's response to October 7 have appealed explicitly to the lessons of history, and in particular, to the post-Holocaust injunction to "never forget." Extrapolating from different aspects of the same collective trauma, they have come to starkly different conclusions about its implications—arguing on one side that the failure of the international community to intercede on behalf of Europe's slaughtered Jews counsels a swift and forceful campaign against Hamas; and on the other side, that the complicity of the German people and the global community during the Holocaust highlights the perils of ethnic nationalism and the moral urgency of humanitarian assistance. Extending a similar set of moves into the debate over campus speech, some have cited it to stress how quickly antisemitic rhetoric can turn to anti-Jewish violence, and others to emphasize the necessity of protesting humanitarian harms. Ultimately, these arguments must be resolved by reference to present-day circumstances, not by appealing to the heroic acts, misdeeds, or missed opportunities of past actors. There is simply too much distance between their world and ours, between the conditions that structured their lives as opposed to our own.

Nonetheless, when I reflect on the motivations of the interwar lawyers and advocates who struggled to articulate their vision of a just society as well as their own place within it, I cannot help but find some parallels profoundly resonant. As in the 1930s, the current debate among Jews over the limits of free speech and the role of law in countering antisemitism is about the nature of freedom and the terms of democratic participation. It is also, fundamentally, about what it means to be Jewish in America—about how American Jews understand their status as minorities historically and today, and also about how non-Jews have situated them, and will continue to situate them, within American society. Now, as in the 1930s, the First Amendment serves as a flashpoint in a conflict over liberty, equality, and security. Once again, departures from accepted orthodoxies are met with accusations of disloyalty on all sides. To be sure, the content of those orthodoxies has not been static. Yet even as the politics of free speech have shifted back and forth, an underlying preoccupation with American Jewish identity has endured.

For the Jewish lawyers engaged in this ongoing conversation, there is no escaping these deeply personal dimensions. Yes, Jews have adopted opposing positions on recent events, and with differing degrees of ambivalence or assurance; as commentators and comedians have long observed, impassioned disagreement is itself a core component of Jewish identity. Yet the current moment has seemingly produced a rare point of convergence. In prescribing a path forward, on the floor of Congress or in the opinion pages of major newspapers, few Jews have disclaimed the relevance of their Jewishness. What unifies the Jewish response to October 7 and its aftermath is recognition of the entangled relationship between advocacy and identity.

That my own reaction to the current moment is bound up with my Jewishness is, to me, self-evident. What was not obvious to me, and has only now come into focus, is how much my Jewishness infused my personal and professional identity even before this most recent chapter began. More than half a decade ago, in a post-Charlottesville exercise of historical distancing, I questioned the ACLU's decision to defend white supremacists, observing in an op-ed that the circumstances that made the organization's defense of Nazi speech attractive to the organization in the 1930s no longer pertained.[172] At the time, I did not see my position as a distinctively Jewish one. Notwithstanding the overt antisemitism of the Unite the Right rally, it never occurred to me that my intervention would be perceived as special pleading. In retrospect, however, my assumption that my reflections on hate speech could be detached from my Jewish identity appears naïve. In fact, the visceral response my op-ed provoked bears a strong, if ironic, resemblance to the reception of the 1930s Jewish lawyers who promoted unfettered speech. The flood of phone calls, email, and tweets that followed reveals the fluidity of some tropes and the stickiness of others. Like Ernst before me, I stirred up antisemitism and antiradicalism; my analysis prompted cautionary notes from worried "co-religionists" along with antisemitic rants. "Go back to Russia," one tweet advised me, in language chillingly reminiscent of the 1938 letter Ernst received. "They don't like free speech either."[173]

[172] Laura Weinrib, "The ACLU's Free Speech Stance Should Be about Social Justice, Not 'Timeless' Principles," *Los Angeles Times*, Aug. 30, 2017, https://www.latimes.com/opinion/op-ed/la-oe-weinrib-aclu-speech-history-20170830-story.html. The headline was not mine.

[173] 30 August 2017. Like Ernst, I was born and raised in the United States.

During the 1930s, the ACLU's Jewish lawyers were struggling to pin down a productive approach to constitutionalism and the courts in the face of a hostile judiciary, a global wave of totalitarianism, and an upsurge of antisemitism. In a period when Jews increasingly recoiled from attempts to define them in racial as opposed to religious terms, the appeal to the universal was alluring.[174] In celebrating civil liberties, it was tempting to imagine that they were fighting exclusively over principle, as opposed to a badge of belonging.

In drawing attention to those less visible stakes, I find myself writing, like Hartog, about my own life, in a way that is simultaneously deeply connected to and deeply estranged from the past. If law is an arena of conflict, the insolubility of a struggle may be more revealing than its resolution.

174 Leora Batnitsky, *How Judaism Became a Religion* (Princeton: Princeton University Press, 2011).

# Major Publication List: Hendrik Hartog

## Books

*Nobody's Boy and His Pals: The Story of Jack Robbins and the Boys' Brotherhood Republic.* Chicago: University of Chicago Press, 2024.

*The Trouble with Minna: A Case of Slavery and Emancipation in the Antebellum North.* Chapel Hill: University of North Carolina Press, 2018. Paperback edition, 2020.

*Someday All This Will Be Yours: A History of Inheritance and Old Age.* Cambridge: Harvard University Press, 2012.

*Man and Wife in America, A History.* Cambridge: Harvard University Press, 2000. Paperback edition, 2002.

*Public Property and Private Power: The Corporation of the City of New York in American Law, 1730 to 1870.* Chapel Hill: University of North Carolina Press, 1983. Paperback edition, Ithaca: Cornell University Press, 1989.

Editor (with Wendy Gamber and Michael Grossberg) and contributor, *American Public Life and the Historical Imagination.* Notre Dame: University of Notre Dame Press, 2003.

Editor (with William Nelson) and contributor, *Law as Culture and Culture as Law: Essays in Honor of John Philip Reid.* Madison: Madison House, 2000.

Editor and contributor, *Law in the American Revolution and the Revolution in the Law.* New York: New York University Press, 1981.

## Articles and Chapters

"Four Fragments on Doing Legal History, or Thinking with and against Willard Hurst." *Law and History Review* 39 (2021): 835–65.

"Three Fragments on Doing Legal History, or Willard Hurst and Me," in William Clune, ed., *Legal Realism to Law in Action: Innovative Courses at UW-Madison.* New Orleans: Quid Pro Books, 2021, 43–77, 100–21 (earlier version of "Four Fragments," along with interview with William Clune).

"Response: A Muddle in the Middle." *Law and Social Inquiry* 44 (2019): 534–47.

"Somedays, I Have Second Thoughts." *Law and Social Inquiry* 40 (2015): 519–30. (Reflections, following a Symposium devoted to *Someday All This Will Be Yours: A History of Inheritance and Old Age.* 2012)

"Coverture and Dignity: A Comment." *Law and Social Inquiry* 41 (2016): 833–40, in symposium on "Dignity Takings and Dignity Restoration."

"Two Stories About Two Currencies of Care." *Buffalo Law Review*, 61 (2013): 269–91. (The Mitchell Lecture of 2012)

"Introduction to Symposium on 'Critical Legal Histories.'" *Law and Social Inquiry* 37 (2012): 147–54.

"Comment on Appleby." *Historically Speaking*, 12 (2011): 13–14.

"Horwitz and the End of Socio-Legal History: 1975." Daniel W. Hamilton and Alfred L. Brophy, eds. *Transformations in American Legal History: Essays in Honor of Professor Morton J. Horwitz, Volume II.* Cambridge: Harvard University Press, 2010.

Welke, Barbara Young. "Glimmers of Life: A Conversation with Hendrik Hartog." *Law and History Review*, 27 (2009): 629–55.

"The Scene of a Marriage: McGuire v. McGuire." Carol Sanger, ed. *Family Law Stories.* St. Paul: Foundation Press, 2008.

"Someday All This Will Be Yours: Inheritance, Adoption, and Obligation in Capitalist America." *Indiana Law Journal* 79 (2004): 345–62 (revised version of Addison C. Harris Lecture)

"Romancing the Quotation." Austin Sarat, ed. *Law in the Liberal Arts.* Ithaca: Cornell University Press, 2004.

"What Gay Marriage Teaches about the History of Marriage." History News Network (http://hnn.us/articles/4400.html, April 2004).

"Interchange: The Practice of History." *Journal of American History* 90 (2003): 576–611.

"Llewellyn, Divorce, and Description." Wendy Gamber, Michael Grossberg, and Hendrik Hartog, eds. *American Public Life and the Historical Imagination.* Notre Dame: University of Notre Dame Press, 2003, 68–90.

"Stone's Transitions." *University of Connecticut Law Review* 34: (2002): 821–32.

"Divorce and Separation." "Marriage." Stanley I. Kutler. *Dictionary of American History.* Vol. 2. 3rd ed. New York: Charles Scribner's Sons, 2003.

"Rights Disputes in American History." Leonard Levy, Kenneth Karst, and Adam Winkler, eds. *Encyclopedia of the American Constitution, Supplement II.* New York: Macmillan, 2003.

"Wives as Favorites." Hendrik Hartog and William Nelson. *Law as Culture and Culture as Law: Essays in Honor of John Philip Reid.* Madison: Madison House, 2000, 292–321.

"Lawyering, Husbands' Rights, and 'The Unwritten Law,' in Nineteenth-Century America." *Journal of American History* 84 (1997): 67–96.

"John Barry's Custodial Rights: Of Power, Justice, and Coverture." Bryant G. Garth and Austin Sarat, eds. *Justice and Power in Sociolegal Studies.* Evanston: Northwestern University Press, 1997.

"Snakes in Ireland: A Conversation with Willard Hurst." *Law and History Review* 12 (1994): 370–90.

"Abigail Bailey's Coverture: Law in a Married Woman's Consciousness." Austin Sarat and Thomas R. Kearns, eds. *Law in Everyday Life.* Ann Arbor: University of Michigan Press, 1993, 63–108.

"Marital Exits and Marital Expectations in 19th Century America." *Georgetown Law Journal* 80 (1991): 95–129.

"Partial Readings." *Focus* (ABA) (1990); reprinted *Canadian Newsletter of Law and Society* (1990).

"Mrs. Packard on Dependency." *Yale Journal of Law and Humanities* 1 (1988): 79–103.

"The End(s) of Critical Empiricism." *Law and Social Inquiry* 14 (1989): 53–9.

"The Constitution of Aspiration and 'The Rights that Belong to Us All.'" *Journal of American History* 74 (1987): 1013–34. Reprinted in David Thelen, ed. *The Constitution and American Life* (Ithaca: Cornell University Press,1988).

"Imposing Constitutional Traditions." *William and Mary Law Review* 29 (1987): 75–82.
"Introduction: Legal Histories from Below." 1985 *Wisconsin Law Review* (1985): 759–66. (with William E. Forbath and Martha Minow)
"Pigs and Positivism." *Wisconsin Law Review* 1985: 899–935.
"The Conclusions of Urban History and Those of Lord Bryce." *Reviews in American History.* 13 (1985): 374–79. Reviewing Jon C. Teaford, *The Unheralded Triumph: City Government in America, 1870–1900.*
"The Politics of The Politics of Law." *American Bar Foundation Research Journal* 9 (1984): 851–57. Reviewing David Kairys, editor, *The Politics of Law: A Progressive Critique.*
"The Significance of a Singular Legal Career; Reflections on Daniel Webster's Legal Papers." *Wisconsin Law Review* 1984: 1105–19. Reviewing Alfred S. Konefsky and Andrew J. King, editors, *The Papers of Daniel Webster: Legal Papers.* Vol. 1 & 2.
"Property as Government in Eighteenth Century America: The Case of New York City." *Journal of Legal Studies* 10 (1981): 305–48.
"Distancing Oneself from the Eighteenth Century: A Commentary on Changing Pictures of American Legal History." Hendrik Hartog, ed. *Law in the American Revolution and the Revolution in the Law.* New York: New York University Press, 1981, 234–57.
"Because all the World Was not New York City: Governance, Property Rights, and the State in the Changing Definition of a Corporation, 1730–1860." *Buffalo Law Review* 28 (1979): 91–109.
Book Review. John Phillip Reid. *In a Defiant Stance. Indiana Law Journal* 54 (1978–9): 65–81. Reprinted as "Losing the World of the Massachusetts Whig." Hendrik Hartog, ed. *Law in the American Revolution and the Revolution in the Law.* New York: New York University Press, 1981. (review essay)
"The Public Law of a County Court: Judicial Government in Eighteenth Century Massachusetts." *American Journal of Legal History* 20 (1976): 282–329.

# Completed Doctoral Dissertations Directed by Hendrik Hartog

Thomas Johnson, S.J.D., University of Wisconsin, 1986
Yusuf Aboki, S.J.D., University of Wisconsin, 1986
Michael Millender, Ph.D., Princeton University, 1996
Felicia Kornbluh, Ph.D., Princeton University, 2000
Jacob Katz Cogan, Ph.D., Princeton University, 2002
Todd Stevens, Ph.D., Princeton University, 2003
Risa Goluboff, Ph.D., Princeton University, 2003
Donna Dennis, Ph.D., Princeton University, 2005
Kenneth Mack, Ph.D., Princeton University, 2005
Mitra Sharafi, Ph.D., Princeton University, 2006 (co-advisor)
Kunal Parker, Ph.D., Princeton University, 2007
Christina (Burnett) Ponsa, Ph.D., Princeton University, 2010
Laura Weinrib, Ph.D., Princeton University, 2011
Anne Twitty, Ph.D., Princeton University, 2012 (co-advisor)
Maribel Morey, Ph.D., Princeton University, 2013 (co-advisor)
Rohit De, Ph.D., Princeton University, 2013 (co-advisor)
Jessica Lowe, Ph.D., Princeton University, 2013
Farah Peterson, Ph.D., Princeton University, 2015
Catherine Evans, Ph.D., Princeton University, 2015
Matthew Axtell, Ph.D., Princeton University, 2016
Sarah A. Seo, Ph.D., Princeton University, 2016
Maeve Glass, Ph. D., Princeton University 2016
Alix Lerner, Ph.D., Princeton University, 2016
Kellen Funk, Ph.D., Princeton University, 2018
Jane Manners, Ph.D., Princeton University, 2018
Emily Prifogle, Ph.D., Princeton University, 2019
Craig Green, Ph.D., Princeton University, 2019
Kalyani Ramnath, Ph.D., Princeton University, 2019 (co-advisor)
Katharina Schmidt, Ph.D., Princeton University, 2021 (co-advisor)
Tara Suri, Ph.D., Princeton University, 2022 (co-advisor)
José Argueta Funes, Ph.D., Princeton University, 2024

Still to come:
Geneva Smith (co-advisor), Caitlin Tully, Manav Kapur (co-advisor), Haris Durrani (co-advisor)

# Index

*For the benefit of digital users, indexed terms that span two pages (e.g., 52–53) may, on occasion, appear on only one of those pages.*